Governmental Accounting, Auditing and Financial Reporting

Government Finance Officers Association

Copyright 1988 by the
Government Finance Officers Association
180 N. Michigan Avenue
Suite 800
Chicago, Illinois 60601

Library of Congress catalog card number 88–80315

ISBN 0–89125–122–7

Printed in the United States of America

First printing, June 1988

FOREWORD

The Government Finance Officers Association (GFOA) has actively supported the advancement of governmental accounting, auditing and financial reporting since the organization was founded in 1906. The GFOA served as the publisher for the National Council on Governmental Accounting (NCGA) and its predecessor bodies for over 50 years and currently is a primary financial supporter of the Governmental Accounting Standards Board (GASB). In keeping with this tradition of commitment to government finance, we are proud to release the 1988 *Governmental Accounting, Auditing and Financial Reporting* (GAAFR).

This new publication was written and published at a time when the practice of governmental accounting, auditing and financial reporting is facing many changes. Since 1980 when the predecessor *GAAFR* was published, the NCGA issued 15 authoritative pronouncements, the GASB issued 9 authoritative pronouncements, the American Institute of Certified Public Accountants issued a new accounting and audit guide for state and local governments, the Single Audit Act of 1984 was passed by Congress, and the U.S. General Accounting Office (GAO) is in the process of issuing its second revision to the *Standards for Audit of Governmental Organizations, Programs, Activities and Functions* (yellow book).

Information on all of these GASB pronouncements, the new GAO yellow book, single audit and other important changes has been included in the 1988 *GAAFR* to provide readers with the most up-to-date guidance in an easy-to-use format to help them meet the challenges of government's complex environment.

The contents of this publication represent a complete revision of the 1980 *GAAFR*. This project only could have been accomplished with the combined efforts of dedicated GFOA staff and members. David R. Bean, Stephen J. Gauthier and Paul E. Glick, the authors of 1988 *GAAFR,* were supported by a three-member Executive Review Committee, a 40-member review committee and other GFOA staff. David Bean, Director of GFOA's Technical Services Center, served as the lead author of this publication. Before joining GFOA, Bean worked in government and public accounting. He also is editor of our monthly accounting newsletter, *GAAFR Review,* and served as a director of the NCGA. Stephen Gauthier, an Assistant Director in GFOA's Technical Services Center, served as a primary author and technical editor of the 1988 *GAAFR*. He joined GFOA from the State of Tennessee's Office of the Comptroller of the Treasury, Division of State Audit. Gauthier is a senior contributor to *GAAFR Review* and serves as a lead instructor in GFOA's training programs. Paul E. Glick also served as a contributing author of the 1988 *GAAFR*. Glick was an Assistant Director in the GFOA's Technical Services Center before joining the University of Georgia as a Senior Financial Management Associate in the governmental training division of the Carl Vinson Institute of Government, Georgia Center for Continuing Education.

The Executive Review Committee was composed of Patrick F. Hardiman, Chief of the Bureau of Management Audit, City of New York, New York; James M. Patton, Associate Professor of Business Administration, Graduate School of Business, University of Pittsburgh; and James M. Williams, Partner, Ernst & Whinney. Their support and guidance throughout this project are greatly appreciated.

GFOA staff members who assisted the authors include Rebecca Russum, Director, Publications Center; Frederick G. Lantz, Manager, GFOA Technical Services Center; Dorothy Ray, Secretary, Technical Services Center; and Sharon Fucone, Secretary, Publications Center. I appreciate the special efforts of everyone who participated in the development and production of the 1988 *GAAFR*.

As we head into the 1990s, accountability remains an important objective of all governments. The GFOA's mission is to enhance and promote the professional management of governmental financial resources by identifying, developing and advancing fiscal strategies, policies and practices for the public benefit. We believe that the 1988 *GAAFR* and GFOA's other publications play a major role in fulfilling this mission.

Finally, David Bean, Stephen Gauthier and Paul Glick would like to join me in dedicating the 1988 *GAAFR* to Frank L. Greathouse, Director, Division of State Audit, State of Tennessee, who served as Chairman of the NCGA and as an officer of the GFOA and member of our Executive Board. Frank Greathouse has been a mentor to each of us and has given us and our colleagues in the government finance profession the benefit of his friendship, wisdom and leadership.

Jeffrey L. Esser
Executive Director
June 1988

PREFACE

Today the complex and ever-changing government finance environment brings with it a challenge to finance practitioners at all levels. The establishment of the Governmental Accounting Standards Board (GASB) as the primary governmental accounting standard setter has brought about an increased emphasis on "staying current." New standards are continually being issued to resolve past problems and to address the new transactions and situations that appear in practice every day. This changing environment compounds the difficulties faced by finance officials who account for these transactions and prepare reports, by auditors of government financial reports and programs, and by users of government financial reports. The challenge, then, is for government finance practitioners to obtain a working knowledge of these changes so that government accountability can be maintained. This step is paramount to the evolution of the government accounting model.

Governmental accounting has made substantial progress in the past 50 years, but there is much work still to be accomplished. Everyone has a part and must play a role in the process of achieving the goal of better financial management in government. Staying current with the standards is just one element in this process. The 1988 *Governmental Accounting, Auditing and Financial Reporting* (*GAAFR*) has been developed as a foundation upon which finance officials or auditors can build their knowledge of governmental accounting, auditing and financial reporting. By understanding the model from which standards evolve, the ability to shape and apply future standards is greatly enhanced. The GASB only issues standards that change this model after considerable deliberations and input from financial statement preparers, attestors and users. When potential respondents to GASB due process documents understand the underlying objectives and specific principles of the government accounting model, due process can work and the government model can evolve on a steady course.

No publication can present guidance on every transaction that could occur in the government accounting model. The authors have taken the approach with the 1988 *GAAFR* of presenting normal transactions found in a government's daily operations, while emphasizing certain transactions addressed in recent authoritative accounting literature and unique transactions that continually raise questions in practice. This approach should enable readers to expand their knowledge of government finance, and then use that knowledge to improve the government environment.

As was the case for the 1980 *GAAFR,* this publication neither establishes nor authoritatively interprets generally accepted accounting principles (GAAP). However, the 1988 *GAAFR* does provide detailed professional guidance on the practical applications of GAAP for governments. Several new features have been incorporated into this publication to enhance its usefulness. The 1988 *GAAFR* contains journal entries that provide sufficient detail to understand the nature and effect of specific transactions. These transactions can be traced to a model comprehensive annual financial report (CAFR) that has been prepared in accordance with the Government Finance Officers Association's (GFOA) Certificate of Achievement for Excellence in Financial Reporting Program standards.

A detailed index also has been added to the 1988 *GAAFR* to enhance the book's value as an easily accessible reference tool. This index has been divided into two sections (topical and journal entries) to further its usefulness to readers.

Finally, a section on how to use the 1988 *GAAFR* has been developed. These instructions have been written to meet the needs of two different groups of readers: the experienced public-sector finance practitioners and their private-sector colleagues, and individuals who are new to the government environment.

Some say that governmental accounting and auditing cannot change the government environment. In a direct sense this may be true; however, without accountability, government officials, governing bodies and citizens are forced to make critical decisions without adequate information. It is the finance practitioners' role to provide the best financial data possible so that legislative bodies and citizens can understand the complete financial circumstances surrounding the decisions to be made. Only then can the financial consequences of those decisions be properly assessed.

The 1988 *GAAFR* was significantly enhanced by the comments and suggestions of the Executive Review Committee, the review committee, production associates and other GFOA members and staff. These individuals include: Wendell H. Bowerman, Seattle, Washington; Edward P. Chait, Price Waterhouse; Stanley Y. Chang, University of Houston; Frederick W. Clarke, Houston, Texas; Donald H. Cormie, Grant Thornton; James L. Craig Jr., Peat Marwick Main; Gilbert W. Crain, Montana State University; Terry W. Drake, Kansas City Board of Public Utilities, Missouri; James A. Davis, Commonwealth of Virginia; Bert T. Edwards, Arthur Andersen; Robert J. Freeman, Texas Tech University; Sharon Fucone, GFOA staff;

Richard J. Haas; J. Dwight Hadley, State of New York; Patrick F. Hardiman, New York, New York; Rhett D. Harrell, Touche Ross; Leon E. Hay, University of Arkansas; Margaret M. Heimbach, GFOA staff; Harold H. Hensold, Jr., University of Illinois at Chicago; Jesse W. Hughes, Old Dominion University; North Jersild, GFOA staff; Jan M. Jutte, State of Washington; Louis G. Karrison, Karrison and Byrne; Walter F. Kelley, Arthur Young; Daniel L. Kovlak, Peat Marwick Main; Frederick G. Lantz, GFOA staff; John S. Linderman, State of Michigan; John B. Lilja, Deloitte Haskins & Sells; Mary Lou Lyle, Chesterfield County, Virginia; Roland M. Malan, Jr., State of New York; Stanley C. Martens, DePaul University; G. Michael Miller, Orlando, Florida; John R. Miller, Peat Marwick Main; Susan M. Miller, Boca Raton, Florida; Barbara G. Mollo, GFOA staff; Karen H. Nelson, GFOA staff; James M. Patton, University of Pittsburgh; Franklin C. Pinkelman, State of Michigan; Ronald J. Points, Price Waterhouse; Dorothy D. Ray, GFOA staff; Jane Russ, State of Tennessee; Rebecca Russum, GFOA staff; Paul M. Sachs, Arthur Andersen; William R. Schwartz, Missouri Local Government Employees Retirement System; Wilbert H. Schwotzer, Georgia State University; Karen Utterback Siegert, GFOA staff; Gary L. Sidelman, Coopers & Lybrand; William R. Snodgrass, State of Tennessee; Samuel E. Stiles, State of Illinois; Marcia L. Taylor, City of Mt. Lebanon, Pennsylvania; Ralph L. Turner, Salt Lake City School District, Utah; Barbara K. White, State of Tennessee; and James M. Williams, Ernst & Whinney.

We also would like to give a special thank you to Pat Hardiman, Jim Patton and Jim Williams of the Executive Review Committee for their expert guidance, to Bob Freeman and Paul Sachs for support above and beyond that expected from our review committee and to William M. Funk, Arthur Andersen, for referencing the 1988 *GAAFR*. We also would like to thank Jane Russ, State of Tennessee, for her invaluable contribution as editor of this work.

Several GFOA staff provided substantial contributions to this publication. We especially would like to thank Rebecca Russum who coordinated the production activities, Dorothy Ray and Sharon Fucone for production support, and Fred Lantz for the Certificate of Achievement for Excellence in Financial Reporting review of the model CAFR. Finally, we are grateful for the support of our wives and our families throughout this project.

David R. Bean
Stephen J. Gauthier
Paul E. Glick

CONTENTS

HOW TO USE
THE 1988 GAAFR

The 1988 *Governmental Accounting, Auditing and Financial Reporting (GAAFR)* is designed to meet the needs of two different, and often overlapping, groups of readers. On the one hand, the 1988 *GAAFR* can serve as an introductory text for those needing to familiarize themselves with accounting, auditing and financial reporting in the public sector. Such users include accountants and auditors new to state and local government, students, elected officials, and members of citizens' groups. On the other hand, the 1988 GAAFR can aid those already proficient in these disciplines by serving as a reference tool that provides quick access to needed information.

Structure. The structure of the 1988 *GAAFR* is designed to facilitate use by both groups. The 1988 *GAAFR* can be divided into the following general sections:

I. *Table of Contents.* The contents page entries represent the first two text subhead levels. In addition to these two levels, the 1988 *GAAFR* incorporates six *additional* levels of headings to further aid the reader. The following chart illustrates the headings used in the 1988 *GAAFR:*

Level	Example
1	**COMPREHENSIVE ANNUAL FINANCIAL REPORT**
2	**Financial Section**
3	***General Purpose Financial Statements***
4	*Notes to the Financial Statements*
5	Detailed Notes
6	Cash and Investments
7	Balance Sheet Data—
8	Deposits:

II. *Introduction.* A discussion of the state and local government accounting and financial reporting environment and objectives (chapter 1).

III. *Basic principles.* An examination of the basic principles that underlie the governmental accounting and financial reporting model (chapter 2). The structure and contents of financial reports are the subject of section VI.

IV. *Fund types and account groups.* A detailed discussion of each of the fund types and account groups, that highlights accounting issues commonly encountered in practice (chapters 3–10). The discussion is supplemented by a complete set of journal entries for the different fund types and account groups for a fiscal year. These entries provide the basis for the model comprehensive annual financial report (CAFR) presented in appendix D.

V. *Applications to specialized units.* An examination of how the generally accepted accounting principles (GAAP) described in sections II and III can be applied to special government units (chapter 11), school districts (chapter 12) and state governments (chapter 13).

VI. *Financial reporting.* A description of the structure and content of financial reports in the public sector (chapter 14). Covered are comprehensive annual financial reports (CAFRs) and component unit financial reports (CUFRs); public employee retirement system (PERS) financial reports; interim reports and condensed or "popular" reports. Information on the Government Finance Officers Association's Certificate of Achievement for Excellence in Financial Reporting program also is presented.

VII. *Auditing.* An examination of the types of auditors and audits encountered in the public sector, as well as a discussion of the applicable professional standards for such engagements (chapter 15). As part of this examination, the provisions of the Single Audit Act and Office of Management and Budget Circular A-128, *Audits of State and Local Governments*, are considered. The discussion also reviews a government's responsibility for audit management.

VIII. *Appendices.* The four appendices to the 1988 GAAFR are an integral part of the work:
  A. Acronyms and Pronouncements
  B. Terminology
  C. Illustrative Accounts, Classifications and Descriptions
  D. Illustrative Comprehensive Annual Financial Report

IX. *Indexes.* Easy-to-use guides to all of the important concepts, terms and journal entries of the 1988 *GAAFR.*

Using *GAAFR* as an Introductory Text. Although the 1988 *GAAFR's* chapters are relatively self-contained, a certain order should be used in approaching the chapters to enhance an understanding of the material. Chapters devoted to individual fund types and account groups (chapters 3–10) assume that the reader is familiar with the basic principles of governmental accounting and financial reporting outlined in chapter 2. Therefore, readers using the 1988 *GAAFR* as a text should assure themselves that they have an understanding of chapter 2 before approaching any of these chapters. Similarly, the section devoted to applications to specialized units (chapters 11–13) assumes that the reader is already familiar with both the basic principles (chapter 2), and with the application of these principles to the various fund types and account groups (chapters 3–10).

The sample journal entries presented in the chapters devoted to individual funds and account groups are *not* arranged chronologically. Instead, entries for the period are grouped into four categories. The first category presents the formal integration of the budget into the government's accounts. CAPITAL LETTERS are used for all budgetary accounts. The second category contains all entries that result in the recognition of revenues or other financing sources; receipts of cash; or increases in assets through nonmonetary transactions. The third category generally presents expenditures, expenses and other financing uses; disbursements of cash; or the recognition of encumbrances. The final category presents the closing entries for both budgetary and operating statement accounts. For example, the entry reflecting interest earned on investments would be presented before the entry showing the purchase of those investments. Accordingly, the reader should examine the entire set of entries to obtain a complete view of the transactions presented. Moreover, because transactions often affect more than a single fund or account group, the reader should refer to related entries in other chapters to gain an understanding of the ramifications of a given transaction or set of transactions. A separate index has been prepared for the journal entries to assist in identifying these situations.

Also, because all of the transactions set forth in the journal entries tie to the model CAFR presented in appendix D, the reader may wish to examine this appendix while studying the journal entries. By doing so, the reader can obtain a clear view of how a given transaction will finally be reflected in the financial statements, including the related notes to the financial statements.

Using the 1988 *GAAFR* as a Reference Guide. The 1988 *GAAFR* is designed to provide those interested in governmental accounting, auditing and financial reporting with quick reference to the information needed to resolve problems encountered in practice. Various approaches should be taken to each of the following research problems:

1. *Illustrative journal entries.* The reader should look to the journal entry index for a list of all the illustrative journal entries relating to a given topic. For example, the index reference for capital leases refers the reader to entries in the general fund, the general fixed assets account group and the general long-term debt account group. If the reader fails to use the journal entry index and instead refers directly to one of the chapters devoted to the fund types and account groups, the reader risks missing related entries in other funds and account groups.

2. *Particular topics.* The reader is advised to refer to the general index. Readers choosing not to use the index should keep in mind that accounting treatments affecting a number of fund types are primarily addressed in chapter 2 rather than repeated in the chapters devoted to fund types and account groups (chapters 3–10). Also, disclosure guidance generally will be found in chapter 14 rather than in chapters 3–10.

3. *Note disclosures.* Descriptions of required note disclosures are presented in chapter 14. Examples of the note disclosures can be found in the model CAFR provided in appendix D. Again, the reader is advised to consult the general index. Readers choosing not to use the index should keep in mind that some of the sample note disclosures related to a given topic (e.g., cash and investments) are divided between the summary of significant accounting policies and the remaining notes.

4. *Definitions of terms.* Appendix B provides the reader with a glossary of some of the most commonly used terminology for governmental accounting, auditing and financial reporting.

5. *Acronyms and abbreviations.* Acronyms and abbreviations are only used after being identified at least once in a given chapter. However, for the reader's convenience, a complete list of all acronyms and abbreviations is provided in appendix A.

Finally, the reader wishing to use the 1988 *GAAFR* as a reference tool should take advantage of the numerous references to the authoritative literature, including the Governmental Accounting Standards Board's 1987 *Codification of Governmental Accounting and Financial Reporting Standards,* as a basis for further research.

Chapter 1
INTRODUCTION

Governmental accounting, auditing and financial reporting have evolved through the decades as has this publication, *Governmental Accounting, Auditing and Financial Reporting (GAAFR)*. When the National Committee on Municipal Accounting (NCMA) was established by the Government Finance Officers Association (GFOA) and began to promulgate formal standards for governments in 1934, a publication of this type did not exist. The NCMA issued the first "blue book" in 1936 (Bulletin No. 6, *Municipal Accounting Statements*). NCMA Bulletin No. 6 codified and updated many previous NCMA bulletins.

In 1951, the NCMA's successor body, the National Committee on Governmental Accounting (the committee) issued Bulletin No. 14, *Municipal Accounting and Auditing*. The committee's Bulletin No. 14 advanced governmental accounting standards and introduced the basic format of the current blue book. The final authoritative blue book was issued in 1968 by the committee. With its widespread acceptance, the 1968 *GAAFR* established generally accepted accounting principles (GAAP) for government.

AUTHORITATIVE STATUS

Rather than revising and updating the 1968 *GAAFR,* the National Council on Governmental Accounting (NCGA) decided instead to issue a restatement of the 1968 *GAAFR* principles. This decision resulted in the discontinuance of the blue book as an authoritative publication. However, the GFOA decided to issue a revised blue book as nonauthoritative guidance for practitioners.

The nonauthoritative blue book made its entrance with the 1980 *GAAFR*. It neither established nor authoritatively interpreted GAAP. The 1988 *GAAFR* has been developed based on the same premise. Although nonauthoritative in status, this publication continues in the tradition of the 1980 *GAAFR* by providing detailed professional guidance on the practical applications of GAAP for governments.

STRUCTURE OF AUTHORITATIVE STANDARD SETTING

In the past, questions were raised as to who set the standards that constituted GAAP for governments. This question rose to prominence when the American Institute of Certified Public Accountants (AICPA) in 1974 issued an industry audit guide, *Audits of State and Local Governmental Units*. Although the audit guide endorsed most of the principles in the 1968 *GAAFR,* it also modified certain of its principles. The conflicts between the two documents, however, were resolved primarily by the issuance of NCGA Statement 1, *Governmental Accounting and Financial Reporting Principles*. This pronouncement was formally recognized without modification by the AICPA in Statement of Position 80–2, *Accounting and Financial Reporting by Governmental Units*.

After the release of NCGA Statement 1, questions still arose in practice as to who established GAAP for governments. Conflicts with NCGA standards generally were associated with pronouncements issued by the Financial Accounting Standards Board (FASB). The application of FASB pronouncements to governments, when they conflicted with an NCGA pronouncement or addressed a situation not specifically covered by an NCGA pronouncement, was not officially addressed until the Governmental Accounting Standards Board (GASB) was established in 1984.

The negotiations leading to the creation of the GASB resulted in a structural agreement that clearly establishes the GASB as the primary standard setter for government. This agreement clarified the relationship between GASB and FASB standards; however, the agreement did not completely eliminate all jurisdictional issues. These issues are being resolved on an ongoing basis.

The GASB was created as a five-member board under the auspices of the Financial Accounting Foundation (FAF). The current GASB includes a full-time chairman, a part-time vice chairman, three other part-time board members and a full-time staff. The FAF also established the Governmental Accounting Standards Advisory Council (GASAC) to advise the GASB of its members' views and those of the organizations they represent. The GASAC has 23 members, representing various organizations including the GFOA, that participate with the FAF in the formal approval process of GASB member appointments. An overview of the current accounting standard-setting structure is presented in Illustration 1–1.

FINANCIAL REPORT USERS

The GASB has the responsibility to establish and improve accounting and financial reporting standards at the state and

ILLUSTRATION 1–1

Standard-setting Structure

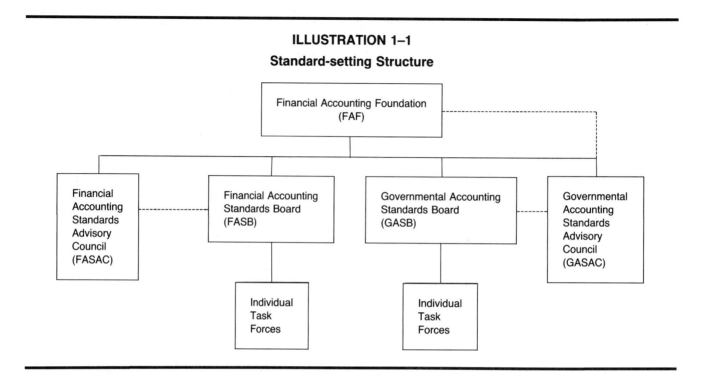

local government level. In developing a theoretical base for the creation of future standards, the GASB established external financial reporting objectives. Although the GASB's focus for these objectives was limited to external financial reporting, it should be remembered that a primary objective of any accounting system is to provide information that can be disseminated to users through financial reports. Therefore, a financial reporting objective can directly influence the accounting system from which the information was derived.

The GASB identified "accountability" in its 1987 *Codification of Governmental Accounting and Financial Reporting Standards* (1987 *Codification*), Section 100.176, as "the paramount objective from which all other objectives must flow." Accountability is defined in the 1987 *Codification,* Section 100.156, as the requirement for "governments to answer to the citizenry—to justify the raising of public resources and the purposes for which they are used." In establishing financial reporting objectives that emphasize accountability the GASB believes that, "financial reporting plays a major role in fulfilling government's duty to be publicly accountable in a democratic society."

Within the context of being publicly accountable for external financial reporting purposes, the GASB identifies three groups of primary users of external financial reports:

- Citizens—taxpayers, voters, public interest groups, the media;
- Legislative and oversight bodies—state legislatures, county boards, city councils, school boards, boards of trustees; and
- Investors and creditors—individual and institutional inves-

tors, securities underwriters, bond rating agencies, bond insurers.

Governments' management was not identified by the GASB as a primary user group of external financial reports because of its ability to obtain information from other sources. However, this is not to say that management does not use external financial reports. In fact, management is one of the primary users because a financial report can provide quick access to certain key information. Some believe that legislative and oversight bodies should be classified in the same category as management in defining financial statement users. Legislative and oversight bodies, however, hold a unique position within government. In effect, they may be treated as insiders by citizens groups and investors and creditors, and as outsiders by management.

USES OF FINANCIAL REPORTS

The 1987 *Codification,* Section 100.132, identifies several different uses of external financial reports in assessing accountability and making social and economic decisions.

a. Comparing actual financial results with the legally adopted budget
b. Assessing financial condition and results of operations
c. Assisting in determining compliance with finance-related laws, rules, and regulations
d. Assisting in evaluating efficiency and effectiveness.

Budgetary Comparisons. As discussed later in this chapter, the budget document is viewed by some as the primary source of government financial information. Although this view generally is considered to be too narrowly focused, the results of a GASB survey indicated that all three user groups are interested in comparing originally adopted budgets and budgets after final amendments with the actual results of the current year's activities on a budgetary basis.

Financial Condition and Results of Operations. Government financial reporting in the past has not emphasized the balance-sheet effects of operations because of the view that, if need be, current-year costs can be paid with future-years' revenues. However, there is a growing acceptance among users of the need for information on the government's ability to "live within its means." The GASB introduced the term "interperiod equity" to describe whether future years' taxpayers will be called upon to pay the liabilities incurred in the current period.

Although there may be an increased emphasis on the balance sheet, the operating statements remain a focal point in government financial reports. This statement provides information on the inflows and outflows of current financial resources (for governmental-type activities) and economic resources (for business-type activities). The results of operations can be compared by users to prior years' results and also to those of governments that provide similar services.

A significant drawback in the attempt to make intergovernmental comparisons is the dissimilarity of functions between governments. For example, one government may incorporate park and recreational activities as a separate department whereas another community may account for all park and recreational activities in a separate park district. This park district may have separately elected officials, a separate budget and an independent accounting system. Therefore, two governments that appear similar may be quite different.

Compliance. When the issue of government compliance is raised one automatically envisions the budget. However, within the complex government environment, a wide array of legal and contractual provisions are found. Because the failure to comply with any of these provisions may have severe financial consequences, all financial report users should be concerned with adherence to laws and regulations. Examples of common compliance items include bond indentures, grant provisions and debt limitations.

Efficiency and Effectiveness. In the GASB survey of user needs, the users of financial reports identified government service efforts and accomplishments information as a necessary element of financial reports. This information provides a basis for assessing the efficiency and effectiveness of government through performance measures. However, a wide range of information currently does not exist from which to make service efforts and accomplishments comparisons.

FINANCIAL REPORTING CHARACTERISTICS

To ensure that the financial report users' need for quality information is met, the GASB in the 1987 *Codification*, Section 100.162, identified six basic characteristics that should be inherent in any report that effectively communicates financial information. These characteristics are:

- Understandability,
- Reliability,
- Relevance,
- Timeliness,
- Consistency and
- Comparability.

Understandability. To demonstrate public accountability effectively, the government should not only issue financial reports for use by knowledgeable financial report users, but also should prepare reports that the citizenry can understand. The preparation of popular reports for the citizenry is discussed in chapter 14.

Reliability. Information presented in external financial reports should be verifiable and free from bias. The GASB stated that for a report to be reliable it "needs to be comprehensive."

Relevance. For a financial report to be relevant it should contain information that meets the needs of the financial statement users. Relevance also encompasses several other basic characteristics (e.g., timeliness, reliability).

Timeliness. A financial report should be issued on a timely basis to be useful to financial statement readers. The time period within which a report should be issued depends on the type of information presented. For example, the GFOA's Certificate of Achievement for Excellence in Financial Reporting Program policy currently considers a comprehensive annual financial report (CAFR) to be timely if it is issued within six months of the government's fiscal year end. However, the GFOA and other organizations strongly encourage that reports be issued in a shorter period of time (e.g., three to five months).

Consistency. Financial reports should be prepared using a basis of accounting consistent from transaction to transaction and from period to period. Any change in accounting principles should be disclosed.

Comparability. The GASB provides that "differences between financial reports should be due to substantive differences in the underlying transactions or in the governmental structure rather than due to the selection of different alternatives in accounting procedures or practices." No two governments' annual reports are identical from a pure comparability standpoint; however, reasonable comparability can be achieved within the context of standard procedures and practices.

LIMITATIONS OF FINANCIAL REPORTING

Financial report users also should be aware of limitations that affect all financial reports. Financial reports cannot be prepared that meet all the needs of every user. If governments were to attempt to meet that goal, the financial report would be so excessively detailed as to confuse readers.

Another limitation that should be taken into consideration when financial reports are prepared is the cost of accumulating certain information, compared to the benefit the users derive from that information. The GASB states that "cost-benefit relationships will be carefully considered" in the establishment of standards.

GOVERNMENT ENVIRONMENT

To properly assess the government accounting and financial reporting model and the GASB's financial reporting objectives, the environment that influences decisions must be understood. The basic premise behind the creation of a separate government accounting and financial reporting model and the subsequent establishment of the GASB is that governments have objectives that differ from those of the private sector. In many respects, the governmental objectives reflect the environment in which governments operate.

As mentioned earlier, accountability is the GASB's primary objective of external financial reporting. The GASB identified three environmental characteristics of government that underscore the need for government accountability. These characteristics are:

- Structure of government,
- Nature of resource providers and
- Political process.

Structure of Government. Governments are founded to protect and serve the needs of their citizens. In the United States, the structure of government is based on a system of checks and balances achieved through the separation of powers. The three branches of government (i.e., executive, legislative and judicial) function within a framework of controls guaranteed by the Constitution that effectively prevents any one branch from controlling the entire government.

The effect of these checks and balances is limited by several factors inherent in the government environment. In the private sector the focus of attention is on the "bottom line" or the maximization of profits. Government's "success" or "failure" is not measured by a bottom line. The question of whether a government has fared better or worse financially compared to the previous period cannot be answered easily within the confines of the current accounting and financial reporting model.

In addition, all three branches of government can arrive at different conclusions on how citizen needs can best be served. This apparent absence of coordinated direction is sometimes compounded by the lack of continuity in government leadership. The periodic election of government officials is an integral part of the system of checks and balances that provides accountability to the citizenry. However, the knowledge that elected officials will be replaced after as little as two years of service sometimes prevents governments from establishing long-range goals and objectives.

Although this system has its imperfections, it has served the United States well over the past 200 years. Accounting and financial reporting can provide valuable information to decision makers and provide a mechanism for the establishment of controls to enable this system to operate more efficiently and effectively.

Government in the United States can be divided into three levels: federal, state and local. The federal system of government significantly affects the manner in which state and local governments operate. State and local governments continually rely on the federal government for financial support of social and economic programs. The federal government maintains a broader revenue base and, therefore, revenues in many instances can be raised for these programs in a politically acceptable manner. By distributing these resources through grants, entitlements and shared revenues, the ability to provide a minimal level of government services to *all* citizens also is greatly

enhanced. The same relationship often exists between state and local governments.

Along with these resources has come an increased level of oversight from the federal and state governments. As resources are filtered down through the various levels of government, accountability becomes increasingly difficult.

Nature of Resource Providers. In the commercial sector there is a direct relationship between the goods or services provided by a company and the price paid by the customer. A different relationship exists for some government activities (e.g., basic government services such as public safety and education) supported primarily by tax revenues. Although an exchange relationship may exist at the aggregate level (i.e., the citizenry as a whole provides resources and the citizenry as a whole receives goods and services), the ability to identify an exchange relationship for a specific tax-supported transaction does not exist. An individual rarely would receive an amount of government-provided goods and services equal to the amount of taxes paid. This occurrence would only be by chance because resources are collected based on entirely different measures (e.g., property values, income) than goods or services provided. The GASB in the 1987 *Codification,* Section 100.117, concluded that a "match" between resources provided and goods and services received occurs at an aggregate level within a specific period of time; however, an actual exchange transaction does not exist.

The GASB identified other factors that complicate the relationship between the taxpayer and the government, including the nature of taxpayers and the types and extent of services provided by the government. Taxpayers by their nature are "involuntary" resource providers. Some citizens, given the option of paying for government services, may choose not to pay. The lack of the option to pay has an effect on how governments operate and the need to demonstrate accountability to these involuntary resource providers.

Government normally provides services that are either not profitable in the private sector or are more efficiently provided through the function of economies of scale by the ability to spread costs across a broader population. In many cases, the service that the government provides may not be found in the commercial sector within that particular jurisdiction. In addition, the rule of supply and demand becomes moot when services are not directly paid for by the recipient of those services and only one service provider exists. It is often difficult, if not impossible, to judge the "proper supply" (i.e., amount) of police protection or education. Therefore, the efficiency and effectiveness of the services provided cannot be measured by the marketplace.

Political Process. Politics play an important role in the democratic process. Citizens in effect speak through politicians to provide direction to government. A politician is elected by the voters based on his or her views of how governments should be operated. Because of the short time period an elected official remains in office, there is continual pressure to provide the maximum amount of service to the citizens with a minimum amount of revenues. This pressure may, in some circumstances, lead those officials operating in a politically sensitive environment to provide services to citizens in the current period without raising sufficient recurring revenues to pay for those services.

In addition, governments, unlike their commercial sector

counterparts, invest significant amounts of resources into non-revenue-producing assets. Although parks, roads and general services buildings can be used to produce revenues, this is seldom the case. For this reason, the motivation to maintain those assets properly sometimes is significantly decreased. In effect, the maintenance of capital assets frequently is placed in the same tenuous funding category as a social program when budgetary decisions are made. The allocation of scarce resources may result in the deterioration of nonrevenue-producing capital assets to the point where the assets no longer are of any value to the government, well before the end of their expected useful life.

Controlling Characteristics. Although some may believe that the previously mentioned influences on the government environment are negative, they can be viewed positively when balanced with some form of control. Three major controlling factors are the budget, fund accounting and internal control structure elements.

Budget. The formal budgetary process can be a major controlling influence in the government environment. Budgets also are prepared in the private sector and are used in both sectors as an expression of policy and financial intent and as a method for evaluating performance. The factor that sets government budgets apart from commercial budgets is the extent they are used as control devices. A government's budget generally carries the force of law when spending limits are established in a legally adopted budget. The government must operate within those confines.

Fund Accounting. The history of fund accounting can be traced back to a time well before formalized governmental accounting standards were established. Fund accounting has always been used as a control device to segregate financial resources and ensure that the segregated resources were only used for their intended purposes. As accounting systems have grown more sophisticated, the reliance on fund accounting as a primary method of control has been reduced; however, the use of funds for financial reporting is still necessary to adequately demonstrate accountability.

Internal Control Structure Elements. The development of a government's internal control structure is essential so that the other control characteristics can operate effectively. Therefore, to ensure that the government's objectives will be achieved within its environment, internal control structure policies and procedures should be established. The AICPA's Statement on Auditing Standards (SAS) No. 55, *Consideration of the Internal Control Structure in a Financial Statement Audit,* states that an internal control structure consists of three elements:

- Control environment,
- Accounting system and
- Control procedures.

Control Environment. A government's control environment consists of the "overall attitude, awareness and actions" of the governing body and management. Several factors influence the control environment, including the presence of an audit committee, effective management control methods (e.g., establishing and monitoring policies for developing and modifying accounting systems and control procedures) and a foresighted management philosophy toward financial reporting.

Accounting System. SAS No. 55 provides that methods and records of an effective accounting system will result in the:

- Identification and recording of all valid transactions.
- Description on a timely basis of the type of transaction in sufficient detail to permit proper classification of the transaction for financial reporting.
- Measurement of the transaction's value in a manner that permits recording of its monetary value in the financial statements.
- Determination of the time period in which the transaction occurred to permit recording of the transaction in the proper accounting period.
- Proper presentation of the transaction and related disclosures in the financial statements.

Control Procedures. The government's accounting and administrative internal controls are now referred to as control procedures. These policies and procedures, addressed in SAS No. 55, generally include:

- Proper authorization of transactions and activities.
- Adequate segregation of duties.
- Adequate documents and records.
- Adequate safeguards over access and use of assets and records.
- Independent checks on performance.

Business-type Activities. The previous discussion has been devoted primarily to tax-supported activities. Governments also may be involved in activities that emulate private-sector businesses. Many of these services are offered by the private sector in different communities or, in some instances, within the same community. Business-type activity services are provided to customers on an exchange basis. This exchange relationship creates an environment different from that of the tax-supported activities. Business-type activities are faced with involuntary resource providers only to the extent the government has a monopoly on the service it provides to the customer. In addition, fixed assets acquired and maintained by business-type activities generally are revenue-producing in nature. Maintenance of these assets normally is required to produce an adequate level of service.

These activities may differ from their commercial-sector counterparts because of the political process. The influence of this process becomes prevalent in rate-setting and allocation of subsidies either to or from business-type activities. The political environment also affects business-type activities when they are subject to the budget process. Although the budget process should not be considered a negative influence, it may affect how the activity's operations are conducted.

The GASB concluded in the 1987 *Codification,* Section 100.175, that:

. . . there are no major differences in the financial reporting objectives of governmental-type and business-type activities. This is because business-type activities, whether performed through a separate legally constituted entity or through a department of government, are nevertheless a part of government and are publicly accountable. To the extent that there are differences in financial reporting objectives, they tend to be differences in emphasis caused by differences in the operating environment of each.

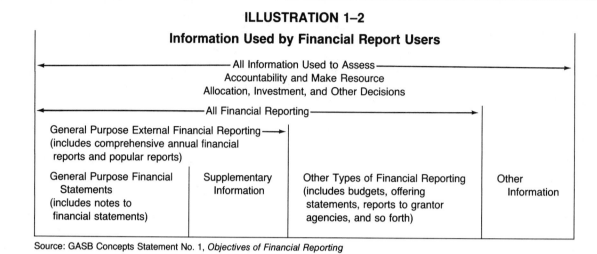

ILLUSTRATION 1–2

Information Used by Financial Report Users

←————————— All Information Used to Assess —————————→
Accountability and Make Resource
Allocation, Investment, and Other Decisions

←————————— All Financial Reporting —————————→

General Purpose External Financial Reporting →
(includes comprehensive annual financial
reports and popular reports)

General Purpose Financial Statements (includes notes to financial statements)	Supplementary Information	Other Types of Financial Reporting (includes budgets, offering statements, reports to grantor agencies, and so forth)	Other Information

Source: GASB Concepts Statement No. 1, *Objectives of Financial Reporting*

FINANCIAL REPORTING OBJECTIVES

Financial reporting objectives effectively are a road map that future accounting and financial reporting standards should follow. By analyzing these objectives, the reader may be able to anticipate where accounting and financial reporting may be in the 1990s. The scope of the financial reporting objectives extends beyond general purpose external financial reporting to encompass all forms of external financial reporting (e.g., CAFRs, official statements, grant reports). Illustration 1–2 presents information needed by financial report users, including the financial information covered by the objectives, within the context of all information used to assess accountability and make resource allocation, investment and other decisions.

The 1987 *Codification,* Sections 100.177–.179, establishes three primary financial reporting objectives including the paramount objective of accountability for external financial reporting.

- Financial reporting should assist in fulfilling government's duty to be publicly accountable and should enable users to assess that accountability.
- Financial reporting should assist users in evaluating the operating results of the governmental entity for the year.
- Financial reporting should assist users in assessing the level of services that can be provided by the governmental entity and its ability to meet its obligations as they become due.

These primary objectives are divided further into nine basic objectives of financial reporting:

1. Financial reporting should provide information to determine whether current-year revenues were sufficient to pay for current-year services.
2. Financial reporting should demonstrate whether resources were obtained and used in accordance with the entity's legally adopted budget; it should also demonstrate compliance with other finance-related legal or contractual requirements.
3. Financial reporting should provide information to assist users in assessing the service efforts, costs and accomplishments of the governmental entity.
4. Financial reporting should provide information about sources and uses of financial resources.
5. Financial reporting should provide information about how the governmental entity financed its activities and met its cash requirements.
6. Financial reporting should provide information necessary to determine whether the entity's financial position improved or deteriorated as a result of the year's operations.
7. Financial reporting should provide information about the financial position and condition of a governmental entity.
8. Financial reporting should provide information about a governmental entity's physical and other nonfinancial resources having useful lives that extend beyond the current year, including information that can be used to assess the service potential of those resources.
9. Financial reporting should disclose legal or contractual restrictions on resources and risks of potential loss of resources.

The following analysis of the nine basic objectives includes both additional explanations of the objectives and *observations* on how the GASB *may* adopt standards designed to achieve these objectives.

The first of the nine basic objectives embraces the concept of interperiod equity. As mentioned earlier, the GASB provides a broad-scope definition of interperiod equity. This measure attempts to determine if the current year's citizens have received services in excess of revenues provided, or if the revenues provided exceeded the services received. The effect of these events could be either that future taxpayers will have an additional burden, or that potential future taxpayers will receive additional benefits from past actions.

The first application of this concept is expected to occur in the GASB's measurement focus and basis of accounting project. This project, and other significant GASB projects introduced later in this chapter, are addressed in chapter 16.

As described earlier, the GASB defines the concept of interperiod equity in terms of "services received." The real impact of interperiod equity on financial reporting cannot be articulated within any individual governmental fund. The GASB realizes this limitation but recognizes that "each individual fund should contribute to measuring interperiod equity as much as possible."

The second objective highlights the continued need for compliance with finance-related legal and contractual provisions. The GASB's identification of compliance with the legally adopted budget appears to give some indication that the current budget-to-actual comparison's level of importance will not be significantly diminished. A footnote to this principle, however, indicates that for some nonbudgetary legal compliance matters "it may be sufficient to demonstrate compliance by identifying items or instances of noncompliance." With the considerable volume of compliance requirements now facing governments, the GASB, as part of its financial reporting project, may address the method of demonstrating legal compliance for items other than the budget.

The GASB's financial reporting project is also tied to the third objective. As stated earlier, the issue of service efforts and accomplishments is a topic of increased interest to the government financial community. The results of a GASB research project are expected to provide a foundation of performance measures upon which to base experimentation, and ultimately standards, for service-effort reporting and accomplishment reporting.

Another important issue introduced in this objective relates to costs of services information. Although the GASB does not appear to be leaning toward a business-type model for all activities, this concept identifies the potential need for costs of services data for comparative purposes.

The GASB appears to use a portion of the fourth objective to announce its intentions on the measurement focus for the new model expected to be implemented in the early 1990s. Chapter 2 of this publication includes a discussion of the current model and, as previously stated, chapter 16 briefly discusses changes proposed as part of the measurement focus and basis of accounting project.

Cash flow and other cash-related information are the focus of the fifth objective. If the proposed accounting model moves the operating statement away from a current financial resources measurement focus, the need for additional information related to the government's cash inflows and outflows increases significantly. Recent developments regarding a cash flow statement are reviewed in chapters 14 and 16.

The fifth objective also focuses on how the government entity's activities were financed. This information is of the type normally set forth in a statement of changes in financial position.

The sixth objective addresses the government's financial position. The primary issue is whether the government's financial position has "improved or deteriorated" as a result of the current year's operations. Although financial position currently is measured at the fund and fund-type levels, the GASB may explore further aggregation to supplement these measures and to provide an overview of the financial position of the government as a whole.

The government's ability to raise resources through the issuance of debt and the ability to tax its citizens is discussed as part of the seventh objective. The GASB user needs survey identified support for providing additional information on tax resources (e.g., property tax, sales tax), tax burden (e.g., overlapping tax rates), tax limitations (i.e., caps) and debt limitations (i.e., legal debt margin). Some of this information currently is presented in annual financial reports. The placement of the disclosures may be the only issue in these instances.

In addition, this objective may provide the basis for the introduction of a classified balance sheet, as the GASB does make reference to "current and noncurrent" resources and obligations. Continued emphasis on debt and its impact on the future (e.g., debt service to maturity schedules) also is included in this basic objective.

Capital assets are the focus of the eighth objective. The GASB's explanation of the objective specifically identified both the service potential of capital assets and the government's short- and long-term capital requirements as needed information. In its capital assets project, the GASB is examining several issues in an effort to address the needs of report users for information on capital assets.

The final basic objective is a combination of objectives. Disclosures of legal and contractual restrictions are an integral part of the current accounting and financial reporting model (e.g. funds, restricted assets, fund balance reserves) and are expected to continue in the future. Disclosure of the potential loss of resources can be viewed from two separate aspects. The potential loss of accumulated resources is being addressed in part by the GASB's risk management project. The other potential loss that could occur is with the reduction or elimination of certain resources in the future.

These objectives have been established to guide the GASB in the future. The GASB is continually reviewing its proposed pronouncements to determine if they are in keeping with the basic concepts of the objectives. At the same time, these objectives are not considered to be static. Changes are to be expected as user needs change or as the need for additional financial reporting information emerges.

Chapter 2
PRINCIPLES OF GOVERNMENTAL ACCOUNTING AND FINANCIAL REPORTING

SOURCES OF GAAP

Any discussion of governmental accounting and financial reporting principles should begin with the source of those principles. As noted in chapter 1, *Governmental Accounting, Auditing and Financial Reporting (GAAFR)* has evolved in conjunction with governmental accounting principles.

Formal standard setting in the governmental accounting and financial reporting arena began in 1934 with the National Committee on Municipal Accounting and has evolved through the establishment of the Governmental Accounting Standards Board (GASB) in June 1984. The GASB, like its private-sector counterpart, the Financial Accounting Standards Board (FASB), functions under the auspices of the Financial Accounting Foundation (FAF). The GASB was established in accordance with an *Agreement Concerning the Structure for a Governmental Accounting Standards Board* (structural agreement), presented in the GASB's *Rules of Procedure,* which sets forth the relative jurisdictions of the two boards.

The structural agreement clearly establishes the GASB as the primary accounting and financial reporting standard-setting body for state and local governments. Moreover, the American Institute of Certified Public Accountants (AICPA) reaffirmed the GASB's authority by designating the GASB as the "body to establish financial accounting principles for state and local governmental entities," pursuant to the AICPA's Ethics Rule 203.

ACCOUNTING PRINCIPLES

The structural agreement defines the GASB's jurisdiction:

The GASB will establish standards for activities and transactions of state and local governmental entities, and the FASB will establish standards for activities and transactions of all other entities.

Separately issued financial statements of certain units in the public sector (e.g., utilities, hospitals, colleges and universities), prepared in accordance with generally accepted accounting principles (GAAP), should be guided by FASB standards unless the GASB has issued a pronouncement applicable to such units. To clarify the status of individual GASB statements and interpretations for these units, the GASB has incorporated application language into its pronouncements.

The structural agreement also establishes guidelines on defining GAAP for financial statements issued by state and local government units, including those entities previously noted (see Illustration 2–1). The "hierarchy" of GAAP established by that agreement is outlined below:

Category 1   Pronouncements of the GASB, as well as statements and interpretations of the National Council on Governmental Accounting (NCGA) adopted by the GASB.

Category 2   Pronouncements of the FASB applicable to transactions or events not addressed in category 1 literature. In addition, the standards established by the Accounting Principles Board (APB) and the Committee on Accounting Procedure (i.e., FASB's predecessor bodies) often apply to state and local government units. These standards include the APB's Opinions and the Committee on Accounting Procedure's Accounting Research Bulletins (ARB).

Category 3   Pronouncements of bodies composed of expert accountants (e.g., AICPA) that follow a due-process procedure. This category of literature includes audit and accounting guides and statements of position (SOP) issued by the AICPA. Due process normally is accomplished through the broad distribution of a proposed standard (e.g., exposure draft) for public comment. The 1986 revision of the AICPA's *Audits of State and Local Governmental Units (ASLGU)* is a prominent example of category 3 literature. The 1986 *ASLGU* establishes accounting principles and describes existing practices. This category also includes technical bulletins issued by the GASB and FASB staffs.

Category 4   Practices or pronouncements that are widely recognized as being generally accepted because they represent prevalent practice in a particular industry or the knowledgeable application of pronouncements to specific circumstances. This category includes studies of current practice that incorporate data regarding the treatment of specific transactions.

ILLUSTRATION 2–1

Hierarchy of Government GAAP

	GASB	NCGA	FASB	AICPA	GFOA	OTHERS
CATEGORY 1	Statements Interpretations	Statements Interpretations				
CATEGORY 2			Statements Interpretations	APB Opinions ARB Bulletins		
CATEGORY 3	Technical Bulletins		Technical Bulletins	Industry audit guides Industry accounting guides Statements of position		
CATEGORY 4				Accounting intrepretations		Recognized and prevalent industry practices or pronouncements
CATEGORY 5	Concepts Statements Action Report	Concepts Statement	Concepts Statements Status Report	APB Statements Issues papers	1988 GAAFR GAAFR Review Accounting Topics Series Financial Reporting Series	Textbooks Articles

Category 5 Other accounting literature encompassing a vast array of documents, including this publication and other textbooks and articles.

Authoritative guidance on the application of GAAP for state and local governments can be categorized within the 12 basic principles set forth in the GASB's 1987 *Codification of Governmental Accounting and Financial Reporting Standards* (1987 *Codification*).

Principle 1—Accounting and Reporting Capabilities. The first principle, *Accounting and Reporting Capabilities* (1987 *Codification,* Section 1100.101), serves as a foundation for the 11 remaining principles:

A governmental accounting system must make it possible both: (a) to present fairly and with full disclosure the financial position and results of financial operations of the funds and account groups of the governmental unit in conformity with generally accepted accounting principles, and (b) to determine and demonstrate compliance with finance-related legal and contractual provisions.

The need to determine and demonstrate legal compliance should be considered in the design and implementation of any government's accounting system. Many of the individual control procedures integrated into a government's accounting system are designed primarily to ensure compliance with legal and contractual provisions.

A government's accounting system should allow the government to comply with legal and contractual provisions and either prepare reports in conformity with GAAP or compile GAAP-conversion information within the system at year end. If a GAAP-conversion approach is used, selected data are collected to adjust non-GAAP (e.g., cash, budgetary) information to determined GAAP amounts.

Since the issuance of NCGA Statement 1, *Governmental Accounting and Financial Reporting Principles,* in 1979, there has been a movement in some states toward a closer alignment of those principles on which budgets are prepared and accounting systems are maintained with GAAP. Although authoritative literature encourages governments to design accounting systems based on GAAP, the standards also stress the principle that GAAP and legal or contractual considerations are both essential. Therefore, GAAP and legal or contractual considerations are not mutually exclusive. Budgets can be prepared, and accounting systems maintained, on a basis that differs from GAAP, as long as GAAP-basis financial reports are issued by the government.

As noted previously, an integral part of GAAP in the government environment is the demonstration of compliance with legal and contractual provisions. Most governments now face the issue of demonstrating compliance with an ever-increasing number of legal and contractual requirements. Indeed, with the increase in these compliance requirements the preparation of a separate legal- or contractual-basis report may be necessary in certain cases.

Principles 2 through 4—Fund Accounting. As previously discussed in chapter 1, governmental accounting systems are established on a fund basis. Specifically, principle two, *Fund Accounting Systems* (1987 *Codification,* Section 1300), provides:

Governmental accounting systems should be organized and operated on a fund basis. A fund is defined as a fiscal and accounting entity with a self-balancing set of accounts recording cash and other financial resources, together with all related liabilities and residual equities or balances, and changes therein, which are segregated for the purpose of carrying on specific activities or attaining certain objectives in accordance with special regulations, restrictions, or limitations.

Funds used in the government model are classified into three broad categories: governmental, proprietary and fiduciary. These funds are supplemented in the model by account groups. Account groups are self-balancing groups of accounts established to account for general fixed assets and unmatured general long-term debt not reported in the funds. Two account groups are provided for in this model: the general fixed assets account group (GFAAG) and the general long-term debt account group (GLTDAG).

The governmental fund category includes activities usually associated with a typical state or local government's operations (e.g., public safety, public health). The focus (i.e., what is being measured) of the funds within this category is on the measurement of the sources and uses (i.e., flow) of current financial resources. This measurement focus is unique in that generally only current expendable financial resources are accounted for in the governmental fund category. Therefore, the flow of current financial resources measurement focus requires the use of account groups to account for noncurrent or nonfinancial resources such as general fixed assets and unmatured general long-term liabilities.

The proprietary fund category often emulates the private sector. Activities found in this category are many times seen in the private sector and are operated in a manner similar to their counterparts in the commercial world. Because of the nature of the operations accounted for in this category, the measurement focus prescribed for proprietary funds is based on the commercial model, which uses a flow of economic resources approach. With this approach, the focus of the proprietary funds is on the measurement of net income (e.g., revenues, expenses). This measurement focus allows the proprietary funds to report all assets and liabilities associated with an activity.

The fiduciary fund category shares similar characteristics with both the governmental and proprietary fund types. However, this category was created for situations in which the government is acting in a fiduciary capacity as a trustee or agent (i.e., in these situations the government usually is acting directly on behalf of another party). Although the fiduciary funds are distinct, they share common features with both the proprietary and governmental categories. Accordingly, the measurement focus more closely associated with the related activity is used for the fiduciary funds.

Fund Types. The three broad fund categories are subdivided into seven fund types for accounting and financial reporting purposes in principle three (1987 *Codification,* Section 1300.104):

a. **Governmental Funds**
   (1) *The General Fund*—to account for all financial resources except those required to be accounted for in another fund.

   (2) *Special Revenue Funds*—to account for the proceeds of specific revenue sources (other than expendable trusts or for major capital projects) that are legally restricted to expenditure for specified purposes.
   (3) *Capital Projects Funds*—to account for financial resources to be used for the acquisition or construction of major capital facilities (other than those financed by proprietary funds and trust funds).
   (4) *Debt Service Funds*—to account for the accumulation of resources for, and the payment of, general long-term debt principal and interest.
   [*Special Assessment Funds*—discontinued for GAAP reporting purposes.]

b. **Proprietary Funds**
   (1) *Enterprise Funds*—to account for operations (a) that are financed and operated in a manner similar to private business enterprises—where the intent of the governing body is that the costs (expenses, including depreciation) of providing goods or services to the general public on a continuing basis be financed or recovered primarily through user charges; or (b) where the governing body has decided that periodic determination of revenues earned, expenses incurred, and/or net income is appropriate for capital maintenance, public policy, management control, accountability, or other purposes.
   (2) *Internal Service Funds*—to account for the financing of goods or services provided by one department or agency to other departments or agencies of the governmental unit, or to other governmental units, on a cost-reimbursement basis.

c. **Fiduciary Funds**
   (1) *Trust and Agency Funds*—to account for assets held by a governmental unit in a trustee capacity or as an agent for individuals, private organizations, other governmental units, and/or other funds. These include (a) expendable trust funds, (b) nonexpendable trust funds, (c) pension trust funds, and (d) agency funds

Number of Funds. The "number of funds" principle (1987 *Codification,* Section 1300) provides general guidance in determining how many funds should be used by a government:

Governmental units should establish and maintain those funds required by law and sound financial administration. Only the minimum number of funds consistent with legal and operating requirements should be established, however, because unnecessary funds result in inflexibility, undue complexity, and inefficient financial administration.

The general fund of most units accounts for the basic operating functions of a government. The 1987 *Codification,* Section 1300.106, provides that the definition of the general fund precludes the reporting of multiple general funds. Therefore, governments should use only one general fund for financial reporting purposes.

A common fund classification approach, often successfully applied in practice, calls for all activities to be accounted for in the general fund unless specifically required by law or GAAP to be accounted for in another fund. However, if an activity is legally mandated to be reported in a separate fund, the use of a special revenue fund should be considered. Also in certain circumstances (e.g., inability to account for grant revenues separately in the general fund), sound financial administration may require the use of a special revenue fund even when it is not legally required.

As financial accounting systems become more effective in controlling revenues and expenditures for specific activities without the use of separate funds, the use of special revenue funds is expected to diminish. General and special revenue funds are discussed further in chapter 3.

Debt service funds should be used if they are legally mandated and/or if financial resources are being accumulated for principal and interest payments maturing in future years.

In 1987, the GASB released GASB Statement No. 6, *Accounting and Financial Reporting for Special Assessments,* which eliminates the special assessment fund type for GAAP reporting purposes. The provisions of GASB Statement No. 6 are effective for periods beginning after June 15, 1987. This pronouncement, as incorporated into the 1987 *Codification,* Section S40.115, states:

> If the government is obligated in some manner to assume the payment of related debt service in the event of default by the property owners . . . transactions of the debt service phase should be reported in a debt service fund, if one is required . . .

Chapter 4 addresses the repayment of certain special assessment debt and other issues associated with debt service funds.

The acquisition or construction of major general government capital facilities (e.g., administrative buildings) should be accounted for in a capital projects fund. As with the debt service fund, the GASB recently expanded the scope of this fund type to include certain special assessment activities. The 1987 *Codification,* Sections S40.115 and S40.119, provides that the construction phase of a capital improvement financed by special assessment debt should, in most instances, be reported in a capital projects fund. Chapter 5 provides a detailed discussion of all capital projects fund activities.

Enterprise funds should account for activities in which goods and/or services are provided to the general public in a manner similar to that found in the private sector. Generally, there is a direct relationship between the benefit received by the customer and the fee charged by the government. Chapter 8 provides a complete discussion of enterprise fund activities.

Internal service funds also are operated in a manner similar to that in the private sector. However, internal service funds differ from enterprise funds in that the customer base is generally the government itself (e.g., other departments, agencies) and the activities normally are operated on a break-even or cost-reimbursement basis. Internal service funds are discussed in chapter 9.

The fiduciary funds are divided into four subclassifications: expendable trust, nonexpendable trust, pension trust and agency. Of the three trust fund subclassifications, the expendable trust is associated most closely with government activities. Generally, what distinguishes an expendable trust fund from a special revenue fund is a formal trust agreement. When trust agreements provide governments with the flexibility of using both the trust principal or corpus and interest in the course of normal operations, the activities should be classified in the expendable trust funds subclassification. These operations are measured using the flow of current financial resources measurement focus.

Activities associated with trust agreements that restrict governments from using the principal or corpus in the normal course of operations should be classified in the nonexpendable trust subclassification. Because these funds are created to maintain trust principal, the focus of operations is on the measurement of economic resources. Pension trust funds, used to account for public employee retirement systems that are a part of the government reporting entity, share the flow of economic resources measurement focus with nonexpendable trust funds.

Agency funds should be used to account for activities in which the government is acting in an agent capacity for some other organization, government, individual or fund. Agency funds are purely custodial in nature (i.e., assets equal liabilities) and thus do not focus on the measurement of operations.

Trust and agency funds are discussed in chapter 10.

Principles 5 through 7—Fixed Assets and Long-term Liabilities. Accounting for fixed assets and long-term liabilities is affected directly by the flow of current financial resources measurement focus model used for governmental funds. Likewise, the proprietary funds model also affects the reporting of long-term assets and liabilities with its flow of economic resources measurement focus.

Principle five, *Accounting for Fixed Assets and Long-term Liabilities* (1987 *Codification,* Section 1100.105), states:

> A clear distinction should be made between (a) fund fixed assets and general fixed assets and (b) fund long-term liabilities and general long-term debt.
> a. Fixed assets related to specific proprietary funds or trust funds should be accounted for through those funds. All other fixed assets of a governmental unit should be accounted for through the general fixed assets account group.
> b. Long-term liabilities of proprietary funds and trust funds should be accounted for through those funds. All other unmatured general long-term liabilities of the governmental unit . . . should be accounted for through the general long-term debt account group.

This principle introduces the concept of fund assets and liabilities. The proprietary and trust funds report all assets and liabilities within the individual funds; however, governmental funds, with their current financial resources measurement focus, generally report only current assets and liabilities.

Therefore, the primary purpose of accounting for governmental funds is to reflect the sources and uses of their current expendable financial resources (e.g., revenues, expenditures, other financing sources and other financing uses) and their assets, related liabilities and net current financial resources available for subsequent appropriation and expenditure.

Fixed Assets. All fixed assets, including infrastructure, used in proprietary fund activities or associated with trust funds should be accounted for through those respective funds. All other fixed assets are classified as general fixed assets, including those acquired under governmental fund capital leases. However, public domain or infrastructure assets are *not* required to be reported in the GFAAG.

Authoritative guidance (1987 *Codification,* Section 1400.109) provides that general government infrastructure assets (e.g., roads, bridges, sidewalks, lighting systems) that are immovable and of value only to the government are not required to be reported in the GFAAG. Because of this optional treatment, many governments have not reported infrastructure general fixed assets. However, the 1987 *Codification*, Section 1400.109, requires that appropriate legal and descriptive records be maintained for *all* fixed assets, including infrastructure. General fixed assets are discussed further in chapter 6.

Long-term Liabilities. Debt instruments and other long-term liabilities directly related to and expected to be paid from proprietary and trust funds should be reported in those funds as liabilities. These liabilities can include revenue bonds, general obligation bonds, capital leases, compensated absences, claims and judgments, and pension liabilities. Other unmatured long-term indebtedness of the government normally is general long-term debt and should be displayed in the GLTDAG.

What constitutes a liability that should be reported in the GLTDAG has been the subject of much debate. As originally defined, general long-term debt encompassed only the unmatured principal of debt instruments and other forms of noncurrent or long-term *general obligation* liabilities that were not specific liabilities of any proprietary or trust fund and were not current liabilities properly recorded in the governmental funds. The application of this definition has been modified somewhat in recent years. The other side of the government model equation, the basis of accounting which determines when a transaction should be recognized, should be reviewed to assess this issue adequately. Accordingly, discussion of both current liabilities and long-term liabilities will be continued in the basis of accounting section of this chapter.

Fixed Assets Valuation. The sixth principle, *Valuation of Fixed Assets* (1987 *Codification*, Section 1400), states:

> Fixed assets should be accounted for at cost or, if the cost is not practicably determinable, at estimated cost. Donated fixed assets should be recorded at their estimated fair value at the time received.

Determining the cost of fixed assets also is affected by their classification. All fixed assets should be reported based on the consideration given or received, including ancillary charges, whichever can more objectively be determined. Normal ancillary charges include freight and transportation charges, closing costs, title and legal fees and installation charges. However, the ancillary charges beyond the construction costs for certain assets reported in the proprietary or trust funds must include capitalized interest. The effect of required capitalization of interest for proprietary and trust funds, based on FASB Statement of Financial Accounting Standards (SFAS) No. 34, *Capitalization of Interest* and SFAS No. 62, *Capitalization of Interest Cost in Situations Involving Certain Tax-Exempt Borrowings and Certain Gifts and Grants*, is discussed in chapter 8. However, the guidance provided in the 1987 *Codification*, Section 1400.111, and the objectives of SFAS No. 34 appear to support the optional treatment of interest capitalization on general fixed assets.

If the historical cost of fixed assets cannot be determined because of the lack of adequate fixed asset records, other appropriate methods may be employed to estimate their original historical cost. Acceptable estimation methods are explored further in chapter 6.

Depreciation. The seventh principle, *Depreciation of Fixed Assets* (1987 *Codification*, Section 1400), provides:

> a. Depreciation of general fixed assets should not be recorded in the accounts of governmental funds. Depreciation of general fixed assets may be recorded in cost accounting systems or calculated for cost finding analyses; and accumulated depreciation may be recorded in the general fixed assets account group.
> b. Depreciation of fixed assets accounted for in a proprietary fund should be recorded in the accounts of that fund. Depreciation is also recognized in those trust funds where expenses, net income, and/or capital maintenance is measured.

Again, the measurement focus used for governmental funds plays an important role with this principle. Depreciation is an allocation of the net costs of the fixed asset over its estimated useful life. Depreciation expense is a measure of the exhaustion of economic resources. It has no effect on the flow of current financial resources measurement focus used for the governmental funds because it neither provides financial resources nor requires the use of financial resources. This distinction is one of the fundamental differences between the models for the governmental and proprietary funds. The cost of a fixed asset is allocated systematically and rationally to the period in which the asset is used within the flow of economic resources model. The flow of current financial resources model, however, measures the financial resources used in the acquisition of a fixed asset as an expenditure and measures any financial resources provided when the asset is disposed as an other financing source.

Principle 8—Basis of Accounting. In addition to the measurement focus, the other major element in the current model is introduced in principle eight, *Accrual Basis in Governmental Accounting* (1987 *Codification*, Section 1600). This principle states:

> The modified accrual or accrual basis of accounting, as appropriate, should be used in measuring financial position and operating results.
> a. *Governmental fund* revenues and expenditures should be recognized on the modified accrual basis. Revenues should be recognized in the accounting period in which they become available and measurable. Expenditures should be recognized in the accounting period in which the fund liability is incurred, if measurable, except for unmatured interest on general long-term debt, which should be recognized when due.
> b. *Proprietary fund* revenues and expenses should be recognized on the accrual basis. Revenues should be recognized in the accounting period in which they are earned and become measurable; expenses should be recognized in the period incurred, if measurable.
> c. *Fiduciary fund* revenues and expenses or expenditures (as appropriate) should be recognized on the basis consistent with the fund's accounting measurement objective. Nonexpendable trust and pension trust funds should be accounted for on the accrual basis; expendable trust funds should be accounted for on the modified accrual basis. Agency fund assets and liabilities should be accounted for on the modified accrual basis.
> d. *Transfers* should be recognized in the accounting pe-

ILLUSTRATION 2-2

Fund Accounting Summary

Fund Type	Fund Category	Measurement Focus	Basis of Accounting
General	Governmental	Flow of current financial resources	Modified accrual
Special Revenue	Governmental	Flow of current financial resources	Modified accrual
Debt Service	Governmental	Flow of current financial resources	Modified accrual
Capital Projects	Governmental	Flow of current financial resources	Modified accrual
Enterprise	Proprietary	Flow of economic resources	Accrual
Internal Service	Proprietary	Flow of economic resources	Accrual
Trust and Agency:	Fiduciary		
Expendable Trust		Flow of current financial resources	Modified accrual
Nonexpendable Trust		Flow of economic resources	Accrual
Pension Trust		Flow of economic resources	Accrual
Agency		Not applicable	Modified accrual

riod in which the interfund receivable and payable arise.

Illustration 2-2 summarizes the measurement focus and basis of accounting applied to each fund type.

Governmental Funds—Revenue Recognition. Governmental fund revenues should be recognized when they become measurable and available. Although measurability is a factor that affects all transactions, the availability criterion is unique to the governmental fund model. The 1987 *Codification*, Section 1600.106, states " 'Available' means collectible within the current period or soon enough thereafter to be used to pay liabilities of the current period."

The meaning of the phrase "soon enough thereafter" has been subject to debate. In practice, this provision has been interpreted as meaning one year, 90 days, 60 days and even zero days (i.e., cash basis accounting). Different availability periods also have been applied to various revenue sources. The different time applications of the available criterion for property taxes led to the issuance of NCGA Interpretation 3, *Revenue Recognition—Property Taxes*. Incorporated into the 1987 *Codification*, Section P70.103, the guidance for property taxes provides:

Available means then due, or past due and receivable within the current period, and collected within the current period or expected to be collected soon enough thereafter to be used to pay liabilities of the current period. Such time thereafter should not exceed 60 days.

Although the 60-day period has been applied by some governments to all governmental fund revenue sources, another pronouncement embodied in GAAP, AICPA Statement of Position 75-3, *Accrual of Revenues and Expenditures by State and Local Governmental Units*, establishes a different period for certain revenue sources (i.e., income taxes, sales taxes). The guidance for these revenue sources is reviewed in chapter 3.

Governmental Funds—Expenditure Recognition. Governmental fund expenditures should be recognized in the accounting period in which the *fund* liability is incurred, if measurable.

As noted previously, the question of what is a fund liability has been addressed in several authoritative pronouncements related to specific issues, but has never received general attention from an authoritative body. These pronouncements introduce the concept that expenditure recognition includes amounts that normally would be "liquidated with expendable available financial resources." This concept is explained further in chapter 3.

The primary exception to the general rule of expenditure accrual relates to unmatured principal and interest on general obligation long-term debt. The 1987 *Codification*, Section 1600.121, provides:

Financial resources usually are appropriated in other funds for transfer to a debt service fund in the period in which maturing debt principal and interest must be paid. Such amounts thus are not current liabilities of the debt service fund as their settlement will not require expenditure of existing fund assets. Further, to accrue the debt service fund expenditure and liability in one period but record the transfer of financial resources for debt service purposes in a later period would be confusing and would result in overstatement of debt service fund expenditures and liabilities and understatement of the fund balance. Thus, disclosure of subsequent year debt service requirements is appropriate, but they usually are appropriately accounted for as expenditures in the year of payment. On the other hand, if debt service fund resources have been provided during the current year for payment of principal and interest due early in the following year, the expenditure and related liability may be recognized in the debt service fund and the debt principal amount removed from the GLTDAG.

Proprietary Funds—Revenue Recognition. The underlying concept for recognizing revenue of proprietary funds currently is provided in FASB Statement of Financial Accounting Concepts (SFAC) No. 5, *Recognition and Measurement in Financial Statements of Business Enterprises*. The criteria used with proprietary fund revenue recognition require that the revenues be both realized or realizable and earned. The most difficult issue associated with proprietary fund revenue is classification (e.g., operating, nonoperating). Classification is discussed in chapter 14.

Proprietary Fund—Expense Recognition. As with revenue recognition, SFAC No. 5 provides the conceptual foundation for the proprietary fund expense recognition criteria. Expenses generally are recognized when economic benefits are used in providing goods or services. Again, the classification issue (e.g., operating, nonoperating) is a primary consideration when expense issues are discussed.

Principle 9—The Budget and Budgetary Accounting. Principle nine, *Budgeting, Budgetary Control, and Budgetary Reporting* (1987 *Codification*, Section 1100.109), provides:

a. An annual budget(s) should be adopted by every governmental unit.
b. The accounting system should provide the basis for appropriate budgetary control.
c. Budgetary comparisons should be included in the appropriate financial statements and schedules for governmental funds for which an annual budget has been adopted.

Budgeting. Budgeting is an essential element of the financial planning, control and evaluation processes of governments. Indeed, the 1987 *Codification*, Section 100.119, states "Many believe the budget is the most significant financial document produced by a governmental entity."

The importance of budgeting in the government environment has been a controversial subject over the years. Budgeting is addressed in the authoritative standards in a manner that goes beyond providing guidance in accounting and financial reporting. Although authoritative standards now provide that the scope and method of state and local government budgetary practices are outside the scope of financial reporting standards, the original budgetary recommendations have not been rescinded.

The 1987 *Codification*, Section 1700.101, specifically provides, "Every governmental unit should prepare a comprehensive budget covering all governmental, proprietary, and fiduciary funds for each annual (or, in some states, biennial) fiscal period." This comprehensive budget can be developed by using a number of budgetary approaches.

A general fund budget generally is developed each year. It follows the normal budgetary procedures in which departments and/or agencies submit requests to the chief executive or budget office; an executive budget is prepared and submitted to the legislative body; and the legislative body acts on the budget through the passage of appropriation bills or ordinances. These bills or ordinances may be subject to subsequent executive veto or amendatory veto. However, when signed into law, they establish revenue, expenditure/expense and obligation authority. In addition, this authority may be extended to budgetary execution and management in the form of allotments, suballocations, contingency reserves, encumbrance controls and transfers.

If the general fund budget is subject to the normal annual budgetary process, it is classified as an appropriated budget. The 1987 *Codification*, Section 1700.114, defines an appropriated budget:

The expenditure authority created by the appropriation bills or ordinances that are signed into law and related estimated revenues. The appropriated budget would include all reserves, transfers, allocations, supplemental appropriations, and other legally authorized legislative and executive changes.

Special revenue funds generally follow an identical process, although some differences may exist. For example, a budget associated with a grant may fall outside the category of an annual appropriated budget for several reasons. One possibility is that the grant may extend beyond the fiscal year, in which case a long-term (e.g., grant-length) budget may be approved by the legislative body. Also, in certain situations the grant document itself may serve as a financial plan for budgetary purposes. A plan of this type is referred to as a nonappropriated budget. The 1987 *Codification*, Section 1700.114 defines a nonappropriated budget:

A financial plan for an organization, program, activity, or function approved in a manner authorized by constitution, charter, statute, or ordinance but not subject to appropriation and therefore outside the boundaries of the definition of "appropriated budget."

Although certain special revenue funds may not require the appropriation process or are subject to alternative budgetary methods, as noted above, it appears that most special revenue fund budgets are adopted annually.

Debt service funds also may be subject to the annual appropriation process. However, legal or contractual provisions sometimes serve as a surrogate. Bond indentures often require specific payments to and from the debt service fund each year and transfers are budgeted in the general fund to comply with this provision. Some believe that the indenture and general fund appropriation supply adequate controls over the debt service transactions; therefore, annual appropriations are not considered necessary. If tax revenues are deposited directly in the debt service funds or if the fund receives resources directly from another source, annual appropriations are considered appropriate. Further, in some circumstances, statutes or ordinances may require an annual appropriated budget even when resources are received through transfers.

Capital projects funds may be subject to either annual or long-term (i.e., project-length) budgets. Long-term budgets associated with capital outlays and the method of financing those plans sometimes are referred to as capital budgets. These budgets generally are adopted for a period of more than one year, and many extend from two to ten years, depending on the complexity of the projects. These capital budgets may be legally adopted.

Annual budgets usually are prepared for proprietary funds because of the nature of their operating cycle. Unlike governmental fund budgets which generally are limited to fixed-dollar amounts, proprietary fund budgets may be flexible budgets or financial plans, based on several levels of activity. Flexible budgets are viewed by many as the appropriate control device in a private-sector-oriented environment. However, governments that adopt annual appropriated budgets generally retain the fixed-dollar amount feature in proprietary fund annual budgets.

Annual appropriated budgets are not commonplace for fiduciary funds although some governments adopt annual budgets for expendable, nonexpendable and pension trust fund administrative activities. Because of their custodial nature, agency funds generally are not subject to the budgetary process.

Budget to GAAP Differences. The 1987 *Codification,* Section 1700.117, provides:

> Preparation of the budget on the cash basis or another basis not consistent with generally accepted accounting principles (GAAP) complicates financial management and reporting. Where legal requirements dictate another basis, governmental units typically (a) maintain the accounts and prepare budgetary reports on the legally prescribed budgetary basis to determine and to demonstrate legal compliance, and (b) maintain sufficient supplemental records to permit presentation of financial statements in conformity with GAAP.

Many governments adopt annual budgets in conformity with GAAP for both governmental and proprietary funds. However, other governments adopt their annual budget on a basis different from GAAP. Because of the nature of budgeting, several common types of differences between budget and GAAP have been identified in practice. These differences are classified into four categories in the 1987 *Codification,* Sections 2400.114–.120: basis, timing, perspective and entity differences.

Basis differences arise when the cash basis or another basis that differs from GAAP is used for budgetary purposes. This type of difference may result from such factors as the budgetary treatment of encumbrances as expenditures, which are not reported as GAAP expenditures; the failure to recognize expenditures at the inception of a capital lease, as required by GAAP; the recognition of tax or revenue anticipation note proceeds as an other financing source for budgetary purposes, a practice prohibited for GAAP reporting purposes, and the adoption of a proprietary fund budget using the modified accrual (non-GAAP) basis of accounting.

Timing differences may result from the adoption of long-term capital budgets and grant-length budgets and the use of a lapse period that extend the budgetary period beyond one year.

Perspective differences result from the adoption of a budgetary structure that differs from GAAP. A number of structure perspectives are used for budgetary purposes, including fund structure, organizational structure or program structure. Differences may arise with the continued adoption of a special assessment fund-type budget, for example, even though that fund type has been eliminated for GAAP reporting purposes.

Entity differences occur when budgets include or exclude organizations, programs, activities and functions that differ from the GAAP entity. This type of difference occurs primarily when a government does not adopt a budget for each fund within a particular fund type or incorporates a component unit that does not adopt an annual appropriated budget.

As discussed in chapter 14, these differences should be reconciled for financial reporting purposes.

Budgetary Control. When an annual appropriated budget is adopted by the legislative body and subsequently signed into law it carries with it maximum expenditure authorizations that cannot be exceeded legally. This limitation level generally is established in a separate budgetary statute or ordinance. However, individual appropriated budgets also may establish the legal level of control. The level at which expenditures legally are controlled varies widely in practice, but the department or agency level is common. At this level, a department or agency head can be held accountable for expenditures incurred without subjecting the department or agency to undue constraints. Other control levels may be established at the function level, fund level or even the fund-type level, where little actual control is exercised. At the other end of the spectrum, controls can be established legally at the department's division level or even at the object level within a department's division. These methods, while creating a high level of assurance that monies are being spent in conformance with legislative intent, provide management with little flexibility.

To ensure budgetary compliance, annual appropriated budgets should be integrated formally into the accounting system. The 1987 *Codification,* Section 1700.119, states:

ILLUSTRATION 2–3

Combined Estimated Revenues and Actual Revenues Subsidiary Ledger
Property Taxes

Account No. _____

Date	Explanation	Estimated Revenues DR	Estimated Revenues CR	Actual Revenues DR	Actual Revenues CR	Unrealized Revenues
Jan. 1	To record budget	$15,000				$15,000
Jan. 15	To record levy				$14,750	250
Dec. 31	To record revenue deferral			$ 250		500
Dec. 31	To close		$15,000	14,500		0
		$15,000	$15,000	$14,750	$14,750	$ 0

ILLUSTRATION 2–4

**Combined Appropriations, Encumbrances and Expenditures Subsidiary Ledger
Maintenance Supplies**

Account No. _____

Date	Explanation	Appropriation		Encumbrances		Expenditures		Unencumbered Balance
		DR	CR	DR	CR	DR	CR	
Jan. 1	To record budget		$2,000					$2,000
11	To record encumbrance			$ 900				1,100
14	To record goods received				$ 900	$ 900		1,100
21	To record encumbrances			1,000				100
22	To record goods received				1,000	950		150
24	To record encumbrances			100				50
31	To close	$2,000			100		$1,850	0
		$2,000	$2,000	$2,000	$2,000	$1,850	$1,850	$ 0

The extent to which budgetary accounts should be integrated in the formal accounting system varies among governmental fund types and according to the nature of fund transactions. Integration is essential in general, special revenue, and other annually budgeted governmental funds that have numerous types of revenues, expenditures, and transfers. Judgment should be used in other circumstances. For example, full or partial budgetary account integration would be essential where numerous construction projects are being financed through a capital projects fund or where such projects are being constructed by the government's labor force.

Illustration 2–3 and Illustration 2–4 present examples of formal budgetary integration for specific revenue and expenditure accounts.

The use of encumbrance accounting as an element of control in formal budgetary integration is widespread in the government sector. Encumbrances are defined in the 1987 *Codification,* Section 1700.129, as "commitments related to unperformed (executory) contracts for goods or services." Authoritative literature endorses the use of encumbrance accounting for general and special revenue funds; it also is used commonly in capital projects funds. Accounting for encumbrances often provides effective budgetary control and facilitates cash management.

In effect, an encumbrance accounting system acts as an early warning device. By controlling expenditure commitments, the government significantly reduces the opportunity to overexpend an appropriation. Even with its control advantages, encumbrances are not recorded for certain expenditures and are recorded only to a limited extent for others. For example, encumbrances normally are not used to control salary expenditures. These expenditures generally are fixed for the entire year and therefore are ascertainable in advance. Because of fixed salaries and other additional administrative and personnel controls (e.g., employment agreements), recording encumbrances for salaries generally is not considered necessary.

An unmodified encumbrance accounting system may prove

to be too much of a burden for other expenditure objects. For example, an encumbrance need not be established when an employee orders a box of pencils. Rather, blanket purchase orders with a maximum dollar limit may be issued and encumbered for small, routine supply purchases.

Because an encumbrance is only a commitment, it does not meet the expenditure or liability recognition criteria. Encumbrances outstanding at year end that do not lapse should be displayed as reservations of fund balance for subsequent years' expenditure. Encumbrances that lapse should be displayed either as a reservation of fund balance or disclosed in the notes to the financial statements if the government intends to honor the commitment.

In addition to encumbrances, the government may use allotments to control budgetary expenditures. Allotments are subdivisions of the appropriation that limit expenditures during a specified period of time (e.g., monthly, quarterly).

Budgetary Reporting. At a minimum, budgetary comparisons should be presented in the general purpose financial statements for governmental funds with annual appropriated budgets. These comparisons should be presented using the basis on which the budgets were adopted (e.g., cash). In addition, budgetary comparisons for all appropriated funds should be presented as individual statements or schedules to demonstrate legal compliance. Additional information on budgetary reporting is presented in chapter 14.

Principles 10 and 11—Classification and Terminology. Principle 10, *Transfer, Revenue, Expenditure, and Expense Account Classification* (1987 *Codification,* Section 1800), provides:

a. Interfund transfers and proceeds of general long-term debt issues should be classified separately from fund revenues and expenditures or expenses.

b. Governmental fund revenues should be classified by fund and source. Expenditures should be classified by fund, function (or program), organization unit, activity, character, and principal classes of objects.

c. Proprietary fund revenues and expenses should be classified in essentially the same manner as those of similar business organizations, functions, or activities.

Within the governmental model, several classifications have similar characteristics but entirely different meanings. For example, other financing sources should be distinguished from revenues and residual equity transfers in. To clarify this issue, the 1987 *Codification,* Section 1800, provides definitions of the various transaction classifications used in the governmental accounting and financial reporting model.

Governmental Funds—Revenues. The primary level of governmental fund revenue classification is by fund and source. Normally, the governmental funds recognize several sources of revenue, including taxes, licenses and permits, intergovernmental revenues, charges for services, fines and forfeits and miscellaneous revenues. Examples of specific sources within these classifications are presented in appendix C.

Governmental Funds—Expenditures. Several levels of classification are used to present governmental fund expenditure data. The major classifications are by fund, function (or program), organizational unit, activity, character and object class. The function level provides information for a group of related activities. Standard function classifications include general government, public safety, highways and streets, sanitation, health and welfare, culture and recreation, and education. These functions vary in importance and nature, based on the government's activities. If program budgets are adopted, program classifications may be used at this level.

The organizational-unit level corresponds to the government's organizational chart. This level of reporting is useful from both control and accountability perspectives. Organization directors not only are held accountable for performance of all activities assigned, but also may be legally responsible for compliance with the appropriated budget if the level of control is at the department or agency level.

Various performance measures can be evaluted at the activity level. By evaluating the economy and efficiency of an activity, government officials are in a better position to make decisions on important issues such as privatization.

The character classification is based primarily on the period the expenditures are expected to benefit. There are four major character classifications: current, capital outlay, debt service and intergovernmental. The current classification represents benefits for the current period; capital outlays represent benefits for the current and future periods; and debt service is presumably for prior, current and future benefits. Intergovernmental expenditures represent transfers of resources to another government unit outside the reporting entity.

The object classification is a grouping of types of items purchased or services obtained. For example, operating expenditures could include personal services, contractual services and commodities.

Proprietary Funds—Revenues. The proprietary funds share the same primary revenue classifications as the governmental funds—by source. One important distinction is that governments also should look to similar business organizations for industry practice and other guidance in classifying proprietary fund revenue sources.

Proprietary Funds—Expenses. Expenses of proprietary funds also should be classified in a logical manner consistent with industry practices and standards. Emphasis should be placed on displaying a cost of sales/services amount and the appropriate display of operating and nonoperating expenses. As previously noted, classification issues associated with operating vs. nonoperating revenues/expenses are discussed in chapter 14.

Interfund Transactions. Transactions between funds can be classified within three broad categories. The first category includes "quasi-external" transactions that are reported as revenues or expenditures/expenses for both the fund and the government as a whole. The 1987 *Codification,* Section 1800.103, defines quasi-external interfund transactions:

> Transactions that would be treated as revenues, expenditures, or expenses if they involved organizations *external* to the governmental unit—for example, payments in lieu of taxes from an enterprise fund to the general fund; internal service fund billings to departments; routine employer contributions from the general fund to a pension trust fund; and routine service charges for inspection, engineering, utilities, or similar services provided by a department financed from one fund to a department financed from another fund—should be accounted for as revenues, expenditures, or expenses in the funds involved.

The second category includes transactions that should be reflected only once for the government as a whole. These transactions are referred to as reimbursements. The 1987 *Codification,* Section 1800.113, defines reimbursements:

> Transactions that constitute reimbursements of a fund for expenditures or expenses initially made from it that are properly applicable to another fund—for example, an expenditure properly chargeable to a special revenue fund was initially made from the general fund, which is subsequently reimbursed—should be recorded as expenditures or expenses (as appropriate) in the reimbursing fund and as reductions of the expenditure or expense in the fund that is reimbursed.

A reimbursement should result only from improper classification or clearing-account payments made for expediency in a controlled environment. A reimbursement should not be used to disguise an interfund loan to a fund with inadequate resources at the time of the transaction, nor should it be confused with an interfund transfer.

The final category includes all interfund transactions except for loans, advances, quasi-external transactions and reimbursements. These transactions, referred to as interfund transfers, are divided into two major categories: residual equity transfers and operating transfers. The 1987 *Codification,* Section 1800.106, defines residual equity transfers:

> Nonrecurring or nonroutine transfers of equity between funds—for example, contribution of enterprise fund or internal service fund capital by the general fund, subsequent return of all or part of such contribution to the general fund, and transfers of residual balances of discontinued funds to the general fund or a debt service fund.

Residual equity transfers should be reported as additions to or deductions from beginning fund balance in governmental funds. Proprietary funds should present residual equity transfers in as additions to contributed capital. Similar transfers from proprietary funds should be reported as reductions of the proprietary fund contributed capital if the transfers represent a return or disposition of the contributed capital or of retained earnings, if appropriate. Care should be taken not to confuse the infusion or return of capital with subsidies (i.e., operating transfers). Generally, if amounts are regularly transferred to or from a proprietary fund, the transactions should not be classified as residual equity transfers. In addition, a government cannot "return" capital from a proprietary fund to a governmental fund when the original contribution was not transferred from the governmental fund. However, distribution of discontinued funds' remaining balances should be reported as a residual equity transfer, regardless of the original source of capital.

The 1987 *Codification*, Section 1800.106, defines operating transfers:

All other interfund transfers—for example, legally authorized transfers from a fund receiving revenue to the fund through which the resources are to be expended, transfers of tax revenues from a special revenue fund to a debt service fund, transfers from the general fund to a special revenue or capital projects fund, operating subsidy transfers from the general or a special revenue fund to an enterprise fund, and transfers from an enterprise fund other than payments in lieu of taxes to finance general fund expenditures.

Governmental Funds—Long-term Debt Issue Proceeds and Extinguishments. Accounting for long-term debt proceeds was relatively straightforward until the recent influx of new debt instruments. The 1987 *Codification*, Sections 1800.109–.112 addresses traditional and contemporary issue proceeds as follows:

Proceeds of long-term debt issues not recorded as fund liabilities—for example, proceeds of bonds or notes expended through capital projects or debt service funds—normally should be reflected as "other financing sources" in the operating statement of the recipient fund. Such proceeds should be reported in captions such as "bond issue proceeds" or "proceeds of long-term notes." The proceeds of a special assessment issue for which the government is *not* obligated in any manner should be identified by a description other than "bond proceeds". . .

For advance refundings resulting in defeasance of debt reported in the GLTDAG, the proceeds of the new debt should be reported as an "other financing source—proceeds of refunding bonds" in the fund receiving the proceeds. Payments to the escrow agent from resources provided by the new debt should be reported as an "other financing use—payment to refunded bond escrow agent." Payments to the escrow agent made from other resources of the entity should be reported as debt service expenditures.

As required by [1987 *Codification*] Section D30, "Demand Bonds," if certain conditions are not met when demand bonds are issued, the liability for those bonds should be reported as a liability of the fund used to account for the proceeds of the bond issue. If those conditions change and it is necessary to report a fund liability for demand bonds previously reported as general long-term debt, the liability should be recorded as a liability of the fund in which the proceeds of the issue were initially recorded with a corresponding debit to "other financing uses." Redemptions of demand bonds reported as fund liabilities should be reported as a credit to "other financing sources."

When a capital lease represents the acquisition or construction of a general fixed asset in accordance with [1987 *Codification*] Section L20, "Leases," the acquisition or construction of the general fixed asset should be reflected as an expenditure and other financing source, consistent with the accounting and financial reporting for general obligation bonded debt.

Governmental Funds—Equity. The equity section of the governmental fund balance sheet is comprised of three major fund balance elements: reserved; unreserved, designated; and unreserved, undesignated. When used in association with the governmental funds, the term "reserved" should be limited to describing the portion of fund balance that is (1) not available for appropriation or expenditure and/or (2) is segregated legally for a specific future use.

A common example of the first type of reservation within the governmental funds is "reserved for inventories." Another example, "reserved for loans receivable," represents amounts expected to be collected in the future. Therefore, this receivable is not available for expenditure or appropriation at the balance sheet date. In this instance, the loans receivable amount is not associated with revenue recognition. However, if outstanding receivables (e.g., property taxes) are related to revenue that is not available, deferred revenue should be reported, *not* a reservation of fund balance.

"Reserved for encumbrances" is a common example of the second reserve type. This type of reserve is legally earmarked for a specific purpose. Generally, the reservations are based on third-party restrictions (e.g., contract with vendor).

A designation of unreserved fund balance can be established by a government to indicate tentative plans for the use of current financial resources in the future. Examples of designations include equipment replacement and contingencies.

These designations should not cause the government to report a deficit unreserved, undesignated fund balance. In addition, a government should not report a deficit unreserved, designated fund balance. In effect, a government cannot designate resources that are not available for expenditure.

The final element, "unreserved, undesignated fund balance," represents financial resources available to finance expenditures other than those tentatively planned by the government.

Proprietary Funds—Equity. There are two primary elements of a proprietary fund's equity: contributed capital and retained earnings. Contributed capital has never been defined adequately in authoritative literature, thus leading to numerous classification inconsistencies in practice. The 1987 *Codification*, Section G60.110, does provide limited guidance:

Grants, entitlements, or shared revenues received for proprietary fund operating purposes, or that may be used for either operations or capital expenditures at the discretion of the recipient government, should be recognized as "nonoperating" revenues in the accounting period in which they are earned and become measurable (accrual basis). Such resources restricted for the acquisition or construction of capital assets should be recorded as contributed equity.

The retained earnings section of the proprietary fund balance sheet is subdivided into two sections: reserved and unreserved. The reserved portion represents amounts that are legally segregated for a specific use. Common examples include accounts associated with debt service sinking funds (e.g., reserved for current debt service). The remaining portion of retained earnings should be reported as unreserved.

Common Terminology and Classification. Principle 11, *Common Terminology and Classification* (1987 *Codification,* Section 1800), states "A common terminology and classification should be used consistently throughout the budget, the accounts, and the financial reports of each fund."

Consistency is a primary factor in enhancing readability. Therefore, it is imperative that a standard chart of accounts be applied to all phases of internal and external budgeting, accounting and financial reporting. A sample chart of accounts is presented in appendix C.

Principle 12—Financial Reporting. The final principle, *Interim and Annual Financial Reports* (1987 *Codification,* Section 1900), provides:

a. Appropriate interim financial statements and reports of financial position, operating results, and other pertinent information should be prepared to facilitate management control of financial operations, legislative oversight, and, where necessary or desired, for external reporting purposes.

b. A comprehensive annual financial report covering all funds and account groups of the reporting entity—including introductory section; appropriate combined, combining, and individual fund statements; notes to the financial statements; required supplementary information; schedules; narrative explanations; and statistical tables—should be prepared and published . . .

c. General purpose financial statements of the reporting entity may be issued separately from the comprehensive annual financial report. Such statements should include the basic financial statements and notes to the financial statements that are essential to fair presentation of financial position and results of operations (and changes in financial position of proprietary funds and similar trust funds). Those statements may also be required to be accompanied by required supplementary information, essential to financial reporting of certain entities.

d. A component unit financial report covering all funds and account groups of a component unit—including introductory section; appropriate combined, combining, and individual fund statements; notes to the financial statements; required supplementary information; schedules; narrative explanations; and statistical tables—may be prepared and published, as necessary.

e. Component unit financial statements of a component unit may be issued separately from the component unit financial report. Such statements should include the basic financial statements and notes to the financial statements that are essential to the fair presentation of financial position and results of operations (and changes in financial

position of proprietary funds and similar trust funds). Those statements may also be required to be accompanied by required supplementary information, essential to financial reporting of certain entities.

Defining the Reporting Entity. Activities included in the reporting entity, as properly defined, have a significant effect on financial reporting. Criteria for defining the reporting entity are set forth in the 1987 *Codification,* Section 2100. Government financial reports should be comprehensive and comparable, and should identify the government's responsibility and control over certain activities. The 1987 *Codification,* Section 2100.107, establishes as an underlying concept ". . . that all functions of government are considered to be responsible to elected officials at the federal, state, or local level. Therefore, all functions of government must be a part of either federal state, or local government and should be reported at the lowest level of legislative authority . . . However, the criteria . . . were intended to exclude certain potential component units from the reporting entity . . ."

In order to apply this underlying concept, it is important to understand certain definitions included in 1987 *Codification,* Section 2600, related to the reporting entity. The following are definitions of a component unit, oversight unit and the reporting entity.

● *Component unit*—A separate governmental unit, agency or nonprofit corporation which, pursuant to the criteria in the 1987 *Codification,* Section 2100, is combined with an oversight unit and other component units to constitute the reporting entity.

● *Oversight unit*—The component unit which has the ability to exercise the basic criterion of oversight responsibility, as defined in the 1987 *Codification,* Section 2100, over the component units.

● *Reporting entity*—The oversight unit and all related component units, if any, combined to constitute the governmental reporting entity.

To determine if potential component units should be included in the reporting entity, all the pertinent facts should be evaluated using the criteria included in the 1987 *Codification,* Section 2100. If there are positive responses to the criteria, then the potential component unit should be *considered* for inclusion as part of the reporting entity. However, these criteria cannot be applied mechanically; professional judgment should be used when determining whether a potential component unit should be included in or excluded from the reporting entity.

Manifestations of Oversight. The 1987 *Codification,* Sections 2100.108–.110, includes five primary manifestations of oversight that should be considered when evaluating potential component units: financial interdependency, selection of governing authority, designation of management, ability to significantly influence operations and accountability for fiscal matters.

Financial Interdependency. The presence of financial interdependency has been identified as the most significant manifestation of oversight. Characteristics of financial interdependency identified in the 1987 *Codification,* Section 2100.109, include:

a. Responsibility for financing deficits
b. Entitlements to surpluses
c. Guarantees of or ''moral'' responsibility for debt.

Selection of Governing Authority. Statutes, ordinances and other related documents should be reviewed to establish who selects the governing board, commission, authority or other body that is held primarily accountable for actions taken by the potential component unit. Once this has been established, it must be determined whether the appointments are ceremonial (i.e., nonauthoritative) or whether there is a significant continuing relationship between the oversight unit and the potential component unit's governing board with respect to carrying out important public functions (i.e., authoritative).

Designation of Management. Management designation is another indication of oversight responsibility. Although in most instances the oversight unit is not directly involved in the hiring process, it may exercise a degree of oversight through the final approval of the potential component unit's executive management appointments.

Ability to Significantly Influence Operations. The ability to significantly influence operations relates directly to the other criteria. The level of influence is the product of many forms of interaction. The oversight unit may have the authority to review and approve contracts and budgets, the ability to retain or terminate either governing board members or key managerial personnel, or the authority to determine the scope of services provided by the potential component unit.

Accountability for Fiscal Matters. The final significant manifestation of oversight is accountability for fiscal matters. When the oversight unit is responsible for reviewing and approving a potential component unit's budget and/or the oversight unit has a legal or moral obligation to fund deficits or controls the use of surpluses, an oversight relationship, to a degree, has been established. Bond and other debt indentures should be reviewed to determine if the oversight unit has either a legal or moral responsibility for the potential component unit's debt.

The government unit reviewing the reporting entity criteria may exercise oversight responsibility if it either controls the collection and disbursement of funds, holds title to the potential component unit's assets or can require an audit of the component unit. If the potential component unit derived a portion of its revenue through a public levy or user charges versus grant receipts, this again may be considered a part of an oversight relationship if the power to set the levy or user charge lies with the oversight unit or has been delegated to the potential component unit.

Scope of Public Service and Special Financing Relationships. There may be circumstances in which factors other than oversight responsibility are so significant in the relationship between an oversight unit and a potential component unit that exclusion of the component unit from the reporting entity's financial statements would be misleading. These factors include scope of public service and special financing relationships.

Scope of Public Service. When the activity is for the benefit of the reporting entity and/or its residents, or the activity is conducted within the geographical boundaries of the reporting entity and is generally available to the entity's citizens, the scope of public service criterion should be taken into account.

Special Financing Relationships. When a potential component unit has a funding relationship because of the issuance of bonds by the oversight unit, or the oversight unit is a significant user of the potential component unit's services (e.g., capital leases) a special financing relationship may exist.

A practical guide in determining the reporting entity is found in the illustrations presented in the 1987 *Codification,* Sections 2100.603–.611. These illustrations provide examples of the exercise of professional judgment in the review of potential component units. However, the examples do not imply that similar activities necessarily should be reported as in these nonauthoritative illustrations. When it has been decided that the government exercises responsibility over the potential component unit pursuant to the criteria, the government would be considered the oversight unit, as that term was defined earlier in this chapter, and the potential component unit would be classified officially as a component unit. The combination of the government and component unit would be defined as the reporting entity. The oversight unit then should incorporate the component unit into the reporting entity's financial statement presentation.

Additional concepts and principles of financial reporting are explored in chapter 14.

Chapter 3
GENERAL AND SPECIAL REVENUE FUNDS

NATURE AND PURPOSE

The general fund of a government unit serves as the primary reporting vehicle for current government operations. The general fund, by definition, accounts for all current financial resources not required by law or administrative action to be accounted for in another fund. Accordingly, the general fund conceivably could be used to account for *all* government activities and normally should be used to account for all general government functions.

By its nature and as required by the Governmental Accounting Standards Board's (GASB) 1987 *Codification of Governmental Accounting and Financial Reporting Standards* (1987 *Codification*), Section 1300.106, "Governments shall report only one general fund." Although some governments are required to segregate certain general fund activities for budgetary reporting and other purposes (see chapter 12), normally these activities can be incorporated into the general fund's subaccounts for accounting and financial reporting purposes.

Some governments may face legal requirements restricting specific resources to expenditure for specified purposes. In these situations, except for trusts, capital projects or debt service, a special revenue fund may be used.

When assessing whether to use a special revenue fund, a government always should take into consideration the "number of funds" principle introduced in chapter 2. Authoritative standards require the use of a special revenue fund only for a component unit's general fund that is to be incorporated into a government reporting entity's comprehensive annual financial report (CAFR) or general purpose financial statements (GPFS). The optional use of a special revenue fund also is discussed for grants, entitlements and shared revenues. If, however, legal restrictions and sound financial management can be met without the segregation of an activity into a separate fund, the number of funds principle, as stated previously, should be followed.

BUDGETARY ISSUES

When statutes or ordinances require the adoption of an annual appropriated (i.e., legal) budget, the two most common fund types identified are general and special revenue. Although theoretical arguments arise on the issue of whether an appropriated budget is required for the general fund, sound financial management warrants such action. Special revenue funds also generally require annual appropriations to ensure sound financial management. However, under certain circumstances, governments may choose to budget only a portion of their special revenue funds. Normally, unbudgeted funds arise when the budget cycle differs from the government's budgeting process (e.g., a project-length grant) or when the notice of impending receipt of legally restricted resources is received after the budget has been adopted.

Those general and special revenue funds with annual appropriated budgets should be formally integrated into the accounting system. As required in the 1987 *Codification*, Section 2400.102, the final budget and actual data for general and special revenue funds' annual appropriated budgets should be presented in the Combined Statement of Revenues, Expenditures and Changes in Fund Balances—Budget and Actual of the GPFS or component unit financial statements (CUFS). To demonstrate legal compliance, individual fund budgetary (i.e., budget to actual) comparisons may be required in the preparation of either a CAFR or a component unit financial report. The individual budgetary comparisons would be required if the level of legal control has not been displayed at the combined fund-type level or if more than one special revenue fund has an annual appropriated budget. As discussed further in chapter 14, compliance at the legal level of budgetary control at least should be demonstrated in the individual budgetary comparison statements (i.e., GAAP basis) or schedules (i.e., non-GAAP budgetary basis).

ACCOUNTING ISSUES

The general and special revenue funds share the same basic accounting model. These fund types use a flow of current financial resources measurement focus and the modified accrual basis of accounting.

The use of this model has resulted in the emergence of several accounting issues that have been addressed in authoritative literature. These issues include taxes, grants, service-type special assessments, capital leases, expenditure recognition, claims and judgments, compensated absences, pension costs, inventories, prepayments and anticipation notes.

Taxes. Tax resources generally are accounted for in the general and special revenue funds. Several factors affect when tax revenues and related receivables are reported. Property tax receivable recognition is based on the levy date. Property taxes assessed by a government, in accordance with the 1987

Codification, Section P70.106, "typically can be determined and recorded in the accounts when levied." Any amounts determined to be uncollectible should be directly offset against the receivables as an allowance for uncollectible accounts (i.e., revenues are reduced and no bad debt expenditure is reported).

Property tax revenue recognition is based on three dates or periods (see Illustration 3–1). The first is the period for which the taxes are levied, in other words, the fiscal year for which the property taxes are used to fund budgetary expenditures. Property tax revenues should not be recognized before the fiscal year for which the taxes were levied. If the property taxes are collected beforehand, the cash collected and any remaining receivable should be offset by a "deferred revenue" liability.

When the first criterion has been met, the second period to be considered by the government should be the date on which the taxes are due. Although authoritative literature has not defined the "due" date, at least two alternatives exist in practice. The first alternative treats taxes as due when the tax bills are mailed. Normally tax bills, in accordance with statutes or ordinances, contain language stating they are "due on receipt." However, tax bills are often mailed several weeks, and in some cases several months, before the penalty period. The second approach defines the due date as the day before any penalties arise from the nonpayment of the property taxes. Taxpayers often look upon the due date as the last possible date a payment can be made without penalty. Because the second approach focuses on a date generally fixed by statute and ordinance, rather than a date affected by the mailing of a bill, it appears to be the more appropriate definition to use in determining whether property taxes are due before the end of the current fiscal year.

The third and final period results from the "availability" criterion incorporated into the current model. This date is the day or days on which collections actually are received. When the first two criteria have been met and the taxes have been collected before the current fiscal year end, or within 60 days thereafter, the property tax revenue should be recognized by the government. Although property taxes normally are recorded in the general fund, these taxes may be reported in the special revenue, debt service, capital projects or even the enterprise fund. (The same reporting pattern also holds true for income and sales taxes.)

The measurability criterion for revenue recognition is a major consideration with income and sales taxes. However, in practice, the convention of conservatism generally has limited the use of estimates for revenue recognition. Income tax revenue recognition generally is limited to collections made during the current fiscal year. Sales taxes, however, should be recognized if the taxes have been forwarded to an intermediary government collection agency (e.g., state revenue department) during the fiscal year.

Specifically, the 1987 *Codification*, Section 1600.110, provides:

> It is neither necessary nor practical to attempt to accrue taxpayer-assessed income and gross receipts taxes unless taxpayer liability and collectibility have been clearly established—as when tax returns have been filed but collection, while assured, is delayed beyond the normal time of receipt. Such items are best recognized as cash is received.

ILLUSTRATION 3–1

Property Tax Revenue Recognition

A government has a fiscal year end of June 30, 19X8. Property taxes are levied based on a calendar year (January 1–December 31). The property tax assessment is formally levied on December 15, 19X7. Property tax bills are mailed twice a year, each billing is equal to one-half the assessment. The first bill is mailed on February 15, 19X8. Although the bill states the property taxes are due upon receipt of the bill, penalties are assessed for any payment not received by May 15, 19X8. The second bill is mailed on June 15, 19X8 with a September 15, 19X8 penalty date. Amounts expected to be collected from the second billing are budgeted in the following year (19X9). Based on these assumptions, the following table illustrates the application of the property tax revenue recognition criteria.

	Levy Date— Receivable Recognized	Due Date Within Current Fiscal Year	Availability Period for Collections
First billing	12/15/X7	Yes	8/29/X8
Second billing	12/15/X7	No	N/A

Property tax collections resulting from the first billing would be recognized as revenue in the current period to the extent that the collections occur by August 29, 19X8. The entire second billing (based on the due date) including amounts collected before June 30, 19X8 would be deferred.

This guidance results in an apparent conflict with other sections of the 1987 *Codification* and highlights the difficulty of establishing a single period for revenue recognition. The underlying principle "collectible . . . soon enough thereafter to be used to pay liabilities of the current period" has led some governments to ignore the authoritative guidance on sales and income taxes in an attempt to achieve a more uniform application of the availability criterion.

The issue of sales tax revenue recognition is complicated further by the guidance provided in the American Institute of Certified Public Accountants' Statement of Position 75–3, *Accrual of Revenues and Expenditures by State and Local Governments*. This pronouncement, which is incorporated in the 1987 *Codification*, Section S10.103, provides that "Sales taxes collected by merchants but not yet required to be remitted to the taxing authority at the end of the fiscal year should not be accrued." Although this guidance is clear, many governments, particularly at the state level, have again chosen to adopt a uniform revenue recognition policy.

Grants. The accounting and financial reporting of grants, entitlements and shared revenues also are addressed in authoritative literature. The 1987 *Codification*, Section G60.109, provides:

> Grants, entitlements, or shared revenues recorded in governmental funds should be recognized as revenue in the accounting period when they become susceptible to accrual, that is, both measurable and available (modified accrual basis) . . . In applying this definition, legal and contractual requirements should be carefully reviewed for guidance. Some such resources, usually entitlements or shared reve-

nues, are restricted more in form than in substance. Only a failure on the part of the recipient to comply with prescribed regulations will cause a forfeiture of the resources. Such resources should be recorded as revenue at the time of receipt or earlier if the susceptible to accrual criteria are met. For other such resources, usually grants, expenditure is the prime factor for determining eligibility, and revenue should be recognized when the expenditure is made. Similarly, if cost sharing or matching requirements exist, revenue recognition depends on compliance with these requirements.

With some grants, a reimburseable expenditure is incurred; however, it may be several years before the revenue becomes available. Therefore, the availability criterion can become a factor in grant revenue recognition. In those instances, the 1987 *Codification,* Section G60.112, provides that the receivable "should not be reported on the balance sheet, but may be disclosed in the notes to the financial statements."

Service-type Special Assessments. Since the elimination of the special assessment fund type, the general fund or special revenue fund types now may be used to account for certain service-type special assessment activities. In addition, these activities also may be reported in the enterprise fund type. The 1987 *Codification,* Section S40.104, provides, "Service-type special assessment projects are for operating activities and do not result in the purchase or construction of fixed assets." Examples of service-type special assessments include street lighting, weed cutting and snow plowing services when only those property owners affected are charged for additional services received.

Service-type special assessment receivables should be recorded when the services are billed. Unbilled amounts also should be accrued at year end. Revenue for service-type special assessment activities should be recognized to the extent that collections meet the availability criterion.

Capital Leases. Lease arrangements from the perspective of both the lessee and lessor raise display issues in the government environment. The 1987 *Codification,* Section L20, adopts the criteria set forth in the Financial Accounting Standards Board's (FASB) Statement of Financial Accounting Standards (SFAS) No. 13, *Accounting for Leases,* for the classification of a lease from the standpoint of the government lessee and lessor.

Lessee. SFAS No. 13 sets forth four criteria for determining capital leases. At least one of the following criteria should be met in the lease agreement provisions for the agreement to be classified as a capital lease:

a. The lease transfers ownership of the property to the lessee by the end of the lease term . . .

b. The lease contains a bargain purchase option . . .

c. The lease term . . . is equal to 75 percent or more of the estimated economic life of the leased property . . . However, if the beginning of the lease term falls within the last 25 percent of the total estimated economic life of the leased property, including earlier years of use, this criterion shall not be used for purposes of classifying the lease.

d. The present value at the beginning of the lease term of the minimum lease payments . . . excluding that portion of the payments representing executory costs . . . to be paid by the lessor, including any profit thereon, equals or exceeds 90 percent of the excess of the fair value of the leased property . . . to the lessor at the inception of the lease . . . However, if the beginning of the lease term falls within the last 25 percent of the total estimated economic life of the leased property, including earlier years of use, this criterion shall not be used for purposes of classifying the lease . . . A lessee shall compute the present value of the minimum lease payments using [the lessee's] incremental borrowing rate . . . unless (i) it is practicable for [the lessee] to learn the implicit rate computed by the lessor and (ii) the implicit rate computed by the lessor is less than the lessee's incremental borrowing rate. If both of those conditions are met, the lessee shall use the implicit rate.

The FASB also provides a glossary in SFAS No. 13 to assist in the application of the criteria.

In practice, both the first and third criteria normally can be applied to government lease agreements without much difficulty because the lease term and the estimated economic life of the leased property generally are readily determinable.

The 1987 *Codification,* Section L20.118, does provide that if a fiscal funding or cancellation clause has an effect on the lease term, this clause would not necessarily prohibit a lease agreement from being capitalized. If it is determined after evaluation of the clause that the possibility of cancellation is remote and that the lease meets the SFAS No. 13 criteria, the lease should be capitalized.

The second criterion is more difficult to determine because the FASB does not quantify a bargain purchase option when it is defined as "a price which is sufficiently lower than the expected fair value of the property at the date the option becomes exercisable that exercise of the option appears, at the inception of the lease, to be reasonably assured." The absence of such guidance does not affect many leases entered into by governments because the purchase options are often for a nominal amount ($1). In such cases, the lessor and lessee normally would be reasonably assured at the inception of the lease that the "bargain purchase option" would be exercised.

The final criterion often appears the most difficult to determine because the amount for minimum lease payments must be calculated. Generally, in government leases, if the lessee is obligated to make the following payments in connection with the leased property, they should be incorporated into this calculation.

1. Minimum rental payments required by the lease over the lease term.

2. Any guarantee by the lessee for the payment of the estimated fair value of the property at the expiration of the lease term, including "bargain purchase options" that will be exercised.

3. Any payment the lessee must make or can be required to make on failure to renew or extend the lease at the expiration of the lease term. The payment would not be included if the penalty would effectively prohibit the termination of the lease. In these cases, the lease term would include the renewal period affected by the penalty.

Executory costs (e.g., insurance, maintenance) paid by the lessee are excluded from this calculation.

In computing the present value of the minimum lease payments, the lessee often is aware of the implicit rate of interest computed by the lessor because many leases include a stated rate in the agreement. Because of the nontaxable nature of most government debt issues, the incremental borrowing rate for a similar period is likely to be lower than the lessor's implicit interest rate. Therefore, the incremental rate in most instances should be used to determine the present value of the minimum lease payments.

By entering into a capital lease, the government has obtained financial resources similar to those raised through the issuance of general obligation bonded debt, and these resources should be reported in a similar manner. The acquisition of the general fixed assets also should be presented in a manner similar to an outright purchase. These amounts are recorded simultaneously at the net present value of the minimum lease payments. Lease payments, including any down payment, should be reported consistently with the principles set forth for general obligation debt. Therefore, capital lease principal and interest payments generally are reported when due.

A general misunderstanding associated with capital lease transactions paid from governmental resources involves the use of debt service funds for lease payments. A debt service fund should *not* be established for lease payments unless a specific legal requirement exists to do so. Normally, such a requirement does not exist, and payment can be recorded directly in the fund making the payment (e.g., general, special revenue).

Lessor. Although governments in the past generally have not functioned as lessors, this type of financial arrangement is increasing. In addition to the four criteria previously presented, a government lessor also should assess the following two criteria set forth in SFAS No. 13 to determine if the lease is to be classified as a capital lease. Otherwise, it should be classified as an operating lease.

    a. Collectibility of the minimum lease payments is reasonably predictable . . .
    b. No important uncertainties surround the amount of unreimbursable costs yet to be incurred by the lessor under the lease . . .

When the property covered by the lease is yet to be constructed or has not been acquired by the lessor at the date of the lease agreement or commitment, the classification criteria should be applied at the date construction of the property is completed or the date property is acquired by the lessor.

For lessor transactions recorded in governmental funds, the distinction between sales and direct financing leases is not a relevant factor because all lease receipts are reported as revenues. When the lease is initially entered into, the net present value of future lease payments should be reported as a receivable and offset by deferred revenue. Revenues (i.e., principal and interest payments) for lessor transactions should be reported when they are considered available.

Expenditure Recognition. Other accounting issues arise for certain specific expenditures and liabilities, such as claims and judgments, compensated absences and pension costs. Expenditures are only recognized under the modified accrual basis

of accounting for liabilities expected to be liquidated through the use of "expendable available financial resources." Of the several methods used to interpret the meaning of this term, the approach that most closely follows the flow of current financial resources measurement focus is to consider expendable available financial resources to be synonymous with "unreserved, undesignated fund balance." Therefore, the amounts recognized as fund liabilities and expenditures for these items generally should not exceed the amount of unreserved, undesignated fund balance. However, if these liabilities are due on demand without additional action (e.g., adjudicated or settled claims), the liabilities and expenditures should be reported in the governmental funds, regardless of the status of the unreserved, undesignated fund balance. While setting a general "ceiling" for fund liability and expenditure recognition, this approach still leaves open the important questions of how the amount of such expenditures should be calculated and in which funds these liabilities should be reported.

To determine the amount of expenditures to be accrued, a government may attempt model symmetry by recognizing as expenditures liabilities paid during the year, plus amounts expected to be liquidated with expendable available financial resources during a specific period of time after year end. This period generally equals the availability period (e.g., 60 days) established for revenue recognition.

The issue of the funds to be used to record the liability also can be perplexing. Although many special revenue funds may have expendable available financial resources, the question of what fund the liability ultimately will be paid from must be considered. For example, during an employee's tenure with a government, the employee may work for several departments and be paid from several funds. Many times the fund the employee will be paid from when the compensated absence is used or the pension costs are paid cannot be determined. In addition, other factors may have an impact on the proper financial reporting. One such case involves special revenue funds established for grant administration. When the grantor will only reimburse the government for actual vacation time taken, the government is forced to make a decision. It must either require employees to use compensated absences during the grant period or provide for future payments from other resources (e.g., general fund). The latter approach is often the basis for reporting the entire governmental fund liability in the general fund.

In addition to determining where these liabilities are to be recorded, guidance also is provided regarding how these liabilities are to be calculated. Specific guidance for claims and judgments, compensated absences and pension costs follows.

Claims and Judgments. Guidance for determining the government's liability for claims and judgments is found in the 1987 *Codification,* Section C50.112, which is based on SFAS No. 5, *Accounting for Contingencies.*

SFAS No. 5 provides:

An estimated loss from a loss contingency [i.e., an existing condition, situation, or set of circumstances involving uncertainty as to possible . . . loss . . . to an enterprise that will ultimately be resolved when one or more future events occur or fail to occur] shall be accrued by a charge to income if *both* of the following conditions are met:

a. Information available prior to issuance of the financial statements indicates that it is probable that an asset had been impaired or a liability had been incurred at the date of the financial statements. It is implicit in this condition that it must be probable that one or more future events will occur confirming the fact of the loss.
b. The amount of loss can be reasonably estimated.*

The FASB defines "probable" in SFAS No. 5 as "the future event or events . . . are likely to occur."

A government may face several types of claims during normal operations. These claims include personal injuries and workers' compensation. The 1987 *Codification,* Section C50.111, presents two primary methods for estimating claims and judgments liabilities. The first method is based on a case-by-case review of all claims by the government to determine if any would meet the SFAS No. 5 criteria. The second method involves the stratification of claims and application of historical claim adjudication or settlement experience by type and amount of claim. The standards also provide that these two methods can be combined in some manner. For example, a government may review all claims over $1 million on a case-by-case basis and apply historical experience to the remaining cases.

Compensated Absences. The 1987 *Codification,* Section C60.108, refers to SFAS No. 43, *Accounting for Compensated Absences,* for governments determining when a compensated absences liability should be recorded. SFAS No. 43 introduces four conditions that should be met before a liability for compensated absences is accrued:

a. The employer's obligation relating to employees' rights to receive compensation for future absences is attributable to employees' services already rendered,
b. The obligation relates to rights that vest or accumulate,
c. Payment of the compensation is probable, and
d. The amount can be reasonably estimated.

SFAS No. 43 also provides specific guidance regarding sick pay benefits. Those benefits that only accumulate, do not vest and cannot be converted to terminal leave are *not* required to be accrued. In addition, governments with incurred liabilities for compensated absences that meet the first three criteria but cannot be reasonably estimated are required to disclose that fact in the notes to the financial statements.

A government's liability for compensated absences generally is calculated by multiplying the number of days and/or hours of eligible compensation time, based on the SFAS No. 43 criteria, by the employee's compensation rate at year end. For example, if an employee had 40 hours of eligible vacation time at year end and the employee's compensation rate at year end was $12 per hour, the liability for compensated absences associated with that employee would be $480.

Pension Costs. The government's pension costs generally are based on an actuarially determined amount calculated within the guidelines established by Accounting Principles Board (APB) Opinion No. 8, *Accounting for the Costs of Pension Plans.* Acceptable actuarial cost methods include entry-age,

attained-age, unit-credit and aggregate. The APB Opinion No. 8 guidelines provide that the pension cost should fall between minimum (normal cost, interest on unfunded prior service cost, and a provision for vested benefits which is generally 2.5 percent of past and prior service cost) and maximum (normal cost, interest, and 10 percent of past and prior service cost) provisions.

Inventories. Accounting for inventories also gives rise to certain issues. Inventory items may be reported as expenditures either when purchased or when consumed. Under both methods, significant amounts of inventory at year end should be reported on the balance sheet. The purchases method is aligned with the flow of current financial resources measurement focus because an expenditure is incurred when financial resources are used. When the purchases method is used, any significant amounts of inventories reported on the balance sheet should be offset by a reservation of fund balance to identify that these assets do not represent expendable available financial resources.

Governments often choose the consumption method for inventory control and other purposes. A reservation of fund balance is not required under this method unless the purchases method is used for budgetary purposes and inventory is accounted for on the consumption basis for GAAP reporting purposes.

Prepayments. Prepaid items also fall within the optional treatment category (i.e., purchases or consumption). Expenditures for insurance and other prepayments need not be allocated between periods, although authoritative literature does not prohibit this practice. If these prepayments are displayed on the balance sheet, a reservation of fund balance is not required unless the purchases method of expenditure recognition is used for budgetary purposes.

Anticipation Notes. The final accounting issue that primarily affects the general and special revenue funds concerns the issuance of tax, revenue or grant anticipation notes. Based on the nature of these transactions (i.e., funding current operating deficits/deficiencies), the 1987 *Codification,* Section B50.101, provides that transactions of this type "should be reported as a fund liability in the fund receiving proceeds." The unresolved issue for this type of transaction arises when the proceeds are received by one fund (e.g., special revenue) and repaid with the resources of another fund (e.g., general). This issue normally is resolved through an operating transfer from the paying fund to the fund that originally reported this liability.

ILLUSTRATIVE JOURNAL ENTRIES

The journal entries included in the remainder of this chapter illustrate the accounting operations of the general fund of a sample government. If these entries are posted to the accounts listed in the beginning of the year trial balance presented as Illustration 3–2 and to the additional accounts indicated, the year-end balances presented in Illustration 3–4 will agree with the CAFR in appendix D. All amounts are expressed in thousands.

Formal Budgetary Integration. CAPITAL LETTERS are used for all budgetary accounts presented to highlight formal budgetary integration in the sample government's accounts.

---

*The government in determining a loss may estimate a range for the contingency liability. If the contingency meets the first condition of the SFAS No. 5 guidance, the government should consider recording at least the lowest amount of the range as a liability.

Also, budgetary and actual transactions are not presented in control accounts (e.g., revenues). These control accounts in accounting systems are reflected in the general ledger either as a separate entry from the subsidiary ledger or as a simultaneous entry.

ILLUSTRATION 3–2

Name of Government
General Fund
Trial Balance
January 1, 19X8
(amounts expressed in thousands)

	DR	CR
Cash	$ 557	
Investments	1,226	
Interest receivable—investments	48	
Taxes receivable—delinquent—property taxes	90	
Allowance for uncollectible delinquent taxes—property taxes		$ 16
Interest and penalties receivable—property taxes	5	
Allowance for uncollectible interest and penalties—property taxes		1
Tax liens receivable—property taxes	25	
Allowance for uncollectible tax liens—property taxes		6
Taxes receivable—sales taxes	800	
Accounts receivable	61	
Allowance for uncollectible accounts receivable		2
Intergovernmental receivable—federal	150	
Intergovernmental receivable—county	127	
Due from other funds—water and sewer fund	193	
Due from other funds—transportation fund	38	
Inventories	37	
Advance to other funds—management information systems fund	50	
Vouchers payable		454
Accounts payable		420
Compensated absences payable		201
Contracts payable		151
Due to other funds—water and sewer fund		21
Due to other funds—management information systems fund		98
Deferred revenue—interest receivable—investments		48
Deferred revenue—taxes receivable—delinquent property taxes		75
Deferred revenue—interest and penalties receivable—property taxes		3
Deferred revenue—tax liens receivable—property taxes		19
Deferred revenue—federal government		85
Fund balance—reserved for encumbrances		211
Fund balance—reserved for advances		50
Fund balance—unreserved, undesignated		1,546
	$ 3,407	$ 3,407

The following journal entry reverses prior-year encumbered amounts the government intends to honor. These amounts will be included in the current year's budget.

	DR	CR
1. Fund balance—reserved for encumbrances	$ 211	
Fund balance—unreserved, undesignated		$ 211
(To reverse prior-year encumbrance reserves)		

The following journal entry illustrates the integration of the $36,956 annual appropriated budget into the government's accounts.

	DR	CR
2. ESTIMATED REVENUES—PROPERTY TAXES	$ 14,487	
ESTIMATED REVENUES—SALES TAXES	6,767	
ESTIMATED REVENUES—FRANCHISE TAXES	4,312	
ESTIMATED REVENUES—LICENSES AND PERMITS	1,827	
ESTIMATED REVENUES—INTERGOVERNMENTAL	5,661	
ESTIMATED REVENUES—CHARGES FOR SERVICES	2,158	
ESTIMATED REVENUES—FINES	810	
ESTIMATED REVENUES—INTEREST	555	
ESTIMATED REVENUES—MISCELLANEOUS	345	
ESTIMATED OTHER FINANCING SOURCES—CAPITAL LEASES	34	
APPROPRIATIONS—GENERAL GOVERNMENT—COUNCIL		$ 98
APPROPRIATIONS—GENERAL GOVERNMENT—COMMISSIONS		70
APPROPRIATIONS—GENERAL GOVERNMENT—MANAGER		521
APPROPRIATIONS—GENERAL GOVERNMENT—ATTORNEY		391
APPROPRIATIONS—GENERAL GOVERNMENT—CLERK		264
APPROPRIATIONS—GENERAL GOVERNMENT—PERSONNEL		325
APPROPRIATIONS—GENERAL GOVERNMENT—FINANCE AND ADMINISTRATION		904
APPROPRIATIONS—GENERAL GOVERNMENT—OTHER—UNCLASSIFIED		2,205
APPROPRIATIONS—PUBLIC SAFETY—POLICE		6,513
APPROPRIATIONS—PUBLIC SAFETY—FIRE		6,040
APPROPRIATIONS—PUBLIC SAFETY—INSPECTION		1,092
APPROPRIATIONS—HIGHWAYS AND STREETS—MAINTENANCE		3,052
APPROPRIATIONS—HIGHWAYS AND STREETS—ENGINEERING		814
APPROPRIATIONS—SANITATION		3,848
APPROPRIATIONS—CULTURE AND RECREATION		5,950
APPROPRIATIONS—OTHER FINANCING USES—OPERATING TRANSFERS OUT		4,700
APPROPRIATIONS—RESIDUAL EQUITY TRANSFERS OUT		60
BUDGETARY FUND BALANCE		109
(To record the annual appropriated budget)		

The following discussion and journal entries illustrate general fund revenues, financing sources, receipts affecting balance sheet accounts and related nonmonetary transactions for the current year.

The government levies $14,097 of property taxes during the current year to provide resources for budgetary expenditures. Payment of the taxes is due before year end. Prior experience provides that .01 percent of the levy should be classified as uncollectible.

	DR	CR
3. Taxes receivable—current property taxes	$ 14,097	
Allowance for uncollectible current taxes—property taxes		$ 14
Deferred revenue—taxes receivable—current property taxes		14,083
(To record property tax levy)		

Note: Property taxes may be recognized as revenue in the accounting system at the time of levy. Under this method, a deferral associated with property taxes receivable that do not meet the revenue recognition availability criterion should be calculated at year end. See Illustration 2–3 for an example.

The government collects $14,000 of the current year's tax levy before year end.

	DR	CR
4. Cash	$ 14,000	
Taxes receivable—current property taxes		$ 14,000
(To record collection of current year's property taxes)		

	DR	CR
5. Deferred revenue—taxes receivable—current property taxes	$ 14,000	
Revenues—property taxes		$ 14,000
(To recognize revenue for current property tax levy)		

The government collects $70 of delinquent property taxes and related interest, penalties and liens receivable. The entire amount of delinquent taxes, interest, penalties and tax liens remitted had been accrued and deferred previously.

	DR	CR
6. Cash	$ 70	
Taxes receivable—delinquent property taxes		$ 65
Interest and penalties receivable—property taxes		3
Tax liens receivable—property taxes		2
(To record collection of property tax-related receivables)		

	DR	CR
7. Deferred revenue—taxes receivable—delinquent property taxes	$ 65	
Deferred revenue—interest and penalties receivable—property taxes	3	
Deferred revenue—tax liens receivable—property taxes	2	
Revenues—property taxes		$ 70
(To recognize revenue from the collection of property taxes, interest, penalties and liens)		

Interest and penalty charges begin immediately after the taxes are deemed delinquent. The penalty rate is 1 percent per year of the delinquent taxes outstanding. The interest rate is based on the yield of the three-month treasury bill (8 percent).

	DR	CR
8. Interest and penalties receivable—property taxes	$ 14	
Allowance for interest and penalties receivable—property taxes		$ 2
Deferred revenue—interest and penalties receivable—property taxes		12
(To record interest and penalties on delinquent property taxes)		

When delinquent property taxes are not paid within a specified period of time as established by statute, a lien is attached to the properties. The property is then subject to sale for the delinquent taxes. During the year, the government places a lien on property for $10 of uncollected taxes, interest and penalties.

	DR	CR
9. Tax liens receivable—property taxes	$ 10	
Taxes receivable—delinquent property taxes		$ 8
Interest and penalties receivable—property taxes		2
(To reclassify property tax liens)		

	DR	CR
10. Deferred revenue—taxes receivable—delinquent property taxes	$ 6	
Deferred revenue—interest and penalties receivable—property taxes	2	
Deferred revenue—tax liens receivable—property taxes		$ 8
(To reclassify deferred revenues related to property tax liens)		

	DR	CR
11. Allowance for uncollectible delinquent taxes—property taxes	$ 2	
Allowance for uncollectible tax liens—property taxes		$ 2
(To reclassify allowance accounts related to property tax liens)		

In addition to property taxes levied on property owners, the government also assesses the water and sewer fund for an amount in lieu of property taxes. The water and sewer fund is assessed $345 in the current year. In the current year, the water and sewer fund remits $473, which includes $193 from the prior year.

	DR	CR
12. Due from other funds—water and sewer fund	$ 345	
Revenues—miscellaneous—payments in lieu of taxes		$ 345
(To record assessments for payments in lieu of taxes from the water and sewer fund)		

Note: Payments in lieu of taxes should only be reported as revenues when the assessment is based on established levy rates applied to similar businesses.

	DR	CR
13. Cash	$ 473	
Due from other funds—water and sewer fund		$ 473
(To record receipt of payments in lieu of taxes)		

The government provides various services financed in part by user charges (e.g., garbage, recreation, administration). Total billings for the year amounted to $2,300, of which $2,292 is collected during the year. In addition, $25 is collected from the prior year's outstanding amount.

	DR	CR
14. Accounts receivable	$ 2,276	
Due from other funds—fleet management fund	8	
Due from other funds—management information systems fund	16	
Revenues—charges for services		$ 2,300
(To record user-charge billings)		

	DR	CR
15. Cash	$ 2,317	
Accounts receivable		$ 2,263
Due from other funds—management information systems fund		16
Due from other funds—transportation fund		38
(To record collection of user charges)		

During the year, the general fund receives $5,928 in grant and shared revenue receipts. Of this amount, $3,323 is from the county's shared-revenue program, included in this amount is $127 recognized as revenue in the prior year. Federal grants of $150 are received for expenditures incurred in the prior year. Drawdowns of $2,455 for federal grants also are received. Drawdowns are made when the government establishes an encumbrance or pays salaries and benefits related to the grants. Finally, previously deferred grant revenue, related to $2,359 of qualifying expenditures incurred for expenditure-driven grants (without matching requirements) is recognized.

	DR	CR
16. Cash	$ 3,323	
Intergovernmental receivable—county		$ 127
Revenues—intergovernmental		3,196
(To record county revenue sharing receipts)		

	DR	CR
17. Cash	$ 150	
Intergovernmental receivable—federal		$ 150
(To record receipt of federal grant monies related to eligible grant expenditures incurred in the prior year)		

	DR	CR
18. Cash	$ 2,455	
Deferred revenue—federal government		$ 2,455
(To recognize cash received from federal government grant drawdowns)		

	DR	CR
19. Deferred revenue—federal government	$ 2,359	
Revenues—intergovernmental		$ 2,359
(To recognize revenue based on eligible federal grant-related expenditures)		

Note: Revenue from grants should only be recognized to the extent that eligible expenditures have been incurred and the revenue meets the availability criterion.

Revenues not previously susceptible to accrual are received from several sources. Amounts collected during the year equal $7,142.

	DR	CR
20. Cash	$ 7,142	
Revenues—franchise taxes		$ 4,293
Revenues—licenses and permits		2,041
Revenues—fines		808
(To record receipt of franchise taxes, license and permit fees, and fines)		

The government levies a 1 percent sales tax that is collected by merchants and forwarded to the state. The state distributes the taxes to the government approximately one month after collection as part of its normal processing cycle. The government receives $800 of sales taxes in January 19X8 that had been accrued in December 19X7.

	DR	CR
21. Cash	$ 800	
Taxes receivable—sales taxes		$ 800
(To record collection of December 19X7 sales tax receipts)		

	DR	CR
22. Cash	$ 5,812	
Revenues—sales taxes		$ 5,812
(To record the receipt of the current year's sales taxes)		

During the year, the government sells general fixed assets originally costing $42 for $5.

	DR	CR
23. Cash	$ 5	
Other financing sources—sales of general fixed assets		$ 5
(To record proceeds from the sales of general fixed assets)		

During the year, the general fund receives a $3 reimbursement for current-year expenditures properly applicable to the fleet management fund.

	DR	CR
24. Cash	$ 3	
Expenditures—general government—other—unclassified		$ 3
(To record reimbursement from the fleet management fund)		

The government, based on its revenue collection cycle, can maintain a significant investment portfolio through most of the year. During the year, the government collects $531 in investment income. In addition, investments are rolled over so that the entire interest accrual at year end would be considered available for revenue recognition.

	DR	CR
25. Cash	$ 531	
Interest receivable—investments		$ 48
Revenues—interest		483
(To record interest receipts for the year)		

	DR	CR
26. Deferred revenue—interest receivable— investments	$ 48	
Revenues—interest		$ 48
(To recognize interest revenue that had been deferred in the prior year)		

	DR	CR
27. Interest receivable—investments	$ 92	
Revenues—interest		$ 92
(To record interest accrued at year end)		

In addition to the $14,000 of property taxes collected during the year, $63 is collected by the government in the 60-day period immediately following year end.

	DR	CR
28. Deferred revenue—taxes receivable—current property taxes	$ 63	
Revenues—property taxes		$ 63
(To recognize revenue for current property tax levy)		

Note: Property tax revenue is only considered available if it meets the criteria set forth in the 1987 *Codification*, Section P70.103, as discussed in this chapter.

At year end, statutes require unpaid current property taxes to be classified as delinquent.

	DR	CR
29. Taxes receivable—delinquent property taxes	$ 97	
Allowance for uncollectible current property taxes	14	
Taxes receivable—current property taxes		$ 97
Allowance for uncollectible delinquent taxes—property taxes		14
(To reclassify delinquent property taxes at year end)		

	DR	CR
30. Deferred revenue—taxes receivable—current property taxes	$ 18	
Deferred revenue—taxes receivable— delinquent property taxes		$ 18
(To reclassify deferred revenue related to delinquent property taxes)		

The government receives a delayed shared-revenue payment of $215 from the county soon after the current year end. It was not recognized previously as a receivable.

	DR	CR
31. Intergovernmental receivable—county	$ 215	
Revenues—intergovernmental		$ 215
(To record delayed shared-revenue payment)		

The government obtains reports from the state that provide information on sales tax remittance during December 19X8.

The state had collected $830 on the government's behalf during this period.

	DR	CR
32. Taxes receivable—sales tax	$ 830	
Revenues—sales taxes		$ 830
(To accrue December 19X8 sales taxes collected by the state)		

The following discussion and journal entries illustrate general fund expenditures, financing uses, encumbrances and disbursements affecting balance sheet accounts.

The government uses an encumbrance accounting system and during the year records $9,613 of encumbrances on purchase orders and contracts.

	DR	CR
33. ENCUMBRANCES—GENERAL GOVERNMENT—COUNCIL	$ 18	
ENCUMBRANCES—GENERAL GOVERNMENT—COMMISSIONS	30	
ENCUMBRANCES—GENERAL GOVERNMENT—MANAGER	191	
ENCUMBRANCES—GENERAL GOVERNMENT—ATTORNEY	219	
ENCUMBRANCES—GENERAL GOVERNMENT—CLERK	71	
ENCUMBRANCES—GENERAL GOVERNMENT—PERSONNEL	139	
ENCUMBRANCES—GENERAL GOVERNMENT—FINANCE AND ADMINISTRATION	237	
ENCUMBRANCES—GENERAL GOVERNMENT—OTHER— UNCLASSIFIED	1,222	
ENCUMBRANCES—GENERAL GOVERNMENT—POLICE	1,789	
ENCUMBRANCES—GENERAL GOVERNMENT—FIRE	1,054	
ENCUMBRANCES—GENERAL GOVERNMENT—INSPECTION	233	
ENCUMBRANCES—HIGHWAYS AND STREETS—MAINTENANCE	1,272	
ENCUMBRANCES—HIGHWAYS AND STREETS—ENGINEERING	207	
ENCUMBRANCES—SANITATION	1,590	
ENCUMBRANCES—CULTURE AND RECREATION	1,341	
BUDGETARY FUND BALANCE— RESERVED FOR ENCUMBRANCES		$ 9,613
(To record encumbrances for purchase orders and contracts)		

The government receives $7,658 in billings during the year for expenditures related to $8,017 of encumbrances.

	DR	CR
34. BUDGETARY FUND BALANCE— RESERVED FOR ENCUMBRANCES	$ 8,017	
ENCUMBRANCES—GENERAL GOVERNMENT—COUNCIL		$ 16
ENCUMBRANCES—GENERAL GOVERNMENT—COMMISSIONS		27
ENCUMBRANCES—GENERAL GOVERNMENT—MANAGER		173
ENCUMBRANCES—GENERAL GOVERNMENT—ATTORNEY		216
ENCUMBRANCES—GENERAL GOVERNMENT—CLERK		57

ENCUMBRANCES—GENERAL GOVERNMENT—PERSONNEL	130	
ENCUMBRANCES—GENERAL GOVERNMENT—FINANCE AND ADMINISTRATION	205	
ENCUMBRANCES—GENERAL GOVERNMENT—OTHER— UNCLASSIFIED	1,092	
ENCUMBRANCES—PUBLIC SAFETY—POLICE	1,264	
ENCUMBRANCES—PUBLIC SAFETY—FIRE	763	
ENCUMBRANCES—PUBLIC SAFETY—INSPECTION	199	
ENCUMBRANCES—HIGHWAYS AND STREETS—MAINTENANCE	1,073	
ENCUMBRANCES—HIGHWAYS AND STREETS—ENGINEERING	157	
ENCUMBRANCES—SANITATION	1,558	
ENCUMBRANCES—CULTURE AND RECREATION	1,087	

(To cancel encumbrances related to billings for goods and services received)

Note: The amount canceled should equal the actual amount encumbered for the purchase order or contract. Therefore, the expenditure may not equal the amount of the original encumbrance.

	DR	CR
35. Expenditures—general government—council	$ 12	
Expenditures—general government—commissions	22	
Expenditures—general government—manager	169	
Expenditures—general government—attorney	214	
Expenditures—general government—clerk	47	
Expenditures—general government—personnel	111	
Expenditures—general government—finance and administration	200	
Expenditures—general government—other—unclassified	956	
Expenditures—public safety—police	1,253	
Expenditures—public safety—fire	750	
Expenditures—public safety—inspection	193	
Expenditures—highways and streets—maintenance	1,071	
Expenditures—highways and streets—engineering	150	
Expenditures—sanitation	1,490	
Expenditures—culture and recreation	1,020	
Vouchers payable		$ 4,120
Accounts payable		687
Contracts payable		1,363
Due to other funds—water and sewer fund		175
Due to other funds—fleet management fund		872
Due to other funds—management information systems fund		441

(To record billings for goods and services received except for materials and supplies inventories)

The government records material and supplies inventories on a consumption basis. During the year, the government purchases $863 of inventories related to $950 of encumbrances and consumes $861.

	DR	CR
36. BUDGETARY FUND BALANCE— RESERVED FOR ENCUMBRANCES	$ 950	
ENCUMBRANCES—GENERAL		

GOVERNMENT—COUNCIL	$ 2	
ENCUMBRANCES—GENERAL GOVERNMENT—COMMISSIONS	3	
ENCUMBRANCES—GENERAL GOVERNMENT—MANAGER	8	
ENCUMBRANCES—GENERAL GOVERNMENT—ATTORNEY	3	
ENCUMBRANCES—GENERAL GOVERNMENT—CLERK	14	
ENCUMBRANCES—GENERAL GOVERNMENT—PERSONNEL	9	
ENCUMBRANCES—GENERAL GOVERNMENT—FINANCE AND ADMINISTRATION	32	
ENCUMBRANCES—GENERAL GOVERNMENT—OTHER— UNCLASSIFIED	35	
ENCUMBRANCES—PUBLIC SAFETY—POLICE	144	
ENCUMBRANCES—PUBLIC SAFETY—FIRE	191	
ENCUMBRANCES—PUBLIC SAFETY—INSPECTION	14	
ENCUMBRANCES—HIGHWAYS AND STREETS—MAINTENANCE	159	
ENCUMBRANCES—HIGHWAYS AND STREETS—ENGINEERING	50	
ENCUMBRANCES—SANITATION	32	
ENCUMBRANCES—CULTURE AND RECREATION	254	

(To cancel encumbrances related to materials and supplies inventories received)

	DR	CR
37. Inventories	$ 863	
Vouchers payable		$ 863

(To record billings for materials and supplies inventories received)

	DR	CR
38. Expenditures—general government—council	$ 2	
Expenditures—general government—commissions	3	
Expenditures—general government—manager	8	
Expenditures—general government—attorney	3	
Expenditures—general government—clerk	14	
Expenditures—general government—personnel	7	
Expenditures—general government—finance and administration	25	
Expenditures—general government—other—unclassified	30	
Expenditures—public safety—police	134	
Expenditures—public safety—fire	151	
Expenditures—public safety—inspection	14	
Expenditures—highways and streets—maintenance	145	
Expenditures—highways and streets—engineering	47	
Expenditures—sanitation	30	
Expenditures—culture and recreation	248	
Inventories		$ 861

(To record consumption of materials and supplies inventories during the year)

In addition to encumbered billings, the government also records vouchers totaling $22,369 for unencumbered transactions (i.e., primary payroll).

	DR	CR
39. Expenditures—general government—council	$ 78	
Expenditures—general government—commissions	39	

Expenditures—general government—manager	328	
Expenditures—general government—attorney	170	
Expenditures—general government—clerk	189	
Expenditures—general government—personnel	186	
Expenditures—general government—finance and administration	655	
Expenditures—general government—other—unclassified	779	
Expenditures—public safety—police	4,827	
Expenditures—public safety—fire	5,130	
Expenditures—public safety—inspection	846	
Expenditures—highways and streets—maintenance	1,723	
Expenditures—highways and streets—engineering	599	
Expenditures—sanitation	2,206	
Expenditures—culture and recreation	4,614	
Vouchers payable		$ 17,824
Compensated absences payable		670
Due to other funds—public safety pension system fund		1,780
Due to other funds—deferred compensation fund		208
Intergovernmental payable—state		1,887

(To record salaries and other unencumbered benefit liabilities)

Note: The establishment of a compensated absences payable account gives the government the ability to track increases and decreases accurately for related note disclosures.

Outstanding liabilities of $30,932 are paid.

	DR	CR
40. Vouchers payable	$ 22,556	
Accounts payable	942	
Compensated absences payable	646	
Contracts payable	1,447	
Due to other funds—water and sewer fund	159	
Due to other funds—fleet management fund	825	
Due to other funds—management information systems fund	482	
Due to other funds—public safety pension system fund	1,780	
Due to other funds—deferred compensation fund	208	
Intergovernmental payable—state	1,887	
Cash		$ 30,932

(To record payment of liabilities incurred during the year)

During the year, the government agrees to participate in a special assessment pipeline construction project at an estimated cost of $1,200 before change orders.

	DR	CR
41. Other financing uses—operating transfers out—pipeline construction fund	$ 1,200	
Due to other funds—pipeline construction fund		$ 1,200

(To record the government's portion of special assessment project)

	DR	CR
42. Due to other funds—pipeline construction fund	$ 1,025	
Cash		$ 1,025

(To record partial payment of project construction costs)

As part of the special assessment construction project agreement, the government committed to provide additional resources in the event of a shortfall due to a bond discount. The special assessment bonds are sold at $10 discount; therefore, the government is obligated to transfer an amount equal to the discount to the capital projects fund. In addition, the government agreed to pay the special assessment bond issuance costs of $150 from general fund resources. The assumption of this liability also requires a $150 transfer of expenditure authority.

	DR	CR
43. Other financing uses—operating transfers out—pipeline construction fund	$ 10	
Due to other funds—pipeline construction fund		$ 10

(To record government commitment to provide additional resources)

	DR	CR
44. APPROPRIATIONS—GENERAL GOVERNMENT—OTHER—UNCLASSIFIED	$ 150	
APPROPRIATIONS—DEBT SERVICE—OTHER—BOND ISSUANCE COSTS		$ 150

(To record budget transfer)

	DR	CR
45. Expenditures—debt service—other—bond issuance costs	$ 150	
Due to other funds—pipeline construction fund		$ 150

(To record amount due to pipeline construction fund for reimbursement of bond issuance costs)

During the year, the general fund transfers $3,327 to the debt service fund for the retirement of general obligation debt.

	DR	CR
46. Other financing uses—operating transfers out—debt service fund	$ 3,327	
Cash		$ 3,327

(To record operating transfers to debt service fund for the retirement of debt)

During the year, the government enters into capital leases for the acquisition of police communication equipment for $140. Originally, $296 had been encumbered for the purchase of these assets. The lease payment requires a down payment of $15. Originally, $30 had been encumbered for the down payment. Scheduled lease payments are not due until the following year.

	DR	CR
47. BUDGETARY FUND BALANCE—RESERVED FOR ENCUMBRANCES	$ 326	
ENCUMBRANCES—PUBLIC SAFETY—POLICE		$ 326

(To cancel encumbrances related to capital lease acquisition)

	DR	CR
48. Expenditures—public safety—police	$ 140	
Other financing sources—capital leases		$ 140

(To record capital lease acquisition)

	DR	CR
49. Expenditures—debt service—principal	$ 15	
Cash		$ 15
(To record capital lease down payment)		

Note: Some lease arrangements require a down payment. Pursuant to the 1987 *Codification*, Section L20.111, a down payment and subsequent lease payments should be accounted for in a manner consistent with general obligation debt (i.e., when due). In practice, the lease payment may be classified as either debt service or current expenditure. The payment generally is budgeted within a current expenditure function (e.g., public safety).

The government puchases an additional $865 of investments during the year.

	DR	CR
50. Investments	$ 865	
Cash		$ 865
(To record purchase of additional investments)		

In addition to an original advance of $50 that has not been repaid, the general fund advances $20 to the management information systems fund and $40 to the fleet management fund.

	DR	CR
51. Advance to other funds—management information systems fund	$ 20	
Advance to other funds—fleet management fund	40	
Cash		$ 60
(To record advances to the management information systems and fleet management funds)		

At year end, the government classifies the portion of advances expected to be repaid in the following year. The amount is calculated based on a repayment schedule.

	DR	CR
52. Interfund receivable—management information systems fund	$ 24	
Interfund receivable—fleet management fund	8	
Advance to other funds—management information systems fund		$ 24
Advance to other funds—fleet management fund		8
(To reclassify current portions of long-term loans to other funds)		

ILLUSTRATION 3–3

Name of Government
General Fund
Preclosing Trial Balance
December 31, 19X8
(amounts expressed in thousands)

	DR	CR		DR	CR
Cash	$ 1,369		Inventories	39	
Investments	2,091		Advance to other funds—fleet management fund	32	
Interest receivable—investments	92		Advance to other funds—management information systems fund	46	
Taxes receivable—delinquent—property taxes	114		Vouchers payable		705
Allowance for uncollectible delinquent property taxes		$ 28	Accounts payable		165
Interest and penalties receivable—property taxes	14		Compensated absences payable		225
Allowance for uncollectible interest and penalties—property taxes		3	Contracts payable		67
			Due to other funds—pipeline construction fund		335
Tax liens receivable—property taxes	33		Due to other funds—water and sewer fund		37
Allowance for uncollectible tax liens—property taxes		8	Due to other funds—fleet management fund		47
Taxes receivable—sales taxes	830		Due to other funds—management information systems fund		57
Accounts receivable	74				
Allowance for uncollectible accounts receivable		2	Deferred revenue—taxes receivable—delinquent property taxes		24
Intergovernmental receivable—county	215		Deferred revenue—interest and penalties receivable—property taxes		10
Due from other funds—water and sewer fund	65		Deferred revenue—tax liens receivable—property taxes		25
Due from other funds—fleet management fund	8		Deferred revenue—federal government		181
Interfund receivable—fleet management fund	8		Fund balance—reserved for advances		78
Interfund receivable—management information systems fund	24		Fund balance—unreserved, undesignated		1,729
			ESTIMATED REVENUES—PROPERTY TAXES	14,487	

	DR	CR		DR	CR
ESTIMATED REVENUES—SALES TAXES	6,767		APPROPRIATIONS—DEBT SERVICE—OTHER—BOND ISSUANCE COSTS		150
ESTIMATED REVENUES—FRANCHISE TAXES	4,312		ENCUMBRANCES—GENERAL GOVERNMENT—MANAGER	10	
ESTIMATED REVENUES—LICENSES AND PERMITS	1,827		ENCUMBRANCES—GENERAL GOVERNMENT—OTHER—UNCLASSIFIED	95	
ESTIMATED REVENUES—INTERGOVERNMENTAL	5,661		ENCUMBRANCES—PUBLIC SAFETY—POLICE	55	
ESTIMATED REVENUES—CHARGES FOR SERVICES	2,158		ENCUMBRANCES—PUBLIC SAFETY—FIRE	100	
ESTIMATED REVENUES—FINES	810		ENCUMBRANCES—PUBLIC SAFETY—INSPECTION	20	
ESTIMATED REVENUES—INTEREST	555		ENCUMBRANCES—HIGHWAYS AND STREETS—ENGINEERING	40	
ESTIMATED REVENUES—MISCELLANEOUS	345		Expenditures—general government—council	92	
Revenues—property taxes		14,133	Expenditures—general government—commissions	64	
Revenues—sales taxes		6,642	Expenditures—general government—manager	505	
Revenues—franchise taxes		4,293	Expenditures—general government—attorney	387	
Revenues—licenses and permits		2,041	Expenditures—general government—clerk	250	
Revenues—intergovernmental		5,770	Expenditures—general government—personnel	304	
Revenues—charges for services		2,300	Expenditures—general government—finance and administration	880	
Revenues—fines		808	Expenditures—general government—other—unclassified	1,762	
Revenues—interest		623	Expenditures—public safety—police	6,354	
Revenues—miscellaneous—payments in lieu of taxes		345	Expenditures—public safety—fire	6,031	
ESTIMATED OTHER FINANCING SOURCES—CAPITAL LEASES	34		Expenditures—public safety—inspection	1,053	
Other financing sources—sales of general fixed assets		5	Expenditures—highways and streets—maintenance	2,939	
Other financing sources—capital leases		140	Expenditures—highways and streets—engineering	796	
APPROPRIATIONS—GENERAL GOVERNMENT—COUNCIL		98	Expenditures—sanitation	3,726	
APPROPRIATIONS—GENERAL GOVERNMENT—COMMISSIONS		70	Expenditures—culture and recreation	5,882	
APPROPRIATIONS—GENERAL GOVERNMENT—MANAGER		521	Expenditures—debt service—principal	15	
APPROPRIATIONS—GENERAL GOVERNMENT—ATTORNEY		391	Expenditures—debt service—other—bond issuance costs	150	
APPROPRIATIONS—GENERAL GOVERNMENT—CLERK		264	APPROPRIATIONS—OTHER FINANCING USES—OPERATING TRANSFERS OUT		4,700
APPROPRIATIONS—GENERAL GOVERNMENT—PERSONNEL		325	Other financing uses—operating transfers out—debt service fund	3,327	
APPROPRIATIONS—GENERAL GOVERNMENT—FINANCE AND ADMINISTRATION		904	Other financing uses—operating transfers out—pipeline construction fund	1,210	
APPROPRIATIONS—GENERAL GOVERNMENT—OTHER—UNCLASSIFIED		2,055	APPROPRIATIONS—RESIDUAL EQUITY TRANSFERS OUT		60
APPROPRIATIONS—PUBLIC SAFETY—POLICE		6,513	Residual equity transfers out—fleet management fund	45	
APPROPRIATIONS—PUBLIC SAFETY—FIRE		6,040	BUDGETARY FUND BALANCE—RESERVED FOR ENCUMBRANCES		320
APPROPRIATIONS—PUBLIC SAFETY—INSPECTION		1,092	BUDGETARY FUND BALANCE—UNRESERVED		109
APPROPRIATIONS—HIGHWAYS AND STREETS—MAINTENANCE		3,052		$ 78,102	$ 78,102
APPROPRIATIONS—HIGHWAYS AND STREETS—ENGINEERING		814			
APPROPRIATIONS—SANITATION		3,848			
APPROPRIATIONS—CULTURE AND RECREATION		5,950			

The remaining long-term portion of the interfund loans is not considered expendable available financial resources.

	DR	CR
53. Fund balance—unreserved, undesignated	$ 28	
Fund balance—reserved for advances		$ 28
(To reclassify fund balance for outstanding advances)		

The general fund also provides the fleet management fund with a capital contribution of $45 in its start-up period.

	DR	CR
54. Residual equity transfer out—fleet management fund	$ 45	
Cash		$ 45
(To record equity transfer to the fleet management fund)		

The following journal entry illustrates the closing of the general fund budgetary accounts.

	DR	CR
55. APPROPRIATIONS—GENERAL GOVERNMENT—COUNCIL	$ 98	
APPROPRIATIONS—GENERAL GOVERNMENT—COMMISSIONS	70	
APPROPRIATIONS—GENERAL GOVERNMENT—MANAGER	521	
APPROPRIATIONS—GENERAL GOVERNMENT—ATTORNEY	391	
APPROPRIATIONS—GENERAL GOVERNMENT—CLERK	264	
APPROPRIATIONS—GENERAL GOVERNMENT—PERSONNEL	325	
APPROPRIATIONS—GENERAL GOVERNMENT—FINANCE AND ADMINISTRATION	904	
APPROPRIATIONS—GENERAL GOVERNMENT—OTHER—UNCLASSIFIED	2,055	
APPROPRIATIONS—PUBLIC SAFETY—POLICE	6,513	
APPROPRIATIONS—PUBLIC SAFETY—FIRE	6,040	
APPROPRIATIONS—PUBLIC SAFETY—INSPECTION	1,092	
APPROPRIATIONS—HIGHWAYS AND STREETS—MAINTENANCE	3,052	
APPROPRIATIONS—HIGHWAYS AND STREETS—ENGINEERING	814	
APPROPRIATIONS—SANITATION	3,848	
APPROPRIATIONS—CULTURE AND RECREATION	5,950	
APPROPRIATIONS—DEBT SERVICE—BOND ISSUANCE COSTS	150	
APPROPRIATIONS—OTHER FINANCING USES—OPERATING TRANSFERS OUT	4,700	
APPROPRIATIONS—RESIDUAL EQUITY TRANSFERS OUT	60	
BUDGETARY FUND BALANCE—UNRESERVED	109	
ESTIMATED REVENUES—PROPERTY TAXES		$ 14,487
ESTIMATED REVENUES—SALES TAXES		6,767
ESTIMATED REVENUES—FRANCHISE TAXES		4,312
ESTIMATED REVENUES—LICENSES AND PERMITS		1,827
ESTIMATED REVENUES—INTERGOVERNMENTAL		5,661
ESTIMATED REVENUES—CHARGES FOR SERVICES		2,158
ESTIMATED REVENUES—FINES		810
ESTIMATED REVENUES—INTEREST		555
ESTIMATED REVENUES—MISCELLANEOUS		345
ESTIMATED OTHER FINANCING SOURCES—CAPITAL LEASES		34
(To close budgetary accounts)		

Pursuant to budgetary procedures, outstanding encumbrances of $320 are canceled at year end.

	DR	CR
56. BUDGETARY FUND BALANCE—RESERVED FOR ENCUMBRANCES	$ 320	
ENCUMBRANCES—GENERAL GOVERNMENT—MANAGER		$ 10
ENCUMBRANCES—GENERAL GOVERNMENT—OTHER—UNCLASSIFIED		95
ENCUMBRANCES—PUBLIC SAFETY—POLICE		55
ENCUMBRANCES—PUBLIC SAFETY—FIRE		100
ENCUMBRANCES—PUBLIC SAFETY—INSPECTION		20
ENCUMBRANCES—HIGHWAYS AND STREETS—MAINTENANCE		40
(To cancel encumbrances at year end for outstanding purchase orders and contracts)		

The $320 of canceled encumbrances are expected to be honored in the next year.

	DR	CR
57. Fund balance—unreserved, undesignated	$ 320	
Fund balance—reserved for encumbrances		$ 320
(To reclassify fund balance for purchase orders and contracts expected to be honored in the following year)		

Note: This entry would be reversed at the beginning of the subsequent year.

The following journal entry illustrates the closing of the general fund operating statement accounts.

	DR	CR
58. Revenues—property taxes	$ 14,133	
Revenues—sales taxes	6,642	
Revenues—franchise taxes	4,293	
Revenues—licenses and permits	2,041	
Revenues—intergovernmental	5,770	
Revenues—charges for services	2,300	
Revenues—fines	808	
Revenues—interest	623	
Revenues—miscellaneous—payments in lieu of property taxes	345	
Other financing sources—sales of general fixed assets	5	
Other financing sources—capital leases	140	
Expenditures—general government—council		$ 92
Expenditures—general government—commissions		64

Expenditures—general government—
  manager   505

Expenditures—general government—
  attorney   387

Expenditures—general government—clerk   250

Expenditures—general government—
  personnel   304

Expenditures—general government—
  finance and administration   880

Expenditures—general government—
  other—unclassified   1,762

Expenditures—public safety—police   6,354

Expenditures—public safety—fire   6,031

Expenditures—public safety—inspection   1,053

Expenditures—highways and streets—
  maintenance   2,939

Expenditures—highways and streets—
  engineering   796

Expenditures—sanitation   3,726

Expenditures—culture and recreation   5,882

Expenditures—debt service—principal   15

Expenditures—debt service—bond
  issuance costs   150

Other financing uses—operating transfers
  out—debt service fund   3,327

Other financing uses—operating transfers
  out—pipeline construction fund   1,210

Fund balance—unreserved, undesignated   1,373

(To close operating statement accounts)

	DR	CR
59. Fund balance—unreserved, undesignated	$ 45	
Residual equity transfers out—fleet management fund		$ 45
(To close residual equity transfers)		

ILLUSTRATION 3–4

**Name of Government
General Fund
Trial Balance
December 31, 19X8
(amounts expressed in thousands)**

	DR	CR
Cash	$ 1,369	
Investments	2,091	
Interest receivable—investments	92	
Taxes receivable—delinquent—property taxes	114	
Allowance for uncollectible delinquent property taxes		$ 28
Interest and penalties receivable—property taxes	14	
Allowance for uncollectible interest and penalties—property taxes		3
Tax liens receivable—property taxes	33	
Allowance for uncollectible property tax liens		8
Taxes receivable—sales tax	830	
Accounts receivable	74	
Allowance for uncollectible accounts receivable		2
Intergovernmental receivable—county	215	
Due from other funds—water and sewer fund	65	
Due from other funds—fleet management fund	8	
Interfund receivable—fleet management fund	8	
Interfund receivable—management information systems fund	24	
Inventories	39	
Advance to other funds—fleet management fund	32	
Advance to other funds—management information systems fund	46	
Vouchers payable		705
Accounts payable		165
Compensated absences payable		225
Contracts payable		67
Due to other funds—pipeline construction fund		335
Due to other funds—water and sewer fund		37
Due to other funds—fleet management fund		47
Due to other funds—management information systems fund		57
Deferred revenue—taxes receivable—delinquent property taxes		24
Deferred revenue—interest and penalties—property taxes		10
Deferred revenue—tax liens receivable—property taxes		25
Deferred revenue—federal government		181
Fund balance—reserved for encumbrances		320
Fund balance—reserved for advances		78
Fund balance—unreserved, undesignated		2,737
	$ 5,054	$ 5,054

Chapter 4
DEBT SERVICE FUNDS

NATURE AND PURPOSE

Debt service funds are used to account for the accumulation of resources for, and the payment of, general long-term debt principal and interest. The Governmental Accounting Standards Board's 1987 *Codification of Governmental Accounting and Financial Reporting Standards* (1987 *Codification*), Section 1500.109, states, "Debt service funds are required if they are legally mandated and/or if financial resources are being accumulated for principal and interest payments maturing in future years."

In the past, separate debt service funds often were established for each bond issue. Governments needed these separate funds to ensure that monies accumulated for debt service on individual debt issues were adequately segregated. However, many governments now have accounting systems that are able to segregate these sources without establishing separate funds. In such cases, governments should consider using separate subaccounts for each bond issue, either within the general fund or within a single debt service fund, for financial reporting purposes. Typically, such subaccounts are sufficient to meet the legal requirement for separate "funds" contained in statutes, ordinances or bond resolutions. This approach also is considered consistent with the "number of funds" principle discussed in chapter 2.

Governments also should consider changing the language in future legislation for bond issues and indentures to refer to "accounts" rather than to "funds." Management would then have more flexibility regarding the establishment of debt service funds for financial reporting purposes. However, because there may be additional legal considerations associated with interpreting current legal and contractual requirements, these factors should be explored thoroughly before an individual debt service fund is eliminated for financial reporting purposes.

In addition to legal requirements, the other criterion that would require the use of a debt service fund is the accumulation of financial resources for future years' principal and interest. Not all resources set aside for debt service, however, should be considered an "accumulation" in applying the "accumulation of financial resources" criterion. Such accumulations should be recurring and should represent more than year-end transfers to provide for debt service payments due early in the subsequent year. For example, if a payment on a general obligation bond is due on July 2 for a government with a June 30 year end and if the payment to the escrow agent is made from the general fund on June 29, such a payment would *not* be considered an accumulation of resources. Therefore, the establishment of a debt service fund would not be warranted. A different conclusion could be reached, however, if the bond indenture requires the establishment of a sinking fund for the entire next year's bond payments. In this instance, the sinking fund could be considered an accumulation when applying the accumulation of financial resources criterion.

With the expanded use of the general long-term debt account group (GLTDAG), governments often have established debt service funds for the repayment of capital leases and claims. In most circumstances, these funds are *not* required. Generally, expenditures for capital leases and claims can be accounted for in another fund (e.g., general fund).

Also, since the elimination of the special assessment fund type, debt service funds are now used when the government is "obligated in some manner" for the repayment of special assessment debt. In this instance, a debt service fund normally is established for the repayment of debt and a special assessments receivable and corresponding deferred revenue should be recognized in this fund at the time of the levy. Revenues would be recognized only as the assessments meet the revenue recognition availability criterion. The repayment of special assessment debt, when the government is obligated in some manner, would be accounted for in the same manner as the repayment of general obligation debt. Additional special assessment debt guidance is explored in chapter 7.

BUDGETARY ISSUES

Debt service funds often are included in the budgetary process as mandated by state statute or local ordinance. Although appropriated budgets are adopted by the governing bodies (based on expenditure control provisions within the bond indenture provisions), some governments have chosen not to integrate the appropriated budget formally into their accounting system for debt service funds. This approach may be considered acceptable when resources for the repayment of debt are derived primarily from interfund operating transfers. A government, however, should consider integration of an appropriated budget when resources (e.g., property taxes) are deposited directly into the debt service fund. Such integration provides additional accountability for the revenue sources and related debt service expenditures.

As required by the 1987 *Codification,* Section 2400.102, the budget and actual data for annual appropriated budgets of the debt service funds should be presented in the Combined Statement of Revenues, Expenditures and Changes in Fund Balances—Budget and Actual of the general purpose financial statements or component unit financial statements. Individual budgetary comparisons would be required for the comprehensive annual financial report (CAFR) or component unit financial report if the government adopts an annual appropriated budget for more than one debt service fund.

ACCOUNTING ISSUES

Debt service funds are accounted for on the modified accrual basis of accounting using the flow of current financial resources measurement focus. Several accounting issues are associated with debt service funds. These issues include expenditure recognition and advance refundings.

Expenditure Recognition. The primary exception to recording expenditure accruals relates to unmatured principal and interest associated with long-term general obligation debt. Debt service principal and interest expenditures generally are recorded when the payment is due. The "when due" exception to expenditure recognition was established to "match" debt service expenditures with resources accumulated to repay the debt. This approach prevents an understatement or overstatement of debt service fund balance. For example, if debt service principal and interest expenditures were accrued at year end and the resources for the payment (e.g., transfers) were provided in the following year when the payment was due, an expenditure accrual would result in an understatement of fund balance.

On the other hand, when resources are provided to the debt service fund *before* year end, for debt service payments due *early* in the next year, an expenditure *may* be recognized for debt service principal and interest. This treatment is permitted to avoid an overstatement of fund balance in the debt service fund. Nevertheless, governments should ensure that the application of this alternative does not lead to inconsistent financial reporting (see Illustration 4–1).

With the emergence of new debt instruments, the expenditure recognition issue is being raised again. In the past, governments limited debt issuances to serial or term bonds. Serial bond principal payments generally are due annually with interest payments due semiannually. Term bond interest payments generally are also due semiannually, but bond principal is due only at maturity. With the appearance of zero-coupon bonds (i.e., both principal and interest payments are not due until the end of the bond's term), a new element has been introduced to the expenditure recognition issue. Although sinking funds generally are established for this type of debt issue, principal and interest payments are not due early in the following year. Therefore, accrual of principal and interest is not recommended for zero-coupon bonds and other deep-discount debt because the requirement that payments be due "early in the next year" is not met. Accounting for these types of debt issues is discussed further in chapter 7.

Advance Refundings. In addition to normal repayment, debt may be extinguished through an advance refunding. An advance refunding takes place when monies are provided (at least in part by a new debt issuance) to retire previously issued

---

ILLUSTRATION 4–1
Debt Service Expenditure Recognition

A government has a fiscal year end of June 30 and is required to make principal payments of $100,000 on July 7 of each year. Interest and principal are paid on July 7 and interest alone is paid on January 2. On July 1, 19X1, the government transfers the resources for the payment of the July 7 principal and interest payment. In the second year, the government continues its practice of providing resources on July 1 for the year 19X2 principal and interest payment. In addition to this transfer, another transfer is made on June 29 for the following year's (i.e., year 19X3) July 7 principal and interest payment. The government then reverts to funding the July 7 payment on July 1 of the following fiscal year (i.e., year 19X4). This sequence of events would result in the following operating results, if expenditures are recognized when the resources are temporarily accumulated in year 19X2:

	19X1	19X2	19X3
Debt service:			
Principal	$100,000	$200,000	—
Interest	10,000	13,000	$ 4,000
	$110,000	$213,000	$ 4,000

Therefore, to prevent an overstatement of expenditures in year 19X2 and an understatement of expenditures in year 19X3, the government should not recognize expenditures for this type of accumulation unless the change in funding pattern is permanent.

---

debt as it matures or at call date. The Financial Accounting Standards Board's Statement of Financial Accounting Standards (SFAS) No. 76, *Extinguishment of Debt,* provides that debt may be considered extinguished, and both debt and related assets may be removed from the balance sheet, when an advance refunding results in a legal or an in-substance defeasance. An advance refunding results in a legal defeasance when the government is released as the primary obligor of the debt and when it is probable the government will not be required to make future debt service payments. A legal defeasance is rare in the government environment and generally would occur only when an amount sufficient to pay both principal and interest *at the time of deposit* is placed in an irrevocable trust with an independent escrow agent.

SFAS No. 76 also establishes specific criteria that define an in-substance defeasance. To achieve an in-substance defeasance, a government is required to deposit cash or other assets that qualify as "essentially risk free as to amount, timing and collection of principal and interest" in an irrevocable trust. These assets should provide cash flows that "approximately coincide, as to timing and amount, with the scheduled *interest* and *principal* payments on the debt that is being extinguished" (emphasis added).

For an asset to qualify as essentially risk free, it should be either a direct obligation of the U.S. Government, an obligation guaranteed by U.S. Government obligations or securities backed by U.S. Government obligations. Generally, in-substance defeasances for government debt are accomplished through the purchase of state and local government series (SLGS) securities. SLGS securities can provide adequate cash flows that coincide with the refunded obligation's debt service

ILLUSTRATION 4–2

Crossover Refunding

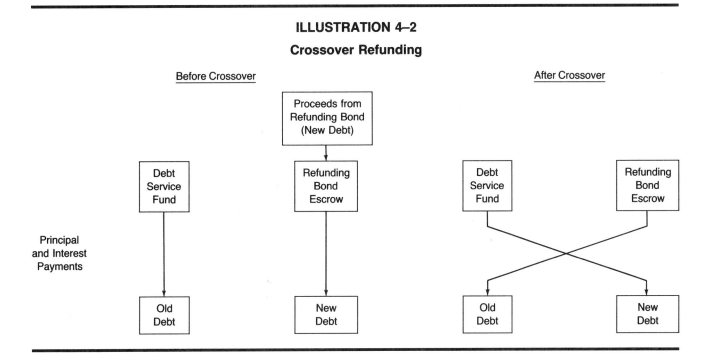

schedule without exceeding the Internal Revenue Code arbitrage limits established by the 1986 Tax Reform Act.

When an advance refunding results in the defeasance of debt reported in the GLTDAG, the 1987 *Codification,* Section D20.108, provides specific guidance. The proceeds from the refunding debt (i.e., new debt) should be reported as an "other financing source—proceeds of refunding bonds" in the fund receiving the proceeds. This fund generally is a debt service fund. The classification of payments to the escrow agent is dependent on the resources used. Payments to the escrow agent from resources provided by the refunding issue should be classified as "other financing use—payment to refunded bond escrow agent." Payments to the escrow agent from other resources (e.g., transfers, sinking fund) should be reported as debt service expenditures. Because the payment to the escrow agent does not represent a direct repayment of bond principal or interest, a third account should be established for the debt service expenditure character classification on the operating statement. "Advance refunding escrow" is a suggested title for the debt service expenditure account.

A crossover refunding does not result in the defeasance of debt. This type of refunding generally produces resources for escrow that are sufficient to pay all or a portion of the new debt's principal and interest until a crossover date when the amount accumulated in escrow is sufficient to repay the old debt. Until the crossover date, both the old and the new debt would be reported in the financial statements. Illustration 4–2 depicts a crossover refunding. Crossover refunding debt was addressed in the American Institute of Certified Public Accountants' Statement of Position (SOP) 78–5, *Accounting for Advance Refundings of Tax-exempt Debt.* SOP 78–5 provided that "the old debt is never defeased at the time of the advance refunding." SOP 78–5 was superseded by SFAS No. 76. Although SFAS No. 76 does not specifically address the crossover refunding issue, application of the guidance provided in this pronouncement also would prohibit the defeasance of the old

debt at the time of the advance refunding. (It should be noted that SOP 78–5 only considered crossover refundings that resulted in the retirement of the old debt at the time of the crossover. The provisions of SFAS No. 76 would apply *at crossover date* to such refundings resulting in an in-substance defeasance at that time.)

The effect on the GLTDAG of an advance refunding and the related note disclosures are discussed in chapters 7 and 14.

ILLUSTRATIVE JOURNAL ENTRIES

The journal entries included in the remainder of this chapter illustrate the accounting operations of the debt service fund of a sample government. If these entries are posted to the accounts listed in the beginning of the year trial balance presented as Illustration 4–3 and to the additional accounts indi-

ILLUSTRATION 4–3

Name of Government
Debt Service Fund
Trial Balance
January 1, 19X8
(amounts expressed in thousands)

	DR	CR
Cash	$ 2	
Investments	8	
Fund balance—reserved for debt service		$ 10
	$ 10	$ 10

cated, the year-end balances presented in Illustration 4–5 will agree with the CAFR in appendix D. All dollar amounts are expressed in thousands.

Formal Budgetary Integration. CAPITAL LETTERS are used for all budgetary accounts presented to highlight formal budgetary integration in the sample government's accounts. Also, budgetary and actual transactions are not presented in control accounts (e.g., revenues). These control accounts in accounting systems are reflected in the general ledger either as a separate entry from the subsidiary ledger or as a simultaneous entry.

The following journal entry illustrates the integration of the $5,060 annual appropriated budget into the government's accounts.

	DR	CR
1. ESTIMATED REVENUES—PROPERTY TAXES	$ 1,500	
ESTIMATED REVENUES—SPECIAL ASSESSMENTS	470	
ESTIMATED REVENUES—INTEREST	220	
ESTIMATED OTHER FINANCING SOURCES—OPERATING TRANSFERS IN	3,500	
APPROPRIATIONS—DEBT SERVICE—PRINCIPAL		$ 2,060
APPROPRIATIONS—DEBT SERVICE—INTEREST		2,950
BUDGETARY FUND BALANCE		680
(To record the annual appropriated budget)		

The following discussion and journal entries illustrate debt service fund revenues, financing sources and receipts affecting balance sheet accounts for the current year.

The government levies $1,595 of property taxes during the current year to provide resources for budgetary expenditures. Payment of the taxes is due before year end.

	DR	CR
2. Taxes receivable—current property taxes	$ 1,595	
Deferred revenue—taxes receivable—current property taxes		$ 1,595
(To record property tax levy)		

Note: Property taxes may be recognized as revenue in the accounting system at the time of levy. Under this method, a deferral associated with property taxes receivable that do not meet the revenue recognition availability criterion should be calculated at year end. See Illustration 2–3 for an example.

The government collects $1,585 of the current year's tax levy before year end.

	DR	CR
3. Cash	$ 1,585	
Taxes receivable—current property taxes		$ 1,585
(To record collection of current year's property taxes)		

	DR	CR
4. Deferred revenue—taxes receivable—current property taxes	$ 1,585	
Revenues—property taxes		$ 1,585
(To recognize revenue for current property tax levy)		

Investments of property tax revenues mature. Proceeds of $1,557 include $62 of interest.

	DR	CR
5. Cash	$ 1,557	
Investments		$ 1,495
Revenues—interest		62
(To record proceeds including interest revenue from matured investments)		

The government debt service fund receives a $3,327 operating transfer from the general fund for the retirement of general obligation debt.

	DR	CR
6. Cash	$ 3,327	
Other financing sources—operating transfers in—general fund		$ 3,327
(To record operating transfer from the general fund for debt service payment)		

The government receives $846 from the pipeline construction capital projects fund to establish a subaccount for the payment of special assessment debt. Debt service payments are scheduled to begin in the following year.

	DR	CR
7. Cash	$ 846	
Other financing sources—operating transfers in—pipeline construction fund		$ 846
(To record transfer of debt service reserve from the pipeline construction fund)		

The government approves a special assessment levy of $4,700 in the current year to repay the special assessment debt. Eight percent interest accrues on outstanding balances assessed to property owners at year end.

	DR	CR
8. Special assessments receivable	$ 4,700	
Deferred revenue—special assessments		$ 4,700
(To record special assessment levy)		

The government collects the $658 first installment of the special assessment levy from property owners. Of this amount, $188 represents interest on the outstanding assessment balance.

	DR	CR
9. Cash	$ 658	
Special assessments receivable		$ 470
Revenues—interest		188
(To record annual collection of special assessment levy)		

	DR	CR
10. Deferred revenue—special assessments	$ 470	
Revenues—special assessments		$ 470
(To recognize revenues associated with special assessment collections)		

The government determines during the year that a $3,000 advance refunding of general obligation bonds (refunded bonds) can be achieved with a $3,300 payment into an escrow account. The advance refunding will result in a $105 economic gain (i.e., difference between the present values of the refunding and refunded bonds, adjusted for additional cash paid). Resources for the advance refunding are obtained through the sale of $3,365 in general obligation bonds (refunding bonds) and the use of $15 in other debt service fund resources. Issuance costs associated with the refunding bonds amount to $65. The advance refunding is approved by the governing body through the adoption of a $3,365 supplemental appropriation and a $15 budget transfer.

	DR	CR
11. ESTIMATED OTHER FINANCING SOURCES—PROCEEDS OF REFUNDING BONDS	$ 3,365	
APPROPRIATIONS—OTHER FINANCING USES—PAYMENT TO REFUNDED BOND ESCROW AGENT		$ 3,300
APPROPRIATIONS—DEBT SERVICE—OTHER—REFUNDING BOND ISSUANCE COSTS		65
(To record budget amendment related to advance refunding)		

	DR	CR
12. APPROPRIATIONS—DEBT SERVICE—PRINCIPAL	$ 6	
APPROPRIATIONS—DEBT SERVICE—INTEREST	9	
APPROPRIATIONS—DEBT SERVICE—OTHER—ADVANCE REFUNDING ESCROW		$ 15
(To record transfer of appropriated budget related to advance refunding)		

The government sells $3,365 of general obligation refunding bonds and incurs $65 of bond issuance costs.

	DR	CR
13. Cash	$ 3,300	
Expenditures—debt service—other—refunding bond issuance costs	65	
Other financing sources—proceeds of refunding bonds		$ 3,365
(To record refunding bond proceeds and related costs)		

Note: Some governments may never directly receive the proceeds from an advance refunding issue. In these instances, the proceeds from the refunding bonds and payments to the escrow agent from the refunding bond proceeds should be combined into one entry.

At year end, statutes require unpaid current property taxes to be classified as delinquent.

	DR	CR
14. Taxes receivable—delinquent—property taxes	$ 10	
Taxes receivable—current property taxes		$ 10
(To reclassify delinquent property taxes at year end)		

	DR	CR
15. Deferred revenue—taxes receivable—current property taxes	$ 10	
Deferred revenue—taxes receivable—delinquent property taxes		$ 10
(To reclassify deferred revenue related to delinquent property taxes)		

At year end, $30 of interest is accrued on outstanding investments.

	DR	CR
16. Interest receivable—investments	$ 30	
Revenues—interest		$ 30
(To record accrued interest revenue)		

The following discussion and journal entries illustrate debt service fund expenditures, financing uses and disbursements affecting balance sheet accounts.

The government invests $1,500 of the property tax revenues and $1,500 of collections and/or transfers related to special assessments.

	DR	CR
17. Investments	$ 3,000	
Cash		$ 3,000
(To record purchase of investments)		

The government remits to its fiscal agent semiannual bond interest payments of $1,450. The entire amount is paid by the fiscal agent to bondholders.

	DR	CR
18. Cash with fiscal agent	$ 1,450	
Cash		$ 1,450
(To record transmittal of cash to fiscal agent for payment of semiannual bond interest)		

	DR	CR
19. Expenditures—debt service—interest	$ 1,450	
Matured interest payable		$ 1,450
(To record expenditures for semiannual bond interest)		

	DR	CR
20. Matured interest payable	$ 1,450	
Cash with fiscal agent		$ 1,450
(To record payments to bondholders by fiscal agent)		

The government remits $3,315 to the refunded bond escrow agent from refunding bond proceeds ($3,300) and other debt service fund resources ($15).

	DR	CR
21. Expenditures—debt service—other—advance refunding escrow	$ 15	
Other financing uses—payment to refunded bond escrow agent	3,300	
Cash		$ 3,315
(To record payment to refunded bond escrow agent)		

The government remits to its fiscal agent annual bond principal payments of $2,030 and semiannual interest payments of $1,478. Of the $3,508 remitted, $3,500 ($2,025 principal and $1,475 interest) was paid to bondholders by the escrow agent.

	DR	CR
22. Cash with fiscal agent	$ 3,508	
Cash		$ 3,508
(To record transmittal of cash to fiscal agent for payment of annual bond principal and semiannual bond interest)		

	DR	CR
23. Expenditures—debt service—principal	$ 2,030	
Expenditures—debt service—interest	1,478	
Matured bonds payable		$ 2,030
Matured interest payable		1,478
(To record expenditures for annual bond principal and semiannual bond interest)		

ILLUSTRATION 4–4

Name of Government
Debt Service Fund
Preclosing Trial Balance
December 31, 19X8
(amounts expressed in thousands)

	DR	CR
Cash	$ 2	
Cash with fiscal agent	8	
Investments	1,513	
Interest receivable—investments	30	
Taxes receivable—delinquent—property taxes	10	
Special assessments receivable	4,230	
Matured bonds payable		$ 5
Matured interest payable		3
Deferred revenue—taxes receivable—delinquent—property taxes		10
Deferred revenue—special assessments		4,230
Fund balance—reserved for debt service		10
ESTIMATED REVENUES—PROPERTY TAXES	1,500	
ESTIMATED REVENUES—SPECIAL ASSESSMENTS	470	
ESTIMATED REVENUES—INTEREST	220	
Revenues—property taxes		1,585
Revenues—special assessments		470
Revenues—interest		280
ESTIMATED OTHER FINANCING SOURCES—PROCEEDS OF REFUNDING BONDS	3,365	
ESTIMATED OTHER FINANCING SOURCES—OPERATING TRANSFERS IN	3,500	
Other financing sources—operating transfers in—general fund		3,327
Other financing sources—operating transfers in—pipeline construction fund		846
Other financing sources—proceeds of refunding bonds		3,365
APPROPRIATIONS—DEBT SERVICE—PRINCIPAL		2,054
APPROPRIATIONS—DEBT SERVICE—INTEREST		2,941
APPROPRIATIONS—DEBT SERVICE—OTHER—ADVANCE REFUNDING ESCROW		15
APPROPRIATIONS—DEBT SERVICE—OTHER—REFUNDING BONDS ISSUANCE COSTS		65
Expenditures—debt service—principal	2,030	
Expenditures—debt service—interest	2,928	
Expenditures—debt service—other—advance refunding escrow	15	
Expenditures—debt service—other—refunding bond issuance costs	65	
APPROPRIATIONS—OTHER FINANCING USES—PAYMENT TO REFUNDED BOND ESCROW AGENT		3,300
Other financing uses—payment to refunded bond escrow agent	3,300	
BUDGETARY FUND BALANCE		680
	$ 23,186	$ 23,186

	DR	CR
24. Matured bonds payable	$ 2,025	
Matured interest payable	1,475	
Cash with fiscal agent		$ 3,500
(To record payments to bondholders by fiscal agent)		

The following journal entry illustrates the closing of the debt service fund budgetary accounts.

	DR	CR
25. APPROPRIATIONS—DEBT SERVICE—PRINCIPAL	$ 2,054	
APPROPRIATIONS—DEBT SERVICE—INTEREST	2,941	
APPROPRIATIONS—DEBT SERVICE—OTHER—ADVANCE REFUNDING ESCROW	15	
APPROPRIATIONS—DEBT SERVICE—OTHER—REFUNDING BOND ISSUANCE COSTS	65	
APPROPRIATIONS—OTHER FINANCING USES—PAYMENT TO REFUNDED BOND ESCROW AGENT	3,300	
BUDGETARY FUND BALANCE	680	
ESTIMATED REVENUES—PROPERTY TAXES		$ 1,500
ESTIMATED REVENUES—SPECIAL ASSESSMENTS		470
ESTIMATED REVENUES—INTEREST		220
ESTIMATED OTHER FINANCING SOURCES—PROCEEDS OF REFUNDING BONDS		3,365
ESTIMATED OTHER FINANCING SOURCES—OPERATING TRANSFERS IN		3,500
(To close budgetary accounts)		

The following journal entry illustrates the closing of the debt service fund operating statement accounts.

	DR	CR
26. Revenues—property taxes	$ 1,585	
Revenues—special assessments	470	
Revenues—interest	280	
Other financing sources—operating transfers in—general fund	3,327	
Other financing sources—operating transfers in—pipeline construction fund	846	
Other financing sources—proceeds of refunding bonds	3,365	
Expenditures—debt service—principal		$ 2,030
Expenditures—debt service—interest		2,928
Expenditures—debt service—other—advance refunding escrow		15
Expenditures—debt service—other—refunding bond issuance costs		65
Other financing uses—payment to refunded bond escrow agent		3,300
Fund balance—reserved for debt service		1,535
(To close operating statement accounts at year end)		

ILLUSTRATION 4–5

Name of Government
Debt Service Fund
Trial Balance
December 31, 19X8
(amounts expressed in thousands)

	DR	CR
Cash	$ 2	
Cash with fiscal agent	8	
Investments	1,513	
Interest receivable—investments	30	
Taxes receivable—delinquent—property taxes	10	
Special assessments receivable	4,230	
Matured bonds payable		$ 5
Matured interest payable		3
Deferred revenue—taxes receivable—delinquent—property taxes		10
Deferred revenue—special assessments		4,230
Fund balance—reserved for debt service		1,545
	$ 5,793	$ 5,793

Chapter 5
CAPITAL PROJECTS FUNDS

NATURE AND PURPOSE

Governments often acquire or construct major capital facilities. Such facilities either can help the government provide services to its citizens (e.g., construction of a police station) or can serve the needs of citizens directly (e.g., establishment of a new park). In addition, governments sometimes acquire or construct assets that primarily benefit the properties of certain citizens, the costs of which are borne by those citizens (i.e., special assessments). In each case, a financial reporting vehicle often is needed to demonstrate compliance with legal and contractual provisions and to compile certain cost data. The capital projects fund type provides such a mechanism and is used, according to the Governmental Accounting Standards Board's 1987 *Codification of Governmental Accounting and Financial Reporting Standards* (1987 *Codification*), Section 1300.104, "to account for the financial resources to be used for the acquisition or construction of major capital facilities other than those financed by proprietary funds and trust funds."[*]

Capital projects funds should be established when legally mandated. They also could be used when capital acquisition or construction is financed, in whole or in part, through bonds, intergovernmental revenues, major private donations or special assessments. In addition, capital projects funds can be useful when capital acquisition or construction is financed by several funds or over several accounting periods.

The "number of funds" principle, as discussed in chapter 2, directs governments to maintain "only the minimum number of funds consistent with legal and operating requirements." Therefore, governments should deliberate carefully before establishing capital projects funds to ensure that this basic principle is followed.

When a government issues debt to finance capital acquisition or construction, it normally needs to demonstrate that the proceeds have been used in accordance with the related debt agreement. Therefore, governments in the past ordinarily established separate capital projects funds for each bond issue. Likewise, when capital acquisition or construction was not financed by debt, governments often established separate funds for each project or closely related group of projects to provide additional controls over expenditures. However, with the information systems now available, many governments no longer need to establish separate funds for individual bond issues or projects. Instead, these governments now use subaccounts within a single capital projects fund to maintain the integrity of the data on individual projects and bond issues. Insofar as this practice can be used to eliminate unnecessary funds, it conforms to the number of funds principle and is to be encouraged. However, governments should evaluate carefully the needs of users of their financial statements for information on individual bond issues and projects before adopting such an approach.

Capital projects funds report capital outlays as expenditures rather than as assets. Accordingly, construction in progress never appears in a capital projects fund. Instead, construction in progress is reported in either the general fixed assets account group (GFAAG) or the appropriate proprietary fund, with a related credit reported as an "investment in general fixed assets" or "contributed capital." However, when a government exercises the option of *not* reporting infrastructure assets in the GFAAG, no construction in progress is reported for construction of the general government's infrastructure. Instead, such infrastructure construction ceases to be reflected in the financial statements once an expenditure has been recognized in the capital projects fund.

Assets remaining in a capital projects fund after the completion of a project normally are conveyed to the debt service fund as a residual equity transfer if debt related to the project is still outstanding. If not, a residual equity transfer typically is made to the fund that provided the resources for the project. Deficits related to completed projects are eliminated most often by residual equity transfers to the capital projects fund from the general fund. Nevertheless, the disposition of the surplus or deficit of a discontinued capital projects fund is often a legal, as well as an accounting, matter. Therefore, whenever a government closes one of its capital projects funds, any related bond indenture should be examined closely to ensure that the disposition of assets is in keeping with the provisions of the indenture.

BUDGETARY ISSUES

Many governments establish capital improvement programs to plan for their capital needs and the means of financing them over a number of years. Often such governments review

---

[*] When acquisition or construction of major capital assets is financed by proprietary or trust funds, it is accounted for in those funds rather than in a capital projects fund. For example, if construction is to be financed through a general obligation bond issue that is to be repaid out of proprietary fund revenues, the construction would be accounted for in the proprietary funds.

the portion of the capital plan related to the coming fiscal year when preparing the annual budget and incorporate all or part of it as a "capital budget" component of the broader annual appropriated budget. Other governments, however, do not provide for capital projects in their annual appropriated budgets. Instead, such governments adopt project-length budgets for their capital projects and rely on mechanisms such as bond indentures to ensure proper control over expenditures. This project-length focus is in keeping with the natural life cycle of capital projects. No matter which method is chosen, governments need to ensure that budgetary compliance is demonstrated in their financial reports.

Annual appropriated budgets for capital projects funds are treated the same as similar budgets for other governmental funds. They should be presented as part of the Combined Statement of Revenues, Expenditures and Changes in Fund Balances—Budget and Actual in the general purpose financial statements or component unit financial statements for fair presentation in conformity with generally accepted accounting principles (GAAP). Moreover, if the legal level of budgetary control is not demonstrated at the combined fund-type level (i.e., annual appropriated budgets are adopted for individual funds), additional reporting is needed. In such cases, a budgetary comparison statement (i.e., GAAP-basis budget) or budgetary comparison schedule (i.e., non-GAAP-basis budget) should be presented in the capital projects fund subsection of the comprehensive annual financial report (CAFR) or component unit financial report (CUFR) for each fund for which an annual appropriated budget has been adopted.

When a project-length budget is adopted, the government should consider whether the need to demonstrate legal compliance would require presentation of budget and actual data since the inception of the project. If such information is necessary, it could be presented in the capital projects fund subsection of the CAFR/CUFR.

Formal budgetary integration is often useful for capital projects funds. Indeed, such integration is essential when an annual appropriated budget is enacted, just as it would be for any other governmental fund type in the same situation. Budgetary integration is also useful when numerous capital projects are accounted for in a single fund or when the government is using its own labor force on a project.

ACCOUNTING ISSUES

The capital projects fund type uses the modified accrual basis of accounting and the flow of current financial resources measurement focus. Therefore, accounting for capital projects funds is essentially similar to the accounting used by other governmental fund types. Nevertheless, questions still arise regarding the classification of financial resources, temporary deficits, premiums and discounts, and interest capitalization.

Classification of Financial Resources. Financial resources used for capital acquisition and construction are classified based on their source. Operating transfers from other funds, as well as the proceeds of most bond issuances, are reported as "other financing sources" and are shown in a subsection of the statement of revenues, expenditures and changes in fund balances, following the excess of revenues over expenditures. Residual equity transfers in, however, are reported as direct additions to beginning fund balance. Interest on investments, intergovern-

mental grants and private donations, on the other hand, are reported as revenues.

Also, the proceeds of special assessment debt with no government commitment (see chapter 10) are reported as revenue rather than as an other financing source. This latter category should be limited to items that provide financial resources to a given fund, but that do not increase the net economic resources of the reporting entity as a whole. To avoid confusion between the proceeds of special assessment debt with no government commitment (which are revenues) and the proceeds of other types of debt (which are *not* revenues), the GASB mandated that the term "bond proceeds" not be applied to the former (1987 *Codification,* Section S40.119).

Temporary Deficits. Sometimes capital projects funds report a temporary deficit if, for instance, a government uses short-term borrowing to finance the early stages of construction. For example, a government decides to finance a three-year capital project with bonds that will be issued in the third year. To begin the project, the government issues short-term bond anticipation notes (BANs). If the BANs do not meet the criteria set forth in the 1987 *Codification,* Section B50.101, for inclusion in the general long-term debt account group (GLTDAG), as discussed in chapter 7, they are reported as a liability of the capital projects fund. Because the debt is reported in the fund along with the proceeds, any expenditures incurred during the first year would create a deficit. This deficit is temporary because it will be eliminated when the bond proceeds budgeted for the project are received in the third year. Concern over such deficits ought to be tempered by consideration of the measurement focus and basis of accounting applicable to the capital projects fund type. Unlike "retained earnings" in the commercial model, the unreserved fund balance of governmental funds is designed to reflect only net expendable, *available* financial resources. A deficit in a capital projects fund, therefore, demonstrates only that uses of expendable available financial resources have exceeded sources. A deficit does *not* necessarily indicate that the government is facing financial difficulties.

Premiums and Discounts. Another accounting issue for capital projects funds is the proper treatment of premiums or discounts on bond issuances. As noted earlier, capital projects funds use the flow of current financial resources measurement focus. Amortization is not appropriate under this measurement focus because the amounts so recognized would not represent an increase or decrease in expendable available financial resources. Therefore, bonds issued generally are reported at their face value in the GLTDAG (i.e., without any applicable discounts or premiums), and the net proceeds of the issuance are reported as an other financing source in the capital projects fund's statement of revenues, expenditures and changes in fund balances. Care should be taken to ensure that the amount reported as "proceeds" is computed correctly. Sometimes issuance costs are withheld from bond proceeds as an additional discount or reduction of premium. In such instances, only the amount representing an adjustment of the face value of the bonds to their present value should be subtracted or added to determine the amount of the proceeds, which are then accounted for as an other financing source. Any amounts withheld for issuance costs should be included in the calculation of proceeds and then reported separately as an expenditure under the debt service character classification on the statement of revenues, expenditures and changes in fund balances.

Interest Capitalization. Capitalization of interest on capital projects also demands consideration. The Financial Accounting Standards Board's (FASB) Statement of Financial Accounting Standards (SFAS) No. 34, *Capitalization of Interest Cost,* requires that interest costs incurred during the construction phase of certain qualified assets be capitalized as part of their cost. According to the 1987 *Codification,* Section 1400.111, the application of this standard to assets that are to be reported in the GFAAG appears optional. However, the 1987 *Codification* left open the question of interest capitalization when capital projects funds are used for construction undertaken on behalf of a proprietary fund. Those favoring interest capitalization in such cases argue that the value of an asset should not depend upon the fund used to account for its construction. Because interest capitalization is required for asset construction reported in proprietary funds, they support extending the same treatment to assets constructed on behalf of proprietary funds. Such an approach, however, can lead to both practical and theoretical problems. Interest capitalization results in higher depreciation expense and can lead to higher user charges. Yet, when construction is reported in a capital projects fund, the responsibility for debt service remains with the general government, not with the proprietary fund. Therefore, a proprietary fund could recover a "cost" that is, in fact, borne by another fund. For this reason, it is recommended that interest not be capitalized on assets constructed on behalf of proprietary funds.

If a government determines that interest capitalization is appropriate for assets reported in the GFAAG, care should be taken that the amount of interest capitalized is computed correctly. In particular, governments must ensure that the provisions of SFAS No. 62, *Capitalization of Interest Cost in Situations Involving Certain Tax-Exempt Borrowings and Certain Gifts and Grants,* are met. This pronouncement requires that interest costs be netted in certain instances against interest earned on the invested proceeds of tax-exempt borrowings when determining the amount of interest to be capitalized. For governments, this approach means that, in most cases, the information needed for the calculation must be drawn from two separate funds (i.e., the debt service fund and the capital projects fund). Accordingly, the calculation of interest to be capitalized normally is performed outside the government's accounting system.

Also, at no time should any amount of capitalized interest appear in the capital projects fund. Instead, the capitalized interest should be reflected in the GFAAG or proprietary fund, as appropriate.

ILLUSTRATIVE JOURNAL ENTRIES

The government establishes a new capital projects fund to account for pipeline construction in a newly developed portion of the government's service area. The construction will take place over the current year and the subsequent year. All amounts are presented in thousands.

Projected sources of funds:

Special assessment debt	$ 4,700
State grant	248
General fund	1,200
Total sources of funds	$ 6,148

Projected uses of funds:

Appropriation for special assessments:		
Contract	$ 3,815	
Projected change orders	39	
Operating transfer to establish mandatory "reserve"	846	
		$ 4,700
Appropriation for public purpose portion of project:		
Contract	1,146	
Projected change orders	12	
Other costs (to be borne directly by government)	290	
		1,448
Total uses of funds		$ 6,148

Issuance costs on the special assessment debt will be paid by the general fund. Also, the general fund will be responsible for transferring an amount equal to any proceeds shortfall if the special assessment debt is issued at a discount. If the issuance of the special assessment debt results in a premium, that amount will be transferred to the debt service fund. The state grant is expenditure-driven, with one half of the total amount to be advanced at the beginning of each of the two fiscal years of the project. Both contracts contain retainage provisions allowing the government to withhold payment of up to 5 percent of progress billings until the project is completed satisfactorily. The special assessment debt issue calls for even, annual payments of principal and semiannual payments of interest at 8 percent over ten years, and requires that a "reserve" be established in the debt service fund equal to the following year's total payments of principal and interest.

Formal Budgetary Integration. CAPITAL LETTERS are used for all budgetary accounts presented in the journal entries to highlight formal budgetary integration in the sample government's accounts. Also, budgetary and actual transactions are not presented in control accounts (e.g., revenues). These control accounts in accounting systems are reflected in the general ledger either as a separate entry from the subsidiary ledger or as a simultaneous entry.

Except for the budgetary accounts, which are not presented in the financial statements, the amounts reported in Illustration 5–2 agree with the CAFR in appendix D.

The following journal entry illustrates the integration of the project budget into the government's accounts.

	DR	CR
1. ESTIMATED REVENUES—INTERGOVERNMENTAL—STATE	$ 248	
ESTIMATED OTHER FINANCING SOURCES—OPERATING TRANSFERS IN—GENERAL FUND	1,200	
ESTIMATED OTHER FINANCING SOURCES—BOND PROCEEDS—SPECIAL ASSESSMENT DEBT	4,700	
APPROPRIATIONS—CAPITAL OUTLAY—PUBLIC WORKS		$ 1,448
APPROPRIATIONS—CAPITAL OUTLAY—SPECIAL ASSESSMENTS		3,854
APPROPRIATIONS—OTHER FINANCING USES—OPERATING TRANSFERS OUT—DEBT SERVICE FUND		846
(To record the project budget)		

The following discussion and journal entries illustrate capital projects fund revenues, financing sources, receipts affecting balance sheet accounts and related nonmonetary transactions for the first year of the project.

The government receives an advance of $124 from the state to cover the state's portion of project expenditures for the first year. The state's participation is in the form of an expenditure-driven grant. Therefore, revenue can be recognized only as expenditures are incurred in conformity with the grant agreement.

	DR	CR
2. Cash	$ 124	
Deferred revenue—intergovernmental—state		$ 124
(To record the state portion of project costs)		

An interfund receivable of $1,200 is established in the capital projects fund for the general fund's portion of the project costs.

	DR	CR
3. Due from other funds—general fund	$ 1,200	
Other financing sources—operating transfers in—general fund		$ 1,200
(To record the general fund's portion of project costs)		

The capital projects fund receives $1,025 as partial payment from the general fund for its portion of project costs.

	DR	CR
4. Cash	$ 1,025	
Due from other funds—general fund		$ 1,025
(To record collection of part of the amount receivable from the general fund)		

The government issues special assessment debt with a face value of $4,700. The government receives bond proceeds of $4,540 (i.e., net of a $160 discount). Of this $160, only $10 represents an adjustment of the face value of the bonds to their present value. The remaining discount of $150 is issuance costs withheld from the proceeds by the underwriter.

	DR	CR
5. Cash	$ 4,540	
Due from other funds—general fund	150	
Other financing sources—bond proceeds—special assessment debt		$ 4,690
(To record the issuance of special assessment bonds)		

Note: The face amount of the debt less the present value adjustment is the amount reported as proceeds. The amount withheld for issuance costs still is considered part of the proceeds even though it was never, in fact, received by the government. No expenditure for issuance costs is reported in the capital projects fund because the general fund is committed to reimburse these costs.

The government records the general fund's obligation to make up the $10 difference between the face value of the

special assessment bonds and their present value (i.e., bond discount).

	DR	CR
6. Due from other funds—general fund	$ 10	
Other financing sources—operating transfers in—general fund		$ 10
(To record the general fund's commitment to make up the difference between the face value of the special assessment bonds and their present value)		

The capital projects fund sells investments that originally cost the government $2,004. The sales price of $2,149 includes $145 of accrued interest.

	DR	CR
7. Cash	$ 2,149	
Investments		$ 2,004
Revenues—interest		145
(To record the sale of investments)		

The government accrues interest of $64 on its capital projects fund investments at year end.

	DR	CR
8. Interest receivable—investments	$ 64	
Revenues—interest		$ 64
(To record the year-end accrual of interest on investments)		

The government recognizes that it has earned the $124 advanced by the state because qualified expenditures have been incurred and matching requirements have been met.

	DR	CR
9. Deferred revenue—intergovernmental—state	$ 124	
Revenues—intergovernmental—state		$ 124
(To recognize revenue for expenditure-driven grant from the state)		

Note: The 1987 *Codification*, Section G60.109, clarifies that revenue from expenditure-driven grants is recognized when the expenditure is made and when any cost-sharing or matching requirements are met, provided the revenue is then measurable and available.

The following discussion and journal entries illustrate capital projects fund expenditures, financing uses, encumbrances and disbursements affecting balance sheet accounts.

The government transfers to a "reserve" established in the debt service fund an amount equal to the following year's principal and interest requirements for special assessment debt.

	DR	CR
10. Other financing uses—operating transfers out—debt service fund	$ 846	
Cash		$ 846
(To record transfer to debt service fund to establish mandatory "reserve" of one year's principal and interest)		

Note: An alternative approach would be to record the proceeds designated for the "reserve" directly in the debt service fund as an "other financing source."

The government records $5,161 of encumbrances on purchase orders issued and contracts approved.

	DR	CR
11. ENCUMBRANCES—CAPITAL OUTLAY—PUBLIC WORKS—CONTRACTS	$ 1,146	
ENCUMBRANCES—CAPITAL OUTLAY—PUBLIC WORKS—PURCHASE ORDERS	253	
ENCUMBRANCES—CAPITAL OUTLAY—SPECIAL ASSESSMENTS	3,762	
BUDGETARY FUND BALANCE—RESERVED FOR ENCUMBRANCES		$ 5,161
(To record encumbrances for purchase orders and contracts)		

The government agrees to a change-order request from the contractor that will raise by $15 the contract amount related to the special assessment project.

	DR	CR
12. ENCUMBRANCES—CAPITAL OUTLAY—SPECIAL ASSESSMENTS	$ 15	
BUDGETARY FUND BALANCE—RESERVED FOR ENCUMBRANCES		$ 15
(To record change order to a special assessment-related contract)		

The government receives progress billings of $2,979 ($2,225 related to the special assessment contract and $754 related to the contract for the general public benefit portion). These amounts have been encumbered. The government also receives invoices for goods and services totaling $251. However, the related purchase orders used to establish the encumbrance amounted to $253. Of the $2,979 of progress billings, $149 is to be withheld, in accordance with the provisions of the contracts, until the projects are completed satisfactorily.

	DR	CR
13. BUDGETARY FUND BALANCE—RESERVED FOR ENCUMBRANCES	$ 3,232	
ENCUMBRANCES—CAPITAL OUTLAY—PUBLIC WORKS—CONTRACTS		$ 754
ENCUMBRANCES—CAPITAL OUTLAY—PUBLIC WORKS—PURCHASE ORDERS		253
ENCUMBRANCES—CAPITAL OUTLAY—SPECIAL ASSESSMENTS		2,225
(To cancel encumbrances related to progress billings and invoices for goods and services received)		

	DR	CR
14. Expenditures—capital outlay—public works	$ 1,005	
Expenditures—capital outlay—special assessments	2,225	
Contracts payable—public works		$ 716
Contracts payable—special assessments		2,114
Accounts payable—public works		251
Retainage payable—public works		38
Retainage payable—special assessments		111
(To record progress billings and invoices for goods and services received)		

The government pays the $2,830 due on contracts payable.

ILLUSTRATION 5–1

**Name of Government
Pipeline Construction Capital Projects Fund
Preclosing Trial Balance
December 31, 19X8
(amounts expressed in thousands)**

	DR	CR
Cash	$ 323	
Investments	1,835	
Interest receivable—investments	64	
Due from other funds—general fund	335	
Accounts payable—public works		$ 251
Retainage payable—public works		38
Retainage payable—special assessments		111
ESTIMATED REVENUES—INTERGOVERNMENTAL—STATE	248	
Revenues—intergovernmental—state		124
Revenues—interest		209
APPROPRIATIONS—CAPITAL OUTLAY—PUBLIC WORKS		1,448
APPROPRIATIONS—CAPITAL OUTLAY—SPECIAL ASSESSMENTS		3,854
ENCUMBRANCES—CAPITAL OUTLAY—PUBLIC WORKS—CONTRACTS	392	
ENCUMBRANCES—CAPITAL OUTLAY—SPECIAL ASSESSMENTS	1,552	
Expenditures—capital outlay—public works	1,005	
Expenditures—capital outlay—special assessments	2,225	
ESTIMATED OTHER FINANCING SOURCES—BOND PROCEEDS—SPECIAL ASSESSMENT DEBT	4,700	
ESTIMATED OTHER FINANCING SOURCES—OPERATING TRANSFERS IN—GENERAL FUND	1,200	
Other financing sources—bond proceeds—special assessment debt		4,690
Other financing sources—operating transfers in—general fund		1,210
APPROPRIATIONS—OTHER FINANCING USES—OPERATING TRANSFERS OUT—DEBT SERVICE FUND		846
Other financing uses—operating transfers out—debt service fund	846	
BUDGETARY FUND BALANCE—RESERVED FOR ENCUMBRANCES		1,944
	$ 14,725	$ 14,725

	DR	CR
15. Contracts payable—public works	$ 716	
Contracts payable—special assessments	2,114	
Cash		$ 2,830
(To record the payment of progress billings less retainage)		

The government determines that it can invest $3,839 of the cash in the capital projects fund and still meet its cash needs for the immediate future.

	DR	CR
16. Investments	$ 3,839	
Cash		$ 3,839
(To record the purchase of investments)		

The following discussion and journal entries illustrate the capital projects fund year-end closing process.

	DR	CR
17. Revenues—intergovernmental—state	$ 124	
Revenues—interest	209	
Other financing sources—operating transfers in—general fund	1,210	
Other financing sources—bond proceeds—special assessment debt	4,690	
Expenditures—capital outlay—public works		$ 1,005
Expenditures—capital outlay—special assessments		2,225
Other financing uses—operating transfers out—debt service fund		846
Fund balance—unreserved, undesignated		2,157
(To close operating statement accounts)		

	DR	CR
18. APPROPRIATIONS—CAPITAL OUTLAY—PUBLIC WORKS	$ 1,005	
APPROPRIATIONS—CAPITAL OUTLAY—SPECIAL ASSESSMENTS	2,225	
APPROPRIATIONS—OTHER FINANCING USES—OPERATING TRANSFERS OUT—DEBT SERVICE FUND	846	
BUDGETARY FUND BALANCE—UNRESERVED	1,948	
ESTIMATED REVENUES—INTERGOVERNMENTAL—STATE		$ 124
ESTIMATED OTHER FINANCING SOURCES—OPERATING TRANSFERS IN—GENERAL FUND		1,200
ESTIMATED OTHER FINANCING SOURCES—BOND PROCEEDS—SPECIAL ASSESSMENT DEBT		4,700
(To close out the portion of budgetary revenues, other financing sources and appropriations related to the actual revenues, other financing sources/uses and expenditures of the first year of the project)		

Note: The budgetary accounts established at the beginning of the project are closed only in amounts equal to actual revenues, other financing sources and expenditures at year end because the budgetary authority remains in force until the end of the project. Closing out amounts in the budgetary accounts used in the first year is necessary to ensure that the subsequent year's results are compared to remaining budgetary authority.

The government establishes a $1,944 reserve for encumbrances to indicate the amount of fund balance in the capital projects fund that does not represent expendable available financial resources.

	DR	CR
19. Fund balance—unreserved, undesignated	$ 1,944	
Fund balance—reserved for encumbrances		$ 1,944
(To establish a reserve for actual encumbrances open at year end)		

Note: This entry would be reversed at the beginning of the subsequent year.

ILLUSTRATION 5–2

**Name of Government
Pipeline Construction Capital Projects Fund
Trial Balance
December 31, 19X8
(amounts expressed in thousands)**

	DR	CR
Cash	$ 323	
Investments	1,835	
Interest receivable—investments	64	
Due from other funds—general fund	335	
Accounts payable—public works		$ 251
Retainage payable—public works		38
Retainage payable—special assessments		111
Fund balance—reserved for encumbrances		1,944
Fund balance—unreserved, undesignated		213
ESTIMATED REVENUES—INTERGOVERNMENTAL—STATE	124	
APPROPRIATIONS—CAPITAL OUTLAY—PUBLIC WORKS		443
APPROPRIATIONS—CAPITAL OUTLAY—SPECIAL ASSESSMENTS		1,629
ENCUMBRANCES—CAPITAL OUTLAY—PUBLIC WORKS		392
ENCUMBRANCES—CAPITAL OUTLAY—SPECIAL ASSESSMENTS		1,552
BUDGETARY FUND BALANCE—RESERVED FOR ENCUMBRANCES	1,944	
BUDGETARY FUND BALANCE—UNRESERVED	1,948	
	$ 6,573	$ 6,573

Chapter 6
GENERAL FIXED ASSETS ACCOUNT GROUP

NATURE AND PURPOSE

Governmental funds use the flow of current financial resources measurement focus. Except for certain limited cases (e.g., inventories) and in keeping with the aims of that measurement focus, only "financial" assets (i.e., assets that will be converted into cash in the course of normal operations) are reported in those funds. Therefore, fixed assets, because they are not financial in nature, are excluded. Yet, accountability requires that adequate control be maintained over fixed assets. Accordingly, generally accepted accounting principles (GAAP) require that those fixed assets of a government not reported in a proprietary fund or a trust fund be reported in a general fixed assets account group (GFAAG). This account group is not a fund; it does not have a balance sheet as such, nor does it report operations. Instead, the GFAAG serves as a list of the government's fixed assets and is designed to ensure accountability. Because the account group does not report operations, all additions and deletions to the GFAAG should be recorded by direct adjustments to the accounts appearing on the entity's combined balance sheet.

The Governmental Accounting Standards Board's 1987 *Codification of Governmental Accounting and Financial Reporting Standards* (1987 *Codification*), Section 1400.109, specifically allows governments the option of *not* reporting "infrastructure" fixed assets in the GFAAG. By definition, infrastructure assets are "immovable and of value only to the governmental unit" (e.g., sidewalks, gutters, bridges). Therefore, some have argued that there is less need for an "accountability listing" of such assets because the risk of their being lost or stolen is considerably less than that of other fixed assets. Such an argument, however, fails to take into account the potential losses that can result from poor maintenance or general neglect.

The assets reported in the GFAAG normally are presented by class (i.e., land, buildings, improvements other than buildings, equipment). The total amount of these assets is offset by "investment in general fixed assets" accounts that normally provide details on the sources of funding for these assets (e.g., other governments, individuals, capital projects, grants). The investment in general fixed assets account is presented as an "other credit" with the government's equity accounts.

Because an account group does not report operations, as described above, no charge for depreciation can be reported in the account group. Therefore, assets reported in the GFAAG normally continue to be reported at their original cost (or fair market value at the time of donation) until disposal. However, GAAP provide governments with the option of reporting "accumulated depreciation" on these assets. Because no charge for depreciation can be reported, this account is established by directly reducing the investment in general fixed assets account and crediting accumulated depreciation for the same amount.

ACCOUNTING ISSUES

A number of practical issues arise in connection with fixed assets reported in the GFAAG. These issues include the proper valuation of the assets, trade-ins, asset "transfers," deletions, adjustments for the results of physical inventories and revision of capitalization policies.

Valuation of Assets. Fixed assets should be recorded at historical (i.e., original) cost. Normally, by applying this rule, governments will report an amount in the GFAAG for fixed assets that equals the related governmental fund expenditures incurred to purchase or construct the fixed asset. Such expenditures include not only the purchase price or construction costs of the asset, but also any other reasonable and necessary costs incurred to place the asset in its intended location and prepare it for its intended use. Such costs could include the following:

- Legal and title fees;
- Closing costs;
- Appraisal and negotiation fees;
- Surveying fees;
- Damage payments;
- Land-preparation costs;
- Demolition cost;
- Architect and accounting fees;
- Insurance premiums during the construction phase;
- Transportation charges; and
- Interest costs during construction (see related discussion in chapters 2 and 5).

Donated or contributed assets should be recorded at their fair market value on the date donated.

When governments establish general fixed assets records for the first time, it is sometimes impossible to determine the original cost of the assets. In such instances, governments may use "estimated historical cost" to value the fixed assets.

One method of estimating historical cost is to establish the average installed cost for a like unit at the estimated date of acquisition. For example, if a government is unable to locate invoices or other similar documentation to establish the cost of a machine acquired ten years ago, the government could try to determine the average cost of such a unit at that time and use that amount as the estimated historical cost of the machine.

A second method of estimating historical cost is known as normal costing or back trending. Under this method, a government would estimate the historical cost of an asset by taking the current cost of reproduction and dividing that amount by the price index (i.e., the percentage of the price increase plus one) since acquisition for that specific asset or class of assets. For example, if a government had a five-year-old offset press that would now cost $5,750 to replace, the government would divide the $5,750 by the appropriate price index. In this case, appraisal manuals indicate that the price of that class of equipment increased by 18.7 percent over the five years since the offset press was acquired; therefore, the historical cost of the asset can be estimated to be $4,844 (i.e., $5,750 divided by 1.187). Contractors, such as appraisal firms, normally have computer software that includes information on price indexes for each class of assets, reducing the effort needed to apply this method.

When general fixed assets are acquired through leases meeting the capitalization requirements of the Financial Accounting Standards Board's Statement of Financial Accounting Standards (SFAS) No. 13, *Accounting for Leases,* they should be reported at the net present value of future minimum lease payments. The requirements of SFAS No. 13 are discussed in chapter 3.

Assets acquired through the use of eminent domain should be valued at the amount of compensation paid to the property owner. Assets acquired through foreclosure actions should be treated in conformity with the government's plans for their eventual disposition. When a government intends to retain assets obtained in foreclosure actions, the assets should be reported in the GFAAG at their fair value on the date of foreclosure. On the other hand, if the government expects to resell the assets in the near future, they should be accounted for in the fund to which the taxes or assessments are owed, rather than in the GFAAG. These assets should be reported at fair market value with a liability to the property owner, if needed, to reflect any excess of the value of the asset over the government's tax or assessment lien.

Trade-ins. When an asset reported in the GFAAG is traded in to obtain a new asset, the old asset's value has no effect upon the value of the new. Instead, the old asset simply is removed from the GFAAG, and the new asset is reported there at its fair market value. For example, if a government trades in a machine reported in the GFAAG at $8,000 to obtain a new machine with a fair market value of $9,000 ($5,000 cash plus $4,000 trade-in allowance), the new asset would be valued in the GFAAG at $9,000, and the old asset would be removed from the account group.

Because account groups do not report operations, the only operating statement effect would be in the governmental fund purchasing the new asset. In that fund, the government could choose to use either the "gross" or the "net" method. Using the gross method and the example above, the government would report the entire $9,000 fair market value of the asset as an expenditure, even though only $5,000 of cash was actually spent. The trade-in allowance would then be reported as an other financing source of the governmental fund. On the other hand, if the net method were used, the governmental fund would only report a $5,000 expenditure for the cash paid in the transaction. Although both methods are acceptable under GAAP, the gross method generally is considered preferable because it shows the entire transaction, rather than only the cash portion.

Asset Transfers. As mentioned earlier, account groups cannot engage in "transfers" as that term normally is used because an account group is not a fund and, therefore, does not report operations. However, fixed assets sometimes are "transferred" to the general government from a proprietary fund or trust fund. In such cases, the asset is recorded in the GFAAG simply by making an entry to both the appropriate asset and investment in general fixed assets accounts.

The appropriate valuation of such a transferred asset, however, is less clear. Some argue that the asset should be reported at its original cost, even if it had been depreciated in the proprietary fund. They believe there is no reason the general rule requiring fixed assets to be valued at original cost should not be interpreted literally in this case. Others, however, believe that a literal interpretation of this rule distorts the financial statements by increasing the value of an asset through an intraentity transaction. Therefore, they favor reporting only the depreciated value of the asset in the GFAAG. In practice, both approaches commonly are followed.

Deletions. As mentioned earlier, additions to or deletions from the GFAAG should be reflected by direct adjustments to the appropriate accounts appearing on the entity's combined balance sheet. Often, however, all deletions are not properly reported. Although governments normally provide for the reporting of all formal asset retirements, "effective retirements" resulting from the loss, theft or obsolescence of assets often may be overlooked. Governments need to establish accounting systems and a schedule of physical inventories to ensure that these effective retirements are included among the deletions of general fixed assets reported in the financial statements.

Adjustments for the Results of Physical Inventories. As previously mentioned, physical inventories need to be taken periodically to provide support for the amounts of general fixed assets reported in the financial statements. Sometimes, however, rather than supporting the amounts reported in the GFAAG, physical inventories indicate the need for adjustments to those amounts. When adjustments are required, they should be reflected in the notes to the financial statements, as described in chapter 14. No changes should be made to the amounts reported in the "memorandum only" total column for the prior year, if presented.

Revision of Capitalization Policies. In an effort to ensure that the benefits of maintaining fixed asset records exceed the related cost, many governments have reexamined their capitalization policies. Often, the result of such a reexamination is that a government will choose to institute a higher capitalization threshold. For example, a government that had been capitalizing all items with more than a one-year useful life and a value greater than $100 could choose to raise the $100 threshold to $200. If such a change is made, amounts previously reported for fixed assets should be adjusted to reflect the new capitalization policy. This adjustment then could be reported in the same manner as adjustments made to reflect the results of physical inventories. Although sometimes encountered in practice, the prospective implementation of a new capitalization threshold (i.e., previously acquired assets not meeting the new threshold continue to be reported in the GFAAG) is not conducive to comparability and is not appropriate for financial reporting.

ILLUSTRATIVE JOURNAL ENTRIES

ILLUSTRATION 6–1

Name of Government
General Fixed Assets Account Group
Trial Balance
January 1, 19X8
(amounts expressed in thousands)

	DR	CR
Land	$ 38,775	
Buildings	7,875	
Improvements other than buildings	4,604	
Machinery and equipment	7,401	
Construction in progress	722	
Investments in general fixed assets—general fund		$ 11,744
Investments in general fixed assets—special revenue funds		3,497
Investments in general fixed assets—capital projects funds		42,442
Investments in general fixed assets—donations		1,694
	$ 59,377	$ 59,377

The following journal entries and discussion, where applicable, illustrate acquisitions and dispositions of general fixed assets reported in the GFAAG. All of the following journal entries are expressed in thousands.

General fixed assets of $659 (i.e., machinery and equipment) are purchased outright with general fund resources.

	DR	CR
1. Machinery and equipment	$ 659	
Investment in general fixed assets—general fund		$ 659
(To record purchase of general fixed assets with general fund resources)		

General fixed assets of $376 (i.e., machinery and equipment) are purchased outright with special revenue fund resources.

	DR	CR
2. Machinery and equipment	$ 376	
Investment in general fixed assets—special revenue funds		$ 376
(To record purchase of general fixed assets with special revenue fund resources)		

A general fixed asset (e.g., a truck) is purchased with general fund resources for $15 (i.e., cost $17 less trade-in of $2 for a general fixed asset originally purchased for $14 from general fund resources).

	DR	CR
3. Machinery and equipment	$ 17	
Investment in general fixed assets—general fund		$ 17
(To record purchase of general fixed assets with trade-in from general fund resources)		
4. Investment in general fixed assets—general fund	$ 14	
Machinery and equipment		$ 14
(To record retirement of traded-in fixed asset)		

Police communication equipment is acquired by the general fund through a capital lease at a cost of $140. The net present value of the minimum lease payments is $140.

	DR	CR
5. Machinery and equipment	$ 140	
Investment in general fixed assets—general fund		$ 140
(To record assets acquired through a capital lease transaction)		

The capital projects fund incurs expenditures of $2,058 for the construction of a general fixed asset (i.e., a building) not yet complete.

	DR	CR
6. Construction in progress	$ 2,058	
Investment in general fixed assets—capital projects fund		$ 2,058
(To record expenditures incurred in the capital projects fund for partially completed building project)		

Note: This transaction is not illustrated in chapter 5.

The capital projects fund incurs expenditures of $31 on a building project completed during the year. Expenditures charged in the previous year totaled $472.

	DR	CR
7. Buildings	$ 503	
Construction in progress		$ 472
Investment in general fixed assets—capital projects fund		31
(To record expenditures incurred in the capital projects fund for completed building project)		

Note: This transaction is not illustrated in chapter 5.

General fixed assets costing $42 originally purchased with general fund resources are sold for $5.

	DR	CR
8. Investment in general fixed assets—general fund	$ 42	
Machinery and equipment		$ 42
(To record sale of general fixed assets originally purchased with general fund resources)		

General fixed assets costing $8 originally purchased with general fund resources are considered obsolete and scrapped.

	DR	CR
9. Investment in general fixed assets—general fund	$ 8	
Machinery and equipment		$ 8
(To record disposal of general fixed assets originally purchased with general fund resources)		

Through the government's power of eminent domain, land is acquired at a cost of $558 from general fund resources, as determined by the courts.

	DR	CR
10. Land	$ 558	
Investment in general fixed assets—general fund		$ 558
(To record purchase of land acquired through the government's power of eminent domain)		

The government receives a donation of equipment with a fair market value of $13 to be used in the police department.

	DR	CR
11. Machinery and equipment	$ 13	
Investment in general fixed assets—donations		$ 13
(To record receipt of equipment donation)		

Fixed assets (i.e., vehicles and a maintenance garage) previously used for this activity in the general fund are transferred from the GFAAG to the new fleet management internal service fund. The fixed assets transferred originally cost $4,253 (i.e., building $87 and machinery and equipment $4,166).

	DR	CR
12. Investment in general fixed assets—general fund	$ 4,253	
Buildings		$ 87
Machinery and equipment		4,166
(To record contribution of general fixed assets to the fleet management internal service fund)		

ILLUSTRATION 6–2

Name of Government
General Fixed Assets Account Group
Trial Balance
December 31, 19X8
(amounts expressed in thousands)

	DR	CR
Land	$ 39,333	
Buildings	8,291	
Improvements other than buildings	4,604	
Machinery and equipment	4,376	
Construction in progress	2,308	
Investment in general fixed assets—general fund		$ 8,801
Investment in general fixed assets—special revenue funds		3,873
Investment in general fixed assets—capital projects funds		44,531
Investment in general fixed assets—donations		1,707
	$ 58,912	$ 58,912

Chapter 7
GENERAL LONG-TERM DEBT ACCOUNT GROUP

NATURE AND PURPOSE

The general long-term debt account group (GLTDAG) should be used to account for a government's unmatured long-term indebtedness that has not been identified as a specific fund liability of a proprietary or trust fund. Besides general obligation debt instruments (e.g., bonds, notes, warrants), the GLTDAG also is used to report revenue bonds that will be repaid from general government resources, special assessment debt when the government is "obligated in some manner," special revenue bonds and certain liabilities that normally are not expected to be liquidated with expendable available financial resources (e.g., compensated absences, claims and judgments, unfunded pension costs).

On the other hand, certain liabilities (e.g., tax anticipation notes, matured debt) have been identified in authoritative literature as fund liabilities and, therefore, should not be reported in the GLTDAG. Moreover, it is recommended that long-term liabilities that are obligations of a fund rather than of the entity (e.g., advances from other funds) *not* be reported in the GLTDAG.

As noted in previous chapters, the GLTDAG is not a fund. It does not present results of operations or reflect the financial position of general long-term liabilities. Instead, those liabilities are simply offset by "other debits" to balance the account group presentation.

There are two primary accounts in the other debits category: "amounts available" and "amounts to be provided." The amounts available account represents current financial resources available to retire liabilities presented in the GLTDAG (typically amounts reported as debt service fund balance). If current financial resources are not available (e.g., debt service fund deficit), this account should not be presented. The amounts to be provided account represents the difference between the liabilities reported in the GLTDAG and the amounts available. The amounts available account can be subdivided to display where current financial resources have been accumulated to repay the liabilities (e.g., amount available in debt service fund). Similarly, the amounts to be provided account can be subdivided to indicate which financial resources will be used to liquidate liabilities (e.g., amounts to be provided from state grants).

It should be noted that other debit accounts do not represent assets. Therefore, financial statements should identify these accounts clearly as "other debits."

ACCOUNTING ISSUES

Several accounting issues associated with the GLTDAG have been identified. These issues include deep-discount debt, bond anticipation notes, demand bonds, special assessment debt and special revenue bonds. Disclosures related to liabilities presented in the GLTDAG are discussed in chapter 14.

Deep-discount Debt. A general limitation on the use of the GLTDAG is presented in the Governmental Accounting Standards Board's 1987 *Codification of Governmental Accounting and Financial Reporting Standards* (1987 *Codification*), Section 1500.103: "General long-term debt is the *unmatured principal* of bonds . . . or other forms of noncurrent or long-term *general obligation* debt . . ."

Because the GLTDAG is limited to unmatured principal, and because the flow of current financial resources measurement focus of governmental funds is incompatible with the deferral and amortization of bond premiums and discounts, bonds generally are reported in the GLTDAG at their face value. The introduction of deep-discount debt instruments (e.g., zero-coupon bonds), however, raises serious questions about the appropriateness of recording debt at face value in all instances. Deep-discount instruments are issued at stated interest rates that are significantly below their effective interest rate, resulting in a substantial (i.e., deep) discount when the securities are issued. A stated interest rate of less than 75 percent of the effective interest rate generally is a benchmark for classifying debt in the deep-discount category.

As discussed in chapter 4, the treatment of the bond discount related to deep-discount debt has not been addressed specifically in authoritative literature. To provide full disclosure within the confines of the model, the debt should be reflected at its face amount less the discount presented as a direct deduction. Generally, the implicit interest (i.e., discount) is not paid until the bond matures; therefore, the net value of the bonds should be accreted (i.e., the discount reduced) over the life of the bonds. The interest method, as set forth in Accounting Principles Board Opinion No. 12, *Omnibus Opinion – 1967*, provides an acceptable means of amortizing the discount. However, the straight-line amortization method also may be used if its application would not produce amounts that would differ materially from those that would be achieved if the interest method were applied.

Bond Anticipation Notes. Notes of various maturities issued in anticipation of future bond sales commonly are referred to as bond anticipation notes (BANs). BANs generally are issued because a government either is waiting for more favorable interest rates or has additional projects that also require financing which would warrant a bond issue. Accounting for BANs is addressed in the 1987 *Codification*, Section B50.101:

> For governmental funds, if all legal steps have been taken to refinance the bond anticipation notes and the intent is supported by an ability to consummate refinancing the short-term note on a long-term basis in accordance with the criteria set forth in FASB Statement No. 6 [SFAS No. 6], *Classification of Short-Term Obligations Expected to Be Refinanced,* they should be shown as part of the general long-term debt account group. If the necessary legal steps and the ability to consummate refinancing criteria have not been met, then the bond anticipation notes should be reported as a fund liability in the fund receiving proceeds.

As outlined in SFAS No. 6, the "ability to consummate the refinancing" can be demonstrated in one of two ways. On the one hand, BANs should be reported in the GLTDAG if, during the period between the balance sheet date and the issuance of the financial report, the government does, in fact, issue obligations that meet the criterion of Accounting Research Bulletin No. 43, *Restatement and Revision of Accounting Research Bulletins,* for classification as long-term liabilities (i.e., mature more than 12 months following the balance sheet date). Therefore, if BANs are to be replaced by other BANs that mature more than 12 months after the balance sheet date, the BANs should be reported in the GLTDAG.

SFAS No. 6 also provides that obligations can be classified as long-term if a financing agreement exists that allows the government to refinance the BANs on a long-term basis even if such a refinancing has not occurred by the time the financial statements are issued. Although rarely found in conjunction with the refinancing of BANs, such financing agreements are encountered commonly with the issuance of demand bonds.

Demand Bonds. Issues similar to those encountered with BANs are faced with demand bonds as well. Authoritative literature defines demand bonds as debt instruments that contain demand (i.e., "put") provisions that are exercisable within a one-year period beginning at the balance sheet date. Specific classification guidance is set forth in the 1987 *Codification*, Section D30.108. It provides that bonds should be reported by governments as general long-term debt or excluded from current liabilities of proprietary funds if all of the following conditions are met.

a. Before the financial statements are issued, the issuer has entered into an arm's-length financing (take out) agreement to convert bonds "put" but not resold into some other form of long-term obligation.
b. The take out agreement does not expire within one year from the date of the issuer's balance sheet.
c. The take out agreement is not cancelable by the lender or the prospective lender during that year, and obligations incurred under the take out agreement are not callable by the lender during that year.
d. The lender or the prospective lender or investor is expected to be financially capable of honoring the take out agreement.

Demand bonds should be reported as fund liabilities or as current liabilities when the preceding conditions are not met.

Government demand bonds generally contain a "take out" provision. These provisions normally are for a period greater than one year. Therefore, demand bonds would be reported in the GLTDAG in most instances.

Special Assessment Debt. The elimination of the special assessment fund type has resulted in the reporting of certain special assessment debt in the GLTDAG. The 1987 *Codification*, Section S40.117, provides specific guidance on the classification of special assessment debt issued to finance capital projects that will be repaid, at least in part, by the benefiting property owners:

a. General obligation debt that will be repaid, in part, from special assessments should be reported like any other general obligation debt.
b. Special assessment debt for which the government is obligated in some manner . . . should be reported in the GLTDAG, except for the portion, if any, that is a direct obligation of an enterprise fund, or that is expected to be repaid from operating revenues of an enterprise fund.

The debt that is reported in the GLTDAG and that will be repaid from special assessment revenues should be reported as "special assessment debt with governmental commitment." Any portion that will be repaid from the government's general resources should be reported like any other general obligation debt.

The phrase "obligated in some manner" associated with special assessment debt is referred to throughout this text. The 1987 *Codification*, Section S40.116, specifically provides:

> Conditions that indicate that a government is obligated in some manner include:
> a. The government is obligated to honor deficiencies to the extent that lien foreclosure proceeds are insufficient.
> b. The government is required to establish a reserve, guarantee, or sinking fund with other resources.
> c. The government is required to cover delinquencies with other resources until foreclosure proceeds are received.
> d. The government must purchase all properties ("sold" for delinquent assessments) that were not sold at public auction.
> e. The government *is authorized* to establish a reserve, guarantee, or sinking fund, *and* it establishes such a fund. (If a fund is not established, the considerations in subparagraphs g and h may nevertheless provide evidence that the government is obligated in some manner.)
> f. The government *may* establish a separate fund with other resources for the purpose of purchasing or redeeming special assessment debt, *and* it establishes such a fund. (If a fund is not established, the considerations in subparagraphs g and h may nevertheless provide evidence that the government is obligated in some manner.)

g. The government explicitly indicates by contract, such as the bond agreement or offering statement, that in the event of default it *may* cover delinquencies, although it has no legal obligation to do so.

h. Legal decisions within the state or previous actions by the government related to defaults on other special assessment projects make it probable that the government will assume responsibility for the debt in the event of default.

Stated differently, the phrase *obligated in some manner* as used in this section is intended to include all situations *other than* those in which (a) the government is *prohibited* (by constitution, charter, statute, ordinance, or contract) from assuming the debt in the event of default by the property owner or (b) the government is not legally liable for assuming the debt and makes no statement or gives no indication, that it will, or may, honor the debt in the event of default.

It should be noted that when the government is *not* "obligated in some manner," the special assessment debt should not be reported on the government's balance sheet.

Special Revenue Bonds. Bonds that are not considered general obligations of the government, but that are to be repaid through specific government resources (e.g., sales taxes) are classified as special revenue bonds. Even though special revenue bonds are *not* considered a general obligation of the government, the bonds should be reported in the GLTDAG. This classification helps create symmetry within the financial reporting model because the proceeds of special revenue bonds normally are used to purchase or construct general fixed assets.

ILLUSTRATIVE JOURNAL ENTRIES

The journal entries included in the remainder of this chapter illustrate the activities of the GLTDAG of a sample government. If these entries are posted to the accounts listed in the beginning of the year trial balance presented in Illustration 7–1 and to the additional accounts indicated, the year-end balances presented in Illustration 7–2 will agree with the comprehensive

---

ILLUSTRATION 7–1

**Name of Government
General Long-term Debt Account Group
Trial Balance
January 1, 19X8
(amounts expressed in thousands)**

	DR	CR
Amount available in debt service fund for the retirement of general obligation bonds	$ 10	
Amount to be provided from general government resources	39,256	
Compensated absences payable		$ 1,811
General obligation bonds payable		37,455
	$ 39,266	$ 39,266

---

annual financial report in appendix D. All dollar amounts are expressed in thousands.

The following discussion and journal entries illustrate issuance, accrual and retirement of general long-term liabilities reported in the GLTDAG.

The government enters into capital leases for the acquisition of police communication equipment. The net present value of future minimum lease payments is $140.

	DR	CR
1. Amount to be provided from general government resources	$ 140	
Capital leases payable		$ 140
(To record capital lease liability)		

Special assessment debt is issued for a water and sewer pipeline project. Although property owners are primarily responsible for repayment, the government is considered obligated for the $4,700 debt issue.

	DR	CR
2. Amount to be provided from special assessments	$ 4,700	
Special assessment debt with governmental commitment		$ 4,700
(To record issuance of special assessment debt)		

During the year, the government incurs $857 of additional liability for compensated absences. The liability is not expected to be liquidated with expendable available financial resources.

	DR	CR
3. Amount to be provided from general government resources	$ 857	
Compensated absences payable		$ 857
(To record long-term compensated absences liabilities)		

The government issues $3,365 of refunding bonds to defease $3,000 of outstanding bonds.

	DR	CR
4. Amount to be provided from general government resources	$ 3,365	
General obligation bonds payable		$ 3,365
(To record issuance of general obligation refunding bonds)		

	DR	CR
5. General obligation bonds payable	$ 3,000	
Amount to be provided from general government resources		$ 3,000
(To reflect payment to escrow agent for bond defeasance)		

The government remits annual bond principal payments of $2,030 to fiscal agent.

	DR	CR
6. General obligation bonds payable	$ 2,030	
Amount to be provided from general government resources		$ 2,030
(To reflect payment to fiscal agent for bond retirement)		

As part of the capital lease arrangements, down payments of $15 are required.

	DR	CR
7. Capital leases payable	$ 15	
Amount to be provided from general government resources		$ 15
(To reflect down payments on capital lease obligations)		

The government liquidates $646 of long-term compensated absences liabilities during the year.

	DR	CR
8. Compensated absences payable	$ 646	
Amounts to be provided from general government resources		$ 646
(To reflect the partial liquidation of the compensated absences liability)		

During the year, the amount available in the debt service fund for the payment of bond principal increased by $1,374. This amount includes $1,346 reserved for the payment of special assessment debt.

	DR	CR
9. Amount available in the debt service fund for the retirement of general obligation bonds	$ 28	
Amount to be provided from general government resources		$ 28
(To reflect increase in financial resources available to retire general obligation bond principal)		

	DR	CR
10. Amount available in the debt service fund for the retirement of special assessment bonds	$ 1,346	
Amounts to be provided from special assessments		$ 1,346
(To reflect increase in financial resources available to retire special assessment bond principal)		

Note: As in this example, the amount available account sometimes may reflect an amount less than the debt service fund balance. This difference normally occurs when financial resources have been accumulated in the debt service fund for interest payments.

The government determines that $220 of workers' compensation claims have been incurred but not reported as of year end.

	DR	CR
11. Amount to be provided from general government resources	$ 220	
Claims and judgments payable		$ 220
(To record workers' compensation claims incurred but not reported)		

ILLUSTRATION 7–2

Name of Government
General Long-term Debt Account Group
Trial Balance
December 31, 19X8
(amounts expressed in thousands)

	DR	CR
Amount available in debt service fund for the retirement of general obligation bonds	$ 38	
Amount available in debt service fund for the retirement of special assessment bonds	1,346	
Amount to be provided from general government resources	38,119	
Amount to be provided from special assessments	3,354	
Claims and judgments payable		$ 220
Compensated absences payable		2,022
General obligation bonds payable		35,790
Special assessment debt with government commitment		4,700
Capital leases payable		125
	$ 42,857	$ 42,857

Chapter 8
ENTERPRISE FUNDS

NATURE AND PURPOSE

Certain government services traditionally have been financed through user charges. These activities include water, sewer, electric and gas utilities; airports; hospitals; ports; parking facilities; mass transit districts; housing authorities and golf courses.

In addition, because the need for government services has outpaced a finite tax base, governments increasingly have turned to user charges as an alternative revenue source to recover all or part of the cost of goods or services from those directly benefiting from them. However, the recovery of cost and the need for information on the cost of services are not compatible with the flow of current financial resources measurement focus of governmental funds. Therefore, enterprise funds, which focus on the flow of economic resources, are typically used to account for such activities.

According to the Governmental Accounting Standards Board's 1987 *Codification of Governmental Accounting and Financial Reporting Standards* (1987 *Codification*), Section 1300.104, enterprise funds should be used to account for operations:

a. that are financed and operated in a manner similar to private business enterprises—where the intent of the governing body is that costs (expenses, including depreciation) of providing goods or services to the general public on a continuing basis be financed or recovered primarily through user charges; or

b. where the governing body has decided that periodic determination of revenues earned, expenses incurred, and/or net income is appropriate for capital maintenance, public policy, management control, accountability, or other purposes.

This definition is intended to provide continuity in the use of the enterprise fund classification. Before this definition was developed, practice dictated that an activity should be classified as an enterprise fund only if more than 50 percent of the activity's costs were recovered through user charges. This practice led to arbitrary changes in the classification used to account for a single activity. For example, if an activity recovered 52 percent of its cost in one year, it would be classified as an enterprise fund. However, if only 48 percent of its costs were recovered through user charges in the next year, it would *not* be classified as an enterprise fund. The current definition,

therefore, stabilized the use of the enterprise fund classification and expanded some governments' use of this fund type.

Because of the increasing reliance many governments place on user charges, the definition has resulted in an increased use of enterprise funds for a variety of activities. However, the definition also has limited the use of enterprise funds because some have interpreted the provision "where the intent of government is that the costs (expenses, including depreciation) of providing goods or services . . . be financed or recovered primarily through user charges . . ." as emphasizing the *stated* intent of the government. For example, an activity's user charges may represent more than 95 percent of the total revenues of a fund so that the activity is funded primarily through these charges. If the government's stated intent is not to fund all cost primarily through user charges, even though user charges are the primary source of revenue, this activity still may be classified in the governmental funds. However, if the government's *implied* intent, as judged by its actual recovery of cost through user charges, is to *primarily*, not *totally*, fund costs, the use of the enterprise fund classification is encouraged.

Enterprise activities are operated either as separate units or within a government. Therefore, in certain cases (e.g., special districts or authorities without potential oversight from another governing body), enterprise funds may be reported as a standalone activity.

Normally, there is a direct correlation between an enterprise activity and an individual fund. Although this approach may result in numerous enterprise funds for certain governments, it is consistent with the "number of funds" principle introduced in chapter 2. Establishing a separate fund for each activity allows the government to report the costs associated with each activity and the extent the user charges cover those costs. In addition, revenue bond indentures usually contain a legal requirement that revenues derived from the activities be pledged for the repayment of the debt. Such revenues should not be diverted to other activities until the enterprise activity obligations under the indenture have been met. A separate fund to account for each activity can assist in demonstrating compliance with these provisions.

There are exceptions to the general rule of one activity/one fund. If activities are closely related (e.g., water and sewer operations) or revenues from all the activities can be used to repay revenue bonds, the related activities can be presented in one enterprise fund.

BUDGETARY ISSUES

Sound financial management in the government environment warrants some form of budgetary control for all enterprise funds. There are several different methods for monitoring enterprise budgetary activities. Although not recommended in the 1987 *Codification,* Section 1700.122, fixed dollar annual appropriated budgets often are adopted for enterprise funds. Generally, this method of budgeting is used to comply with statutory requirements. However, there are instances (e.g., refuse collection) where the service level is *not* expected to fluctuate during the year because of the weather or other factors. In these instances, fixed-dollar budgeting would be recommended.

An alternative to an appropriated budget is the adoption of a nonappropriated budget. This type of budget (i.e., financial plan) should be considered for various reasons. Many consider the adoption of a financial plan based on flexible versus fixed budgets more appropriate within the enterprise fund environment. The use of flexible budgets allows management to establish various plans based on several levels of activity. In other cases, however, an enterprise activity may use a financial plan with fixed dollar amounts simply because it does not have the statutory authority to adopt an appropriated budget.

When a government does adopt an annual appropriated budget, statutes or ordinances may require the enterprise activity to demonstrate legal compliance with the budget authorizations. In this case, individual budgetary comparison statements/schedules should be presented in the comprehensive annual financial report (CAFR) or component unit financial report (CUFR). In addition, the 1987 *Codification,* Section 2400.111, states that "more comprehensive budget presentations are generally to be preferred over the minimum standards." Therefore, a government can choose to present enterprise fund appropriated budgets in the general purpose financial statements (GPFS) or component unit financial statements (CUFS). This budgetary comparison can be presented as part of the Combined Statement of Revenues, Expenditures and Changes in Fund Balances—Budget and Actual, if the budgetary basis is consistent with that of the governmental funds. When the budget basis for enterprise funds differs from the budget basis for governmental funds (e.g., accrual versus modified accrual), a separate budgetary comparison statement for the enterprise funds should be presented if the statement is included in the GPFS/CUFS.

Although not required, nonappropriated budgets can be included in the CAFR/CUFR. In addition, the 1987 *Codification,* Section 2400.111, also allows nonappropriated budgets to be presented in the GPFS/CUFS. If this option is chosen, nonappropriated budget information should be clearly identified.

Both fixed and flexible budgeting and related financial reporting for proprietary funds are discussed in greater detail in chapter 9.

ACCOUNTING ISSUES

Several accounting issues are faced in the proprietary fund types, particularly in the enterprise funds. These issues include restricted assets, nonmonetary transactions, interest capitalization for constructed fixed assets, joint ventures, bonds payable, contributed capital, payments in lieu of taxes and regulation.

Restricted Assets. Bond indentures and other legal requirements sometimes mandate that governments establish separate accounts within an enterprise fund to report assets (e.g., cash, investments) restricted to specific uses. Although these accounts often are referred to improperly in bond indentures as funds, they should be reported as accounts within an enterprise fund to meet generally accepted accounting principles. To demonstrate compliance with the provisions of bond indentures, account information may be presented in combining and/or individual schedules in the CAFR/CUFR.

Five accounts normally are associated with revenue bond indentures: revenue bond construction; revenue bond operations and maintenance; revenue bond current debt service; revenue bond future debt service; and revenue bond renewal and replacement. The revenue bond construction account normally represents cash and investments (including interest receivable) segregated by the bond indenture for construction. Construction liabilities payable from restricted assets should be reported as contracts payable—restricted assets. As with all restricted accounts, construction assets, and the liabilities to be paid from them, generally should not be classified as current assets and liabilities, pursuant to Accounting Research Bulletin No. 43, *Restatement and Revision of Accounting Research Bulletins.* The difference between the restricted construction asset and liability accounts is not required to be reported as a reserve in retained earnings.

A revenue bond operations and maintenance account often is established pursuant to a bond indenture. Resources for this account are provided through bond proceeds and/or operating income or net income. This account generally accumulates assets equal to operating costs for one month. Once this account has been established, additional proceeds from future bond issues generally are necessary only to the extent the costs associated with these expanded operations are expected to increase. This account is normally balanced by a reserved for revenue bond operations and maintenance account in retained earnings.

Bond indentures also may include a covenant requiring the establishment of a restricted account for the repayment of bond principal and interest. Resources for this account also are provided through bond proceeds and/or operating income or net income. Normally, assets accumulated for debt service payments (i.e., principal and interest) due within one year are classified in the revenue bond current debt service account. This account is at least partially associated with bonds payable—current and accrued interest payable accounts. Any difference between the revenue bond current debt service account and related current bonds payable and accrued interest payable should be reported as reserved retained earnings. When accounts are restricted for debt service payments beyond the next twelve months, a revenue bond future debt service account should be established.

The final restricted account established pursuant to a covenant within a bond indenture is the revenue bond renewal and replacement account. Bond proceeds and/or net income often are restricted for payments of unforeseen repairs and replacements of assets originally acquired with bond proceeds. Provided that liabilities have not been incurred for this purpose, the revenue bond renewal and replacement account is balanced by the reserved for revenue bond renewal and replacement account in retained earnings.

There is a general rule that should be considered when determining the amount of retained earnings that should be reserved related to restricted asset accounts. Unless otherwise required by the bond indenture, retained earnings should only be reserved for amounts of restricted assets in excess of related liabilities.

Customer deposits also should be classified as restricted assets. Utilities, housing authorities and other enterprise activities often require deposits to insure against nonpayment of billings and/or property damage. Because the deposit remains the property of the customer, governments establish restricted accounts to distinguish these assets from current assets available for operations. The asset account is balanced by a customer deposits payable liability account to demonstrate the fiduciary relationship with the customers. The customer deposit account also may include a provision, based on statute or policy, for accruing interest payable to the customers upon return of the deposit.

Nonmonetary Transactions. Accounting Principles Board (APB) Opinion No. 29, *Accounting for Nonmonetary Transactions* addresses exchanges with another entity involving nonmonetary assets or liabilities. Nonmonetary assets and liabilities are defined in APB Opinion No. 29 as assets or liabilities whose amounts are *not* fixed in terms of units of currency. The most common nonmonetary transaction governments involved in enterprise activities encounter is the acquisition of fixed assets with trade-ins.

The underlying principle of APB Opinion No. 29 is that nonmonetary transactions should be valued on the same basis (i.e., fair value) as monetary transactions. A major exception is made for exchanges that are not part of the completion of the government's earning cycle. Fixed asset trade-ins generally would be classified in this latter category.

Based on the guidance provided in APB Opinion No. 29, if an enterprise activity trades in a "productive" fixed asset (i.e., asset used in the production of revenue) for a similar asset, the acquired asset generally would be valued at the net book value of the traded asset, plus any monetary consideration. No gain is recognized on this type of transaction. However, if the net book value of a traded asset exceeds its fair value, the loss would be recognized at the time of the transaction. An example of a fixed asset trade-in is presented in chapter 9.

Interest Capitalization for Constructed Fixed Assets. When a government chooses to construct a fixed asset for an enterprise fund, a significant accounting issue that arises is the calculation of interest to be capitalized. Guidance on the capitalization of interest is contained in two pronouncements of the Financial Accounting Standards Board (FASB): Statement of Financial Accounting Standards (SFAS) No. 34, *Capitalization of Interest Cost*, and SFAS No. 62, *Capitalization of Interest Costs in Situations Involving Certain Tax-Exempt Borrowings and Certain Gifts and Grants.*

When SFAS No. 34 was issued, governments identified problems with one of the pronouncement's underlying principles. SFAS No. 34 provides that the interest capitalization period should begin only when construction expenses are incurred. Before the Tax Reform Act of 1986, many governments would borrow funds well in advance of actual construction. The timing of the borrowing often played an integral role in the government's capital budgeting decisions. Because interest was earned on the bond proceeds and paid on the debt outstanding before actual construction costs were incurred, many governments believe that SFAS No. 34 did not properly address construction factors in the government environment.

The Tax Reform Act of 1986, which limits both the time that the government can take before starting construction and interest earnings on bond proceeds, has reduced the effect of these concerns. However, the FASB addressed governmental unit's initial concerns in 1982 with the release of SFAS No. 62. This pronouncement, which provides that interest expense should be capitalized, net of interest revenue earned on the proceeds, from the time of the borrowing until the completion of the project, applies to "specified qualifying assets." SFAS No. 34 defined *qualifying* assets in part as, "assets that are constructed or otherwise produced for an enterprise's own use . . ." SFAS No. 62 provides that a *specified* qualifying asset is one where proceeds are externally restricted to finance the acquisition of that particular asset. Therefore, in instances where constructed assets are not specifically identified as part of the bond indenture, governments would apply SFAS No. 34 for the purpose of enterprise fund interest capitalization without modification. In addition, SFAS No. 34 would be applied to assets constructed with taxable debt proceeds because of the limited scope of SFAS No. 62.

Joint Ventures. In certain situations an enterprise fund may participate in a joint venture. The 1987 *Codification*, Section J50.101, defines a joint venture as:

. . . a legal entity or other contractual arrangement participated in by a government as a separate and specific activity for the benefit of the public or service recipients in which the government retains an ongoing financial interest (for example, an equity interest in either assets or liabilities) and/or responsibility.

Examples of joint ventures related to an enterprise fund include regional transportation authorities and water treatment plants.

The 1987 *Codification*, Section J50.102, provides that for enterprise funds, "the joint venture should be included in the investing fund's financial statements using the equity method of accounting." APB Opinion No. 18, *The Equity Method of Accounting for Investments in Common Stock*, provides guidance regarding the initial capitalization of the investment and subsequent investments, distributions and the investor's share of the earnings or losses of the joint venture. This guidance should be followed even though most government joint ventures do not issue common stock. Changes in the government's equity position based on the joint venture's earnings or losses should be reported as nonoperating revenues/expenses.

Bonds Payable. Several specific issues are associated with bonds payable reported in an enterprise fund. These issues include determining the debt to be reported in the enterprise fund, bond issuance costs, bond premiums and discounts, and extinguishment of debt.

Debt to be Reported in an Enterprise Fund. Several types of debt can be reported in an enterprise fund, including revenue bonds, general obligation bonds and special assessment bonds. Revenue bonds are a common capital resource for enterprise activities. The primary, or in some cases sole, resources for the repayment of these obligations are the "net revenues" generated by the enterprise activity. Often, the bond indenture defines net revenues as gross revenues less costs of services, or costs of goods sold and administrative expenses. This definition may exclude depreciation or related capital outlay and debt service payments from the calculation of net revenues.

General obligation bonds issued to finance enterprise fund capital acquisition or construction can be reported in an enterprise fund. When the debt is expected to be repaid from resources generated by the enterprise fund, consideration should be given to reporting the debt in the enterprise fund. The decision, however, should be based on the level of resource commitment over the life of the bonds. If the debt will not be paid from enterprise fund resources, the bond proceeds (i.e., cash) and "contributed capital—government" could be reported in the enterprise fund. When the proceeds are used to construct a major facility and the debt will not be paid from enterprise resources, the capital projects fund's capitalizable expenditures should be reported as an asset (e.g., buildings) and contributed capital—government.

In certain cases, proceeds from a general obligation bond issue are used for both enterprise and general government activities. In this instance, the government should consider dividing the debt between the enterprise fund and the general long-term debt account group (GLTDAG). This allocation should be based on the amount of debt expected to be liquidated with enterprise fund resources.

Special assessment debt also can be reported in the enterprise fund, based on guidance provided in the 1987 *Codification*, Section S40.123. Special assessment debt that is a direct obligation of the enterprise fund and/or is expected to be repaid from enterprise fund resources should be reported as a liability of the enterprise fund. In addition, if a project is administered by an enterprise activity a government may report the special assessment transactions in an enterprise fund.

Bond Issuance Costs. Significant costs of a bond issue (e.g., fees, insurance, underwriting spreads) should be reported as a deferred charge and amortized over the life of the bonds. Authoritative guidance for amortizing the deferred charge is contained in APB Opinion No. 21, *Interest on Receivables and Payables,* and APB Opinion No. 12, *Omnibus Opinion— 1967.* These pronouncements provide that the interest method, defined in APB Opinion No. 12, should be used to amortize bond issuance costs. However, a straight-line amortization method can be used if the results are not significantly different from the interest method.

Bond Premiums and Discounts. When market conditions change before a bond with a stated interest rate is issued, a premium or discount may result from the sale. If a bond is first acquired by an underwriter and then marketed, it may be difficult for the government to distinguish market-related premiums or discounts from bond issuance costs. In these instances, unless a change in the market rate was known at the date the bonds were issued, the difference between the face value of the bonds (plus any premiums) and the actual proceeds received should be reported as issuance costs.

Bond premiums and discounts are subject to the same guidance (i.e., APB Opinion No. 12) as bond issuance costs. In addition, the amortization basis (i.e., amortization period and method) should be consistent with the basis applied to any related bond issuance costs, if both are considered material.

Extinguishment of Debt. Several authoritative pronouncements provide guidance for the accounting and financial reporting of the extinguishment of debt. The 1987 *Codification*,

Section D20, specifies applicable standards for circumstances that result in extinguishments and provides disclosure and display requirements. Disclosure requirements are discussed in chapter 14.

SFAS No. 76, *Extinguishment of Debt,* amended APB Opinion No. 26, *Early Extinguishment of Debt,* to expand application of that guidance to all defeasances (e.g., legal, in-substance), other than debt originally excluded from the scope of APB Opinion No. 26. SFAS No. 76 clarifies what events culminate in an extinguishment.

Specifically, this pronouncement sets forth three circumstances that result in the extinguishment of debt for financial reporting purposes. The first two circumstances reflect payment and forgiveness of debt. The final circumstance involves what is commonly referred to as an in-substance defeasance. In this instance, the debt has not been defeased legally; however, it is reported as an extinguishment in the financial statements.

To achieve an in-substance defeasance of debt, the government must deposit into an irrevocable trust cash or qualifying assets (i.e., direct obligations of the federal government or obligations guaranteed by or securities backed by the federal government with payment to the holder). This deposit must provide sufficient cash flows in order to virtually guarantee the payment of the defeased debt's principal and interest as scheduled.

An early extinguishment of debt, primarily due to refunding issues for enterprise fund activities, often will result in the reporting of a gain or loss in the financial statements. APB Opinion No. 26 includes guidance on the calculation of the gain or loss and provides that the difference between the reacquisition price (i.e., amount paid to trustee) and the net carrying amount of the extinguished debt should be recognized as a gain or loss. SFAS No. 4, *Reporting Gains and Losses from Extinguishment of Debt,* as amended by SFAS No. 64, *Extinguishments of Debt Made to Satisfy Sinking-Fund Requirements,* provides guidance on the display of the gain or loss. If material, gains or losses from the extinguishment of debt should be classified as an extraordinary item.

In determining materiality a government should use the guidance in APB Opinion No. 30, *Reporting the Results of Operations—Reporting the Effects of Disposal of a Segment of a Business, and Extraordinary, Unusual and Infrequently Occurring Events and Transactions:* "The effect of an extraordinary event or transaction should be classified separately . . . if it is material in relation to income before extraordinary items or to the trend of annual earnings before extraordinary items, or is material by other appropriate criteria." When the sinking-fund requirement calls for payment within one year of the date of the extinguishment, the extraordinary-item treatment would not be applied to the transaction.

Contributed Capital. The contributed capital accounts of an enterprise fund generally can be defined as its "permanent" fund capital. These accounts normally are divided into four classifications: government, developer, customer and intergovernmental contributions.

The intergovernmental account resources usually are derived from grants, entitlements and shared revenues externally restricted to capital acquisition or construction. Residual equity transfers from other funds and "transfers" of fixed assets from the GLTDAG are identified as government contributions. The developer and customer account resources are provided through contributions of fixed assets, donations restricted to the acquisition of fixed assets, and contributions and system-connection-related fees (e.g., impact, tap) in excess of related costs.

A significant accounting issue related to contributed capital was addressed in the 1987 *Codification,* Section G60.116. This section states that "depreciation recognized on assets acquired or constructed through such resources externally restricted for capital acquisitions may be closed to the appropriate contributed capital account. . ." Such "resources" are identified in the 1987 *Codification,* Section G60.116. These resources include grants, entitlements and shared revenues externally restricted for capital acquisitions or construction. The optional close-out of depreciation to the contributed capital account should not be netted against the depreciation expense account. Instead, it should be presented as a separate account after net income as shown in Illustration 8–1.

Payments in Lieu of Taxes. Governments often assess enterprise activities for payments in lieu of various taxes (e.g., property taxes, sales taxes). These taxes should be reported as an operating expense only when the assessment is based on criteria applied to similar activities in the private sector. For example, if an enterprise activity is assessed for an amount equivalent to a general sales tax and the payment is based on a percentage equal to that found in the private sector (1 percent of sales), the payment should be classified as an operating expense. When there is no direct relationship, the payment should be classified as an operating transfer out.

Regulation. Sometimes government enterprise funds (e.g., electric utilities) are subject to rate regulation. SFAS No. 71, *Accounting for the Effects of Certain Types of Regulation* (as amended by SFAS No. 90, *Regulated Enterprises—Accounting for Abandonments and Disallowances of Plant Costs*) applies to enterprise funds that meet *all* of the following criteria:

(a) The enterprise's rates for regulated services or products provided to its customers are established by or are subject to approval by an independent, third-party regulator or by its own governing board empowered by statute or contract to establish rates that bind customers.

(b) The regulated rates are designed to recover the specific enterprise's costs of providing the regulated services or products.

(c) In view of the demand for the regulated services or products and the level of competition, direct and indirect, it is reasonable to assume that rates set at levels that will recover the enterprise's costs can be charged to and collected from customers. This criterion requires consideration of anticipated changes in levels of demand or competition during the recovery period for any capitalized costs.

ILLUSTRATION 8–1

Optional Add-back of Qualifying Depreciation

Net income	$ 1,250
Add depreciation on fixed assets acquired by grants externally restricted for capital acquisitions and construction	25
Increase in retained earnings	$ 1,275

Although some may conclude that any enterprise fund with rates approved by a governing body is subject to the provisions of SFAS No. 71, generally only enterprise funds that do not receive subsidies (i.e., those with rates designed to cover cost) should adopt these provisions.

Authoritative pronouncements that apply to nonregulated enterprise funds also apply to regulated enterprise funds. However, regulated enterprise funds should apply SFAS No. 71 when its provisions conflict with other authoritative pronouncements.

Regulation of an enterprise fund's prices is sometimes based on the enterprise fund's costs. Regulators use a variety of mechanisms to estimate a regulated enterprise's allowable costs, and they allow the enterprise to charge rates that are intended to produce revenue approximately equal to those allowable costs.

Regulators sometimes include costs in allowable costs in a period other than the period in which the costs would be charged to expense by an unregulated enterprise. That procedure can create assets (future cash inflows that will result from the rate-making process), reduce assets (reductions of future cash inflows that result from the rate-making process) or create liabilities (future cash outflows that will result from the rate-making process) for the regulated enterprise. An incurred cost for which a regulator permits recovery in a future period is accounted for like an incurred cost that is reimbursable under a cost reimbursement-type contract.

Rate actions of a regulator can provide reasonable assurance of the existence of an asset. An enterprise fund should capitalize all or part of an incurred cost that would otherwise be charged to expense if both of the following criteria set forth in SFAS No. 71 are met:

(a) It is probable that future revenue in an amount at least equal to capitalized cost will result from inclusion of that cost in allowable cost for rate-making purposes.

(b) Based on available evidence, the future revenue will be provided to permit recovery of the previously incurred cost rather than to provide for expected levels of future costs. If the revenue will be provided through an automatic rate adjustment clause, this criterion requires that the regulator's intent clearly be to permit recovery of the previously incurred cost.

Rate actions of a regulator can reduce or eliminate the value of an asset. If a regulator excludes all or part of the cost from allowable cost and it is not probable that the cost will be included as an allowable cost in a future period, the cost cannot be expected to result in future revenue through the rate-making process. Accordingly, the carrying amount of any related asset should be reduced to the extent that the asset has been impaired. Subsequent FASB pronouncements further define when an asset has been impaired and at what value the asset should be carried in the enterprise fund.

Rate actions of a regulator can impose a liability on a regulated enterprise fund. Such liabilities are usually obligations to the enterprise fund's customers. SFAS No. 71 states that the following are the usual ways in which liabilities can be imposed and the resulting accounting:

(a) A regulator may require refunds to customers. Refunds that meet the criteria of . . . FASB Statement [SFAS] No. 5, *Accounting for Contingencies,* shall be recorded as liabilities and as reductions of revenue or as expenses of the regulated enterprise.

(b) A regulator can provide current rates intended to recover costs that are expected to be incurred in the future with the understanding that if those costs are not incurred future rates will be reduced by corresponding amounts. If current rates are intended to recover such costs and the regulator requires the enterprise to remain accountable for any amounts charged pursuant to such rates and not yet expended for the intended purpose, the enterprise shall not recognize as revenues amounts charged pursuant to such rates. Those amounts shall be recognized as deferred revenue and taken to income only when the associated costs are incurred.

(c) A regulator can require that a gain or other reduction of net allowable costs be given to customers over future periods. That would be accomplished, for rate-making purposes, by amortizing the gain or other reduction of net allowable costs over those future periods and reducing rates to reduce revenues in approximately the amount of the amortization. If a gain or other reduction of net allowable costs is to be amortized over future periods for rate-making purposes, the regulated enterprise shall not recognize that gain or other reduction of net allowable costs in income of the current period. Instead, it shall record it as a liability for future reductions of charges to customers that are expected to result.

In general, if an enterprise fund qualifies as a regulated operation under the criteria previously noted, the government needs to ensure that its accounting follows the provisions of the regulator in establishing customer rates. These provisions may defer costs and/or revenues to future periods consistent with the intent of the regulators.

ILLUSTRATIVE JOURNAL ENTRIES

The journal entries included in the remainder of the chapter illustrate the accounting operations of the water and sewer authority enterprise fund of a sample government. If these entries are posted to the accounts listed in the beginning of the year trial balance presented as Illustration 8–2 and to the additional accounts indicated, the year-end balances presented in Illustration 8–4 will agree with the CAFR in appendix D. All amounts are expressed in thousands.

The following discussion and journal entries illustrate revenues and receipts affecting balance sheet accounts.

The authority issues bills for services totaling $14,046 during the year. Water sales amounted to $8,699 and sewer charges equaled $5,347. Approximately 1 percent of the billings are expected to be uncollectible.

	DR	CR
1. Accounts receivable	$ 13,842	
Due from other funds—general fund	175	
Due from other funds—golf course fund	27	
Due from other funds—fleet management fund	2	
Operating expenses—costs of sales and services	138	
Allowance for uncollectible accounts receivable		$ 138
Operating revenues—water sales		8,699
Operating revenues—sewer charges		5,347
(To record billings for water sales and sewer charges and related allowance for uncollectible amount)		

During the year the authority connects various customers and developers to water and sewer lines. Billings for these services amount to $5,815, which exceeds actual connection costs by $4,294.

	DR	CR
2. Accounts receivable	$ 5,815	
Operating revenues—tap fees		$ 1,521
Contributed capital—customers		208
Contributed capital—developers		4,086
(To record charges for tap fees)		

The authority collects $20,195 of the outstanding accounts during the year including a portion of accounts receivable outstanding at the beginning of the year.

	DR	CR
3. Cash	$ 20,195	
Accounts receivable		$ 19,991
Due from other funds—general fund		159
Due from other funds—golf course fund		45
(To record the collection of outstanding amounts)		

The authority writes off $10 of accounts receivable for which allowances had been previously established.

	DR	CR
4. Allowance for uncollectible accounts receivable	$ 10	
Accounts receivable		$ 10
(To write off uncollectible accounts receivable)		

During the year, the authority collects $250 of deposits from new customers.

	DR	CR
5. Restricted assets—customer deposits	$ 250	
Customer deposits payable—restricted assets		$ 250
(To record collection of new customer deposits)		

The authority issues $34,600 of revenue bonds. The bonds are sold at a discount. Issuance costs of $150 were incurred with the sale.

	DR	CR
6. Cash	$ 34,150	
Deferred charge—revenue bond issuance costs	150	
Unamortized bond discount—revenue bonds	300	
Revenue bonds payable		$ 34,600
(To record sale of revenue bonds and related discount and issuance costs)		

The cash received from the issuance of revenue bonds is allocated to the restricted asset accounts in accordance with bond indenture provisions.

ILLUSTRATION 8–2

Name of Government
Water and Sewer Authority Enterprise Fund
Trial Balance
January 1, 19X8
(amounts expressed in thousands)

	DR	CR		DR	CR
Cash	$ 823		Vouchers payable		851
Investments—current	7,322		Accounts payable		253
Interest receivable—investments	316		Compensated absences payable		359
Accounts receivable	2,585		Accrued interest payable		1,100
Allowance for uncollectible accounts			Intergovernmental payable—state		11
receivable		$ 259	Due to other funds—general fund		193
Due from other funds—general fund	21		Due to other funds—management		
Due from other funds—golf course fund	18		information systems fund		14
Inventories	461		General obligation bonds payable—		
Restricted assets—customer deposits	1,199		current		1,360
Restricted assets—revenue bond			Customer deposits payable—restricted		
operations and maintenance account	1,023		assets		1,199
Restricted assets—revenue bond current			Revenue bonds payable—restricted		
debt service account	1,380		assets		530
Restricted assets—revenue bond future			Accrued interest payable—restricted		
debt service account	523		assets		448
Restricted assets—revenue bond renewal			General obligation bonds payable		23,798
and replacement account	1,165		Revenue bonds payable		8,580
Deferred charge—general obligation bond			Contributed capital—government		803
issuance costs	366		Contributed capital—customers		13,854
Deferred charge—revenue bond issuance			Contributed capital—developers		31,155
costs	103		Contributed capital—intergovernmental		5,588
Land	604		Retained earnings—reserved for revenue		
Buildings	13,100		bond operations and maintenance		1,023
Accumulated depreciation—buildings		1,964	Retained earnings—reserved for revenue		
Improvements other than buildings	1,250		bond current debt service		402
Accumulated depreciation—			Retained earnings—reserved for revenue		
improvements other than buildings		188	bond renewal and replacement		1,165
Machinery and equipment	103,825		Retained earnings—unreserved		28,014
Accumulated depreciation—machinery				$136,084	$136,084
and equipment		12,973			

	DR	CR
7. Restricted assets—revenue bond construction account	$ 28,200	
Restricted assets—revenue bond operations and maintenance account	200	
Restricted assets—revenue bond current debt service account	3,500	
Restricted assets—revenue bond future debt service account	700	
Restricted assets—revenue bond renewal and replacement account	1,550	
Cash		$ 34,150
(To record allocation of revenue bond proceeds to restricted accounts)		

The authority determines that to remove restrictive bond covenants, $8,580 of revenue bonds should be defeased through an advance refunding. To advance refund the old debt, the government sells $7,060 of general obligation bonds at par with related issuance costs of $55. The general obligation bonds are expected to be repaid with the water and sewer authority's resources.

	DR	CR
8. Cash	$ 7,005	
Deferred charge—general obligation bond issuance costs	55	
General obligation bonds payable		$ 7,060
(To record sale of general obligation bonds for advance refunding)		

The $8,580 defeasance of revenue bonds lifts the restrictions on amounts held in the revenue bond renewal and replacement account ($1,165) associated with this bond issue.

	DR	CR
9. Cash	$ 1,165	
Restricted assets—revenue bond renewal and replacement account		$ 1,165
(To reclassify assets no longer restricted by a bond covenant)		

Interest of $1,347 is collected on investments during the year. The amount collected includes $316 of interest receivable at the prior year end and $609 for restricted asset accounts.

	DR	CR
10. Cash	$ 738	
Restricted assets—customer deposits	59	
Restricted assets—revenue bond construction account	324	
Restricted assets—revenue bond operations and maintenance account	43	
Restricted assets—revenue bond current debt service account	112	
Restricted assets—revenue bond future debt service account	22	
Restricted assets—revenue bond renewal and replacement account	49	
Customer deposits payable—restricted assets		$ 59
Nonoperating revenues—interest		972
Interest receivable—investments		316
(To record collection of interest on investments)		

At year end, the authority accrues $833 of interest on outstanding investments, including $424 for investments held in restricted assets accounts.

	DR	CR
11. Interest receivable—investments	$ 409	
Restricted assets—customer deposits	52	
Restricted assets—revenue bond construction account	220	
Restricted assets—revenue bond operations and maintenance account	28	
Restricted assets—revenue bond current debt service account	76	
Restricted assets—revenue bond future debt service account	15	
Restricted assets—revenue bond renewal and replacement account	33	
Customer deposits payable—restricted assets		$ 52
Nonoperating revenues—interest		781
(To accrue interest income at year end)		

The authority determines that $528 of water sales and $324 of sewer charges have not been billed at year end. Approximately 1 percent of the unbilled amounts are expected to be uncollectible.

	DR	CR
12. Accounts receivable	$ 852	
Operating expenses—costs of sales and services	85	
Operating revenues—water sales		$ 528
Operating revenues—sewer charges		324
Allowance for uncollectible accounts receivable		85
(To record unbilled accounts at year end and related allowance for uncollectible amounts)		

Fixed assets of $35 ($20 accumulated depreciation) scheduled to be replaced as part of a modernization project are sold by the government for $5.

	DR	CR
13. Cash	$ 5	
Accumulated depreciation—machinery and equipment	20	
Nonoperating expenses—loss on sale of fixed assets	10	
Machinery and equipment		$ 35
(To record sale of fixed assets)		

Note: If depreciation is calculated based on a component unit (e.g., average life groups, equal life groups), the loss on the disposal would be considered an adjustment of the carrying value of the remaining assets. Therefore, under this acceptable depreciation method gains or losses from the disposal of individual fixed assets generally would not be recognized.

The authority reclassifies $575 to the revenue bond current debt service account for the subsequent year's revenue bond principal and interest payments.

	DR	CR
14. Restricted assets—revenue bond current debt service account	$ 575	
Cash		$ 575
(To reclassify cash to restricted assets account)		

The authority recognizes $3,230 of construction in progress from the pipeline construction project undertaken by the government.

	DR	CR
15. Construction in progress	$ 3,230	
Contributed capital—government		$ 3,230
(To record assets being constructed in the pipeline construction capital projects fund on behalf of the water and sewer fund)		

The following discussion and journal entries illustrate expenses and disbursements affecting balance sheet accounts.

The authority acquires $374 of machinery and equipment during the year.

	DR	CR
16. Machinery and equipment	$ 374	
Accounts payable		$ 374
(To record purchase of fixed assets)		

The authority undertakes a two-phase construction project with $28,200 of proceeds from the sale of revenue bonds. Progress billings of $10,738 are received. Of this amount, $536 is to be withheld, in accordance with the provisions of the contracts, until both phases of the project are completed satisfactorily.

	DR	CR
17. Construction in progress	$ 10,738	
Contracts payable		$ 10,202
Retainage payable		536
(To record construction in progress billings)		

	DR	CR
18. Construction in progress	$ 978	
Nonoperating expense—interest		$ 978
(To record capitalization of net interest expense related to tax-exempt revenue bonds)		

The contractor completes the $7,828 first phase of the construction project.

	DR	CR
19. Buildings	$ 7,828	
Construction in progress		$ 7,828
(To record completion of first phase of the construction project)		

The authority enters into capital lease agreements for the acquisition of wastewater trucks. The actual present value of future lease payments is $119. The lessor requires a 5 percent down payment. During the year, the authority remits $17 (including $5 of interest) for the capital lease payments. Payments are due in six-month intervals.

	DR	CR
20. Machinery and equipment	$ 119	
Cash		$ 6
Capital lease payable		113
(To record acquisition of trucks under capital lease agreements and related down payments)		

	DR	CR
21. Capital lease payable	$ 12	
Nonoperating expenses—interest	5	
Cash		$ 17
(To record capital lease payments)		

Payroll vouchers totaling $3,162 are received during the year, including $477 of pension contributions due to the statewide retirement system. In addition, a $15 increase in accumulated compensated absences, based on salary rates at year end, was authorized to be carried over into the following year.

	DR	CR
22. Operating expenses—costs of sales and services	$ 2,037	
Operating expenses—administration	1,140	
Vouchers payable		$ 2,685
Compensated absences payable		15
Intergovernmental payable—state		477
(To record payroll and benefits)		

The authority purchases $1,497 of consumable materials and supplies for inventory stock. During the year, the government uses $1,650 of inventory stock.

	DR	CR
23. Inventories	$ 1,497	
Accounts payable		$ 1,497
(To record purchase of inventories)		

	DR	CR
24. Operating expenses—costs of sales and services	$ 1,650	
Inventories		$ 1,650
(To record consumption of inventories)		

The authority purchases $5,084 of various goods and services during the normal course of operations, including $659 of services from other funds.

	DR	CR
25. Operating expenses—costs of sales and services	$ 3,087	
Operating expenses—administration	1,997	
Accounts payable		$ 4,425
Due to other funds—general fund		345
Due to other funds—fleet management fund		264
Due to other funds—management information systems fund		50
(To record operating expenses incurred)		

The authority pays $20,317 of outstanding liabilities; $10,202 of the payments are related to the capital construction project.

	DR	CR
26. Vouchers payable	$ 2,629	
Accounts payable	6,219	
Contracts payable	10,202	
Due to other funds—general fund	473	
Due to other funds—fleet management fund	247	
Due to other funds—management information systems fund	59	
Intergovernmental payable—state	488	
Cash		$ 10,115
Restricted assets—revenue bond construction account		10,202
(To record payment of liabilities incurred during the year)		

During the year, the authority returns $17 of deposits to customers who have moved from the service area.

	DR	CR
27. Customer deposits payable—restricted assets	$ 17	
Restricted assets—customer deposits		$ 17
(To record return of customer deposits)		

The authority purchases investments of $7,288 with cash generated from operations and contributions.

	DR	CR
28. Investments	$ 7,288	
Cash		$ 7,288
(To record purchase of investments)		

The authority defeases $8,580 of revenue bonds and $448 of related accrued interest with proceeds from the advance refunding revenue bond issue. At the date of the advance refunding, issuance costs of $103 for the defeased debt remain unamortized. The advance refunding results in an accounting gain of $547; however, no economic gain or loss was realized from this transaction.

	DR	CR
29. Revenue bonds payable—restricted assets	$ 530	
Accrued interest payable—restricted assets	448	
Revenue bonds payable	8,580	
Cash		$ 7,005
Restricted assets—revenue bond current debt service account		1,380
Restricted assets—revenue bond future debt service account		523
Deferred charge—revenue bond issuance costs		103
Extraordinary item—gain on defeasance of debt		547
(To record defeasance of revenue bonds)		

The authority remits to its fiscal agent semiannual revenue and general obligation bond interest payments of $1,857. The entire amount is paid by the fiscal agent to bondholders.

	DR	CR
30. Cash with fiscal agent	$ 1,857	
Restricted assets—revenue bond current debt service account		$ 557
Cash		1,300
(To record transmittal of cash to fiscal agent for payment of semiannual revenue and general obligation bond interest)		

	DR	CR
31. Nonoperating expenses—interest	$ 757	
Accrued interest payable	1,100	
Matured general obligation bond interest payable		$ 1,300
Matured revenue bond interest payable		557
(To recognize semiannual revenue and general obligation bond interest)		

	DR	CR
32. Matured general obligation bond interest payable	$ 1,300	
Matured revenue bond interest payable	557	
Cash with fiscal agent		$ 1,857
(To record interest payment to bondholders by fiscal agent)		

The authority remits to its fiscal agent a bond principal payment of $1,360 for general obligation bonds. Revenue bond principal and interest payments are not due until the following year. The semiannual interest payment totaled $1,249 for the general obligation bonds. The fiscal agent pays $2,486 to the bondholders. The bondholders did not remit $123 of general obligation coupon bonds to the fiscal agent.

	DR	CR
33. Cash with fiscal agent	2,609	
Cash		$ 2,609
(To record transmittal of cash to fiscal agent for payment of annual principal and semiannual interest for general obligation bonds)		

	DR	CR
34. Nonoperating expenses—interest	$ 1,249	
Matured general obligation bond interest payable		$ 1,249
(To record accrual of general obligation interest due)		

	DR	CR
35. General obligation bonds payable—current	$ 1,360	
Matured general obligation bonds payable		$ 1,360
(To record maturation of general obligation bonds)		

	DR	CR
36. Matured general obligation bonds payable	$ 1,292	
Matured general obligation bond interest payable	1,194	
Cash with fiscal agent		$ 2,486
(To record payment to bondholders by fiscal agent)		

At year end, the authority adjusts bond-related accounts to reclassify current principal portions of general obligation bonds payable ($1,480) and revenue bonds payable ($1,484).

	DR	CR
37. General obligation bonds payable	$ 1,480	
Revenue bonds payable	1,484	
General obligation bonds payable—current		$ 1,480
Revenue bonds payable—restricted assets		1,484
(To reclassify current portion of general obligation and revenue bonds payable)		

At year end, the authority reclassifies the $23 current portion of capital leases payable.

	DR	CR
38. Capital leases payable	$ 23	
Capital leases payable—current		$ 23
(To reclassify current portion of capital leases payable)		

At year end, the authority accrues interest expense on outstanding general obligation ($1,045) and revenue ($1,331) bonds.

	DR	CR
39. Nonoperating expenses—interest	$ 2,376	
Accrued interest payable		$ 1,045
Accrued interest payable—restricted assets		1,331
(To accrue interest expense on general obligation and revenue bonds at year end)		

The authority determines that depreciation expense for the year is $2,436 (i.e., building $512, improvements other than buildings $154, and machinery and equipment $1,770).

	DR	CR
40. Operating expenses—depreciation	$ 2,436	
Accumulated depreciation—buildings		$ 512
Accumulated depreciation—improvements other than buildings		154
Accumulated depreciation—machinery and equipment		1,770
(To record depreciation expense)		

At year end, the authority amortizes a portion of deferred charges related to bond issuance costs. The amortization amounts to $25.

	DR	CR
41. Nonoperating expenses—issuance costs	$ 25	
Deferred charge—general obligation bond issuance costs		$ 20
Deferred charge—revenue bond issuance costs		5
(To record amortization of bond issuance costs)		

At year end, the authority amortizes a portion of bond discounts. The amortization amounts to $12.

	DR	CR
42. Nonoperating expenses—interest	$ 12	
Unamortized bond discount—revenue bonds		$ 12
(To record amortization on bond discount)		

ILLUSTRATION 8–3

Name of Government
Water and Sewer Authority Enterprise Fund
Preclosing Trial Balance
December 31, 19X8
(amounts expressed in thousands)

	DR	CR		DR	CR
Cash	$ 1,016		Due to other funds—management information systems fund		5
Cash with fiscal agent	123		General obligation bonds payable—current		1,480
Investments—current	14,610		Capital leases payable—current		23
Interest receivable—investments	409		Customer deposits payable—restricted assets		1,543
Accounts receivable	3,093		Revenue bonds payable—restricted assets		1,484
Allowance for uncollectible accounts receivable		$ 472	Accrued interest payable—restricted assets		1,331
Due from other funds—general fund	37		General obligation bonds payable		29,378
Due from other funds—fleet management fund	2		Revenue bonds payable		33,116
Inventories	308		Unamortized discounts on bonds—revenue bonds	288	
Restricted assets—customer deposits	1,543		Capital leases payable		78
Restricted assets—revenue bond operations and maintenance account	1,294		Contributed capital—government		4,033
Restricted assets—revenue bond construction account	18,542		Contributed capital—customers		14,062
Restricted assets—revenue bond current debt service account	3,706		Contributed capital—developers		35,241
Restricted assets—revenue bond future debt service account	737		Contributed capital—intergovernmental		5,588
Restricted assets—revenue bond renewal and replacement account	1,632		Retained earnings reserved for revenue bond operations and maintenance		1,023
Deferred charge—general obligation bond issuance costs	401		Retained earnings—reserved for revenue bond current debt service		402
Deferred charge—revenue bond issuance costs	145		Retained earnings—reserved for revenue bond renewal and replacement		1,165
Land	604		Retained earnings—unreserved		28,014
Buildings	20,928		Operating revenues—water sales		9,227
Accumulated depreciation—buildings		2,476	Operating revenues—sewer charges		5,671
Improvements other than buildings	1,250		Operating revenues—tap fees		1,521
Accumulated depreciation—improvements other than buildings		342	Operating expenses—costs of sales and services	6,997	
Machinery and equipment	104,283		Operating expenses—administration	3,137	
Accumulated depreciation—machinery and equipment		14,723	Operating expenses—depreciation	2,436	
Construction in progress	7,118		Nonoperating revenues—interest		1,753
Vouchers payable		907	Nonoperating expenses—interest	3,421	
Accounts payable		330	Nonoperating expenses—bond issuance costs	25	
Compensated absences payable		374	Nonoperating expenses—loss on sale of fixed assets	10	
Matured bonds payable		68	Extraordinary item—gain on retirement of debt		547
Matured interest payable		55		$198,095	$198,095
Accrued interest payable		1,045			
Retainage payable		536			
Due to other funds—general fund		65			
Due to other funds—fleet management fund		17			

The following journal entries illustrate the water and sewer authority enterprise fund year-end closing process.

		DR	CR
43.	Operating revenues—water sales	$ 9,227	
	Operating revenues—sewer charges	5,671	
	Operating revenues—tap fees	1,521	
	Nonoperating revenues—interest	1,753	
	Extraordinary item—gain on retirement of debt	547	
	Operating expenses—costs of sales and services		$ 6,997
	Operating expenses—administration		3,137
	Operating expenses—depreciation		2,436
	Nonoperating expenses—interest		3,421

	DR	CR		DR	CR
Nonoperating expenses—bond issuance costs		25	Retained earnings—reserved for revenue bond renewal and replacement		467
Nonoperating expenses—loss on sale of fixed assets		10	(To reclassify retained earnings reserved accounts)		
Retained earnings—unreserved		2,693			
(To close operating accounts at year end)					

	DR	CR
44. Retained earnings—unreserved	$ 1,227	
Retained earnings—reserved for operations and maintenance		$ 271
Retained earnings—reserved for revenue bond current debt service		489

ILLUSTRATION 8–4

Name of Government
Water and Sewer Authority Enterprise Fund
Trial Balance
December 31, 19X8
(amounts expressed in thousands)

	DR	CR		DR	CR
Cash	$ 1,016		Matured bonds payable		68
Cash with fiscal agent	123		Matured interest payble		55
Investments—current	14,610		Accrued interest payable		1,045
Interest receivable—investments	409		Retainage payable		536
Accounts receivable	3,093		Due to other funds—general fund		65
Allowance for uncollectible accounts receivable		$ 472	Due to other funds—fleet management fund		17
Due from other funds—general fund	37		Due to other funds—management information systems fund		5
Due from other funds—fleet management fund	2		General obligation bonds payable—current		1,480
Inventories	308		Capital leases payable—current		23
Restricted assets—customer deposits	1,543		Customer deposits payable—restricted assets		1,543
Restricted assets—revenue bonds operations and maintenance account	1,294		Revenue bonds payable—restricted assets		1,484
Restricted assets—revenue bond construction account	18,542		Accrued interest payable—restricted assets		1,331
Restricted assets—revenue bond current debt service account	3,706		General obligation bonds payable		29,378
Restricted assets—revenue bond future debt service account	737		Revenue bonds payable		33,116
Restricted assets—revenue bond renewal and replacement account	1,632		Unamoritized discounts on bonds—revenue bonds	288	
Deferred charge—general obligation bond issuance costs	401		Capital leases payable		78
Deferred charge—revenue bond issuance costs	145		Contributed capital—government		4,033
Land	604		Contributed capital—customers		14,062
Buildings	20,928		Contributed capital—developers		35,241
Accumulated depreciation—buildings		2,476	Contributed capital—intergovernmental		5,588
Improvements other than buildings	1,250		Retained earnings—reserved for revenue bond operations and maintenance		1,294
Accumulated depreciation—improvements other than buildings		342	Retained earnings—reserved for revenue bond current debt service		891
Machinery and equipment	104,283		Retained earnings—reserved for revenue bond renewal and replacement		1,632
Accumulated depreciation—machinery and equipment		14,723	Retained earnings—unreserved		29,480
Construction in progress	7,118			$182,069	$182,069
Vouchers payable		907			
Accounts payable		330			
Compensated absences payable		374			

Chapter 9
INTERNAL SERVICE FUNDS

NATURE AND PURPOSE

The internal service fund classification should be used to account for the financing on a cost-reimbursement basis of goods or services provided by one department or agency to other departments or agencies within the same government or to other governments or not-for-profit organizations.

Generally accepted accounting principles (GAAP) do not require the use of internal service funds unless legally mandated. However, in recent years, state and local governments have increased the use of this fund. Governments choose to use internal service funds for a variety of reasons, including a desire to:

- Account for the total cost of each activity;
- Provide greater ease in costing and pricing services;
- Accumulate resources for replacing fixed assets;
- Combine certain governmental fund-type overhead costs so they can be redistributed to the benefitting programs; and
- Isolate interfund services so that governmental fund types do not display revenues and expenditures related to interfund transactions twice within the same fund type (i.e., usually the general fund)—once by the department furnishing the goods or services and once by the department receiving the goods or services.

Many governments have interdepartmental charges for the costs of certain goods or services, and the general fund is often used to account for these charges. One consideration in determining the proper fund classification for such transactions should be whether the charge to the user departments is intended to recover total cost, including the cost of the fixed assets used in providing the goods or services (i.e., depreciation). If the cost of the fixed assets is to be passed on to the user, the internal service fund should be used so that depreciation expense may be included in the user charge. If, however, there is no intent to recover the cost of the fixed assets through user charges, the internal service fund should *not* be used in most cases. Such activities can be accounted for just as well in the general fund, thereby avoiding the creation of an additional fund in accordance with the "number of funds" principle. If an internal service fund is used and depreciation is not recovered through user charges, the retained earnings account usually would report a deficit because depreciation still would

be recognized as an expense. A deficit balance in retained earnings is not consistent with the objective of an internal service fund (i.e., revenues should equal expenses over the life of the fund).

In practice, governments include a wide variety of activities within the internal service fund classification. Although the types of activities that may be so classified are numerous, services accounted for in internal service funds usually are tangible, and the extent to which they benefit individual departments of the government should be possible to determine. Some of the more common activities include central garages and motor pools, duplicating and printing services, data processing services, purchasing, central stores, communications and risk management activities. Some activities found less often in internal service funds include engineering services, personnel services, paving products, microfilm activities and central food facilities.

Individual internal service funds normally should be used to account for each type of service. Such segregation is essential to (1) accumulate the costs of providing a service and (2) ensure that the resources generated by one service are not used improperly for another.

However, administrative services such as communications, office supplies, legal services, purchasing services and printing and duplicating often are included in a single administrative internal service fund. Even in such instances, the accounting system and fund structure should allow for the determination of the total cost of providing each specific service. For example, if a motor pool and a data processing function are included in the same internal service fund, the accounting system should have the capability of distinguishing the costs of each of these applications so that an appropriate price can be set for each specific service. If the government's accounting system does not have this capability, a separate fund should be established for each of these services. Generally, it is suggested that a separate fund be maintained for each nonhomogeneous activity.

Alternatively, a government could use subfunds for each specific activity. In such cases, only one internal service fund would be presented for financial reporting purposes. With this alternative, financial reporting is simplified because combining statements would not be required yet costing and pricing could still be determined separately for each individual activity (e.g., print shop, data processing services) through the use of subfunds for internal accounting and reporting.

BUDGETARY ISSUES

The Governmental Accounting Standards Board's 1987 *Codification of Governmental Accounting and Financial Reporting Standards* (1987 *Codification*), Section 1700.109, provides that a government's budgets should be categorized as either fixed or flexible. Fixed budgets include estimates of specific revenues and expenses whereas flexible budgets include dollar estimates that vary in accordance with the demand for the goods or services.

The 1987 *Codification,* Section 1700.120, suggests that flexible budgeting should be used for internal service funds. However, in practice, fixed dollar budgets usually are adopted for internal service funds either to meet legal requirements or to control costs. If a fixed budget is adopted, it should be integrated into the government's accounting system to enhance budgetary control.

Fixed Budgets. If a fixed budget is legally required, the budgetary basis usually is defined. In many instances, the budget is adopted on the modified accrual basis rather than on the accrual basis (i.e., the GAAP basis for proprietary funds). This type of budget allows a government to better control such costs as capital outlay (e.g., equipment purchases) and debt service payments. In addition, some believe that budgeting for depreciation, required when the accrual basis is used for budget, serves no practical purpose.

From a management viewpoint, rigid fixed budgetary controls often may not be appropriate for proprietary fund types because user demand for services may affect actual revenues and expenses. This observation, however, applies more to enterprise funds than to most internal service funds because a government's management usually has control over the use of internal service funds. The critical issue, therefore, is whether the government's departments are required to use the internal service fund instead of procuring goods or services from an outside source.

If the use of the services provided by the internal service fund is mandatory, the internal service fund's revenue budget should be based upon the anticipated users' expenditure budgets. These amounts should agree unless services also are provided to other governments. The internal service fund's expense budget should be based upon estimated revenues. However, because most internal service funds are financed on a cost-reimbursement basis, the anticipated total cost could be budgeted, and then a cost allocation model could be developed to finance the costs from user departments.

At times, an internal service fund may fail to meet the demands for services from other funds and departments because of the timing of their requirements (i.e., many departments want services at the same time, exceeding the fund's capacity to provide the services at a given moment). In these instances, departments may need to procure services from an outside source, thereby reducing the potential revenues of the internal service fund. Therefore, the timing of the services to be provided should be considered when developing the budget. A fixed budget for an internal service fund requires careful monitoring to ensure that resources are available to cover the fund's fixed costs to reduce the possibility of a deficit balance in retained earnings.

If a government is required legally to adopt an annual budget (i.e., appropriated budget) for its internal service funds and also is required legally to report on such budgets, budgetary data for these funds may be presented in the general purpose financial statements (GPFS) or component unit financial statements (CUFS). Budgets adopted on compatible bases (i.e., flow of current financial resources measurement focus and modified accrual basis of accounting) may be presented within the Combined Statement of Revenues, Expenditures and Changes in Fund Balances—Budget and Actual. GAAP-based budgetary comparisons may be presented in a separate budgetary comparison statement within the GPFS or CUFS. At a minimum, annual appropriated budgets should be incorporated within the internal service fund-type subsection of the comprehensive annual financial report or component unit financial report.

Flexible Budgets. When formally adopted, the expense estimates of flexible budgets typically are not viewed as appropriations but as approved financial plans (i.e., nonappropriated budgets). Budgetary control and evaluation are achieved by comparing actual interim or annual revenues and expenses with planned revenues and expenses at the actual level of activity for that period.

With flexible budgets, there generally is a direct correlation between revenues and expenses. As the demand for services increases, certain variable costs increase proportionally. When formulating a flexible budget, planning in units of service precedes planning in dollars. For example, an internal service fund providing data processing services may use machine time as a unit of service (i.e., the number of hours of computer time available for the provision of services). The revenue and expense standards appropriate to each type of physical unit are then established. The cost per hour to operate the computer is one example. The estimated number of units to be provided can then be compared to the unit cost to provide data for the preparation of a budget.

A flexible budget generally is not formally integrated into a government's accounting system; however, if not integrated, interim analyses would be necessary to control costs and avoid potential deficits.

Absence of Budgets. Even though a budget is not always required, some type of control should be established over internal service funds to ensure that they are managed properly. As indicated earlier, certain cost analyses are necessary to determine the budgets of the user funds. Interim comparisons with the original cost analysis are essential for adequate monitoring of financial activities.

ACCOUNTING ISSUES

Internal service funds use the flow of economic resources measurement focus and the accrual basis of accounting. Although internal service funds face accounting issues similar to those encountered by enterprise funds, there are other issues that warrant specific discussion. These issues are grouped by revenue and expense classifications.

Revenues. Most sources of revenues for internal service funds are charges for goods and/or services to other individual funds within the reporting entity or to other government entities. These revenues are recognized in the period they are earned. That is, as soon as a service is performed or a product is provided, a receivable and revenue should be reported. In practice, the reporting of this transaction typically is delayed until the actual billing is completed, usually monthly. However, unbilled amounts should be accrued for financial reporting purposes.

For those services provided to other funds, a receivable account captioned "due from other funds" should be used rather than "accounts receivable" for financial reporting purposes. This classification helps underscore the special nature of the debtor-creditor relationship resulting from this related-party transaction. During the year, for purposes of bookkeeping, these amounts could be recorded as "accounts receivable" just as if the transaction involved an organization external to the reporting entity. At year end, amounts outstanding should be reclassified as "due from other funds." Similarly, the asset account "intergovernmental receivable" should be used for receivables resulting from goods or services provided to other government entities. Normally, deferred revenue would not be reflected in an internal service fund because the receivables would not be reported until the service is provided (i.e., the revenue recognition criteria are met). However, if any user fund has been paying a fixed monthly charge to the internal service fund and an adjustment is to be made at year end to reflect actual charges, the user may have overpaid. In such a case, deferred revenue would be reported.

Expenses. Internal service fund expenses are recognized in the period they are incurred. For services rendered to the internal service fund, the expense is reported when the service has been performed and the amount of the liability can be estimated. Practically, this type of transaction usually is recorded upon receipt of a vendor invoice, which is payable. Inventories of consumable materials and supplies are recognized as expenses when they are consumed in providing the service. For example, repair parts are reported as an expense in a vehicle maintenance internal service fund when the parts are used to repair a vehicle. Again, for practical reasons, the cost of supplies and materials usually is reported as an expense when the inventory is withdrawn from stock.

For additional reading on internal service funds, see volume 2 of the Government Finance Officers Association's Accounting Topics Series, *Internal Service Funds: Government Accounting & Financial Reporting*.

ILLUSTRATIVE JOURNAL ENTRIES

The following discussion and journal entries, where applicable, illustrate the financial transactions required for the establishment and operation of an internal service fund. All amounts are expressed in thousands.

A new fleet management internal service fund is being established to account for the cost of operating a maintenance facility and providing vehicles used by other government departments for activities formerly included in the general fund. The general fund provides $85 of working capital to this internal service fund. Of this amount, $40 is scheduled to be repaid in equal annual installments over a five-year period (i.e., $8 per year), and the remaining $45 is considered a contribution, which will not be repaid. The amount to be repaid is reported as an advance payable, and the balance is reported as contributed capital.

	DR	CR
1. Cash	$ 85	
Advance from other funds—general fund		$ 40
Contributed capital—government		45
(To record advance and contribution from general fund)		

Fixed assets (e.g., vehicles, tools and a maintenance garage) previously used for this activity in the general fund are transferred from the general fixed assets account group (GFAAG) to this internal service fund. The fixed assets transferred have an original cost of $4,253 (i.e., building $87 and vehicles and tools $4,166). The fair market value at the time of transfer is $2,160 (i.e., building $83 and vehicles and tools $2,077). Depreciation was not reported in the GFAAG. The $2,160 fair market value approximates what would have been the book value of the assets if depreciation had been recorded since their acquisition (i.e., cost of $4,253 less accumulated depreciation of $2,093).

	DR	CR
2. Buildings	$ 87	
Machinery and equipment	4,166	
Accumulated depreciation—buildings		$ 4
Accumulated depreciation—machinery and equipment		2,089
Contributed capital—government		2,160
(To record contribution of general fixed assets)		

Note: The fixed assets should be capitalized and recorded as contributed capital at the original cost less an amount equivalent to the depreciation that would have been recorded had the fixed asset been recorded initially in the internal service fund. However, in no instance should the net book value recorded in the internal service fund be greater than the current market value of the transferred assets. The value of the equipment is treated as contributed capital from the government because this equipment was purchased originally from governmental fund resources. The cost of the fixed assets would be deleted from the GFAAG. No entry should be made in the governmental funds for this equipment transfer.

The following discussion and journal entries illustrate revenues and receipts affecting balance sheet accounts.

Billings for services totaling $1,264 are issued; $128 is sent to various governments receiving the services; $872, to the general fund and $264, to the water and sewer enterprise fund.

	DR	CR
3. Intergovernmental receivable	$ 128	
Due from other funds—general fund	872	
Due from other funds—water and sewer fund	264	
Operating revenues—charges for services		$ 1,264
(To record billings)		

Cash of $825 is received on account from the general fund; $247, from the water and sewer fund and $124, from other governments.

	DR	CR
4. Cash	$ 1,196	
Intergovernmental receivable		$ 124
Due from other funds—general fund		825
Due from other funds—water and sewer fund		247
(To record cash receipts for services rendered)		

Investments costing $31 are sold. Proceeds of $35 include $4 of interest.

	DR	CR
5. Cash	$ 35	
Investments		$ 31
Nonoperating revenues—interest		4
(To record sale of investment and interest revenue earned)		

Note: In most internal service funds, interest revenue is classified as nonoperating revenue.

Interest of $2 is earned on investments, but has not been received at year end.

	DR	CR
6. Interest receivable—investments	$ 2	
Nonoperating revenues—interest		$ 2
(To record accrued interest on investments)		

The following discussion and journal entries illustrate expenses, disbursements affecting balance sheet accounts and related nonmonetary transactions.

Vehicles are purchased for $572 (fair market value of $663 less trade-in allowance of $91). The traded-in vehicles originally cost $452 and had a book value of $48.

	DR	CR
7. Machinery and equipment	$ 620	
Accumulated depreciation—machinery and equipment	404	
Accounts payable		$ 572
Machinery and equipment		452
(To record acquisition of vehicles and disposal of traded-in vehicles)		

Note: Determining the proper amount at which the new vehicles should be capitalized is addressed in Accounting Principles Board Opinion No. 29, *Accounting for Nonmonetary Transactions.* According to this guidance, no gain is recognized when nonmonetary assets are exchanged, with additional monetary consideration, to obtain similar assets.

Various goods and services totaling $81 are received from outside vendors.

	DR	CR
8. Operating expenses—costs of services	$ 81	
Accounts payable		$ 81
(To record operating expenses on account)		

A $2 billing is received from the water and sewer fund and a $8 billing is received from the general fund for various administrative services.

	DR	CR
9. Operating expenses—costs of services	$ 2	
Operating expenses—administration	8	
Due to other funds—general fund		$ 8
Due to other funds—water and sewer fund		2
(To record interfund billings)		

Note: This transaction could be recorded as accounts payable provided any unpaid amounts were reclassified at year end as due to other funds.

Consumable materials and supplies costing $153 are purchased and delivered. Inventories valued at $130 are withdrawn from stock and used.

	DR	CR
10. Inventories	$ 153	
Accounts payable		$ 153
(To record purchase of inventories)		

	DR	CR
11. Operating expenses—costs of services	$ 130	
Inventories		$ 130
(To record inventories withdrawn and used)		

Payroll vouchers of $533 are received during the year. Also, the government makes a $47 pension contribution to the state-wide retirement system. In addition, $5 of accumulated compensated absences, based on salary rates at year end, are authorized to be carried over into the following year.

	DR	CR
12. Operating expenses—costs of services	$ 561	
Operating expenses—administration	24	
Vouchers payable		$ 533
Compensated absences payable		5
Intergovernmental payable—state		47
(To record payroll and benefits)		

Outstanding liabilities of $1,159 are paid.

	DR	CR
13. Vouchers payable	$ 533	
Accounts payable	579	
Intergovernmental payable—state	47	
Cash		$ 1,159
(To record payment of liabilities incurred during the year)		

A reimbursement of $3 for expenditures paid from the fleet management internal service fund is received from the general fund.

	DR	CR
14. Cash	$ 3	
Operating expenses—costs of services		$ 3
(To record reimbursement from general fund)		

Note: This transaction is reported as a reimbursement (i.e., as a reduction of expenditures rather than as revenue).

A $76 two-year insurance policy is acquired. One-half of the insurance premium expires and is charged to operations.

	DR	CR
15. Prepaid items	$ 76	
Cash		$ 76
(To record prepaid insurance)		

	DR	CR
16. Operating expenses—administration	$ 38	
Prepaid items		$ 38
(To adjust prepaid items at year end)		

Excess cash of $48 is placed in short-term investments.

	DR	CR
17. Investments	$ 48	
Cash		$ 48
(To record purchase of short-term investments)		

Depreciation expense for the year totals $419 (i.e., building $4, machinery and equipment $415).

	DR	CR
18. Operating expenses—depreciation	$ 419	
Accumulated depreciation—buildings		$ 4
Accumulated depreciation—machinery and equipment		415
(To record depreciation expense)		

ILLUSTRATION 9–1

**Name of Government
Fleet Management Internal Service Fund
Preclosing Trial Balance
December 31, 19X8
(amounts expressed in thousands)**

	DR	CR
Cash	$ 36	
Investments	17	
Interest receivable—investments	2	
Intergovernmental receivable	4	
Due from other funds—general fund	47	
Due from other funds—water and sewer fund	17	
Inventories	23	
Prepaid items	38	
Buildings	87	
Machinery and equipment	4,334	
Accumulated depreciation—buildings		$ 8
Accumulated depreciation—machinery and equipment		2,100
Accounts payable		227
Compensated absences payable		5
Due to other funds—general fund		8
Due to other funds—water and sewer fund		2
Interfund payable—general fund		8
Advance from other funds—general fund		32
Contributed capital—government		2,205
Operating revenues—charges for services		1,264
Operating expenses—costs of services	771	
Operating expenses—administration	70	
Operating expenses—depreciation	419	
Nonoperating revenues—interest		6
	$ 5,865	$ 5,865

Twenty percent of the advance due to the general fund is classified as current.

	DR	CR
19. Advance from other funds—general fund	$ 8	
Interfund payable—general fund		$ 8
(To reclassify current portion of long-term loan from general fund)		

Note: Because this amount ($40 at 20 percent = $8) is now a current liability, it should be reclassified from an advance to an interfund payable.

The following journal entry illustrates the fleet management internal service fund year-end closing process.

	DR	CR
20. Operating revenues—charges for services	$ 1,264	
Nonoperating revenues—interest	6	
Operating expenses—costs of services		$ 771
Operating expenses—administration		70
Operating expenses—depreciation		419
Retained earnings—unreserved		10
(To close operating statement accounts)		

ILLUSTRATION 9–2

**Name of Government
Fleet Management Internal Service Fund
Trial Balance
December 31, 19X8
(amounts expressed in thousands)**

	DR	CR
Cash	$ 36	
Investments	17	
Interest receivable—investments	2	
Intergovernmental receivable	4	
Due from other funds—general fund	47	
Due from other funds—water and sewer fund	17	
Inventories	23	
Prepaid items	38	
Buildings	87	
Machinery and equipment	4,334	
Accumulated depreciation—buildings		$ 8
Accumulated depreciation—machinery and equipment		2,100
Accounts payable		227
Compensated absences payable		5
Due to other funds—general fund		8
Due to other funds—water and sewer fund		2
Interfund payable—general fund		8
Advance from other funds—general fund		32
Contributed capital—government		2,205
Retained earnings—unreserved		10
	$ 4,605	$ 4,605

Chapter 10
TRUST AND AGENCY FUNDS

NATURE AND PURPOSE

The trust and agency fund type generally is used to account for assets held by a government in a trustee or agent capacity for others and is the only fund type included in the fiduciary category, pursuant to the Governmental Accounting Standards Board's (GASB) 1987 *Codification of Governmental Accounting and Financial Reporting Standards* (1987 *Codification*). The trust and agency fund type is different from the other fund types in that it includes four different subclassifications: expendable trust funds, nonexpendable trust funds, pension trust funds and agency funds.

In most instances, the use of expendable and nonexpendable trust funds should be limited to formal legal trusts. Trust fund spending is controlled primarily through legal trust agreements and applicable state laws.

Expendable Trust Funds. This fund type subclassification should be used when both the principal and revenues earned on that principal may be expended for purposes designated by the trust agreement (e.g., donations received for specific expendable purposes). Expendable trust funds sometimes are used to account for revenues earned in nonexpendable trust funds and transferred to this fund type. In such a case, however, an expendable trust fund should not be established if all resources can be accounted for adequately in a nonexpendable trust fund. The 1987 *Codification*, Section U50.101, identifies one instance where an expendable trust fund should be reported. This section requires state government unemployment compensation benefit plans be accounted for as expendable trust funds.

Governments often classify activities as expendable trust funds when they could be accounted for either in the general fund or in a special revenue fund. As previously noted, if a formal trust agreement is not established, the trust fund classification generally should not be used.

Nonexpendable Trust Funds. This fund-type subclassification is similar to expendable trust funds; however, the principal (i.e., corpus) of the trust must be preserved intact. Common activities that have trust restrictions precluding expenditure of the principal of the fund include cemetery perpetual care funds, land trusts and endowments. For example, this classification often is used to account for the principal portion of endowments provided by private donors with the stipulation that the principal balance not be disbursed. In another example, a

government could be allowed the use of any net income resulting from the operation of a donated farm but would not be able to sell the property pursuant to the trust agreement attached to the donation.

Pension Trust Funds. This fund type subclassification is used primarily to account for the activities of a government's single-employer public employee retirement system (PERS). Some governments include a multiple-employer PERS that meets the reporting entity definition discussed in chapter 2. PERS represent the single largest fund(s) for a significant portion of governments that include a PERS either as a part of the oversight unit or as a component unit of the reporting entity. An individual fund should be maintained for each PERS the government operates (e.g., if a government maintains one PERS for its general employees and a separate PERS for its public safety employees, two pension trust funds should be reported).

If a government contributes to a multiple-employer PERS, it should not use this fund classification to report the contributions. In this instance, the contributions to a PERS should be reported in the fund where the cost and/or employee deduction occurs.

Agency Funds. An agency fund is used to account for assets held for other funds, governments or individuals. The 1987 *Codification*, Section 1300.102, provides that agency funds are custodial in nature (i.e., assets equal liabilities) and do not involve measurement of operations. Therefore, agency funds generally serve as clearing accounts, and, with few exceptions, these activities could be reported in another fund type.

The most common uses of agency funds include taxes billed and collected by one government on behalf of other governments; certain deferred compensation plans pursuant to the 1987 *Codification*, Section D25.109; special assessment collections when the government is not obligated in some manner for special assessment debt; and performance deposit funds, such as refundable construction bid bonds and deposits required of various licensees.

Separate agency funds generally are used for individual agent relationships. However, a single agency fund may be used to account for several closely related activities (e.g., if a county government is collecting property taxes for other governments, a single fund may be used for this purpose with separate liability accounts for each government).

BUDGETARY ISSUES

Legally adopted budgets and formal budgetary integration usually are not required for trust funds. Trust fund spending is controlled primarily through legal trust agreements and applicable state laws. However, if legally required, or if formal budgetary integration is considered necessary to ensure acceptable control over trust fund spending, this accounting convention should be used (e.g., it may be necessary to adopt a budget for the administrative operating costs of a pension trust fund).

The 1987 *Codification,* Section 1700.124, indicates that formal budgetary integration is considered essential in controlling expendable trust funds that are similar to special revenue funds, but rarely appropriate for other fiduciary fund types. The appropriation of administrative expenses for certain trust fund activities (e.g., PERS) is an exception to this general rule. Because agency funds are custodial in nature, formal budgetary integration is not necessary.

If an annual appropriated budget is adopted for a trust fund, a budgetary comparison (i.e., budget to actual) statement should be prepared and presented within the trust and agency fund-type subsection of the comprehensive annual financial report (CAFR). In addition, a government may chose to present the budgetary comparison statement within the general purpose financial statements (GPFS). In this instance, if the presentation of the governmental fund types on the combined budgetary comparison statement is consistent with that of the trust fund budgetary comparison, the statements may be combined. However, a separate trust fund budgetary comparison statement within the GPFS is considered acceptable.

ACCOUNTING ISSUES

As indicated in chapter 2, funds of a government reporting entity generally use the measurement focus and basis of accounting of either governmental or proprietary fund types.

Expendable Trust Funds. Like the governmental fund types, expendable trust funds are accounted for on a flow of current financial resources measurement focus, using the modified accrual basis of accounting. Most of the revenues of expendable trust funds are donations, which normally are not susceptible to accrual until received in cash. Occasionally, resources may be pledged but the actual donation will not be received until early in the next year. The guidance provided in the American Institute of Certified Public Accountants' industry audit guide, *Audits of Certain Nonprofit Organizations* can be applied within the context of the governmental model. Therefore, such a pledge would be reported as revenue in the current year only if legally enforceable and collectible soon enough after year end to pay liabilities of the current year. Normally, any interest earnings at year end also would be accrued. Expenditures would be recognized in the same manner as for governmental fund types.

Expendable trust funds are unique in that fixed assets and long-term liabilities are reported within the fund in certain instances. Although authoritative standards appear to require fixed assets to be reported within an expendable trust fund, there is no method for allocating the cost of these assets over future periods. Therefore, any fixed assets accounted for in

an expendable trust fund would be reported at historical or estimated historical cost until the assets' disposal.

Another issue is the treatment of certain liabilities, such as claims, judgments and compensated absences. Exceptions to the general rule of reporting these long-term liabilities as *fund* liabilities are established in the 1987 *Codification,* Sections C50 and C60. In these instances, liabilities not normally expected to be liquidated with expendable available financial resources would be reported in the general long-term debt account group, not as fund liabilities. An example of a liability that would be reported in the expendable trust fund is the amount owed to the federal government for unemployment compensation benefit advances.

The 1987 *Codification,* Section U50.101, also provides specific guidance for administrative costs and fees of state unemployment programs. Resources provided for these administrative costs and fees should be accounted for in the general fund unless the accounting and financial reporting of those resources in another fund are legally required.

Nonexpendable Trust Funds. Like all proprietary fund types, nonexpendable trust funds are accounted for using a flow of economic resources measurement focus and the accrual basis of accounting. Interest earnings on the principal normally are the primary revenue source for these funds and should be accrued. The accounting for expenses is similar to that of proprietary fund types: therefore, depreciation is recorded for nonexpendable trust fund fixed assets.

Pension Trust Funds. This section discusses the accounting and financial reporting principles applicable to government employers maintaining a pension trust fund (separate PERS reporting is discussed in chapter 14). PERS are categorized as either defined benefit plans or defined contribution plans. A defined benefit plan generally bases the pension benefit on age, years of service and/or compensation. A defined contribution plan bases benefits solely on amounts contributed to the participant's account. The 1987 *Codification,* Section P20.117, further classifies defined benefit PERS as single-employer or multiple-employer. Only one employer (e.g., component unit) contributes to a single-employer PERS and more than one employer contributes to a multiple-employer PERS. Some multiple-employer PERS are aggregations of single-employer PERS and have separate complete actuarial valuations for each participating government. These PERS are classified as agent PERS. Other multiple-employer PERS are essentially one large pension plan with cost-sharing arrangements, and one actuarial valuation is performed for the PERS as a whole. These PERS are classified as cost-sharing PERS.

The 1987 *Codification,* Section P20.102, recognizes three alternative sources of authoritative guidance: National Council on Governmental Accounting (NCGA) Statement 1, *Governmental Accounting and Financial Reporting Principles;* NCGA Statement 6, *Pension Accounting and Financial Reporting: Public Employee Retirement Systems and State and Local Government Employers* and the Financial Accounting Standards Board's (FASB) Statement of Financial Accounting Standards (SFAS) No. 35, *Accounting For Pensions.* These three pronouncements differ in both the accounting and financial reporting guidance offered. The GASB provided this interim guidance because the effective dates of both NCGA Statement 6 and SFAS No. 35 had been extended indefinitely for governments.

In 1985, the FASB issued SFAS No. 87, *Employers' Accounting for Pensions,* providing guidance to employers on recognizing and measuring expenses and liabilities resulting from pension plans. The GASB responded in 1986 by issuing GASB Statement No. 4, *Applicability of FASB Statement No. 87, "Employers' Accounting for Pensions," to State and Local Governmental Employers* which provides that government employers should not change their pension accounting practices to conform to SFAS No. 87, pending issuance of a future GASB statement or statements on pension recognition, measurement and display. Until this guidance is issued the three pronouncements (i.e., NCGA Statement 1, NCGA Statement 6 and SFAS No. 35) remain authoritative sources of guidance for pension accounting.

NCGA Statement 1. The 1987 *Codification,* Section 1300.104, does not provide specific guidance on the valuation methods for pension trust fund assets and benefit obligations. However, this guidance does require the fund to be accounted for using the flow of economic resources measurement focus and the accrual basis of accounting. The illustrations included in the 1968 *Governmental Accounting, Auditing, and Financial Reporting* (1968 *GAAFR*) are considered to represent the principles of NCGA Statement 1, to the extent such material is consistent. The 1968 *GAAFR* supports a cost-based method (i.e., cost/amortized cost) for investment valuation.

In practice, an unfunded accrued liability most often is not reported on the balance sheet as a fund deficit, following NCGA Statement 1. The pension plan assets usually are offset in the fund equity section of the PERS balance sheet by a reserved for employees' retirement system. The combined balance sheet illustration in the 1987 *Codification,* Section 2200.603, exhibit 1, displays both a reserved for employees' retirement system account and a deficit unreserved, undesignated fund balance account, that appears to imply an unfunded actuarial deficiency. Therefore, the actuarial reserves preferably should be presented in the equity section as a reserved for employees' retirement system account. The difference between the assets, liabilities and reserves should be reported in the unreserved, undesignated fund balance. In addition, an explanation of the Combined Statement of Revenues, Expenses and Changes in Retained Earnings/Fund Balances (1987 *Codification,* Section 2200.606) suggests that changes in the various reserves of pension trust funds be disclosed in the notes to the financial statements or in a separate statement.

NCGA Statement 6. Although the application of the accounting principles included in NCGA Statement 6 is optional, this pronouncement does provide specific guidance on pension trust fund accounting. The 1987 *Codification,* Section Pe5.108, indicates that equity securities should "be reported at cost, subject to adjustment for market value declines judged to be other than temporary," pursuant to SFAS No. 12, *Accounting for Certain Marketable Securities.* The 1987 *Codification,* Section Pe5.109, provides that fixed-income securities should be reported at amortized cost, subject to adjustment for market value declines judged to be other than temporary. Premiums and discounts should be amortized using the effective interest method. If a government plans to hold a fixed-income security until maturity, however, any decline in value should be considered temporary and the security should not be adjusted. Liabilities on PERS balance sheets should be reported as a reduction of assets and the difference between assets and liabilities should be captioned "net assets available for benefits," pursuant to the 1987 *Codification,* Section Pe5.115.

If governments follow the guidance provided in NCGA Statement 6 (1987 *Codification,* Section P20.109) and the PERS financial statements are incorporated into the GPFS, the format of the balance sheet should be consistent with that illustrated in the 1968 *GAAFR* (i.e., assets equal liabilities and fund balance). The fund balance should be presented as a single amount, appropriately captioned "reserved for employees' retirement system." However, when the PERS financial statements are reflected in the pension trust fund subsection of the CAFR, the reporting guidance for PERS presented in chapter 14 should be followed.

GAAP have required that gains and losses on sales of fixed-income securities be recognized using the completed transaction method of accounting (i.e., the difference between the selling price and the book value of the fixed-income security is recognized as a gain or loss at the time of sale). However, the 1987 *Codification,* Section Pe5.118, allows the use of the deferral-and-amortization method of accounting for gains and losses on the exchange of fixed-income securities when the transaction is classified as an exchange, rather than as a sale.

The 1987 *Codification,* Section Pe5.118, recognizes that sales of fixed-income securities and the reinvestment of the proceeds may take place under circumstances that warrant the deferral and amortization of the gains and losses over a future period. Therefore, criteria are established to define an exchange as follows:

a) Both the sale and purchase must be planned simultaneously; that is, each half undertaken in contemplation of the other and each half executed conditioned upon execution of the other.
b) Both the sale and purchase must be made on the same day, although settlement of the two transactions may occur on different dates.
c) The sale and purchase must increase the net yield to maturity and/or an improvement of the quality of the bond held.
d) The purchase must involve an investment-grade bond that is better rated, equally rated or rated no worse than one investment grade lower than the bond sold.

Unless all of the foregoing criteria are met, the transaction is considered a sale, not an exchange. Once adopted, the deferral-and-amortization method should be used consistently for both gains and losses. This method recognizes a deferred gain or loss at the time of the sale, amortizing the deferral over the remaining life of the security sold or the security purchased, whichever is shorter.

Again, it should be noted that the deferral-and-amortization method may be used only with pension plans.

SFAS No. 35. Major differences between SFAS No. 35 and NCGA requirements arise in the valuation of investments and the actuarial liability. SFAS No. 35 requires the use of market value for investments. This valuation method may differ significantly from the cost/amortized cost investment valuation method established by the NCGA. The other major difference arises from the required use of the actuarial present value of accumulated plan benefits in SFAS No. 35. This method primarily differs from other actuarial liabilities in that it does not consider any potential salary increases from the date of the actuarial valuation. Additional pension reporting requirements are outlined in chapter 14.

Agency Funds. Even though agency funds do not report operations, the modified accrual basis of accounting is followed for recognizing assets and liabilities. Assets always should equal liabilities. If resources are accumulated from an agency fund's assets (e.g., interest), the assets are increased and a liability is reported to whomever will receive these resources. Because agency funds do not have operations per se, it is necessary to present the additions and deductions to these funds in the combining and individual fund section of a CAFR. The statement of changes in assets and liabilities enables financial statement users to determine the fund activity for the year.

The 1987 *Codification*, Section D25, provides guidance for the financial reporting of deferred compensation plans adopted under the provisions of Internal Revenue Code Section 457. The 1987 *Codification*, Section D25.109, requires most employers to report these plans in agency funds. The agency fund balance sheet generally should display the plan assets at market value, with a corresponding liability to employees for deferred compensation pursuant to the 1987 *Codification*, Section D25.111. If a government provides both governmental and proprietary type services, the agency fund classification is appropriate. However, employers using proprietary fund accounting for separately constituted public authorities (e.g., utilities) should display the plan's assets and liabilities in the enterprise fund.

There is a possibility of duplicate reporting when a PERS that is a component unit of a reporting entity also is the administrator of the reporting entity's plan. The 1987 *Codification*, Section D25.114, permits only one presentation of the oversight unit's plan in the trust and agency fund column on the combined balance sheet. In this instance, the component unit's share of the plan would be eliminated from the oversight unit's agency fund at the combined financial reporting level. Both would be presented (with an elimination) at the combining level.

Agency funds also should be used to account for debt service transactions of special assessment debt issues where the government is *not* obligated in some manner. The 1987 *Codification*, Section S40.119, provides an agency fund should be used, "to reflect the fact that the government's duties are limited to acting as an agent for the assessed property owners and the bondholders."

If the entire receivable from the property owners were reported in the agency fund, a corresponding liability for the amounts due to bondholders also would have to be reported. However, to comply with the 1987 *Codification*, Section S40.117, provision that, "special assessment debt for which the government is not obligated in some manner should not be displayed in the government's financial statements," the agency fund activities should be limited to cash collected from the property owners and the related interest on investments.

ILLUSTRATIVE JOURNAL ENTRIES

The following discussion and journal entries illustrate the financial transactions required for the establishment of an expendable trust fund, a nonexpendable trust fund (e.g., a perpetual care fund), a general employees' pension plan and an

agency fund (e.g., to collect property taxes for other governmental agencies) during a year. All of the following amounts are expressed in thousand dollars.

Expendable Trust Fund. The balances of the senior citizens transportation expendable trust fund at January 1, 19X8, are as follows:

ILLUSTRATION 10–1

Name of Government
Senior Citizens Transportation
Expendable Trust Fund
Trial Balance
January 1, 19X8
(amounts expressed in thousands)

	DR	CR
Cash	$ 16	
Investments	33	
Interest receivable—investments	2	
Accounts payable		$ 2
Fund balance—unreserved, undesignated		49
	$ 51	$ 51

The following discussion and journal entries illustrate revenues and receipts affecting balance sheet accounts.

Donations of $82 are received and held in trust.

	DR	CR
1. Cash	$ 82	
Revenues—donations		$ 82
(To record donations received)		

Investments costing $30 are sold for $32. The sales price includes $2 of accrued interest earned to the date of sale.

	DR	CR
2. Cash	$ 32	
Investments		$ 30
Revenues—interest		2
(To record sale of investment and interest revenue earned)		

Interest earned on investments, but not yet received, totaled $4.

	DR	CR
3. Interest receivable—investments	$ 4	
Revenues—interest		$ 4
(To record accrued interest on investments)		

The following discussion and journal entries illustrate expenditures and disbursements affecting balance sheet accounts.

Various services are provided by outside vendors and invoices are received totaling $86.

	DR	CR
4. Expenditures—general government	$ 86	
Accounts payable		$ 86
(To record operating expenditures on account)		

Excess cash of $38 is placed in short-term investments.

	DR	CR
5. Investments	$ 38	
Cash		$ 38
(To record purchase of short-term investments)		

Outstanding accounts payable of $81 are paid.

	DR	CR
6. Accounts payable	$ 81	
Cash		$ 81
(To record the payment of accounts payable)		

The trial balance for the senior citizens transportation expendable trust fund at December 31, 19X8, before the closing entries is as follows:

ILLUSTRATION 10–2

Name of Government
Senior Citizens Transportation
Expendable Trust Fund
Preclosing Trial Balance
December 31, 19X8
(amounts expressed in thousands)

	DR	CR
Cash	$ 11	
Investments	41	
Interest receivable—investments	6	
Accounts payable		$ 7
Fund balance—unreserved, undesignated		49
Revenues—donations		82
Revenues—interest		6
Expenditures—general government	86	
	$ 144	$ 144

The following journal entry illustrates the senior citizens transportation expendable trust fund year-end closing process.

	DR	CR
7. Revenues—donations	$ 82	
Revenues—interest	6	
Expenditures—general government		$ 86
Fund balance—unreserved, undesignated		2
(To close operating statement accounts at year end)		

The following trial balance is presented after the closing entry:

ILLUSTRATION 10–3

Name of Government
Senior Citizens Transportation
Expendable Trust Fund
Trial Balance
December 31, 19X8
(amounts expressed in thousands)

	DR	CR
Cash	$ 11	
Investments	41	
Interest receivable—investments	6	
Accounts payable		$ 7
Fund balance—unreserved, undesignated		51
	$ 58	$ 58

Nonexpendable Trust Fund. The balances of the perpetual care nonexpendable trust fund at January 1, 19X8, are as follows:

ILLUSTRATION 10–4

Name of Government
Perpetual Care Nonexpendable Trust Fund
Trial Balance
January 1, 19X8
(amounts expressed in thousands)

	DR	CR
Cash	$ 16	
Investments	1,848	
Interest receivable—investments	41	
Accounts payable		$ 18
Fund balance—reserved for perpetual care		1,102
Fund balance—unreserved, undesignated		785
	$ 1,905	$ 1,905

The following discussion and journal entries illustrate revenues and receipts affecting balance sheet accounts.

Investments costing $1,650 are sold for $1,788. The sale price includes a $138 gain.

	DR	CR
8. Cash	$ 1,788	
Investments		$ 1,650
Nonoperating revenues—gain on sale of investments		138
(To record sale of investments and the gain on the sale)		

Interest earned on investments, but not yet received, totaled $41.

	DR	CR
9. Interest receivable on investments	$ 41	
Operating revenues—interest		$ 41
(To record accrued interest on investments)		

The following journal entries and discussion, where applicable, illustrate expenses and disbursements affecting balance sheet accounts.

Various services are provided by outside vendors and invoices are received totaling $13.

	DR	CR
10. Operating expenses—costs of services	$ 13	
Accounts payable		$ 13
(To record operating expenses on account)		

Outstanding accounts payable of $18 were paid.

	DR	CR
11. Accounts payable	$ 18	
Cash		$ 18
(To record payment of outstanding payables)		

Excess cash of $1,555 is placed in short-term investments.

	DR	CR
12. Investments	$ 1,555	
Cash		$ 1,555

(To record purchase of short-term investments)

The trial balance for the perpetual care nonexpendable trust fund at December 31, 19X8, before the closing entries is as follows:

ILLUSTRATION 10–5

Name of Government
Perpetual Care Nonexpendable Trust Fund
Preclosing Trial Balance
December 31, 19X8
(amounts expressed in thousands)

	DR	CR
Cash	$ 231	
Investments	1,753	
Interest receivable—investments	82	
Accounts payable		$ 13
Fund balance—reserved for perpetual care		1,102
Fund balance—unreserved, undesignated		785
Operating revenues—interest		41
Operating expenses—costs of services	13	
Nonoperating revenues—gain on sale of investments		138
	$ 2,079	$ 2,079

The following journal entry illustrates the perpetual care nonexpendable trust fund year-end closing process.

	DR	CR
13. Operating revenues—interest	$ 41	
Nonoperating revenues—gain on investments	138	
Operating expenses—costs of service		$ 13
Fund balance—unreserved, undesignated		166

(To close operating statement accounts at year end)

The following trial balance is presented after the closing entry:

ILLUSTRATION 10–6

Name of Government
Perpetual Care Nonexpendable Trust Fund
Trial Balance
December 31, 19X8
(amounts expressed in thousands)

	DR	CR
Cash	$ 231	
Investments	1,753	
Interest receivable—investments	82	
Accounts payable		$ 13
Fund balance—reserved for perpetual care		1,102
Fund balance—unreserved, undesignated		951
	$ 2,066	$ 2,066

Pension Trust Fund. The balances of the public safety employees pension trust fund at January 1, 19X8, are as follows:

ILLUSTRATION 10–7
NCGA Statement No. 1 Method

Name of Government
Public Safety Employees Pension Trust Fund
Trial Balance
January 1, 19X8
(amounts expressed in thousands)

	DR	CR
Cash	$ 55	
Investments	12,615	
Interest receivable—investments	118	
Accounts payable		$ 16
Fund balance—member contributions		5,893
Fund balance—employer contributions		6,142
Fund balance—benefit reserve		1,129
Fund balance—disability reserve		842
Fund balance—undistributed investment earnings reserve		242
Fund balance—unreserved, undesignated	1,476	
	$ 14,264	$ 14,264

The following discussion and journal entries illustrate revenues and receipts affecting balance sheet accounts.

Investments costing $1,650 are sold for $1,788. The sale price included $138 of accrued interest that was earned to the date of sale.

	DR	CR
14. Cash	$ 1,788	
Investments		$ 1,650
Operating revenues—interest		138

(To record sale of investments and interest revenue earned)

Interest of $115 accrued on investments was received.

	DR	CR
15. Cash	$ 115	
Interest receivable—investments		$ 115

(To record receipt of interest)

Interest earned and received in cash during the year totaled $295.

	DR	CR
16. Cash	$ 295	
Operating revenues—interest		$ 295

(To record interest earnings)

Interest earned on investments, but not yet received, totaled $341.

	DR	CR
17. Interest receivable—investments	$ 341	
Operating revenues—interest		$ 341

(To record accrued interest on investments)

Pension contributions of $1,051 and $729 withheld from general fund and public safety employees were received from the general fund.

	DR	CR
18. Cash	$ 1,780	
Operating revenues—member contributions		$ 729
Operating revenues—employer contributions		1,051
(To record receipt of employer and employee contributions)		

The following discussion and journal entries illustrate expenses and disbursements affecting balance sheet accounts. Investments of $2,700 are purchased at par value.

	DR	CR
19. Investments	$ 2,700	
Cash		$ 2,700
(To record purchase of investments)		

Investments of $670 are purchased with accrued interest of $2.

	DR	CR
20. Investments	$ 670	
Interest receivable—investments	2	
Cash		$ 672
(To record the purchase of investments with accrued interest)		

Benefits of $455 are paid to retired employees.

	DR	CR
21. Operating expenses—benefits	$ 455	
Cash		$ 455
(To record payment of benefits)		

Refunds of $15 are paid to terminated employees.

	DR	CR
22. Operating expenses—refunds	$ 15	
Cash		$ 15
(To record payment of refunds to terminated employees)		

Administrative costs of $160 were incurred during the year; $158 of this amount was paid.

	DR	CR
23. Operating expenses—administration	$ 160	
Accounts payable		$ 160
(To record administrative expenses incurred)		

	DR	CR
24. Accounts payable	$ 158	
Cash		$ 158
(To record payment of administrative expenses)		

The trial balance of the public safety employees pension trust fund at December 31, 19X8, before the closing entries is as follows:

ILLUSTRATION 10–8

Name of Government
Public Safety Employees Pension Trust Fund
Preclosing Trial Balance
December 31, 19X8
(amounts expressed in thousands)

	DR	CR
Cash	$ 33	
Investments	14,335	
Interest receivable—investments	346	
Accounts payable		$ 18
Fund balance—member contributions		5,893
Fund balance—employer contributions		6,142
Fund balance—benefit reserve		1,129
Fund balance—disability reserve		842
Fund balance—undistributed investment earnings reserve		242
Fund balance—unreserved, undesignated	1,476	
Operating revenues—interest		774
Operating revenues—member contributions		729
Operating revenues—employer contributions		1,051
Operating expenses—benefits	455	
Operating expenses—refunds	15	
Operating expenses—administration	160	
	$ 16,820	$ 16,820

The following journal entry illustrates the pension trust fund year-end closing entries.

	DR	CR
25. Operating revenues—interest	$ 774	
Operating revenues—member contributions	729	
Operating revenues—employer contributions	1,051	
Operating expenses—benefits		$ 455
Operating expenses—refunds		15
Operating expenses—administration		160
Fund balance—unreserved, undesignated		1,924
(To close operating statement accounts at year end)		

The following entries are necessary to adjust the fund balance reserves.

The fund balance reserved for member and employer contributions is adjusted for current-year contributions.

	DR	CR
26. Fund balance—unreserved, undesignated	$ 1,780	
Fund balance—member contributions		$ 729
Fund balance—employer contributions		1,051
(To adjust fund balance reserved for member and employer contributions)		

Interest earnings in the amount of $774 are allocated consistent with the pension plan policies.

	DR	CR
27. Fund balance—unreserved, undesignated	$ 774	
Fund balance—member contributions		$ 341
Fund balance—employer contributions		282
Fund balance—benefit reserve		86
Fund balance—disability reserve		51
Fund balance—undistributed investment earnings reserve		14
(To allocate interest earnings)		

The following trial balance is presented after closing entries:

ILLUSTRATION 10–9

Name of Government
Public Safety Employees Pension Trust Fund
Trial Balance
December 31, 19X8
(amounts expressed in thousands)

	DR	CR
Cash	$ 33	
Investments	14,335	
Interest receivable—investments	346	
Accounts payable		$ 18
Fund balance—member contributions		6,963
Fund balance—employer contributions		7,475
Fund balance—benefit reserve		1,215
Fund balance—disability reserve		893
Fund balance—undistributed investment earnings reserve		256
Fund balance—unreserved, undesignated	2,106	
	$ 16,820	$ 16,820

Agency Fund. The balances of the deferred compensation agency fund at January 1, 19X8, are as follows:

ILLUSTRATION 10–10

Name of Government
Deferred Compensation Agency Fund
Trial Balance
January 1, 19X8
(amounts expressed in thousands)

	DR	CR
Investments	$ 898	
Interest receivable—investments	2	
Deferred compensation benefits payable		$ 900
	$ 900	$ 900

The following discussion and journal entries illustrate the changes in the assets and liabilities.

Payments of $287 are withheld from employees' payroll.

	DR	CR
28. Cash	$ 287	
Deferred compensation benefits payable		$ 287
(To record amounts withheld from employees' payroll)		

Payments of $29 are made to employees.

	DR	CR
29. Deferred compensation benefits payable	$ 29	
Cash		$ 29
(To record payment of deferred compensation benefits payable)		

Interest receivable of $2 is received.

	DR	CR
30. Cash	$ 2	
Interest receivable—investments		$ 2
(To record receipt of accrued interest)		

Interest of $58 on investment is received.

	DR	CR
31. Cash	$ 58	
Deferred compensation benefits payable		$ 58
(To record interest received on investments)		

Investments of $300 are puchased.

	DR	CR
32. Investments	$ 300	
Cash		$ 300
(To record purchase of investments)		

The trial balance for the deferred compensation agency fund at December 31, 19X8, is as follows:

ILLUSTRATION 10–11

Name of Government
Deferred Compensation Agency Fund
Trial Balance
December 31, 19X8
(amounts expressed in thousands)

	DR	CR
Cash	$ 18	
Investments	1,198	
Deferred compensation benefits payable		$ 1,216
	$ 1,216	$ 1,216

Chapter 11
SPECIAL GOVERNMENT UNITS

NATURE AND PURPOSE

Governments have grown increasingly complex as citizens have turned more and more to the public sector for a wide variety of services. Often, separate new units of government are formed to meet the demand. These special government units usually are established solely to perform one or more services and, in effect, function as limited-purpose governments. They encompass a wide array of entities including state colleges and universities, community colleges, hospitals, utility districts, public benefit corporations/authorities, special districts and councils of government (e.g., regional planning commissions and economic development districts).* Indeed, the majority of government units in the United States are of this type.

There are many different reasons the choice is made to establish new units of government rather than to expand the scope of services provided by general-purpose government units (i.e., states, counties, cities, towns and villages). Reasons for creating new units of government include:

1. *Geographical limitations.* The limited geographical jurisdiction of traditional units of government can hamper their dealing effectively with certain issues. For example, flood control and irrigation often can be better addressed by a single river basin authority than by individual governments in the watershed.

2. *Independence.* Sometimes it is considered preferable to remove certain services, as much as possible, from the pressures inherent in the political process. For example, state colleges and universities, although receiving considerable resources from taxpayers, normally are not organized as departments within the state government, but are established as separate units.

3. *Local autonomy.* Citizens may wish to share one or more services with a larger neighboring government, but may not wish to lose their autonomy. A special government unit can provide one or more benefits without requiring incorporation into the larger government. For example, residents of outlying subdivisions may wish to be connected to a neighboring city's sewer system, but do not wish to be annexed by the city. A special sewerage district could provide them with the needed service without annexation.

4. *Financial restrictions.* Sometimes governments have to work within a framework of debt or investment limitations. Such limitations may not allow a traditional government to take on new responsibilities. For example, special bond authorities may be used to avoid the requirement that all bond issuances be subject to a special vote of the people.

5. *Political considerations.* Sometimes citizens of a traditional unit of government may not be willing to consider any broadening of the scope of service unless they receive immediate and direct benefit individually. In such cases, special government units may be the only politically acceptable expedient for providing a needed service. For example, a majority of citizens living in a heavily urbanized area could prove unwilling to extend sewer lines to new subdivisions. A special district, issuing its own debt and relying solely on user charges, could be a politically acceptable method of providing sewers to these residents.

All special units of government are subject to the financial reporting jurisdiction of the Governmental Accounting Standards Board (GASB), just as are the more traditional government units. Nonetheless, particular care must be taken in applying generally accepted accounting principles (GAAP) to these units because of specialized industry practices.

ACCOUNTING ISSUES

Many special government units face potential financial reporting issues when evaluating their relations with other government units. This chapter will address this situation as well as the unique problems facing preparers of financial statements of colleges and universities, hospitals, and public utilities. Accounting and financial reporting for special districts and councils of government also will be considered.

Relation to Other Government Units. One important consideration in accounting and financial reporting for special government units is their relation to other governments. The provisions of the GASB's 1987 *Codification of Governmental Accounting and Financial Reporting Standards* (1987 *Codification*), Sections 2100 and 2600, provide the necessary guidance

---

*One of the more common types of special government units, the school district, is the subject of chapter 12.

on defining the reporting entity and on component unit financial reporting.

Some special government units typically do not qualify for inclusion as part of a larger reporting entity (e.g., councils of government). Other special government units often, if not ordinarily, are treated as component units of other governments (e.g., public utilities). Still other special government units should be accounted for as joint ventures by each of the participating governments.

Governments commonly fail to account for and disclose properly those special government units that meet the definition of a joint venture in the 1987 *Codification,* Section J50. For example, if two cities establish a separate legal entity to build and maintain a bridge between them, this separate legal entity may qualify as a joint venture of both governments. In that case, both of the governments would need to account for their individual participation in the joint venture in their financial statements. In addition, GAAP would require both governments to provide a general description of the joint venture in the notes to their financial statements, as well as to provide certain condensed financial information. The government reporting entity and joint ventures are discussed at greater length in chapter 2 and chapter 14.

Colleges and Universities. Colleges and universities, both government and private, generally subscribe to specialized accounting and financial reporting principles set forth in the National Association of College and University Business Officers' (NACUBO) publication *College and University Business Administration.* Government colleges and universities also should adhere to the guidance set forth in the GASB's statements and interpretations. The 1987 *Codification,* Section Co5, indicates that the following sections, unless otherwise specified, are applicable to government colleges and universities:

C20 "Cash Deposits with Financial Institutions"
D20 "Debt Extinguishments"
D25 "Deferred Compensation Plans"
D30 "Demand Bonds"
I50 "Investments, including Repurchase Agreements"
P20 "Pension Activities—Employer Reporting"
R10 "Reverse Repurchase Agreements"
S40 "Special Assessments"
Pe6 "Pension Funds—Disclosure"

Moreover, depreciation accounting, required by the Financial Accounting Standards Board (FASB) Statement of Financial Accounting Standards (SFAS) No. 93, *Recognition of Depreciation by Not-For-Profit Organizations,* is still optional for government institutions because of GASB Statement No. 8, *Applicability of FASB Statement No. 93, Recognition of Depreciation by Not-for-Profit Organizations, to Certain State and Local Governmental Entities.* Similarly, GASB Statement No. 4, *Applicability of FASB Statement No. 87, Employers' Accounting for Pensions, to State and Local Governmental Employers* prohibits government colleges and universities from adopting the accounting and financial reporting guidance for pensions offered in SFAS No. 87.

Government colleges and universities commonly are component units of larger governments, such as states. Because colleges and universities use specialized accounting principles,

oversight governments ordinarily cannot integrate college and university financial information into their own funds and account groups.

The 1987 *Codification,* Section 2600.109, therefore, provides for "discrete" presentation of college and university financial information in the financial statements of the government reporting entity. With discrete presentation, all of the separate fund information that appears in college and university balance sheets is combined into a single column in the combined balance sheet of the government reporting entity. An extra column, however, does *not* appear in the combined operating statements of the government reporting entity. Instead, separate statements of changes in fund balances and current funds revenues, expenditures and other changes are provided in the government reporting entity's general purpose financial statements (GPFS).*

These separate statements should use the appropriate NACUBO terminology (e.g., mandatory transfers, nonmandatory transfers) rather than government terminology (e.g., operating transfers). These separate statements also should provide information on a fund basis, in conformity with NACUBO principles. The NACUBO fund structure provides for the following fund groups: current funds (unrestricted and restricted), loan funds, endowment and similar funds, annuity and life income funds, plant funds (unexpended plant funds, funds for renewals and replacements, funds for retirement of indebtedness and investment in plant) and agency funds.

In addition, governments need to disclose that they are using the NACUBO principles to account for their colleges and universities and to explain briefly how NACUBO accounting differs from that used by the oversight unit for its other activities. Also, governments should provide a separate college and university subsection in their comprehensive annual financial reports so that readers can have access to balance sheet information presented on a fund basis.

Another potential problem for government universities is the proper financial reporting for affiliated hospitals. GAAP for hospitals are not compatible with GAAP for colleges and universities (e.g., hospitals are required to use depreciation). Yet, there is no clear guidance on how affiliated hospitals should be reported in the universities' financial statements. One method used in practice incorporates hospitals separately within the college's or university's financial statements. Following this method, hospital operations are reported separately in the unrestricted current fund in a manner similar to auxiliary enterprises. When this method is followed, however, appropriate adjustments should be made to the hospital data so that it is comparable to other data in the unrestricted current funds. For example, depreciation expense and the capitalization of property, plant and equipment would not be appropriate for a current fund, even though this treatment would be necessary in separately issued hospital financial statements.

Hospitals. Government hospitals, like public-sector colleges and universities, follow some specialized industry practices. These practices are set forth in the American Institute of Certi-

---

* NACUBO standards allow for the information on these two statements to be combined into a single statement provided that no information is deleted from the combined statement that would have appeared on the separate statements.

fied Public Accountants' audit and accounting guide, *Audits of Providers of Health Care Services.* In addition, the 1987 *Codification,* Section Ho5, indicates that the following sections, unless otherwise indicated, apply to government hospitals as well as to governments:

C20 "Cash Deposits with Financial Institutions"
D20 "Debt Extinguishments"
D25 "Deferred Compensation Plans"
D30 "Demand Bonds"
I50 "Investments, including Repurchase Agreements"
P20 "Pension Activities—Employer Reporting"
R10 "Reverse Repurchase Agreements"
S40 "Special Assessments"
Pe6 "Pension Funds—Disclosure"

Like government colleges and universities, government hospitals may *not* follow the pension guidance provided by SFAS No. 87 even though this guidance applies to similar institutions in the private sector. Unlike government colleges and universities, however, government hospitals should follow the private-sector practice of capitalizing and depreciating their property, plant and equipment (GASB Statement No. 8 is not applicable to government hospitals).

Also, data for government hospitals ordinarily are presented differently in the financial statements of an oversight government from that presented in a separately issued report. Separately issued hospital reports provide information on a fund basis whereas hospitals ordinarily appear in a single enterprise fund column in the government's financial statements.

Public Utilities. The measurement of net income and the maintenance of capital are important to most users of the financial statements of public utilities. Therefore, public utilities normally are classified as enterprise funds in government financial statements and are subject to the same GAAP applicable to similar businesses in the private sector. In addition, the 1987 *Codification,* Section Ut5, indicates that the following sections, unless specified otherwise, are applicable to public utilities.

C20 "Cash Deposits with Financial Institutions"
D20 "Debt Extinguishments"

D25 "Deferred Compensation Plans"
D30 "Demand Bonds"
I50 "Investments, including Repurchase Agreements"
P20 "Pension Activities—Employer Reporting"
R10 "Reverse Repurchase Agreements"
S40 "Special Assessments"
Pe6 "Pension Funds—Disclosure"

Questions also arise concerning how to treat capital contributions and when to charge depreciation directly to contributed capital. The publication *Enterprise Funds: Government Accounting & Financial Reporting* in the Government Finance Officers Association's Accounting Topics Series provides guidance on applying GAAP in these and similar situations.

Moreover, the guidelines of the Federal Energy Regulatory Commission and the National Association of Regulatory Utility Commissioners should be followed, when appropriate, so long as they do not conflict with GAAP promulgated by authoritative standard-setting bodies.

Finally, the effects of regulation on certain public utilities are addressed in SFAS No. 71, *Accounting for the Effects of Certain Types of Regulation* (see chapter 8).

Special Districts and Councils of Government. Besides the special government units described above, numerous "special districts" have been created to provide any one of a large number of specialized services to the public. Examples of these special districts include conservation, fire protection, forest preserve, library, road and sanitary districts. Also, governments often form councils of governments to allow for regional planning and economic development. Both special districts and councils of government use the same GASB accounting and financial reporting principles applicable to other governments.

Governments should exercise special caution when incorporating data from component unit special districts into their reporting entity financial statements. The general fund of a component unit should *not* be aggregated into the general fund of the oversight unit, but rather should be reported as a special revenue fund (1987 *Codification,* Section 2600.102). Other fund types and account groups of a component unit special district should be aggregated into the government reporting entity's corresponding fund types and account groups reported in the GPFS.

Chapter 12
SCHOOL DISTRICTS

NATURE AND PURPOSE

Public school systems are one of the most common types of special government units (see chapter 11) and numerically form a significant portion of the total number of governments in the United States. As units of local government, public school districts are subject to generally accepted accounting principles (GAAP) as promulgated by the Governmental Accounting Standards Board (GASB). Because most of the accounting and financial reporting activities of school districts are similar to those already described for other local governments, they will not be addressed again in this chapter. Instead, this chapter will discuss accounting and financial reporting issues unique to school districts, as well as the proper application of GAAP in these situations.

GENERAL PRINCIPLES

Each of the general principles, introduced in chapter 2, that applies specifically to school districts is discussed below.

GAAP and Legal Compliance. In cities and counties, local ordinances providing specific regulations are common. In school districts, local ordinances are uncommon. However, policies formally adopted by the school board act as a surrogate for ordinances in many jurisdictions. In addition, state laws and regulations also govern the fiscal affairs of school districts. In most states, it is the responsibility of the state department of education to establish regulations to implement applicable state statutes.

For example, most school districts are required to file annual financial reports with the state department of education. Often, these reports are used to determine the amounts of state aid to be distributed. Also, a chart of accounts, which provides the necessary data needed by the state department of education, is often mandated. In such cases, the accounting system should be capable of maintaining information on a basis compatible with both the regulatory chart of accounts and the GAAP financial reporting classifications.

Many states provide a high percentage of their school districts' financing; therefore, the school districts must meet many related legal requirements. For instance, one state implemented a new quality basic education program that provides funding based upon enrollments in specifically defined student categories on various dates. These school districts must file an annual financial form indicating that the funding was used specifically for those categories. In this case, the accounting system should be designed to provide the information needed to demonstrate compliance with these spending requirements, as well as the information needed to prepare financial statements in conformity with GAAP.

Finally, the federal government provides various grants to school districts for specific purposes, such as special or vocational education. These grants also include spending limitations and financial reporting requirements that school districts must adhere to. School districts should take care to ensure that their accounting systems are capable of providing the information necessary to demonstrate legal compliance, as well as the information needed for financial reporting purposes.

Fund Accounting. The generic fund types included in the GASB's 1987 *Codification of Governmental Accounting and Financial Reporting Standards* (1987 *Codification*) provide an adequate framework for classifying funds of school districts. The 1987 *Codification,* Section 1300.106, states that governments should report only one general fund. However, in some states, school districts are required to maintain multiple "general funds" to meet legal requirements. Because only one general fund may be reported in the financial statements, it is recommended that school districts classify these multiple general funds as accounts or "subfunds," rather than as funds, and prepare a general fund schedule, like the example in Illustration 12–1, to demonstrate legal compliance.

As indicated previously, school districts receive numerous state and federal grants. Often, these grants are reported in

---

ILLUSTRATION 12–1

Name of School District
Combining Schedule of General Fund Accounts
(amounts expressed in thousands)

Assets	Educational	Maintenance	Total
Cash	$ 218	$ 74	$ 292
Investments	14,600	400	15,000
Taxes receivable (net)	1,498	335	1,833
Intergovernmental receivable	777	—	777
Inventories	792	—	792
Total assets	$17,885	$809	$18,694

---

special revenue funds. An effort should be made, in keeping with the "number of funds" principle, to examine the legal restrictions in laws or grant agreements to ensure that special revenue funds are, in fact, required. In many instances, existing legislation mandates certain accountability requirements but does not require the use of separate special revenue funds for each grant. In these cases, grants could be accounted for in the general fund as long as the school district's accounting system is capable of distinguishing between the activities of each grant.

As a group, school districts maintain few enterprise funds. The activity accounted for most frequently as an enterprise fund is the food service program. The U.S. Department of Agriculture and various state departments of education routinely subsidize school lunch and breakfast programs to help ensure that students receive low-cost, nutritionally balanced meals. In addition, the federal government provides food service programs with commodities. These commodities should be reported as inventories and appropriately recognized as nonoperating revenues and operating expenses when consumed. Because most local school boards do not intend to recover the full cost of each meal through user charges, the first criterion for the enterprise fund definition (included in the 1987 *Codification,* Section 1300.104) is not met. Yet, many governments choose to use this classification to monitor the costs of such programs, in keeping with the second criterion for enterprise fund definition (see chapter 8).

In many states, the department of education provides regulations for the classification of school food service programs. Some states require that food service programs be classified as special revenue funds. This classification is acceptable under GAAP. In other situations, however, food service programs may be classified in the general fund; this classification is also an acceptable treatment under GAAP. In either case, once a decision has been made concerning the appropriate fund classification for school food service operations, it should be followed consistently. Although the measurement focus is different for governmental funds, federal food service commodities should be similarly accounted for regardless of fund classification.

Another school district activity that may be accounted for in an enterprise fund is a building trades program. Under the supervision of an instructor, students in this program build houses and then sell them, usually at cost. The proceeds from the sale are used to finance further construction activities. Because the intent of such programs is usually to recover the cost of materials (and sometimes the cost of the instructor's salary and benefits), the enterprise fund classification is appropriate.

Student activity funds also are unique to school districts. These funds are used to account for those resources owned, operated and managed by the student body, under the guidance of a staff member or another adult, for educational, recreational or cultural purposes. These funds are used for a wide range of activities that can include the school yearbook, the student council, athletics or various student clubs.

The appropriate fund classification for student activity funds is determined by their legal status. If resources accounted for in student activity funds are legally owned by students or student groups, these funds should be classified as agency funds. However, if the school district legally owns the resources accounted for in student activity funds, they should be accounted for in the general or special revenue fund type.

Because most school districts operate numerous student activities at each school, it is suggested that each activity be classified as a subaccount, not as an individual fund. Also, a single, separate student activity fund could be established for each school. The use of subaccounts for each activity within a single school, rather than funds, facilitates annual reporting.

A final fund classification consideration is the use of trust funds. Often, school districts receive gifts or bequests. If a bequest is formalized with a trust agreement, the trust fund classification is appropriate. However, if a monetary gift is received with no specific intended purpose, the general fund classification is recommended. The distinction between the use of expendable and nonexpendable trust funds for school districts is the same as for any other government.

Fixed Assets. As with most governments, school districts build or purchase land, buildings and equipment. Infrastructure accounting, however, is not usually a consideration for schools. Normally, textbooks are not capitalized as fixed assets because they can become obsolete in a short time. Some school districts do, however, capitalize library books and reference books because they have an extended life.

School districts often receive fixed assets as gifts from organizations outside the school district (e.g., parent-teacher organizations). These fixed assets should be reported at their estimated fair value on the date donated. To maintain accurate fixed asset records, school district personnel should determine the fair value of these contributed gifts. These donated fixed assets should be reported in either the general fixed assets account group or the proprietary fund type, as appropriate.

Long-term Liabilities. Decreasing enrollments can lead school districts to seek ways to reduce costs. When this occurs, teachers may be given the option of retiring before their normal retirement age. Usually, a special benefit is determined based on a planned formula and is payable in installments over a short period (e.g., three years). The 1987 *Codification,* Section T25.101, indicates that the Financial Accounting Standards Board's Statement of Financial Accounting Standards (SFAS) No. 74, *Accounting for Special Termination Benefits Paid to Employees,* provides the authoritative guidance for reporting special termination benefits, subject to the distinctions applicable to governmental fund types.

Following this guidance, school districts should report a liability in connection with special termination benefit arrangements as soon as employees accept the offer, provided that the amount can be reasonably estimated. This liability should reflect both lump-sum payments and the present value of any expected future benefits. However, because these special termination benefit arrangements may affect the estimated costs of other employee benefits (e.g., pensions), complications in computing the liability can arise. SFAS No. 74 specifically requires that "if reliably measurable the effects of such changes on an employer's previously accrued expenses . . . that result directly from the termination of employees shall be included in measuring the termination expense." Accordingly, the services of an actuary may be necessary to calculate this liability.

As explained in chapter 2, only the portion of the liability expected to be liquidated from expendable available financial resources would be reported as a fund liability (with a corresponding expenditure). The remaining portion of the liability would be reported in the general long-term debt account group.

Basis of Accounting. One revenue source that requires special consideration is the amount of state aid school districts should accrue in a fiscal year. Many states base the aid on some variable, often student enrollments or attendance. Payments are calculated by using estimates for the current year or by relying on experience from previous periods. These calculations are then adjusted during the period, as necessary, by comparison with current-year data.

A problem arises because the adjustment normally is made in the next fiscal year. The issue then is whether this adjustment should be recognized as revenue (if an underpayment has been made) or whether current-year revenue should be reduced (if an overpayment has been made). For example, after the year ends, the state department of education gathers the actual data and calculates the adjustment. This adjustment can be added or deducted from the subsequent year's state aid and prorated over payments for the next 12 months. In the case of underpayment, is the underpayment collected soon enough after year end to pay liabilities of the year? Because state aid commonly is provided to pay salaries that have been accrued at year end, it is recommended that the state aid adjustment also be accrued. In other words, the available period for state aid in such cases should be considered to be 12 months. Likewise, an overpayment should be reported as deferred revenue, reducing revenues for the period.

Budgets. Generally, budgets for school districts are not much different from those of other governments. However, school districts often must submit their budgets to their state departments of education for approval before the beginning of the fiscal year. The state department of education usually indicates which funds should have appropriated (i.e., legally adopted) annual budgets. In addition, the legal level of budgetary control often is detailed (e.g., object within function within program) and is established by the state department of education. The classification and terminology for school districts' budgets differ from other local governments and are discussed in the next section of this chapter.

Classification and Terminology. As indicated previously, the classifications used by school districts can be prescribed by the annual reporting requirements of the state department of education. These reporting requirements usually follow closely the chart of accounts illustrated in the handbook *Financial Accounting for Local and State School Systems* because the U.S. Department of Education requires states to accumulate financial statistics consistent with this chart of accounts.

Revenues should be classified by fund and revenue source. Revenue sources include the following:

- Local sources
- State sources
- Federal sources
- Other sources.

Expenditures may be classified at various detailed levels. Some are required by state departments of education, and others are optional for local management purposes:

- Fund
- Program
- Function
- Object
- Project
- Instructional organization
- Operational unit
- Subject matter
- Job classification
- Special cost center.

The handbook, revised in 1980, provides a detailed chart of accounts with numeric designations and account descriptions and is available from the Superintendent of Documents, U.S. Government Printing Office, Washington, D.C. 20402.

Financial Reporting. One financial reporting issue relating to school districts is that of the reporting entity. Generally, there are two types of school districts in the United States, independent and dependent. Independent school districts operate like any other independent government: they levy their own property taxes, adopt their own budgets and issue their own debt. These types of school districts are considered reporting entities and issue comprehensive annual financial reports (CAFRs) or general purpose financial statements.

Dependent school districts rely upon other governments, usually a city or county, for certain fiscal activities, such as the levying of property taxes, the adoption of budgets and the issuance of debt. In these instances, the dependent school districts could be considered component units and should issue only component unit financial reports (CUFRs) and component unit financial statements.

Generally, independent school districts do not have oversight responsibility for other component units. On occasion a school district will participate with other school districts in a special education or vocational education project (e.g., a vocational education center). In such instances, however, none of the school districts usually exercises oversight responsibility and so a joint-venture treatment of the project is normally appropriate. In these instances, the 1987 *Codification,* Section J50, provides the relevant reporting guidance, as indicated in chapter 14.

School districts are able to complete the majority of the 15 statistical tables recommended by the 1987 *Codification,* Section 2800.103 (see chapter 14); however, some of these tables clearly do not apply to many school districts. For example, tables on special assessments and revenue bonds typically are absent from school district reports. However, school districts can and do use the statistical section of the CAFR/CUFR to communicate other information more relevant to their situation (e.g., enrollment and attendance data).

Often school districts are unable to provide demographic information compiled specifically for their service area. In such cases, data compiled for a city, county or region could be used instead. When such alternative data are provided, however, they should be clearly labeled to avoid misleading users of the report.

Under miscellaneous statistics, school districts may present data regarding pupil transportation (e.g., number of buses, number of miles driven), follow-up studies of high school graduates, square footage and capacity of buildings, personnel information (e.g., current salary schedule, number of personnel by employment class) and achievement test results.

Chapter 13
STATE
GOVERNMENT
ACCOUNTING

State governments share a common body of generally accepted accounting principles (GAAP) with their local counterparts. These primarily are the principles set forth in the Governmental Accounting Standards Board's (GASB) 1987 *Codification of Governmental Accounting and Financial Reporting Standards* (1987 *Codification*). Still, questions arise in practice about the proper application of these principles to situations encountered only at the state level.

In two instances, the 1987 *Codification* specifically addresses specialized state accounting and financial reporting issues. Also, the American Institute of Certified Public Accountants' 1986 industry audit and accounting guide, *Audits of State and Local Governmental Units* (1986 *ASLGU*), provides some guidance on the application of GAAP to certain situations unique to state government. Other questions, however, have yet to be addressed in the authoritative literature.

ACCOUNTING ISSUES

This chapter will review several state accounting and financial reporting issues:

- State unemployment compensation benefit plans
- Escheat property
- Medicaid
- Lotteries
- Federal pass-through monies
- Grants to local governments for capital acquisition
- Matching state and local receivables and payables
- Financing authorities using no-commitment debt
- Federal commodities
- Food stamps
- Statistical section of state comprehensive annual financial reports (CAFRs).

State Unemployment Compensation Benefit Plans. The 1987 *Codification*, Section U50, provides definitive guidance on accounting for state unemployment compensation benefit plans:

State unemployment compensation benefit plans are to be accounted for in an expendable trust fund. Resources that are provided for administrative costs and fees of the state unemployment programs are to be accounted for in the general fund unless legal requirements exist that require

the accounting and financial reporting of the resources in another fund.

Care should be taken, however, not to draw a general principle from this particular application. Legal restrictions do not allow states to use unemployment compensation benefit plan assets to pay administrative costs and fees. Requiring that these costs and fees not be reported in the trust fund was designed to reflect this legal limitation and to address the previous practice of reporting transfers from other funds to the trust fund to cover such costs. Unfortunately, some have reasoned by analogy that administrative costs and fees should be excluded from other trust funds as well, even when the resources of those trust funds can be legally used to meet these obligations. Such an approach is not in keeping with the spirit of this guidance because it leads to the reporting of "transfers" from the trust funds to the general fund to cover expenditures that, in reality, are those of the trust funds.

Escheat Property. The 1987 *Codification*, Section E70, also provides state governments with guidance on the proper accounting and financial reporting treatment to be applied to escheat property:

Escheat property should be accounted for in either an expendable trust fund or the fund to which the property ultimately escheats, since principally all escheat property eventually escheats permanently to the government. Further, fund balance should be reserved for that portion of the escheat property that under law is held in perpetuity for its owners. Escheat property held for another government should be accounted for in an agency fund.

Medicaid. Another concern of state governments is the proper accounting for receivables and payables related to Medicaid service providers. This issue was addressed in the 1986 *ASLGU*. If audits of provider cost reports indicate before the issuance of the financial statements that money is owed to the state, a receivable should be reported on the state's balance sheet. Although this receivable may not have been known as of the balance sheet date, it still should be reported because the best information before the issuance of the financial statements indicates that the receivable does, in fact, exist and that the events giving rise to it occurred as of or before the balance sheet date.

Also, it is important for states to apply the criteria of the

Financial Accounting Standards Board's Statement of Financial Accounting Standards (SFAS) No. 5, *Accounting for Contingencies,* to claims providers will file after the balance sheet date for services rendered during the accounting period. SFAS No. 5 provides that such claims should be reported as a liability if it is probable they have been incurred and the amount of the eventual settlement is measurable (i.e., at least estimable within a range). States should base their estimates of such a liability on their historical experience with Medicaid provider claims, taking care to make appropriate adjustments to reflect changed conditions (e.g., significant new providers, rule changes likely to result in delayed submission of claims). Finally, states should be sure to report a receivable for Medicaid costs eligible for federal reimbursement.

Lotteries. Another issue addressed by the 1986 *ASLGU* is the proper accounting and financial reporting for lotteries. Normally, lotteries are accounted for in an enterprise fund because accrual accounting is needed to match revenues and expenses properly to determine net income from the operation. At year end, the government should accrue an expense and liability, using the criteria of SFAS No. 5, for prizes yet to be awarded for games in progress as of the date of the balance sheet. Failure to do so would result in an overstatement of income on lottery operations. Governments also should report receivables from sales agents and related revenues as of the balance sheet date in their financial statements.

In addition, it should be noted that annuities purchased on behalf of prize recipients are accounted for differently, depending upon the type of annuity purchased. An annuity purchased in the name of a prize recipient would *not* be reported on the balance sheet. Instead, the liability related to the annuity would be removed from the balance sheet. This treatment is appropriate because the state would no longer be directly responsible for paying the prize recipient, but would be only contingently liable if the issuer of the annuity defaulted on the obligation. On the other hand, if the annuity is purchased in the name of the government on behalf of a prize winner, both the annuity and the related liability would be retained on the balance sheet. In this latter case, the state would remain directly liable to the prize winner, and the annuity would represent only the setting aside of assets to meet that obligation.

Federal Pass-through Monies. A third issue treated by the 1986 *ASLGU* is the matter of federal pass-through monies. In some instances, the state is little more than a conduit for federal monies. In these cases, federal monies are best accounted for in an agency fund. On the other hand, states sometimes exercise considerable latitude in dispensing federal monies to local governments; they may even have the choice of spending the money themselves or passing it on to the local governments. In such instances, the general or special revenue fund type, not an agency fund, would be appropriate. For example, if the federal government were to provide a state with grant monies to aid handicapped elementary school students, and the state was required to distribute the monies to local districts solely on the basis of their population of such students, the grant monies would be accounted for in an agency fund. On the other hand, if the federal government were to provide the state with grant monies for handicapped elementary school students, but the state was free either to distribute the money to local school districts or to use it for a centralized state program, the general or special revenue fund type would be used to account for the grant.

Grants to Local Governments for Capital Acquisition. Another issue at the state level is the proper character classification for grants that local governments will use for capital acquisition. For example, if a state provides resources to a school district to build a new school building, should the state report the item as a "capital outlay" or in some other character classification on the operating statement? Although the school district eventually will make a capital outlay in connection with these funds, it does not appear that such expenditures are truly "capital" from the state's perspective because no capital assets are acquired for the state's use. Accordingly, it would seem more appropriate in such instances not to classify the amounts as capital outlays, but to report them in the same category used for other grants to local governments.

Matching State and Local Receivables and Payables. Another issue involves intergovernmental receivables and payables. Should an intergovernmental receivable of one government always be matched by an intergovernmental payable of another? Under the modified accrual basis of accounting, intergovernmental expenditures and revenues do not always match because revenues must be both earned and available to be recognized. Can the same be said for the related receivables and payables? In fact, the reporting of a receivable or a payable is independent of revenue or expenditure recognition, although the two situations often overlap. A receivable is reported whenever the definition of an asset has been met. Similarly, a payable is reported whenever the definition of a liability has been met. Generally, the same situation that creates a receivable for one government can be considered to create a liability for another. Therefore, amounts reported on the balance sheets of local governments as payable to the state normally should be reported on the state's balance sheet as receivables. These amounts should be accompanied, if necessary, by a liability for deferred revenue.

Financing Authorities Using No-commitment Debt. Sometimes as a result of applying the entity criteria in the 1987 *Codification,* Section 2100, a state reporting entity will include a financing authority that issues no-commitment debt. How should such an authority be reported in the financial statements of the state's reporting entity? In such cases, the authority's activity, after issuance of the no-commitment debt, usually is limited to administrative matters. Accordingly, only the administrative costs of such financing authorities normally appear in the state's financial statements (most often in a separate enterprise fund). Because the no-commitment debt does not meet the definition of a liability for the state's reporting entity it would not be reported.

Federal Commodities. An important, and as of yet unresolved, issue for state governments is the proper accounting and financial reporting for commodities received from the federal government. Current practice varies widely. As stated in chapter 12, commodities used to operate meal programs should be reported in the operating statement and on the balance sheet. There is, however, considerable disagreement over the appropriate treatment for surplus commodities, such as cheese and butter, provided by the federal government for distribution to designated portions of the general population (e.g., citizens over 65).

One view holds that these surplus commodities should be reported as both revenues and expenditures of the government and that inventories at year end should be reported on the face of the balance sheet. Using this approach, any surplus commodities received would be offset initially by a deferred revenue liability. Revenue then would be recognized only when the commodities actually were distributed to the intended recipients. Those who support this position believe that programs for distributing surplus commodities are like other government programs and should be reported in the same manner in the financial statements.

A second, very different view sometimes taken is that surplus commodities should not appear either on the government's balance sheet or in its operating statement, but should be disclosed only in the notes to the financial statements. Those who advocate this position believe that reporting these nonfinancial items as revenues, expenditures and assets would violate the government accounting model with its emphasis on current financial resources. Moreover, they do not see an inconsistency in such treatment, as some charge, because they believe commodities distribution programs are fundamentally different from other government programs. They argue that without federal assistance states probably would not purchase commodities such as cheese and butter for distribution.

Yet a third view holds that surplus commodities should be reported in an agency fund. Proponents of this approach do not believe that receipts and distributions of commodities are revenues and expenditures under the current financial resources reporting model for governmental funds. However, they still hold that accountability requires inventories of these items to be reported on the balance sheet.

Food Stamps. In many ways, the issue of the proper accounting and financial reporting for food stamps is similar to the question of how to report federal surplus commodities. Some governments report food stamps as both revenues and expenditures of the government and present food stamps on the balance sheet. They argue that food stamp programs probably would be operated by the states even in the absence of federal assistance and so should be accounted for like any other government program. Moreover, they contend that food stamps, unlike commodities for distribution, are a near-cash financial asset and so can be reported in the financial statements without violating the current financial resources model. Others, however, propose that food stamps be reported in the notes rather than on the face of the financial statements. They argue that food stamps are a contingent liability and not an asset of the state. Still others do not support reporting food stamps as revenues and expenditures, but believe an agency fund is desirable to ensure adequate accountability.

The issues of federal commodities and food stamps are important to state governments, but will not be resolved definitively until the GASB undertakes an examination of the issues involved. In the meantime, state governments should disclose information on surplus commodities and food stamps at least in the notes to the financial statements and on the schedule of federal financial assistance required by the Single Audit Act of 1984.

Statistical Sections of State CAFRs. Although states usually are able to complete the majority of the 15 statistical tables recommended by the 1987 *Codification,* Section 2800.103 (see chapter 14), some of these tables clearly do not apply to many state governments. For example, tables on property tax rates and collections, assessed valuations, legal debt margin, special assessments and overlapping debt are typically absent from state CAFRs. However, state governments can and do use the statistical section of the CAFR to communicate other information more relevant to their situation. In fact, states are often in an excellent position to provide a variety of data from federal and state collection efforts that is not available to local governments. Most commonly, states choose to expand the types of information provided in the portion of the statistical section dedicated to demographic and miscellaneous data.

For example, the state's population can be separated into its urban and rural components. It also can be stratified by age and compared with similar information available for the total U.S. population. In addition, a presentation of changes in the population that reports migration separately from other changes can be useful to bond analysts.

Because many states have income taxes, information may be available on the personal income of state residents. One possible presentation to consider would be total state personal income divided by the state's population to calculate per capita personal income. This figure could then in turn be compared with prior periods or with the per capita personal income figures for the region or for the United States as a whole.

Normally, more detail is available at the state level than at the city or county level for employment data. Useful information that could be presented includes the total number of employed and unemployed, with a comparison of the state's rate of unemployment to the national rate. Also, a state could present data on the work force employed in specific industries to disclose reliance upon those industries. The average annual wage is also an important piece of economic information.

Other potentially useful information that could be included in the statistical section of a state CAFR includes the following:

- School enrollments, including five- and ten-year projections
- Expansion and growth in manufacturing and industry
- Gross state product for each major industry
- Sales tax by type of sales or by industry
- Livestock and crop information (if the state is heavily agricultural)
- Imports and exports (for states with significant international trade).

Providing such information in the statistical section can help to make the state's CAFR a more useful tool for bond analysts and other financial statement users.

Chapter 14
FINANCIAL REPORTING

Broadly defined, financial reporting is the process of communicating information concerning a government's financial position and financial activities. Financial information often is dissiminated through financial reports which can be classified according to their content and the purposes for which they are issued. Different types of financial reports may be issued according to the reports' intended use (i.e., internal or external) or according to the reports' timing (i.e., interim and annual).

This chapter reviews various types of financial reporting including the comprehensive annual financial report (CAFR)/component unit financial report (CUFR), the unique reporting requirements for public employee retirement systems (PERS), interim reports and condensed summary data (including popular reports). In addition, requirements of the Government Finance Officers Association's (GFOA) Certificate of Achievement for Excellence in Financial Reporting program also are contained in this chapter.

COMPREHENSIVE ANNUAL FINANCIAL REPORT/COMPONENT UNIT FINANCIAL REPORT

The Governmental Accounting Standards Board's (GASB) 1987 *Codification of Governmental Accounting and Financial Reporting Standards* (1987 *Codification*), Section 2200.101, provides that "every government should prepare and publish, as a matter of public record, a comprehensive annual financial report (CAFR) . . ."

The CAFR/CUFR generally contains three distinct sections: introductory, financial and statistical. These sections may be supplemented by certain specialized sections as the need arises.

Introductory Section. The introductory section (and related front matter) is the first section of a CAFR/CUFR. It is intended to familiarize the reader with the organizational structure of the government, the nature and scope of the services it provides, and a summary of a government's financial activities and the factors that influence these activities. Some of the introductory section material is subjective in nature in contrast to the relatively objective information reported in the financial and statistical sections. The introductory section also includes future-oriented predictive information such as economic forecasts and discussions of future initiatives. Because of the subjective and predictive nature of the introductory section material, it

is ordinarily excluded from the scope of the independent auditor's examination.

The recommended front matter of the CAFR/CUFR includes:

* Report cover
* Title page
* Table of contents.

The report cover should indicate the city and state in which the government is located, as well as the month and day of its fiscal year end. The report cover should identify the report as either a CAFR or as a CUFR. The title page should include the name of the government, the fiscal year covered by the report and the department preparing the report.

A detailed table of contents should be located immediately behind the title page. The table of contents should segregate clearly the CAFR/CUFR into its three distinct sections. It should contrast the general purpose financial statements (GPFS)/component unit financial statements (CUFS) with the financial statements and schedules of individual funds and make it clear that the notes to the financial statements are an integral part of the "liftable" GPFS/CUFS.

The table of contents also should describe sufficiently the information (e.g., statements, schedules, tables) presented in the CAFR/CUFR. It specifies the presence and location of individual component elements of the report and gives page references for them. The table of contents should distinguish the basic financial statements and schedules (i.e., within the scope of the audit) from supplementary data presentations. Governments with complex reports also should employ exhibit and schedule references.

The recommended contents of the CAFR's/CUFR's introductory section include:

* Letter of transmittal
* A current Certificate of Achievement for Excellence in Financial Reporting (if applicable)
* Listing of principal officials
* Organizational chart
* Other material deemed appropriate by management.

Each government and the needs of its financial report users are unique, thus, presentations of introductory section materials will vary from government to government. Report preparers should use all resources available to convey adequately the financial condition of the government.

Letter of Transmittal. The introductory section of the CAFR/CUFR should include, at a minimum, a letter of transmittal from the government's chief finance officer. Depending on the circumstances, other forms of this letter may be produced. For example, if the chief finance officer is not integrally involved in either the government's major initiatives for the future or the government's economic forecasting, the government's chief executive officer (e.g., mayor, county board president) or chief operating officer (e.g., city manager, county executive) should become involved in the process. The role of the chief executive or operating officer can be either that of an additional signatory to a single letter of transmittal or the author of a separate letter.

The CAFR's/CUFR's introductory section is important to certain report users (e.g., citizens) because they may read only the letter of transmittal. The letter should be prepared with this audience in mind. However, the needs of the other financial statement users should not be ignored.

To effectively communicate the information contained in the letter of transmittal for all report readers, the following items should be considered during the letter's development stage.

- Target a perceived audience and address the letter to that audience.
- Consider the reader's attention span.
- Avoid long and complex sentences, the use of accounting jargon or the use of unnecessarily formal language.
- Incorporate appropriate captions in the text.
- Incorporate pictures, graphs and charts.

The letter of transmittal should be printed on the official stationery of the government and dated with the approximate date that the report is made available or "transmitted" to the public. There is no "right length" for the letter of transmittal. Normally, it takes six to ten pages to cover the suggested letter topics presented below.

The contents of the letter can be categorized into five subsections: introduction, economic condition and outlook, major initiatives, financial information and other information. The following outline is recommended as a basis for preparing the letter of transmittal:

  I. Introduction
     A. Management responsibility for financial information
     B. Explanation of CAFR/CUFR sections
     C. Definition of the reporting entity
 II. Economic Condition and Outlook
     A. Summary of local economy
     B. Data regarding major industries affecting the local economy
     C. Future economic outlook
III. Major Initiatives
     A. Current year projects
        1. Goals
        2. Results
     B. Future projects
     C. Department or activity service efforts and accomplishments

 IV. Financial Information
     A. Discussion of controls
        1. Internal control structure
        2. Budgetary controls
     B. General government functions
        1. Summary schedule of revenues
        2. Summary schedule of expenditures
        3. Discussion of significant changes in revenues and expenditures
        4. Effect of revenue limitations
        5. Status of fund balances
     C. Proprietary operations
        1. Discussion of financial condition and results of operations
        2. Relationship with general government operations
     D. Fiduciary operations
        1. Level of pension plan funding
        2. Status of pension plan obligation
        3. Other fiduciary activities
     E. Debt administration
        1. Summary of outstanding debt
        2. Review of current year's debt issuances
        3. Information on advance refundings
        4. Discussion of debt limitation
        5. Debt ratings
        6. Per capita debt levels
     F. Cash management
        1. Investment policies
        2. Safeguarding activities
        3. Yield information
     G. Risk management
        1. Types and level of risk assumed
        2. Risk control policies
  V. Other Information
     A. Independent audit
        1. Scope of the audit
        2. Additional audit requirements
           a. Federal—single audit
           b. State
     B. Awards
        1. GFOA Certificate of Achievement for Excellence in Financial Reporting
        2. GFOA Distinguished Budget Presentation Award
        3. Other awards
     C. Acknowledgements
        1. Governing body
        2. Staff

Introduction. The introductory subsection of the letter of transmittal should acquaint the report reader with the operations of the government and acknowledge the fact that the information contained in the CAFR/CUFR are management's assertions.

The first paragraph should identify the report and officially transmit it to the appropriate officials. This paragraph should be followed by a discussion of management's responsibility for the contents of the CAFR/CUFR. This statement clearly places the reader on notice that the accuracy of the data presented and the responsibility for the CAFR's/CUFR's completeness and accuracy rests with management.

Given the emphasis on the financial statement user who generally is not knowledgeable in governmental accounting and financial reporting, certain basic elements of the CAFR/CUFR (e.g., introductory, financial and statistical sections) should be explained. The extent of this explanation is vital to the achievement of the letter of the transmittal's objectives. The fine line between educating less knowledgeable financial statement users and losing the interest of those familiar with the contents of the CAFR/CUFR often can be difficult to determine. However, as a general rule, a short sentence on each of the sections of the CAFR/CUFR should be sufficient.

A discussion of the government's reporting entity also is necessary to provide the reader with an understanding of what information has been included in the report. For example, if a government has the ability to exercise oversight responsibility over a park district established within the government's boundaries, the fact that the park district has been included as a component unit within the reporting entity should be stated. Although each section of the CAFR/CUFR should be able to stand alone, duplicating the reporting entity disclosure presented in the notes to the financial statements is not warranted. Highlighting key criteria that were applied to potential component units and specific responses (e.g., appointment of governing body) that influenced the government's decision in determining the reporting entity is one method of communicating this information. Again, a concise presentation (i.e., one paragraph) generally enhances the readability of the letter of transmittal.

Economic Condition and Outlook. The section on economic condition and outlook provides the government with a means of highlighting certain features of the economy that may directly influence the government's operations. Although finance officials generally are not economic forecasters, a considerable amount of data on the government's economic condition exists at the federal, state and local government levels. Because government services are influenced heavily by the economic environment, this information is useful to report users. Information on economic conditions that can affect the government may include economic indicators such as increases/decreases in retail sales, industry employment information and the unemployment rate for the community as a whole. These rates can be compared with governments of similar size, and/or state and nationwide averages. Specific references to events that significantly influenced the economy also should be made. Such events include new construction activities in the private sector, plant closings, and federal and state mandates to improve the environment.

The community's short- and long-term economic outlook should be assessed by the government. Although the government may not have personnel with economic forecasting expertise, a wide range of information that may benefit the users also can be obtained from both the public and private sectors.

Major Initiatives. A discussion of the major initiatives or programs that the government has undertaken or plans to take in the future is beneficial to the report users. This subsection should be divided into two categories: current initiatives including ongoing projects, and future or planned initiatives. It also should focus on the government's service efforts and accomplishments.

This discussion provides the reader with an overview of the activities that the government considers to be high priority items. Therefore, major initiatives can be defined not only in terms of financial or economic impact but also social impact. Major initiatives include expansion of services (e.g., public safety, health and welfare) and capital projects. The public's concern over the maintenance of government's capital assets (i.e., fixed assets and infrastructure) may warrant discussion of the government's capital policy and future capital plans in addition to current capital projects.

Service efforts and accomplishments can be addressed for the entire government by highlighting an individual department or activity each year in the letter of transmittal. By focusing on a particular department or activity, the government could establish a theme for the CAFR/CUFR that could be carried throughout the report (e.g., cover, divider pages). Although specific performance measures are not abundant for many topics, both the GASB and the GFOA encourage governments to experiment with this form of reporting. Because performance measures often contain nonfinancial information, care should be taken to ensure the accuracy of the information and the validity of the conclusions drawn.

Financial Information. This subsection provides readers with an overview of the information presented in the financial section of the CAFR/CUFR. It should be prepared in a fashion that raises the level of understanding for financial statement users who may not be familiar with the government's operations or the financial environment (e.g., fund structure, accounting standards, controls) in which the government functions.

The public's perception of how government conducts its business may be enhanced by a discussion of the government's internal control structure. In addition, the government's budgetary system and its relationship with the generally accepted accounting principles (GAAP) financial statements should be addressed. Although care should be taken not to duplicate the notes to the financial statements, discussion of budgetary control should include the extent of budgetary integration, the type(s) of budgets adopted (annual, project length), the basis (i.e., GAAP, non-GAAP) on which budgets are adopted, the level at which expenditures cannot legally exceed appropriations and additional controls through the use of an encumbrance accounting system.

A brief discussion of the government's general functions gives the report user the opportunity to assess the government's financial position and results of operations from a broad perspective. This discussion generally is preceded by tables that summarize the government's revenues and expenditures for the year. These tables may include any or all of the four governmental fund types (i.e., general, special revenue, debt service, capital projects). In addition, the government can select varying degrees of revenue and expenditure information for this presentation. Normally, revenues are presented by source (e.g., taxes, intergovernmental revenues) and expenditures are presented by function (e.g., general government, public safety). In certain instances, the government may consider the presentation of other financing sources and uses necessary to convey the overall results of the government's operations. This generally should occur when significant interfund transfers take place.

To assess the progress that a government has made during the past year, comparative data from the previous year are useful to the financial statement users. The comparisons may be presented in tables as described above or in charts and graphs.

In addition to the presentation of revenue and expenditure data, narrative explanations highlighting the major changes in revenues and expenditures and indicating the reasons for the variances should be included. Narratives are important for the reader to understand why changes occurred. A discussion of current taxing levels (e.g., income tax rates, property tax rates) should be presented for the major tax revenue sources. Some governments also may be faced with caps on either property tax rates, revenue growth rates or other limitations on the government's potential resources. If these limitations exist, there should be discussion within the letter of the current and potential effects on the government's ongoing operations.

The status of the general fund and other governmental fund type fund balances also may be discussed. Because various factors (e.g., timing of revenues and expenditures) could influence the amount of fund balance necessary to sustain operations without short-term borrowing, these factors should be clearly identified. Some governments have created formulas to calculate what they consider an adequate fund balance to maintain operations. If target balances have been established, comparisons should be made and significant variations explained.

Some governments present their financial data in graphs and charts to supplement numeric tables. This type of presentation often enhances understanding of the data. However, care should be taken not to significantly lengthen the letter by including numerous charts and graphs.

The government's proprietary and fiduciary funds also should be analyzed in the letter of transmittal. The government's proprietary operations presentations should include an analysis of relevant financial information. Many proprietary activities (e.g., utilities) are a vital part of government services, therefore, this segment of the government's operations should receive attention. The proprietary activity's financial relationship with the governmental funds also should be reviewed. If significant subsidies are either provided to or provided from the governmental funds, this should be highlighted. Discussion of the fiduciary funds should focus on the government's pension funding policies and the current status of net assets accumulated for the payment of plan benefits versus actuarially determined liabilities.

The administration of the government's debt is another category within the financial information subsection. A summary of the various types of outstanding debt provides a base for further analysis. Discussions of debt administration should include the government's current bond rating(s), new bond issuances (including refinancing of any outstanding debt) and debt per capita calculations. A discussion of the government's legal debt limitations and the effect that this limitation may have on future bond issues (or debt alternatives) also is beneficial.

Another topic of discussion that should be included in the financial information subsection is cash management. The letter of transmittal should present an overview of the government's investment policies and the effect that these policies have on the credit risk categories identified in the 1987 *Codification*, Sections I50.163 and I50.164. This subsection can provide the readers with an explanation of the categories and the reason why the government has selected a particular investment strat-

egy. Additional data on the government's investment yield vs. average market yield also may be included in this section.

Information on the government's risk management activities also should be incorporated into the financial information subsection. The government should consider presenting information on type (e.g., workers' compensation) and level (e.g., claims under $150,000) of exposure assumed under the government's risk management program. Although a detailed discussion of risk control policies (i.e., procedures implemented to reduce risk) generally is not conducive to financial reporting, a general discussion of the government's effort to reduce losses may be useful to the report reader.

Other Information. The final portion of the letter of transmittal generally includes discussion of the independent audit. Although reference may have been made to the single audit in previous sections, the scope of the audit, including any additional audit requirements at the federal, state or local level should be reviewed.

This section also provides a vehicle for recognizing and acknowledging certain achievements or awards received by the government. It is important to properly recognize all parties that were involved in preparing materials that won the awards and discuss the significance of those awards. If the award is subject to annual review (e.g., GFOA Certificate of Achievement for Excellence in Financial Reporting) the number of consecutive years that the award has been received could be mentioned.

The balance of the introductory section should include a reproduction of the prior year's Certificate of Achievement for Excellence in Financial Reporting, if applicable, a list of principal officials and an organizational chart. The list of principal officials can be included on a separate page or included on the title page. The list of principal officials can be presented by classification such as elected, appointed and principal department directors.

The introductory section also should include an organizational chart. An organizational chart provides the CAFR/CUFR reader with a visual overview of the government's organization. The illustration may simply include each department presented in the traditional hierarchical line-and-box organizational chart.

For detailed examples of introductory section presentations, see GFOA's Financial Reporting Series (FRS), Volume 2, *Illustrations of Introductory Sections of Comprehensive Annual Financial Reports of State and Local Governments.*

Financial Section. The financial section should be segregated into separate subsections employing the pyramid approach to government financial reporting. The financial reporting pyramid owes its name to the pattern of reporting financial information at different levels of increasing detail.

Financial Reporting Pyramid. Using the pyramid, the beginning of the financial section (top of the pyramid) contains relatively narrowly focused and less detailed data. Subsequent portions of the financial section (moving down the reporting pyramid) include gradually increasing levels of reporting detail.

The four primary advantages to the pyramid approach include:

- Organizing by fund type to identify clearly the nature and purpose of each fund;
- Providing an overview and broad perspective of financial

ILLUSTRATION 14–1
The Financial Reporting "Pyramid"

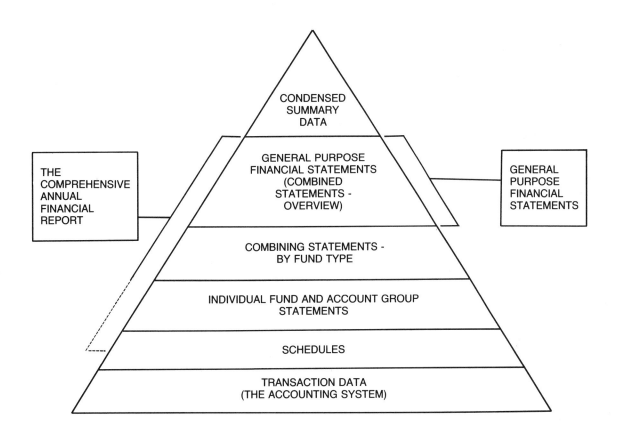

— Required
-- May be necessary

position and results of operations in a standardized, labeled format;

- Streamlining the CAFR's financial section; and
- Facilitating tracing from one reporting level to another.

The financial reporting section is divided into four specific levels:

- General Purpose Financial Statements (GPFS),
- Combining statements—by fund type,
- Individual fund and account group statements, and
- Schedules.

General Purpose Financial Statements. Under the pyramid approach, the first level within the financial section contains the GPFS which are intended to provide report users with an overview and broad perspective of the financial position and results of operations of the government as a whole.

The GPFS normally do not present data for individual funds, rather, they report aggregated data by each fund type and for both account groups in separate, adjacent columns, captioned with fund type and account group titles. When the reporting entity maintains only one individual fund for a specific fund type (e.g., general fund), the individual fund will be presented in the appropriate column in the GPFS.

The data contained in the following three levels should be presented by fund type and not by type of financial statement.

Combining Statements—By Fund Type. Combining statements should be presented in the second level, after the GPFS for each fund type for which the government maintains more than one individual fund. These statements include separate, adjacent columns for each individual fund of a given fund type, which effectively serve as separate financial statements for each of the individual funds. They also include a total for all such funds, which carries forward to the presentation of that fund type in the GPFS.

Individual Fund and Account Group Statements and Schedules. The third level of a CAFR's financial section contains individual fund and account group statements and schedules. These statements and schedules present information on the individual funds and account groups where such data could not be readily presented in the combining or combined statements (e.g., comparative financial statements).

Schedules. The CAFR's financial section also includes appropriate supporting schedule presentations of data that have been prepared on a legal compliance or other required basis differing from GAAP. Supporting schedules often include multifund information (e.g., fixed asset schedules).

Discrete Presentations. The 1987 *Codification,* Section 2600.109, authorizes the use of discrete presentations. A discrete presentation is a reporting convention that allows a government to present a separate column on the GPFS balance sheet for activities that cannot be classified appropriately in the seven generic fund types and two account groups. More specifically, the 1987 *Codification,* Section 2600.109, authorizes the use of a discrete presentation column only when both of the following criteria are met:

- A component unit has adopted accounting principles that are not in conformity with governmental accounting and reporting standards but those principles are considered to be generally accepted, and

- Where the inclusion of the component unit data would distort a fund type of the reporting entity.

This type of presentation should be displayed only on rare occasions. For example, a college or university component unit that is part of a state reporting entity, or a junior college component unit that is part of a city or county reporting entity, may follow the accounting principles established by the National Association of College and University Business Officers (NACUBO). In these instances, it would be appropriate to present a separate column for college and university data on the combined balance sheet because NACUBO standards are considered GAAP.

Joint Ventures. The 1987 *Codification* Section J50.102, provides the option for governmental fund types to use the equity method of accounting, as presented in Accounting Principles Board (APB) Opinion No. 18, *Equity Method for Investments in Common Stock,* to account for joint ventures. Using this method, the initial investment would be reported as an asset, captioned "investment in joint venture." However, the 1987 *Codification,* Section J50.102, does not indicate how subsequent changes in the investment should be reported. The change could be reported as revenue or expenditure; or as an other financing source or other financing use. Optionally, this investment could be reported in the notes only, which appears more consistent with the flow of current financial resources measurement focus. In practice, this latter alternative is prevalent for governmental fund-type investments. Proprietary fund types always should use the above-described equity method of accounting, reporting activity for the year as nonoperating revenue or expense.

Functional Basis Combining Concept. The 1987 *Codification,* Section 2600.108, introduces the functional grouping accounting principle. Because complex reporting entities may be required to include a significant number of component units within the reporting entity, consideration should be given to the grouping or combining of similar funds (e.g., economic development) on a functional basis in the combining statements. This form of functional combining may be accomplished by combining similar funds where it enhances communication and understanding of the financial statements. However, it should not be used to combine all funds within a specific fund type (e.g., pension trust funds).

A question often arises in regard to the application of functional reporting to functional-type activities of the reporting entity when no component units are included. Functional grouping may be used when the funds incorporated into the functional columns are immaterial to the total combining statement presentation. However, GAAP do not address this issue specifically.

Single Audit. With the passage of the Single Audit Act of 1984, affected governments are implementing the single audit concept. As part of this implementation process, a decision must be made regarding the format and location of the required single audit financial data if the government decides to incorporate this information into the CAFR/CUFR. Although authoritative pronouncements do not provide guidance, the presentation of single audit information in a separate (i.e., fourth) section of the CAFR/CUFR is recommended. This section would include the schedule of federal financial assistance, auditor's reports related to the single audit requirements, and single audit findings, recommendations, and questioned costs.

General Purpose Financial Statements/Component Unit Financial Statements. The GPFS/CUFS provides the financial statement reader with an overview of the government at the fund type/account group level. The GPFS/CUFS, which are necessary for fair presentation in conformity with GAAP, include:

1. Combined Balance Sheet—All Fund Types and Account Groups;
2. Combined Statement of Revenues, Expenditures and Changes in Fund Balances—All Governmental Fund Types and Similar Trust Funds;
3. Combined Statement of Revenues, Expenditures and Changes in Fund Balances—Budget and Actual—General and Special Revenue Fund Types (and other governmental fund types for which annual budgets have been legally adopted);
4. Combined Statement of Revenues, Expenses and Changes in Retained Earnings (or Equity) and Fund Balances—All Proprietary Fund Types and Similar Trust Funds;
5. Combined Statement of Changes in Financial Position—All Proprietary Fund Types and Similar Trust Funds; and
6. Notes to the financial statements.

The GPFS/CUFS originally were designed for inclusion in official statements and for widespread distribution to financial statement users requiring less information than is presented in the CAFR/CUFR. Although the GPFS/CUFS do provide the basic information for a fair presentation, every attempt should be made to prepare a CAFR/CUFR.

The following discussion analyzes each combined financial statement contained in the GPFS/CUFS.

Combined Balance Sheet. The 1987 *Codification,* Section 2200.106, requires the presentation of a combined balance sheet in the GPFS/CUFS for all fund types and account groups used by the government. The proper title for this statement, Combined Balance Sheet—All Fund Types and Account Groups, should be used except where only one fund of a single fund type is presented (e.g., utility fund). The title "Balance Sheet" is appropriate in that situation.

The combined balance sheet should present information at the fund-type level (e.g., general, special revenue) for all funds. In addition, separate columns should be presented for the general fixed assets account group (GFAAG) and general long-term debt account group (GLTDAG). No fund type or account group should include more than one column at the combined balance sheet level.

The combined balance sheet is organized using the following categories: assets and other debits, liabilities, equity and other credits. These categories should include totals for assets and other debits as well as for liabilities, equity and other credits. Subtotals should be presented for the liabilities section and for the equity and other credits section. All account descriptions presented on the combined balance sheet should be detailed enough to be meaningful.

Assets and Other Debits. The debit side of the balance sheet generally presents assets; however, given the unique nature of the governmental model the debit side of the balance sheet also contains certain accounts that do not meet the definition of an asset. These "other debits" (e.g., amounts to be provided) are used to offset liabilities reported in the GLTDAG.

Although a government balance sheet contains many accounts that are found in the commercial sector, it also includes other accounts that warrant further clarification. These accounts include: equity in pooled cash and investments, due from other funds, interfund receivables, advances to other funds, fixed assets, amounts available and amounts to be provided.

A government will often pool its investments to maximize return. The equity in pooled cash and investments account is essentially cash, cash equivalents (e.g., time deposits) and short-term investments. This account is used to inform the financial statement user that a pooling method is used and that these assets (e.g., cash) are not held by any specific fund. It should be noted that under the pooling approach a fund may overdraw its account in the pool. These overdrafts should be reported as liabilities, with a corresponding receivable (i.e., due to/from other funds), on the balance sheet. Overdrafts should not be offset against the positive balances of other funds of the same fund type or be reported as a credit balance (i.e., "negative cash") in the account. Because the receivables and liabilities connected with pooled cash overdrafts do not affect the balance of the pooled cash account, the notes should provide a reconciliation of the account as reported on the balance sheet to its true balance (i.e., less overdraft liabilities).

Assets arising from interfund transactions can be classified in several different accounts depending on their nature and duration. The due from other funds account is used to reflect receivables that are associated with quasi-external transactions and transfers. If an amount is owed by one fund to another as a result of a short-term loan, the amount should be reflected as an interfund receivable/payable. Although government balances generally are not classified as to short- and long-term categories, if an interfund loan is considered long-term in nature the loan should be classified as an advance to other funds.

As noted in chapter 2, fixed assets generally are reported only in the proprietary and trust funds and the GFAAG. However, fixed assets acquired for resale by governmental funds should be reported as assets held for resale in these funds. In certain circumstances, because of the nature of a fund's activities, (e.g., redevelopment authority) fixed assets may be reported as an investment.

As mentioned earlier, certain accounts presented in the debit side of the balance sheet do not meet the definition of an asset. These other debit accounts include "amounts available" and "amounts to be provided" that are associated with liabilities reported in the GLTDAG. Therefore, these accounts should not be reported outside the GLTDAG. The amounts available account (e.g., amount available in debt service funds) generally represents amounts available in debt service and other governmental funds for the repayment of GLTDAG liabilities. In practice, the account normally is equal to the fund balance reported in the debt service fund. It should be noted, however, that the definition provided in the 1987 *Codification,* Section 1500.105, states that only amounts available for the repayment of debt service *principal* should be reflected in this account. The amount to be provided account(s) (e.g., amount to be provided for the retirement of long-term debt) represents the difference between the liabilities reported in the GLTDAG and amounts available.

Liabilities. Governmental liability accounts (e.g., accounts payable, vouchers payable, contracts payable) generally are reflected as fund liabilities. As noted in chapter 2, certain liabilities (e.g., compensated absences payable, claims and judgments payable) that are not expected to be liquidated with expendable available financial resources should be reported in the GLTDAG.

Liability accounts that have unique characteristics in the governmental model include deferred revenue and interfund transactions. The deferred revenue accounts are considered unique from the viewpoint that in the commercial sector this account generally represents amounts that have been collected in advance of the event that results in revenue recognition. For governments, however, this account also is used for amounts that have been recognized as receivables, but are not "available" to finance current operations.

Interfund liabilities should be classified using the same criteria previously discussed in relation to the assets and other debits.

Equity and Other Credits. The equity and other credits accounts generally are grouped into four categories: investment in fixed assets, contributed capital, retained earnings and fund balance.

Investment in Fixed Assets. The investment in fixed assets account should be limited to use as a counter balancing account for fixed assets reported in the GFAAG and a NACUBO model discrete presentation. If the use of this amount is limited to counterbalancing the GFAAG, the title "investment in general fixed assets" should be used. Although this account is presented in the equity section, the nature of the account groups prevents the GFAAG from reporting equity. Thus, the term "other credits" is used to identify such amounts.

At the combined level the investment in fixed assets account generally is presented as a single line. However, if a government does not wish to supplement this display with additional schedules presenting the sources of funds (e.g., by fund or revenue source) it should provide this detail on the combined balance sheet. As with any account, the overall level of detail and the needs of the financial statement users must be assessed before a level of display detail can be selected by the preparer.

Contributed Capital. The contributed capital account represents amounts "contributed" to the proprietary funds. This account normally is presented as a single line at the combined level; however, information regarding the source of the contribution (e.g., developer, intergovernmental, customer) should be presented elsewhere in the CAFR/CUFR.

What constitutes a contribution has not been adequately defined in authoritative literature except in limited instances. For example, the 1987 *Codification,* Section G60.110, provides that capital grants from another government should be recorded as a contribution. In addition, residual equity transfers in are reported as a contribution based on the guidance provided in the 1987 *Codification,* Section 1800.107.

A major point of contention related to contributed capital involves the proper treatment of systems development or "tap" fees. As discussed in chapter 8, generally a portion of these fees also should be reported as contributed capital. In addition to these items, fixed assets provided to the government proprietary fund by developers (e.g., sewer lines) are considered contributed capital.

Retained Earnings. The proprietary funds' retained earnings generally parallel private sector reporting. Retained earnings can be divided into two subcategories: reserved and unreserved.

Although the presentation of reserved retained earnings is not prominent in the private sector, many governments display reserves related to assets and liabilities restricted by bond indentures to demonstrate legal compliance. Chapter 8 includes an expanded discussion of the individual reserve accounts.

"Designation" of retained earnings also has been a point of contention. The 1987 *Codification,* Section 1800.124, defines designations as "tentative plans for financial resource utilization in a future period." The 1987 *Codification* specifically identified fund balance designations and refers to financial resources (i.e., governmental fund measurement focus). Based on authoritative guidance provided, the designation of retained earnings does not appear appropriate.

Fund Balance. The final category within equity and other credits, fund balance, is utilized for governmental and trust funds. This balance is classified into two subcategories: reserved and unreserved. The unreserved fund balance can be subdivided further into designated and undesignated portions.

Reserved fund balance is reported to denote portions of fund balance that are either (1) legally restricted to a specific future use or (2) not available for appropriation or expenditure. Examples of the first category include "fund balance—reserved for encumbrances," "fund balance—reserved for debt service," and fund balance reserved for the principal portion of a nonexpendable trust fund. The second category identifies the portion of fund balance representing assets that are not considered "expendable available financial resources." Examples of this category include advances to other funds and noncurrent loans receivable.

Designations, as discussed above, represent tentative management plans. The 1986 American Institute of Certified Public Accountants (AICPA) audit and accounting guide, *Audits of State and Local Governmental Units,* provides that "such designations should be supported by definitive plans and approved by either the government's chief executive officer or the legislature."

Combined Statement of Revenues, Expenditures and Changes in Fund Balances—All Governmental Fund Types and Similar Trust Funds. The GPFS/CUFS should contain an all-inclusive operating statement for the governmental and similar trust funds. Several presentation options for this statement are highlighted in the 1987 *Codification,* Section 2200. The first presentation decision that the preparer must make concerns the type of funds to be included in the statement. The governmental and fiduciary fund types may be either incorporated into one statement or presented in two separate statements.

Once this decision has been made, four format alternatives can be used for this statement. The most common format found in practice presents revenues first, followed by expenditures, other financing sources (uses) and finally by a reconciliation of beginning and ending fund equity. This format is illustrated in appendix D.

The second alternative format begins with revenues and other financing sources, followed by expenditures and other financing uses and concludes with a reconciliation of beginning and ending equity.

A third alternative format allows governments to open the statement with the beginning fund equity and end the statement with the ending fund equity.

The final reporting format alternative addressed by the 1987

Codification, Section 2200, allows governments to present the combined operating statement with a focus on unreserved fund balance rather than on total fund balance. If this format is used, any changes in reserves during the year should be presented separately in the statement.

The combined governmental operating statement should present revenue and expenditure accounts at a level that provides the report user with information on the overall operations of the government. Revenues should be presented by major source (e.g., taxes, intergovernmental) and expenditures by major function (e.g., general government, public safety).

The governmental operating statements also may include information that affects the financial resources of a given fund but not the net economic resources of the overall reporting entity. These transactions generally are reported as other financing sources and other financing uses.

This classification should reflect interfund operating transfers and the receipt of long-term debt proceeds. Operating transfers in and operating transfers out should be presented in separate line captions and not netted. This section also includes payments to the escrow agent from refunding bond proceeds made as part of an in-substance defeasance of debt. Although not addressed specifically in authoritative literature, the proceeds from the sale of general fixed assets often are included in this section of the governmental operating statement because they do not increase the net economic resources of the overall reporting entity.

Generally, any direct changes to fund equity should be reported in conformity with APB Opinion No. 20, *Accounting Changes,* and Statement of Financial Accounting Standards (SFAS) No. 16, *Prior Period Adjustments.* Essentially, only prior period adjustments and residual equity transfers should be presented as adjustments to fund equity. The only prior period adjustment identified in SFAS No. 16 that applies to governments is "a correction of an error in the financial statements of a prior period." In addition to the prior period adjustments allowed by the FASB literature, the GASB transition language requires the restatement of beginning equity when a change in accounting principle cannot be applied retroactively.

Residual equity transfers should be reported gross (i.e., separate captions for transfers in and transfers out) rather than netted. When a government reports inventories in its governmental fund types using the purchases method, reporting the change in the carrying amount of the inventory in the fund equity reconciliation is appropriate. For example, when a government purchases the inventory, it is charged to the appropriate expenditure accounts. At year end, however, any material inventories on hand should be reported on the balance sheet with an appropriate reserved fund balance account. Therefore, the operating statement should reflect the change in the reserve for inventories from the beginning of the year to the end of the year in order to have fund balance equity on the combined operating statement reconcile to the combined balance sheet.

Combined Statement of Revenues, Expenditures and Changes in Fund Balances—Budget and Actual. The GPFS/CUFS should contain, at a minimum, an all-inclusive Combined Statement of Revenues, Expenditures and Changes in Fund Balances—Budget and Actual for all governmental fund types with annual appropriated budgets. The caption for this statement should indicate clearly which funds are included. In addition to governmental funds, the presentation of proprietary or trust funds on this statement is not prohibited. However, the measurement focus of their budget should be compatible (e.g., flow of current financial resources) with the governmental fund types. Governments that choose to present proprietary and similar fund type budgetary comparisons in the GPFS/CUFS that were adopted using a flow of economic resources measurement focus, should present the comparison in a separate statement within the GPFS/CUFS.

The column headings should include the applicable fund types. Columns for the budget data, actual data and the variance between the budget and actual data usually are included. The variance column is not required by GAAP; however, it provides additional information to the financial statement user.

Also, when annual appropriated budgets are adopted for some, but not all, funds of a specific fund type (e.g., special revenue funds), data for only those budgeted funds should be included on this statement. The column captions should indicate the omission of any fund (e.g., budgeted special revenue funds).

The account format of this statement generally is identical to that of the Combined Statement of Revenues, Expenditures and Changes in Fund Balances—All Governmental Fund Types and Expendable Trust Funds. The budget column should present the final budget after all amendments and supplemental appropriations. The budget and actual columns should include data presented on the budgetary basis used to control operations. For example, if the government legally adopts a modified cash basis (i.e., cash receipts and disbursements plus encumbrances recorded as expenditures) budget, the budget and actual data columns should include modified cash basis data.

It is not necessary to present the data in the combined budgetary comparison statement (i.e., budget to actual) at the legal level of budgetary control (e.g., function, activity or object levels). The legal level of budgetary control generally is that level which cannot be exceeded without action by the governing body. However, a comparison of the budget and actual results at the legal level of budgetary control for each individual fund should be presented elsewhere within the CAFR/CUFR.

If the budgetary basis used to control operations is consistent with GAAP, the actual data on the combined budgetary comparison statement would be the same data that appear on the combined GAAP operating statement. However, some governments are required to adopt a legal budget on a basis that differs from GAAP. In these instances, the differences between the budgetary basis and GAAP should be reconciled, either in the notes to the financial statements or on the face of the combined budgetary comparison statement. Generally, it is recommended that these differences be reconciled in the notes unless the differences are not considered complex and can be reconciled easily. For example, if the only budget/GAAP difference is the inclusion of encumbrances as expenditures, the reconciliation may be presented in the fund equity reconciliation section of the combined budgetary comparison statement. Budgetary-GAAP reporting differences are explored further in chapter 2.

Combined Statement of Revenues, Expenses and Changes in Retained Earnings (Equity)/Fund Balances. The GPFS/

CUFS should contain an all-inclusive Combined Statement of Revenues, Expenses and Changes in Retained Earnings (Equity)/Fund Balances—All Proprietary Fund Types and Similar Trust Funds. This statement should include separate columns for the proprietary fund type (e.g., enterprise) and the nonexpendable trust fund and pension trust fund subclassifications in use. The government's nonexpendable trust funds and pension trust funds may be presented either on the Combined Statement of Revenues, Expenses and Changes in Retained Earnings (Equity)—All Proprietary Fund Types or on a separate statement.

This statement can be divided into as many as seven categories: operating revenues, operating expenses, nonoperating revenues and/or expenses, operating transfers, extraordinary items, add back of depreciation, and changes in equity.

In addition to the decision that must be reached regarding trust fund presentation, the preparer should assess an alternative presentation format for the proprietary operating statement addressed in the 1987 *Codification,* Section 2500.108. This alternative was prompted by the need to include within the GPFS/CUFS certain segment information for enterprise funds. The 1987 *Codification,* Section 2500.108, allows governments to present segment information (e.g., individual funds) for the enterprise fund type on the Combined Statement of Revenues, Expenses and Changes in Retained Earnings (Equity)—All Proprietary Fund Types. This alternative eliminates the need to include the majority of the required segment information disclosure in the notes to the financial statements. Unless the government has only a few enterprise funds, however, this format is not practicable.

Operating Revenues. Operating revenues for proprietary fund types should be classified in essentially the same accounts used in similar commercial sector businesses. Interest earned for financing authorities and pension trust funds should be classified as operating revenue but interest earned for most proprietary funds should be reported as nonoperating revenue. The nonoperating revenue classification is used because the primary source of operating revenues for these funds is *not* interest earnings.

Operating Expenses. As with revenue reporting, the classification of operating expenses should be consistent with the accounts used by similar businesses operating in the commercial sector. Normally, depreciation expense should be presented as a separate caption within the operating expense section of the statement. Because both proprietary and fiduciary fund-type data generally are presented on a single statement, the classifications usually become somewhat varied (e.g., costs of sales and services, pension benefits).

Nonoperating Revenues and/or Expenses. Nonoperating revenues and expenses should be presented in a separate category after the operating income or loss. Transactions that should be reported in the nonoperating category include those that do not arise from the activities of primary ongoing operations. The 1987 *Codification,* Section G60.110, requires that operating grants be reported as nonoperating revenues on this statement. In addition, tax revenue, interest revenue and interest expense (except as mentioned previously) and the gain or loss on the sale of fixed assets also are classified as nonoperating revenues and expenses.

Operating Transfers. Operating transfers in and out should be reported in a separate category after the reported "income or loss before operating transfers." Operating transfers in and operating transfers out should be presented separately and not netted.

Extraordinary Items. As in the commercial sector, when a government incurs a gain or loss that is both unusual in nature and infrequent in occurrence it should be reported as an extraordinary item pursuant to APB Opinion No. 30, *Reporting the Results of Operations—Reporting the Effects of Disposal of a Segment of a Business, and Extraordinary, Unusual and Infrequently Occurring Events and Transactions* and SFAS No. 4, *Reporting Gains and Losses from Extinguishment of Debt.* Extraordinary items normally are formatted as the last item before net income on the proprietary operating statement.

Add Back of Depreciation. As discussed in chapter 8, depreciation recognized on assets acquired or constructed through capital grants, entitlements and shared revenues externally restricted for capital acquisition may be closed to the appropriate contributed capital account after being recognized in operations pursuant to guidance provided in the 1987 *Codification,* Section G60.116 (see Illustration 8–1).

Changes in Equity. The last category of the proprietary operating statement is the changes in fund equity. This category should include the net income or loss for the period and the beginning and ending retained earnings/fund balance. In addition, residual equity transfers, any changes in equity identified pursuant to APB Opinion No. 20 and SFAS No. 16 (i.e., correction of prior years' errors) and restatements resulting from a change in accounting principles should be reported as adjustments to beginning fund equity.

Three reconciliation formats currently are acceptable for the proprietary operating statements. Governments can reconcile to total retained earnings, total fund equity (i.e., retained earnings and contributed capital) or unreserved retained earnings.

The first alternative limits the reconciliation to total retained earnings. When this method is chosen, the government should either identify changes in contributed capital in the statement of changes in financial position or disclose the changes separately in the notes. This format is illustrated in appendix D.

The second alternative includes a reconciliation of both contributed capital and retained earnings. This format can either include a reconcilation of total equity or present separate reconciliations of contributed capital and retained earnings.

The final alternative allows the government to reconcile unreserved retained earnings. When this alternative is chosen, any changes in reserved retained earnings during the year should be presented as "other changes in unreserved retained earnings" after net income but before the beginning and ending equity.

Combined Statement of Changes in Financial Position. The GPFS/CUFS also should include a Combined Statement of Changes in Financial Position—All Proprietary Fund Types and Similar Trust Funds. This statement should include proprietary, nonexpendable and pension trust funds, as applicable. The statement caption should indicate which funds are presented. As mentioned previously, governments may include separate columns presenting individual enterprise funds in order to present a portion of the required segment information disclosure. In addition, the same option for reporting trust funds, explained above for the proprietary operating statement, is applicable. Guidance regarding the presentation of this statement is in a state of flux within the governmental financial reporting model. Therefore, several different options exist for reporting changes in financial position. These options are based on approaches set forth in SFAS No. 95, *Statement of Cash Flows* and APB Opinion No. 19, *Reporting Changes in Financial Position*.

SFAS No. 95 Format. In 1988, SFAS No. 95 superseded APB Opinion No. 19 in the commercial sector. However, based on the hierarchy of GAAP for governments, because APB Opinion No. 19 is addressed in the 1987 *Codification,* Section 2200.112, SFAS No. 95 would not immediately apply to governments. In 1988, the GASB added a project to its technical agenda on cash flows that encompass both the governmental and proprietary funds (see Chapter 16). In the interim, SFAS No. 95 with some minor modifications can be applied to the enterprise and similar trust funds. The modifications address the APB Opinion No. 19 requirement that the statement of changes in financial position report the financial effects of noncash transactions (e.g., trade-in of equipment).

SFAS No. 95 contains several other departures from the working cash format allowed by APB Opinion No. 19. Therefore, to apply the basic SFAS No. 95 model, certain terminology must be reviewed for application to the public sector. For example, the FASB specifically defined both "cash" and "cash equivalents" in SFAS No. 95. These definitions are not consistent with the manner in which these terms have been used in government. Cash is defined in SFAS No. 95 as "not only currency on hand but demand deposits with banks or other financial institutions. Cash also includes other kinds of accounts that have the general characteristics of demand deposits in that the customer may deposit additional funds at any time and also effectively may withdraw funds at any time without prior notice or penalty." Cash equivalents are defined in SFAS No. 95 as liquid investments that are both:

a. Readily convertible to known amounts of cash.
b. So near their maturity that they present insignificant risk of changes in value because of changes in interest rates.

SFAS No. 95 further states that "only investments with original maturities of three months or less" would qualify under this definition of cash equivalents. However, SFAS No. 95 does provide the option of reporting cash equivalents as investments. The entity's policy regarding the treatment of cash equivalents should be disclosed.

The presentation of cash flows is divided by the FASB in SFAS No. 95 into three categories: operating activities, investing activities and financing activities. Presentation of amounts for all activities in most cases should be displayed at gross and not netted.

Operating Activities. The operating activities category includes most "transactions, and other events that enter into the determination of net income." SFAS No. 95 does provide an option in reporting cash flows from operating activities. Entities may use either a direct method or indirect method in presenting the cash flows from operations. The direct method divides cash inflows and outflows from operating activities into various captions such as "cash received from customers" and "interest paid." Entities that choose the direct method option also should prepare a reconciliation of net cash flows from operating activities to net income. This reconciliation generally is presented with the cash flow statement. The FASB encourages the use of the direct method because it is "more comprehensive and presumably more useful" than the indirect method.

The indirect method begins with the entity's net income or loss and reconciles to net cash flows from operating activities. The method eliminates the need for a separate reconciliation; however, interest payments (net of capitalized amounts) should be included in the disclosures associated with this presentation.

In reviewing the cash flows from the operating activities category, one must realize that the term "operating" is being used in the broad sense of the term. In other words, this category does not exclude nonoperating items but incorporates activities that are presented in the "operating" statement. This results in nonoperating items such as interest revenue and expense being presented in this category.

Investing Activities. The second category in the cash flow statement, cash flows from investing activities, is used to report cash receipts and disbursements related to the acquisition or disposal of fixed assets; loans to others (including advances to other funds); and investments in debt and equity securities. Down payments for capital leases would be reported as an investing activity. Again, following the general approach set forth in SFAS No. 95, investment activities (i.e., buy/sell) should not be netted.

Financing Activities. The third category identified in SFAS No. 95, financing activities, includes cash receipts and disbursements related to the principal portion of the entity's debt and investments by others in the entity (including the contribution and subsequent return of contributed capital). Principal payments on capital leases would be reported as a financing activity.

A category that itemizes noncash transactions affecting financial position is necessary to meet the noncash transaction reporting requirement of APB Opinion No. 19. Transactions that can be classified in this category include "borrowings" related to capital leases and "transfers" associated with the government's account groups.

This method of adapting the SFAS No. 95 format to the requirements of APB Opinion No. 19 is illustrated in appendix D.

In addition to the modified SFAS No. 95 approach, there are various alternatives that may be used for formatting changes in financial position within the traditional APB Opinion No. 19 guidance. A traditional statement of changes in financial position may be presented in a form expressing changes in financial position in terms of cash, cash and temporary investments combined, or working capital. It may also be presented in a balanced format.

Working Capital Format. The changes in working capital format is a common presentation method used by governments. This alternative includes three primary categories: sources of working capital, uses of working capital and elements of net increase (decrease) in working capital.

Generally, the sources of working capital include two subcategories, sources from operations and other sources. The sources from operations subcategory begins with the net income before extraordinary items from the combined proprietary operating statement. Items recognized in determining net income, but which do not provide or require the use of working capital, are then subtracted from or added to net income. These items normally include depreciation and amortization expense.

The second subcategory of the sources of working capital includes ''other sources.'' The most commonly reported other sources are the gross proceeds from disposal or retirement of noncurrent assets, the proceeds from long-term borrowing, residual equity transfers in and capital contributions.

The second category of the combined statement of changes in financial position should be the uses of working capital. For governments, the uses of working capital category would include such items as acquisition of noncurrent assets, retirement of long-term debt or reclassification of long-term debt as current debt, and residual equity transfers out.

The final section of the working capital format is the elements of net increase (decrease) in working capital. This section should be captioned as ''net changes'' because that is the data presented. APB Opinion No. 19 requires that the net changes in working capital be analyzed in appropriate detail. The level of detail presented should be consistent with captions presented on the combined balance sheet.

A government also may present the combined statement of changes in financial position in the ''balanced format.'' That is, the increase (decrease) in working capital is reported as a source or use resulting in the sources and uses being equal.

Notes to the Financial Statements. Financial statements alone do not provide all of the information required for fair presentation of the government's financial position and results of operations in conformity with GAAP. Additional information is needed, often too detailed in nature or otherwise unsuitable for presentation on the face of the financial statements. The notes to the financial statements provide this additional information, and so form an integral part of the basic financial statements.

GAAP require that the notes to the financial statements contain all disclosures necessary to prevent the financial statements from being misleading. Such a concept is qualitative, and cannot be reduced to a simple checklist of required disclosures. Nevertheless, the authoritative literature, described in chapter 2, does set forth certain minimum standards essential to fair presentation.

The 1987 *Codification,* Section 2300, provides a list of note disclosures that is specifically tailored to public sector financial reporting. This list forms a good starting point for the financial statement preparer wishing to evaluate the adequacy of the notes to the financial statements. Nevertheless, the proper exercise of professional judgment is essential. Materiality and the particular circumstances of each case must be carefully evaluated to avoid unnecessary or excessive note disclosure that complicates rather than clarifies the financial statements.

Organization and Presentation of Note Disclosures. The notes to the financial statements are an integral part of the liftable GPFS/CUFS. Therefore, they should be included as part of the CAFR/CUFR financial section directly after the Combined Statements—Overview. Moreover, the format of the table of contents should indicate clearly that the notes are part of the GPFS/CUFS, and each basic financial statement should contain a reference to the notes (e.g., ''the notes to the financial statements are an integral part of the financial statements''). When combining and individual fund and account group financial statements and schedules fall within the scope of the auditor's opinion, they too should refer to the notes to the financial statements, as illustrated in appendix D.

Note disclosures should be organized and presented in a logical order. The order of presentation will vary depending on each individual government's disclosures. The 1987 *Codification,* Section 2300.601, provides guidance on one possible sequence of note disclosures. Financial statement preparers, however, are free to modify this suggested sequence, as needed, to provide the most meaningful disclosure in a given set of circumstances.

GAAP are established under the presumption that the notes contain any material information needed to present fairly the financial statements. Therefore, as a general rule, governments should *not* present notes that indicate only that a given type of disclosure is not necessary. For example, if the government has no related party transactions, a note is not needed stating that there were no such transactions during the period.

The GPFS/CUFS, including the notes, also are presumed by GAAP to be ''liftable.'' Accordingly, the notes should not contain references to financial statements and schedules outside of the GPFS/CUFS. Similarly, statements and schedules elsewhere in the financial section should not refer to the notes as being ''an integral part of the financial statements'' unless these statements and schedules themselves fall within the scope of the auditor's opinion.

Summary of Significant Accounting Policies. A government's accounting policies are the specific accounting principles—and methods of applying those principles—judged by the government's management to be appropriate in the circumstances to present fairly the financial position and results of operations in conformity with GAAP. APB Opinion No. 22, *Disclosure of Accounting Policies,* requires financial statement preparers to include a description of all significant accounting policies as an integral part of the financial statements. For governments, this summary of significant accounting policies (SSAP) most often takes the form of a group of separate ''subnotes'' addressing a variety of topics. Because the SSAP is designed to provide the reader with information on the government's accounting policies rather than on specific transactions, amounts normally are not presented in the SSAP.

Although this SSAP normally is presented as the first of the notes to the financial statements, it may also be presented as a separate, integral part of the basic financial statements. If presented separately, the basic financial statements should contain a reference to the SSAP as well as to the notes to the financial statements.

APB Opinion No. 22, as applied to state and local governments, requires that the SSAP disclose those accounting principles and methods that involve:

1) The selection of an accounting principle or method from several acceptable alternatives (e.g., method used to depreciate fixed assets);
2) Principles and practices peculiar to state and local government accounting (e.g., modified accrual basis of accounting); and
3) Unusual or innovative applications of GAAP (e.g., reporting deep-discount debt in the GLTDAG at net or accreted value rather than at face value).

Reporting Entity. The 1987 *Codification,* Section 2100, provides note disclosure requirements related to the reporting entity. This note should be presented as the first subnote in the SSAP. If not presented in the SSAP, this disclosure should be formatted as the first note. This approach allows the reader to gain an understanding of the reporting entity before reading the other notes to the financial statements.

All governments are required to present an "entity note" regardless of whether any component units are included within the reporting entity. This disclosure should describe the criteria used in determining the reporting entity. Although these criteria normally are taken directly from the 1987 *Codification,* Sections 2100.108–.112, they should be described rather than just referenced.

In any instances when potential component units meeting any of the criteria of the 1987 *Codification,* Sections 2100.108–.112, are *not* included in the reporting entity, governments are required to disclose the specific reasons for excluding the potential component units. One acceptable approach is to include a paragraph in the entity note about each potential component unit that was omitted with an explanation of why it was not included within the reporting entity.

The 1987 *Codification,* Section 2100.122, requires the disclosure of any component units included within the reporting entity. Many governments include a discussion about each component unit and why it has been included in the reporting entity. This disclosure may become somewhat detailed when the reporting entity includes a number of component units.

If any component units' fiscal years differ from the oversight unit's fiscal year, this fact should be disclosed. The existence of different fiscal years also could require a reconciliation of interfund receivables and payables and transfers in and out if they do not equal. Usually, fiscal year differences are disclosed in the entity note while the reconciliation normally is presented in a separate disclosure on interfund transactions.

Fund Accounting. A subnote identifying the basis of presentation is not specifically required by GAAP. Such a disclosure, however, can help the financial report reader to gain a better understanding of governmental accounting.

Because fund accounting is unique to governments and certain limited types of entities (e.g., hospitals, colleges and universities), a brief explanation of this convention is appropriate. All of a government's individual funds are classified by the three fund categories, governmental, proprietary and fiduciary. A brief description of these categories, as well as an explanation of the account groups, is appropriate. Also, any fund types used by the reporting entity should be described.

Basis of Accounting. Because governmental accounting requires the use of both accrual and modified accrual accounting, depending upon the types of funds used, the SSAP should include a description of the measurement focus that applies to each fund type followed by an explanation of the basis of accounting used.

Revenues Susceptible to Accrual. The 1987 *Codification,* Section 1600.108, requires that the SSAP indicate clearly which primary revenue sources have been treated as "susceptible to accrual" under the modified accrual basis of accounting.

Budgetary Data. The SSAP should include various disclosures about the reporting entity's budget and budget process. The SSAP for budgets should provide:

- A description of the budgetary basis of accounting,
- An indication of the funds for which appropriated budgets have been adopted,
- A brief description of the budget process,
- Details regarding appropriations,
- An indication of the legal level of budgetary control and
- Information on encumbrances

The budgetary basis of accounting normally is mandated by either state statute or local ordinance. If the budgets are adopted on a basis consistent with GAAP, this fact should be indicated. If the budgetary basis differs from GAAP, the disclosure should indicate that a difference exists and provide a brief explanation of the difference. Normally, the reconciliation of differences between GAAP-basis amounts and non-GAAP budget basis amounts should be presented separately, outside of the SSAP. If a government has legally adopted annual budgets for some, but not all funds of a specific fund type, the disclosure should make this fact clear.

Although not required by GAAP, it is suggested that the government present a brief overview of its budgetary process. When appropriations lapse at year end, the disclosure should so indicate. If a portion of the appropriations carry forward to the subsequent year, this fact should be made clear. If supplemental appropriations were necessary during the year, the disclosure should indicate this fact.

Because GAAP require that expenditures exceeding appropriations at the legal level of budgetary control be reported within the GPFS/CUFS, it is important to present the legal level of budgetary control in the SSAP. When doing so, care should be taken to avoid ambiguity. For example, the use of the term "line item" is generic rather than specific.

Encumbrances are unique to government; therefore, the disclosure should include an explanation of this special accounting convention. Some governments use a separate subnote within the SSAP to present this information. However, because encumbrances relate to budgetary control, it is also appropriate to present this information within the budgetary disclosure. If outstanding encumbrances will be honored in the subsequent year, the amounts should be disclosed in the detailed notes, rather than the SSAP, if not reserved in the fund equity section of the combined balance sheet.

Cash and Investments. If a government participates in a cash and investment pool, the accounting policy should explain this arrangement, which could include information on how interest earnings are allocated. Although the 1987 *Codification,* Section I50, requires detailed disclosures for deposits and investments (this disclosure is discussed later in this chapter), the stated basis for investments should be disclosed in the SSAP.

Receivables. Normally, the basis of accounting subnote, included within the SSAP, discloses when receivables and revenues are recorded and reported. The receivables subnote should disclose the government's policy regarding the allowance for uncollectible receivables.

Advances to Other Funds. Governments often advance resources to other funds that will not be repaid in the current period. In these instances, the SSAP should explain that the fund balance of the loaning governmental fund is reserved to indicate it is not available for appropriation.

Inventories. ARB No. 43, *Restatement and Revision of Accounting Research Bulletins,* Chapter 4, requires a disclosure of the valuation basis of inventories (i.e., cost). In addition, the method used to determine the value should be presented (e.g., first-in, first-out; last-in, first-out). Finally, because governmental funds may use either the purchases or consumption method for recognizing inventory expenditures, the method chosen should be disclosed in the SSAP. When the purchases method is used for budgeting purposes, the subnote also should indicate that the inventory asset amount is not available for appropriation because it has been charged to expenditures when purchased rather than when used.

Prepaid Items. Although not required by GAAP for governmental fund types, governments may capitalize prepaid items and charge them to the appropriate fiscal period. When prepaid items are capitalized, a subnote could explain this policy and indicate that a portion of fund balance equal to the prepaid items is reserved to indicate that it is not available for appropriation.

Restricted Assets. When the government presents restricted asset accounts on its proprietary fund balance sheets, it is suggested that a subnote be provided in the SSAP to indicate the functions of the restricted asset accounts so presented.

Fixed Assets. The SSAP needs to include various disclosures regarding a government's fixed assets. Many of the disclosures are required because of the variety of accounting treatments allowed. Because fixed assets purchased by governmental fund types are reported differently from those purchased by proprietary fund types, the subnote should explain both accounting treatments. Sometimes this disclosure is provided when defining the GFAAG rather than in a policy subnote. This disclosure also may include the government's accounting for betterments.

Because it is optional for governments to capitalize infrastructure, the government's accounting policy on infrastructure capitalization should be disclosed. The valuation bases for purchased fixed assets and donated fixed assets also should be disclosed. In addition, GAAP require various disclosures regarding a government's depreciation policy (e.g., useful lives).

The 1987 *Codification,* Section G60, allows for depreciation on certain assets (i.e., acquired or constructed with resources externally restricted for capital acquisition) to be closed to the appropriate contributed capital account after being recognized in operations. When this option is used, the subnote should indicate this fact.

Compensated Absences. The 1987 *Codification,* Section C60, provides guidance regarding the accounting treatment for compensated absences. Because different approaches are used in dividing the liability between the funds and the GLTDAG, an accounting policy subnote is appropriate. The compensated absences liability for proprietary fund types should be accrued as earned, consistent with the accrual basis of accounting, and the disclosure should indicate this fact when both governmental and proprietary fund types are included in the financial statements.

Long-term Obligations. It is suggested that the SSAP contain an explanation of the rationale for classifying long-term obligations either in the GLTDAG, the debt service fund, or the proprietary or trust funds. Also, the accounting treatment accorded zero-coupon and other deep-discount debt should be explained.

Fund Equity. An explanation of the components of fund equity often is included in the SSAP. However, the details of the reserves and designations should be presented in a separate disclosure.

Bond Discounts, Bond Premiums and Issuance Costs. The SSAP should include an explanation of the treatment accorded bond discounts, bond premiums and issuance costs, for governmental and proprietary fund types, as appropriate. For proprietary funds, APB Opinion No. 21, *Interest on Receivables and Payables,* provides the appropriate guidance on display and amortization.

Interfund Transactions. When a government maintains numerous funds within the reporting entity, the SSAP may explain the various types of interfund transactions. The 1987 *Codification,* Sections 1800.103 and 1800.106, provide the classification for the various types of interfund transactions. Only those types of transactions included in the government's financial statements should be defined in the SSAP.

"Memorandum Only" Total Columns. When a government presents total columns on the GPFS/CUFS, a subnote should be presented to explain the nature of such total columns and to state that they do not present GAAP data and do not represent consolidated financial information.

Comparative Data. Although not required by GAAP, a subnote could be included in the SSAP explaining that comparative data are presented in the financial statements to allow the reader to make appropriate comparisons with prior periods.

Stewardship, Compliance and Responsibility. Financial statement preparers are required by GAAP to provide certain disclosures to demonstrate compliance with finance-related legal and contractual provisions. Because of the importance of legal compliance in the public sector, it is appropriate that such disclosures immediately follow the SSAP. The 1987 *Codification,* Section 1200.112, requires the disclosure of material violations of legal requirements. Such violations can occur, for example, if sufficient care is not taken to ensure compliance with detailed revenue bond indentures. Since appropriated budgets limit the amount a government may legally expend, certain budgetary disclosures also are required to demonstrate compliance or to report noncompliance.

When a government adopts a budget on a basis which differs from GAAP, the 1987 *Codification,* Section 2400.123, requires that the nature and amount of the adjustments necessary to convert the actual GAAP data to the budgetary basis be reported either on the combined budgetary comparison statement or in the notes. Unless the reconciliation is quite simple, note disclosure is the more appropriate alternative. When the reconciliation is required, it is suggested that the differences be classified in a manner consistent with the 1987 *Codification,* Section 2400.114–.122 (i.e., basis, timing, entity and perspective differences), although this specific terminology need not be used.

The data that should be reconciled are not clearly indicated in GAAP. Generally, there are two alternatives for this presentation.

- operating statement approach (i.e., excess (deficiency) of revenues and other financial sources over (under) expenditures and other financing uses)
- balance sheet approach (i.e., fund balance)

An example of a budget-GAAP reconciliation using the operating statement approach is presented in Illustration 14–2.

The 1987 *Codification,* Section 2300.104, requires the note disclosure of any individual funds that have expenditures over appropriations at the legal level of budgetary control (e.g., the fund total, the object classification). The individual fund, the level of control and the amount of overexpenditure should be disclosed.

Detailed Notes—All Fund Types and Account Groups. The notes to the financial statements should include detailed disclosures of all assets, liabilities and fund equities essential for fair presentation at the GPFS/CUFS level. It also may be neces-

---

ILLUSTRATION 14–2

Budget to GAAP Reconciliation
Operating Statement Approach
(amounts expressed in thousands)

Assumptions. The government adopts an annual appropriated modified cash basis budget for its general fund and certain special revenue funds. The government for GAAP reporting purposes accrues $44 of sales tax in the general fund and defers $11 of grant receipts in the special revenue funds. This compares with an accrual of $23 in the general fund and a deferral of $6 in the special revenue funds in the prior year. Salaries at year end of $15 for the general fund and $6 for the special revenue funds are accrued on the GAAP basis of accounting versus $8 in the general fund and $4 in the special revenue funds in the prior year.

The budgetary basis accounts for encumbrances as expenditures. Current year's encumbrances of $7 did not meet the GAAP criteria for expenditures, as compared with $3 in the prior year for the general fund and $4 in the current year, as compared with $3 in the prior year for the special revenue funds. The excess of revenues and other financing sources over expenditures and other financing uses for nonbudgeted special revenue funds is $9.

	General	Special Revenue
Excess of revenues and other financing sources over expenditures and other financing uses (budgetary basis)	$75	$22
Adjustments:		
To record accrual of sales tax revenues	21	—
To record deferral of grant receipts	—	(5)
To record accrual of salary expenditures	(7)	(2)
To adjust for encumbrances not recognized as expenditures	4	1
Excess of revenues and other financing sources over expenditures and other financing uses (GAAP basis-budgeted funds)	93	16
Other adjustments:		
To record excess of revenues and other financing sources over expenditures and other financing uses for nonbudgeted funds	—	9
Excess of revenues and other financing sources over expenditures and other financing uses (GAAP basis)	$93	$25

---

sary to provide details of selected accounts to give the reader of the financial statements a better understanding of the statement disclosures. The following discussion reviews disclosures that should be presented in the notes to the financial statements but is not intended to represent a preferred order or grouping of those disclosures.

Cash and Investments. The 1987 *Codification,* Section I50, requires governments to disclose data regarding deposits and investments in order that financial statement users may assess certain risks inherent in these assets. These note disclosures generally are provided for the government as a whole and can be segregated into three categories: legal and contractual provisions, balance sheet date data and activity information.

Legal and Contractual Provisions—The first category of disclosures includes a brief description of the authorized types of investments the government can hold. In addition, any unauthorized investments held during the year should be disclosed. Authorized investments can be determined through a review of the state constitution or statutes, local government charters or resolutions, and grant provisions. When investments are not addressed in these types of documents, the government's formal investment policy should be used as a basis for this disclosure.

Compliance with legal and contractual provisions also is demonstrated by the disclosure of significant violations of such provisions during the year. These provisions also may include collateral requirements. For example, when the state statute requires that a public deposit be collateralized at 102 percent of the total deposits and the collateral level falls to 85 percent during the year, this fact should be disclosed.

Balance Sheet Data—The second category of disclosures addresses deposit and investment balance sheet data information.

Deposits: The 1987 *Codification,* Section I50.163, provides:

If the bank balances of deposits as of the balance sheet date are entirely insured or collateralized with securities held by the entity or by its agent in the entity's name, that fact should be stated. If not, these disclosures should be made:
a. Carrying amount of total deposits, if not separately displayed on the balance sheet.
b. The amount of the total bank balance classified in these three categories of credit risk:
  1. Insured or collateralized with securities held by the entity or by its agent in the entity's name
  2. Collateralized with securities held by the pledging financial institution's trust department or agent in the entity's name
  3. Uncollateralized. (This includes any bank balance that is collateralized with securities held by the pledging financial institution or its trust department or agent but not in the entity's name.)

To properly disclose deposits, the definitions and applications of several terms must first be understood. These terms include deposits, bank balances, insured, "held in the entity's name" and agent. Deposits encompass the government's cash on deposit with financial institutions and several cash equivalents, including money market accounts with financial institutions and certificates of deposit. All accounts including cash equivalents that are subject to federal or state depository insurance generally are classified as deposits.

Bank balance can be defined in terms of the amount that is eligible for collateralization or depository insurance. It should not be confused with the carrying amount of deposits on the government's accounting records. Bank balance has been interpreted in practice as the deposits that have been "collected" by the financial institution. Therefore, cash in transit and deposits that have not cleared through the banking system (e.g., Federal Reserve) would not be considered a part of bank balance. This interpretation was based on an informal Federal Deposit Insurance Corporation (FDIC) staff response related to an inquiry on depository insurance coverage and should be reviewed with regional officials before implementation.

The FDIC, Federal Savings and Loan Insurance Corporation (FSLIC) and some state government sponsored programs provide insurance for government deposits. Federal depository insurance generally is limited to $100,000 per institution; however, additional coverage may be available in certain cases. Additional coverage is normally available when public deposits with a financial institution are separated into demand and time deposits (i.e., $100,000 for each *type* of deposit). Also, cases where the law requires separate official custodians (e.g., treasurer and clerk), each custodian may be separately insured by the FDIC or FSLIC. Finally, when deposits are held in trust (e.g., bondholders, PERS members), the FDIC and FSLIC generally have established the coverage on the individual level. However, this insurance has been reduced when it was determined the PERS assets exceeded the pension obligation. The rules establishing federal depository insurance coverage are contained within the Code of Federal Regulations (e.g., 12*CFR*330) and can be referred to for additional clarification of this issue.

The 1987 *Codification,* Section I50.110, also identifies certain multiple-institution collateral pools as potentially meeting the insurance criterion in the classification of deposits. These pools require that when a financial institution fails, the entire pool assumes the claims for the deposits. There may be instances when the pool's resources are inadequate to cover the claims. When the entire shortfall can be assessed to the members of the pool, the deposits are considered insured.

Those cases where the members cannot be assessed, the deposits are considered to be collateralized to the extent of the pool's value to deposits. For example, when a collateral pool cannot assess members for excess claims and holds collateral equal to 75 percent of the uninsured deposits, the government's deposits are considered to be only 75 percent collateralized.

When collateralized deposits are assessed for classification into the three categories of risk, the predominant factor in the classification is the "name" in which the collateral is being held. For collateral to be considered for classification in category 1 or category 2, it should be held by the government (i.e., category 1), by the government's agent (i.e., category 1) or by the financial institution's trust department or agent in the entity's name (i.e., category 2). Held in the entity's name does not mean that the collateral security has been registered in the government's name as this would represent a purchase of that security. However, the phrase held in the entity's name does imply that certain custodial procedures are in place that identify the government's right to the securities in the event of a default. Those custodial procedures may differ based on the form of securities held (i.e., physical securities or book-entry system).

A book-entry system (e.g., depository trust company, federal reserve banks) poses some unique problems in that a government normally does not have an account within the system. A government's right to collateral normally is identified through the use of custodial subaccounts. The presence of custodial agreements that only allow the withdrawal of securities after the approval of the government is received and periodic safekeeping reporting assist in identifying this right in the event of default. When physical securities are involved, the placement of this collateral in the government's account, as evidenced by the custodial records, normally leaves an adequate audit trail of safekeeping receipts and confirmations. As mentioned above, a custodial agreement for this type of collateral should limit the access to these securities without prior approval of the government.

Once the government's rights to the securities have been established, the classification is based solely on who is holding the collateral. Often it is difficult to determine when a third party is acting on behalf of the government or the financial institution as an agent. In the case of three-party relationships, prior approval by the government before any transfer of securities may take place establishes the identification of securities in the account and helps establish the agency relationship between the government and the third party. Reducing this relationship to a written contract is encouraged but not required to prove agency.

Investments: The carrying value of each type of investment also should be disclosed at the balance sheet date. In addition, the market value for each type of investment should be disclosed. The 1987 *Codification,* Section I50.164, requires:

> The disclosure of carrying amounts by type of investment should be classified in these three categories of credit risk:
> a. Insured or registered, or securities held by the entity or its agent in the entity's name
> b. Uninsured and unregistered, with securities held by the counterparty's trust department or agent in the entity's name
> c. Uninsured and unregistered, with securities held by the counterparty, or by its trust department or agent but not in the entity's name.

All of the government's investments held at the balance sheet date are subject to classification, except for investment pools (e.g., state treasurer) and mutual funds (e.g., some deferred compensation plans) where specific securities related to the government cannot be identified. Securities underlying reverse repurchase agreements also would not be classified because they are held by the buyer-lender. Under the broad scope of this classification investments held in restricted accounts and by fiscal agents would be subject to classification; however, investments held by escrow agents, as part of an in-substance defeasance, would not be considered subject to classification.

Clarification of certain terminology also may be necessary to properly classify investments held by the government. These terms include insured, trust department and counterparty. Certain investments (excluding repurchase agreements) may be subject to insurance by the Securities Investor Protection Corporation (SIPC). The SIPC insurance (maximum of $500,000, including up to $100,000 on cash claims) generally is available through Securities and Exchange Commission registered broker-dealers.

Because the trust departments of financial institutions are legally separated and regulated, the GASB recognizes these departments for the second category of credit risk. A safekeeping department or broker-dealer's "trust department" would be classified with the counterparty (i.e., category 3).

For certain transactions it may be difficult to determine who is a counterparty versus an agent. For example, if an agent holds investments for a PERS and is called upon to provide settlement for a securities purchase, the agent remains within the confines of an agency relationship. However, when an agent places an order for the purchase of securities, the agent is acting as a counterparty for that particular transaction. This transaction should not jeopardize the agency relationship for the other investments.

When the credit risk of the oversight unit for deposits and investments is not apparent because of significant balances of component units or the "mix" of component units' credit risk categories differs significantly from that of the oversight unit, additional disclosure should be considered (e.g., 75 percent of investments classified in category 3 are held by the PERS). In addition, when unrealized losses of a fund or component unit are not apparent from the disclosure of market and carrying values by type of investment; the unrealized loss, carrying value and market value for that component unit or fund should be disclosed separately.

A government may choose to provide additional information on the categorization of credit risk either through a narrative explanation of the deposit and investment balances without a categorization table or through additional subcategorization (e.g., collateralized and held by the counterparty). These options are acceptable as long as the integrity of the categories is not compromised.

Activity Information—The final category of disclosures includes information on deposit and investment activity during the year. When the amounts of deposits and investments classified in category 3 during the year significantly exceed the amounts classified in this category at year end, that fact and the causes should be briefly disclosed.

In addition, the government is required to disclose the types of investments that were held during the year (e.g., repurchase agreement) but not at year end. Also, any losses because of counterparty default that occurred during the year should be disclosed.

Receivables. Although not required by GAAP, the detailed components of the receivables accounts presented on the combined balance sheet may be disclosed. The amount of the allowance for uncollectibles also could be itemized.

Leases Receivable. The government may be involved in leasing fixed assets to others. The 1987 *Codification*, Section L20.124 states that the disclosure requirements of SFAS No. 13, *Accounting for Leases,* should be used by governments for both capital and operating leases. In addition to a general description of the government's capital and operating lease arrangements, SFAS No. 13 requires the following disclosures of sales-type and direct financing capital leases:

i. The components of the net investment in sales-type and direct financing leases as of the date of each balance sheet presented:
   a. Future *minimum lease payments* to be received, with separate deductions for (i) amounts representing *executory costs,* including any profit thereon, included in the minimum lease payments and (ii) the accumulated allowance for uncollectible *minimum lease payments* receivable.
   b. The *unguaranteed residual values* accruing to the benefit of the lessor.
   c. Unearned income.
ii. Future *minimum lease payments* to be received for each of the five succeeding fiscal years as of the date of the latest balance sheet presented.
iii. The amount of unearned income included in income to offset *initial direct costs* charged against income for each period for which an income statement is presented. (For direct financing leases only.)
iv. Total *contingent rentals* included in income for each period for which an income statement is presented.

SFAS No. 13 also requires the following disclosures for governments participating in operating leases as a lessor:

i. The cost and carrying amount, if different, of property on lease or held for leasing by major classes of property according to nature or function, and the amount of accumulated depreciation in total as of the date of the latest balance sheet presented [if applicable].
ii. Minimum future rentals on noncancelable leases as of the date of the lastest balance sheet presented, in the aggregate and for each of the five succeeding fiscal years.
iii. Total *contingent rentals* included in income for each period for which an income statement is presented.

Restricted Assets. When a single line caption is presented on the combined balance sheet for restricted assets, more detailed data may be presented in the notes, usually organized by the type of accounts included in the revenue bond indenture (e.g., restricted assets—revenue bond renewal and replacement account).

Fixed Assets. In addition to the inclusion of accounting policies for fixed assets, some additional disclosures for fixed assets are required. The 1987 *Codification,* Section 2300.104, requires a disclosure of changes in general fixed assets. In addition, APB Opinion No. 12, *Omnibus Opinion,* requires disclosure in the notes of the separate classes of fixed assets and the amount of accumulated depreciation, if not disclosed in the combined balance sheet. The disclosure of changes in general fixed assets may be more specific and include separate columns for the transfer from the construction in progress account to the other asset classes. In addition, the disclosure could present fixed assets transferred to other fund types.

Risk Management. Many governments have been choosing to finance all or a portion of their risks rather than to seek traditional commercial insurance coverage. A disclosure explaining this activity is appropriate. The following information could be included:

- The fact that certain risks are financed by the government, rather than insured;
- The types of risks retained by the government (e.g., general liability, employee medical coverage);
- The amount of risk that is assumed (i.e., the difference between the total risk and the amount of risk covered by third parties);
- The fund classification used to account for the government's risk management activities;
- The accounting policy for interfund premiums (e.g., reported as quasi-external transactions);
- The fact that claims incurred but not reported (IBNRs) have been considered when determining the claims liability; and
- An indication that an actuary was used, if applicable.

The GASB is now studying various accounting and disclosure issues related to risk management, as discussed further in chapter 16.

Deferred Revenues. Although not required by GAAP, a definition of deferred revenues may be provided in a separate disclosure. Often, however, this definition is included in the revenue recognition accounting policy. The disclosure also could include the amount of deferred revenues by type, if not presented on the balance sheet.

Construction and Other Significant Commitments. Disclosure is required by the 1987 Codification, Section 2300.104, of significant long-term commitments not recognized in the financial statements. The most common disclosures of this type are construction commitments. Construction commitment disclosures should identify the type of project and selected details (e.g., project authorization, remaining commitment, required future financing) regarding the commitments.

Lease Obligations. The 1987 Codification, Section L20.124, also provides authoritative guidance on lessee disclosures. Governments are required to provide disclosures for capital lease agreements in accordance with SFAS No. 13. The disclosure requirements of SFAS No. 13 for capital leases include:

- General leasing arrangements;
- The gross amount of assets recorded under capital leases presented by major asset classes; and
- Minimum future lease payments in total and for each of the next five years, presenting a deduction for the amount of imputed interest to reduce the net minimum future lease payments to their present value.

SFAS No. 13 also requires the following disclosures for governments participating as lessees in operating leases:

- General leasing arrangements;
- The future minimum rental payments in total and for each of the next five years*;
- Total minimum rentals to be received in the future under noncancelable subleases*; and
- Current year rental costs.

Long-term Debt. In most instances, governments are required to present detailed disclosures relating to their long-term debt. Some of the topics that should be included are:

---
* This disclosure applies only to noncancelable arrangements of more than one year.

- A description of issues,
- Changes in long-term debt,
- Debt service requirements to maturity,
- Details regarding advance refunding of debt,
- Bonds authorized but unissued and
- Revenue bond indenture information.

Normally, these disclosures are included as part of the long-term debt detailed note. However, the presentation of separate notes for each topic is also acceptable.

It is suggested that a government include a brief description of each outstanding bond issue that could include the following:

- Purpose of bonds,
- Original amount of the issue,
- Type of bond (e.g., general obligation, revenue),
- Amount of installments,
- Interest rates and
- Maturity date range.

Governments with a significant number of individual bond issues outstanding should consider combining the disclosure previously outlined into meaningful categories (e.g., original issue general obligation bonds, refunding revenue bonds, special assessment debt with government commitment).

The 1987 Codification, Section 2300.104, requires that changes in all general long-term debt be included within the GPFS/CUFS, usually in the notes to the financial statements. Changes in all general long-term debt should include not only bonded debt, but capital leases, compensated absences, claims and judgments, and any unfunded pension plan liability that appear in the GLTDAG.

The 1987 Codification, Section 2300.104, mandates the disclosure of debt service requirements to maturity for all long-term debt. At a minimum, this disclosure should report the combined payments of principal and interest for each of the succeeding five years and a single amount representing principal and interest payments over the remaining life of the debt. This disclosure could be expanded to report principal and interest payments separately. In addition, this disclosure could report debt service for each five-year period following the initial five years, rather than provide a single figure for all remaining debt service. Debt service to maturity is normally presented by type of debt (e.g., general obligation bonds, revenue bonds). The debt service requirements for capital lease obligations may be combined with this disclosure or be presented with other lease information. The amounts reported for the long-term portion of compensated absences, claims and judgments, and for unfunded pension contributions usually are not included in this disclosure because the repayment dates are unknown.

The 1987 Codification, Section D20, provides guidance on disclosure requirements in the year of an advance refunding as well as in subsequent years. The required disclosures in the year of the advance refunding include:

- The difference between the cash flows required to service the old debt and the cash flows required to service the new debt, adjusted for additional cash (e.g., for issuance costs or payments to the escrow agent), but unadjusted for the time value of money.
- The economic gain or loss resulting from the refunding transaction (i.e., the difference between the present value

of the old debt service requirements and the present value of the new debt service requirements, discounted at the effective interest rate and adjusted for additional cash paid).

When the advance refunding results in an in-substance rather than a legal defeasance of debt, the amount of the defeased debt outstanding at year end should be reported in the notes in all periods following the advance refunding for which the debt remains outstanding.

Finally, when bonds have been authorized at year end but remain unissued, a disclosure explaining this fact is suggested.

Fund Equity. When the nature and purpose of all reserves or designations are not described sufficiently on the combined balance sheet, the notes should provide an adequate description. For example, a government could explain the reserve for inventory required by the 1987 *Codification,* Section 1800.122.

The 1986 *ASLGU* also suggests that significant changes to reserves and designations be disclosed in the notes to the financial statements.

Interfund Transactions. Two primary types of interfund transactions occur, loans and transfers. The 1987 *Codification,* Section 2300.104, requires the disclosure within the GPFS/CUFS of the amounts of interfund receivables and payables for each individual fund. Normally this disclosure is presented in the notes. Although not required by GAAP, the details of a government's operating transfers also could be disclosed.

Other Disclosures. In addition to the SSAP and detailed notes on all funds and account groups, other disclosures should be presented that are essential for a fair presentation of a government's financial position and results of operations in conformity with GAAP.

Segment Information—Enterprise Funds. The 1987 *Codification,* Section 2500, requires the inclusion of summary segment financial information when a government maintains non-homogeneous enterprise funds or when an enterprise fund has debt outstanding. The following disclosures should be presented in either of these situations for each enterprise fund:

- Types of goods or services provided,
- Operating revenues (total revenues from sales of goods or services),
- Depreciation, depletion, and amortization expense,
- Operating income or loss (operating revenues less operating expenses),
- Operating grants, entitlements, and shared revenues,
- Operating interfund transfers in and out,
- Tax revenues,
- Net income or loss (total revenues less total expenses),
- Current capital contributions and transfers,
- Property, plant, and equipment additions and deletions,
- Net working capital (current assets less current liabilities),
- Total assets,
- Bonds and other material long-term liabilities outstanding,
- Total equity and
- Other material facts necessary to make the GPFS/CUFS not misleading.

Related Party Transactions. SFAS No. 57, *Related Party Disclosures,* requires certain disclosures of related party transactions. SFAS No. 57 requires disclosure of a description of the relationship and of the transactions, their dollar amounts, and the amounts due from or due to the related party. When the report preparer believes a related party transaction exists, the relationship between the reporting entity and the related party first should be evaluated using the criteria of the 1987 *Codification,* Section 2100, to ensure that the related party is not to be included as part of the reporting entity.

Contingent Liabilities. The 1987 *Codification,* Section C50.108, recognizes the requirements of SFAS No. 5, *Accounting for Contingencies,* for the disclosure of loss contingencies. When a loss contingency exists, the likelihood that the future event or events will confirm the loss or impairment of an asset, or the incurrence of a liability, can range from probable to remote. SFAS No. 5 classifies the ranges as follows:

Probable—the future event or events are likely to occur.

Reasonably possible—the chance of the future event or events occurring is more than remote but less than likely.

Remote—the chance of the future event or events occurring is slight.

Under SFAS No. 5, when it is reasonably possible that a contingent liability may result in a loss, this fact should be disclosed in the notes to the financial statements. Generally, pending litigation and the potential loss of grant funds resulting from a pending grant audit are the most common contingencies disclosed.

When the chance of a contingent liability resulting in a loss is only remote, no disclosure is ordinarily necessary. Nevertheless, when a government guarantees indebtedness, this fact should be disclosed even if the chance of actual loss is considered remote when applying the criteria of SFAS No. 5.

Joint Ventures. The 1987 *Codification,* Section J50.103, requires the inclusion of the following disclosures within the notes to the financial statements when this information is not displayed on the financial statements.

- A general description of each joint venture that includes:
  —Identifying the participants and their percentage shares.
  —Describing the arrangements for selecting the governing body or management.
  —Disclosing the degree of control the participants have over budgeting and financing.
- Condensed or summary financial information for each joint venture, including:
  —Balance sheet date
  —Total assets, liabilities and equity
  —Total revenues, expenditures/expenses, other financing sources (uses), and net increase (decrease) in fund balance/retained earnings
  —Reporting entity's share of assets, liabilities, equity, and changes therein during the year, if known
- Joint venture debt, both current and long-term, and the security for the debt.

Extraordinary Items. APB Opinion No. 30, provides guidance regarding what data need to be reported as extraordinary items. When such events or transactions occur, they should be explained in the notes. The most common extraordinary items applicable to governments are advance bond refundings which are normally presented with the other debt disclosures.

Prior Period Adjustments. SFAS No. 16 and the GASB pronouncement transition language provide general guidance on the proper use of prior period adjustments. Such adjustments, whether resulting from the correction of an error or the implementation of a new authoritative standard, should be explained in the notes.

Subsequent Events. The government should disclose any significant events directly affecting it that occur between the end of the period covered by the financial statements and the statement completion date. The two items normally included in this disclosure are the issuance of debt and the settlement of material litigation.

Other Employee Benefits. Governments often disclose details of various employee benefits other than the pension plans.

Deferred Compensation Plans—The 1987 *Codification*, Section D25, requires the following disclosures of governments participating in a deferred compensation plan under the provisions of Internal Revenue Code (IRC) Section 457:

- The IRC Section 457 requirement that the plan assets remain the property of the employer, subject to the claims of the employer's general creditors, until paid or made available to the participating employees;
- A statement of the employer's fiduciary responsibilities under the plan;
- Any use of plan assets for purposes other than the payment of benefits; and
- Those plan assets to which the administering government has legal access in multi-jurisdictional plans.

A summary of requirements for eligibility is also an appropriate disclosure for such plans.

Postretirement Benefits—SFAS No. 81, *Disclosure of Postretirement Health Care and Life Insurance Benefits*, requires that governments offering their employees certain postretirement health and life insurance benefits provide the following disclosures:

- A description of the benefits and employee groups covered;
- The employer's accounting and funding policies for the benefits; and
- The cost of benefits recognized during the period.

As discussed earlier, the SSAP should include the accounting policy for compensated absences, consistent with the 1987 *Codification*, Section C60. However, a detailed disclosure could be presented that explains how employees earn benefits and when they are paid. Optionally, this additional information could be joined with the accounting policy disclosure in the SSAP.

Pensions. Current practice allows PERS considerable latitude in the selection of a method of financial information presentation. As discussed later in this chapter, the 1987 *Codification*, Section P20.102, provides PERS with three different options for reporting pension-related balances and activities in their financial statements. Regardless of the method of pension presentation selected, all PERS and government employers are subject to a common set of disclosure requirements set forth in the 1987 *Codification*, Sections P20 and Pe6.

Standardized Measure of Pension Obligation—Several important features of this guidance should be noted. First, the GASB mandates the use of a standardized measure of the

pension obligation for disclosure in the notes to the financial statements. This measure, known as the actuarial present value (APV) of credited projected benefits or pension benefit obligation (PBO), is calculated using the projected unit credit actuarial cost method. Previous to this guidance, pension note disclosures have included information from whatever actuarial method was used to determine funding levels. Because governments generally do *not* use the projected unit credit method for funding purposes, actuarial valuations will have to be expanded in many instances to provide the additional information. Therefore, to avoid placing an undue burden on smaller plans and employers, the 1987 *Codification*, Sections P20 and Pe6, exempt certain single-employer PERS and related employers from the requirement to use the standardized measure of the pension obligation. When a single-employer PERS covers less than 100 current employees, and the employer has fewer than 200 total current employees, the actuarial accrued liability measure may be produced as a by-product of the actuarial funding method, provided one of three acceptable alternatives is used for funding (i.e., projected unit credit, entry age normal, attained age).

Timing of Actuarial Valuation and Updating—A second important feature of the guidance on disclosure provided in the 1987 *Codification*, Sections P20 and Pe6, is the provision regarding the timing of actuarial valuations and updates. The GASB's disclosure guidance requires that an actuarial valuation be performed at least once every two years. In years when an actuarial valuation is not required, an actuarial update is mandated. Actuarial valuations must always be performed in years when actuarial assumptions or plan benefits change. Once again, to avoid unduly burdening smaller plans and employers, the GASB chose to waive the requirement for actuarial updates when the PERS covers less than 100 current employees and the employer has less than 200 total current employees.

Trend Data—A third notable feature of the disclosure requirements set forth in the 1987 *Codification*, Sections P20 and Pe6, is the provision requiring the presentation of, or reference to, certain 10-year trend data. Also, in certain cases, three years of trend data is required to be presented in the notes to the financial statements. The board has designated the 10-year trend data as required supplementary information. Although outside the scope of the auditor's opinion, it is still subject to certain prescribed procedures. Trend data presented in the notes to the financial statements, on the other hand, is within the scope of the auditor's opinion on the basic financial statements.

Disclosure Categories—The detail of required pension disclosures varies greatly, depending on the character of the PERS and the type of benefit provided to employees. Therefore, it is important for financial statement preparers to clearly identify which of the four major categories is applicable to their particular situation before attempting to prepare note disclosures.

The first variable in determining the proper disclosure category is the type of benefit provided to employees. Most traditional plans promise employees some sort of defined benefit upon retirement (e.g., annuity based on salary and years of service). Such "defined benefit" plans can serve either a single employer or several employers. Multiple-employer PERS, in turn, are of two types. In some situations, the employees of all participating governments are placed in a common pool and a single actuarial valuation is made of the entire PERS.

These arrangements are known in the GASB literature as "cost-sharing" PERS. In other multiple-employer PERS, there is a separate actuarial valuation for each employer so that the PERS essentially functions as an aggregation of separate plans. These plans are referred to as "agent" PERS by the GASB.

Defined contribution plans have become increasingly popular in the public sector. Under these plans, the employer's commitment is not to a defined benefit upon retirement, but only to provide regular contributions. The benefits payable upon retirement depend upon the performance of the PERS' portfolio.

Having identified pension plans by the type of benefit offered, number of participating employers and number of actuarial valuations, the financial statement preparer should be able to classify pension arrangements into one of the following four disclosure categories:

1. An employer participating in a single-employer PERS or in a multiple-employer agent PERS;
2. An employer participating in a multiple-employer cost-sharing PERS;
3. An employer participating in a defined contribution plan; or
4. Separately issued reports of PERS and single-employer PERS included in an employer's CAFR as part of the reporting entity.

Disclosure requirements for categories 1 through 3 will be discussed in the remainder of this section. The special disclosure requirements of category 4 will be dealt with later in this chapter.

Category 1: The disclosure requirements for employers contributing to single-employer PERS and multiple-employer agent PERS are similar to those discussed later in this chapter applicable to PERS reporting.

To provide the reader of the financial statements with the background needed to understand these plans, the first section of the disclosure should contain:

- An identification of the PERS to which contributions are made as single employer or agent multiple-employer PERS;
- The amount of the employer's current-year covered payroll and the employer's total current-year payroll for all employees;
- A brief statement about types of employees covered, benefit provisions, employee eligibility requirements including eligibility for vesting and the authority under which benefit provisions are established; and
- Employee and employer obligations to contribute to the plan and the authority under which those obligations are established.

The next major section of the disclosure is devoted to providing the reader with an understanding of the funding status and progress of the plans. This goal is achieved by comparing obligations and resources associated with the plans to determine if the PERS are adequately funded.

This section should contain an explanation of the PBO. The 1987 *Codification*, Section P20.123 c (1), provides language that can be used in the notes for this purpose. This section should also contain the date of the actuarial valuation that was used to calculate the PBO, as well as significant actuarial assumptions that were used, including:

- The rate of return on investment of present and future assets and
- Projected salary increases due to inflation, merit or seniority, and postretirement benefit increases.

The PBO should then be presented, both in total and divided into the following categories:

- Retirees and beneficiaries currently receiving benefits and terminated employees entitled to benefits but not yet receiving them;
- Accumulated employee contributions for current employees, including allocated investment income, if any;
- Employer-financed vested benefits for current employees; and
- Employer-financed nonvested benefits for current employees.

Net assets available for benefits should also be presented, as of the same date as the PBO, valued as on the PERS' balance sheet (with the method disclosed). When market value is not used to value the assets, it still must be disclosed.

The difference between the net assets available for benefits and the PBO should then be disclosed. This should produce either an amount of "assets in excess" of the PBO, or an "unfunded" PBO.

Finally, the separate dollar effect on the PBO of any current-year changes in either actuarial assumptions or benefit provisions should be reported.

The third major section of the disclosure is designed to provide readers with information on the contribution required and the contribution actually made by the employer and employees. When an actuarial funding method is used to establish the contribution requirements for a plan, the following should be disclosed:

- The actuarial funding method and the period for amortizing any unfunded actuarial accrued liability;
- A statement that significant actuarial assumptions used to compute actuarially determined contribution requirements are the same as those used to compute the pension benefits earned or an explanation of the differences;
- The actuarially determined contribution requirements and amounts intended to cover normal cost and amortize any unfunded actuarial accrued liability. Also, the contributions actually made by the employer and employees, expressed in both dollar amounts and as percentages of current-year covered payroll; and
- Separate dollar effects on contribution requirements of any current-year change in actuarial assumptions, actuarial funding methods or benefit provisions.

When contribution requirements are *not* actuarially determined, the following alternative disclosures would be made:

- The fact that the contribution requirement was not actuarially determined;
- How the requirement was established;
- Whether an actuary was used to determine the actuarial

implications of the requirement and what those implications are;

- The amount of the contribution requirement and the contributions actually made by employers and employees expressed as percentages of current-year covered payroll;
- The separate dollar effects on contributions required, of any current-year changes in the method used to calculate or establish contribution requirements, for example, a change in the law.

The 1987 *Codification*, Section P20.123, also requires three years of certain trend data in the notes to the financial statements in most instances (see 1987 *Codification*, Section P20.128):

- Net assets available for benefits, expressed as percentages of the PBO applicable to the entity's employees;
- The unfunded PBO or the assets in excess of the PBO, expressed as percentages of annual covered payroll; and
- Employer contributions expressed as percentages of annual covered payroll. This disclosure should state whether contributions were made in accordance with actuarially determined requirements.

As mentioned earlier, most governments would not be expected to have information on the PBO for years prior to the enactment of this disclosure guidance. Therefore, the GASB requires presentation of the three year's of trend data on a *prospective* basis (i.e., one year's information in the first year of implementation, two years' information in the second year, etc.).

The 1987 *Codification*, Section P20.124, also requires that the reader have access, on a prospective basis, to 10 years of certain trend information:

- Net assets available for benefits (as of date of the PBO), using the same asset valuation method (e.g., cost, market) as the PERS' balance sheet;
- The PBO;
- Net assets available for benefits as a percentage of the PBO;
- Unfunded PBO or assets in excess of the PBO;
- Annual covered payroll; and
- Unfunded PBO or assets in excess of the PBO, expressed as a percentage of annual covered payroll.

Access to this information can be provided to the reader in one of three ways. First, when this information is presented in a publicly available, separately issued PERS report, reference can be made in the government's notes to the availability of that report. When a separate PERS report does not contain the information, it could be presented in the statistical section of the CAFR/CUFR. When a CAFR/CUFR is not issued, the information should be presented with the GPFS/CUFS, immediately following the notes to the financial statements as required supplementary information. Whether this required supplementary information is presented in the statistical section of the CAFR/CUFR or immediately following the notes to the financial statements in the GPFS/CUFS, the auditor still is required to perform certain prescribed procedures. Illustration 14-3 presents an example of this trend information.

When an employer includes a single-employer PERS as a pension trust fund of its reporting entity, both the category 1

disclosures, just described, and the category 4 disclosures, described later in this chapter, would apply. Because the disclosure requirements are largely similar for the two categories, these disclosures should be combined rather than duplicated.

Category 2: Employers contributing to a cost-sharing multiple-employer PERS are required to provide the following summarized disclosures:

- Identification of the PERS as a cost-sharing multiple-employer PERS;
- Amount of employer's current-year covered payroll and the employer's total current-year payroll for all employees;
- Brief statement about employees covered, benefit provisions and employee eligibility requirements;
- Employer's and employee's obligations to contribute and the authority under which those obligations are established;
- The actuarially determined employer's contribution requirement and the employer and employee contribution actually made, expressed in both dollar amounts and percentages of the employer's current-year payroll; also, disclose any current-year changes in actuarial assumptions, benefit provisions, and actuarial funding method or other significant factors and the aggregate effect on the employer's contribution rate;
- An explanation of the PBO;
- The total PERS' PBO and the total PERS' net assets available for benefits as of the same date;
- The employer's actuarially determined contribution requirement, expressed as a percentage of the total of the current-year actuarially determined employer contribution requirement for all employers;
- Reference to 10-year historical trend data in separately issued PERS report.

Category 3: The note disclosures required for employers contributing to a defined contribution plan are as follows:

- Identification of the plan to which contributions are made as a defined contribution plan;
- The employer's total current-year payroll for all employees and its current-year covered payroll for employees covered by the plan;
- Employee and employer obligations to contribute and the authority under which those obligations are established including a brief statement about plan provisions and eligibility requirements;
- Employer contribution requirement and the contribution actually made, expressed both in dollar amounts and percentages of the employer's current-year covered payroll;
- The effects of any current-year changes in plan provisions.

Pension—Other Required Disclosures. The 1987 *Codification*, Section P20, also includes disclosure requirements for special PERS funding situations. Those situations include the following:

- Government employers that are not legally responsible for making contributions to a PERS, but whose employees are covered by a PERS because of contributions made by another entity;
- Government entities legally responsible for making contri-

ILLUSTRATION 14–3

Statewide PERS
Required Supplementary Information
Analysis of Funding Progress
(in millions of dollars)

Fiscal Year	(1) Net Assets Available for Benefits*	(2) Pension Benefit Obligation	(3) Percentage Funded (1) ÷ (2)	(4) Unfunded Pension Benefit Obligation (2) − (1)	(5) Annual Covered Payroll	(6) Unfunded Pension Benefit Obligation as a Percentage of Covered Payroll (4) ÷ (5)
19W2	$ 15.0	$ 34.4	43.6%	$19.4	$ 50.6	38.3%
19W3	21.8	42.6	51.2	20.8	60.1	34.6
19W4	29.1	54.0	53.9	24.9	69.5	35.8
19W5	37.4	64.0	58.4	26.6	82.0	32.4
19W6	48.1	75.8	63.5	27.7	97.3	28.5
19W7	60.5	88.2	68.6	27.7	108.4	25.6
19W8**	76.8	109.0	70.5	32.2	124.4	25.9
19W9	94.8	124.5	76.1	29.7	142.3	20.9
19X0	118.2	147.0	80.4	28.8	169.4	17.0
19X1	148.6	167.6	88.7	19.0	191.9	9.8

Analysis of the dollar amounts of net assets available for benefits, pension benefit obligation, and unfunded pension benefit obligation in isolation can be misleading. Expressing the net assets available for benefits as a percentage of the pension benefit obligation provides one indication of Statewide's funding status on a going-concern basis. Analysis of this percentage over time indicates whether the system is becoming financially stronger or weaker. Generally, the greater this percentage, the stronger the PERS. Trends in unfunded pension benefit obligation and annual covered payroll are both affected by inflation. Expressing the unfunded pension benefit obligation as a percentage of annual covered payroll approximately adjusts for the effects of inflation and aids analysis of Statewide's progress made in accumulating sufficient assets to pay benefits when due. Generally, the smaller this percentage, the stronger the PERS.

* At cost.

** In fiscal year 19W8, plan benefit provisions were amended to retroactively increase benefits from 0.9 percent of final average salary to 1.0 percent. The amendment had the effect of increasing the pension benefit obligation in 19W8 by $4.5 million.

Source: GASB Statement No. 5.

butions to a PERS to cover the employees of another employer; and

• Employers that maintain defined benefit pension arrangements which are not funded.

Other Note Disclosure Illustrations. In addition to the illustrative note disclosures included in appendix D, see GFOA's Financial Reporting Series Volume 1, *Illustrations of Notes to the Financial Statements of State and Local Governments.*

Combining and Individual Fund Statements and Schedules. The remainder of the financial section of a CAFR/CUFR, following the GPFS/CUFS, is segregated into separate subsections for each fund type in use and both account groups. Financial data for all funds included in each fund type should be presented within a specific subsection of the CAFR/CUFR for that fund type. Even if some of the data are outside the scope of the audit and only receive "in relation to" coverage (see chapter 15) by the auditor, the data generally should be presented within the subsection.

Combining Statements—General. Columnar combining statements should be presented for each fund type (e.g., special revenue fund) for which the government maintains more than one individual fund. Combining statements are required for balance sheets, operating statements and statements of changes in financial position. However, combining statements are not required for the budgetary comparison presentations (i.e., budget to actual). All of the combining statements for a particular fund type should be presented first in the subsection devoted to that fund type and followed by separate statements and schedules presented for any of the individual funds. For example, if a government has two internal service funds, a fleet management fund and a management information systems fund, the three combining statements (i.e., balance sheet, operating statement and statement of changes in financial position) should be presented before those of the individual funds. Individual statements of the fleet management fund should be grouped separately from those of the management information systems fund. The individual fund statements should only be presented in the GPFS/CUFS when a government chooses to take the option of limiting the disclosure of enterprise fund segment information in the notes by reporting multiple enterprise funds in the combined proprietary operating statement and combined statement of changes in financial position. Total columns should be included on all combining statements by fund type and should agree with the amounts reported for that fund type in the GPFS/CUFS. The government should refrain from caption-ing such total columns "memorandum only." Prior year's amounts for the fund type may be presented for comparative purposes.

The government may present more detailed account caption information on the combining statements than is presented on the GPFS/CUFS. In these instances, it may be appropriate in certain circumstances (e.g., details presented for a number of accounts) to subtotal the additional detail. These subtotals facilitate the tracing of related amounts from the combining statements by fund type to the GPFS/CUFS. The titles for these statements also should be consistent with the related GPFS/CUFS.

When many funds of one fund type are in use, or there are distinctions within fund types, it may be useful to have an intermediate combining statement presentation. Trust and agency funds are an example of the latter situation since they comprise accrual basis pension and nonexpendable trust funds, modified accrual basis expendable trust funds and nonoperating agency funds. If intermediate combining statements are not needed for each subtype, each individual fund column on the combining statement should be labeled so the reader can determine the subtype of which it is a part. In any event, totals appearing in the GPFS/CUFS should be traceable to the total columns on a combining statement.

Although no operating statement is applicable to agency funds, a combining statement of changes in assets and liabilities should be presented for agency funds. The presentation provides the financial statement user with the information necessary to assess the volume of agency fund activities.

Individual Fund Statements and Schedules. The individual fund statements and schedules should be sequenced in the same order as they appear from left to right on the combining statements. For example, if a water and sewer fund is presented before the golf course fund in the combining statements, the individual statements of the water and sewer fund would be presented before those of the golf course.. Governments, however, need not present physically separate individual fund financial statements that display only duplicate information already available on the combined or combining fund statements.

Individual fund statements and schedules generally are only presented for budgetary comparisons, comparative data and when additional detail is not presented on one of the higher levels of reporting.

The 1987 *Codification,* Section 2400.112, allows governments to prepare separately bound budgetary reports when the level of budgetary control is so detailed that its presentation would detract from the CAFR/CUFR presentation. When a separate budgetary report is prepared, the notes to the GPFS/CUFS should make reference to that report and its availability. In these instances, the CAFR/CUFR still should contain individual fund budgetary comparison statements or schedules with account classifications aggregated beyond the legal level of budgetary control but not beyond the level presented in the GPFS/CUFS. This type of aggregated presentation is limited primarily to state governments and complex local governments where budgetary comparison statements or schedules presenting the legal level of budgetary control would significantly increase (e.g., double) the size of the CAFR/CUFR.

Statistical Section. The third section of the CAFR/CUFR contains comprehensive statistical data for the government.

It is intended to provide CAFR/CUFR users with a broader understanding of the government and the trends in its financial affairs than is possible from the financial statements and supporting schedules included in the financial section alone. Most of the data included in the statistical section are easily convertible to official statement use for governments issuing debt.

A distinguishing characteristic of the statistical section is the fact that its data usually will cover a period of time up to 10 years. Another distinguishing feature is that some of the data—physical, economic and social in nature—are derived from sources outside the formal accounts maintained by the government. In contrast to financial section information, statistical section data usually are not susceptible to independent audit.

The 1987 *Codification,* Section 2800.103, identifies 15 statistical tables that should be included in the CAFR/CUFR unless they clearly are inapplicable in the circumstances.

1. General governmental expenditures by function—last 10 fiscal years
2. General governmental revenues by source—last 10 fiscal years
3. Property tax levies and collections—last 10 fiscal years
4. Assessed and estimated actual value of taxable property—last 10 fiscal years
5. Property tax rates—all overlapping governments—last 10 fiscal years
6. Principal taxpayers
7. Special assessment billings and collections—last 10 fiscal years (if the government is obligated in some manner for related special assessment debt)
8. Computation of legal debt margin
9. Ratio of net general bonded debt to assessed value and net bonded debt per capita—last 10 fiscal years
10. Ratio of annual debt service for general bonded debt to total general expenditures—last 10 fiscal years
11. Computation of overlapping debt
12. Revenue bond coverage—last 10 fiscal years
13. Demographic statistics
14. Property value, construction and bank deposits—last 10 fiscal years
15. Miscellaneous statistics

These tables often are referred to by these numbers throughout this discussion.

As previously mentioned, governments should include only those tables that are applicable. For example, when a government has no legal debt margin, it is not necessary that a separate page be included in the CAFR/CUFR indicating that no legal debt margin exists. When disclosure is considered desirable, a comment on the statistical section divider page indicating that a particular required table is not applicable is appropriate.

Although most governments currently present statistical section tables in the same order as listed in the 1987 *Codification,* Section 2800.103, consideration should be given to organizing the statistical section by topic (e.g., revenue /expenditures, taxes, and assessments, long-term debt and other) for a more coherent presentation. Appendix D of this text illustrates the topical approach.

The first two tables identified in the 1987 *Codification,* Section 2800.103, present 10-year trend data for general governmental expenditures and general governmental revenues. The first table highlights changes in the government's spending patterns. The table should indicate clearly the source of the "general governmental" expenditure data presented (e.g., government's general fund only, all of its governmental funds). The inclusion of a total column in the expenditure table is recommended. Normally, the data in this table is classified by major function.

When other financing uses are presented, this distinction should be made in the formatting of the data and be reflected in the table caption. If the basis of accounting has changed or the expenditure classifications have changed during the 10 years presented, these changes should be noted clearly on the table.

The second table presents 10-year trend data for recurring general revenues by source. This table highlights changes in the composition of the government's revenue sources (e.g., change from reliance on state and federal aid to increased dependence on local sources). When a single revenue source constitutes a major portion of the government's revenues, a more detailed disclosure in a separate table is appropriate (e.g., taxes). An example of general governmental tax revenues by source—last 10 fiscal years table is presented in appendix D. A total column for both these revenue tables assists reader analysis.

When other financing sources are presented, this distinction should be made in the formatting of the data and be reflected in the table caption. If the basis of accounting has changed or the revenue sources have changed during the 10 years presented, these changes should be noted clearly on the table.

Another table not required by the 1987 *Codification* but of particular interest to bond analysts presents year-end unreserved fund balances compared to annual expenditures for the general fund. This presentation illustrates the relationship of the appropriable fund equity as compared to the current year's expenditure amounts. This table is *not* presented in appendix D.

The next group of tables normally included in the statistical section presents data on property taxes and special assessments that are useful to investors and potential investors in assessing the relative attractiveness of the reporting government's securities compared to alternative investment possibilities.

Table 3 includes property tax levies and collections for the past 10 years. Only taxes levied for the reporting entity should be included in this table. Sometimes this table is presented by tax year rather than fiscal year when the years differ. In this instance, the period presented (tax year) should be clearly identified in the table's title. This table usually includes the percentage of current year's taxes collected in the current year, the total and percentage of delinquent taxes collected and the total outstanding delinquent taxes in the years reported. The outstanding delinquent taxes should agree with the presentation in the financial statements and normally are calculated by taking the prior year's outstanding amount plus the current year's levy minus current and delinquent tax collections during the year. This amount may differ when the delinquent receivables are written off during the year.

Table 4 includes the assessed and estimated actual value of taxable property. This table should include the ratio of total assessed value to estimated actual value for real and personal property. Any property tax exemptions also should

be included in this calculation. When the property is assessed at 100 percent of market value, the estimated actual value column may be eliminated if the assessed value column clearly is identified as representing market value.

Table 5 includes property tax rates for all overlapping governments. The table should indicate clearly if tax rates are expressed in "per $100" or "per $1,000" of assessed valuation. Often the government presents its own tax rates in this table. When the government's tax rates are presented, the tables should identify that "direct" rates have been incorporated. In addition, the government's rates presented on this table multiplied by the adjusted assessed valuation should equal the total tax levy for the year. When separate tax rates are levied for special purposes (e.g., operating versus debt service), this fact may be disclosed on the table. Also, when a number of overlapping governments have insignificant tax rates, they may be grouped in a single column under the caption "other." All of these variations are illustrated in appendix D.

Table 6 lists the 10 largest taxpayers in the reporting government's jurisdiction. This table is intended to indicate the extent to which the government is dependent upon a limited number of taxpayers for its operating resources. This table generally presents data on property taxpayers, because property taxes are usually the single largest tax revenue source of local governments. Both the amount of assessed valuation and percentage of total assessed valuation for each primary taxpayer should be presented. When a government (e.g., state) is dependent upon a limited number of income taxpayers or sales taxpayers, then comparable tables representing information for those types of taxes would be appropriate, when the statutes allow the publication of such information. A table of the 10 largest employers, presenting the number of employees in the government's jurisdiction, may be substituted if income or sales tax information cannot be disclosed.

Table 7 presents 10-year trend data reflecting the government's historical experience with special assessment financing. The 1987 *Codification*, Section S40.125, requires the table to include special assessment billings and collections of those billings for the past 10 fiscal years. This table should be presented only when the government is obligated in some manner for the related special assessment debt.

Table 8 illustrates the computation of a government's legal debt margin, which is the maximum amount of debt that a government legally is permitted to issue. A local government's legal debt margin is its debt limitation (normally a percentage of assessed valuation) less the net amount of debt applicable to the limitation (i.e., gross debt less nonapplicable debt and debt service fund amounts available for debt repayment). Statutes and/or ordinances should be reviewed as to the status of capital leases, special revenue debt and other debt in relation to the debt limitations.

Table 9 presents the ratio of net general bonded debt to assessed value and net bonded debt per capita. This table includes a calculation of net bonded debt (i.e., gross general obligation debt less amounts available for repayment of the debt in the governmental funds and general obligation debt payable not expected to be repaid through general governmental resources) that should be traceable to the appropriate amounts in the financial statements. In addition, the population used in the debt per capita computation should agree with the presentation in Table 13 and the assessed value should agree with Table 4.

Table 10 includes the ratio of annual debt service (i.e., debt service principal and interest) for general bonded debt to total general expenditures. This table should indicate clearly the fund or fund types comprising the total "general" expenditure data. The general expenditures here normally will agree with a related amount in the "general governmental expenditures" table disclosed earlier in this chapter. The debt principal and interest expenditures included in this table should be for debt which is tax supported. When general obligation debt is supported fully by enterprise fund revenues, it should not be included in this table.

The CAFR/CUFR debt statistical tables should indicate clearly what reported general obligation debt amounts are included (e.g., only bonded debt, thereby excluding long-term general obligation notes and warrants, and lease/purchase agreements; only general obligation debt intended to be repaid with property tax proceeds).

Table 11 presents the computation of direct and overlapping debt. This table includes the debt for the reporting entity as well as any debt from overlapping governments. The computation is intended to demonstrate the total property tax burden on the taxpayers within the reporting government's geographic jurisdiction and the total debt that their property taxes will be expected to repay. A common format includes the columns presenting the government's and overlapping jurisdictions' net outstanding debt and the percentage and amount of debt applicable to the government. The table should specify consistently either gross debt or net debt. When the reporting entity has numerous overlapping entities with insignificant amounts of debt, they may be grouped as long as the overlapping debt has been computed separately for each unit of government and then totaled for the presentation.

Table 12 indicates the past performance of the government's enterprise operations in meeting outstanding revenue bond repayment requirements. The revenue bond indenture ordinarily includes a pledge by the issuer to establish and maintain rates and charges at levels at least sufficient to meet specified debt service coverage requirements. Often, excess coverage is required. This required coverage customarily is expressed in terms of annual debt service (i.e., principal and interest), either for the succeeding year, the peak year, or the average annual debt service. Generally, net revenues represent the regular recurring operating income remaining after provisions for operating and maintenance expenses. It is customary to begin with net income and add back depreciation and interest expense. However, nonrecurring items of revenue or expense generally are not included in determining net revenue available for debt service. A revenue bond coverage table is normally required for each revenue bond issuance unless the bonds are paid from combined revenue sources.

The balance of the required tables are considered miscellaneous tables. Table 13 presents demographic statistics useful in analyzing the social and economic characteristics of the government's constituency. The demographic data should include the population, per capita income, the median age of the population, the years of formal schooling, school enrollment and the government's unemployment rate. This information is intended to indicate whether a community is expanding or contracting, becoming older or younger, and becoming wealthier or poorer. Some governments may have difficulty obtaining demographic information corresponding exactly to their geographic boundaries. Such data often are compiled only for standard metropolitan statistical areas. In such instances, governments should disclose the best available information, and clearly explain the extent to which the data relate to areas not sharing the same boundaries.

Table 14 presents information on property values (i.e., taxable less exemptions), the estimated value of new commercial and residential construction, and bank deposits within the reporting government's jurisdiction. This information is intended to indicate the growth or contraction of the government's property tax base and the relative wealth of the community. The bank deposits information should include amounts on deposit in financial institutions located within the geographic boundaries of the reporting entity. The amount of bank deposits reported should be those as of the end of the reporting entity's fiscal year, or monthly or quarterly averages.

The miscellaneous statistics (i.e., Table 15) present data on the physical, historical, geographic, social, census and economic statistical data that reflect the scope of the government's activities and functions, its organizational structure and legal environment. This nonfinancial data is intended for use in combination with the CAFR's/CUFR's financial data to facilitate economic and fiscal analysis of management and organizational performance and the government's financial viability.

The CAFR/CUFR should indicate clearly the source of statistical section data presented. This is especially important where data for different years has been derived from different sources. The CAFR/CUFR also should indicate clearly the extent to which presented data includes estimates.

For detailed examples of statistical section presentations, see GFOA's Financial Reporting Series Volume 3, *Illustrations of Statistical Sections of Comprehensive Annual Financial Reports of State and Local Governments*.

PUBLIC EMPLOYEE RETIREMENT SYSTEM (PERS) FINANCIAL REPORTING

Pension system financial reporting has received a significant amount of attention from both the GASB and the FASB during the past several years. Although a basic model has been developed in the commercial sector after 10 years of deliberations, a final set of standards has not yet been developed in the public sector. Based on the 1987 *Codification*, Section Pe5.102, the following three pronouncements are considered sources of authoritative accounting guidance for PERS.

a. NCGA Statement 1, *Governmental Accounting and Financial Reporting Principles*. (The material contained in the 1968 *GAAFR* may be considered illustrative of NCGA Statement 1 to the extent such material is consistent with NCGA Statement 1.)
b. NCGA Statement 6, *Pension Accounting and Financial Reporting: Public Employee Retirement Systems and State and Local Government Employers*.
c. SFAS No. 35, *Accounting and Reporting by Defined Benefit Pension Plans*.

The basic elements of these pronouncements were reviewed in chapter 10. This section primarily will highlight the variations between a separately issued PERS CAFR/CUFR and the general government's CAFR/CUFR.

Financial Section. Although the contents of the PERS letter of transmittal will be different from that of a general government, the first major variation is encountered in the supplementary statements and schedules included in the CAFR's/CUFR's financial section.

Required Supplementary Information. PERS reports are required by the 1987 *Codification*, Section Pe6.131, to include 10-year historical trend information as required supplementary information immediately after the notes to the financial statements.

The 1987 *Codification*, Section Pe6.132, provides: The 10-year historical trend information required to be disclosed is:

a. Net assets available for benefits (as of the same date as the pension benefit obligation, and as valued for PERS balance sheet purposes), the pension benefit obligation, and the former expressed as a percentage of the latter; also unfunded [assets in excess of] pension benefit obligation, annual covered payroll, and the former expressed as a percentage of the latter.

b. Revenues by source (employer contributions, employee contributions, investment income, and other income) and expenses by type (benefit payments, administrative expenses, refunds of employee contributions, and other expenses). Except for agent multiple-employer PERS, employer contributions should be expressed both as dollar amounts and as percentages of annual covered payroll. The disclosure should state whether contributions were made in accordance with actuarial requirements. If contributions actually made for particular years differed from actuarial or legal requirements, both the contribution made and the contribution required should be presented for those years.

The timing, nature, and total dollar effect of any changes in actuarial assumptions, benefit provisions, actuarial funding methods, accounting policies, or other factors that significantly affect the information presented in the trend information should be disclosed for the year in which the changes are made.

These tables are required for fiscal years beginning after December 15, 1986. The first table should be prepared on a prospective basis unless the PERS previously calculated the PBO using the actuarial present value of credited projected benefits. Those PERS exempt from the standardized measure requirement (i.e., covering fewer than 100 current employees, the employer has fewer than 200 total current employees and the PERS uses the projected unit credit, entry-age normal or attained-age actuarial funding methods to compute contribution requirements) may use the obligation calculated based on their funding method for these disclosures. If a substitute method is used, it should be disclosed clearly on the table. Revenue and expense data, however, should be presented for the past 10 years.

Schedules. Additional schedules generally included as part of the PERS CAFR/CUFR include Schedule of Administrative Expenses, Investment Summary, Summary Schedule of Cash Receipts and Disbursements and a Summary Schedule of Compensation of Administrative Officials and Commissions and Payments to Brokers and Consultants.

Schedule of Administrative Expenses. The Schedule of Administrative Expenses should include the costs by major category of expense and object of expense (e.g., professional services/actuarial). This schedule may be presented on a comparative basis and should be prepared in a manner that facilitates tracing to the operating statement.

Investment Summary. The Investment Summary schedule provides an overview of the PERS investment activity during the year by significant types of investments (e.g., fixed income/government bonds, short-term investments/commercial paper). The schedule should begin with the carrying amount and market value at the beginning of the year, present the purchases and sales/redemptions of securities during the year, and arrive at the ending balances for carrying and market values. In addition to this activity report, the percentages of the securities held at year end in relation to total market value and yield at market value also should be presented as part of this table.

Summary Schedule of Cash Receipts and Disbursements. The Summary Schedule of Cash Receipts and Disbursements provides details of cash inflows and outflows during the year by major revenue and expense categories (e.g., member contribution refunds). If the PERS Statement of Changes in Financial Position is prepared based on the modified SFAS No. 95 method illustrated in appendix D, the presentation of this schedule would not be necessary.

Summary Schedules of Compensation of Administrative Officials and Commissions and Payments to Brokers and Consultants. The final schedule, Summary Schedule of Compensation of Administrative Officials and Commissions and Payments to Brokers and Consultants, presents information by individual and firm. Administrative officials' titles and salary allowances should be disclosed, along with nature of the brokers' and consultants' services and their fees or commissions.

Actuarial Section. The actuarial section, which normally is presented as the third section of a PERS CAFR/CUFR, should include:

- Actuarial certification letter (including a summary of actuarial assumptions and methods).
- Schedule of Active Member Valuation Data
- Schedule of Retirants and Beneficiaries Added to and Removed from Rolls
- Summary of Accrued and Unfunded Accrued Liabilities (based on actuarial method use for funding purposes)
- Solvency Test
- Schedule of Recommended versus Actual Contributions
- Analysis of Financial Experience (when applicable)

Actuary's Certification Letter (including a Summary of Actuarial Assumptions and Methods). The actuary's certification letter, summary of assumptions and methods, and notes thereto are an integral part of the actuarial section. The combination of the letter and related summary of assumptions and methods should present the overall funding objective of the plan and the progress being made toward that objective. Information regarding the actuarial assumptions and methods also should be presented. This information should include:

- Rate of return on investments;
- Projected salary increases (including inflation and merit portions);
- Acturial method used;
- Mortality table used;
- Assumed retirement age(s);
- Probabilities of withdrawal before retirement at sample ages; and
- Assumed annual percentage rate of increase of active member payroll (if applicable) including growth and inflation portions.

The date that actuarial assumptions were adopted, the determination process (i.e., who approved or selected) and the affect of any assumption changes adopted in the current year also should be disclosed. In addition, the frequency of the actuarial valuations and updates and the date(s) of the latest complete valuation and/or update should be included in this section.

Schedule of Active Member Valuation Data. The Schedule of Active Member Valuation Data should present for the last 10 years the number of active members, the employer's annual payroll for covered employees, the annual average pay and the percentage increase in the average pay from the previous year. This table provides trend information on the growth (reduction) of active member payroll including the percentage rate increase of active member payroll and number of members. This information provides a basis for comparison with the assumed growth rates (if applicable).

Schedule of Retirants and Beneficiaries Added to and Removed from Rolls. Information on the Schedule of Retirants and Beneficiaries Added to and Removed from Rolls provides relevant information on the demographics of the plan. Data for the past 10 years presented in this schedule not only include the number and annual allowances of retirants and beneficiaries added to and deleted from the rolls during the year, but also provides information on the total number and amount of allowances at year end, the percentage of increase in annual allowances from the prior year and the average annual allowance.

Summary of Accrued and Unfunded Liabilities. The Summary of Accrued and Unfunded Liabilities should be presented based on the actuarial funding method (e.g., entry-age normal). This summary provides for the past 10 years the actuarial determined liabilities, the plan assets valued in accordance with the method used for the actuarial valuation (e.g., five-year moving average), plus assets as a percentage of the actuarial liability, the unfunded actuarial liability (i.e., actuarial liability less plan assets), the annual active member payroll for the year and the unfunded actuarial liability as a percentage of active member payroll. The results of this summary provide a basis to assess funding progress for the plan.

Solvency Test. The Solvency Test also should be prepared for the past 10 years using amounts calculated as part of the actuarial valuation. The actuarial liability is divided into amounts related to active member contributions, retirants and beneficiaries, and employer contributions associated with active members. These amounts are then compared to the plan assets and the percentage covered by these assets is presented for all three liability amounts. This test when analyzed also provides information on the plan's funding status.

Schedule of Recommended versus Actual Contributions. The Schedule of Recommended versus Actual Contributions presents for the past five years a comparison of the actual employer contribution rate (employer contributions divided by covered payroll) to the actuarially recommended contribution rate also is presented. These five-year comparisons provide another basis for assessing the funding status of the plan.

Analysis of Financial Experience. The Analysis of Financial Experience is presented in fiscal periods when actuarial gains and losses by activity (e.g., age and service retirants, investment income) are calculated. These gains and losses, which occur when experience differs from the actuarial assumptions that had been used, are segregated from nonrecurring amounts (e.g., adjustments for plan amendments).

Statistical Section. The scope of the PERS CAFR/CUFR statistical section has been reduced with the introduction of the required supplementary information. The statistical section of a PERS should now include the following tables:

- Schedule of Retired Members by Type of Benefit
- Schedule of Investment Results
- Schedule of Average Benefit Payment Amounts
- Schedule of Participating Employers (if applicable)

Schedule of Retired Members by Type of Benefit. The Schedule of Retired Members by Type of Benefit presents the number of retirants at year end by type of retirement (e.g., early retirement, normal retirement, disability retirement) and by the amount of monthly or yearly benefit. Based on the benefit options available this table should be customized to the individual PERS.

Schedule of Investment Results. A schedule of the plan's investment rate of return should be presented for the last five years. This rate should be compared to equivalent industry averages and other relevant information to provide a basis for judging investment return performance. A five-year average comparison also may be presented as part of this table.

Schedule of Average Benefit Payment Amounts. A Schedule of Average Benefit Payment Amounts presents average benefit payments by years of credited service (e.g., 5–10 years). This table also can include the average salary on which benefits are based and the number of retirants by years of credited service. Payments can be presented by annual or monthly amounts and can be compared as a percentage of the benefit base salary.

Schedule of Participating Employers. Multiple-employer PERS should include a listing of the employers that participate in the plan. The listing also could present information on active members and retirants by employer.

CERTIFICATE OF ACHIEVEMENT FOR EXCELLENCE IN FINANCIAL REPORTING

The Certificate of Achievement for Excellence in Financial Reporting Program (certificate program) was established in 1945 by the GFOA to encourage government units to produce and publish excellent CAFRs/CUFRs and to provide educational assistance and well deserved peer recognition to the report preparers. The certificate program is recognized as the highest award in governmental financial reporting.

Government units choosing to participate in the program submit copies of their CAFRs/CUFRs for review by an impartial Special Review Committee (SRC) of qualified judges. Reports meeting program standards are awarded Certificates of Achievement. The CAFR/CUFR generally should demonstrate a constructive "spirit of full disclosure" effort to clearly communicate its financial picture, to enhance understanding of the logic underlying the traditional governmental financial reporting model and to address CAFR/CUFR user needs.

The certificate program is not an accreditation program. Therefore, a unit can neither "lose" a certificate nor can a certificate be "revoked," "cancelled" or "withdrawn." However, the fact that a unit has received a Certificate of Achievement in one or more years is not a guarantee that its subsequent reports will be similarly honored.

A certificate, unlike an independent auditor's report, covers the preceding year's CAFR/CUFR. The program's review of a CAFR/CUFR begins after the unit's report is published. A reproduction of a certificate published in a CAFR/CUFR therefore bears no direct relation to that report's contents. Government units receiving certificates are permitted to reproduce them only in their immediately succeeding CAFR/CUFR provided they also include standard program text to explain the period a certificate covers to the report users.

Benefits of Certificate Program. Benefits likely to be realized by a government unit which submits its CAFR/CUFR to the certificate program include:

Education. Government units participating in the certificate program are provided with a confidential list of detailed comments and suggestions for improvements in their financial reporting techniques.

Recognition. Because the certificate is the highest form of recognition in governmental accounting and financial reporting, its attainment represents a significant accomplishment by a government unit and its management.

Securities Marketing Aid. Reports qualifying for a certificate provide detailed information from which market analysts, investors, potential investors and others may assess the relative attractiveness of a government unit's securities compared to alternative investment possibilities.

Clarity. CAFRs/CUFRs satisfying certificate program requirements are likely to be free of ambiguities and the potential for misleading inferences.

Comparability. Because reports qualifying for a certificate employ standardized terminology and formatting conventions, this comparison is facilitated both from one year to the next and among different units.

Completeness. The financial statements, supporting schedules, statistical tables and narrative explanations required by the certificate program help to assure that information needed by the CAFR/CUFR users is provided. These users include oversight bodies, investors and creditors, citizens, and others.

Eligibility for a Certificate of Achievement. To be eligible for a Certificate of Achievement, a report submitted to the program must be the published CAFR/CUFR of the government unit. A government unit's CAFR/CUFR must include all of its funds and account groups meeting the entity definition criteria and required disclosures set forth in the 1987 *Codification*, Section 2100.

The CAFR/CUFR must be examined by an independent

auditor in accordance with generally accepted auditing standards or generally accepted government auditing standards. Reproductions of the report(s) of the auditor must be incorporated as an integral part of the CAFR/CUFR. The auditor's examination must have included the GFPS/CUFS, and the auditor must have accepted at least "in relation to" responsibility for supplementary data in the financial section.

Disclaimers of opinion on any of the fund types or account groups and auditor's report qualifications resulting from client-imposed scope limitations or the exclusion of a fund type, individual fund or account group will render a CAFR/CUFR ineligible. Report qualifications rendered on the general fixed assets account group, as a result of a lack of detailed fixed asset accounting records, will likewise render a CAFR/CUFR ineligible. The CAFR/CUFR must be mailed to the GFOA within six months of the government unit's fiscal year end to be eligible for review.

Judging the CAFR/CUFR. After a preliminary screening, eligible CAFRs/CUFRs are assigned to two judges who are members of the certificate program's SRC. The SRC membership includes government officials, independent certified public accountants, academicians and others with particular expertise in governmental accounting and financial reporting. The judges operate independently of the GFOA officers and staff.

To qualify for a certificate, a report must receive the approval of both reviewers. Upon the completion of their reviews, the SRC members return their reviews to the GFOA where a program professional staff member conducts an in-house review to assure consistency in the application of program standards.

Results of the Review Process. If a CAFR/CUFR is judged to achieve the highest standards in government accounting and financial reporting, a certificate is awarded to the government unit. When a certificate is awarded to a government unit, an Award of Financial Reporting Achievement also is presented to the individual(s) designated as primarily responsible for the government's having earned the certificate. Additional information on the certificate program is available on request from the GFOA's Technical Services Center.

INTERIM FINANCIAL REPORTS

Interim reports can be defined as financial reports prepared at regular intervals that cover periods shorter than the fiscal year. In the public sector, the most common interim reports are statements presenting financial position at the end of a month or quarter, and comparisons of actual results to budget for a month, quarter or for the year to date. Typically, such reports are prepared primarily for internal use rather than for external financial reporting.

Authoritative literature strongly recommends the use of interim budgetary reports as a means of exercising management control and legislative oversight (1987 *Codification,* Section 2900.102). However, because such reports are typically prepared primarily for internal use, they normally are not subject to GAAP and should take whichever form best serves management and legislative needs. Accordingly, most governments prepare their interim reports on a budgetary basis.

Purposes and Users. The primary purpose of most interim reports is to serve the needs of management. Therefore, a government's interim financial reporting should be judged by how well it functions as a management tool. Sound interim reporting should aid management, not only by providing a basis for evaluating the government's current financial status and results of operations to date, but also by providing information that can be useful in planning future operations.

The principal focus of interim financial statements should be directed toward the control of revenues and expenditures in the primary operating funds. Interim reports should allow government administrators to ensure that estimated revenues are being sufficiently realized to support current operations and that actual expenditures do not exceed legal appropriations. The financial position of these funds during the fiscal year, while also potentially important, is normally of less concern to management in controlling current operations.

Interim budgetary reporting allows management to determine whether curtailments appear necessary for certain budget items or whether transfers or additional appropriations should be sought. A secondary purpose of interim financial reporting is to aid in the preparation of the subsequent year's budget, which is likely to be prepared several months before the next fiscal year begins.

The primary internal users of interim reports are the chief executive officer, the chief operating officer, government managers held accountable for a portion of the budget (e.g., director of public works, police chief, fire chief), the financial accounting administrators and budget department personnel. However, elected officials not involved in the day-to-day management of the government also depend upon interim financial reports to provide them with the information they need to monitor the administration's compliance with budgetary, legal and contractual provisions. In addition, although these reports are not distributed ordinarily beyond the administration and the governing body, they can sometimes be of use to certain parties outside of the government. For example, the securities industry often is interested in interim reports, particularly as these reports relate to proposed government bond offerings.

Types of Interim Reports. Although the interim reporting needs of governments differ, the primary type of interim financial report is an operating statement for governmental fund types that compares estimated revenues with actual, year-to-date revenues and appropriations with actual, year-to-date expenditures and outstanding encumbrances. Many governments prepare all-inclusive budgetary operating statements which include revenues, expenditures, encumbrances and changes in fund equity in a single statement. Other governments present separate statements for revenues and for expenditures supplemented by narratives highlighting and explaining any major variances.

Some governments also prepare analysis of selective balance sheet accounts for informational purposes (e.g., cash and investments by type and location). As previously mentioned, balance sheets are not as important for management control during interim periods for governmental type funds. Interim balance sheets for governmental funds would not usually be pertinent because these funds operate within an annual operating cycle. Nonetheless, governments should consider presenting balance sheets for their proprietary fund types. The use of full accrual accounting in proprietary funds permits meaningful comparisons with prior years. Moreover, the preparation of a balance sheet allows the calculation of selected ratios (e.g.,

working capital) that may be particularly useful for internal management purposes.

Governments also present a wide variety of specialized interim reports, primarily for management's use. These reports may emphasize construction, personnel staffing, utility operating data and miscellaneous data on receivables. Other data commonly presented include cash and investments, cash flow projections, interest earnings, percentage of cash invested, specific revenue sources and grants.

Formats of Interim Reports. The formats and level of detail of interim financial reports should be tailored to meet report users' needs. For instance, the governing body needs information that will allow it to monitor compliance with the budget. Therefore, the level of detail in interim reports prepared for governing bodies should be at least the legal level of budgetary control. When the legal level of budgetary control is by activity and function, the interim financial information should be reported in similar detail. Providing more detailed information would normally not be warranted for governing bodies. Internal budget managers, on the other hand, typically could be expected to need the most detailed level of information available (e.g., function, activity and detailed object classification).

Beside the issue of the appropriate level of detail to present, preparers of interim reports need to consider how formatting the presentation of additional data can enhance the usefulness of their reports. For example, variance columns are normally helpful in conjunction with budgetary comparisons. Also, presenting the percentage of the revenue budget realized and the percentage of the appropriation budget expended and encumbered can facilitate analysis of the information.

Sometimes governments with automated data processing systems use computer printouts as their interim financial reports. Although using computer printouts for interim financial reporting can have distinct advantages, experience has shown that all too often the result can be voluminous, excessively detailed reports that serve more to obscure than to enlighten. Ideally, using computers to generate reports should allow management to provide different users with the varying levels of detail needed for their differing purposes. Used in this way, computer printouts can be an invaluable aid in interim financial reporting.

Narrative Explanations and Graphics Presentations. A narrative supplementing interim financial statement presentations definitely improves the potential for a clear understanding of the data presented. Moreover, such a narrative can assist the finance officer when making presentations at public meetings.

The types of narratives presented will vary based on the financial presentations. The narrative should be organized by fund type, with revenue and expenditure analyses normally placed in a single presentation. The narrative could highlight differences in major revenue sources with detailed explanations describing these differences. The expenditure section of the narrative could be used to describe differences for each functional area.

An emerging trend in both interim and annual financial reporting is the inclusion of graphic presentations. For a nonaccountant, graphic presentations may be easier to understand than financial statements and schedules.

Frequency. Although interim financial reports normally are prepared monthly, in some instances they may be prepared quarterly, semiannually or on some other basis. However, most interim financial statements (particularly the budget-to-actual comparison statements) should be prepared at least monthly.

Interim financial reporting alone is not sufficient to ensure compliance with the budget. Accounting systems should have some type of budgetary control component which will not allow actual expenditures to exceed budgets. A government may control expenditures by reviewing the details of an account at a computer terminal, by reviewing a manual list of purchase orders or just by relying on the responsible individual manager not to exceed the budget.

Timeliness of the interim reports is essential to meet the objectives of interim financial reporting. For example, when a specific line item has been overexpended by the end of the month and the interim report is not prepared for 30 days after the close of the fiscal period, the reporting delay may result in an account being even further overexpended. Therefore, most larger governments try to complete their interim financial statements within 10 to 15 days of the close of the fiscal period. Often interim report preparation is dictated by the meeting cycle of the governing body.

Generally Accepted Accounting Principles. As stated earlier, most interim financial statements are prepared primarily for internal use by management and legislative bodies, and are presented on the budgetary basis rather than in conformity with GAAP. Nonetheless, sometimes governments do choose to issue GAAP-basis interim financial statements for external use. When such external reports are prepared, the guidelines set forth in APB Opinion No. 28, *Interim Financial Reporting,* should be followed. The most important principle set forth in APB Opinion No. 28 is that interim periods are to be treated as integral parts of the fiscal year rather than as separate, autonomous accounting periods. For example, the cumulative effect of a change in accounting principles always would be reported as a change of the first interim period, regardless of the interim period in which the change was actually made. APB Opinion No. 28 also requires that seasonal fluctuations in activity be disclosed.

For detailed examples of interim financial statements see GFOA's Financial Reporting Series Volume 5, *Illustrations of Interim Financial Statement of State and Local Governments.*

CONDENSED SUMMARY DATA (INCLUDING "POPULAR" REPORTS)

Many governments prepare CAFRs/CUFRs as recommended in the 1987 *Codification,* Section 1900.109. In addition to publishing and distributing a CAFR/CUFR, some governments also separately issue their "liftable" GPFS/CUFS. These separately issued GPFS/CUFS are useful for inclusion in official statements related to bond offerings. They also sometimes may be helpful to certain users of the government's financial statements who have less need of detailed information. Few governments, however, avail themselves of a third option, provided in the 1987 *Codification,* Section 2700.104, of reporting financial information on a still higher, more condensed, level. This reluctance to provide condensed summary data or "top of the pyramid" information is unfortunate. For while condensed

summary data are not sufficient to meet the requirements of GAAP, they can be an invaluable means of conveying financial information to the public and to others unfamiliar with government accounting and financial reporting.

Reports presenting condensed summary data, therefore, are designed to meet a special need not satisfied by the more traditional CAFR/CUFR or GPFS/CUFS presentations. These reports by no means should be considered as eliminating the need for GAAP financial reporting; they supplement, rather than supplant, traditional financial statements. To underscore this point, the 1987 *Codification,* Section 2700.104, states that condensed summary data should be reconcilable with the GAAP financial statements and that the reader of these reports should be referred to the CAFR/CUFR or GPFS/CUFS.

Condensed Popular Reports. Reports on condensed summary data, commonly referred to as "popular reports," can take a variety of forms. For example, a few governments issue consolidated financial statements, similar to those proposed by the American Institute of Certified Public Accountants (AICPA) in a project on experimental financial reporting (see *Accounting and Financial Reporting by State and Local Governments—An Experiment.*) Such a consolidated approach replaced the funds and account groups by a single "fund" that is used to report the financial position and results of operations of the entire oversight unit or reporting entity. Intragovernmental transactions are eliminated in the consolidation process and a single basis of accounting (normally accrual) is used for all transactions.

Consolidated financial statements typically include a balance sheet, operating statement and statement of changes in financial position. Because the accrual basis of accounting is normally used, fixed assets are reported in the single fund and depreciated. Also, long-term obligations are reported in the single fund with the result that debt service principal payments are treated as balance sheet rather than operating statement transactions.

A second type of popular report presents condensed, rather than consolidated, financial statements. In some instances, such condensed government financial statements may be simply the "memorandum only" total columns that appear in the GPFS/CUFS. In other cases, a government may choose to eliminate significant interfund transactions from these totals. Whichever approach is taken, the "other debits" reported in the GLTDAG and the "investment in general fixed assets" reported in the GFAAG are *not* eliminated, to avoid a change in total fund equity.

Other types of popular reports also are found at the top of the financial reporting pyramid. These reports may contain detailed narratives of specific activities that occurred during the fiscal period as well as a "state of the government" message. The financial data found in these reports can vary widely. Some present limited financial information in graphic form. Others make use of consolidated financial information, described earlier. Still others use the GPFS/CUFS and other financial presentations to highlight particular financial aspects of the government (e.g., cash flow, tax rates).

Presentation. Glossy report covers, the use of color illustrations and pictures, and typesetting are standard in many popular reports. An attractive report not only can serve as a source of pride for the government and its citizens, but its physical qualities also may be a factor encouraging use of the report by some groups. In addition, a well-produced popular report can have public relations value when dealing with potential employers and residents of the government's geographic area.

A notable trend in popular report preparation is the growing use of charts and graphs to portray the reporting entity's financial position and activities. Graphs are used primarily to depict trends and compare actual and projected data or different aspects of the reporting entity's activities. A number of publications are available to help the report preparer use graphics effectively.

Graphics are particularly useful in extremely condensed popular reports (e.g., four pages) that highlight financial resources and uses.

Although not required by GAAP, reports presenting condensed summary financial data, such as popular reports, can play an important role in a government's financial reporting strategy. While not replacing the need for CAFRs/CUFRs or GPFS/CUFS, these reports do allow governments to convey financial information effectively to groups and individuals less familiar with traditional GAAP financial reporting.

Chapter 15
AUDITING GOVERNMENT ENTITIES

Many groups and individuals have an interest in the financial position, results of operations and performance of government organizations. Audits can provide citizens, legislators, oversight bodies, grantors, creditors and investors with the reasonable assurance they need that a government's financial assertions can be relied upon and that the government is efficiently and effectively carrying out its responsibilities. Audits also can be used to provide management with the information it needs to evaluate its own performance and to take appropriate corrective action to remedy deficiencies in its internal control structure.

An audit* can be defined as a systematic collection of the sufficient, competent evidential matter needed to attest to the fairness of management's assertions in the financial statements, or to evaluate management's efficiency and effectiveness in carrying out its responsibilities. The auditor obtains this evidential matter through inspection, observation, inquiries and confirmations from third parties.

Of course, a knowledge of government auditing standards and of the government audit process is critical for auditors performing engagements in the public sector. But this information also is of great importance to state and local officials responsible for the finances of their governments. Only a thorough familiarity with the audit process and the standards that govern it can provide finance officials with the information they need to obtain the type and quality of audit services their governments require.

ROLE OF THE AUDITOR

Types of Auditors. In the private sector, the distinction between internal and external auditors appears clear. An auditor normally serves either as the internal auditor of a concern or as an independent public accountant. In the public sector, on the other hand, the distinction is often less clear; an auditor can serve in both capacities. For example, an auditor who is an employee of a social welfare agency may regularly perform examinations of the agency's internal control structure to identify weaknesses and to suggest improvements. When performing such examinations, the auditor would be acting as an internal

auditor. The same auditor, on another occasion, could be asked to perform an audit of one of the agency's service providers, perhaps a private concern providing job training to the unemployed. In this capacity, the auditor would be acting as an external auditor. Adding to the potential for ambiguity, auditors in governments sometimes hold the legal title of "internal auditor" even though much or most of their work may be, in fact, external auditing. Therefore, the following definitions should be taken only as an indication of the two conceptually different roles of an auditor in the public sector, not as a description of the work of any given auditor, regardless of title.

"Internal auditors" are employed by the organization they audit and function as an integral part of the organization's control environment. As such, they help management to measure and evaluate the effectiveness of the entity's internal control structure.

"External auditors" are independent of the entities they audit and serve third parties by providing them with an unbiased appraisal of the fairness of management's assertions and the economy and efficiency of its performance.

Independence. Generally accepted government auditing standards (GAGAS), discussed later, make it clear that both the internal and the external auditor need considerable, though differing, degrees of independence from management to perform their roles properly.

Internal auditors, for example, should be free from political pressures that could compromise the impartiality of their audit work and the reports they prepare. To achieve this goal, internal auditors should be provided with the greatest degree of organizational independence possible within the entity they serve. They should be organizationally outside the staff or line management function, and they should be accountable and report directly to the entity's chief executive or deputy chief executive. Moreover, the internal audit function's independence and effectiveness can be enhanced when internal auditors are part of a personnel system that bases compensation, training, job tenure and advancement solely on merit.

External auditors may be either independent public accountants or elected or appointed government officials. In either case, they must be independent, in both fact *and appearance,* to achieve and maintain the confidence of the third parties who will rely on their work. Therefore, both independent public accountants and government auditors must avoid *personal* or

---

*The term "audit" is used in this chapter only to refer to what have traditionally been known as post-audits, the examination of past transactions and events. Pre-audits, the examination of transactions before their completion, are not within the scope of this chapter.

external impairments that reasonably may cause third parties to question their independence. A spouse who serves as an accountant in an agency to be audited would be an example of a personal impairment. Unreasonable restrictions on the time allowed to complete an audit would be an example of an external impairment.

In addition, external government auditors also should avoid *organizational* impairments. A government auditor is considered to be organizationally independent for an engagement if that auditor meets one of the following tests:

1. The entity under audit is on a different level of government from that of the auditor. For example, a federal auditor conducting a performance audit of a state-administered grant program would be considered independent because the auditor represents the federal government and the government being audited is a state. Similarly, an internal auditor of a state agency examining a county or municipality would be considered independent.

2. The entity under audit is a different branch of the government from that of the auditor. For example, an auditor from the legislative branch of a government would be considered independent if auditing an agency in the executive branch of the same government.

3. The auditor is elected by the citizens of the auditor's jurisdiction. For example, a state auditor elected by a vote of the people would be considered independent if auditing any branch of the government.

4. The auditor is elected or appointed by the legislative body of the auditor's level of government and is accountable, and reports the results of the audit, to this same legislative body. For example, if the city council appoints the city auditor, that auditor would be considered independent.

5. The auditor is appointed by the chief executive but is confirmed by the legislative body of the auditor's level of government and is accountable and reports to this same legislative body. For example, if the mayor or city manager nominates the city auditor, who is then confirmed by the city council, that auditor would be considered independent provided the auditor reports and is accountable to the legislative body.

Cooperation Between Internal and External Auditors. Internal auditors lack sufficient independence to be able to attest to third parties that the government's financial statements are presented fairly. However, external auditors may and *should,* to the greatest extent possible, make use of the work of internal auditors to determine the nature, timing and extent of their own auditing procedures. Using the work of internal auditors avoids needless duplication of audit effort and allows for the more efficient use of scarce audit resources. For example, if internal auditors have examined the internal control structure related to a particular grant program, the external auditors should build upon that work when possible, instead of duplicating it. When external auditors make use of the work of internal auditors in this way, the American Institute of Certified Public Accountants' (AICPA) Statement on Auditing Standards (SAS) No. 9, *The Effect of an Internal Audit Function on the Scope of the Independent Auditor's Examination,* provides that they should:

1. Determine that the internal audit staff is competent and qualified,
2. Determine whether the internal audit function is located within the government in such a way as to allow the internal audit staff to perform their work objectively,
3. Determine that the work is acceptable by examining on a test basis the documentary evidence of the work performed.

The external auditor can meet this last requirement either by reexamining some of the items already examined by the internal audit staff or by examining similar items not selected previously by the internal auditor.

Sometimes the request for proposal (RFP), prepared to obtain the services of the external auditor, may offer the direct assistance of internal audit staff. When the internal audit staff is to assist the external auditors directly, SAS No. 9 provides that the external auditors should assure themselves of the internal audit staff's competence and objectivity. Also, the external auditors are responsible for properly supervising and testing the internal auditors' work to the extent they consider appropriate in the circumstances.

NATURE OF THE AUDIT

Types of Audits. Government audits may be classified as either financial audits or performance audits. Traditionally, financial audits have been designed to provide external auditors the sufficient, competent evidential matter they need to form an opinion on the fairness of the presentation of a government's financial statements. Because a government's activities normally are subject to strict legal and regulatory control, the auditor must consider specifically whether the government has complied with those laws and regulations that could have a material adverse effect on the government's financial statements. This special concern with the government's compliance with laws and regulations explains why financial audits of government previously were referred to as financial and compliance audits. Although the terminology has changed, the responsibility has not. In fact, the need to determine compliance with laws and regulations actually has been expanded in certain instances, as will be discussed below.

It is important for users of financial audits to be aware of the audits' limitations. Financial audits are designed to provide *reasonable assurance* that the financial statements are free from material misstatements (intentional or unintentional). Auditors do not assert the absolute accuracy of the information presented, nor do they claim that an audit will disclose all instances of illegal acts.

Performance audits are designed to provide auditors with the sufficient, competent evidential matter needed to assess a government's effectiveness in meeting its responsibilities economically and efficiently. As part of this process, performance auditors seek to determine the cause and suggest potential remedies for ineffectiveness, inefficiencies or uneconomical practices. Because of the special environment of the public sector, the performance auditor, like the financial auditor, should pay special attention to the government's compliance with laws and regulations, especially those concerned with the administration of assistance programs.

Single Audits. One particular type of financial audit is the single audit, mandated for many governments by the provisions of the Single Audit Act of 1984 (Single Audit Act) and its implementing circular, Office of Management and Budget (OMB) Circular A–128, *Audits of State and Local Governments*. Before the acceptance and implementation of the single audit concept, a government receiving aid from several grantor agencies was subject to audit by each grantor. Because of these separate audits, many different auditors could examine and reexamine a single set of financial records and internal control structure for the same period. Single audits are intended to eliminate such duplication of audit effort by providing for only one entitywide audit, specifically designed to meet the needs of all interested parties. Although individual federal grantor agencies still may arrange for additional audit work if they consider it necessary for their purposes, the law requires that any additional work be built upon the single audit. Also, a federal agency that performs or contracts for additional audit work must arrange to fund the costs.

The Single Audit Act specifically applies only to financial audits. Performance auditing is *not* required.

Scope of the Financial Audit. Because the costs involved in a financial audit should not outweigh the benefits to be gained, auditors do not attempt to attest to the absolute accuracy of financial information. Instead, the financial auditor gathers the evidential matter needed to ensure that the financial statements are not *materially* misstated. A problem arises, however, because materiality is normally a relative criterion, i.e., in most instances, something is not material or immaterial in and of itself, but only in relation to something else. What standard or focus then should be used to gauge materiality in audits of government entities? What should be the scope of the financial audit?

In the private sector, the focus of financial audits is traditionally the financial statements "taken as a whole." Using this focus for the audit, an item is material if it would change the overall picture the financial statements present of the entity's financial position and results of operations.

In the public sector, however, the proper focus of the audit has been debated. Appendix B of the Governmental Accounting Standards Board's (GASB) 1987 *Codification of Governmental Accounting and Financial Reporting Standards* recommends that:

. . . the scope of the annual audit also encompass the combining and individual financial statements of the funds and account groups included in the comprehensive annual financial report. Although presentation of individual fund data of homogeneous funds is not necessary for fair presentation in conformity with generally accepted accounting principles, the individual funds should be subjected to the audit tests and other procedures.

The Government Finance Officers Association (GFOA) has long supported this position, which represented the only acceptable practice prior to the issuance of the National Council on Governmental Accounting's Statement 1, *Governmental Accounting and Financial Reporting Principles*. In its policy statement "Audit Coverage of Individual Funds," the association explains its position:

In the absence of definite legal requirements, governmental entities are faced with a choice in selecting appropriate audit coverage. Audit tests based on the combined statements are narrower than tests based on individual fund statements. The level of materiality affecting audit tests is raised substantially when the auditor extends his or her opinion only to the combined statements—overview. Thus a greater degree of assurance is provided to citizens, governing board members, oversight bodies and others if the audit tests and the auditor's opinion are extended to the individual fund statements.

These facts led the association to take the following position:

The Government Finance Officers Association recommends that governments give consideration to subjecting their individual fund financial statements to a full scope audit similar to the audit required of the combined statements—overview. We believe that any additional audit cost resulting from the full scope audit would be more than offset by the benefit of providing full assurance to all users with regard to the financial statements of every government.

Others believe the proper focus of the audit should be the general purpose financial statements (GPFS) because this level of coverage is the minimum required for fair presentation in conformity with generally accepted accounting principles (GAAP).

The 1986 AICPA industry audit and accounting guide, *Audits of State and Local Governmental Units* (1986 *ASLGU*), allows both approaches. This guide also clarifies that if the GPFS are selected as the audit focus, materiality judgments still should be made at the fund type and account group level rather than for the GPFS "taken as a whole." However, as mentioned earlier, the GFOA believes a government is usually best advised to choose the former or "full scope" approach.

AUDITING STANDARDS FOR FINANCIAL AUDITS

Sources of Auditing Standards. An audit is made up of various tests and procedures designed to meet the objectives of the audit. *Auditing standards* define those objectives and provide measures of quality that can be used to judge the effectiveness of the tests and procedures used to meet them.

Standards for traditional financial audits are known as generally accepted auditing standards (GAAS) and are promulgated by the AICPA through the institute's Auditing Standards Board. The institute also provides guidance as needed on the proper application of GAAS through the promulgation of Statements on Auditing Standards (SAS).

Supplemental standards for financial audits of governments, as well as standards for public-sector performance auditing, have been established by the U.S. General Accounting Office (GAO) in its publication *Standards for Audit of Governmental Organizations, Programs, Activities and Functions* (revised 1988)*, commonly referred to as the "yellow book." These standards form generally accepted *government* auditing standards (GAGAS).

---

* Citations are from an advance draft and are subject to editorial revision.

In addition, the Single Audit Act and Circular A–128 set forth specific requirements for single audits that go beyond both GAAS and GAGAS.

All the standards applicable to financial audits will be discussed in the remaining portion of this section. The GAGAS applicable to performance auditing are the subject of the section that follows.

General Standards. The AICPA has set three general standards for audits that are to be performed in accordance with GAAS:

1. The examination is to be performed by a person or persons having adequate technical training and proficiency as an auditor.
2. In all matters relating to the assignment, an independence in mental attitude is to be maintained by the auditor or auditors.
3. Due professional care is to be exercised in the performance of the examination and the preparation of the report.

GAGAS provide a separate but similar set of general standards that apply to single audit and other yellow book engagements. These standards address qualifications, independence, due professional care and quality control:

1. *Qualifications.* The staff assigned to conduct the audit should collectively possess adequate professional proficiency for the tasks required.
2. *Independence.* In all matters relating to the audit work, the audit organization and the individual auditors, whether government or public, should be free from personal or external impairments to independence, should be organizationally independent, and should maintain an independent attitude and appearance.
3. *Due Professional Care.* Due professional care should be used in conducting the audit and in preparing related reports.
4. *Quality Control.* Audit organizations conducting government audits should have an appropriate internal quality control system in place and participate in an external quality control review program.

Although they are similar, the GAAS and GAGAS general standards differ in significant ways. The GAGAS on quality control, unlike GAAS, requires auditors to participate in specific types of continuing education and training to maintain their professional proficiency. Starting January 1, 1989, auditors must complete at least 80 hours of continuing education and training every two years. All 80 hours of this training must contribute to the auditor's professional proficiency. For individuals responsible for planning, directing, conducting substantial portions of the field work or reporting on the audit, at least 24 of these hours should relate directly to the government environment and to government auditing. This GAGAS also goes beyond GAAS in requiring auditors to participate in an external quality control review (peer review) program at least once every three years, beginning January 1, 1989.

Recently, the AICPA has taken action in this same direction. A successful 1987 referendum on a plan to restructure professional standards gained approval for, among other proposals, the adoption of new membership requirements for continuing professional education and practice monitoring.

Standards for Field Work in Financial Audits. The AICPA's GAAS establish three standards for field work to guide auditors in planning and performing the audit:

1. The work is to be adequately planned and assistants, if any, are to be properly supervised.
2. A sufficient understanding of the internal control structure is to be obtained to plan the audit and to determine the nature, timing and extent of tests to be performed.
3. Sufficient competent evidential matter is to be obtained through inspection, observation, inquiries, and confirmations to afford a reasonable basis for an opinion regarding the financial statements under examination.

The AICPA provides additional guidance, as needed, on the application of these standards by issuing SAS.

The field work standards of GAGAS incorporate the AICPA standards. To meet the special needs and interests of the public sector, however, the yellow book also sets forth certain supplemental standards for field work:

1. *Audit Requirements.* Planning should include consideration of the audit requirements of all levels of government.
2. *Legal and Regulatory Requirements.* A test should be made of compliance with applicable laws and regulations.
3. *Illegal Acts.* The auditor should design audit steps and procedures to provide reasonable assurance of detecting errors, irregularities, and illegal acts that could have a direct and material effect on the financial statement amounts or the results of financial-related audits. The auditor should be aware of the possibility of illegal acts from noncompliance with laws and regulations that could have an indirect and material effect on the financial statements or results of financial-related audits.
4. *Evidence.* A record of the auditor's work is to be retained in the form of working papers. Supplemental working paper requirements for financial audits are that working papers should:
   a. contain a written audit program cross-referenced to the working papers,
   b. contain the objective, scope, methodology and results of the audit,
   c. contain sufficient information so that supplementary oral explanations are not required,
   d. be legible with adequate indexing and cross-referencing and include summaries and lead schedules as appropriate,
   e. restrict information included to matters that are materially important and relevant to the objectives of the audit, and
   f. contain evidence of supervisory reviews of the work conducted.
5. *Internal Control.* A sufficient understanding of the internal control structure is to be obtained to plan the audit and to determine the nature, timing, and extent of tests to be performed.

The AICPA, in SAS No. 41, *Working Papers,* followed the lead set by GAGAS and now requires auditors in GAAS engagements to prepare and maintain working papers. However, differences in emphasis still remain between GAAS and GAGAS. SAS No. 41 does not "imply that the auditor would be precluded from supporting his report by other means in addition to working papers." The GAGAS on working papers, on the other hand, underscores the need for working papers to be complete. According to this yellow book standard, working papers should "contain sufficient information so that supplementary oral explanations are not required."

Similarly, the AICPA has acted recently to strengthen its standard on illegal acts. SAS No. 53, *The Auditor's Responsibility to Detect and Report Errors and Irregularities* provides that auditors following GAAS will be required, among other things, to design the audit to detect errors and irregularities that are material to the financial statements.

Standards for Reporting the Results of Financial Audits. The AICPA's GAAS set forth four standards of reporting:

1. The report shall state whether the financial statements are presented in accordance with generally accepted accounting principles.
2. The report shall identify those circumstances in which such principles have not been consistently observed in the current period in relation to the preceding period.
3. Informative disclosures in the financial statements are to be regarded as reasonably adequate unless otherwise stated in the report.
4. The report shall either contain an expression of opinion regarding the financial statements, taken as a whole, or an assertion to the effect that an opinion cannot be expressed. When an overall opinion cannot be expressed, the reasons therefor should be stated. In all cases where an auditor's name is associated with financial statements, the report should contain a clear-cut indication of the character of the auditor's examination, if any, and the degree of responsibility he is taking.

As in the case of the GAAS on field work, the AICPA provides additional guidance, as needed, on the application of these standards by issuing SAS.

Because GAAP consider every fund to be a separate accounting entity, some have raised the question of whether it is appropriate for an auditor to express an opinion on the combined financial statements of a government if the auditor has not performed any audit work on one or more individual fund types. For example, can an auditor opine on a city's combined financial statements, but rely entirely on the work of another auditor for the city's one enterprise fund, a separately audited utility? The 1986 *ASLGU* resolves this question in favor of the traditional approach that allows auditors to give opinions on the combined financial statements in such situations. However, the 1986 *ASLGU* clarifies that this "principal auditor" should meet two criteria:

1. The auditor should be engaged by the oversight unit as the principal auditor for the reporting entity.
2. The auditor should be responsible for examining at least the general fund of the oversight unit, or the primary operating fund type if no general fund exists.

Normally, GAAS do not allow different auditors to sign an audit report in their individual capacities. Therefore, it generally would not be appropriate for any but the principal auditor, as just defined, to sign the audit report on the entity's financial statements.

In addition to the GAAS guidance on reporting just described, GAGAS set forth additional reporting standards to meet the special needs and interests of the public sector:

1. *Statement on Auditing Standards.* A statement should be included in the auditors' report that the audit was made in accordance with generally accepted government auditing standards.
2. *Report on Compliance.* The auditors should prepare a written report on their tests of compliance with applicable laws and regulations. This report, which may be included in either the report on the financial audit or a separate report, should contain a statement of positive assurance on those items which were tested for compliance and negative assurance on those items not tested. It should include all material instances of noncompliance, and all instances and indications of illegal acts that could result in the entity, or an officer or an employee of the entity, being subject to criminal prosecution.
3. *Report on Internal Controls.* The auditors should prepare a written report on their understanding of the entity's internal control structure and the assessment of control risk made as part of a financial statement audit or financial-related audit. This report may be included in either the auditors' report on the financial audit or a separate report. The auditors' report should include as a minimum:
   a. the scope of the auditors' work in obtaining an understanding of the internal control structure and assessing the control risk,
   b. the entity's significant internal controls or control structure including the controls established to ensure compliance with laws and regulations that have a material impact on the financial statements and the results of the financial-related audit, and
   c. the reportable conditions, including the identification of material weaknesses identified as a result of the auditors' work.
4. *Reporting on Financial-related Audits.* Written audit reports are to be prepared giving the results of each financial-related audit.
5. *Privileged and Confidential Information.* If certain information is prohibited from general disclosure, the report should state the nature of the information omitted and the requirement that makes the omission necessary.
6. *Distribution.* Written audit reports are to be submitted by the audit organization to the appropriate officials of the organization audited and to the appropriate officials of the organizations requiring or arranging for the audits, including external funding organizations unless legal restrictions, ethical considerations or other arrangements prevent it. Copies of the reports should also be sent to other officials who have legal oversight authority or who may be responsible for taking action and to others authorized to receive such reports. Unless restricted by law or regulation, copies should be made available for public inspection.

Although GAAS only require one auditors' report on the fairness of the presentation of the financial statements, GAGAS normally require two additional reports: a report on the auditors' understanding of the entity's internal control structure and related assessment of levels of control risk and a report on compliance with applicable laws and regulations. Also, GAGAS require the auditor to issue a report on any instances or indications of illegal acts related to compliance. This requirement is met normally by issuing a separate report.

Special Field Work and Reporting Requirements Arising from the Single Audit Act and OMB Circular A–128. The requirements for conducting and reporting the results of a single audit, set forth in the Single Audit Act and OMB Circular A–128, go beyond those contained in GAAS and GAGAS. These additional requirements, related both to the auditor's consideration of the internal control structure and to the auditor's determination of compliance with applicable laws and regulations, are designed to meet the needs of federal grantor agencies that must rely on the results of the single audit.

Under the GAAS for field work, as applied by SAS No. 55, *Consideration of the Internal Control Structure in a Financial Statement Audit,* an auditor's obligation to perform tests of controls can be limited in some instances. For example, if the auditor knew there were not sufficient personnel to allow for the proper separation of incompatible duties, the auditor could choose not to rely upon the internal control structure at all. Instead, the auditor could choose to assess control risk at the maximum level (i.e., decide *not* to rely on the internal control structure's operating effectiveness) and to expand substantive test work to determine that the financial statements were presented fairly. In another instance, the auditor could choose not to perform tests of controls simply because it would be more efficient to rely solely upon substantive testing. For example, if only a small number of transactions occurred in a given transaction cycle, the auditor could choose to examine each of the transactions rather than to test the government's controls over the transaction cycle. In each case, the auditor would still be required to gain an understanding of the internal control structure (through past experience, inspection, observation, etc.) and to document that understanding in a manner appropriate to the size and complexity of the audited government. Although auditors *are required* to document their decision to assess control risk at the maximum level, they are *not* required to document the basis for that decision.

This approach is based on the financial audit's primary emphasis on the fairness of the presentation of the financial statements. However, such an approach does not always answer important concerns of certain users of the audit reports, such as federal grantors. For example, an auditor performing a financial audit ordinarily would be satisfied if substantive test work demonstrated that students who received aid in a particular student assistance program were eligible. A federal grantor, on the other hand, may be equally if not more concerned to determine that such compliance resulted from effective eligibility controls rather than from a failure of ineligible students to apply for the assistance. The federal grantor's concerns cannot be satisfied by substantive testing alone.

To meet the special needs of federal grantor agencies, the Single Audit Act and OMB Circular A–128 require that auditors do more than obtain and document an understanding of the audited government's internal control structure as it relates to major federal financial assistance programs. Auditors also must test whether controls are functioning in accordance with prescribed procedures, regardless of whether or not the auditor

intends to place reliance on them. Moreover, the AICPA's 1986 *ASLGU* clarifies that this expanded requirement should cover control systems through which at least one-half of the total federal financial assistance expenditures of the government are processed. If expenditures for all major federal financial assistance programs do not account for at least one-half of the total federal financial assistance expenditures, the auditor should extend tests of controls to include controls over the largest nonmajor programs so that controls over at least 50 percent of federal financial assistance program expenditures are tested.

Similarly, the Single Audit Act and OMB Circular A–128 expand the auditor's responsibilities related to the government's compliance with applicable laws and regulations. The AICPA's 1986 *ASLGU* clarifies that auditors, subject to the provisions of the Single Audit Act and OMB Circular A–128, should give an opinion on compliance for the major federal financial assistance programs. This opinion is to state that the government has complied with all applicable laws and regulations, noncompliance with which could have a material effect on the allowability of program expenditures. It is important to note that the materiality focus for compliance opinions is the individual major federal financial assistance program. In addition, OMB Circular A–128 requires that the auditor report *all* instances of noncompliance discovered during the audit, regardless of materiality, for both major and nonmajor federal financial assistance programs. This reporting of instances of noncompliance, however, can be in summary form.

To aid auditors in their determination of whether a government has or has not complied with applicable laws and regulations, the OMB has prepared the *Compliance Supplement for Single Audits of State and Local Governments* (*Compliance Supplement*) containing general compliance features common to all federal assistance programs, as well as specific compliance features of individual programs. Although use of the *Compliance Supplement* is not mandatory, it does provide auditors with a useful source of information on the more important compliance features of various federal assistance programs, and it does serve as a ''safe harbor'' for the auditor should a federal agency choose to question the scope of the compliance testing performed for a given program.

Because of these additional requirements concerning internal control structures related to federal financial assistance and concerning compliance with applicable laws and regulations, and also because of the requirement that auditors give an ''in relation to'' opinion on the schedule of federal financial assistance that must be presented, auditors could issue up to six separate reports on the results of their audit work:

1. Report on the fairness of the presentation of the financial statements (required by GAAS and GAGAS)
2. Report on the fairness of the presentation of the schedule of federal financial assistance in relation to the financial statements (required by the Single Audit Act and OMB Circular A–128)
3. Report on the internal control structure (required by GAGAS)
4. Report on the internal control structure related to federal financial assistance programs (required by the Single Audit Act and OMB Circular A–128)

5. Report on compliance with applicable laws and regulations (required by GAGAS)
6. Report on compliance with applicable laws and regulations related to federal financial assistance programs (required by the Single Audit Act and OMB Circular A–128).

Although up to six auditors' reports may be produced as a result of the single audit, as few as three reports can be issued to meet all of the special requirements described above. The auditor may issue a single report on the fairness of the presentation of the financial statements and the schedule of federal financial assistance, another report on the internal control structure, including controls related to federal financial assistance programs, and, finally, a single report on the entity's compliance with applicable laws and regulations, including an opinion on compliance for each of the major federal financial assistance programs. When an auditor does decide to issue only three reports, however, care should be taken to ensure that the three reports meet all the special reporting requirements of the single audit. Examples of the six separate reports can be found in appendix A to the 1986 *ASLGU* and in the sample comprehensive annual financial report provided in appendix D of this book.*

Because the Single Audit Act mandates the use of GAGAS, the auditor would be required, as stated earlier, to issue an additional report on any instances or indications of illegal acts.

AUDITING STANDARDS FOR PERFORMANCE AUDITS

Auditors, both financial and performance, share much common ground in the methods they use to collect and evaluate evidential matter. Yet, despite the many similarities between financial and performance auditing, there are important differences.

For example, although management makes assertions in both financial and performance audits, the assertions made in a financial audit are *explicit* whereas those made in a performance audit are mostly *implicit*. In a financial audit, management's assertions take the concrete form of financial statements. In a performance audit, there are few or no specific management assertions as such, only the implicit understanding that management claims to be meeting its responsibilities as economically and efficiently as possible. As a result, the financial auditor has direct control over only a small part of the typical annual financial report. Changes to the financial statements only can be made with the consent of management because they are management's assertions, not the auditor's. On the other hand, the performance auditor has direct control over almost all of the contents of the performance audit report. Management can respond to audit findings, but cannot otherwise directly affect the final report.

Another difference between financial and performance audits is their scope. While most financial statement audits encompass all of the activities of a government, ordinarily it is not feasible for performance audits to do so. Instead, performance audits

* These examples are likely to be amended to make them consistent with the provisions of SAS No. 55 and SAS No. 58, *Reports on Audited Financial Statements*.

focus on individual departments, agencies, activities or functions, rather than on the government as a whole.

Yet another difference between financial and performance audits is the lack of standard criteria for the latter. In a financial audit, both the auditor and management agree (at least in principle) that "fairness" requires conformity with GAAP. A widely accepted body of literature, including the pronouncements of the GASB and the Financial Accounting Standards Board (FASB), provides much detailed guidance on difficult points. No such commonly accepted criteria exist, however, for determining what is "economical," "efficient" or "effective." Therefore, the performance auditor must establish for each audit the criteria to be used to judge economy, efficiency and effectiveness and must do so in a way that makes these criteria persuasive to the users of the report.

Therefore, although the general standards set forth in the yellow book apply equally to performance audits and financial audits, separate field work and reporting standards apply to performance audit engagements.

The following standards constitute the GAGAS for field work in performance audit engagements:

1. *Planning.* Work is to be adequately planned.
2. *Supervision.* Staff are to be properly supervised.
3. *Legal and Regulatory Requirements.* An assessment is to be made of compliance with applicable requirements of laws and regulations when necessary to satisfy the audit objectives.
4. *Internal Control.* An assessment should be made of applicable internal controls when necessary to satisfy the audit objectives.
5. *Evidence.* Sufficient, competent and relevant evidence is to be obtained to afford a reasonable basis for the auditors' judgments and conclusions regarding the organization, program, activity or function under audit. A record of the auditors' work is to be retained in the form of working papers. Working papers may include tapes, films, and disks.

The GAGAS for reporting the results of a performance audit are as follows:

1. *Form.* Written audit reports are to be prepared communicating the results of each government audit.
2. *Timeliness.* Reports are to be issued promptly so as to make the information available for timely use by management and legislative officials, and by other interested parties.
3. *Report Contents.* The report should:
   a. include a statement of the audit objectives and a description of the audit scope and methodology.
   b. include a full discussion of the audit findings, and where applicable, the auditor's conclusions.
   c. include the underlying cause of problem areas noted in the audit, and recommendations for actions to correct the problem areas and to improve operations when called for by the audit objectives.
   d. include a statement that the audit was made in accordance with generally accepted government auditing standards and disclose when applicable standards were not followed.
   e. identify the significant internal controls that were as-

sessed, the scope of the auditor's assessment work, and any significant weaknesses found during the audit.

   f. include all significant instances of noncompliance and abuse and all indications and instances of illegal acts that were found during or in connection with the audit that could result in the entity, or an officer or an employee of the entity, being subject to criminal prosecution.

   g. include pertinent views of responsible officials of the organization, program, activity, or function audited concerning the auditors' findings, conclusions, and recommendations, and what corrective action is planned.

   h. include a description of any significant noteworthy accomplishments, particularly when management improvements in one area may be applicable elsewhere.

   i. include a listing of any significant issues needing further study and consideration.

   j. include a statement about any pertinent information that was omitted because it is deemed privileged or confidential. The nature of such information should be described, and the basis under which it is withheld should be stated.

4. *Presentation.* The report should be complete, accurate, objective, and convincing and be as clear and concise as the subject matter permits.

5. *Distribution.* Written audit reports are to be submitted by the audit organization to the appropriate officials of the organization audited, and to the appropriate officials of the organizations requiring or arranging for the audits, including external funding organizations, unless legal restrictions, ethical considerations or other arrangements prevent it. Copies of the report should also be sent to other officials who have legal oversight authority or who may be responsible for taking action and to others authorized to receive such reports. Unless restricted by law or regulation, copies should be made available for public inspection.

Detailed information on various aspects of performance auditing, including establishing the performance audit function, managing the performance audit unit and its work, data gathering, analysis, sampling techniques and operational issues can be found in the GFOA publication *Performance Auditing in Local Government.*

MANAGING THE AUDIT

Procuring Financial Audits. Much recent attention has been devoted to the problem of substandard audits of governments. For instance, two GAO reports (December 1985 and March 1986) indicated that there were significant problems with the quality of many audits of governments performed by certified public accountants (CPAs). A subsequent study by the GAO, *CPA Audit Quality: A Framework for Procuring Audit Services* (August 1987), determined further that there was an identifiable relationship between the audit procurement process used by a government and the quality of the audit eventually performed. Therefore, governments need to establish sound audit procurement practices to ensure that they obtain the quality audits they need.

The GAO study on procurement identifies four critical attributes of an effective audit procurement process. First, the procurement process should be designed to ensure there is adequate *competition.* Second, governments need to use effective *solicitation* procedures to ensure that auditors have all the information they need about the nature of the government and its audit requirements to make an informed proposal. Third, the selection of an audit firm from among a number of firms proposing to perform the engagement should be made on the basis of a *technical evaluation* of the auditor's qualifications to perform the audit successfully. Price alone cannot be allowed to determine the choice of an auditor any more than price alone should be allowed to determine the choice of other professionals, such as doctors and lawyers. Fourth, the final *written agreement* with the auditor should establish a common and legally binding understanding between the government and the auditor concerning mutual accountability and the conduct of the audit.

Those in the government with special expertise in accounting and auditing, such as internal auditors, are in an excellent position to provide the technical advice needed to establish and apply sound procurement policies. These individuals should work with management in preparing the RFP. Besides providing information about the government and the audit period needed by proposers to prepare a response, an acceptable RFP also will address the following:

1. *The scope of the audit.* The RFP should designate the funds, account groups and component units to be included in the audit. The RFP also should indicate clearly whether the auditor's scope is to be the combined, combining and individual fund and account group statements and schedules or only the combined financial statements.

2. *The auditing standards to be used.* The RFP should indicate clearly whether the audit is to be performed in accordance with GAAS, GAGAS or GAGAS and the additional provisions of the Single Audit Act and OMB Circular A–128. Also, the RFP should outline any additional auditing standards that must be followed (e.g., standards set by the state to supplement GAAS and GAGAS).

3. *The type and extent of assistance to be provided to the auditor.* The RFP should specify what types and amounts of services the government is ready to provide the auditor, both clerical and professional. If the government plans to offer the direct assistance of members of the internal audit staff, the nature and extent of this assistance should be defined clearly (e.g., will internal audit staff only perform isolated procedures for the auditor or will they complete sections of the audit work program under the auditor's supervision?). Also, if internal auditors are to assist the external auditor directly, how is their performance to be evaluated?

4. The reports that will be required, as well as related distribution and timing.

5. The need to retain working papers for an adequate period and the right to have these working papers reviewed by appropriate third parties.

When responses to the RFP are received, individuals knowledgeable in accounting and auditing, in cooperation with bureau managers should screen and evaluate them. As mentioned above, a technical evaluation of qualitative factors, such as the expertise and experience of the proposers, should weigh more heavily in the final selection than cost. One possible procedure for weighing these factors would be to use technical factors alone to isolate the most promising proposers and then to consider cost only within this select group.

Preparing for the Financial Audit. Auditors' services, like those of other professionals, can be relatively costly. Therefore, a government normally is well advised to close its own books, prepare its own financial statements, and use its own staff to prepare schedules and provide clerical services rather than to rely upon the auditor for such assistance. The government's staff, for example, should:

1. Gather documents needed by the auditors (e.g., minutes, lease agreements, lists of depositories, bank reconciliations, organizational charts, formally adopted annual budgets and amendments, tax levies);
2. Prepare general schedules needed by the auditors (e.g., insurance, litigation, interfund loans and advances, investment transactions, fixed asset acquisitions and disposals, deposits and investments as of balance sheet date); and
3. Prepare a schedule of federal financial assistance (if required by the Single Audit Act and OMB Circular A–128). Programs should be listed by their number as it appears in the *Catalog of Federal Domestic Assistance* (CFDA).

Moreover, governments can facilitate the audit greatly by carefully documenting throughout the period under audit the workings of certain internal controls that ordinarily may not provide an "audit trail." For example, a government should document:

1. The monitoring of federal grant subrecipients' compliance with applicable laws and regulations;
2. The monitoring of collateralization requirements for uninsured deposits and investments; and
3. The proper functioning of controls related to compliance with laws and regulations affecting federal financial assistance programs.

The government's planning and preparation can greatly increase the prospects of achieving the best possible audit at the lowest possible cost to the government.

Audit Committees. As mentioned earlier, auditor independence is critical if the financial audit is to be effective. Yet, governments always face the danger of management's attempting to exercise undue influence over the audit process. To avoid this possibility, many governments now are choosing to follow the common private-sector practice of establishing audit committees. Moreover, by providing governments with access to the views of a separate group of individuals knowledgeable in accounting and auditing matters, audit committees help prevent governments from placing excessive reliance on the technical expertise of the auditor.

An audit committee should provide both the auditor and the governing body a means to communicate directly with each other on all matters related to the audit. To serve this function, the audit committee itself must be protected from management influence. Normally, this goal can be achieved

by ensuring that a majority of committee members exercise no administrative or managerial responsibilities within the government (e.g., a practicing CPA or corporate comptroller residing in the community).

Once in place, the audit committee should be responsible for reviewing and advising the governing body on all matters related to the audit. For example, the audit committee should:

1. Satisfy itself that the auditor selected is both independent and competent;
2. Recommend the proper scope of the audit;
3. Determine if the level of nonaudit services (e.g., management advisory services) to be provided by the auditor is appropriate;
4. Monitor the progress of the audit;
5. Examine carefully the control weaknesses discovered during the audit and reported in the audit findings and recommendations (for a GAGAS audit) and in the auditor's "management letter;" and
6. Satisfy itself that management has taken appropriate action to correct any deficiencies discovered during the audit.

The importance of audit committees has been underscored by the AICPA's SAS No. 61, *Communication with Audit Committees* which requires auditors to assure themselves that audit committees are informed about a number of specific items related to the audit. With this increased emphasis on audit committees, it is likely that their use in the public sector will become even more common.

Audit Findings. In a GAGAS audit, weaknesses in the internal control structure and instances of noncompliance are reported most often in the form of audit findings. An audit finding typically is composed of four elements:

1. *Condition.* What is the weakness in controls or instance of noncompliance that has been discovered during the audit?
2. *Criterion/Criteria.* What is the basis for asserting that a certain condition constitutes a weakness in controls or represents an instance of noncompliance?
3. *Cause.* Why has the condition come into being or been allowed to continue?
4. *Result.* What harm is caused or could be caused by the condition?

As the yellow book points out, all of these elements will not be present in every audit finding. What is important is that the finding be tailored to meet the specific objectives of the individual audit. Moreover, in practice it is sometimes difficult to distinguish among the four elements of an audit finding. In certain instances, the criterion and the result can be the same. For example, lax security over portable computers is a weakness in controls (condition) because (criterion) of the danger that the machines could be lost or stolen (result). Additional criteria are not needed when the benefit of avoiding a potential adverse result is self-evident.

Also, findings should be constructive in tone and accompanied by recommendations on how to improve the unsatisfactory conditions they identify. Management should respond to the audit findings in writing, and this response should be reproduced, with the finding, in the final audit report. Management's response should indicate clearly either concurrence or nonconcurrence with the finding, as well as the nature and timing of any specific actions management intends to take to alleviate the unsatisfactory conditions identified.

Audit Resolution. Audits can be a powerful diagnostic tool governments can use to assess and improve their performance. Nonetheless, even the best audit can be of little help if its findings and recommendations do not lead to constructive action. Therefore, the constructive use of the audit cannot be left to chance; management, the auditors and the governing body should all do their part to ensure that appropriate action is taken to resolve the issues raised by the audit.

Management, of course, is primarily responsible for implementing audit recommendations. Auditors, however, have a responsibility under GAGAS to monitor management's implementation of recommendations and to report unsatisfactory resolution of audit findings in subsequent audit reports. Still, unless more is done, a government could easily fall into a cycle in which findings are repeated endlessly without adequate corrective action by management. To avoid this possibility, governments are well advised to establish systems that hold management accountable for any failure to implement correc-

tive action in a timely manner. For example, a governing body could choose to ask the auditors to evaluate the effectiveness of management's corrective action within the six months following the issuance of the audit report. The governing body could then require that those responsible explain any failure on their part to take the actions recommended. The governing body also could require a specific plan to alleviate the unsatisfactory condition in the future. The knowledge that those responsible will be held accountable for resolving audit findings can serve as a strong incentive to management.

CONCLUSION

The public is demanding an ever-increasing degree of accountability from its elected officials and government employees. As GAO and AICPA actions have already indicated, in such an environment, increasing attention is likely to be directed to the quality of government audits. It is, therefore, critical that all parties involved with the audit—management, the governing body and the auditors—be knowledgeable of the audit process so that this demand for accountability can be met.

Chapter 16
CURRENT ISSUES IN GOVERNMENTAL ACCOUNTING AND FINANCIAL REPORTING

Accounting and financial reporting standards for government entities are constantly evolving to meet changing conditions and the increasing demands of financial statement users. The Governmental Accounting Standards Board (GASB) is now actively engaged in research on a variety of projects to meet these needs. The GASB's major current projects, and their status as of Spring 1988, are presented in this chapter:

- Financial reporting
- Measurement focus and basis of accounting for governmental funds
- Risk management
- Pension accounting
- Capital assets
- Cash flow reporting.

FINANCIAL REPORTING

From its inception, the GASB has been committed to a broad-scale reexamination of the framework of governmental financial reporting. Accordingly, the GASB's technical agenda from the beginning has contained a project on financial reporting. This project is made up of five subprojects; two have been completed and three are still in various stages of research.

The first of these subprojects was the development and completion of a user needs survey. Through this survey the GASB attempted to identify the needs of governmental financial statement users, divided into three broad categories: citizen groups, investors/creditors and government oversight groups (e.g., legislature, city council). The publication of the results of the user needs survey, GASB research report, *The Needs of Users of Governmental Financial Reports,* was completed in 1985.

The second subproject, the development of a statement of financial reporting objectives, was designed to help the board set consistent standards by establishing theoretical guidelines for the board to follow in developing and evaluating proposed statements and interpretations. The issuance of GASB Concepts Statement No. 1, *Objectives of Financial Reporting,* marked the completion of this second subproject.

The third subproject, currently being researched, is a reexamination of the criteria used to define the reporting entity and the display of that entity. This subproject began with the preparation of a research report *An Empirical Study of Governmental Financial Reporting Entity Issues,* published in 1987.

Among other findings, the results of this report indicate that preparers tend to emphasize oversight responsibility when considering whether a potential component unit should be included within the reporting entity, while attestors and credit analysts are more concerned with financial interdependency. The board is now preparing a discussion memorandum (DM) that will further explore these issues.

The fourth subproject will address the financial reporting model itself. Potential issues that may be considered include whether trust and agency funds and internal service funds should be retained as part of financial statement display and whether the general purpose financial statements (GPFS) should be supplemented by additional statements at a higher level of aggregation. Also, the possibility of replacing the capital projects fund type, the debt service fund type and the two account groups by a plant fund is also likely to be considered. Research on this project is still in its early stages.

The final subproject will deal with service-level reporting and statistical information. Work on this project is also in its early stages. The GASB hopes that several individual studies now in progress on service-level reporting will provide financial statement preparers with the criteria they need to answer the GASB's 1985 call for experimental reporting of service levels and accomplishments. Such experimental reporting could be of great value to the GASB in its later deliberations.

MEASUREMENT FOCUS AND BASIS OF ACCOUNTING FOR GOVERNMENTAL FUNDS

In 1987, the GASB issued an exposure draft (ED) of the proposed statement *Measurement Focus and Basis of Accounting—Governmental Funds.* The changes proposed in this ED are potentially the most significant to face governments since the adoption of National Council on Governmental Accounting (NCGA) Statement 1 in 1979.

The ED proposes that the present "flow of current financial resources" measurement focus and modified accrual basis of accounting used in governmental funds be replaced by a new "flow of financial resources" measurement focus and an accrual basis of accounting. Although the new measurement focus would still be concerned with *financial* resources (i.e., expendable resources), it would no longer emphasize the availability of these resources, as in the past.

Under the proposed new measurement focus and basis of accounting, governmental funds normally would recognize revenues when they are earned (for exchange transactions) or when the transaction or event occurs that increases net financial resources (for nonexchange transactions). Similarly, expenditures generally would be recognized when the transaction or event occurs that decreases net financial resources. In principle, neither the recognition of revenue nor the recognition of expenditures would depend upon the timing of the related cash flows.

Also, the new measurement focus and basis of accounting would limit significantly the types of obligations that could be classified in the general long-term debt account group (GLTDAG). Only debt related to the acquisition or construction of capital assets would qualify for inclusion in the GLTDAG under the proposed guidance. Other obligations now reported in the GLTDAG (e.g., long-term portion of compensated absences, debt not associated with capital acquisition or construction) would be reported instead as fund liabilities.

Left unchanged by the proposed new measurement focus and basis of accounting, however, would be the current treatment of capital outlay and debt service expenditures. Accordingly, the full effect of capital acquisition or construction would be reported as an expenditure in the year the asset is acquired or constructed. Such costs would not be deferred (i.e., capitalized) and amortized in future periods by the use of depreciation accounting. Similarly, the proceeds of debt issuances related to capital assets would be reported as an "other financing source" on the operating statement of the governmental fund involved and subsequent debt service outlays would be reported as expenditures. This treatment of capital outlays and debt service expenditures, however, could be modified by the GASB as part of its debt and capital assets projects.

The ED also contains specific guidance on the application of the new principles to specific revenue and expenditure items. These items include property tax, income tax, sales tax and bond issuance costs.

RISK MANAGEMENT

In recent years, many governments have faced an insurance "crisis," in which certain types of insurance are either too expensive or impossible to obtain at any price. This situation has brought to the fore, once again, the issue of the proper accounting and financial reporting for a government's risk management activities. Following initial research, the GASB issued a DM on the topic in 1987, identifying several important issues the board needs to resolve.

In the view of many, the central issue the GASB must address is determining when and if a government can indeed be considered to have transferred risk. Without the transference of risk, insurance is not possible, at least as the term "insurance" is normally defined. If governments, in fact, can transfer risk to an insurance pool or a captive insurance company, then an argument can be made that these latter entities need to use the same type of accounting used by other entities in the insurance industry (i.e., Statement of Financial Accounting Standards (SFAS) No. 60, *Accounting and Reporting by Insurance Enterprises*). On the other hand, if risk, in fact, is not transferred, many would argue that insurance accounting is

inappropriate (i.e, the position of SFAS No. 5, *Accounting for Contingencies,* that self-insurance is no insurance).

Another major issue to be resolved is the proper measurement of the liability that may result from not transferring risk to an outside party. Should the liability be limited to the amount of probable and measurable losses (including claims that have not been reported) incurred as of the balance sheet date (i.e., SFAS No. 5)? Should an actuarial method be used to determine the amount of the liability and periodic expenditure expense? Or should the liability (and the corresponding expenditure/ expense) be "smoothed" by recognizing expected catastrophe and shock losses before they actually occur?

Moreover, should the liability be discounted (i.e, reduced to its present value)? If so, what discount rate should be applied? Should the government use its investment rate to discount the liability? Should the government use its incremental borrowing rate? Should the government report the liability as the amount the government would have to pay to an outside party to assume it (i.e., the settlement rate)? Or should the government avoid discounting altogether and report the liability at its gross value?

The DM also addresses issues such as the proper fund classification for risk management activities (i.e., internal service fund, general fund or trust fund) and the proper valuation of assets (e.g., cost, market, SFAS No. 60 valuation method) set aside to meet anticipated claims.

Finally, if the GASB elects to use the internal service fund classification for risk management activities, how should the premiums of participating funds be accounted for? Should the amount of the premium recognized as expenditure/expense be limited to the fund's allocated share of the SFAS No. 5 expenditure/expense? Should the entire amount of an actuarially determined premium be recognized as expenditure/expense even if it exceeds the SFAS No. 5 amount? Should premiums be treated as transfers rather than as expenditure/expense?

PENSION ACCOUNTING

The issue of the proper financial reporting for pensions has been no easier to resolve in the public sector than it has been in the private sector. Indeed, it is the subject of a major current GASB project.

The earliest guidance, applicable to government employers, was furnished by Accounting Principles Board (APB) Opinion No. 8, *Accounting for the Cost of Pension Plans*. This pronouncement not only provided guidance on the determination of the amount of pension expense/expenditure for a period, but also provided guidance on what pension-related liability should be reported (i.e., the difference between the amount charged against operations and the amount paid). In addition, APB Opinion No. 8 mandated certain note disclosures, including the amount of the unfunded actuarial liability. The American Institute of Certified Public Accountants, in its 1974 industry audit guide *Audits of State and Local Governmental Units*, acknowledged the applicability of APB Opinion No. 8 guidance to government entities. This position was affirmed in NCGA Statement 1, *Governmental Accounting and Financial Reporting Principles*.

Later guidance on pensions from the private sector was not

always so well received by governments. In 1980, the Financial Accounting Standards Board (FASB) issued SFAS No. 35, *Accounting and Reporting by Defined Benefit Plans.* Paragraph 2 of this statement specifically extended the pronouncement's scope to the pension plans of state and local governments. The NCGA, however, took exception to some of the guidance provided by SFAS No. 35 (most notably, the issue of the valuation of plan assets) and issued NCGA Interpretation 4, *Accounting and Financial Reporting for Public Employee Retirement Systems and Pension Trust Funds,* in 1981. NCGA Interpretation 4 was issued only to provide interim guidance; the NCGA stated that the issue would be studied further and that additional pronouncements would be forthcoming. Both the FASB and the NCGA agreed to defer implementation of their respective pronouncements by governments to allow time for the two standard-setting bodies to attempt to resolve their differences on the pension issue. (In fact, these differences were still not resolved when the NCGA was dissolved in 1984.)

The NCGA pursued its study of the issues and in April 1983, issued Statement 6, *Pension Accounting and Financial Reporting: Public Employee Retirement Systems and State and Local Governmental Employers,* which superseded NCGA Interpretation 4. However, the NCGA's subsequent Interpretation 8, *Certain Pension Matters* (November 1983), deferred implementation of NCGA Statement 6 guidance indefinitely pending the outcome of discussions with the FASB aimed at reconciling material differences between NCGA Statement 6 and SFAS No. 35.

The series of events just described left it unclear which authoritative guidance should be followed. In GASB Statement No. 1, *Authoritative Status of NCGA Pronouncements and AICPA Industry Audit Guide,* the board clarified the situation by stating that both pension plans and government employers could follow the accounting and reporting guidance of either NCGA Statement No. 1 (i.e., APB Opinion No. 8) as amended by NCGA Interpretation 8, NCGA Statement 6 or SFAS No. 35, pending further board action.

An additional potential complication occurred, however, when the FASB issued SFAS No. 87, *Employers' Accounting for Pensions,* in December 1985. NCGA Statement 1 guidance had referred to APB Opinion No. 8 "or subsequent FASB pronouncements" for proprietary funds. The GASB once again found itself having to clarify the situation. In GASB Statement No. 4, *Applicability of FASB Statement No. 87, "Employers' Accounting for Pensions," to State and Local Governmental Employers,* the board ruled that the FASB guidance was not applicable to government entities. Instead, these entities were advised to await the completion of the GASB pension project for definitive guidance on pension accounting and reporting in the public sector.

The pension issue has been on the GASB's agenda since the board was first formed in June 1984. Because the GASB was aware of the acute need for additional guidance, the board decided early to divide its pension project into two portions to allow for the issuance of at least some guidance before completion of the entire project. One portion was to be concerned with the appropriate note and other disclosures (i.e., required supplementary information) for plans and for government employers. The other portion was to address the account-

ing and financial reporting issues involving the balance sheet and the operating statement for both plans and government employers.

The board completed its work on the first portion of the pension project and issued GASB Statement No. 5, *Disclosure of Pension Information by Public Employee Retirement Systems and State and Local Governmental Employers,* in 1986 (see chapter 14) and is now at work on the second portion of its pension project. The major issues to be resolved will be the proper measurement of expense/expenditure, the proper measurement of any liability, and the appropriate valuation basis for plan assets.

Some argue that the board should choose a single actuarial attribution approach for the measurement of pension expense/expenditure, as the FASB did in SFAS No. 87. They believe comparability demands such a single measure and point to the GASB's own arguments in GASB Statement No. 5 in favor of a standardized measure of the pension benefit obligation. Others, however, reject such an approach and urge that any number of acceptable actuarial approaches within a range should be allowable for the determination of pension expense/expenditure.

A related question concerns the role funding should play in determining which actuarial approach or approaches the board will allow. Some argue that interperiod equity should move the GASB toward a pension expense/expenditure approach that encourages sound funding policies. Others, however, argue that funding is a budgetary, rather than an accounting, issue. They believe a balance sheet approach should be taken toward the measurement of pension expense/expenditure (i.e., pension expense/expenditure essentially should be the difference between the pension obligation at the beginning of the period and the pension obligation at the end of the period).

Another major issue is the liability, if any, that should be reported on the balance sheet. Some argue that the actuarial accrued liability is a true liability and should appear on the balance sheet. Others, however, argue that only unfunded contributions should appear as a liability on the balance sheet. Still others favor a compromise approach similar to that taken in SFAS No. 87 (i.e., the liability on the balance sheet should be the amount of unfunded contributions, provided this amount is at least equal to a certain portion of the actuarial accrued liability).

Finally, the issue of the appropriate valuation basis for plan assets remains unresolved. The NCGA supported the use of cost or amortized cost to value these assets. The NCGA argued that public employee retirement systems are going concerns and that the use of market values for plan assets can result in sizeable fluctuations. These fluctuations can hinder the user's understanding of the overall progress of a government toward accumulating sufficient assets to meet its pension obligations. Others, including the FASB in SFAS No. 35, believe that market is the only meaningful valuation for plan assets.

CAPITAL ASSETS

In the past 15 to 20 years, public concern has grown regarding the condition of governments' capital assets, particularly infrastructure. Numerous reports, many in the popular press, have made a strong case that current maintenance of capital assets is inadequate and that citizens in the not too distant future may have to face the prospect of reconstructing significant portions of governments' infrastructure at tremendous cost.

These concerns have led many interested in government finance to question whether financial reporting by state and local governments is providing the information needed to assess the potential financial impact of governments' maintenance and acquisition policies on capital assets. The GASB, in Concepts Statement No. 1, seemed to share these concerns when it stated, "Financial reporting should provide information about a governmental entity's physical and other nonfinancial resources having useful lives that extend beyond the current year, including information that can be used to assess the service potential of those resources." Accordingly, in an attempt to address these concerns, the GASB added a project on capital assets to its technical agenda and in 1987 issued a DM on the subject. This document seeks to identify financial reporting problems related to capital assets, as well as alternatives for their resolution.

Current GAAP require little in the way of financial reporting for general governmental capital assets. However, the GASB, in its DM, is exploring a number of issues related to capital assets in an attempt to provide more useful information concerning these assets to users of governmental financial statements.

One option the board is considering is requiring infrastructure to be reported in the general fixed assets account group along with other fixed assets. Those in favor of this option point to the significant percentage of capital outlay these assets typically represent. Why, they ask, should other fixed assets be recorded, but not infrastructure? Opponents, however, challenge the value of the historical-cost information that is now required for fixed assets and question whether the benefits of historical-cost information on infrastructure could justify the costs that would be necessary to obtain it.

Another issue being addressed is the proper valuation to use for reporting capital assets on the balance sheet. Current GAAP mandate the use of historical cost, but many critics believe this information is meaningless to users of the financial statements. Should historical cost be replaced or supplemented as a valuation method? Some argue in favor of replacement-cost or constant-dollar valuation. Both of these methods avoid the distortion in value that arises from inflation when historical cost is used. Opponents, however, argue that both of these alternatives are flawed. They consider the replacement-cost method too expensive to be practical and lacking in objectivity. On the other hand, they believe the constant-dollar approach, while inexpensive, is simplistic and alleviates few of the problems of the historical-cost approach.

Depreciation is another issue raised by the board in its DM. State and local governments traditionally have voiced strong support for the current practice of not depreciating capital assets, challenging the usefulness of reporting depreciation charges in the operating statements of governmental funds. The board, however, is exploring whether such charges might best be reported as supplementary information or in the notes to the financial statements.

The board is also questioning whether the option of showing accumulated depreciation in the account group (without a charge to the operating statement) should continue. (This issue is discussed in chapter 6.)

Another important issue being considered is deferred maintenance. Governments sometimes find it politically expedient to defer needed maintenance on capital assets even though this action can lead to shortened useful lives for these assets and a higher overall maintenance cost. Should users of the financial statements somehow be put on notice that needed maintenance is being deferred? If so, how should the amount of deferred maintenance be measured? Should a disclosure of deferred maintenance, if any, be limited to the notes, or should it appear as a liability on the face of the balance sheet?

The GASB is also considering the possibility of requiring additional budgetary information on capital projects. In practice, both project-length and annual appropriated budgets are used to control capital projects. Current GAAP, however, only provide explicit guidance on budgetary reporting for those projects with annual appropriated budgets. Because cost overruns on capital projects can easily lead to potentially serious drains on a government's financial resources, many argue that some type of budgetary information should be required for project-length budgets as well. If the GASB adopts a requirement to present such information, the board will also have to consider whether the original budget or the revised budget (or both) should be presented.

In a similar vein, the GASB is exploring whether governments should be required to provide information on their capital plans. This information could aid users of the financial statements in determining whether the government is planning adequately for its future capital needs. Others, however, claim that information on capital plans is inherently subjective. Moreover, they argue that presenting capital plans in the financial statements would be inconsistent with the traditional approach of using the financial statements to communicate the results of past events.

Finally, many would argue that the most important information users of the financial statements need on capital assets is not their historical cost, but their capacity and condition. They argue, for example, that when trying to determine the future capital needs of an entity and the related demand for financial resources, the price of a school building is not nearly as important as the number of students it can serve and the building's age and condition.

CASH FLOW REPORTING

The 1987 *Codification,* Section 2200.112, requires that proprietary funds present a statement of changes in financial position, prepared in conformity with APB Opinion No. 19, *Reporting Changes in Financial Position.* This statement is designed to provide users of the financial statements with important information on the financing and investing activities of those funds as well as with information on other changes in their financial position during the period. Because of the unique measurement focus used in governmental funds, and the type of information that is reported in their operating statements as a result, such a statement is *not* now required for governmental funds. However, the issuance of both SFAS No. 95, *Statements of Cash Flows,* and the publication of the GASB's ED proposing a new measurement focus and basis of accounting for governmental funds, have led the GASB to reexamine the current guidance.

There are two principal differences between the guidance offered in APB Opinion No. 19 and that provided by SFAS No. 95. APB Opinion No. 19 allows information on changes in financial position to be presented on several bases (e.g., cash basis, working capital basis); SFAS No. 95 requires information to be presented on *cash flows* alone. APB Opinion No. 19 also requires that certain activities be reported in the statement of changes in financial position that do not affect cash flows, but that do affect an entity's financial position (e.g., purchase of a building with a mortgage). SFAS No. 95, on the other hand, *prohibits* the presentation of noncash information in the statement of cash flows. Instead, SFAS No. 95 requires that such information be reported in related disclosures.

Although SFAS No. 95 supersedes the guidance provided by APB Opinion No. 19 for private sector entities, it does *not* do so for governments. The 1987 *Codification,* Section 2200.112, which takes precedence over FASB pronouncements on the GAAP hierarchy, specifically mandates the use of the APB Opinion No. 19 guidance. Many have argued, however, that the GASB should consider requiring cash flow information similar to that required by SFAS No. 95. Accordingly, the GASB has added a project on cash flow reporting to its technical agenda. Until this project is completed, the guidance in APB Opinion No. 19 will continue to be applicable to governments. Nonetheless, governments desiring to do so may implement much of the guidance of SFAS No. 95, provided that they are careful to stay within the boundaries defined the APB guidance, as described in Chapter 14.

Also, as a part of the same project, the GASB will be considering the need for additional cash flow information in governmental funds following its proposed conclusions on the measurement focus and basis of accounting to be used in those funds. Under the current guidance, debt service on all long-term debt of the general government is reported as an expenditure in the governmental funds. However, with the proposed requirement that operating debt be recorded in the governmental funds rather than in the GLTDAG, the possibility exists that information on debt service for such fund debt would not be provided in the financial statements. The GASB, therefore, plans to examine alternative means of providing information on such financing activities.

* *

All of the projects discussed in this chapter could result in the issuance of pronouncements that would change significantly the financial reporting of government entities. A series of important changes in financial reporting practices, however, could pose a danger to the credibility of government financial reports. To allay such concerns, the GASB plans, as much as possible, to combine the effective date of any major changes resulting from these projects.

The process of change in financial reporting is ceaseless and will not end with the implementation of the decisions reached as a result of the projects described in this chapter. As mentioned earlier, financial reporting standards need to change continually to meet new conditions and increased demands for financial information. Financial statement users, preparers and attesters are encouraged to participate in the GASB due process system, so that the GASB's final pronouncements can meet these demands.

Appendix A
ACRONYMS AND PRONOUNCEMENTS

ACTS	Accounting Topics Series
AICPA	American Institute of Certified Public Accountants
APB	Accounting Principles Board
ARB	Accounting Research Bulletin
ASLGU	Audits of State and Local Governmental Units (AICPA, 1986)
BANs	Bond Anticipation Notes
CAFR	Comprehensive Annual Financial Report
CFDA	Catalog of Federal Domestic Assistance
CUFR	Component Unit Financial Report
CUFS	Component Unit Financial Statements
DM	Discussion Memorandum
ED	Exposure Draft
FASB	Financial Accounting Standards Board
FERC	Federal Energy Regulatory Commission
FRS	Financial Reporting Series
GAAFR	Governmental Accounting, Auditing and Financial Reporting
GAAP	Generally Accepted Accounting Principles
GAAS	Generally Accepted Auditing Standards
GAGAS	Generally Accepted Government Auditing Standards (see *Standards for Audit of Governmental Organizations, Programs, Activities and Functions* GAO, 1988, also known as "Yellow Book.")
GAO	U.S. General Accounting Office
GASB	Governmental Accounting Standards Board
GANs	Grant Anticipation Notes
GFAAG	General Fixed Assets Account Group
GFOA	Government Finance Officers Association
GLTDAG	General Long-Term Debt Account Group
GPFS	General Purpose Financial Statements
IRC	Internal Revenue Code
IRS	Internal Revenue Service
NARUC	National Association of Regulatory Utility Commissioners
NCGA	National Council on Governmental Accounting
OMB	U.S. Office of Management and Budget
PERS	Public Employee Retirement System
RANs	Revenue Anticipation Notes
SAS	Statement on Auditing Standards

SFAC	Statement of Financial Accounting Concepts
SFAS	Statement of Financial Accounting Standards
SLGS (or SLUGS)	State and Local Government Series
SOP	Statement of Position
SSAP	Summary of Significant Accounting Policies
TANs	Tax Anticipation Notes
TB	Technical Bulletin

PRONOUNCEMENTS/PUBLICATIONS

American Institute of Certified Public Accountants

Accounting Principles Board

APB Opinion No. 8	Accounting for the Cost of Pension Plans
APB Opinion No. 12	Omnibus Opinion—1967
APB Opinion No. 18	The Equity Method of Accounting for Investments in Common Stock
APB Opinion No. 19	Reporting Changes in Financial Position
APB Opinion No. 20	Accounting Changes
APB Opinion No. 21	Interest on Receivables and Payables
APB Opinion No. 22	Disclosure of Accounting Policies
APB Opinion No. 26	Early Extinguishment of Debt
APB Opinion No. 28	Interim Financial Reporting
APB Opinion No. 29	Accounting for Nonmonetary Transactions
APB Opinion No. 30	Reporting the Results of Operations— Reporting the Effects of Disposal of a Segment of a Business and Extraordinary, Unusual and Infrequently Occurring Events and Transactions

Accounting Research Bulletins

ARB No. 43	Restatement and Revision of Accounting Research Bulletins

Industry Audit and Accounting Guides

Industry Audit Guide	Audits of Certain Nonprofit Organizations
Industry Audit and Accounting Guide	Audits of Providers of Health Care Services

| 1974 Industry Audit Guide | Audits of State and Local Governmental Units |
| 1986 Industry Audit and Accounting Guide | Audits of State and Local Governmental Units |

Statements of Position

SOP 75–3   Accrual of Revenues and Expenditures by State and Local Governments

SOP 78–5   Accounting for Advance Refundings of Tax-exempt Debt

SOP 80–2   Accounting and Financial Reporting by Governmental Units

Statement on Auditing Standards

SAS No. 9   The Effect of an Internal Audit Function on the Scope of the Independent Auditor's Examination

SAS No. 41   Working Papers

SAS No. 53   The Auditor's Responsibility to Detect and Report Errors and Irregularities

SAS No. 55   Consideration of the Internal Control Structure in a Financial Statement Audit

SAS No. 58   Reports on Audited Financial Statements

SAS No. 61   Communication with Audit Committees

Financial Accounting Standards Board

Statement of Financial Accounting Concepts

SFAC No. 5   Recognition and Measurement in Financial Statements of Business Enterprises

Statement of Financial Accounting Standards

SFAS No. 4   Reporting Gains and Losses from Extinguishment of Debt

SFAS No. 5   Accounting for Contingencies

SFAS No. 6   Classification of Short-Term Obligations to Be Refinanced

SFAS No. 12   Accounting for Certain Marketable Securities

SFAS No. 13   Accounting for Leases

SFAS No. 16   Prior Period Adjustments

SFAS No. 34   Capitalization of Interest Cost

SFAS No. 35   Accounting for Pensions

SFAS No. 43   Accounting for Compensated Absences

SFAS No. 57   Related Party Disclosures

SFAS No. 62   Capitalization of Interest Cost in Situations Involving Certain Tax-Exempt Borrowings and Certain Gifts and Grants

SFAS No. 64   Extinguishment of Debt Made to Satisfy Sinking-Fund Requirements

SFAS No. 71   Accounting for the Effects of Certain Types of Regulation

SFAS No. 74   Accounting for Special Termination Benefits Paid to Employees

SFAS No. 76   Extinguishment of Debt

SFAS No. 81   Disclosure of Postretirement Health Care and Life Insurance Benefits

SFAS No. 87   Employers' Accounting for Pensions

SFAS No. 90   Regulated Enterprises—Accounting for Abandonments and Disallowances of Plant Costs

SFAS No. 93   Recognition of Depreciation by Not-for-Profit Oranizations

SFAS No. 95   Statement of Cash Flows

U.S. General Accounting Office

"Yellow Book"   Standards for Audit of Governmental Organizations, Programs, Activities and Functions (1988)

Governmental Accounting Standards Board

Codification of Governmental Accounting and Financial Reporting Standards as of June 15, 1987

100   Objectives of Financial Reporting

1100   Summary Statement of Principles

1200   Generally Accepted Accounting Principles and Legal Compliance

1300   Fund Accounting

1400   Fixed Assets

1500   Long-Term Liabilities

1600   Basis of Accounting

1700   The Budget and Budgetary Accounting

1800   Classification and Terminology

1900   Financial Reporting

2100   Defining the Reporting Entity

2200   Comprehensive Annual Financial Report

2300   Notes to Financial Statements

2400   Budgetary Reporting

2500   Segment Information for Enterprise Funds

2600   Reporting Entity and Component Unit Presentation and Disclosure

2700   Supplemental and Special Purpose Reporting

2800   Statistical Tables

2900   Interim Financial Reporting

B50   Bond, Tax, and Revenue Anticipation Notes

C20   Cash Deposits with Financial Institutions

C50   Claims and Judgments

C60   Compensated Absences

D20   Debt Extinguishments

D25   Deferred Compensation Plans (IRC Section 457)

D30   Demand Bonds

E70   Escheat Property

G60   Grants, Entitlements, and Shared Revenues

H50   Hospitals

I50   Investments, including Repurchase Agreements

J50   Joint Ventures

L20   Leases

P20   Pension Activities—Employer Reporting

P70   Property Taxes

R10   Reverse Repurchase Agreements

S10   Sales Tax

S40   Special Assessments

T25   Termination Benefits (Special)

U50   Unemployment Compensation Benefit Plans

Co5   Colleges and Universities

Ho5   Hospitals

Jo5   Joint Ventures

Pe5   Pension Funds—Accounting

Pe6   Pension Funds—Disclosure

Pu5   Public Benefit Corporations and Authorities

Ut5   Utilities

Concept Statement of Governmental Accounting Standards Board

GASB Concepts Statement No. 1   Objectives of Financial Reporting

Statement of Governmental Accounting Standard Board

GASB
Statement No. 1   Authoritative Status of NCGA Pronouncements and AICPA Industry Audit Guide

GASB
Statement No. 2   Financial Reporting of Deferred Compensation Plans Adopted under the Provisions of Internal Revenue Code Section 457

GASB
Statement No. 3   Deposits with Financial Institutions, Investments (including Repurchase Agreements), and Reverse Repurchase Agreements

GASB
Statement No. 4   Applicability of FASB Statement No. 87, "Employers' Accounting for Pensions," to State and Local Governmental Employers

GASB
Statement No. 5   Disclosure of Pension Information by Public Employee Retirement Systems and State and Local Governmental Employers

GASB
Statement No. 6   Accounting and Financial Reporting for Special Assessments

GASB
Statement No. 7   Advance Refundings Resulting in Defeasance of Debt

GASB
Statement No. 8   Applicability of FASB Statement No. 93, Recognition of Depreciation by Not-for-Profit Organizations, to Certain State and Local Governmental Entities

Interpretation of Governmental Accounting Standards Board

GASB
Interpretation
No. 1   Demand Bonds Issued by State and Local Governmental Entities

Technical Bulletin of Governmental Accounting Standards Board

GASBTB
No. 87-1   Applying Paragraph 68 of GASB Statement 3

Government Finance Officers Association

ACTS 1   Enterprise Funds: Governmental Accounting & Financial Reporting

ACTS 2   Internal Service Funds: Governmental Accounting & Financial Reporting

ACTS 3   Fund Structure Including Interfund Transactions: Governmental Accounting & Financial Reporting

Fixed Asset Inventory Systems: Establishing, Maintaining & Accounting

FRS 1   Illustrations of Notes to the Financial Statements of State and Local Governments

FRS 2   Illustrations of Introductory Sections of Comprehensive Annual Financial Reports of State and Local Governments

FRS 3   Illustrations of Statistical Sections of Comprehensive Annual Financial Reports of State and Local Governments

FRS 5   Illustrations of Interim Financial Statements

FRS 7   Illustrations of Combined, Combining and Individual Fund and Account Group Statements and Schedules of State and Local Governments

Performance Auditing in Local Government

National Council on Governmental Accounting

NCGA
Statement 1   Governmental Accounting and Financial Reporting Principles

NCGA
Statement 2   Grant, Entitlement, and Shared Revenue Accounting by State and Local Governments

NCGA
Statement 3   Defining the Governmental Reporting Entity

NCGA
Statement 4   Accounting and Financial Reporting Principles for Claims and Judgments and Compensated Absences

NCGA
Statement 5   Accounting and Financial Reporting Principles for Lease Agreements of State and Local Governments

NCGA
Statement 6   Pension Accounting and Financial Reporting: Public Employee Retirement Systems and State and Local Government Employers

NCGA
Statement 7   Financial Reporting for Component Units Within the Governmental Reporting Entity

NCGA
Interpretation 1   GAAFR and the AICPA Audit Guide (Superseded)

NCGA
Interpretation 2   Segment Information for Enterprise Funds

NCGA
Interpretation 3   Revenue Recognition—Property Taxes

NCGA
Interpretation 4   Accounting and Financial Reporting for Public Employee Retirement Systems and Pension Trust Funds (Superseded)

NCGA
Interpretation 5   Authoritative Status of Governmental Accounting, Auditing, and Financial Reporting (1968)

NCGA
Interpretation 6   Notes to the Financial Statements Disclosure

NCGA
Interpretation 7   Clarification as to the Application of the Criteria in NCGA Statement 3, "Defining the Governmental Reporting Entity"

NCGA
Interpretation 8   Certain Pension Matters
NCGA
Interpretation 9   Certain Fund Classifications and Balance
                    Sheet Accounts
NCGA
Interpretation 10   State and Local Government Budgetary
                    Reporting
NCGA
Interpretation 11   Claim and Judgment Transactions for
                    Governmental Funds

U.S. Office of Management and Budget
Compliance Supplement for Single Audits of State and Local
    Government Units
Circular
A-128   Audits of State and Local Governments

Appendix B
TERMINOLOGY

The following explanations of terms are presented to aid in understanding the narrative discussions and illustrations included in this text and the terminology generally used in governmental accounting, auditing, financial reporting and budgeting. Synonyms for specific terms also may be presented in this appendix. In such instances, the abbreviation "syn." is used before the term. Acronyms used in the discussion of terms can be found in appendix A.

ABATEMENT. A complete or partial cancellation of a levy imposed by a government. Abatements usually apply to tax levies, special assessments and service charges.

ACCOUNTABILITY. The state of being obliged to explain one's actions, to justify what one does. Accountability requires governments to answer to the citizenry—to justify the raising of public resources and the purposes for which they are used.

ACCOUNT GROUPS. Accounting entities used to establish control over and accountability for the government's general fixed assets and the unmatured principal of its general long-term debt, including special assessment debt for which the government is obligated in some manner. Current authoritative literature provides for two such account groups: the general fixed assets account group (GFAAG) and the general long-term debt account group (GLTDAG). The long-term portions of claims, judgments, compensated absences and unfunded pension contributions not reported in proprietary or trust funds are also usually reported in the GLTDAG. Account groups are dissimilar to funds in that they are not used to account for sources, uses and balances of expendable available financial resources.

ACCOUNTING PERIOD. See **FISCAL PERIOD.**

ACCOUNTING SYSTEM. The methods and records established to identify, assemble, analyze, classify, record and report a government's transactions and to maintain accountability for the related assets and liabilities.

ACCOUNT NUMBER. See **CODING.**

ACCOUNTS PAYABLE. A short-term liability account reflecting amounts owed to private persons or organizations for goods and services received by a government.

ACCOUNTS RECEIVABLE. An asset account reflecting amounts due from private persons or organizations for goods and services furnished by a government (but not including amounts due from other funds or other governments).

ACCRETED VALUE. A valuation basis for certain investments and debt instruments that reports on the balance sheet only that portion of their face value that reflects principal and interest accrued to date.

ACCRUAL BASIS. The recording of the financial effects on a government of transactions and other events and circumstances that have cash consequences for the government in the periods in which those transactions, events and circumstances occur, rather than only in the periods in which cash is received or paid by the government.

ACCRUED BENEFITS. The amount of a pension plan participant's benefit (whether or not vested) as of a specified date, determined in accordance with the terms of the pension plan and based on compensation (if applicable) and service to that date.

ACCRUED INTEREST PAYABLE. A liability account reflecting certain interest cost that has been incurred but is not due until a later date.

ACCRUED SALARIES AND WAGES PAYABLE. A liability account reflecting salaries and wages earned by employees but not due until a later date.

ACCUMULATED BENEFIT OBLIGATION. The actuarial present value of benefits (whether vested or nonvested) attributed by the pension benefit formula to employee service rendered before a specified date and based on employee service and compensation (if applicable) before that date. The accumulated benefit obligation differs from the projected benefit obligation in that it includes no assumption about future compensation levels.

ACCUMULATED DEPRECIATION. A contra-asset account used to report the accumulation of periodic credits to reflect the expiration of the estimated service life of fixed assets.

ACCUMULATED PLAN BENEFITS. Benefits attributable under the provisions of a pension plan to employees for services rendered to the benefit information date.

ACTIVITY. A specific and distinguishable service performed by one or more organizational components of a government to accomplish a function for which the government is responsible (e.g., police is an activity within the public safety function). See also **SUBACTIVITY.**

ACTIVITY CLASSIFICATION. Expenditure classification according to the specific type of work performed by organizational units (e.g., sewage treatment and disposal, waste collection, waste disposal and street cleaning are activities performed in carrying out the function of sanitation).

ACTUARIAL ACCRUED LIABILITY. That portion, as determined by a particular actuarial cost method, of the actuarial present value of pension plan benefits and expenses not provided for by future normal costs.

ACTUARIAL ASSUMPTIONS. Assumptions used in the actuarial valuation process as to the occurrence of future events affecting pension costs, such as mortality, withdrawal, disablement and retirement; changes in compensation and national pension benefits; rates of investment earnings and asset appreciation or depreciation; procedures used to determine the actuarial value of assets; characteristics of future entrants for open group actuarial cost methods and other relevant items.

ACTUARIAL BASIS. A basis used in computing the amount of contributions to be made periodically to a fund or account so that the total contributions plus the compounded earnings thereon will equal the required payments to be made out of the fund or account. The factors considered in arriving at the amount of these contributions include the length of time over which each contribution is to be held and the rate of return compounded on such contribution over its life. A pension trust fund for a PERS is an example of a fund concerned with actuarial basis data.

ACTUARIAL COST METHOD. A procedure for determining the actuarial present value of pension plan benefits and expenses and for developing an actuarially equivalent allocation of such value to individual periods, usually in the form of a normal cost and an actuarial accrued liability.

ACTUARIALLY DETERMINED CONTRIBUTION REQUIREMENTS. Amounts required to be paid annually to a pension plan, based on an actuarial cost method or funding method.

ACTUARIAL PRESENT VALUE (APV). The discounted value of an amount or series of amounts payable or receivable at various times, determined as of a given date by the application of a particular set of actuarial assumptions.

ACTUARIAL UPDATE. An estimate or projection of the pension benefit obligation developed by using techniques and procedures considered necessary by the actuary. If conditions are relatively stable, only a few minor adjustments (such as an accrual of additional interest on the pension benefit obligation since the valuation date, and addition of benefits earned during the year less benefits paid) may be sufficient. If there have been significant changes in one or more relevant factors (e.g., in the size or composition of the population covered by the PERS), the procedures may be more extensive.

AD VALOREM TAX. A tax based on value (e.g., a property tax).

ADVANCE FROM OTHER FUNDS. A liability account used to record noncurrent portions of a long-term debt owed by one fund to another fund within the same reporting entity. See **DUE TO OTHER FUNDS** and **INTERFUND RECEIVABLE/PAYABLE.**

ADVANCE REFUNDING BONDS. Bonds issued to refinance an outstanding bond issue before the date the outstanding bonds become due or callable. Proceeds of the advance refunding bonds are deposited in escrow with a fiduciary, invested in U.S. Treasury Bonds or other authorized securities and used to redeem the underlying bonds at their maturity or call date, to pay interest on the bonds being refunded, or to pay interest on the advance refunding bonds.

ADVANCE TO OTHER FUNDS. An asset account used to record noncurrent portions of a long-term loan from one fund to another fund within the same reporting entity. See **DUE FROM OTHER FUNDS.**

ADVERSE OPINION. An opinion stating the auditor's view that financial statements do not present fairly financial position, results of operations or changes in financial position in conformity with generally accepted accounting principles.

AGENCY FUND. A fund normally used to account for assets held by a government as an agent for individuals, private organizations or other governments and/or other funds. The agency fund also is used to report the assets and liabilities of Internal Revenue Code, Section 457, deferred compensation plans.

AGENT MULTIPLE-EMPLOYER PERS . An aggregation of single-employer PERS with pooled administrative and investment functions (i.e., the PERS acts as a common investment and administrative agent for each employer). Each entity participating in an agent PERS receives a separate actuarial valuation to determine its periodic contribution rate. See **COST-SHARING MULTIPLE-EMPLOYER PERS.**

AGGREGATE ACTUARIAL COST METHOD. A method under which the excess of the actuarial present value of projected benefits of the group included in an actuarial valuation over the actuarial value of assets is allocated on a level basis over the earnings or service of the group between the valuation date and assumed exit. This allocation is performed for the group as a whole, not as a sum of individual allocations. That portion of the actuarial present value allocated to a valuation year is called the normal cost. The actuarial accrued liability is equal to the actuarial value of assets.

"ALL-INCLUSIVE" OPERATING STATEMENT. The financial statement that reports both operating results and changes in fund balance (or fund equity/retained earnings) combined into a single GAAP financial statement

ALLOT. To divide a budgetary appropriation into amounts that may be encumbered or expended during an allotment period (e.g., a government may choose to allot its annual budget to 12 monthly periods). See **ALLOTMENT** and **ALLOTMENT PERIOD.**

ALLOTMENT. A part of an appropriation that may be encumbered or expended during a given period. See **ALLOT** and **ALLOTMENT PERIOD.**

ALLOTMENT LEDGER. A subsidiary ledger containing an account for each allotment, showing the amount allotted, expenditures for the allotment period, outstanding encumbrances and net balance. See **APPROPRIATION LEDGER.**

ALLOTMENT PERIOD. A period of time during which an allotment is effective. Monthly and quarterly allotments are most common. See **ALLOT** and **ALLOTMENT.**

ALLOWANCE FOR UNCOLLECTIBLES. A contra-asset valuation account used to indicate the portion of a receivable not expected to be collected.

AMORTIZATION. (1) The portion of the cost of a limited-life or intangible asset charged as an expense during a particular period. (2) The reduction of debt by regular payments of principal and interest sufficient to retire the debt by maturity.

AMORTIZATION SCHEDULE. A schedule of debt service payments separating the portions of payments attributable to principal and interest.

AMOUNT AVAILABLE IN _____ FUNDS. An "other debit" account in the GLTDAG designating the amount of assets available in other funds for the retirement of outstanding amounts reported in the GLTDAG.

AMOUNT TO BE PROVIDED. An "other debit" account in the GLTDAG representing the amount to be provided from taxes, special assessments or other general revenues to retire outstanding general long-term liabilities.

ANNUAL BUDGET. A budget applicable to a single fiscal year. See **BUDGET** and **OPERATING BUDGET.**

ANNUAL FINANCIAL REPORT. A financial report applicable to a single fiscal year.

ANNUAL OPERATING BUDGET. See **OPERATING BUDGET.**

ANNUITY. A series of equal payments made or received at equal intervals over a designated period.

ANNUITY PERIOD. The designated length of time during which annuity payments are to occur.

APPRAISAL. See **APPRAISE.**

APPRAISE. To estimate the value, particularly the value of property. If the property is valued for taxation, the narrower term "assess" is substituted.

APPROPRIATED BUDGET. The expenditure authority created by the appropriation bills or ordinances, which are signed into law, and the related estimated revenues. The appropriated budget would include all reserves, transfers, allocations, supplemental appropriations and other legally authorized legislative and executive changes

APPROPRIATION. A legal authorization granted by a legislative body to make expenditures and to incur obligations for specific purposes. An appropriation usually is limited in amount and time it may be expended. See **CONTINUING APPROPRIATION** and **INDETERMINATE APPROPRIATION.**

APPROPRIATION ACCOUNT. A budgetary account set up to record spending authorizations for specific purposes. The account is credited with the original appropriation and any supplemental appropriations and is charged with expenditures and encumbrances.

APPROPRIATION BALANCE. See **UNALLOTED BALANCE OF APPROPRIATION, UNENCUMBERED ALLOTMENT** and **UNENCUMBERED APPROPRIATION.**

APPROPRIATION BILL, ORDINANCE, RESOLUTION or ORDER. A bill, ordinance, resolution or order through which appropriations are given legal effect.

APPROPRIATION LEDGER. A subsidiary ledger containing an account for each appropriation. Each account usually includes the amount originally appropriated, transfers to or from the appropriation, amounts charged against the appropriation, the available balance and other related information. See **ALLOTMENT LEDGER.**

ARBITRAGE. Classically, the simultaneous purchase and sale of the same or an equivalent security in order to profit from price discrepancies. In government finance, the most common occurrence of arbitrage involves the investment of the proceeds from the sale of tax-exempt securities in a taxable money market instrument that yields a higher rate, resulting in interest revenue in excess of interest costs.

ASSESS. To establish an official property value for taxation. See **APPRAISE.**

ASSESSED VALUATION. A valuation set upon real estate or other property by a government as a basis for levying taxes.

ASSESSMENT. (1) The process of making the official valuation of property for taxation. (2) The valuation placed upon property as a result of this process. See **SPECIAL ASSESSMENT.**

ASSESSMENT ROLL. With real property, the official list containing the legal description of each parcel of property and its assessed valuation. The name and address of the last known owner usually are listed. With personal property, the assessment roll is the official list containing the name and address of the owner, a description of the personal property and its assessed value.

ASSET. A probable future economic benefit obtained or controlled by a particular entity as a result of past transactions or events.

ATTAINED AGE ACTUARIAL COST METHOD. A method under which the portion of the actuarial present value of projected benefits that exceeds the actuarial accrued liability of each individual in an actuarial valuation is allocated on a level basis over the earnings or service of the individual between the valuation date and assumed exit.

ATTRIBUTION. The process of assigning pension benefits or cost to periods of employee service.

AUDIT. A systematic collection of the sufficient, competent evidential matter needed to attest to the fairness of management's assertions in the financial statements or to evaluate whether management has efficiently and effectively carried out its responsibilities. The auditor obtains this evidential matter through inspection, observation, inquiries and confirmations with third parties. See **INTERNAL AUDITING, FINANCIAL AUDIT, SINGLE AUDIT, PERFORMANCE AUDITING, PRE-AUDIT** and **POST-AUDIT.**

AUDIT COMMITTEE. A group of individuals, selected by the governing body, having specific responsibility for addressing all issues related to the external financial audit. Ideally, audit committees form a direct communications link between the auditor and the governing body; therefore, the majority of the committee's members normally would be expected *not* to have management responsibilities within the entity under audit.

AUDITED CLAIMS PAYABLE. See **ACCOUNTS PAYABLE.**

AUDIT FINDING. In the context of a financial audit, a weakness in internal controls or an instance of noncompliance with applicable laws and regulations that is presented in the audit report in conformity with GAGAS. A typical audit finding is composed of a statement of the condition (i.e., weakness or instance of noncompliance) and the criterion or criteria used to define it, an explanation of the cause of the condition, a discussion of its results and recommendations for improvement. Findings ordinarily are presented together with a response from management, which states management's concurrence or nonconcurrence with each finding and its plan for corrective action.

AUDIT MANAGEMENT. The process used to procure auditing services (See **AUDIT PROCUREMENT**), to monitor the performance of the auditor and to ensure the satisfactory resolution of issues raised by the audit.

AUDIT PROCUREMENT. The process used to obtain auditing services from independent public accountants.

AUDIT PROGRAM. A detailed outline of the work to be done and the procedures to be followed in any given audit.

AUDITOR'S REPORT. In the context of a financial audit, a statement by the auditor describing the scope of the audit and the auditing standards applied in the examination, and setting forth the auditor's opinion on the fairness of presentation of the financial information in conformity with GAAP or some other comprehensive basis of accounting.

AUDIT RESOLUTION. The process whereby corrective action is planned, implemented and monitored to remedy weaknesses discovered and reported in conjunction with an audit.

AUDIT SCOPE. In the context of a financial audit, the focus of audit testing as well as the reference point used by auditors when evaluating the results of audit tests or otherwise exercising their professional judgment. The minimum acceptable audit scope for governments would result in an opinion on the combined (i.e., general purpose) financial statements, with each fund type and account group considered separately when applying materiality evaluations.

AUTHORITY. A government or public agency created to perform a single function or a restricted group of related activities. Usually, such units are financed from service charges, fees and tolls, but in some instances they also have taxing powers. An authority may be completely independent of other governments or be partially dependent upon other governments for its financing or the exercise of certain powers. See **SPECIAL DISTRICT.**

BALANCE SHEET. The financial statement disclosing the assets, liabilities and equity of an entity at a specified date in conformity with GAAP.

BANK BALANCE. In the context of GASB Statement No. 3, *Deposits with Financial Institutions, Investments (including Repurchase Agreements), and Reverse Repurchase Agreements,* the amount credited by a financial institution to the government's account as opposed to the government's own ledger balance for the account (e.g., if checks have been written against an account, but have not yet cleared the bank, the ledger balance would be lower than the bank balance).

BANKER'S ACCEPTANCES. Short-term, noninterest-bearing notes sold at a discount and redeemed by the accepting banks at maturity for face value. Banker's acceptances generally are created based on a letter of credit issued in a foreign trade transaction.

BASIC FINANCIAL STATEMENTS. Those financial statements, including notes thereto, necessary for the fair presentation of the financial position and results of operations of an entity in conformity with GAAP. The basic financial statements include a balance sheet, an ''all-inclusive'' operating statement, a budget comparison statement (for all governmental funds for which annual appropriated budgets are adopted), and a statement of changes in financial position (for proprietary funds, pension trust funds and nonexpendable trust funds). See

FINANCIAL REPORTING PYRAMID, COMBINED STATEMENTS—OVERVIEW, COMBINING STATEMENTS—BY FUND TYPE, INDIVIDUAL FUND STATEMENTS, GENERAL PURPOSE FINANCIAL STATEMENTS and GENERALLY ACCEPTED ACCOUNTING PRINCIPLES.

BASIS OF ACCOUNTING. A term used to refer to *when* revenues, expenditures, expenses, and transfers—and the related assets and liabilities—are recognized in the accounts and reported in the financial statements. Specifically, it relates to the *timing* of the measurements made, regardless of the nature of the measurement, on either the cash or the accrual method.

BASIS POINT. Equal to $\frac{1}{100}$ of one percent. If interest rates rise from 7.50 percent to 7.75 percent, the difference is referred to as an increase of 25 basis points.

BENEFITS. Payments to which participants may be entitled under a pension plan, including pension benefits, death benefits and benefits due on termination of employment.

BETTERMENT. An addition made to, or change made in, a fixed asset, other than maintenance, to prolong its life or to increase its efficiency. The cost of the addition or change is added to the book value of the asset. The term sometimes is applied to sidewalks, sewers and highways, but it is preferable to designate these as improvements.

BIENNIAL BUDGET. A budget applicable to a two-year fiscal period. See BUDGET and OPERATING BUDGET.

BILL. A term used to denote a law or statute passed by certain legislative bodies. A bill has greater legal formality and standing than a resolution. See APPROPRIATION BILL.

BOND. Most often, a written promise to pay a specified sum of money (called the face value or principal amount), at a specified date or dates in the future, called the maturity date(s), together with periodic interest at a specified rate. Sometimes, however, all or a substantial portion of the interest is included in the face value of the security. See DEEP-DISCOUNT DEBT and ZERO-COUPON DEBT. The difference between a note and a bond is that the latter is issued for a longer period and requires greater legal formality. See GENERAL OBLIGATION BONDS PAYABLE and REVENUE BONDS PAYABLE. See also SURETY BOND.

BOND ANTICIPATION NOTES (BANs). Short-term interest-bearing notes issued by a government in anticipation of bonds to be issued at a later date. The notes are retired from proceeds of the bond issue to which they are related. See INTERIM BORROWING.

BOND COVENANT. A legally enforceable promise made by an issuer of bonds to the bondholders, normally contained in the bond resolution or indenture (e.g., pledged revenues).

BOND DISCOUNT. The difference between the present value and the face amount of bonds when the former is less than

the latter. In common usage, the term also often includes issuance costs withheld from the bond proceeds by the underwriter.

BONDED DEBT. The portion of indebtedness represented by outstanding bonds. See GROSS BONDED DEBT and NET BONDED DEBT.

BOND INDENTURE. A formal agreement, also called a deed of trust, between an issuer of bonds and the bondholder.

BOND ORDINANCE OR RESOLUTION. An ordinance or resolution authorizing a bond issue.

BOND PREMIUM. The difference between the present value and the face amount of bonds when the former is greater than the latter.

BONDS AUTHORIZED AND UNISSUED. Bonds that have been authorized legally but not issued and that can be issued and sold without further authorization.

BONDS ISSUED. Bonds sold by the government.

BONDS PAYABLE. Generally, the face value of bonds issued and unpaid. In the case of deep-discount and zero-coupon bonds, however, only the accreted value of the security is reported as bonds payable on the balance sheet.

BOOK ENTRY. A system that eliminates the need to physically transfer bearer-form paper or to register securities by using a central depository facility.

BOOKS OF ORIGINAL ENTRY. The record in which various transactions are recorded formally for the first time (e.g., cash journal, check register or general journal). With automated bookkeeping methods, one transaction may be recorded simultaneously in several records, one of which may be regarded as the book of original entry. Memorandum books, check stubs, files of duplicate sales invoices, etc., on which first or prior business notations may have been made, are not books of original entry in the accepted meaning of the term, unless they also are used as the media for direct posting to the ledgers.

BOOK VALUE. Value as shown by the books of account. In the case of assets subject to reduction by valuation allowances, book value refers to cost or stated value less the appropriate allowance. Sometimes a distinction is made between gross book value and net book value, the former designating value before deduction of related allowances and the latter the value after their deduction. In the absence of any modifiers, however, book value is understood to be synonymous with net book value. Syn. CARRYING AMOUNT.

BUDGET. A plan of financial operation embodying an estimate of proposed expenditures for a given period and the proposed means of financing them. Used without any modifier, the term usually indicates a financial plan for a single fiscal year. The term ''budget'' is used in two senses in practice. Sometimes it designates the financial plan presented to the appropriating governing body for adoption, and sometimes, the plan finally approved by that body. See **ANNUAL BUDGET, CAPITAL BUDGET, CAPITAL PROGRAM, LONG-TERM BUDGET, OPERATING BUDGET, PERFORMANCE BUDGET, PROGRAM BUDGET** and **TRADITIONAL BUDGET.**

BUDGETARY ACCOUNTS. Accounts used to enter the formally adopted annual operating budget into the general ledger as part of the management control technique of formal budgetary integration.

BUDGETARY COMPARISONS. Statements or schedules presenting comparisons between approved budgetary amounts (as amended) and actual results of operations on the budgetary basis.

BUDGETARY CONTROL. The control or management of a government or enterprise in accordance with an approved budget to keep expenditures within the limitations of available appropriations and available revenues.

BUDGETARY EXECUTION AND MANAGEMENT. Suballocations, contingency reserves, rescissions, deferrals, transfers, conversions of language appropriations, encumbrance controls and allotments established by the executive branch, without formal legislative enactment. These transactions may be relevant for various accounting control and internal reporting purposes, but are not part of the appropriated budget.

BUDGET DOCUMENT. The instrument used by the budget-making authority to present a comprehensive financial program to the appropriating governing body. The budget document usually consists of three parts. The first part contains a message from the budget-making authority, together with a summary of the proposed expenditures and the means of financing them. The second consists of schedules supporting the summary. These schedules show in detail the past years' actual revenues, expenditures and other data used in making the estimates. The third part is composed of drafts of the appropriation, revenue and borrowing measures necessary to put the budget into effect. See **BUDGET MESSAGE** and **EXECUTIVE BUDGET.**

BUDGET-GAAP BASIS DIFFERENCES. Differences arising from the use of a basis of accounting for budgetary purposes that differs from the basis of accounting applicable to the fund type when reporting on operations in conformity with GAAP. For example, a cash-basis budget would produce a budget-GAAP basis difference.

BUDGET-GAAP DIFFERENCES. Differences between the GAAP reporting model and a government's budgetary practices.

BUDGET-GAAP ENTITY DIFFERENCES. Differences rising from the inclusion or exclusion in the budget of organizations, programs, activities and functions that may or may not be compatible with the criteria defining the government reporting entity.

BUDGET-GAAP PERSPECTIVE DIFFERENCES. Differences that result when the structure of financial information for budgetary purposes is not compatible with the fund structure prescribed by GAAP (i.e., some governments budget on the basis of organizational or program structures that differ from the funds used for financial reporting purposes).

BUDGET-GAAP TIMING DIFFERENCES. Variations such as continuing appropriations, project appropriations, automatic reappropriations and biennial budgeting that separate budgetary accounting from GAAP.

BUDGET MESSAGE. A general discussion of the proposed budget as presented in writing by the budget-making authority to the legislative body. The budget message should contain an explanation of the principal budget items, an outline of the government's experience during the past period and its financial status at the time of the message and recommendations regarding the financial policy for the coming period. See also **EXECUTIVE BUDGET.**

BUILDINGS AND BUILDING IMPROVEMENTS. A fixed asset account reflecting the acquisition cost of permanent structures owned or held by a government and the improvements thereon.

BUSINESS-TYPE ACTIVITIES. Those activities of a government carried out primarily to provide specific services in exchange for a specific user charge.

CALLABLE BOND. A type of bond with a feature that permits the issuer to pay the obligation before the stated maturity date by giving notice of redemption in a manner specified in the bond contract.

CAPITAL ASSETS. See **FIXED ASSETS.**

CAPITAL BUDGET. A plan of proposed capital outlays and the means of financing them. See **CAPITAL PROGRAM.**

CAPITAL EXPENDITURES. Expenditures resulting in the acquisition of or addition to the government's general fixed assets.

CAPITAL GRANTS. Grants restricted by the grantor for the acquisition and/or construction of fixed assets. See **OPERATING GRANTS.**

CAPITAL IMPROVEMENT PROGRAM. See **CAPITAL PROGRAM.**

CAPITAL IMPROVEMENT SPECIAL ASSESSMENTS. Special assessment projects that are capital in nature and enhance the utility, accessibility or aesthetic value of the affected properties. Usually, the projects also provide improvements or additions to a government's general fixed assets or infrastructure. Typical special assessment capital improvements are streets, sidewalks, parking facilities and curbs and gutters. Sometimes the improvements provide capital assets that become an integral part of a government's enterprise activities (e.g., water or sewer main construction).

CAPITALIZATION POLICY. The criteria used by a government to determine which outlays should be reported as fixed assets.

CAPITAL LEASE. An agreement that conveys the right to use property, plant or equipment, usually for a stated period of time, that meets one or more of the criteria set forth in SFAS No. 13 for lease capitalization.

CAPITAL OUTLAYS. See **CAPITAL EXPENDITURES.**

CAPITAL PROGRAM. A plan for capital expenditures to be incurred each year over a fixed period of years to meet capital needs arising from the long-term work program or other capital needs. It sets forth each project or other contemplated expenditure in which the government is to have a part and specifies the resources estimated to be available to finance the projected expenditures.

CAPITAL PROJECTS FUND. A fund created to account for financial resources to be used for the acquisition or construction of major capital facilities (other than those financed by proprietary funds and trust funds).

CARRYING AMOUNT. The amount at which assets and liabilities are reported in the financial statements. Carrying amount also is known as book value. See **BOOK VALUE.**

CASH BASIS. A basis of accounting under which transactions are recognized only when cash is received or disbursed.

CASH DISCOUNT. An allowance received or given if payment of an account is completed within a stated period of time.

CASH-FLOW UNDERWRITING. The practice of an insurance enterprise depending on investment income rather than on positive underwriting results to achieve a profit.

CASH WITH FISCAL AGENT. An asset account reflecting deposits with fiscal agents, such as commercial banks, for the payment of bond principal and interest.

CERTIFICATE OF ACHIEVEMENT FOR EXCELLENCE IN FINANCIAL REPORTING PROGRAM. A voluntary program administered by the GFOA to encourage governments to publish efficiently organized and easily readable CAFRs/CUFRs and to provide technical assistance and peer recognition to the finance officers preparing them.

CERTIFIED PUBLIC ACCOUNTANT (CPA). An accountant who has met all the statutory and licensing requirements of a given state for use of that designation. All U.S. states require accountants, at a minimum, to complete successfully a uniform national examination before being allowed to designate themselves as CPAs.

CHARACTER CLASSIFICATION. Expenditure classification according to the periods expenditures are presumed to benefit. The four character groupings are (1) current operating expenditures, presumed to benefit the current fiscal period; (2) debt service, presumed to benefit prior fiscal periods as well as current and future periods; (3) capital outlays, presumed to benefit the current and future fiscal periods and (4) intergovernmental, when one government transfers resources to another.

CHECK. A bill of exchange drawn on a bank and payable on demand; a written order on a bank to pay on demand a specified sum of money to a named person, to his or her order, or to bearer out of money on deposit to the credit of the maker. A check differs from a warrant in that the latter is not necessarily payable on demand and may not be negotiable. It differs from a voucher in that the latter is not an order to pay. A voucher-check combines the distinguishing characteristics of a voucher and a check; it shows the propriety of a payment and is an order to pay.

CLAIM. (1) Potential losses that can rise from (a) employment (e.g., worker compensation and unemployment), (b) contractual actions (e.g., delays or inadequate specifications), (c) actions of government personnel (e.g., medical malpractice, damage to privately owned vehicles by government-owned vehicles, improper police arrest) and (d) governmental properties (e.g., personal injuries, property damage). (2) In the context of insurance, a demand for payment of a policy benefit because of the occurrence of an insured event, such as the destruction or damage of property and related deaths or injuries.

CLEARING ACCOUNT. An account used to accumulate total charges or credits so that they can be distributed later among the accounts to which they are allocable or so that the net differences can be transferred to the proper account.

CODE. See **CODING.**

CODING. A system of numbering or otherwise designating accounts, entries, invoices, vouchers, etc., in such a manner that the symbol used reveals quickly certain required information. To illustrate the coding of accounts, numbers in the 400 range could be used for expenditures, numbers between 420 and 430 for expenditures within the public safety function, and the number 421 for expenditures incurred in connection with the police activity classification. Within the police activity classification, the number 421.5 could be used for support services, and the number 421.51 for communications support services. Accordingly, an expenditure for police radios would be classified as 421.51 (i.e., expenditures for communications services, within support services, within the police activity classification, within the public safety function).

COLLATERAL. Assets pledged to secure deposits, investments or loans.

COLLATERAL POOL. As applied to single financial institutions, a group of securities pledged by a single financial institution against all the public deposits it holds. A multiple financial institution collateral pool is a group of securities pledged by various financial institutions to provide common collateral for their deposits of public funds. In such a collateral pool, the assets of the pool and the power to make additional assessments against the members of the pool, if necessary, ensure there will be no loss of public funds because of the default of a member.

COLLECTORS' ROLL. See **TAX ROLL.**

COMBINATION BOND. A bond issued by a government that is payable from the revenues of a government enterprise but that also is backed by the full faith and credit of the government.

COMBINED STATEMENTS—OVERVIEW. See **GENERAL PURPOSE FINANCIAL STATEMENTS.**

COMBINING STATEMENTS—BY FUND TYPE. The second of the financial reporting pyramid's three reporting levels containing GAAP financial statements. Such statements are presented for each fund type (e.g., special revenue funds) for which the government maintains more than one fund. They include GAAP financial statements for each fund of a particular fund type in separate adjacent columns and a total column, which duplicates the column for that fund type in the combined statements—overview.

COMMERCIAL PAPER. An unsecured promissory note issued primarily by corporations for a specific amount and maturing on a specific day. The maximum maturity for commercial paper is 270 days, but most is sold with maturities of up to 30 days. The credit risk of almost all commercial paper is rated by a rating service.

COMMITMENTS. In the context of note disclosure, contingent obligations at the balance sheet date, arising from the terms of executory contracts.

COMPENSATED ABSENCES. Absences, such as vacation, illness and holidays, for which it is expected employees will be paid. The term does not encompass severance or termination pay, postretirement benefits, deferred compensation or other long-term fringe benefits, such as group insurance and long-term disability pay.

COMPLIANCE AUDITING. Auditing for compliance with applicable laws and regulations. Tests of compliance with laws and regulations are *substantive* tests; therefore, the term "compliance auditing" should not be confused with the similar term "compliance testing," which usually refers to testing for compliance with internal control procedures.

COMPONENT UNIT. A separate government unit, agency or nonprofit corporation that is combined with other component units to constitute the reporting entity in conformity with GAAP.

COMPONENT UNIT FINANCIAL REPORT (CUFR). A report covering all funds and account groups of a component

unit—including introductory section; appropriate combined, combining, and individual fund statements; notes to the financial statements; required supplementary information; schedules; narrative explanations; and statistical tables.

COMPONENT UNIT FINANCIAL STATEMENTS (CUFS). Financial statements of a component unit that may be issued separately from the component unit financial report. Such statements should include the financial statements and notes to the financial statements that are essential to the fair presentation of financial position and results of operations (and changes in financial position of proprietary funds and similar trust funds).

COMPREHENSIVE ANNUAL FINANCIAL REPORT (CAFR). The official annual report of a government. It includes (a) the five combined financial statements in the combined statements—overview and their related notes (the "liftable" GPFS) and (b) combining statements by fund type and individual fund and account group financial statements prepared in conformity with GAAP and organized into a financial reporting pyramid. It also includes supporting schedules necessary to demonstrate compliance with finance-related legal and contractual provisions, required supplementary information, extensive introductory material and a detailed statistical section. Every government reporting entity should prepare a CAFR.

CONNECTION FEES. See **SYSTEM DEVELOPMENT FEES.**

CONSTRUCTION IN PROGRESS. A fixed asset account reflecting the cost of construction work for projects not yet completed.

CONSUMPTION METHOD. The method under which inventories are recorded as expenditures/expense when used. See **PURCHASES METHOD.**

CONTINGENT LIABILITY. Items that may become liabilities as a result of conditions undetermined at a given date, such as guarantees, pending lawsuits, judgments under appeal, unsettled disputed claims, unfilled purchase orders and uncompleted contracts. Contingent liabilities should be disclosed within the financial statements (including the notes) when there is a reasonable possibility a loss may have been incurred. Guarantees, however, should be disclosed even though the possibility of loss may be remote.

CONTINUING APPROPRIATION. An appropriation that, once established, is automatically renewed without further legislative action, period after period, until altered or revoked. The term should not be confused with **INDETERMINATE APPROPRIATION.**

CONTRACTS PAYABLE. A liability account reflecting amounts due on contracts of goods or services furnished to a government. Amounts withheld as guarantees on contracts should be classified separately in an account entitled "Retainage payable." See **ACCOUNTS PAYABLE.**

CONTRIBUTED CAPITAL. The permanent fund capital of a proprietary fund. Contributed capital forms one of two classifications of equity found on the balance sheet of a proprietary fund. Contributed capital is created when a residual equity transfer is received by a proprietary fund, when a general fixed asset is "transferred" to a proprietary fund or when a grant is received that is externally restricted to capital acquisition or construction. Contributions restricted to capital acquisition and construction and fixed assets received from developers and customers, as well as amounts of tap fees in excess of related costs, also would be reported in this category.

CONTRIBUTED CAPITAL—CUSTOMERS. An equity account in proprietary fund presenting the amount of permanent fund capital contributed to the fund by its customers.

CONTRIBUTED CAPITAL—DEVELOPERS. An equity account in a proprietary fund presenting the amount of permanent fund capital contributed by developers.

CONTRIBUTED CAPITAL—_____ FUND. An account identical to **CONTRIBUTED CAPITAL—GOVERNMENT,** except the specific fund of origin is indicated.

CONTRIBUTED CAPITAL—GOVERNMENT. An equity account in a proprietary fund presenting the amount of permanent fund capital generally contributed by the government from general government revenues and resources.

CONTRIBUTED CAPITAL—INTERGOVERNMENTAL. An equity account in a proprietary fund presenting the amount of permanent fund capital contributed by other governments.

CONTROL ACCOUNT. An account in the general ledger in which is recorded the aggregate of debit and credit postings to a number of related accounts called subsidiary accounts (e.g., taxes receivable is a control account supported by the aggregate of individual balances in individual property taxpayers' subsidiary accounts). See **GENERAL LEDGER** and **SUBSIDIARY ACCOUNT.**

CONTROL ENVIRONMENT. The collective effect of various factors on establishing, enhancing, or mitigating the effectiveness of specific policies and procedures. Such factors include (1) management philosophy and operating style, (2) organizational structure, (3) the function of the legislative body and its committees, (4) methods of assigning authority and responsibility, (5) management control methods, (6) the internal audit function, (7) personnel policies and procedures, and (8) external influences concerning the entity.

CONTROL PROCEDURES. The policies and procedures in addition to the control environment and accounting system that management has established to provide reasonable assurance that specific entity objectives will be achieved.

CORRECTIVE ACTION PLAN. A plan state and local officials are required to submit to appropriate federal officials under the Single Audit Act. The plan details how material noncompliance or weaknesses found in the audit will be eliminated or why corrective action is not necessary.

COST. The amount of money or other consideration exchanged for goods or services.

COST ACCOUNTING. The method of accounting that provides for the assembling and recording of all the elements of cost incurred to accomplish a purpose, to carry on an activity or operation, or to complete a unit of work or a specific job.

COST LEDGER. A subsidiary record wherein each project, job production center, process, operation, product or service is given a separate account to which all items entering into its cost are posted in the required detail. Such accounts should be arranged and kept so that the results shown in them may be reconciled with and verified by a control account or accounts in the general books.

COST OF REPLACEMENT. See **REPLACEMENT COST.**

COST OF REPRODUCTION. See **REPRODUCTION COST.**

COST RECORDS. All ledgers, supporting records, schedules, reports, invoices, vouchers and other records and documents reflecting the cost of projects, jobs, production centers, processes, operations, products or services, or the cost of any of the component parts thereof.

COST-SHARING MULTIPLE-EMPLOYER PERS. Essentially one large pension plan with cost-sharing arrangements (i.e., all risks and costs, including benefit costs, are shared proportionately by the participating entities). One actuarial valuation is performed for the PERS as a whole, and the same contribution rate generally applies to each participating entity. See **AGENT MULTIPLE EMPLOYER PERS.**

COST UNIT. In cost accounting, the unit of product or service for which cost is computed. These units are selected to compare the actual cost with a standard cost or with actual costs of units produced under different circumstances or at different places and times. See **UNIT COST** and **WORK UNIT.**

COUNTERPARTY. Another party to a transaction. In the case of deposits and investments made by government entities, a counterparty could be the issuer of a security, a financial institution holding a deposit, a broker-dealer selling securities or a third party holding securities or collateral.

COUPON RATE. The interest rate specified on interest coupons attached to a bond. The term "nominal interest rate" is also used in this sense.

COVENANT. See **BOND COVENANT.**

COVERAGE. The ratio of pledged revenues to related debt service for a given year. See **NET REVENUE AVAILABLE FOR DEBT SERVICE.**

COVERED PAYROLL. All compensation that is paid to active employees covered by the PERS and on which contributions are based. Covered payroll also may be referred to as covered compensation.

CREDITED PROJECTED BENEFITS. Those pension plan benefit amounts expected to be paid at various future times under a particular set of actuarial assumptions, taking into account such items as the effect of advancement in age and past and anticipated future compensation and service credits. That portion of an individual's projected benefit allocated to service to date, determined in accordance with the terms of a pension plan and based on future compensation as projected to retirement, is called the credited projected benefit.

CREDIT RISK. The risk that a counterparty to an investment transaction will not fulfill its obligations. Credit risk can be associated with the issuer of a security, with a financial institution holding deposits or with parties holding securities or collateral. Credit risk exposure can be affected by a concentration of deposits or investments in any one investment type or with any one counterparty.

CURRENT. As applied to budgeting and accounting, designates the operations of the present fiscal period as opposed to past or future periods. It usually connotes items likely to be used up or converted into cash within one year.

CUSTODIAL AGREEMENT. A written contract establishing the responsibilities of a custodian who holds collateral for deposits with financial institutions, investment securities or securities underlying repurchase agreements.

CUSTOMER DEPOSITS. A liability account used in an enterprise fund to reflect deposits made by customers as a prerequisite to receiving goods and/or services provided by the fund.

DEBT. An obligation resulting from the borrowing of money or from the purchase of goods and services. Debts of governments include bonds, time warrants and notes. See **ACCOUNTS PAYABLE, BOND, NOTE PAYABLE, LONG-TERM DEBT** and **GENERAL LONG-TERM DEBT.**

DEBT EXTINGUISHMENTS. See **ADVANCE REFUNDING BONDS, DEFEASANCE** and **IN-SUBSTANCE DEFEASANCE.**

DEBT LIMIT. The maximum amount of outstanding gross or net debt legally permitted.

DEBT PROCEEDS. The difference between the face amount of debt and the issuance discount or the sum of the face amount and the issuance premium. Debt proceeds differ from cash receipts to the extent issuance costs, such as underwriters' fees, are withheld by the underwriter.

DEBT RATIOS. Comparative statistics illustrating the relation between the issuer's outstanding debt and such factors as its tax base, income or population. These ratios often are used as part of the process of determining the credit rating of an issue, especially with general obligation bonds.

DEBT SERVICE FUND. A fund established to account for the accumulation of resources for, and the payment of, general long-term debt principal and interest. Sometimes referred to as a **SINKING FUND.**

DEBT SERVICE FUND REQUIREMENTS. The resources which must be provided for a debt service fund so that all principal and interest payments can be made in full and on schedule.

DEBT SERVICE REQUIREMENTS. The amount of money required to pay interest on outstanding debt, serial maturities of principal for serial bonds and required contributions to accumulate monies for future retirement of term bonds.

DEDUCTIBLE. In the context of an insurance policy with a deductible clause, the amount that first must be subtracted from the total loss incurred before determining the insurer's liability. The deductible may be in the form of an amount of dollars, a percentage of the loss, a percentage of the value of the insured property or a period of time (as in health insurance).

DEEP-DISCOUNT DEBT. Debt issued with a stated interest rate significantly less than the effective interest rate (e.g., less than 75 percent of the effective interest rate).

DEFEASANCE. The legal release of a debtor from being the primary obligor under the debt, either by the courts or by the creditor. Also referred to as a legal defeasance. See **IN-SUBSTANCE DEFEASANCE.**

DEFERRED CHARGES. Expenditures that are not chargeable to the fiscal period in which they were made but that are carried as an asset on the balance sheet, pending amortization or other disposition (e.g., bond issuance costs). Deferred charges differ from prepaid items in that they usually extend over a long period of time (more than five years) and are not regularly recurring costs of operation. See **PREPAID ITEMS.**

DEFERRED COMPENSATION PLANS. Plans that offer employees the opportunity to defer receipt of a portion of their salary and the related liability for federal income taxes. Several sections of the Internal Revenue Code authorize certain state and local governments to provide deferred compensation plans for their employees.

DEFERRED MAINTENANCE. The act of not performing (deferring) maintenance at the time it should have been, or was scheduled to be, performed. Maintenance in this context means more than routine preventive maintenance and repairs. It also includes replacement of parts, periodic road resurfacing and other activities needed to maintain the fixed asset at its originally contemplated serviceability for its originally estimated life.

DEFERRED REVENUE. Amounts for which asset recognition criteria have been met, but for which revenue recognition criteria have not been met. Under the modified accrual basis of accounting, amounts that are measurable but not available are one example of deferred revenue.

DEFICIT. (1) The excess of the liabilities of a fund over its assets. (2) The excess of expenditures over revenues during an accounting period or, in the case of proprietary funds, the excess of expenses over revenues during an accounting period.

DEFINED BENEFIT PENSION PLAN. A pension plan that defines an amount of pension benefit to be provided, usually as a function of one or more factors, such as age, years of service or compensation.

DEFINED CONTRIBUTION PENSION PLAN. A plan that provides pension benefits in return for services rendered, provides an individual account for each participant and specifies how contributions to the individual's account are to be determined instead of specifying the amount of benefits the individual is to receive. Under a defined contribution pension plan, the benefits a participant will receive depend solely on the amount contributed to the participant's account, the returns earned on investments of those contributions and forfeitures of other participants' benefits that may be allocated to the participant's account.

DELINQUENT SPECIAL ASSESSMENTS. Special assessments remaining unpaid on and after the date to which a penalty for nonpayment is attached.

DELINQUENT TAXES. Taxes remaining unpaid on and after the date to which a penalty for nonpayment is attached. Even though the penalty may be subsequently waived and a portion of the taxes may be abated or canceled, the unpaid balances continue to be delinquent taxes until abated, canceled, paid or converted into tax liens.

DEMAND BONDS. Long-term debt issuances with demand (''put'') provisions that require the issuer to repurchase the bonds upon notice from the bondholder at a price equal to the principal plus accrued interest. To ensure their ability to redeem the bonds, issuers of demand bonds frequently enter into short-term standby liquidity agreements and long-term ''takeout'' agreements.

DEPLETION. The allocation of the cost of wasting assets (e.g., timber, oil, coal) to the periods benefited by their use.

DEPOSITORY INSURANCE. Insurance on deposits with financial institutions. FDIC, FSLIC and some state governments provide this insurance.

DEPOSITS. In the context of required note disclosures, cash and near cash items placed on account with a financial institution or fiscal agent. Some deposits (e.g., checking accounts) are subject to withdrawal upon demand without notice or penalty (demand deposits) and others (e.g., certificates of deposit) can only be withdrawn without penalty upon completion of a fixed period (time deposits).

DEPRECIATION. (1) Expiration in the service life of fixed assets, other than wasting assets, attributable to wear and tear, deterioration, action of the physical elements, inadequacy and obsolescence. (2) The portion of the cost of a fixed asset, other than a wasting asset, charged as an expense during a particular period. In accounting for depreciation, the cost of a fixed asset, less any salvage value, is prorated over the estimated service life of such an asset, and each period is charged with a portion of such cost. Through this process, the entire cost of the asset is ultimately charged off as an expense.

DEPRECIATION SCHEDULE. A schedule listing the annual allocation of the cost of fixed assets to future periods, using one of the depreciation methods acceptable under GAAP.

DIRECT CHARGES. See **DIRECT EXPENSES.**

DIRECT COSTS. See **DIRECT EXPENSES.**

DIRECT DEBT. The debt a government has incurred in its own name or assumed through the annexation of territory or consolidation with another government. See **OVERLAPPING DEBT.**

DIRECT EXPENSES. Expenses specifically traceable to specific goods, services, units, programs, activities or functions. Direct expenses differ from indirect expenses in that the latter cannot be specifically traced and so must be allocated on some systematic and rational basis.

DISBURSEMENTS. Payments in cash.

DISCLAIMER OF OPINION. A report stating that the auditor does not express an opinion on the financial statements. The disclaimer of opinion is appropriate when the auditor has not performed an examination sufficient in scope to enable him to form an opinion on the financial statements. A disclaimer of opinion should *not* be expressed because the auditor believes, on the basis of the examination, that there are material departures from GAAP. In such circumstances, an adverse opinion would be appropriate. See **ADVERSE OPINION** and **QUALIFIED OPINION.**

DISCOUNT. In the context of bonds payable and investments, the amount by which par value exceeds the price paid for a security. The discount generally represents the difference between the nominal interest rate and the actual or effective rate of return to the investor.

DISCOUNT RATE. The rate used to adjust a series of future payments to reflect the time value of money. For the purpose of calculating the pension benefit obligation defined by the GASB, this rate is equal to the estimated long-term rate of return on current and future investments of the pension plan. For capitalized leases, the discount rate used by the lessee is the lessee's incremental borrowing rate unless the lessee is aware of the lessor's implicit rate and that rate is less than the lessee's incremental borrowing rate.

DISCOUNTED PRESENT VALUE. See **PRESENT VALUE.**

DISCRETE PRESENTATIONS. The inclusion of a separate column for a component unit in the applicable general purpose financial statements. Current GAAP permit discrete presentations if a component unit has adopted accounting principles inconsistent with authoritative governmental pronouncements but considered to be generally accepted, and if the inclusion of the component unit would distort a fund type of the reporting entity. State colleges and universities are often presented by means of discrete presentations.

DISCUSSION MEMORANDUM (DM). A document issued by either the GASB or the FASB as a basis for written comments by respondents, leading to the issuance of one or more GASB or FASB pronouncements. In a DM, neither the GASB nor the FASB attempts to reach any conclusions about the issues and related arguments and implications presented. A DM is not an authoritative document and should not be used to justify departures from GAAP.

DOLLAR REPURCHASE/REVERSE REPURCHASE AGREEMENT. An agreement that involves the transfer of securities and in which the parties agree the securities returned usually will be of the same issuer but will not be the same certificates. Fixed-coupon and yield-maintenance agreements are the most common types of dollar agreements.

DOUBLE ENTRY. A system of bookkeeping requiring that for every entry made to the debit side of an account or accounts, an entry or entries be made for an equal amount to the credit side of another account or accounts.

DUE FROM OTHER FUNDS. An asset account used to indicate amounts owed to a particular fund by another fund for goods sold or services rendered. This account includes only short-term obligations on open account, not interfund loans. See **ADVANCE TO OTHER FUNDS** and **INTERFUND RECEIVABLE/PAYABLE.**

DUE TO FISCAL AGENT. A liability account reflecting amounts due to fiscal agents, such as commercial banks, for servicing a government's maturing interest and principal payments on indebtedness.

DUE TO OTHER FUNDS. A liability account reflecting amounts owed by a particular fund to another fund for goods sold or services rendered. These amounts include only short-term obligations on open account, not interfund loans. See **ADVANCE FROM OTHER FUNDS** and **INTERFUND RECEIVABLE/PAYABLE.**

ECONOMIC GAIN/LOSS. In the context of an advance refunding, the difference between the present value of the old debt service requirements and the present value of the new debt service requirements, discounted at the effective interest rate and adjusted for additional cash paid.

EFFECTIVE INTEREST RATE. The rate of earning on a bond investment, based on the actual price paid for the bond, the coupon rate, the maturity date and the length of time between interest dates, in contrast with the nominal interest rate.

EMINENT DOMAIN. The power of a government to acquire private property for public purposes. It is used frequently to obtain real property that cannot be purchased from owners in a voluntary transaction. When the power of eminent domain is exercised, owners normally are compensated by the government in an amount determined by the courts.

ENCUMBRANCES. Commitments related to unperformed (executory) contracts for goods or services. Used in budgeting, encumbrances are not GAAP expenditures or liabilities, but represent the estimated amount of expenditures ultimately to result if unperformed contracts in process are completed.

ENDOWMENT. Funds or property that are donated with either a temporary or permanent restriction as to the use of principal.

ENTERPRISE FUND. (1) A fund established to account for operations financed and operated in a manner similar to private business enterprises (e.g., water, gas and electric utilities; airports; parking garages; or transit systems). In this case the governing body intends that costs (i.e., expenses, including depreciation) of providing goods or services to the general public on a continuing basis be financed or recovered primarily through user charges. (2) A fund established because the governing body has decided that periodic determination of revenues earned, expenses incurred and/or net income is appropriate for capital maintenance, public policy, management control, accountability or other purposes.

ENTITLEMENT. The amount of payment to which a state or local government is entitled pursuant to an allocation formula contained in applicable statutes.

ENTITY. (1) The basic unit upon which accounting and/or financial reporting activities focus. The basic governmental legal and accounting entity is the individual fund and account group. (2) That combination of funds and account groups that constitutes the reporting entity for financial reporting purposes and alone may issue CAFRs and GPFS.

ENTRY. The record of a financial transaction in the appropriate book of account.

ENTRY-AGE ACTUARIAL COST METHOD. A method under which the actuarial present value of the projected benefits of each individual included in an actuarial valuation is allocated on a level basis over the earnings or service of the individual between entry age and assumed exit age(s). The portion of this actuarial present value allocated to a valuation year is called the normal cost. The portion of this actuarial present value not provided for at a valuation date by the actuarial present value of future normal costs is called the actuarial accrued liability.

EQUIPMENT. See **MACHINERY AND EQUIPMENT.**

EQUITY ACCOUNTS. Those accounts presenting the difference between assets and liabilities of the fund.

EQUITY SECURITIES. Investments that represent an ownership interest in an enterprise.

ESCHEAT. The reversion of private property to a government because there is no one to inherit or because of a breach of condition.

ESTIMATED LIFE. The expected economic useful life of an asset from the date placed in service to the projected retirement date.

EXECUTIVE BUDGET. The aggregate of information, proposals and estimates prepared and submitted to the legislative body by the chief executive and the budget office.

EXPECTED USEFUL LIFE. See **ESTIMATED LIFE.**

EXPENDABLE TRUST FUND. A trust fund whose resources, including both principal and earnings, may be expended. Expendable trust funds are accounted for in essentially the same manner as governmental funds.

EXPENDITURES. Decreases in net financial resources. Expenditures include current operating expenses requiring the present or future use of net current assets, debt service and capital outlays, and intergovernmental grants, entitlements and shared revenues.

EXPENSES. Outflows or other using up of assets or incurrences of liabilities (or a combination of both) from delivering or producing goods, rendering services or carrying out other activities that constitute the entity's ongoing major or central operations.

EXPOSURE DRAFT (ED). A proposed statement or interpretation issued for public comment by the GASB or the FASB.

EXTERNAL AUDIT. See **INDEPENDENT AUDIT.**

FACE VALUE. As applied to securities, the amount of the issuer's liability stated in the security document. See **PAR VALUE.**

FEDERAL DEPOSIT INSURANCE CORPORATION (FDIC). A federal institution that insures deposits of federally chartered banks.

FEDERAL FINANCIAL ASSISTANCE. For purposes of applying the provisions of the Single Audit Act of 1984 and OMB Circular A-128, *Audits of State and Local Governments,* assistance provided by a federal agency in the form of grants, contracts, loans, loan guarantees, property, cooperative agreements, interest subsidies, insurance, or direct appropriations. Federal financial assistance does *not* include direct federal cash assistance to individuals.

FEDERAL SAVINGS AND LOAN INSURANCE CORPORATION (FSLIC). A federal institution that insures deposits of federally chartered savings and loan associations.

FIDELITY BOND. A written promise to indemnify against losses from theft, defalcation and misappropriation of public monies by government officers and employees.

FIDUCIARY FUND TYPE. The trust and agency funds used to account for assets held by a government unit in a trustee capacity or as an agent for individuals, private organizations, other government units and/or other funds.

FINANCIAL ADVISOR. In the context of bond issuances, a consultant who advises the issuer on any of a variety of matters related to the issuance. The financial advisor sometimes also is referred to as the fiscal consultant.

FINANCIAL AUDIT. An audit made to determine whether the financial statements of a government are presented fairly in conformity with GAAP.

FINANCIAL REPORTING PYRAMID. The plan of organization for the financial section of the CAFR/CUFR, as set forth in the 1987 *Codification of Governmental Accounting and Financial Reporting Standards.* The pyramid presents GAAP financial statements on three distinct and progressively more detailed reporting levels: (1) combined statements—overview (the "liftable" GPFS/CUFS), (2) combining statements—by fund type and (where necessary or appropriate) (3) individual fund statements.

FINANCIAL RESOURCES. Cash and other assets that, in the normal course of operations, will become cash.

FINANCIAL STATEMENTS. See **BASIC FINANCIAL STATEMENTS.**

FISCAL AGENT. A fiduciary agent, usually a bank or county treasurer, who performs the function of paying debt principal and interest when due.

FISCAL FUNDING CLAUSE. A clause in a lease agreement providing that the lease is cancelable if the legislature or other funding authority does not appropriate the funds necessary for the government unit to fulfill its obligations under the lease agreement.

FISCAL PERIOD. Any period at the end of which a government determines its financial position and the results of its operations. Syn. **ACCOUNTING PERIOD.**

FISCAL YEAR. A 12-month period to which the annual operating budget applies and at the end of which a government determines its financial position and the results of its operations.

FIXED ASSETS. Long-lived tangible assets obtained or controlled as a result of past transactions, events or circumstances. Fixed assets include buildings, equipment, improvements other than buildings and land. In the private sector, these assets are referred to most often as property, plant and equipment.

FIXED BUDGET. A budget setting forth dollar amounts that are not subject to change based on the volume of goods or services to be provided.

FIXED COSTS. Costs of providing goods or services that do not vary proportionately to the volume of goods or services provided (e.g., insurance and contributions to retirement systems).

FIXED-COUPON REPURCHASE/REVERSE REPURCHASE AGREEMENT. Agreements in which the parties agree that the securities returned will have the same stated interest rate as, and maturities similar to, the securities transferred. See **REPURCHASE AGREEMENT** and **REVERSE REPURCHASE AGREEMENT.**

FIXED-INCOME SECURITIES. Securities that offer a specified, measurable cash flow (e.g., most bonds).

FIXTURES. Attachments to buildings that are not intended to be removed and cannot be removed without damage to the buildings. Those fixtures with a useful life presumed to be as long as that of the building itself are considered a part of the building; all others are classified as equipment.

FLEXIBLE BUDGET. A budget whose dollar amounts vary according to the volume of goods or services to be provided.

FLOW OF CURRENT FINANCIAL RESOURCES. A measurement focus that recognizes the net effect of transactions on current financial resources by recording accruals for those revenue and expenditure transactions which have occurred by year end that are normally expected to result in cash receipt or disbursement early enough in the following year either (a) to provide financial resources to liquidate liabilities recorded in the fund at year end or (b) to require the use of available expendable financial resources reported at year end.

FLOW OF ECONOMIC RESOURCES. The measurement focus used in the commercial model and in proprietary and similar trust funds to measure economic resources, the claims to those economic resources and the effects of transactions, events and circumstances that change economic resources and claims to those resources. This focus includes depreciation of fixed assets, deferral of unearned revenues and prepaid expenses, and amortization of the resulting liabilities and assets. Under this measurement focus, all assets and liabilities are reported on the balance sheet, whether current or noncurrent. Also, the accrual basis of accounting is used, with the result that operating statements report expenses rather than expenditures.

FLOW OF FINANCIAL RESOURCES MEASUREMENT FOCUS. A new measurement focus proposed for governmental funds in the GASB's exposure draft *Measurement Focus and Basis of Accounting—Governmental Funds* (December 1987). It is:

a measure of the extent to which financial resources obtained during a period are sufficient to cover claims incurred during that period against financial resources, and the net financial resources available for future periods. This is accomplished by measuring the increases and decreases in net financial resources and the balances of and claims against financial resources using an accrual basis of accounting.

This definition uses the term ''financial resources'' in a way that differs from its current use. See **FINANCIAL RESOURCES.** In this instance, the term means cash, claims to

cash (e.g., accounts and taxes receivable), and claims to goods or services (e.g., prepaid items) obtained or controlled as a result of past transactions or events. See **FLOW OF CURRENT FINANCIAL RESOURCES.**

FORECLOSURE. The seizure of property as payment for delinquent tax or special assessment obligations. Ordinarily, property foreclosed is resold to liquidate delinquent tax or special assessment obligations, but on occasion governments retain possession for their own needs.

FORFEITURE. The automatic loss of cash or other property as a penalty for not complying with legal provisions and as compensation for the resulting damages or losses. This term should not be confused with confiscation. The latter term designates the actual taking over of the forfeited property by the government. Even after property has been forfeited, it cannot be said to be confiscated until the government claims it.

FORMAL BUDGETARY INTEGRATION. The management control technique through which the annual operating budget is recorded in the general ledger through the use of budgetary accounts. It is intended to facilitate control over revenues and expenditures during the year.

FRANCHISE. A special privilege granted by a government, permitting the continued use of public property, such as city streets, and usually involving the elements of monopoly and regulation.

FROZEN ENTRY AGE ACTUARIAL COST METHOD. A method under which the portion of the actuarial present value of projected benefits of the group included in an actuarial valuation, exceeding the sum of the actuarial value of assets plus the unfunded frozen actuarial accrued liability is allocated on a level basis over the earnings or service of the group between the valuation date and assumed exit. This allocation is performed for the group as a whole, not as a sum of individual allocations. The frozen actuarial accrued liability is determined using the entry-age actuarial cost method. The portion of this actuarial present value allocated to a valuation year is called the normal cost.

FULL FAITH AND CREDIT. A pledge of the general taxing power for the payment of debt obligations. Bonds carrying such pledges are referred to as general obligation bonds or full-faith-and-credit bonds.

FUNCTION. A group of related activities aimed at accomplishing a major service or regulatory program for which a government is responsible (e.g., public safety). See **SUBFUNCTION.**

FUNCTIONAL-BASIS COMBINING. The process of grouping or combining similar funds and/or component units on a functional basis (e.g., transportation, economic development) for financial reporting purposes.

FUNCTIONAL CLASSIFICATION. Expenditure classification according to the principal purposes for which expenditures are made (e.g., public safety).

FUND. A fiscal and accounting entity with a self-balancing set of accounts in which cash and other financial resources, all related liabilities and residual equities, or balances, and changes therein, are recorded and segregated to carry on specific activities or attain certain objectives in accordance with special regulations, restrictions or limitations.

FUND BALANCE. The difference between fund assets and fund liabilities of governmental and similar trust funds.

FUND BALANCE SHEET. A balance sheet for a single fund. See **FUND** and **BALANCE SHEET.**

FUND BALANCE—RESERVED FOR ADVANCE TO OTHER FUNDS. An account used to segregate a portion of fund balance to indicate that noncurrent portions of long-term interfund receivables do not represent expendable available financial resources.

FUND BALANCE—RESERVED FOR DEBT SERVICE. An account used to segregate a portion of fund balance for resources legally restricted to the payment of general long-term debt principal and interest maturing in future years.

FUND BALANCE—RESERVED FOR EMPLOYEES' RETIREMENT SYSTEM. Accounts used to account for PERS and pension trust reserved fund balances. These normally include (1) fund balance—reserved for member contributions, (2) fund balance—reserved for employer contributions, (3) fund balance—reserved for benefits, (4) fund balance—reserved for disability and (5) fund balance—reserved for undistributed interest earnings.

FUND BALANCE—RESERVED FOR ENCUMBRANCES. An account used to segregate a portion of fund balance for expenditure upon vendor performance.

FUND BALANCE—RESERVED FOR ENDOWMENTS. An account used to indicate that trust fund balance amounts representing endowment principal are legally restricted.

FUND BALANCE—RESERVED FOR FIXED ASSETS HELD FOR RESALE. An account used to segregate a portion of fund balance to indicate that fixed assets held for resale do not represent expendable available financial resources.

FUND BALANCE—RESERVED FOR INVENTORIES. An account used to segregate a portion of fund balance to indicate that, under the purchases method, inventories of supplies do not represent expendable available financial resources even though they are a component of net current assets.

FUND BALANCE—RESERVED FOR NONCURRENT LOANS RECEIVABLE. An account used to segregate a portion of fund balance to indicate that noncurrent portions of long-term loans receivable do not represent expendable available financial resources.

FUND BALANCE—RESERVED FOR PREPAID ITEMS. An account used to segregate a portion of fund balance to indicate that prepaid items do not represent expendable available financial resources even though they are a component of net current assets.

FUND CAPITAL ASSETS. Those capital assets associated with proprietary or trust funds. See **FIXED ASSETS.**

FUNDED PENSION PLAN. A pension plan in which contributions are made and assets are accumulated to pay benefits to potential recipients before cash payments to recipients actually are required.

FUNDING POLICY. In the context of pension plans, the policy for the amounts and timing of contributions to be made by the employer(s), participants and any other sources to provide the benefits a pension plan specifies.

FUND TYPE. Any one of seven categories into which all funds are classified in governmental accounting. The seven fund types are: general, special revenue, debt service, capital projects, enterprise, internal service, and trust and agency.

GENERAL FIXED ASSETS. Capital assets that are not assets of any fund, but of the government unit as a whole. Most often these assets arise from the expenditure of the financial resources of governmental funds.

GENERAL FIXED ASSETS ACCOUNT GROUP (GFAAG). A self-balancing group of accounts established to account for fixed assets of a government not accounted for through specific proprietary funds or trust funds.

GENERAL FUND. The fund used to account for all financial resources, except those required to be accounted for in another fund.

GENERAL JOURNAL. A journal in which are recorded all entries not recorded in special journals. See **JOURNAL** and **SPECIAL JOURNAL.**

GENERAL LEDGER. A record containing the accounts needed to reflect the financial position and the results of operations of a government. In double-entry bookkeeping, the debits and credits in the general ledger are equal (i.e., the debit balances equal the credit balances). See **SUBSIDIARY LEDGER, CONTROL ACCOUNT** and **SUBSIDIARY ACCOUNT.**

GENERAL LONG-TERM DEBT. Long-term debt expected to be repaid from governmental funds. See **LONG-TERM DEBT.**

GENERAL LONG-TERM DEBT ACCOUNT GROUP (GLTDAG). A self-balancing group of accounts established to account for the unmatured general long-term debt of a government. See **GENERAL LONG-TERM DEBT.** The GLTDAG is also used to report that portion of the liabilities for claims, judgments, compensated absences and unfunded pension contributions of governmental funds and expendable trust funds not expected to be liquidated through the use of expendable available financial resources.

GENERAL OBLIGATION BONDS PAYABLE. Bonds backed by the full faith and credit of government. See **FULL FAITH AND CREDIT.**

GENERALLY ACCEPTED ACCOUNTING PRINCIPLES (GAAP). Uniform minimum standards and guidelines for financial accounting and reporting. They govern the form and content of the financial statements of an entity. GAAP encompass the conventions, rules and procedures necessary to define accepted accounting practice at a particular time. They include not only broad guidelines of general application, but also detailed practices and procedures. GAAP provide a standard by which to measure financial presentations. The primary authoritative body on the application of GAAP to state and local governments is the GASB.

GENERALLY ACCEPTED AUDITING STANDARDS (GAAS). Standards established by the AICPA for the conduct and reporting of financial audits. There are 10 basic GAAS, classed into three broad categories: general standards, standards of field work and standards of reporting. The Auditing Standards Board of the AICPA publishes SAS to comment and expand upon these basic standards. These SAS, together with the 10 basic standards, constitute GAAS. These GAAS set forth the objectives of the audit and establish measures that can be applied to judge the quality of its performance.

GENERALLY ACCEPTED GOVERNMENT AUDITING STANDARDS (GAGAS). Standards established by the GAO in its publication *Standards for Audit of Governmental Organizations, Programs, Activities and Functions* (''yellow book'') for the conduct and reporting of both financial and performance audits. GAGAS set forth general standards applicable to both types of audits and separate standards of field work and reporting for financial and performance audits. The GAGAS standards of field work and reporting for financial audits incorporate and build upon GAAS.

GENERAL PURPOSE FINANCIAL STATEMENTS (GPFS). Five combined financial statements that, together with the accompanying notes, constitute the minimum financial reporting needed for fair presentation in conformity with GAAP. Syn. **COMBINED STATEMENTS—OVERVIEW.** See **BASIC FINANCIAL STATEMENTS, FINANCIAL REPORTING PYRAMID** and **''LIFTABLE'' GENERAL PURPOSE FINANCIAL STATEMENTS.** These five combined financial statements, with their accompanying notes, make up the first of the financial reporting pyramid's three reporting levels containing financial statements. Known as the combined statements—overview, these statements include (1) combined balance sheet—all fund types and account groups, (2) combined statement of revenues, expenditures and changes in fund balances—all governmental fund types, (3) combined statement of revenues, expenditures and changes in fund balances—budget and actual—general and special revenue fund types (and similar governmental fund types for which annual budgets have been legally adopted), (4) combined statement of revenues, expenses and changes in retained earnings (or equity)—all proprietary fund types and (5) combined statement of changes in financial position—all proprietary fund types. Trust fund operations may be reported in (2), (4) and (5)

above, as appropriate, or separately. The combined statements—overview also are referred to as the ''liftable'' GPFS.

GOVERNMENTAL ACCOUNTING. The composite activity of analyzing, recording, summarizing, reporting and interpreting the financial transactions of governments.

GOVERNMENTAL ACCOUNTING STANDARDS BOARD (GASB). The authoritative accounting and financial reporting standard-setting body for government entities.

GOVERNMENTAL FUND TYPES. Funds used to account for the acquisition, use and balances of expendable financial resources and the related current liabilities—except those accounted for in proprietary funds and fiduciary funds. In essence, these funds are accounting segregations of financial resources. Expendable assets are assigned to a particular governmental fund type according to the purposes for which they may or must be used. Current liabilities are assigned to the fund type from which they are to be paid. The difference between the assets and liabilities of governmental fund types is referred to as fund balance. The measurement focus in these fund types is on the determination of financial position and changes in financial position (sources, uses and balances of financial resources), rather than on net income determination. The statement of revenues, expenditures and changes in fund balance is the primary governmental fund type operating statement. It may be supported or supplemented by more detailed schedules of revenues, expenditures, transfers and other changes in fund balance. Under current GAAP, there are four governmental fund types: general, special revenue, debt service and capital projects.

GOVERNMENTAL-TYPE ACTIVITIES. Those activities of a government that are carried out primarily to provide services to citizens and that are financed primarily through taxes and intergovernmental grants.

GRANT ANTICIPATION NOTES (GANs). Short-term, interest-bearing notes issued by a government in anticipation of grants to be received at a later date. The notes are retired from proceeds of the grants to which they are related. See **INTERIM BORROWING.**

GRANTS. Contributions or gifts of cash or other assets from another government to be used or expended for a specified purpose, activity or facility. See **CAPITAL GRANTS** and **OPERATING GRANTS.**

GRANTS-IN-AID. See **GRANTS.**

GROSS BONDED DEBT. The total amount of direct debt of a government, represented by outstanding bonds before deduction of any assets available and earmarked for their retirement.

HISTORICAL COST. See **COST.**

HOLD-HARMLESS AGREEMENT. A contract under which the liability of one party for damages is assumed by another.

IMPACT FEES. Fees charged to developers to cover, in whole or in part, the anticipated cost of improvements that will be necessary as a result of the development (e.g., parks, sidewalks).

IMPREST ACCOUNT. An account into which a fixed amount of money is placed for minor disbursements or disbursements for a specific purpose (e.g., payroll). When disbursements are made, a voucher is completed to record their date, amount, nature and purpose. From time to time, a report with substantiating vouchers is prepared; the account is replenished for the exact amount of the disbursements and the appropriate general ledger accounts are charged. The total of cash plus substantiating vouchers always should equal the total fixed amount of money set aside in the imprest account. See **PETTY CASH.**

IMPROVEMENTS OTHER THAN BUILDINGS. Attachments or annexations to land that are intended to remain so attached or annexed, such as sidewalks, trees, drives, tunnels, drains and sewers. Sidewalks, curbing, sewers and highways are sometimes referred to as betterments, but the term "improvements" is preferred.

INCOME. A term used in proprietary fund-type accounting to represent (1) revenues or (2) the excess of revenues over expenses. See **OPERATING INCOME, INCOME BEFORE OPERATING TRANSFERS** and **NET INCOME.**

INCOME BEFORE OPERATING TRANSFERS. Proprietary fund operating income plus nonoperating revenues and minus nonoperating expenses.

INCURRED-BUT-NOT-REPORTED (IBNR) CLAIMS/ LOSSES. Claims for insured events that have occurred but have not yet been reported to the government entity, insurer or reinsurer as of the date of the financial statements. IBNR claims also may include expected future developments on claims already reported.

INDEPENDENT AUDIT. An audit performed by an independent auditor.

INDEPENDENT AUDITOR. An auditor meeting the independence criteria set forth in GAAS or GAGAS.

INDETERMINATE APPROPRIATION. An appropriation that is not limited either to any definite period of time or to any definite amount. A distinction must be made between an indeterminate appropriation and a continuing appropriation. First, whereas a continuing appropriation is indefinite only as to time, an indeterminate appropriation is indefinite as to both time and amount. Second, even indeterminate appropriations that are indefinite only as to time are to be distinguished from continuing appropriations in that such indeterminate appropriations may eventually lapse (e.g., an appropriation to construct a building may be made to continue in effect until the building is constructed. Once the building is completed, however, the unexpended balance of the appropriation lapses). A continuing appropriation, on the other hand, may continue forever; it can only be abolished by specific action of the legislative body.

INDIRECT COSTS. See **OVERHEAD.**

INDIRECT EXPENSES. See **OVERHEAD.**

INDIVIDUAL FUND STATEMENTS AND SCHEDULES. The third of the financial reporting pyramid's three reporting levels containing GAAP financial statements. Such statements and schedules should be presented only when necessary or appropriate. Governments should not present physically separate individual fund financial statements and schedules that simply repeat information already presented in columns on the combined statements—overview or combining statements—by fund type. Physically separate individual fund statement and schedule formats normally are used only (1) to present required individual fund budgetary comparisons, (2) to present prior-year comparative data or (3) to present more detailed information than is presented for a fund on one of the higher levels of the financial reporting pyramid.

INDUSTRIAL DEVELOPMENT BONDS. Bonds issued by governments, the proceeds of which are used to construct facilities for a private business enterprise.

INFRASTRUCTURE ASSETS. Public domain fixed assets such as roads, bridges, curbs and gutters, streets and sidewalks, drainage systems, lighting systems and similar assets that are immovable and of value only to the government unit.

IN-SUBSTANCE DEFEASANCE. An advance refunding in which the government is not legally released from being the primary obligor on the refunded bonds, but the possibility of the government having to make additional payments is considered remote under criteria provided by SFAS No. 76. See **ADVANCE REFUNDING BONDS.**

INSURABLE VALUE. The property, or portion of a property, covered by insurance in accordance with the terms of the insurance policy or other agreement. The standard insurance policy provides indemnity for the replacement cost or actual cash value.

INSURANCE. The transfer of risk of loss from one party (the insured) to another party (the insurer) in which the insurer promises (unusually specified in a written contract) to pay the insured (or others on the insured's behalf) an amount of money (or services, or both) for economic losses sustained from an unexpected (accidental) event during a period of time for which the insured makes a premium payment to the insurer.

INTEREST METHOD. In the context of bonds, a method of periodic amortization of issuance costs and premium or discount over the term of the related debt. The objective of the interest method is to arrive at a periodic interest cost (including amortization) that will represent a level effective rate on the sum of the face amount of the debt and (plus or minus) the unamortized premium or discount and issuance costs at the beginning of each period. The difference between the periodic interest cost so calculated and the nominal interest on the outstanding amount of the debt is the amount of periodic amortization.

INTERFUND RECEIVABLE/PAYABLE. Short-term loans made by one fund to another, or the current portion of an advance to or from another fund.

INTERFUND TRANSACTIONS. Transactions between funds of the same government reporting entity. They include (1) **QUASI-EXTERNAL TRANSACTIONS,** (2) **REIMBURSEMENTS,** (3) **RESIDUAL EQUITY TRANSFERS,** (4) **OPERATING TRANSFERS** and (5) interfund loans.

INTERFUND TRANSFERS. All interfund transactions except loans, quasi-external transactions and reimbursements. Transfers can be classified as belonging to one of two major categories: **RESIDUAL EQUITY TRANSFERS** or **OPERATING TRANSFERS.**

INTERGOVERNMENT PAYABLE. A liability account reflecting amounts owed by the reporting government to another government.

INTERGOVERNMENTAL RECEIVABLE. An asset account reflecting amounts due to the reporting government from another government. These amounts may represent grants-in-aid, shared taxes, taxes collected by another unit, loans and charges for services rendered by the government for another government.

INTERGOVERNMENTAL REVENUES. Revenues from other governments in the form of grants, entitlements, shared revenues or payments in lieu of taxes.

INTERIM BORROWING. (1) Short-term loans to be repaid from general revenues during the course of a fiscal year. (2) Short-term loans in anticipation of tax collections, grants or bond issuance. See **BOND ANTICIPATION NOTES, GRANT ANTICIPATION NOTES** and **TAX ANTICIPATION NOTES.**

INTERIM FINANCIAL STATEMENTS. Financial statements prepared as of a date or for a period during the fiscal year and including only financial transactions during the current year to date.

INTERNAL AUDITING. An independent appraisal of the diverse operations and controls within a government entity to determine whether acceptable policies and procedures are followed, established standards are met, resources are used efficiently and economically and the organization's objectives are being achieved. The term covers all forms of appraisal of activities undertaken by auditors working for and within an organization.

INTERNAL CONTROL STRUCTURE. Policies and procedures established to provide reasonable assurance that specific government objectives will be achieved.

INTERNAL SERVICE FUND. A fund used to account for the financing of goods or services provided by one department or agency to other departments or agencies of a government, or to other governments, on a cost-reimbursement basis.

INTERPERIOD EQUITY. The measure of the extent to which current-year revenues are sufficient to pay for the services provided by the government entity during the year, and whether current-year citizens are receiving services by shifting part of the payment burden to future years' citizens or by using up previously accumulated resources.

INVENTORY. (1) A detailed list showing quantities, descriptions and values of property and, frequently, units of measure and unit prices. (2) An asset account reflecting the cost of goods held for resale or for use in operations.

INVESTMENT IN GENERAL FIXED ASSETS. An account in the GFAAG representing the government's investment in general fixed assets. The balance of this account generally is subdivided according to the source of the monies that financed the asset acquisition, such as general fund revenues and special assessments.

INVESTMENTS. Most commonly, securities and real estate held for the production of revenues in the form of interest, dividends, rentals or lease payments. The term does not include fixed assets used in government operations.

JOINT VENTURE. A legal entity or other contractual arrangement in which a government participates as a separate and specific activity for the benefit of the public or service recipients and in which the government retains an ongoing financial interest.

JOURNAL. A book of original entry. See **GENERAL JOURNAL, SPECIAL JOURNAL** and **REGISTER.**

JOURNAL VOUCHER. A standard form provided for the recording of certain transactions or information in place of, or supplementary to, the journals or registers. The journal voucher usually contains an entry or entries, explanations, references to documentary evidence supporting the entry or entries and the signature or initials of one or more properly authorized officials.

JUDGMENT. An amount to be paid or collected by a government as the result of a court decision, including a condemnation award in payment for private property taken for public use.

JUDGMENT BONDS. Bonds issued to finance judgments.

JUDGMENTS PAYABLE. The liability incurred as the result of a judgment.

LAND. A fixed asset account reflecting the cost of land owned by a government.

LAPSE. As applied to appropriations, the automatic termination of an appropriation. Except for indeterminate appropriations and continuing appropriations, an appropriation is made for a certain period of time. At the end of this period, any unexpended or unencumbered balance thereof lapses, unless otherwise provided by law.

LEASEHOLD. The right to the use of real estate by virtue of a lease, usually for a specified term of years, for which consideration is paid.

LEASE-PURCHASE AGREEMENTS. Contractual agreements that are termed leases, but that in substance are purchase contracts. See **CAPITAL LEASES.**

LEASE RENTAL BOND. A bond usually issued by a nonprofit authority and secured by lease payments to be made by the government leasing the project financed by bond proceeds.

LEDGER. A group of accounts in which are recorded the financial transactions of an entity. See **GENERAL LEDGER** and **SUBSIDIARY LEDGER.**

LEGAL DEBT LIMIT. See **DEBT LIMIT.**

LEGAL LEVEL OF BUDGETARY CONTROL. The level at which spending in excess of budgeted amounts would be a violation of law.

LEGAL INVESTMENTS. (1) Investments that savings banks, insurance companies, trustees and other fiduciaries (individual or corporate) are permitted to make by the laws of the state in which they are domiciled, or under the jurisdiction in which they operate or serve. The investments meeting the conditions imposed by law constitute the legal investment list. (2) Investments that governments are permitted to make by law.

LEGAL OPINION. (1) The opinion as to legality of an authorized official, such as an attorney general or city attorney. (2) In the case of government bonds, the opinion of a specialized bond attorney as to the legality of the bond issue.

LETTER OF CREDIT. A financial institution's written guarantee of a customer's drafts, up to a specified amount, for a certain period of time.

LEVEL OF BUDGETARY CONTROL. One of the three possible levels of budgetary control and authority to which organizations, programs, activities and functions may be subject. These levels of budgetary control are (a) appropriated budget, (b) legally authorized nonappropriated budget review and approval process, which is outside the appropriated budget process or (c) nonbudgeted financial activities, which are not subject to the appropriated budget and the appropriation process or to any legally authorized nonappropriated budget review and approval process, but still are relevant for sound financial management and oversight. See **LEGAL LEVEL OF BUDGETARY CONTROL.**

LEVY. (1) (Verb) To impose taxes, special assessments or service charges for the support of government activities. (2) (Noun) The total amount of taxes, special assessments or service charges imposed by a government.

LIABILITIES. Probable future sacrifices of economic benefits, arising from present obligations of a particular entity to transfer assets or provide services to other entities in the future as a result of past transactions or events.

"LIFTABLE" GENERAL PURPOSE FINANCIAL STATEMENTS (GPFS). The GPFS designed to be "liftable" from the financial section of the CAFR for inclusion in official statements for securities offerings or for widespread distribution, along with an independent auditor's opinion, to users requiring less detailed information than is contained in the full CAFR. In order to be "liftable," the GPFS must include all disclosures necessary for their fair presentation in conformity with GAAP including certain specified disclosures related to individual funds. See **GENERAL PURPOSE FINANCIAL STATEMENTS.**

LIQUIDITY. The ability to convert assets to cash quickly, without significant losses.

LOANS RECEIVABLE. An asset account reflecting amounts loaned to individuals or organizations external to a government, including notes taken as security for such loans. Loans to other funds and governments should be recorded and reported separately.

LOCAL IMPROVEMENT TAX. See **SPECIAL ASSESSMENT.**

LONG-TERM BUDGET. A budget prepared for a period longer than a fiscal year; in some state governments, a budget prepared for a period longer than a biennium. Long-term budgets concerned with capital outlay plans and capital improvement programs are referred to as capital budgets.

LONG-TERM DEBT. In the context of the GLTDAG, any unmatured debt that is not a fund liability.

LUMP-SUM APPROPRIATION. An appropriation made for a stated purpose, or for a named department, without specifying further the amounts that may be spent for specific activities or for particular objects of expenditure (e.g., a lump-sum appropriation for the police department would not specify the amounts to be spent for uniform patrol, traffic control, etc., or for salaries and wages, materials and supplies, travel).

MACHINERY AND EQUIPMENT. Property that does not lose its identity when removed from its location and is not changed materially or consumed immediately (e.g., within one year) by use.

MAINTENANCE. The act of keeping capital assets in a state of good repair. It includes preventive maintenance; normal periodic repairs; replacement of parts, structural components and so forth and other activities needed to maintain the asset so that it continues to provide normal services and achieves its optimum life.

MARGIN. In the context of repurchase agreements and reverse repurchase agreements, the excess of the market value including accrued interest of the securities underlying a repurchase-reverse repurchase agreement or a fixed-coupon repurchase-reverse repurchase agreement over the agreement amount including accrued interest. It is common practice for a margin to be built into an agreement to protect against declines in the market value of the underlying securities.

MARKET RISK. The risk that the market value of an investment, collateral protecting a deposit or securities underlying a repurchase agreement will decline. Market risk is affected by the length to maturity of a security, the need to liquidate a security before maturity, the extent to which collateral exceeds the amount invested and how often the amount of collateral is adjusted for changing market values.

MASTER AGREEMENT. A written contract covering all future transactions between the parties to repurchase-reverse repurchase agreements and establishing each party's rights in the transactions. A master agreement often will specify, among other things, the right of the buyer-lender to liquidate the underlying securities in the event of default by the seller-borrower.

MATCHED POSITION. When the proceeds from a reverse repurchase agreement are invested in securities that mature at, or almost at, the same time as the reverse repurchase agreement and the proceeds from those securities will be used to liquidate the agreement.

MATURED BONDS PAYABLE. A liability account reflecting unpaid principal of bonds that have reached or passed their maturity date.

MATURED INTEREST PAYABLE. A liability account reflecting unpaid interest on bonds that have reached or passed their maturity date.

MEASUREMENT FOCUS. The accounting convention that determines (1) which assets and which liabilities are included on a government's balance sheet and where they are reported there, and (2) whether an operating statement presents information on the flow of financial resources (revenues and expenditures) or information on the flow of economic resources (revenues and expenses).

MILL. One one-thousandth of a dollar of assessed value.

MILLAGE. Rate used in calculating taxes based upon the value of property, expressed in mills per dollar of property value.

MODIFIED ACCRUAL BASIS. The accrual basis of accounting adapted to the governmental fund-type measurement focus. Under it, revenues and other financial resource increments (e.g., bond issue proceeds) are recognized when they become susceptible to accrual, that is when they become both "measurable" and "available to finance expenditures of the current period." "Available" means collectible in the current period or soon enough thereafter to be used to pay liabilities of the current period. Expenditures are recognized when the fund liability is incurred except for (1) inventories of materials and supplies that may be considered expenditures either when purchased or when used, and (2) prepaid insurance and similar items that may be considered expenditures either when paid for or when consumed. All governmental funds, expendable trust funds and agency funds are accounted for using the modified accrual basis of accounting.

MORTGAGE BONDS. Bonds secured by a mortgage against specified properties of a government, usually its public utilities or other enterprises. If primarily payable from enterprise revenues, they also are classed as revenue bonds. See **REVENUE BONDS**.

MUNICIPAL. In its broadest sense, an adjective denoting the state and all subordinate units of government. In a more restricted sense, an adjective denoting a city or village as opposed to other local governments.

MUNICIPAL CORPORATION. A political and corporate body established pursuant to state statutes to provide government services and regulations for its inhabitants. A municipal corporation has defined boundaries and a population and usually is organized with the consent of its residents. It usually has a seal and may sue and be sued (e.g., cities and villages). See **QUASI-MUNICIPAL CORPORATION**.

NET BONDED DEBT. Gross bonded debt less any cash or other assets available and earmarked for its retirement and less all self-supporting debt (e.g., revenue bonds).

NET BOOK VALUE. See **BOOK VALUE**.

NET INCOME. Proprietary fund excess of operating revenues, nonoperating revenues and operating transfers in over operating expenses, nonoperating expenses and operating transfers out.

NET INTEREST COST. A method used to calculate a bond issuer's interest cost. The net interest cost (NIC) does not take into account the time value of money. The NIC is equal to the total interest payments plus discount (or minus premium), divided by the number of bond years.

NET PROFIT. See **NET INCOME**.

NET REVENUE. See **NET INCOME** and **NET REVENUES AVAILABLE FOR DEBT SERVICE**.

NET REVENUES AVAILABLE FOR DEBT SERVICE. Proprietary fund gross operating revenues less operating and maintenance expenses (which normally do not include depreciation expense or interest expense on bonds). "Net revenues available for debt service" as thus defined is used to compute "coverage" on revenue bond issues. See **COVERAGE**. Under the laws of some states and the provisions of some revenue bond indentures, to compute revenue bond coverage, net revenues available for debt service must be calculated on a cash basis, rather than in conformity with GAAP.

NOMINAL INTEREST RATE. The contractual interest rate shown on the face and in the body of a bond and used to compute the amount of interest to be paid, in contrast to the effective interest rate. See **COUPON RATE.**

NONAPPROPRIATED BUDGET. A financial plan for an organization, program, activity or function approved in a manner authorized by constitution, charter, statute or ordinance but not subject to appropriation and, therefore, outside the boundaries of the definition of appropriated budget.

NONCONTRIBUTING EMPLOYERS. In the context of pension disclosures for governments, employers that are not legally responsible for making contributions to a PERS but whose employees are covered by a PERS because of contributions made by another entity.

NONEMPLOYER CONTRIBUTOR. In the context of pension disclosures for governments, a government that makes contributions to a PERS to provide benefits to employees of another government (e.g., a state may make the employer's pension contribution for school districts in the state).

NONEXPENDABLE TRUST FUND. A trust fund, the principal of which may not be expended. Nonexpendable trust funds are accounted for in essentially the same manner as proprietary funds.

NONOPERATING EXPENSES. Proprietary fund expenses not directly related to the fund's primary activities (e.g., interest).

NONOPERATING PROPERTIES. Properties owned by an enterprise fund but not used in the provision of the fund's primary service activities.

NONOPERATING REVENUES. Proprietary fund revenues incidental to, or byproducts of, the fund's primary activities.

NORMAL COST. That portion of the actuarial present value of pension plan benefits and expenses allocated to a valuation year by the actuarial cost method. This amount does not include any payment related to an unfunded actuarial accrued liability. For plans financed in part by employee contributions, normal cost ordinarily refers to the total of employee contributions and employer normal cost.

NOTE PAYABLE. In general, an unconditional written promise signed by the maker to pay a certain sum of money on demand or at a fixed or determinable time either to the bearer or to the order of a person designated therein. See **TEMPORARY LOANS.**

NOTE RECEIVABLE. A legal right to receive payment of a certain sum of money on demand or at a fixed or determinable time, based on an unconditional written promise signed by the maker.

NOTES TO THE FINANCIAL STATEMENTS. The SSAP and other disclosures required for a fair presentation of the financial statements of a government in conformity with GAAP and not included on the face of the financial statements themselves. The notes to the financial statements are an integral part of the GPFS/CUFS.

OBJECT. As used in expenditure classification, applies to the article purchased or the service obtained, rather than to the purpose for which the article or service was purchased or obtained (e.g., personal services, contractual services, materials and supplies). See **ACTIVITY, CHARACTER CLASSIFICATION, FUNCTION** and **OBJECT CLASS.**

OBJECT CLASS. Expenditure classification according to the types of items purchased or services obtained (e.g., personal services, materials, supplies and equipment).

OBJECT OF EXPENDITURE. See **OBJECT.**

OBLIGATIONS. Amounts a government may be required legally to meet out of its resources. They include not only actual liabilities, but also unliquidated encumbrances.

OBSOLESCENCE. The decrease in the value of fixed assets, resulting from economic, social, technological or legal changes.

OFFICIAL STATEMENT. A document published by a government planning to issue bonds that provides information on the proposed bond issue, the purpose of the issue, and the means of servicing the indebtedness, as well as other information about the issuer that may be helpful in evaluating creditworthiness.

OPERATING BUDGET. Plans of current expenditures and the proposed means of financing them. The annual operating budget (or, in the case of some state governments, the biennial operating budget) is the primary means by which most of the financing, acquisition, spending and service delivery activities of a government are controlled. The use of annual operating budgets is usually required by law. Even when not required by law, however, annual operating budgets are essential to sound financial management and should be adopted by every government. See **BUDGET.**

OPERATING EXPENSES. Proprietary fund expenses related directly to the fund's primary activities.

OPERATING GRANTS. Grants that are restricted by the grantor to operating purposes or that may be used for either capital or operating purposes at the discretion of the grantee. See **CAPITAL GRANTS.**

OPERATING INCOME. The excess of proprietary fund operating revenues over operating expenses.

OPERATING LEASE. A lease agreement that does not meet the criteria for capitalization set forth in SFAS No. 13.

OPERATING REVENUES. Proprietary fund revenues directly related to the fund's primary activities. They consist primarily of user charges for goods and services.

OPERATING STATEMENT. The financial statement disclosing the financial results of operations of an entity during an accounting period in conformity with GAAP. In governmental financial reporting, operating statements and statements of changes in fund equity are combined into "all-inclusive" operating statement formats.

OPERATING TRANSFERS. All interfund transfers other than residual equity transfers (e.g., legally authorized transfers from a fund receiving revenue to the fund through which the resources are to be expended).

OPTIONAL BOND. See **CALLABLE BOND.**

ORDER. A formal legislative enactment by the governing board of certain local governments; it has the full force and effect of law (e.g., county governing bodies in some states pass orders rather than laws, resolutions or ordinances).

ORDINANCE. A formal legislative enactment by the governing body of a municipality. If it is not in conflict with any higher form of law, such as a state statute or constitutional provision, it has the full force and effect of law within the boundaries of the municipality to which it applies. The difference between an ordinance and a resolution is that the latter requires less legal formality and has a lower legal status. Ordinarily, the statutes or charter will specify or imply those legislative actions that must be by ordinance and those that may be by resolution. Revenue-raising measures, such as the imposition of taxes, special assessments and service charges, universally require ordinances. See **RESOLUTION.**

ORGANIZATIONAL UNIT. A responsibility center within a government.

ORGANIZATIONAL-UNIT CLASSIFICATION. Expenditure classification according to responsibility centers within a government's organizational structure. Classification of expenditures by organizational unit is essential to fulfilling stewardship responsibility for individual government resources.

OTHER FINANCING SOURCES. Governmental fund general long-term debt proceeds, amounts equal to the present value of minimum lease payments arising from capital leases, proceeds from the sale of general fixed assets, and operating transfers in. Such amounts are classified separately from revenues on the governmental operating statement.

OTHER FINANCING USES. Governmental fund operating transfers out and the amount of refunding bond proceeds deposited with the escrow agent. Such amounts are classified separately from expenditures on the governmental operating statement.

OUTLAYS. Syn. **EXPENDITURES.** See **CAPITAL EXPENDITURES.**

OVERDRAFT. (1) The amount by which checks, drafts or other demands for payment on the treasury or on a bank exceed the amount of the credit against which they are drawn. (2) The amount by which requisitions, purchase orders or audited vouchers exceed the appropriation or other credit to which they are chargeable.

OVERHEAD. Those elements of cost necessary in the production of a good or service which are not directly traceable to the product or service. Usually these costs relate to objects of expenditure that do not become an integral part of the finished product or service, such as rent, heat, light, supplies, management and supervision.

OVERLAPPING DEBT. The proportionate share property within each government must bear of the debts of all local governments located wholly or in part within the geographic boundaries of the reporting government. Except for special assessment debt, the amount of debt of each unit applicable to the reporting unit is arrived at by (1) determining what percentage of the total assessed value of the overlapping jurisdiction lies within the limits of the reporting unit, and (2) applying this percentage to the total debt of the overlapping jurisdiction. Special assessment debt is allocated on the basis of the ratio of assessment receivable in each jurisdiction, which will be used wholly or in part to pay off the debt, to total assessments receivable, which will be used wholly or in part for this purpose.

OVERSIGHT RESPONSIBILITY. The basic—but not the only—criterion for including a government department, agency, institution, commission, public authority or other organization in a government unit's reporting entity for general purpose financial reports. Oversight responsibility is derived from the government unit's power and includes, but is not limited to, financial interdependency, selection of governing authority, designation of management, ability to significantly influence operations and accountability for fiscal matters.

OVERSIGHT UNIT. In defining the reporting entity, the component unit that has the ability to exercise oversight responsibility. Typically, an oversight unit is the primary unit of government directly responsible to the chief executive and the elected legislative body.

PAR VALUE. In the case of bonds, the amount of principal that must be paid at maturity. Par value is referred to as the face value of the security.

PAY-AS-YOU-GO BASIS. In the context of pension accounting and risk management, the failure to finance retirement obligations or anticipated losses on a current basis, using an acceptable actuarial funding method.

PAYING AGENT. An entity responsible for paying of bond principal and interest on behalf of the government.

PENSION BENEFIT OBLIGATION (PBO). The standardized measure of funding status and progress required by the GASB to be disclosed in the notes to the financial statements. It is the actuarial present value of credited projected benefits, prorated on service and discounted at a rate equal to the expected return on present and future plan assets.

PENSION CONTRIBUTION. The amount paid into a pension plan by an employer (or employee), pursuant to the terms of the plan, state law, actuarial calculations or some other basis for determinations.

PENSION OBLIGATION. A generic term for that portion of the actuarial present value of total projected benefits estimated to be payable in the future as a result of employee service to date, with the portion attributable to credited service to date calculated with or without projected salary increases. Stated differently, it is benefits attributable to (a) retirees, beneficiaries and terminated employees entitled to benefits and (b) current covered employees, as a result of their credited service to date.

PENSION TRUST FUND. A trust fund used to account for a PERS. Pension trust funds, like nonexpendable trust funds, use the accrual basis of accounting and have a capital maintenance measurement focus.

PER CAPITA DEBT. The amount of a government's debt divided by its population. Per capita debt is used to indicate the government's credit position by reference to the proportionate debt borne per resident.

PERFORMANCE AUDITING. A systematic process of objectively obtaining and evaluating evidence regarding the performance of an organization, program, function or activity. Evaluation is made in terms of its economy and efficiency of operations, effectiveness in achieving desired regulations, for the purpose of ascertaining the degree of correspondence between performance and established criteria and communicating the results to interested users. The performance audit function provides an independent, third-party review of management's performance and the degree to which the performance of the audited entity meets prestated expectations.

PERFORMANCE BUDGET. A budget that bases expenditures primarily upon measurable performance of activities and work programs. A performance budget may also incorporate other bases of expenditure classification, such as character and object class, but these are secondary to activity performance.

PERPETUAL INVENTORY. A system whereby the inventory of units of property at any date may be obtained directly from the records, without resorting to an actual physical count, for each item or group of items to be inventoried. This system provides an ongoing record of goods ordered, received and withdrawn and the balance on hand, in units and frequently also in value.

PETTY CASH. A sum of money set aside on an imprest basis to make change or to pay small obligations for which the issuance of a formal voucher and check would be too expensive and time-consuming. Petty cash accounts are sometimes referred to as petty cash funds. However, they are not "funds" in the sense of governmental accounting individual funds. Petty cash accounts should be reported as assets of the fund of ownership. See **IMPREST ACCOUNT.**

PETTY CASH VOUCHER. A form used to record individual disbursements of petty cash. See **IMPREST ACCOUNT.**

PHYSICAL DETERIORATION. The loss in value of fixed assets resulting from wear and tear in operation and exposure to the elements.

PLEDGED REVENUES. Funds generated from revenues and obligated to debt service or to meet other obligations specified by the bond contract.

POINT. In the context of bond issuances, one percent of the par value of the bond. Because bonds are quoted as a percentage of $1,000, a point is equal to $10. See **BASIS POINT.**

POST-AUDIT. An examination of financial transactions that have been completed or are in various stages of completion at the end of an accounting period. See **PRE-AUDIT.**

POSTING. The act of transferring to an account in a ledger the data, either detailed or summarized, contained in a book or document of original entry.

POTENTIAL COMPONENT UNIT. A separate government unit, agency or nonprofit corporation that needs to be evaluated to determine if it is to be included with other component units and the oversight unit to constitute the reporting entity.

PRE-AUDIT. An examination of financial transactions before their completion.

PREMIUM. The excess of the price of a security over its face value, excluding any amount of accrued interest bought or sold.

PREPAID ITEMS. Payment in advance of the receipt of goods and services in an exchange transaction. Prepaid items (e.g., prepaid rent and unexpired insurance premiums) differ from deferred charges (e.g., unamortized issuance costs) in that they are spread over a shorter period of time than deferred charges and are regularly recurring costs of operations.

PREPAYMENT OF TAXES. The deposit of money with a government on condition that the amount deposited is to be applied against the tax liability of a designated taxpayer after the taxes have been levied and such liability has been established. See **TAXES COLLECTED IN ADVANCE.**

PRESENT VALUE. The discounted value of a future amount or amounts of cash, assuming a given rate of interest.

PRIMARY DEALER. Government securities dealers included in the "List of Government Securities Dealers Reporting to the Market Reports Division of the Federal Reserve Bank of New York (NY Fed)" that submit daily reports of market activity and positions and monthly financial statements to the NY Fed and are subject to its informal oversight. Primary dealers include SEC-registered securities broker-dealers, banks and a few unregulated firms.

PRINCIPAL. In the context of bonds other than deep-discount debt, the face value or par value of a bond or issue of bonds payable on stated dates of maturity. See **FACE VALUE** and **PAR VALUE.**

PROGRAM. Group activities, operations or organizational units directed to attaining specific purposes or objectives.

PROGRAM BUDGET. A budget wherein expenditures are based primarily on programs of work and secondarily on character and object class, on the one hand, and performance, on the other. See **PERFORMANCE BUDGET** and **TRADITIONAL BUDGET.**

PROJECTED BENEFIT OBLIGATION. As used in SFAS No. 87, the actuarial present value as of a date of all benefits attributed by the pension benefit formula to employee service rendered before that date. The projected benefit obligation is measured using assumptions as to future compensation levels if the pension benefit formula is based on those future compensation levels (pay-related, final-pay, final-average-pay or career-average-pay plans).

PROJECTED TOTAL-LIFE COST. The total anticipated costs related to a fixed asset during its estimated useful life. Projected total-life cost normally includes a detailed schedule of maintenance requirements for each year of the asset's life, including preventive maintenance, normal repair and replacement, and replacement of major parts or components needed to achieve the normal (intended) life of the asset. The total-life cost is calculated at the time an asset is acquired or constructed, often as an integral part of capital acquisition or budgeting procedures.

PROJECTED UNIT-CREDIT ACTUARIAL COST METHOD. A method under which the projected benefits of each individual included in an actuarial valuation are allocated by a consistent formula to valuation years. The actuarial present value of benefits allocated to a valuation year is called the normal cost. The actuarial present value of benefits allocated to all periods prior to a valuation year is called the actuarial accrued liability.

PROPRIETARY FUND TYPES. Sometimes referred to as income determination or commercial-type funds, the classification used to account for a government's ongoing organizations and activities that are similar to those often found in the private sector (i.e., enterprise and internal service funds). All assets, liabilities, equities, revenues, expenses and transfers relating to the government's business and quasi-business activities are accounted for through proprietary funds. The GAAP used are generally those applicable to similar businesses in the private sector and the measurement focus is on determination of net income, financial position and changes in financial position. However, where the GASB has issued pronouncements applicable to those entities and activities, they should be guided by these pronouncements.

PUBLIC ACCOUNTING. The practice of holding oneself out to be a CPA or public accountant and at the same time performing for a client one or more types of services rendered by public accountants (e.g., auditing). This term should not be confused with governmental accounting.

PUBLIC AUTHORITY. See **AUTHORITY.**

PUBLIC CORPORATION. See **MUNICIPAL CORPORATION** and **QUASI-MUNICIPAL CORPORATION.**

PURCHASE ORDER. A document authorizing the delivery of specified merchandise or the rendering of certain services and the making of a charge for them.

PURCHASES METHOD. The method under which inventories are recorded as expenditures when acquired. See **CONSUMPTION METHOD.**

"PUT." In the context of demand bonds, a feature in the bond agreement requiring the issuer or its agent (trustee or remarketing agent) to buy back the bonds on the bondholder's demand.

PYRAMID. See **FINANCIAL REPORTING PYRAMID**

QUALIFIED OPINION. An opinion stating that "except for" the effect of the matter to which the qualification relates, the financial statements present fairly the financial position, results of operations and (when applicable) changes in financial position in conformity with GAAP. Such an opinion is expressed when a lack of sufficient, competent evidential matter or restrictions on the scope of the auditor's examination have led the auditor to conclude that an unqualified opinion cannot be expressed, or when the auditor believes, on the basis of his examination, that (1) the financial statements contain a departure from GAAP, the effect of which is material, (2) there has been a material change between periods in accounting principles or in the method of their application or (3) there are significant uncertainties affecting the financial statements, and the auditor has decided not to express an adverse opinion or to disclaim an opinion. See **ADVERSE OPINION** and **DISCLAIMER OF OPINION.**

QUASI-EXTERNAL TRANSACTIONS. Interfund transactions that would be treated as revenues, expenditures or expenses if they involved organizations external to the government unit (e.g., payments in lieu of taxes from an enterprise fund to the general fund; internal service fund billings to departments; routine employer contributions to a pension trust fund and routine service charges for inspection, engineering, utilities or similar services provided by a department financed from one fund to a department financed from another fund). These transactions should be accounted for as revenues, expenditures or expenses in the funds involved.

QUASI-MUNICIPAL CORPORATION. An agency (e.g., a county or school district) established by the state primarily to help the state carry out its functions. Some counties and other agencies ordinarily classified as quasi-municipal corporations have been granted the powers of municipal corporations by their states. See **MUNICIPAL CORPORATION.**

RATINGS. In the context of bonds, normally an evaluation of credit-worthiness performed by an independent rating service.

REBATES. Abatements or refunds.

RECEIPTS. Cash received.

RECOVERABLE EXPENDITURE. An expenditure that is made for or on behalf of another government, fund or department or for a private individual, firm or corporation and that will subsequently be recovered in cash or its equivalent.

REFUND. (1) (Noun) An amount paid back or credit allowed because of an overcollection or because of the return of an object sold. (2) (Verb) To pay back or allow credit for an amount because of an overcollection or because of the return of an object sold. (3) (Verb) To provide for the payment of an obligation through cash or credit secured by a new obligation.

REFUNDING BONDS. Bonds issued to retire bonds already outstanding. The refunding bonds may be used to provide the resources for redeeming outstanding bonds, or the refunding bonds may be exchanged with the holders of the outstanding bonds. See **ADVANCE REFUNDING BONDS.**

REGISTER. A record for the consecutive entry of a certain class of events, documents or transactions, with proper notation of all the required details. See **JOURNAL.**

REGISTERED BOND. A bond whose owner is registered with the issuing government. A registered bond cannot be sold or exchanged without a change of registration.

REGISTERED SECURITY. A security that has the name of the owner written on its face. A registered security cannot be negotiated except by the endorsement of the owner.

REGULAR SERIAL BONDS. Serial bonds in which all periodic installments of principal repayment are equal.

REIMBURSABLE EXPENDITURE. See **RECOVERABLE EXPENDITURE.**

REIMBURSEMENTS. (1) Repayments of amounts remitted on behalf of another party. (2) Interfund transactions that constitute reimbursements to a fund for expenditures or expenses initially made from it but that properly apply to another fund (e.g., an expenditure properly chargeable to a special revenue fund is initially made from the general fund, and is subsequently reimbursed). These transactions are recorded as expenditures or expenses (as appropriate) in the reimbursing fund and as reductions of expenditures or expenses in the fund reimbursed.

REINSURANCE. A transaction in which a reinsurer (assuming enterprise), for a consideration (premium), assumes all or part of a risk undertaken originally by another insurer (ceding enterprise). However, the legal rights of the insured are not affected by the reinsurance transaction, and the insurance enterprise issuing the insurance contract remains liable to the insured for payment of policy benefits.

REPLACEMENT COST. The amount of cash or other consideration that would be required today to obtain the same asset or its equivalent. See **REPRODUCTION COST.**

REPORTING ENTITY. The oversight unit and all of its component units, if any, that are combined in the CAFR/GPFS.

REPORTING PYRAMID. See **FINANCIAL REPORTING PYRAMID.**

REPRODUCTION COST. The cost as of a certain date of reproducing an exactly similar new property in the same place. Sometimes this term is designated as reproduction cost new to distinguish it from depreciated reproduction cost, which is the reproduction cost of a given property less the estimated accumulated depreciation applicable to it. In the absence of any modifier, however, reproduction cost is understood to be synonymous with reproduction cost new. See **REPLACEMENT COST.**

REPURCHASE AGREEMENT. A generic term for an agreement in which a government entity (buyer-lender) transfers cash to a broker-dealer or financial institution (seller-borrower); the broker-dealer or financial institution transfers securities to the entity and promises to repay the cash plus interest in exchange for the same securities or for different securities.

REQUIRED SUPPLEMENTARY INFORMATION. Consists of statements, schedules, statistical data or other information which, according to the GASB, is necessary to supplement, although not required to be a part of, the general purpose financial statements.

REQUISITION. A written demand or request, usually from one department to the purchasing officer or to another department, for specified articles or services.

RESERVED FUND BALANCE. Those portions of fund balance that are not appropriable for expenditure or that are legally segregated for a specific future use.

RESIDUAL EQUITY TRANSFERS. Nonrecurring or nonroutine transfers of equity between funds (e.g., contribution of enterprise fund or internal service fund capital by the general fund, subsequent return of all or part of such contribution to the general fund and transfers of residual balances of discontinued funds to the general fund or a debt service fund).

RESOLUTION. A special or temporary order of a legislative body; an order of a legislative body requiring less legal formality than an ordinance or statute. See **ORDINANCE.**

RESTRICTED ASSETS. Monies or other resources, the use of which is restricted by legal or contractual requirements. In governmental accounting, special treatments are applied to restricted assets arising out of revenue bond indentures in enterprise funds. These are sometimes also called restricted "funds" but such terminology is not preferred.

RETAINAGE PAYABLE. A liability account reflecting amounts due on construction contracts not paid pending final inspection of the project or the lapse of a specified period, or both. The unpaid amount is usually a stated percentage of the contract price.

RETAINED EARNINGS. An equity account reflecting the accumulated earning of an enterprise or internal service fund.

RETAINED EARNINGS—RESERVED FOR REVENUE BOND CURRENT DEBT SERVICE. An account used to segregate a portion of retained earnings, in accordance with the terms of a revenue bond indenture, for amounts that should be accumulated in such a restricted asset account less current liabilities for revenue bond principal and interest.

RETAINED EARNINGS—RESERVED FOR REVENUE BOND OPERATIONS AND MAINTENANCE. An account used to segregate a portion of retained earnings in accordance with the terms of a revenue bond indenture, for amounts that should be accumulated in such a restricted asset account.

RETAINED EARNINGS—RESERVED FOR REVENUE BOND RENEWAL AND REPLACEMENT. An account used to segregate a portion of retained earnings in accordance with the terms of a revenue bond indenture, for amounts that should be accumulated in such a restricted asset account.

RETENTION. In the context of insurance accounting, the amount that an insured or an insurer assumes as its own liability and that is not otherwise insured. Sometimes referred to as self-insured retention.

RETIREMENT ALLOWANCES. Amounts paid to government employees who have retired from active service or to their survivors.

RETIREMENT FUND. See **PENSION TRUST FUND.**

REVENUE BONDS. Bonds whose principal and interest are payable exclusively from earnings of an enterprise fund. In addition to a pledge of revenues, such bonds sometimes contain a mortgage on the enterprise fund's property.

REVENUE BONDS PAYABLE. A liability account reflecting the face value of revenue bonds issued and outstanding.

REVENUES. (1) Increases in the net current assets of a governmental fund type from other than expenditure refunds and residual equity transfers. Also, general long-term debt proceeds and operating transfers in are classified as "other financing sources" rather than as revenues. (2) Increases in the net total assets of a proprietary fund type from other than expense refunds, capital contributions and residual equity transfers. Also, operating transfers in are classified separately from revenues.

REVERSE REPURCHASE AGREEMENT. An agreement in which a broker-dealer or financial institution (buyer-lender) transfers cash to a government entity (seller-borrower); the entity transfers securities to the broker-dealer or financial institution and promises to repay the cash plus interest in exchange for the same securities or different securities.

REVOLVING FUND. (1) An internal service fund. (2) An imprest account accounted for as an asset of a fund.

RISK. In the context of insurance, defined variously as uncertainty of loss, chance of loss or variance of actual from expected results. Also, the subject matter of an insurance contract (e.g., the insured property or liability exposure).

RISK MANAGEMENT. All the ways and means used to avoid accidental loss or to reduce its consequences if it does occur.

SALVAGE VALUE. The amount that could be realized from sale of a dismantled asset to be removed for use elsewhere.

SCHEDULES. See **SUPPORTING SCHEDULES.**

SCOPE OF PUBLIC SERVICE. One of the criteria used to determine whether the statements of a potential component unit should be included in the financial statements of a reporting entity. This criterion embraces two aspects: (1) is the activity for the benefit of the reporting entity and/or its residents? and (2) is the activity conducted within the geographic boundaries of the reporting entity and is it generally available to the citizens of that entity?

SCRAP VALUE. The amount that would be realized if property were sold for its recovery value.

SCRIP. An evidence of indebtedness, usually in small denomination, secured or unsecured, interest-bearing or noninterest-bearing, stating that the government, under conditions set forth, will pay the face value of the certificate or accept it in payment of certain obligations.

SECURITIES. A negotiable or nonnegotiable instrument that signifies an ownership interest, the right to an ownership interest or creditor status.

SECURITIES INVESTOR PROTECTION CORPORATION (SIPC). A nonprofit corporation funded by its member SEC-registered broker-dealers that protects customer accounts in the event of the financial failure of a member. SIPC distributes customer assets and then provides funds for all remaining claims of each customer up to a maximum of $500,000, including up to $100,000 on claims for cash. SIPC does not consider repurchase agreement participants to be customers of its member broker-dealers and does not extend its insurance to repurchase agreements.

SEGMENT INFORMATION. In the context of governmental financial reporting, the presentation within the "liftable" GPFS of selected information on certain individual enterprise funds. Such disclosures are required by GAAP if (1) material long-term liabilities are outstanding, (2) the disclosures are essential to ensure the GPFS are not misleading or (3) they are necessary to ensure interperiod comparability.

SELF-INSURANCE. A term often used to describe the retention by an entity of a risk of loss arising out of the ownership of property or from some other cause, instead of transferring that risk to an independent third party through the purchase of an insurance policy. It is sometimes accompanied by the setting aside of assets to fund any related losses. Because no insurance is involved, the term self-insurance is a misnomer.

SELF-SUPPORTING or LIQUIDATING DEBT. Debt obligations whose principal and interest are payable solely from the earnings of the enterprise for whose construction or improvement the bonds were originally issued. See **REVENUE BONDS.**

SERIAL BONDS. Bonds whose principal is repaid in periodic installments over the life of the issue. See **REGULAR SERIAL BONDS** and **STRAIGHT SERIAL BONDS.**

SERVICE ASSESSMENTS. Special assessment projects for operating activities that do not result in the purchase or construction of fixed assets. Often such service assessments are for services that are normally provided to the public as general government functions and that would otherwise be financed by the general fund or a special revenue fund. Those services include street lighting, street cleaning and snow plowing. Financing for these routine services typically comes from general revenues. However, when routine services are extended to property owners outside the normal service area of the government or are provided at a higher level or at more frequent intervals than that provided the general public, special assessments are sometimes levied. Only the affected property owners are charged for the additional services.

SHARED REVENUES. Revenues levied by one government but shared on a predetermined basis, often in proportion to the amount collected at the local level, with another government or class of governments.

SHARED TAXES. See **SHARED REVENUES.**

SHORT-TERM DEBT. Debt with a maturity of one year or less after the date of issuance. Short-term debt usually includes variable-rate debt, bond anticipation notes, tax anticipation notes and revenue anticipation notes.

SINGLE AUDIT. An audit performed in accordance with the Single Audit Act of 1984 and Office of Management and Budget (OMB) Circular A-128, *Audits of State and Local Governments*. The Single Audit Act allows or requires governments (depending on the amount of federal assistance received) to have one audit performed to meet the needs of all federal grantor agencies.

SINKING FUND. See **DEBT SERVICE FUND.**

SINKING FUND BONDS. Bonds issued under an agreement requiring the government to set aside periodically out of its revenues a sum that, with compound earnings thereon, will be sufficient to redeem the bonds at their stated date of maturity. Sinking fund bonds are usually term bonds

SPECIAL ASSESSMENT. A compulsory levy made against certain properties to defray all or part of the cost of a specific

capital improvement or service deemed to benefit primarily those properties.

SPECIAL ASSESSMENT BONDS. Bonds payable from the proceeds of special assessments. If the bonds are payable only from the collections of special assessments, they are known as special assessment bonds. If, in addition to the assessments, the full faith and credit of the government are pledged, they are known as general obligation special assessment bonds.

SPECIAL ASSESSMENT LIENS RECEIVABLE. Claims a government has upon properties until special assessments levied against them have been paid. The term normally applies to those delinquent special assessments the government has taken legal action to collect through the filing of claims.

SPECIAL ASSESSMENT ROLL. The official list showing the amount of special assessments levied against each property presumed to be benefited by an improvement or service.

SPECIAL ASSESSMENTS RECEIVABLE—CURRENT. Uncollected special assessments that a government has levied and that are due within one year and not yet considered delinquent.

SPECIAL ASSESSMENTS RECEIVABLE—DELINQUENT. Special assessment remaining unpaid on and after the date to which a penalty for nonpayment is attached.

SPECIAL ASSESSMENTS RECEIVABLE—NONCURRENT. Uncollected special assessments that a government has levied but that are not due within one year.

SPECIAL DISTRICT. An independent unit of local government organized to perform a single government function or a restricted number of related functions. Special districts usually have the power to incur debt and levy taxes; however, certain types of special districts are entirely dependent upon enterprise earnings and cannot impose taxes. Examples of special districts are water districts, drainage districts, flood control districts, hospital districts, fire protection districts, transit authorities, port authorities and electric power authorities.

SPECIAL DISTRICT BONDS. Bonds issued by a special district.

SPECIAL JOURNAL. A journal in which are entered all entries of a particular type. Examples include cash receipts journals, cash disbursement journals and purchases journals. See **JOURNAL** and **GENERAL JOURNAL.**

SPECIAL LIEN BONDS. Special assessment bonds that are liens against particular pieces of property.

SPECIAL REVENUE FUND. A fund used to account for the proceeds of specific revenue sources (other than expendable trusts or major capital projects) that are legally restricted to expenditure for specified purposes. GAAP only require the use of special revenue funds when legally mandated.

SPECIAL TERMINATION BENEFITS. See **TERMINATION BENEFITS.**

STANDARD COST. The predetermined cost of performing an operation or producing a product when labor, materials and equipment are used efficiently under reasonable and normal conditions. Normal conditions exist when there is an absence of special or extraordinary factors affecting the quality or quantity of the work performed or the time or method of performing it.

STANDARD COSTING. In the context of the valuation of fixed assets, an estimate of original cost using a known average installed cost for a like unit at the estimated acquisition date.

STANDARDIZED MEASURE. See **PENSION BENEFIT OBLIGATION.**

STATE AND LOCAL GOVERNMENT SERIES (SLGS, "slugs"). Direct obligations of the U.S. government that the U.S. Treasury issues specifically to provide state and local governments with required cash flows at yields that do not exceed Internal Revenue Service arbitrage limits.

STATEMENT OF CASH RECEIPTS AND DISBURSEMENTS. A financial presentation summarizing an entity's cash transactions in an accounting period. This statement is not currently required by GAAP.

STATEMENT OF CHANGES IN FINANCIAL POSITION. A GAAP financial statement for proprietary and similar trust funds that summarizes all important aspects of a government's financing and investing activities, regardless of whether cash or other elements of working capital are directly affected. Governments may also choose, as illustrated in appendix D, to present a modified form of a statement of cash flows.

STATEMENT OF CHANGES IN EQUITY. The financial statement that reconciles the equity balances of an entity at the beginning and end of an accounting period in conformity with GAAP. It explains the relation between the operating statement and the balance sheet. Statements of changes in equity of governments should be combined with operating statements into "all-inclusive" operating statement formats.

STATEMENT OF FINANCIAL POSITION. See **BALANCE SHEET.**

STATEMENT OF REVENUES AND EXPENDITURES. The financial statement that is the governmental fund and expendable trust fund GAAP operating statement. It presents increases (revenues and other financing sources) and decreases (expenditures and other financing uses) in an entity's net current assets. Statements of changes in equity of governments should be combined with operating statements into "all-inclusive" operating statement formats.

STATEMENT OF REVENUES AND EXPENSES. The financial statement that is the proprietary fund, nonexpendable trust fund and pension trust fund GAAP operating statement. It presents increases (revenues, gains and operating transfers in) and decreases (expenses, losses and operating transfers out) in an entity's net total assets. Statements of changes in equity of governments should be combined with operating statements into "all-inclusive" operating statement formats.

STATEMENTS. See **BASIC FINANCIAL STATEMENTS.**

STATISTICAL TABLES. Presentations included in the statistical section of the CAFR/CUFR providing detailed data on the physical, economic, social and political characteristics of the reporting government. They are intended to provide CAFR/CUFR users with a broader and more complete understanding of the government and its financial affairs than is possible from the financial statements and supporting schedules included in the financial section. Statistical tables usually cover more than two fiscal years and often present data from outside the accounting records. Therefore, in contrast to financial section information, statistical section data are not usually susceptible to independent audit.

STATUTE. A written law enacted by a duly organized and constituted legislative body. See **ORDINANCE, RESOLUTION** and **ORDER.**

STEP-RATE BENEFIT FORMULA. In the context of pension accounting, formulas, also known as variable-rate formulas, that define benefits by applying different salary or dollar factors to different years of credited service.

STORES. Goods subject to requisition and use that are on hand in storerooms.

STRAIGHT SERIAL BONDS. Serial bonds in which the annual installments of bond principal are equal or nearly equal.

SUBACTIVITY. A special line of work performed in carrying out a government activity (e.g., cleaning luminaries and replacing defective street lamps would be subactivities under the activity of street light maintenance).

SUBFUNCTION. A grouping of related activities within a particular government function (e.g., police is a subfunction of the function public safety).

SUBSIDIARY ACCOUNT. One of a group of related accounts supporting in detail the debit and credit summaries recorded in a control account (e.g., the individual property taxpayers' accounts for the taxes receivable control account in the general ledger). See **CONTROL ACCOUNT** and **SUBSIDIARY LEDGER.**

SUBSIDIARY LEDGER. A group of subsidiary accounts, the sum of the balances of which should equal the balance of the related control account. See **GENERAL LEDGER** and **SUBSIDIARY ACCOUNT.**

SUMMARY OF SIGNIFICANT ACCOUNTING POLICIES (SSAP). A disclosure of accounting policies, required by GAAP, that should identify and describe the accounting principles followed by the reporting entity and the methods of applying those principles that materially affect the determination of financial position, changes in financial position or results of operations. In general, the disclosure should encompass important judgments as to the appropriateness of principles relating to the recognition of revenue and allocation of asset costs to current and future periods; in particular, it should encompass those accounting principles and methods that involve any of the following: (1) a selection from existing acceptable alternatives, (2) principles and methods peculiar to government and (3) unusual or innovative applications of accounting principles, including those peculiar to government.

SUPPORTING SCHEDULES. Financial presentations used (1) to demonstrate compliance with finance-related legal and contractual provisions, (2) to aggregate and present in greater detail information spread throughout the financial statements (e.g., cash balances, investments, current and delinquent taxes), (3) to present in greater detail information reported in the financial statements (e.g., additional revenue sources, changes in general fixed assets by function and (4) to present information not disclosed in GAAP financial statements (e.g., cash receipts and disbursements, changes in agency fund assets and liabilities). Supporting schedules are included on the fourth level of the financial reporting pyramid.

SURETY BOND. A written promise to pay damages or to indemnify against losses caused by the party or parties named in the document, through nonperformance or through defalcation (e.g., a surety bond may be required of an independent contractor). Surety bonds also include fidelity bonds covering government officials and employees.

SUSPENSE ACCOUNT. An account carrying charges or credits temporarily pending the determination of the proper account or accounts to which they are to be posted. See **CLEARING ACCOUNT.**

SYSTEMS DEVELOPMENT FEES. Fees charged to join or to extend an existing utility system. Syn. **TAP FEES** and **CONNECTION FEES.**

TAKEOUT AGREEMENT. In the context of demand bonds, an arrangement with a financial institution to convert demand bonds to an installment loan payable over a specified period if the remarketing agent is unable to resell the bonds after they are "put" by the bondholders.

TAP FEES. See **SYSTEMS DEVELOPMENT FEES.**

TAX ANTICIPATION NOTES (TANs). Notes (or warrants) issued in anticipation of the collection of taxes, usually retirable only from tax collections, and frequently only from the proceeds of the tax levy whose collection they anticipate. Syn. **TAX NOTES.**

TAX ANTICIPATION WARRANTS. See **TAX ANTICIPATION NOTES.**

TAX CERTIFICATE. A certificate issued by a government as evidence of the conditional transfer of title to tax-delinquent property from the original owner to the holder of the certificate. If the owner does not pay the amount of the tax arrearage and other charges required by law during the specified period of redemption, the holder can foreclose to obtain title. Also called tax sale certificate and tax lien certificate in some jurisdictions. See **TAX DEED.**

TAX DEED. A written instrument by which title to property sold for taxes is transferred unconditionally to the purchaser. A tax deed is issued upon foreclosure of the tax lien and is obtained by the purchaser at the tax sale. The tax lien cannot be foreclosed until the expiration of the period during which the owner may redeem the property by paying the delinquent taxes and other charges. See **TAX CERTIFICATE.**

TAXES. Compulsory charges levied by a government to finance services performed for the common benefit. This term does not include specific charges made against particular persons or property for current or permanent benefits, such as special assessments. Neither does the term include charges for services rendered only to those paying such charges (e.g., sewer service charges).

TAXES LEVIED FOR OTHER GOVERNMENTS. An asset account reflecting taxes that are levied by the reporting government for other governments that, when collected, are to be paid over to those governments.

TAXES RECEIVABLE—DELINQUENT. Taxes remaining unpaid on and after the date on which a penalty for nonpayment attaches. Delinquent taxes receivable are classified as such until paid, abated, canceled or converted into tax liens.

TAX-EXEMPT BONDS. State and local government securities whose interest is exempt from taxation by the federal government or within the jurisdiction issued.

TAX-INCREMENT BOND. A bond secured by the anticipated incremental increase in tax revenues, resulting from the redevelopment of an area.

TAX LEVY ORDINANCE. An ordinance through which taxes are levied.

TAX LIENS. Claims governments have upon properties until the taxes levied against them have been paid. This term is sometimes limited to those delinquent taxes the government has taken legal action to collect through the filing of liens.

TAX LIENS RECEIVABLE. Legal claims against property that have been exercised because of nonpayment of delinquent taxes, interest and penalties. Amounts accumulated in this account include delinquent taxes, interest and penalties receivable thereon and costs of converting delinquent taxes into tax liens.

TAX NOTES. See **TAX ANTICIPATION NOTES.**

TAX RATE. The amount of tax stated in terms of a unit of the tax base (e.g., 25 mills per dollar of assessed valuation of taxable property).

TAX-RATE LIMIT. The maximum rate at which a government may levy a tax. The limit may apply to taxes raised for a particular purpose or to taxes imposed for all purposes and may apply to a single government to a class of governments operating in a particular area. Overall tax-rate limits usually restrict levies for all purposes and of all governments, state and local, having jurisdiction in a given area.

TAX ROLL. The official list showing the amount of taxes levied against each taxpayer or property. Frequently, the tax roll and the assessment roll are combined, but even in these cases the two can be distinguished. Syn. **COLLECTORS' ROLL.**

TAX SUPPLEMENT. A tax levied by a local government having the same base as a similar tax levied by a higher level of government, such as a state. The local tax supplement is frequently administered by the higher level of government along with its own tax (e.g., locally imposed, state-administered sales tax).

TAX TITLE NOTES. Obligations secured by pledges of the government's interest in certain tax liens or tax titles.

TEMPORARY LOANS. Short-term obligations representing amounts borrowed for short periods of time and usually evidenced by notes payable or warrants payable. They may be unsecured or secured by specific revenues to be collected. See **TAX ANTICIPATION NOTES.**

TERM BONDS. Bonds that mature, in total, on one date.

TERMINATION BENEFITS. Benefits provided to employees in connection with their termination of employment. They may be either *special termination benefits* offered only for a short period of time or *contractual termination benefits* required by the terms of a plan only if a specified event occurs.

THIRD-PARTY CLAIM. A claim in which the insurer has agreed to pay, defend or settle claims made by third parties against the insured. A liability claim is a third-party claim.

TIME WARRANT. A negotiable obligation of a government having a term shorter than bonds and frequently tendered to individuals and firms in exchange for contractual services, capital acquisitions or equipment purchases.

TIME WARRANTS PAYABLE. The amount of time warrants outstanding and unpaid.

TOTAL-LIFE COST. See **PROJECTED TOTAL-LIFE COST.**

TRADE DISCOUNT. An allowance, usually varying in percentage with the volume of transactions, made to those engaged in certain businesses and given without respect to when the account is paid. These discounts are commonly considered a reduction of the sales or purchase price, not earnings. The term is not to be confused with cash discount.

TRADITIONAL BUDGET. A term sometimes applied to the budget of a government wherein expenditures are based entirely or primarily on objects of expenditure. See **PROGRAM BUDGET** and **PERFORMANCE BUDGET.**

TRANSFER VOUCHER. A form authorizing transfers of cash or other resources between funds.

TRIAL BALANCE. A list of the balances of the accounts in a ledger kept by double entry, with the debit and credit balances shown in separate columns. If the totals of the debit and credit columns are equal or if their net balance agrees with a control account, the ledger from which the figures are taken is said to be in balance.

TRUST AND AGENCY FUND. One of the seven fund types in governmental accounting. See **TRUST FUNDS** and **AGENCY FUND.**

TRUSTEE. A fiduciary holding property on behalf of another.

TRUST FUNDS. Funds used to account for assets held by a government in a trustee capacity for individuals, private organizations, other governments and/or other funds. See **PENSION TRUST FUND, NONEXPENDABLE TRUST FUND** and **EXPENDABLE TRUST FUND.**

UNALLOTTED BALANCE OF APPROPRIATION. An appropriation balance available for allotment.

UNAMORTIZED DISCOUNTS ON BONDS SOLD. A contra-liability account used to reflect that portion of the face value of bonds exceeding the amount received from their sale (excluding amounts paid for accrued interest) which remains to be amortized over the remaining life of such bonds.

UNAMORTIZED PREMIUMS ON INVESTMENTS. An asset account used to reflect that portion of the excess of the amount paid for investments (excluding amounts paid for accrued interest) over their face value which remains to be amortized over the remaining life of such investments.

UNBILLED ACCOUNTS RECEIVABLE. An account designating the estimated amount of accounts receivable for goods or services that have not yet been billed (e.g., if a utility bills its customers bimonthly but prepares monthly financial statements, the amount of goods sold or services rendered during the first month of the bimonthly period would be reflected in the balance sheet under this account title).

UNDERLYING SECURITIES. Securities transferred in accordance with a repurchase/reverse repurchase agreement.

UNDERWRITER. In the context of bonds, a dealer who purchases a new issue for resale.

UNDERWRITING. The process of selecting, classifying, evaluating, rating and assuming risks.

UNENCUMBERED ALLOTMENT. That portion of an allotment not yet expended or encumbered.

UNENCUMBERED APPROPRIATION. That portion of an appropriation not yet expended or encumbered.

UNFUNDED PENSION PLAN. See **PAY-AS-YOU-GO BASIS.**

UNIT COST. In the context of cost accounting, the cost of producing a unit of product or rendering a unit of service (e.g., the cost of treating and purifying 1,000 gallons of sewage).

UNIT-CREDIT ACTUARIAL COST METHOD. A method under which the benefits (projected or unprojected) of each individual included in an actuarial valuation are allocated by a consistent formula to valuation years. The actuarial present value of benefits allocated to a valuation year is called the normal cost. The actuarial present value of benefits allocated to all periods prior to a valuation year is called the actuarial accrued liability.

UNLIQUIDATED ENCUMBRANCES. Encumbrances outstanding. See **ENCUMBRANCES.**

UNQUALIFIED OPINION. An auditor's opinion stating that the financial statements present fairly the financial position, results of operations and (when applicable) changes in financial position in conformity with GAAP (which include adequate disclosure). This conclusion may be expressed only when the auditor has formed such an opinion on the basis of an examination made in accordance with GAAS or GAGAS.

VALUE. As used in governmental accounting (1) the act of describing anything in terms of money or (2) to measure in terms of money. The term should not be used without further qualification. See also **BOOK VALUE** and **FACE VALUE.**

VARIABLE INTEREST RATE. A rate of interest subject to adjustment (e.g., the rate of interest specified may be a percentage of the prime rate on certain set dates).

VESTED BENEFIT. A benefit for which the employer has an obligation to make payment even if an employee terminates; thus, the benefit is not contingent on an employee's future service.

VOUCHER. A written document that evidences the propriety of transactions and usually indicates the accounts in which they are to be recorded.

VOUCHERS PAYABLE. Liabilities for goods and services evidenced by vouchers that have been pre-audited and approved for payment but that have not been paid.

VOUCHER SYSTEM. A system that calls for the preparation of vouchers for transactions involving payments and for the recording of such vouchers in a special book of original entry, known as a voucher register, in the order in which payment is approved.

WARRANT. An order drawn by the legislative body or an officer of a government upon its treasurer, directing the latter to pay a specified amount to the person named or to the bearer. It may be payable upon demand, in which case it usually circulates the same as a bank check; or it may be payable only out of certain revenues when and if received, in which case it does not circulate as freely.

WARRANTS PAYABLE. The amount of warrants outstanding and unpaid.

WASTING ASSETS. Mines, timberlands, quarries, oil fields and similar assets that diminish in value by the removal of their contents.

WORK ORDER. A written order authorizing and directing the performance of a certain task and issued to the person who is to direct the work. Among the items of information included on the order are the nature and location of the job, specifications of the work to be performed and a job number, which is referred to in reporting the amount of labor, materials and equipment used.

WORK UNIT. A fixed quantity that will measure consistently work effort expended in the performance of an activity or the production of a good.

YIELD. See **EFFECTIVE INTEREST RATE.**

YIELD-MAINTENANCE REPURCHASE/REVERSE REPURCHASE AGREEMENT. A type of dollar repurchase/reverse repurchase agreement in which the securities returned provide the seller-borrower with a yield specified in the agreement. See **REPURCHASE AGREEMENT** and **REVERSE REPURCHASE AGREEMENT.**

ZERO-COUPON DEBT. Deep discount debt issued with a stated interest rate of zero percent.

Appendix C
ILLUSTRATIVE
ACCOUNTS,
CLASSIFICATIONS
AND DESCRIPTIONS

Common terminology and classifications should be used throughout the budgeting, accounting and financial reporting activities of a government. The illustrative chart of accounts presented in this appendix has been designed for this purpose.

The list of account titles in this chart of accounts is not exhaustive. Governments should supplement these classifications as necessary to provide information required for management purposes. For example, this chart of accounts does not include detailed revenue and expense classifications for utilities, transportation systems, airports, hospitals and numerous other activities commonly accounted for in proprietory funds. Neither does it include detailed revenue and expenditure classifications for school districts. However, sources for this information are as follows:

Activity	Source
Airports	*Airports, Accounting and financial Reporting* published by the Government Finance Officers Association (forthcoming)
Electric Utilities	*Public Utilities and Licensees Subject to the Provisions of the Federal Power Act* published by the Federal Energy Regulatory Commission
Gas Utilities	*Uniform System of Accounts Prescribed for Natural Gas Companies Subject to the Provisions of the Natural Gas Act* published by the Federal Energy Regulatory Commission
School Districts	*Financial Accounting for State and Local School Systems* published by the National Center for Education Statistics, U.S. Department of Education
Sewer Utilities	*Uniform System of Accounts for Sewer Utilities* published by the National Association of Regulatory Utility Commissioners

Activity	Source
Transit Systems	*Urban Mass Transportation Industry Uniform System of Accounts and Records and Reporting System* published by the U.S. Department of Transportaton, Urban Mass Transportation Administration
Water Utilities	*Uniform System of Accounts for Water Utilities* published by the National Association of Regulatory Utility Commissioners

In addition, many state governments have established a uniform chart of accounts for local governments. These accounts often are incorporated into prescribed forms that are submitted to a designated state department annually.

The illustrative chart of accounts is by no means the only one acceptable for use by state and local governments. However, if this chart of accounts is used, it is recommended that it be adjusted only when necessary. Similar classifications enhance the comparability of government financial statements and hence their potential usefulness for comparative analysis.

This chart of accounts generally includes only accounts used in accounting and financial reporting. Budgetary accounts necessary for formal budgetary integration are discussed in chapter 2 and illustrated in chapters 3, 4 and 5.

This appendix is divided into three sections. The first contains a summary of the account classifications; the second presents definitions of these account classifications and the third lists balance sheet accounts by fund type and account group.

Accounts in this classification are numbered consecutively. The 100 series are assets and "other debit" accounts. The Governmental Accounting Standards Board's 1987 *Codification of Governmental Accounting and Financial Reporting Standards* provides that other debits may be reported only in the general long-term debt account group. The 200 series are liabilities and equities and "other credits." The 300 series are revenue and "other financing sources" accounts, and those in the 400 series are expenditure and "other financing uses" accounts.

Although the numbering system used is intended primarily for reference, it could become an account coding system, with appropriate modifications. A coding system permits the identification of individual accounts without resorting to their full titles on every occasion. It also simplifies the referencing of entries on documents and records and helps reflect account relationships. For these reasons, each government should devise an account coding system consistent with its own budgeting, accounting and reporting needs.

FUND CLASSIFICATIONS

Governmental accounting systems should be organized and operated on a fund basis. All of a government's individual funds are first classified by category and then by fund type within each category. There are four categories:

- **Governmental funds**—The funds through which most government functions typically are financed.
- **Proprietary funds**—The funds used to account for government activities that are similar to business operations in the commercial sector or the funds used when the reporting focus is on determining net income, financial position and changes in financial position.
- **Fiduciary funds**—The funds used to account for assets held by the government as trustee or agent.
- **Account groups**—The category used to record and control a government's general fixed assets and the unmatured principal of its general long-term liabilities.

The four categories listed above are divided into the following fund types and account groups:

Governmental fund types
1. **General fund**
2. **Special revenue funds**
3. **Capital projects funds**
4. **Debt service funds**
Proprietary fund types
5. **Enterprise funds**
6. **Internal service funds**
Fiduciary fund types
7. **Trust and agency funds**
Account groups
8. **General fixed assets**
9. **General long-term debt**

These nine fund types and account groups are described later in this chapter.

BALANCE SHEET ACCOUNT CLASSIFICATIONS

A summary of balance sheet accounts is presented below. Most of the accounts listed are used in the balance sheets illustrated in the financial statements included in the illustrative comprehensive annual financial report (CAFR) in appendix D. Detailed descriptions of these balance sheet accounts are presented later in this appendix.

Certain valuation accounts that carry credit balances are included among the assets in this list because they are presented with the assets in a balance sheet. For example, the allowance for uncollectible delinquent taxes account appears among the

assets, even though it is not an asset, because on the balance sheet it reduces the amount of reported delinquent taxes receivable to indicate the estimated collectible portion.

Code	Classification
	Assets
101.	Cash (including cash equivalents)
101.1	Petty cash
102.	Cash with fiscal agent
103.	Investments—current
104.	Interest receivable—investments
105.	Taxes receivable—current
105.1	Allowance for uncollectible current taxes (credit)
107.	Taxes receivable—delinquent
107.1	Allowance for uncollectible delinquent taxes (credit)
109.	Interest and penalties receivable—taxes
109.1	Allowance for uncollectible interest and penalties (credit)
111.	Tax liens receivable
111.1	Allowance for uncollectible tax liens (credit)
115.	Accounts receivable
115.1	Allowance for uncollectible accounts receivable (credit)
117.	Unbilled accounts receivable
117.1	Allowance for uncollectible unbilled accounts receivable (credit)
121.	Special assessments receivable—current
121.1	Allowance for uncollectible current special assessments (credit)
122.	Special assessments receivable—noncurrent
122.1	Allowance for uncollectible noncurrent special assessments (credit)
123.	Special assessments receivable—delinquent
123.1	Allowance for uncollectible delinquent special assessments (credit)
124.	Special assessment liens receivable
124.1	Allowance for uncollectible special assessment liens (credit)
125.	Interest receivable—special assessments
125.1	Allowance for uncollectible special assessment interest (credit)
126.	Intergovernmental receivable
127.	Taxes levied for other governments
128.	Notes receivable
128.1	Allowance for uncollectible notes (credit)
129.	Loans receivable
129.1	Allowance for uncollectible loans (credit)
130.	Due from other funds— _____ fund
131.	Interfund receivable— _____ fund
136.	Rent receivable
136.1	Allowance for uncollectible rent (credit)
141.	Inventories—materials and supplies
142.	Inventories—stores for resale
143.	Prepaid items
149.	Deferred charges
151.	Investments—noncurrent
151.1	Unamortized premiums—investments
151.2	Unamortized discounts—investments (credit)

152. Advance to other funds—_____ fund
153. Investments—joint venture
161. Land
162. Buildings
162.1   Accumulated depreciation—buildings (credit)
163. Improvements other than buildings
163.1   Accumulated depreciation—improvements other than buildings (credit)
164. Machinery and equipment
164.1   Accumulated depreciation—machinery and equipment (credit)
165. Construction in progress
170. Other assets

Other Debits

181. Amount available
182. Amount to be provided

Liabilities and Equities and Other Credits

201. Vouchers payable
202. Accounts payable
203. Compensated absences payable
204. Claims and judgments payable
205. Contracts payable
206. Retainage payable
207. Intergovernmental payable
208. Due to other funds—_____ fund
209. Interfund payable—_____ fund
212. Matured bonds payable
213. Matured interest payable
214. Accrued interest payable
222. Deferred revenue
223. Notes payable—current
225. Bonds payable—current
225.1   General obligation bonds payable
225.2   Special assessment bonds payable
225.3   Special assessment debt with government commitment
225.4   Revenue bonds payable
225.5   Other bonds payable
226. Capital leases payable—current
227. Other current liabilities
229. Customer deposits
230. Advance from other funds—_____ fund
231. Bonds payable—noncurrent
231.1   General obligation bonds payable
231.2   Special assessment bonds payable
231.3   Special assessment debt with government commitment
231.4   Revenue bonds payable
231.5   Other bonds payable
232. Unamortized premiums on bonds
233. Unamortized discounts on bonds (debit)
234. Notes payable—noncurrent
237. Capital leases payable—noncurrent
238. Deferred compensation benefits payable
239. Other noncurrent liabilities
241. Fund balance—reserved for debt service
242. Fund balance—reserved for endowments
244. Fund balance—reserved for encumbrances

245. Fund balance—reserved for inventories
246. Fund balance—reserved for prepaid items
247. Fund balance—reserved for noncurrent loans receivable
248. Fund balance—reserved for advance to other funds
249. Fund balance—reserved for fixed assets held for resale
251. Fund balance—reserved for employees' retirement system
251.1   Fund balance—reserved for member contributions
251.2   Fund balance—reserved for employer contributions
251.3   Fund balance—reserved for benefits
251.4   Fund balance—reserved for disability
251.5   Fund balance—reserved for undistributed investment earnings
253. Fund balance—unreserved
253.1   Fund balance—unreserved, designated for ____
253.2   Fund balance—unreserved, undesignated
261. Contributed capital—government
262. Contributed capital—customers
263. Contributed capital—developers
264. Contributed capital—intergovernmental
271. Retained earnings—reserved for revenue bond operations and maintenance
272. Retained earnings—reserved for revenue bond current debt service
273. Retained earnings—reserved for revenue bond renewal and replacement
279. Retained earnings—unreserved
280. Investment in general fixed assets

REVENUES AND OTHER FINANCING SOURCES CLASSIFICATION

Government revenues are classified by fund, type and source. The following classification includes revenues commonly found in a local government's governmental funds. However, many of these revenues also are common to state governments and other types of governments. This revenue list is intended to provide a logically structured and reasonably complete revenue classification that can be adapted to meet the managerial and reporting needs of state and local governments.

Code   *Classification*

311. General property taxes
311.1   Real property
311.2   Personal property
311.21   Tangible personal
311.22   Intangible personal
312. Property taxes on other than assessed valuation
313. General sales and use taxes
314. Selective sales and use taxes
314.1   Motor fuel
314.2   Tobacco products
314.3   Alcoholic beverages
315. Income taxes
315.1   Individual
315.2   Corporate
315.3   Unincorporated business
316. Gross receipts business taxes

316.1	Privately owned public utility
316.2	Publicly owned public utility
316.3	Insurance companies
316.4	Amusements
317.	Death and gift taxes
318.	Other taxes
318.1	Severance taxes
318.2	Franchise taxes
319.	Penalties and interest on delinquent taxes
319.1	General property taxes
319.11	Real property
319.12	Personal property
319.2	Property taxes on other than assessed valuation
319.3	General sales and use taxes
319.4	Selective sales and use taxes
319.5	Income taxes
319.6	Gross receipts business taxes
319.7	Death and gift taxes
320.	Licenses and permits
321.	Business licenses and permits
321.1	Alcoholic beverages
321.2	Health
321.3	Police and protective
321.4	Corporate
321.5	Public utilities
321.6	Professional and occupational
321.7	Amusements
322.	Nonbusiness licenses and permits
322.1	Building structures and equipment
322.2	Motor vehicle
322.3	Motor vehicle operators
322.4	Hunting and fishing
322.5	Marriage licenses
322.6	Animal licenses
330.	Intergovernmental revenues
331.	Federal government grants
331.1	Operating—categorical
331.11	Direct
331.12	Indirect
331.2	Operating—noncategorical
331.21	Direct
331.22	Indirect
331.3	Capital
331.31	Direct
331.32	Indirect
333.	Federal government payments in lieu of taxes
334.	State government grants
334.1	Operating—categorical
334.2	Operating—noncategorical
334.3	Capital
335.	State government shared revenues
335.1	Property taxes
335.2	Income taxes
335.21	Individual income taxes
335.22	Corporate income taxes
335.3	General sales and use taxes
335.4	Motor vehicle fuel taxes
335.5	Motor vehicle licenses
335.6	Tobacco taxes
335.7	Alcoholic beverage taxes

335.8	Death and gift taxes
335.9	Gross receipts business taxes
336.	State government payments in lieu of taxes
337.	Local government unit (specify unit) grants
338.	Local government unit (specify unit) shared revenues
339.	Local government unit (specify unit) payments in lieu of taxes
340.	Charges for services
341.	General government
341.1	Court costs, fees and charges
341.2	Recording of legal instruments
341.3	Zoning and subdivision fees
341.4	Printing and duplicating services
342.	Public safety
342.1	Special police services
342.2	Special fire protection services
342.3	Correctional fees
342.4	Protective inspection fees
344.	Sanitation
344.1	Sewerage charges
344.2	Street sanitation charges
344.3	Refuse collection charges
345.	Health
345.1	Vital statistics
345.2	Health and inspection fees
345.3	Clinic fees
345.4	Animal control and shelter fees
346.	Welfare
346.1	Institutional charges
347.	Culture—recreation
347.1	Golf fees
347.2	Swimming pool fees
347.3	Playground fees
347.4	Park and recreation concessions
347.5	Auditorium use fees
347.6	Library use fees (not fines)
347.7	Zoo charges
351.	Fines
351.1	Court
351.2	Library
352.	Forfeits
355.	Special assessments
355.1	Capital improvement
355.2	Service
361.	Interest revenues
362.	Gain on the sale of investments
363.	Rents and royalties
364.	Escheats
365.	Contributions and donations from private sources
370.	Special assessment financing
390.	Other financing sources
391.	Interfund operating transfers in—_____ fund
392.	Proceeds of general fixed asset dispositions
392.1	Sale of general fixed assets
392.2	Compensation for loss of general fixed assets
393.	Proceeds of general long-term liabilities
393.1	General obligation bond proceeds
393.2	Special assessment bond proceeds
393.3	Special assessment debt with government commitment proceeds

393.4 Other bond proceeds
393.5 Proceeds from refunding bonds
393.6 Premiums on bonds sold
393.7 Capital leases

EXPENDITURES AND OTHER FINANCING USES CLASSIFICATION

Multiple classification of the governmental funds' expenditure data is important for both internal and external management control and accountability. This multiple classification facilitates the collection and analysis of data in different ways for different purposes (e.g., internal evaluation, external reporting and intergovernmental comparison) and in manners that cross fund and organizational lines. The major accounting classifications of expenditures are by fund character, function (or program), activity, organizational unit and object class.

Expenditures should be classified by **character** (i.e., on the basis of the fiscal period they are presumed to benefit). The major character classifications of expenditures are current expenditures, which benefit the current fiscal period; capital outlays, which are presumed to benefit both the present and future fiscal periods and debt service, which presumably benefits prior fiscal periods, as well as current and future periods. Intergovernmental, a fourth character classification, is appropriate when one government unit transfers resources to another, such as when state governments act as an intermediary in federally financed programs.

Function or program classification provides information on the overall purposes or objectives of expenditures. Functions are group-related activities aimed at accomplishing a major service or regulatory responsibility. Programs include group activities, operations or organizational units directed to attaining specific purposes or objectives. Government units employing program budgeting may use the program classifications and subclassifications in addition to or instead of functional classifications.

Activity classification is particularly significant because it facilitates evaluation of the economy and efficiency of operations by providing data for calculating expenditures per unit of activity (i.e., the expenditure requirements to perform a given unit of work can be determined by classifying expenditures by activities and can provide data for measuring performance when such techniques are practicable). These expenditure data, in turn, can be used in preparing future budgets and in setting standards against which future expenditure levels can be evaluated. Further, activity expenditure data provide a convenient starting point for calculating total and/or unit expenses of activities if that is desired (e.g., for "make-or-buy" and "do-or-contract-out" decisions). Current operating expenditures (i.e., total expenditures less those for capital outlay, debt service and intergovernmental) may be adjusted by depreciation and amortization data derived from the account group records to determine activity expense.

Classification of expenditures by **organizational unit** is essential to maintaining accountability. This classification corresponds with the government unit's organizational structure. A particular organizational unit may be charged with carrying out one or several activities or programs. Moreover, the same activity or program is sometimes carried on by several organizational units because of its inherent nature or because of faulty organizational structure.

Finally, expenditures should be classified by **object classes** (i.e., according to the types of items purchased or services obtained). Examples of current operating object of expenditure classifications are personal services, supplies and other services and charges. Capital outlays and debt service also are major objects of expenditure classifications. Excessively detailed object classifications should be avoided because they complicate the accounting procedure and are of limited use in financial management. Few object classifications are needed because the emphasis of budget preparation and control should be on organizational units, functions (or programs) and activities, rather than on objects of expenditure.

CHARACTER CLASSIFICATION

1. **Current operating expenditures** primarily benefit the current fiscal period.
2. **Capital outlays** benefit both the current and future fiscal periods.
3. **Debt service** represents debt principal payments, periodic interest payments and related service charges.
4. **Intergovernmental** expenditures are transfers of resources from one government to another.

FUNCTION, PROGRAM AND ACTIVITY CLASSIFICATION

Code   Classification

410.   General government
411.   Legislative
411.1   Governing body
411.2   Legislative committees and special bodies
411.3   Ordinances and proceedings
411.4   Clerk of council
412.   Judicial
412.1   Criminal courts
412.2   Grand jury
412.3   Public defender
412.4   Civil courts
412.41   Chancery court
412.42   Small claims court
412.43   Civil court
412.44   Domestic relations court
412.5   Law library
413.   Executive
413.1   Mayor
413.2   Chief executive
413.3   Boards and commissions
414.   Elections
415.   Financial administration
415.1   Finance
415.11   General supervision
415.12   Accounting
415.13   Independent audit
415.14   Budget

415.15	Tax administration	424.8	Elevator inspection
415.16	Treasury	424.9	Weights and measures
415.17	Licensing	429.	Other protection
415.18	Purchasing	429.1	Civil defense
415.19	Debt administration	429.2	Militia and armories
415.21	Internal audit	429.3	Traffic engineering
415.3	Law	429.4	Examination of licensed occupations
415.4	Recordings and reporting	429.5	Public scales
415.5	Personnel administration	429.6	Flood control
419.	Other—unclassified	**431**	**Highways and streets**
419.1	Planning and zoning	431.21	Paved streets
419.2	Data processing	431.22	Unpaved streets
419.3	Research and investigation	431.23	Alleys
419.4	General government buildings and plant	431.24	Sidewalks and crosswalks
420.	**Public safety**	431.25	Snow and ice removal
421.	Police	431.3	Bridges, viaducts and grade separations
421.1	Police administration	431.4	Tunnels
421.2	Crime control and investigation	431.5	Storm drainage
421.21	Criminal investigation	431.6	Street lighting
421.22	Vice control	**432.**	**Sanitation**
421.23	Patrol	432.1	Sanitary administration
421.24	Records and identification	432.2	Street cleaning
421.25	Youth investigation and control	432.3	Waste collection
421.26	Custody of prisoners	432.4	Waste disposal
421.27	Custody of property	432.5	Sewage collection and disposal
421.28	Crime laboratory	432.51	Sanitary sewer construction
421.3	Traffic control	432.52	Sanitary sewer maintenance
421.31	Motor vehicle inspection and regulation	432.53	Sanitary sewer cleaning
421.4	Police training	432.54	New sewer services
421.5	Support service	432.55	Sewer lift stations
421.51	Communications services	432.56	Sewage treatment plants
421.52	Automotive services	432.6	Weed control
421.53	Ambulance services	**440.**	**Health and welfare**
421.54	Medical services	441.	Health
421.6	Special detail services	441.1	Public health administration
421.7	Police stations and buildings	441.2	Vital statistics
422.	Fire	441.3	Regulation and inspection
422.1	Fire administration	441.31	Food and drugs
422.2	Fire fighting	441.32	Milk and dairy products
422.3	Fire prevention	441.33	Other sanitary inspection
422.4	Fire training	441.4	Communicable disease control
422.5	Fire communications	441.41	Tuberculosis
422.6	Fire repair services	441.42	Socially transmitted diseases
422.7	Medical services	441.43	Rabies and animal control
422.8	Fire stations and buildings	441.44	Other communicable diseases
423.	Corrections	441.5	Maternal and child health services
423.1	Correctional administration	441.51	Maternal and preschool
423.2	Adult correctional institutions	441.52	School
423.3	Juvenile correctional institutions	441.6	Adult health services
423.4	Delinquents in other institutions	441.7	Health centers and general clinics
423.5	Adult probation and parole	441.8	Laboratory
423.6	Juvenile probation and parole	444.	Welfare
424.	Protective inspection	441.1	Welfare administration
424.1	Protective inspection administration	444.2	Institutional care
424.2	Building inspection	444.3	Direct assistance
424.3	Plumbing inspection	444.31	General assistance
424.4	Electrical inspection	444.32	Old-age assistance
424.5	Gas inspection	444.33	Aid to dependent children
424.6	Air conditioning inspection	444.34	Aid to the blind
424.7	Boiler inspection	444.35	Aid to the disabled

444.36	Other direct assistance		463.4	Other urban redevelopment
444.4	Intergovernmental welfare payments		**465.**	**Economic development and assistance**
444.41	General assistance		465.1	Economic development and assistance administration
444.42	Old-age assistance		465.2	Economic development
444.43	Aid to dependent children		465.3	Employment security
444.44	Aid to the blind		**466.**	**Economic opportunity**
444.45	Aid to the disabled		466.1	Job corps
444.46	Other welfare assistance		466.11	Men's urban training centers
444.5	Vendor welfare payments		466.12	Women's urban training centers
444.51	Vendor medical payments		466.13	Rural conservation centers
444.52	Other vendor payments		466.14	Youth camps
450.	**Culture—recreation**		466.2	Youth work-training programs
451.	Recreation		466.21	In-school projects
451.1	Culture—recreation administration		466.22	Out-of-school projects
451.2	Participant recreation		466.3	Community action programs
451.21	Supervision		466.31	Preschool readiness instruction
451.22	Recreation centers		466.32	Study centers
451.23	Playgrounds		466.33	Day-care centers
451.24	Swimming pools		466.34	Remedial instruction for elementary school students
451.25	Golf courses		466.35	Family health education
451.26	Tennis courts		466.36	Other projects
451.27	Other recreational facilities		466.4	Adult basic education
451.3	Spectator recreation		466.5	Assistance to migrant agricultural workers and families
451.31	Botanical gardens		466.6	Work experience programs for needy persons
451.32	Museums		**470.**	**Debt service**
451.33	Art galleries		471.1	Bond principal
451.34	Zoos		471.2	Other debt principal
451.4	Special recreational facilities		472.1	Interest—bonds
452.	Parks		472.2	Interest—other debt
452.1	Supervision		475.	Fiscal agent's fees
452.2	Park areas		476.	Issuance costs
452.3	Parkways and boulevards		477.	Advance refunding escrow
452.4	Forestry and nursery		**480.**	**Intergovernmental expenditures**
452.5	Park policing		**490.**	**Other financing uses**
452.6	Park lighting		491.	Operating transfers out—_____ fund
455.	Libraries		492.	Payment to refunded bond escrow agent
455.1	Library administration			
455.2	Circulation			
455.3	Catalog			
455.4	Reference			
455.5	Order			
455.6	Periodicals			
455.7	Extension			
455.8	Special collections			
455.9	Branch libraries			

CHARACTER AND OBJECT CLASSIFICATION

461.	**Conservation**		*Code*	*Classification*
461.1	Water resources		100.	Personal services—salaries and wages
461.2	Agricultural resources		110.	Regular employees
461.3	Forest resources		120.	Temporary employees
461.4	Mineral resources		130.	Overtime
461.5	Fish and game resources		200.	Personal services—employee benefits
463.	**Urban redevelopment and housing**		210.	Group insurance
463.1	Urban redevelopment and housing administration		220.	Social security contributions
463.2	Urban redevelopment		230.	Retirement contributions
463.21	Redevelopment administration		240.	Tuition reimbursements
463.22	Conservation projects		250.	Unemployment compensation
463.23	Rehabilitation projects		260.	Workers' compensation
463.24	Clearance projects		290.	Other employee benefits
463.25	Relocation		300.	Purchased professional and technical services
463.3	Public housing		310.	Official/administrative

320.	Professional
330.	Other professional
340.	Technical
400.	Purchased-property services
410.	Utility services
411.	Water/sewerage
420.	Cleaning services
421.	Disposal
422.	Snow plowing
423.	Custodial
424.	Lawn care
430.	Repair and maintenance services
440.	Rentals
441.	Rental of land and buildings
442.	Rental of equipment and vehicles
450.	Construction services
500.	Other purchased services
520.	Insurance, other than employee benefits
530.	Communications
540.	Advertising
550.	Printing and binding
580.	Travel
600.	Supplies
610.	General supplies
620.	Energy
621.	Natural gas
622.	Electricity
623.	Bottled gas
624.	Oil
625.	Coal
626.	Gasoline
630.	Food
640.	Books and periodicals
700.	Property
710.	Land
720.	Buildings
730.	Improvements other than buildings
740.	Machinery and equipment
741.	Machinery
742.	Vehicles
743.	Furniture and fixtures
800.	Other objects

FUND CLASSIFICATION DESCRIPTIONS

Code *Description*

1 **General fund.** Accounts for all financial resources except those required to be accounted for in another fund.

2 **Special revenue funds.** Account for the proceeds of specific revenue sources (other than those from expendable trusts or for major capital projects) that are restricted legally to expenditure for specified purposes.

3 **Capital projects funds.** Account for financial resources to be used for the acquisition or construction of major capital facilities (other than those financed by proprietary funds and trust funds).

4 **Debt service funds.** Account for the accumulation of resources for, and the retirement of, general long-term debt principal and interest.

5 **Enterprise funds.** Account for operations financed and operated in a manner similar to private business enterprises. An enterprise fund should be established if the governing body (1) intends that the costs of providing goods or services to the general public on a continuing basis be financed or recovered primarily through user charges or (2) has decided that periodic determination of revenues earned, expenses incurred and/or net income is appropriate for capital maintenance, public policy, management control, accountability or other purposes.

6 **Internal service funds.** Account for the financing of goods or services provided by one department or agency to other departments or agencies of the reporting entity, or to other government units, on a cost-reimbursement basis.

7 **Trust and agency funds.** Account for assets held by a government in a trustee capacity or as an agent for individuals, private organizations, other government units and/or other funds. These include the following subclassifications:

Expendable trust funds. Account for assets held by a government in a trustee capacity, when both the principal and earnings on principal may be expended.

Nonexpendable trust funds. Account for assets held by a government in a trustee capacity, when only the earnings on principal may be expended and the principal must remain intact.

Pension trust funds. Account for pension assets held by a government in a trustee capacity.

Agency funds. Account for assets held by a government in an agent capacity.

8 **General fixed assets account group.** Records the fixed assets other than those accounted for in proprietary fund types or trust funds.

9 **General long-term debt account group.** Records the principal amount of all general long-term liabilities, excluding those of proprietary fund types and trust funds.

BALANCE SHEET CLASSIFICATION DESCRIPTIONS

Code *Description*

A. **Assets**

101. **Cash (including cash equivalents).** Currency, coin, checks, money orders and bankers' drafts on hand

or on deposit with an official or agent designated as custodian of cash or demand deposits with financial institutions. Cash equivalents are short-term highly liquid investments including treasury bills, commercial paper and money market funds. This account includes certain securities (e.g., treasury bills) that are classified as investments in the notes to the financial statements to disclose credit and market risks.

101.1 **Petty cash.** Currency and coins set aside to make change or pay small obligations when the issuance of a formal voucher or check is not cost-effective.

102. **Cash with fiscal agent.** Deposits with fiscal agents, such as commercial banks, for the payment of matured bonds and interest.

103. **Investments—current.** Securities that are expected to be held for less than one year and that generate revenue in the form of interest or dividends. This account includes certain securities (e.g., certificates of deposit) that are classified as deposits in the notes to the financial statements to disclose credit and market risks.

104. **Interest receivable—investments.** The amount of interest receivable on all investments.

105. **Taxes receivable—current.** The uncollected portion of taxes that a government has levied, that are due within one year and that are not yet considered delinquent.

105.1 **Allowance for uncollectible current taxes** (credit). That portion of current taxes receivable estimated not to be collectible. The balance in this account is reported as a deduction from **taxes receivable—current** to indicate net current taxes receivable.

107. **Taxes receivable—delinquent.** Taxes remaining unpaid on and after the date on which a penalty for nonpayment attaches. Delinquent taxes receivable are classified as such until paid, abated, canceled or converted into tax liens.

107.1 **Allowance for uncollectible delinquent taxes** (credit). That portion of delinquent taxes receivable estimated not to be collectible. The balance in this account is reported as a deduction from **taxes receivable—delinquent** to indicate net delinquent taxes receivable.

109. **Interest and penalties receivable—taxes.** The uncollected portion of interest and penalties receivable on taxes.

109.1 **Allowance for uncollectible interest and penalties** (credit). That portion of interest and penalties receivable on taxes estimated not to be collectible. The balance in this account is reported as a deduction from **interest and penalties receivable—taxes** to indicate net interest and penalties receivable—taxes.

111. **Tax liens receivable.** Legal claims against property that have been exercised because of nonpayment of delinquent taxes, interest and penalties. Amounts accumulated in this account include delinquent taxes, interest and penalties receivable thereon and costs of converting delinquent taxes into tax liens.

111.1 **Allowance for uncollectible tax liens** (credit). That portion of tax liens receivable estimated not to be collectible. The balance in this account is reported as a deduction from **tax liens receivable** to indicate net tax liens receivable.

115. **Accounts receivable.** Amounts owed on open accounts from private individuals or organizations for goods and services furnished by a government (excluding amounts due from other funds or intergovernmental receivables). Although taxes and special assessments receivable could be considered forms of accounts receivable, they should be recorded and reported separately in **taxes receivable** and **special assessments receivable** accounts.

115.1 **Allowance for uncollectible accounts receivable** (credit). That portion of accounts receivable estimated not to be collectible. The balance in this account is reported as a deduction from **accounts receivable** to indicate net accounts receivable.

117. **Unbilled accounts receivable.** The estimated amount of accounts receivable for goods and services rendered but not yet billed to customers.

117.1 **Allowance for uncollectible unbilled accounts receivable** (credit). That portion of unbilled accounts receivable estimated not to be collectible. The balance in this account is reported as a deduction from **unbilled accounts receivable** to indicate net unbilled accounts receivable.

121. **Special assessments receivable—current.** The uncollected portion of special assessments a government unit has levied. This account represents amounts due within one year and not yet considered delinquent.

121.1 **Allowance for uncollectible current special assessments** (credit). That portion of current special assessments receivable estimated not to be collectible. The balance in this account is reported as a deduction from **special assessments receivable—current** to indicate net current special assessments receivable.

122. **Special assessments receivable—noncurrent.** Special assessments that have been levied but that are not due within one year.

122.1 **Allowance for uncollectible noncurrent special assessments** (credit). That portion of noncurrent special assessments receivable estimated not to be collectible. The balance is reported as a deduction from **special assessments receivable—noncurrent** to indicate net noncurrent special assessments receivable.

123. **Special assessments receivable—delinquent.** Special assessments remaining unpaid on and after the date to which a penalty for nonpayment is attached.

123.1 Allowance for uncollectible delinquent special assessments (credit). That portion of delinquent special assessments receivable estimated not to be collectible. The balance in this account is reported as a deduction from **special assessments receivable—delinquent** to indicate net delinquent special assessments receivable.

124. Special assessment liens receivable. Legal claims that have been exercised against property because of nonpayment of delinquent special assessments, interest and penalties. Amounts accumulated in this account include delinquent special assessments, interest and penalties receivable thereon and costs of converting delinquent special assessments into special assessment liens.

124.1 Allowance for uncollectible special assessment liens (credit). That portion of special assessment liens receivable estimated not to be collectible. The balance in this account is reported as a deduction from **special assessment liens receivable** to indicate net special assessment liens receivable.

125. Interest receivable—special assessments. The uncollected portion of interest receivable due on unpaid installments of special assessments.

125.1 Allowance for uncollectible special assessment interest (credit). That portion of special assessment interest estimated not to be collectible. The balance in the account is reported as a deduction from **interest receivable—special assessments** to indicate net special assessment interest.

126. Intergovernmental receivable. Amounts due the reporting government from another government. These amounts may represent intergovernmental grants, entitlements or shared revenues or may represent taxes collected for the reporting government by an intermediary collecting government, loans and charges for goods or services rendered by the reporting government for another government.

127. Taxes levied for other governments. Taxes receivable that have been levied for other governments and that are to be collected and distributed to those governments by the reporting government.

128. Notes receivable. An unconditional written promise, signed by the maker, to pay a certain sum on demand or at a fixed or determinable future time either to the bearer or to the order of a person designated therein.

128.1 Allowance for uncollectible notes (credit). That portion of notes receivable estimated not to be collectible. The balance in this account is reported as a deduction from **notes receivable** to indicate net notes receivable.

129. Loans receivable. Amounts that have been loaned to individuals or organizations external to a government, including notes taken as security for such loans. Loans to other funds and governments should be recorded and reported separately.

129.1 Allowance for uncollectible loans (credit). That portion of loans receivable estimated not to be collectible. The balance in this account is reported as a deduction from **loans receivable** to indicate net loans receivable.

130. Due from other funds (specify fund). Amounts owed for goods and services rendered to a particular fund by another fund in the government reporting entity.

131. Interfund receivable (specify fund). Amounts that are owed, other than charges for goods and services rendered, to a particular fund by another fund in the government reporting entity and that are due within one year.

136. Rent receivable. Amounts due to the government pursuant to operating leases and rental agreements.

136.1 Allowance for uncollectible rent (credit). That portion of rent estimated not to be collectible. The balance in this account is reported as a deduction from rent receivable to indicate net rent receivable.

141. Inventories—materials and supplies. Materials and supplies on hand for future consumption.

142. Inventories—stores for resale. Goods held for resale rather than for use in operations.

143. Prepaid items. Charges entered in the accounts for benefits not yet received. Prepaid items (e.g., prepaid rent and unexpired insurance premiums) differ from deferred charges in that they are spread over a shorter period of time than deferred charges and are regularly recurring costs of operation.

149. Deferred charges. Nonregularly recurring, noncapital costs of operations that benefit future periods. These costs include those incurred in connection with the issuance of fund debt (e.g., underwriting and legal fees). Although bond discounts can be classified as deferred charges, discounts are reported in account 233.

151. Investments—noncurrent. Securities and real estate that are held for more than one year and that generate revenue in the form of interest, dividends, rentals or operating lease payments. This account does not include real estate used in government operations. This account includes certain securities (e.g., certificates of deposit) that are classified as deposits in the notes to the financial statements to disclose credit and market risks.

151.1 Unamortized premiums on investments. The unamortized portion of the excess of the amount paid for securities over their face value (excluding accrued interest).

151.2 Unamortized discounts—investments (credit). The unamortized portion of the excess of the face value of securities over the amount paid for them (excluding accrued interest).

152. **Advance to other funds** (specify fund). Amounts that are owed, other than charges for goods and services rendered, to a particular fund by another fund in the government reporting entity and that are not due within one year.

153. **Investments—joint venture.** Government investments and subsequent allocations of earnings or losses for joint ventures reported using the equity method of accounting.

161. **Land.** Land purchased or otherwise acquired by the government. This account includes costs incurred in preparing land for use (e.g., razing of structures).

162. **Buildings.** Permanent structures purchased or otherwise acquired by the government and improvements thereon. This account includes costs incurred in the acquisition of buildings (e.g., broker's fees).

162.1 **Accumulated depreciation—buildings** (credit). The accumulation of systematic and rational allocations of the estimated cost of using buildings, on an historical cost basis, over the useful lives of the buildings.

163. **Improvements other than buildings.** Permanent improvements, other than buildings, that add value to land (e.g., fences, retaining walls, sidewalks, pavements, gutters, tunnels and bridges).

163.1 **Accumulated depreciation—improvements other than buildings** (credit). The accumulation of systematic and rational allocations of the estimated cost of using improvements, on an historical cost basis, over the useful lives of the improvements.

164. **Machinery and equipment.** Tangible property of a more or less permanent nature, other than land or buildings and improvements thereon (e.g., machinery, tools, trucks and furnishings). This account includes costs incurred in the acquisition of machinery and equipment (e.g., transportation costs).

164.1 **Accumulated depreciation—machinery and equipment** (credit). The accumulation of systematic and rational allocations of the estimated cost of using machinery and equipment, on an historical cost basis, over the useful lives of the machinery and equipment.

165. **Construction in progress.** The cost of construction undertaken but not yet completed.

170. **Other assets.** Intangible assets and other assets not previously classified. Appropriately descriptive account titles should be used for these items.

B. OTHER DEBITS

181. **Amount available.** An account in the general long-term debt account group equal to the amount of fund balance available in the governmental funds (e.g., debt service fund) for the retirement of general long-term liabilities.

182. **Amount to be provided.** An account in the general long-term debt account group representing the amount to be provided from taxes, special assessments or other general revenues to liquidate general long-term liabilities.

C. LIABILITIES AND EQUITIES

201. **Vouchers payable.** Liabilities for goods and services evidenced by vouchers that have been pre-audited and approved for payment but that have not been paid. This account can include salaries and wages and related payroll taxes payable.

202. **Accounts payable.** A short-term liability account reflecting amounts owed to private persons or organizations for goods and services received by a government.

203. **Compensated absences payable.** Amounts owed to employees for unpaid vacation and sick leave liabilities.

204. **Claims and judgments payable.** Amounts owed as the result of administrative or court decisions, including workers' compensation, unemployment, improper arrests, property damage and condemnation awards.

205. **Contracts payable.** Amounts due on contracts for goods or services furnished to a government.

206. **Retainage payable.** Amounts due on construction contracts. Such amounts represent a percentage of the total contract price that is not paid pending final inspection, the lapse of a specified time, or both.

207. **Intergovernmental payable.** Amounts owed by the government reporting entity to another government.

208. **Due to other funds** (specify fund). Amounts owed for goods and services rendered by a particular fund to another fund in the government reporting entity.

209. **Interfund payable** (specify fund). Amounts that are owed, other than charges for goods and services rendered, by a particular fund to another fund in the government reporting entity, and that are due within one year.

212. **Matured bonds payable.** Unpaid bonds that have reached or passed their maturity date.

213. **Matured interest payable.** Unpaid interest on bonds that have reached or passed their maturity date.

214. **Accrued interest payable.** Interest costs related to the current period and prior periods, but not due until a later date.

222. **Deferred revenue.** Amounts for which asset recognition criteria have been met, but for which revenue recognition criteria have not yet been met. Under the modified accrual basis of accounting, such amounts can be measurable but not available for expenditure.

223. **Notes payable—current.** The face value of notes generally due within one year, including all tax anticipation and revenue anticipation notes payable.

225. **Bonds payable—current.** The face value of bonds due within one year, except for deep-discount bonds (e.g., zero-coupon). The accreted value of deep-discount bonds due within one year should be presented in this account.

225.1 **General obligation bonds payable.** The face value of general obligation bonds due within one year.

225.2 **Special assessment bonds payable.** The face value of special assessment bonds due within one year when the government is primarily obligated for the repayment of the bonds.

225.3 **Special assessment debt with government commitment.** The face value of special assessment bonds due within one year when the government is secondarily obligated for the repayment of the bonds.

225.4 **Revenue bonds payable.** The face value of revenue bonds due within one year.

225.5 **Other bonds payable.** The face value of bonds due within one year to be repaid from specific governmental fund revenues.

226. **Capital leases payable—current.** Current portion of the discounted present value of total future stipulated payments on lease agreements that were capitalized.

227. **Other current liabilities.** Current portion of liabilities for unfunded pension obligations and similar items. Appropriately descriptive account titles should be used for such items.

229. **Customer deposits.** Liability for deposits made by customers as a prerequisite to receiving the goods or services the government provides.

230. **Advance from other funds** (specify funds). Amounts that are owed, other than charges for goods and services rendered, by a particular fund to another fund in the government reporting entity and that are not due within one year.

231. **Bonds payable—noncurrent.** The face value of bonds not due within one year, except for deep-discount bonds (e.g., zero-coupon). The accreted value of deep discount bonds not due within one year should be presented in this account.

231.1 **General obligation bonds payable.** The face value of general obligation bonds not due within one year.

231.2 **Special assessment bonds payable.** The face value of special assessment bonds not due within one year when the government is primarily obligated for repayment of the bonds.

231.3 **Special assessment debt with government commitment.** The face value of special assessment bonds not due within one year when the government is obligated in some manner for repayment of the bonds.

231.4 **Revenue bonds payable.** The face value of revenue bonds not due within one year.

231.5 **Other bonds payable.** The face value of bonds that are not due within one year and that are to be repaid from specific governmental fund revenues.

232. **Unamortized premiums on bonds.** The unamortized portion of the excess of bond proceeds over their face value (excluding accrued interest and issuance costs).

233. **Unamortized discounts on bonds** (debit). The unamortized portion of the excess of the face value of bonds over the amount received from their sale (excluding accrued interest and issuance costs).

234. **Notes payable—noncurrent.** The face value of notes not due within one year.

237. **Capital leases payable—noncurrent.** Noncurrent portion of the discounted present value of total future stipulated payments on lease agreements that are capitalized.

238. **Deferred compensation benefits payable.** Amounts held by the government or others on behalf of participants in Internal Revenue Code Section 457 deferred compensation plans.

239. **Other noncurrent liabilities.** Noncurrent portions of liabilities for unfunded pension obligations and similar items. Appropriately descriptive account titles should be used for these items.

241. **Fund balance—reserved for debt service.** Segregation of a portion of fund balance for resources legally restricted to the payment of general long-term debt principal and interest maturing in future years.

242. **Fund balance—reserved for endowments.** Account used to indicate that trust fund balance amounts are legally restricted to endowment purposes.

244. **Fund balance—reserved for encumbrances.** Segregation of a portion of a fund balance for commitments related to unperformed contracts.

245. **Fund balance—reserved for inventories.** Segregation of a portion of a fund balance to indicate, using the purchases method for budgetary purposes, that inventories do not represent expendable available fi-

nancial resources even though they are a component of net current assets.

246. **Fund balance—reserved for prepaid items.** Segregation of a portion of fund balance to indicate that prepaid items do not represent expendable available financial resources even though they are a component of net current assets.

247. **Fund balance—reserved for noncurrent loans receivable.** Segregation of a portion of fund balance to indicate that noncurrent portions of loans receivable do not represent expendable available financial resources.

248. **Fund balance reserved for advance to other funds.** Segregation of a portion of a fund balance to indicate that advances to other funds do not represent expendable available financial resources.

249. **Fund balance—reserved for fixed assets held for resale.** Segregation of a portion of fund balance to indicate that fixed assets held for resale do not represent expendable available financial resources.

251. **Fund balance—reserved for employees' retirement system.** Pension trust fund reserves allocated based on applicable legal or plan provisions.

251.1 **Fund balance—reserved for member contributions.** Pension trust fund reserve for accumulated contributions made by employees as members of a public employees' retirement system, plus interest earnings credited in accordance with applicable legal or plan provisions.

251.2 **Fund balance—reserved for employer contributions.** Pension trust fund reserve for accumulated contributions made by the government as employer, plus interest earnings credited in accordance with applicable legal or plan provisions.

251.3 **Fund balance reserved for benefits.** Pension trust fund reserve for amounts set aside for the payment of benefits to retired members and to beneficiaries. In a contributory system, this reserve is established at the time the employee retires by transfers from accumulations in the **fund balance—reserved for employer contributions** and **fund balance—reserved for member contributions** accounts.

251.4 **Fund balance—reserved for disability.** Pension trust fund reserve for amounts set aside for disability payments to members and beneficiaries.

251.5 **Fund balance—reserved for undistributed investment earnings.** Pension trust fund unallocated reserve representing investment earnings of the employees' retirement system that have not yet been distributed to other reserves.

253. **Fund balance—unreserved.** The excess of the assets of a governmental fund or trust fund over its liabilities and reserved fund balance accounts.

253.1 **Fund balance—unreserved, designated** (specify designation). Segregation of a portion of fund balance to indicate tentative plans for future financial resource use, such as general contingencies or equipment replacement. These designations reflect tentative managerial plans or intent and should be clearly distinguished from reserves.

253.2 **Fund balance—unreserved, undesignated.** Portion of fund balance representing expendable available financial resources.

261. **Contributed capital—government.** Permanent fund capital contributed to a proprietary fund by the government from general government resources.

262. **Contributed capital—customers.** Permanent fund capital contributed to a proprietary fund by customers.

263. **Contributed capital—developers.** Permanent fund capital contributed to a proprietary fund by developers.

264. **Contributed capital—intergovernmental.** Amounts that are contributed to a proprietary fund by other governments and that are restricted by those governments to the acquisition or construction of capital assets.

271. **Retained earnings—reserved for revenue bond operations and maintenance.** Segregation of a portion of retained earnings, in accordance with the terms of a revenue bond indenture, for the revenue bond financed activity's ongoing operations.

272. **Retained earnings—reserved for revenue bond current debt service.** Segregation of a portion of retained earnings, in accordance with the terms of a revenue bond indenture, for amounts that should be accumulated for current debt service payments less current liabilities for revenue bond principal and interest. Additional amounts in such a restricted asset account should also be reserved using this account.

273. **Retained earnings—reserved for revenue bond renewal and replacement.** Segregation of a portion of retained earnings, in accordance with the terms of a revenue bond indenture, for amounts that should be accumulated for the repair and replacement of assets acquired or constructed with revenue bond proceeds.

279. **Retained earnings—unreserved.** The accumulated earnings of a proprietary fund that are not reserved for any specific purpose.

280. **Investment in general fixed assets.** An account representing the government's investment in capital assets reported in the general fixed assets account group. The balance of this account is subdivided according to the source of the monies with which asset acquisitions are financed.

REVENUES AND OTHER FINANCING SOURCES CLASSIFICATION DESCRIPTIONS

Code   *Description*

311. **General property taxes** are ad valorem taxes levied on an assessed valuation of real and/or personal property. The distinguishing characteristics of general property taxes are that the revenues are (1) derived from taxes (2) levied by the government reporting entity and (3) assessed on the general property. From this group are eliminated (1) all nontax revenue (2) all taxes levied by another level of government, such as a county or state or the federal government, even when they are distributed to another government and (3) all taxes levied by the government reporting entity upon subjects or bases other than general property.
  311.1 **Real property**
  311.2 **Personal property**
      311.21 **Tangible personal**
      311.22 **Intangible personal**

312. **Property taxes on other than assessed valuation** are direct taxes (1) assessed and levied on a valuation other than the general assessed valuation usually applied in the case of privately owned real property or (2) calculated at a specified rate per unit. Examples include taxes on a corporation's property levied upon the basis of the amount of corporate stock, corporate indebtedness or some basis other than an assessed valuation applied to all the corporation's property; taxes on banks and savings and loan associations levied in proportion to a certain specified portion of deposits; taxes on life insurance corporations assessed upon the basis of the valuation of their policies and all specific taxes on property, such as taxes on land at a specified amount per acre and taxes on animals at a specified amount per head.

313. **General sales and use taxes** are imposed upon the sale or consumption of goods and/or services, generally with few or limited exemptions. An example of a general sales tax is a tax on the retail price of all goods sold within a taxing jurisdiction, with the exception of food purchased for consumption off the premises.

314. **Selective sales and use taxes** are imposed upon the sale or consumption of selected goods or services.
  314.1 **Motor fuel**
  314.2 **Tobacco products**
  314.3 **Alcoholic beverages**

315. **Income taxes** are measured by net income, (i.e., by gross income less certain deductions permitted by law).
  315.1 **Individual**
  315.2 **Corporate**
  315.3 **Unincorporated business** (when business income is taxed separately from individual income)

316. **Gross receipts business taxes** are levied in proportion to gross receipts on business activities of all or designated types of businesses.
  316.1 **Privately owned public utility**
  316.2 **Publicly owned public utility**
  316.3 **Insurance companies**
  316.4 **Amusements**

317. **Death and gift taxes** are imposed upon the transfer of property at death or gifts made in contemplation of death.

318. **Other taxes**
  318.1 **Severance taxes** are imposed on the privilege of removing designated natural resources from land or water. They are based upon the value and/or amount of resources removed or sold.
  318.2 **Franchise taxes** are imposed on the privilege of using public property for private purposes.

319. **Penalties and interest on delinquent taxes** are amounts assessed as penalties for the payment of taxes after their due date, and the interest charged on delinquent taxes from their due date to the date of actual payment. Separate accounts should be used for penalties and interest on each type of tax.
  319.1 **General property taxes**
      319.11 **Real property**
      319.12 **Personal property**
  319.2 **Property taxes on other than assessed valuation**
  319.3 **General sales and use taxes**
  319.4 **Selective sales and use taxes**
  319.5 **Income taxes**
  319.6 **Gross receipts business taxes**
  319.7 **Death and gift taxes**

320. **Licenses and permits** generally are segregated into business and nonbusiness categories.

321. **Business licenses and permits** are revenues from businesses and occupations that must be licensed before doing business within the government's jurisdiction.
  321.1 **Alcoholic beverages**
  321.2 **Health**
  321.3 **Police and protective**
  321.4 **Corporate**
  321.5 **Public utilities**
  321.6 **Professional and occupational**
  321.7 **Amusements**

322. **Nonbusiness licenses and permits** are revenues from all nonbusiness licenses and permits levied according to the benefits presumably conferred by the license or permit.
  322.1 **Building structures and equipment**
  322.2 **Motor vehicles**
  322.3 **Motor vehicle operators**

322.4 **Hunting and fishing**
322.5 **Marriage licenses**
322.6 **Animal licenses**

330. **Intergovernmental revenues** are revenues from other governments in the form of operating grants, entitlements, shared revenues or payments in lieu of taxes.

An operating grant is a contribution or gift of cash or other assets from another government to be used or expended for a specified purpose, activity or facility. Capital grants are restricted by the grantor for the acquisition and/or construction of fixed (capital) assets. A grant may be received either directly from the granting government or indirectly as a pass-through from another government.

An entitlement is the amount of payment to which a government is entitled pursuant to an allocation formula contained in applicable statutes. A shared revenue is a revenue levied by one government but shared on a predetermined basis, often in proportion to the amount collected at the local level, with another government or class of governments.

Payments in lieu of taxes are payments made from general revenues by one government to another in lieu of taxes it would have to pay, had its property or other tax base been subject to taxation by the recipient government on the same basis as privately owned property or other tax base.

331. **Federal government grants**
331.1 **Operating—categorical**
331.11 **Direct**
331.12 **Indirect**
331.2 **Operating—noncategorical**
331.21 **Direct**
331.22 **Indirect**
331.3 **Capital**
331.31 **Direct**
331.32 **Indirect**

333. **Federal government payments in lieu of taxes**

334. **State government grants**
334.1 **Operating—categorical**
334.2 **Operating—noncategorical**
334.3 **Capital**

335. **State government shared revenues**
335.1 **Property taxes**
335.2 **Income taxes**
335.21 **Individual income taxes**
335.22 **Corporate income taxes**
335.3 **General sales and use taxes**
335.4 **Motor vehicle fuel taxes**
335.5 **Motor vehicle licenses**
335.6 **Tobacco taxes**
335.7 **Alcoholic bevarage taxes**
335.8 **Death and gift taxes**
335.9 **Gross receipts business taxes**

336. **State government payments in lieu of taxes**

337. **Local government unit** (specify unit) **grants**

338. **Local government unit** (specify unit) **shared revenues**

339. **Local government unit** (specify unit) **payments in lieu of taxes**

340. **Charges for services** are charges for current services exclusive of revenues of proprietary funds.

341. **General government**
341.1 **Court costs, fees and charges**
341.2 **Recording of legal instruments**
341.3 **Zoning and subdivision fees**
341.4 **Printing and duplicating services**

342. **Public safety**
342.1 **Special police services**
342.2 **Special fire protection services**
342.3 **Correctional fees**
342.4 **Protective inspection fees**

344. **Sanitation**
344.1 **Sewerage charges**
344.2 **Street sanitation charges**
344.3 **Refuse collection charges**

345. **Health**
345.1 **Vital statistics**
345.2 **Health and inspection fees**
345.3 **Hospital fees**
345.4 **Clinic fees**
345.5 **Animal control and shelter fees**

346. **Welfare**
346.1 **Institutional charges**

347. **Culture—recreation**
347.1 **Golf fees**
347.2 **Swimming pool fees**
347.3 **Playground fees**
347.4 **Park and recreation concessions**
347.5 **Auditorium use fees**
347.6 **Library use fees (not fines)**
347.7 **Zoo charges**

351. **Fines** include monies derived from fines and penalties imposed for the commission of statutory offenses, violation of lawful administrative rules and regulations, and for the neglect of official duty.
351.1 **Court**
351.2 **Library**

352. **Forfeits** include monies derived from confiscating deposits held as performance guarantees.

355. **Special assessments** are amounts levied against certain properties to defray all or part of the cost of a specific capital improvement or service deemed to benefit primarily those properties.

355.1 **Capital improvement**

355.2 **Service**

361. **Interest revenues** are compensation for the use of financial resources over a period of time.

362. **Gains on the sale of investments** are the difference between financial inflows and the carrying value of the disposed investments.

363. **Rents and royalties** are financial resources derived from the use by others of the government's tangible and intangible assets.

364. **Escheats** are the uncompensated acquisition of private property abandoned or otherwise alienated by its owners.

365. **Contributions and donations from private sources** are financial resources provided by private contributors.

390. **Other financing sources**

391. **Interfund operating transfers in** (specify fund) are financial inflows from other funds of the government reporting entity that are not classified as quasi-external transactions, reimbursements, loans, advances or residual equity transfers.

392. **Proceeds of general fixed asset dispositions** are financial inflows provided from the disposition of general fixed assets.

392.1 **Sales of general fixed assets**

392.2 **Compensation for loss of general fixed assets**

393. **Proceeds of general long-term liabilities** generally are gross financial resources provided by the issuance of general long-term liabilities.

393.1 **General obligation bond proceeds**

393.2 **Special assessment bond proceeds**

393.3 **Special assessment debt with government commitment**

393.4 **Other bond proceeds**

393.5 **Proceeds from refunding bonds**

393.6 **Premiums on bonds sold**

393.7 **Capital leases**

EXPENDITURES AND OTHER FINANCING USES CLASSIFICATION DESCRIPTIONS

Function, Program and Activity Classification

Code   *Description*

410. **General government** is charged with all expenditures for the legislative and judicial branches of a govern-ment. It also is charged with expenditures made by the chief executive officer and other top-level auxiliary and staff agencies in the administrative branch of the government. The accounts are subdivided into three groups: legislative, executive and judicial.

411. **Legislative** is charged with expenditures of governing body in the performance of its primary duties and subsidiary activities. A decision whether a given item should be charged to a legislative account is based on whether the item is a direct or an indirect cost. Direct costs are charged to legislative accounts. Indirect costs are charged to another account, usually a staff agency account (e.g., public safety—police).

411.1 **Governing body** is charged with the direct expenditures of the governing body. Direct expenditures, which include salaries and travel costs, represent expenditures incurred by members themselves or by a committee of the governing body. Indirect expenditures represent expenditures incurred for the governing body by a staff agency or official.

If the governing body is composed partly or wholly of administrative officials (e.g., the commission under the commission form of government), their salaries are charged to the departments they direct. (See 413.3 below.) If additional compensation is specifically provided in return for services as members of such body, their regular salaries are charged as explained above, and the remainder is charged to this account (411.1). The salaries of citizen members of such bodies also are charged to this account.

Expenditures of commissions or bodies acting in both a legislative and an executive capacity are classified as executive if their legislative function is incidental and subordinate to the executive function. The most common example of a dual capacity is encountered under the commission form of government. Expenditures of boards composed of exofficio members performing predominantly executive functions, are charged to the respective functions headed by the board members.

411.2 **Legislative committees and special bodies** is charged with expenditures of regular committees of the governing body, special investigating committees, boards or representatives responsible solely to the governing body. Costs of an investigation preliminary to the purchase of equipment or properties for a specific department should be included as a cost of the purchase.

411.3 **Ordinances and proceedings** is charged with expenditures for printing and advertising ordinances and for printing the proceedings of the governing body.

411.4 **Clerk of council** is charged with expenditures

for the office of clerk of council. Where other officials (city clerk) also perform the duty of the clerk of council in addition to their regular duties, their expenditures are usually charged to account 415.4. Although it may not be practicable to allocate their expenditures to accounts other than 415.4, whenever possible these expenditures should be apportioned to 411.4 and 415.4 in proportion to the time required for each office.

412. **Judicial** includes accounts for recording expenditures for judicial activities of the government.

    412.1 **Criminal courts** is charged with expenditures for judicial activities involving criminal cases. When several courts try criminal cases, expenditures should be classified further by each court.

    412.2 **Grand jury** is charged with expenditures for grand jury hearings and includes compensation of jurors, witness fees, investigation costs and clerical costs.

    412.3 **Public defender** is charged with expenditures for the office of public defender. If the public defender is attached to and a part of the law office, it may not be possible to segregate expenditures related to the activities performed as public defender. In such a case, the expenditure should be included in account 415.3.

    412.4 **Civil courts** is charged with expenditures for judicial activities involving civil cases. When several courts try civil cases, expenditures should be classified by each court, such as chancery court (412.41), small claims court (412.42), civil court (412.43) and domestic relations court (412.44).

    412.5 **Law library** is charged with all expenditures for acquiring and maintaining a law library.

413. **Executive** includes accounts for recording expenditures of general executive officers and boards of the government.

    413.1 **Mayor** is charged with expenditures for salaries and other costs of the mayor and employees connected with his or her office in the mayor-council form of government. Expenditures of a mayor under the council-manager form of government are charged to account 411.1 (governing body), and those for a mayor under the commission form are charged to the functions the mayor directs.

    413.2 **Chief executive** is charged with expenditures of the government's chief executive and the employees connected with his or her office. This account title may be changed to indicate the chief executive's specific title, such as **manager** or **administrator.**

    413.3 **Boards and commissions** is charged with expenditures of elected commissioners under the commission form of government and expenditures of other boards and commissions acting primarily in executive capacities to the extent that such expenditures cannot be allocated to the functions the commissioners or board members direct. Expenditures of elected commissioners who are also executive officers should be charged to the functions they direct to reflect the complete cost of each function of government. When a commissioner directs the finance function, the expenditures of his or her office should be charged to account 415.

        Expenditures of a commissioner of utilities should not be charged to an account in the general fund, but to the proper accounts of the government's utility funds. When a commissioner directs two or more departments, the expenditures of that office should be allocated to the functions under the commissioner's direction.

414. **Elections** includes accounts for recording direct expenditures for registering voters and holding general, primary and special elections. Salaries of the officials and police performing election duties recurrently and incidentally as part of their broader duties are not charged to elections but to their respective departmental activities. The salaries of election deputies, judges, tellers, hired watchers or inspectors, special clerks and special police are chargeable to this account.

415. **Financial administration** includes accounts for recording expenditures of central staff agencies performing financial management functions for the government.

    415.1 **Finance** includes individual accounts for each of the following types of financial activities: **general supervision** (415.11), **accounting** (415.12), **independent audit** (415.13), **budget** (415.14), **tax administration** (415.15), **treasury** (415.16), **licensing** (415.17), **purchasing** (415.18), **debt administration** (415.19), and **internal audit** (415.21), if not performed in an independent role.

    415.3 **Law** includes accounts for recording expenditures for legal services required by a government in the discharge of its functions and activities. Included are the costs of the attorney or other attorneys who render legal advice to the governing body or administrative agencies of the government, who draft laws, ordinances or administrative regulations for it and its constituent agencies and who serve as counsel in lawsuits to which the government is a party.

    415.4 **Recording and reporting** includes accounts for recording expenditures of those staff agencies whose main activity is the preparation and recording of government documents, records, proceedings and papers. These include the recording of deeds, mortgages and similar legal documents; and general public reports of the government. The clerical, stenographic and filing costs of individual offices and agencies are not charged to these accounts, but to appropriate accounts elsewhere on the basis of functions and activities performed by such agencies.

415.5 **Personnel administration** includes accounts that record expenditures of the agency or agencies performing central personnel and related services for the entire government. Such services include general supervision of personnel management, classification of positions, recruitment, placement (transfers, promotions, demotions), service ratings, attendance, certification of payrolls, separations, fringe benefits and retirement systems.

419. **Other—unclassified**
419.1 **Planning and zoning**
419.2 **Data processing**
419.3 **Research and investigation**
419.4 **General government buildings and plant**

420. **Public safety,** a major function of government, has as its objective the protection of persons and property. The major subfunctions under public safety are police protection, fire protection, protective inspection and correction.

421. **Police** includes accounts for recording expenditures incurred by the police department in the administration of various law enforcement activities.

421.1 **Police administration** is charged with all expenditures incurred by the chief of police and assistant chiefs in supervising the activities of the police department. In addition to directing departmental personnel and budgetary responsibilities, this supervision may include long-range planning, research into problems of criminal activity and law enforcement, and investigatory and intelligence activities that disclose the integrity and effectiveness of the department's administrative activities and that provide information on known criminals and organized crime.

421.2 **Crime control and investigation**
421.21 **Criminal investigation** is charged with expenditures made by detectives in investigating criminal activities, detecting and arresting criminal offenders, obtaining evidence for prosecution of criminal cases, filing cases, returning fugitive felons from other jurisdictions, testifying in court cases, locating missing persons and recovering lost or stolen property. If a separate organizational unit handles youth and juvenile delinquency problems, its expenditures should not be recorded in this account, but should be recorded in account 421.25

421.22 **Vice control** is charged with expenditures arising out of activities to suppress vice. These include investigation and procurement of evidence necessary for prosecution in gambling, prostitution, narcotics and related cases and for regulation of vice-related businesses.

421.23 **Patrol** is charged with all expenditures for uniformed police patrol of assigned districts and such related police activities as investigating law violations of all kinds, arresting law violators, checking premises for illegal entry, checking open doors and windows, making reports of traffic accidents and other law violations, including suspected criminal activity.

421.24 **Records and identification** is charged with expenditures connected with the maintenance of the records of all police incidents and criminals, such as fingerprints, photographs and case histories.

421.25 **Youth investigation and control** is charged with expenditures arising out of investigations of complaints against juveniles; programs to control juvenile delinquency; law violations involving accessories, accomplices or contributors to the delinquency of minors; programs for self-education, rehabilitation and job placement for reformed youths and location of missing juveniles.

421.26 **Custody of prisoners** is charged with all expenditures for the temporary detention and custody of offenders. Such expenditures include costs of operating a jail and caring for prisoners, pending conviction or permanent disposition of their cases. Maintaining prisoners serving sentences in penal institutions should not be charged to this account, but should be charged to appropriate corrections accounts (423).

421.27 **Custody of property** is charged with expenditures required in caring for property belonging to prisoners, lost and found properties and stolen and recovered properties.

421.28 **Crime laboratory** is charged with all expenditures for laboratory examinations and analyses of physical evidence involved in law enforcement.

421.3 **Traffic control** is charged with expenditures arising out of controlling traffic, enforcing traffic laws, operating radar units, investigating traffic accidents, checking parking meter violations, issuing tickets for such violations, patrolling streets and issuing tickets for moving violations.

421.31 **Motor vehicle inspection and regulation** is charged with expenditures for examining and licensing motor vehicles and motor vehicle operators.

421.4 **Police training** is charged with expenditures for training police officers. This training may include formal basic training for recruits, in-service training for commissioned police officers and maintenance of training facilities.

421.5 **Support service**

421.51 **Communications services** is charged with all expenditures for providing and maintaining police communications, including receipt of calls for police assistance, dispatch of police units and maintenance of police communications equipment.

421.52 **Automotive services** is charged with all expenditures for maintaining and servicing police vehicles, towing for police and confiscated vehicles and equipping police vehicles with special equipment.

421.53 **Ambulance services** is charged with expenditures for emergency ambulance services provided directly by the police department or provided as a contracted service by the government.

421.54 **Medical services** is charged with expenditures for rendering first aid to civilians and for medical examinations, treatment and hospital care of prisoners and policemen, either directly by the government or as a contracted service.

421.6 **Special detail services** is charged with expenditures for police personnel exercising police functions outside of regular police assignments. This account includes special services for which the government receives compensation from private sources or other governments.

421.7 **Police stations and buildings** is charged with

expenditures for police stations and buildings other than the general municipal building. If buildings are rented, rental payments are charged to this account.

422. **Fire** includes accounts for recording the expenditures incurred by the fire department in preventing and fighting fires.

422.1 **Fire administration** is charged with expenditures of the fire chief and immediate assistants in supervising all the activities of the fire department. These activities include general administration of all official policies, budgetary and personnel administration and long-range planning and research.

422.2 **Fire fighting** is charged with expenditures for extinguishing fires and for providing such special services as building and fire-hydrant inspections and assistance to persons and property during a disaster.

422.3 **Fire prevention** is charged with expenditures for such fire prevention activities as inspection of fire hazards, investigation of the causes of fires, investigation and prosecution of persons involved in incendiary fires, fire prevention education, control of inflammable materials and enforcement of fire prevention ordinances.

422.4 **Fire training** is charged with all expenditures for training firemen either in the department or by educational institutions outside the government. This account is also charged with maintenance of special training facilities.

422.5 **Fire communications** is charged with expenditures for the acquisition, operation and maintenance of fire alarm systems and other communication systems used by the fire department in preventing and fighting fires. It also is charged with the maintenance of current coverage maps and assignment schedules for fire apparatus and with the maintenance of records showing the locations of and changes in fire hydrants and sprinkler systems.

422.6 **Fire repair services** is charged with all expenditures for repair of fire apparatus and equipment and for conducting regular equipment tests.

422.7 **Medical services** is charged with all expenditures for the medical examination, treatment and care of sick or injured firemen.

422.8 **Fire stations and buildings** is charged with expenditures for fire stations and buildings other than the general municipal building. If buildings are rented, rental payments are charged to this account.

423. **Corrections** includes accounts for recording expenditures for confinement of law violators and for proba-

tion and parole activities involved in their rehabilitation.

423.1 **Correctional administration** is charged with expenditures of any officer, board or commission having top-level responsibility for correctional activities. Expenditures for supervision of individual institutions are charged to the appropriate institution.

423.2 **Adult correctional institutions** is charged with expenditures for the construction, operation and maintenance of such correctional institutions as prisons, jails, prison factories and prison farms. A separate subsidiary account should be established for each institution operated by the government.

423.3 **Juvenile correctional institutions** is charged with expenditures for the construction, operation and maintenance of correctional institutions for the punishment and rehabilitation of juvenile offenders. Such institutions include jails, detention homes and reformatories. When a government maintains more than one institution of this kind, separate accounts should be established for each institution.

423.4 **Delinquents in other institutions** is charged with expenditures for offenders confined in correctional institutions of other government jurisdictions, including jails, prisons, detention homes, reformatories and foster homes. These expenditures include payments for transporting delinquents to and from such institutions. If both adult and youth offenders are cared for in this manner, this account should be divided into two separate accounts, one for youth and one for adults.

423.5 **Adult probation and parole** is charged with expenditures incurred in the supervision of adult offenders who are paroled or placed on probation.

423.6 **Juvenile probation and parole** is charged with expenditures incurred in the supervision of juvenile offenders who are paroled or placed on probation.

424. **Protective inspection** includes accounts for recording expenditures incurred in making protective inspections, except those related to health and fire and those definitively assigned to other functions.

424.1 **Protective inspection administration** is charged with expenditures for the centralized administration of two or more inspection services.

424.2 **Building inspection** is charged with expenditures incurred in the examination of building plans, inspection of building construction, inspection of existing buildings for structural defects and compliance with minimum housing standards and issuance of building permits.

424.3 **Plumbing inspection** is charged with ex-

penditures incurred in the examination of plumbing plans, inspection of plumbing installations and issuance of building permits.

424.4 **Electrical inspection** is charged with expenditures incurred in the examination of electrical plans, inspection of electrical installations and issuance of electrical permits.

424.5 **Gas inspection** is charged with expenditures incurred in the examination of gas installations and fittings and issuance of gas permits.

424.6 **Air conditioning inspection** is charged with expenditures incurred in the examination of plans for air conditioning installations, inspection of such installations and issuance of permits.

424.7 **Boiler inspection** is charged with expenditures for examining the plans for and the installation and operation of boilers, pressure tanks, steam engines and similar devices.

424.8 **Elevator inspection** is charged with expenditures for examining the plans for and the installation and operation of elevators, dumb waiters and escalators.

424.9 **Weights and measures** is charged with expenditures for determining the accuracy of devices used for weighing and measuring physical objects, checking such devices periodically, investigating complaints and prosecuting violators.

429. **Other protection** includes accounts for protection activities that are not strictly a part of the foregoing major account groupings.

429.1 **Civil defense** is charged with expenditures for the preparation of survival plans to be used in the event of war or natural disaster, for the administration of training programs for protection and survival and for the provision and inspection of shelters, shelter supplies and other civil defense installations and equipment.

429.2 **Militia and armories** is charged with expenditures for the construction and maintenance of armories, support of militias and construction and maintenance of related facilities.

429.3 **Traffic engineering** is charged with expenditures for investigations relating to the design and location of traffic control devices and for the installation and maintenance of such traffic control and parking devices as traffic signals, street and curb markings, street signs and parking meters.

429.4 **Examination of licensed occupations** is charged with the expenditures of boards and other administrative personnel who examine and license individuals to practice certain professions and vocations.

429.5 **Public scales** is charged with all expenditures incurred in the provision and maintenance of public scales.

429.6 **Flood control** is charged with expenditures for walls, levees and other devices that protect persons and property from surface water damage.

431. **Highways and streets** includes accounts for recording expenditures for roadways and walkways, according to the type of facility involved. Roadways and walkways in parks are not charged to this account, but to appropriate accounts under the function of **culture—recreation** (450).

    431.21 **Paved streets** is charged with expenditures for construction, maintenance and repair of street surfaces, curbs and gutters on streets paved with concrete, asphalt or brick.

    431.22 **Unpaved streets** is charged with expenditures incurred for construction, maintenance and repair of unpaved streets, including scraping, grading, graveling, dragging, cindering and oiling.

    431.23 **Alleys** is charged with expenditures for the construction, maintenance and repair of alleys.

    431.24 **Sidewalks and crosswalks** is charged with expenditures for the construction, maintenance and repair of sidewalks, crosswalks, steps and stairs.

    431.25 **Snow and ice removal** is charged with expenditures for removing snow and ice and for sanding or salting streets, alleys, bridges and sidewalks.

431.3 **Bridges, viaducts and grade separations** is charged with expenditures for the construction, maintenance and repair of bridges (stationary and movable), viaducts, grade separations, trestles and railroad crossings.

431.4 **Tunnels** is charged with expenditures for the construction, maintenance and repair of tunnels, including payments to other government jurisdictions for the joint construction and maintenance of tunnels.

431.5 **Storm drainage** is charged with expenditures for the construction, maintenance and repair of storm drainage inlets and collection and disposal systems.

431.6 **Street lighting** is charged with expenditures for street lighting fixtures and for lighting all streets, alleys, bridges, subways and tunnels, except those located in parks.

432. **Sanitation,** a major function of government, includes all activities involved in the removal and disposal of sewage and other types of waste.

    432.1 **Sanitary administration** is charged with all expenditures for the general administrative direction of sanitation activities.

432.2 **Street cleaning** is charged with expenditures for sweeping and washing streets, flushing gutters and underpasses and collecting and disposing of debris from streets and public roadways.

432.3 **Waste collection** is charged with expenditures for collecting garbage and other refuse and delivering it to the place of disposal.

432.4 **Waste disposal** is charged with expenditures for disposing of garbage and other refuse. When several methods of disposal are used, such as sanitary landfill and incineration, appropriate accounts should be set up for each disposal facility.

432.5 **Sewage collection and disposal** includes accounts for recording expenditures incurred in the collection and disposal of sewage.

    432.51 **Sanitary sewer construction** is charged with expenditures for the construction of new sanitary sewer lines.

    432.52 **Sanitary sewer maintenance** is charged with expenditures for repair, reconstruction and maintenance of sanitary sewer lines.

    432.53 **Sanitary sewer cleaning** is charged with expenditures for routine cleaning of sanitary sewer lines.

    432.54 **New sewer services** is charged with expenditures for installing of new sanitary sewer lines, clearing emergency stoppages in sanitary sewer service lateral lines and making taps for service laterals installed by plumbers.

    432.55 **Sewer lift stations** is charged with expenditures for construction and operation of lift stations that pump sewage over geographical elevations prior to disposition into gravity-flow sewer lines.

    432.56 **Sewage treatment plants** is charged with expenditures for the construction and operation of plants that treat and dispose of sewage.

432.6 **Weed control** is charged with expenditures for cutting and removing weeds from private property when the property owners will not and from government property such as parkways, alleys and easements.

440. **Health and welfare**

441. **Health,** a major function of government, includes all activities involved in the conservation and improvement of public health.

    441.1 **Public health administration** is charged with expenditures for the general administration of public health activities.

    441.2 **Vital statistics** is charged with expenditures

for preparing and maintaining vital records of births, deaths, adoptions, marriages and divorces; preparing reports and statistical analyses of such data and issuing certified copies of birth certificates, death certificates and other records, as permitted and required by law.

441.3 **Regulation and inspection** includes expenditure accounts for various inspection and regulatory activities essential to the conservation and improvement of public health.

441.31 **Food and drugs** is charged with expenditures for regulation and inspection of food and drugs. Pertinent activities include licensing; inspection of food stores, factories, markets and restaurants; laboratory tests of food and drugs; examination and licensing of food handlers; meat inspection; inspection of meat markets and enforcement of pure food and drug laws and ordinances.

441.32 **Milk and dairy products** is charged with expenditures incurred in the inspection and regulation of milk, dairy products, dairies, dairy cattle, dairy establishments and dairy delivery facilities.

441.33 **Other sanitary inspection** is charged with expenditures incurred in health inspection and regulatory activities other than those related to milk, food and drugs. Examples of such activities include inspection of barber and beauty shops, hotels, motels, and tourist and trailer parks; inspection of nursing homes and children's institutions; mosquito, fly and other insect inspections; inspections of government-owned and private premises for other types of health hazards; air pollution and radiological inspections and inspection of refuse, water and sewage facilities. If several of these activities are performed by a single government, separate accounts should be set up for each activity.

441.4 **Communicable disease control** includes accounts for expenditures incurred in the prevention and treatment (except hospitalization) of certain defined communicable diseases.

441.41 **Tuberculosis** is charged with expenditures incurred for the prevention and treatment (except hospitalization) of tuberculosis.

441.42 **Socially transmitted diseases** is charged with expenditures incurred for the prevention and treatment (except hospitalization) of socially transmitted diseases.

441.43 **Rabies and animal** control is charged with expenditures incurred for the prevention and treatment (except for hospitalization) of rabies.

441.44 **Other communicable diseases** is charged with expenditures incurred for the prevention and treatment (except hospitalization) of all communicable diseases other than tuberculosis, socially transmitted diseases and rabies. Covered activities include vaccination and immunization against diseases, quarantine and disinfection, extermination of rodents, mosquitos and flies, and operation of clinics and dispensaries.

441.5 **Maternal and child health services** includes accounts for expenditures incurred for various maternal and child health services (except communicable diseases).

441.51 **Maternal and preschool** is charged with all expenditures for child hygiene, except in schools. Pertinent activities include operation of prenatal clinics, nursing visits to expectant mothers, supervision and medicine, operation of preschool clinics and home visits to children by nurses.

441.52. **School** is charged with expenditures for health and hygiene activities in public and private schools. These activities include medical examination of school children and treatment by health officers, dental examination of school children and treatment by health officers, operation of school clinics, school nursing, nutrition nursing, and psychological and psychiatric examinations and treatment of school children.

441.6 **Adult health services** is charged with expenditures for health services for adults other than those rendered in connection with communicable diseases. These services include educational programs aimed at prevention and control of chronic diseases and accidents.

441.7 **Health centers and general clinics** is charged with expenditures for health centers and general clinics furnishing two or more types of clinical services. If the clinic is maintained exclusively for one service, such as tuberculosis, the expenditures should be charged to the appropriate activity account under **communicable disease control.** Dispensaries operated in connection with clinics should be considered as part of the clinic.

441.8 **Laboratory** is charged with expenditures for laboratory tests essential to the maintenance of public health. These tests include serologic tests for syphilis; bacteriological analysis of water, milk and milk products and food products, chemical analysis of milk and dairy products, and bacteriological analysis for tuberculosis and other diseases.

444. **Welfare,** a major function of government, includes all activities designed to provide public assistance and institutional care for individuals economically unable to provide essential needs for themselves.

444.1 **Welfare administration** is charged with expenditures for the general administration of all public welfare activities.

444.2 **Institutional care** is charged with expenditures for the construction and operation of welfare institutions maintained by the government for the care of the indigent. Separate activity accounts should be set up for each type of institution, such as homes for the aged and orphanages.

444.3 **Direct assistance** is charged with expenditures, in cash or in kind, made directly to eligible welfare recipients by the government. If there are several categories of assistance programs, expenditures should be classified under one or more of the following categories.

444.31 **General assistance** is charged with expenditures to families or individuals who meet specified eligibility criteria and who are not classified under one of the other welfare programs. General assistance refers to such forms of welfare as home relief and general emergency relief.

444.32 **Old-age assistance** is charged with expenditures made by the government to persons older than a specified age.

444.33 **Aid to dependent children** is charged with expenditures for the care and support of needy dependent children, including payments made to parents, guardians and foster parents.

444.34 **Aid to the blind** is charged with expenditures made by the government to persons judged legally blind.

444.35 **Aid to the disabled** is charged with expenditures made by the government to persons judged legally disabled.

444.36 **Other direct assistance** is charged with expenditures to needy persons other than those classified under the foregoing categories. If several additional classes of persons are welfare recipients, separate activity accounts should be established for each class.

444.4 **Intergovernmental welfare payments** is charged with expenditures made by the government to another government for welfare programs administered by it. Such expenditures should be classified under one of the following categories:

444.41 **General assistance**
444.42 **Old-age assistance**
444.43 **Aid to dependent children**
444.44 **Aid to the blind**
444.45 **Aid to the disabled**
444.46 **Other welfare assistance**

444.5 **Vendor welfare payments** is charged with expenditures made directly to private individuals and organizations who furnish authorized care, commodities and services to welfare recipients.

444.51 **Vendor medical payments** is charged with expenditures to private individuals and organizations for medical assistance for the aged under federal and/or state programs and for medical assistance payments under general assistance, aid to the blind and other programs.

444.52 **Other vendor payments** is charged with expenditures made to vendors of care, commodities and services for welfare recipients other than those for medical services. Examples include legal services, burial services, rent, food and clothing. If more than one class of vendor payments exists, separate accounts should be established for each class.

450. **Culture—recreation,** a major function of government, includes all cultural and recreational activities maintained for the benefit of residents and visitors.

451. **Recreation**

451.1 **Culture—recreation administration** is charged with expenditures for the general administration of all cultural and recreational activities and facilities.

451.2 **Participant recreation** is charged with expenditures for recreational facilities and activities in which direct participation is the primary attribute. Examples include organized athletics, individual participant sports such as golf, indoor and outdoor games of various kinds and dancing.

451.21 **Supervision** is charged with expenditures for supervision of two or more recreational activities classified under **participant recreation.**

451.22 **Recreation centers** is charged with expenditures for the construction, maintenance and operation of multipurpose recreation centers, which contain a full compliment of recreational facilities such as gymnasiums, athletic fields, craft rooms and swimming pools.

451.23 **Playgrounds** is charged with expenditures for the construction, maintenance and operation of neighborhood playgrounds.

451.24 **Swimming pools** is charged with expenditures for the construction, maintenance and operation of swimming pools. If more than one pool is maintained, a separate account should be established for each one. If a government operates other types of swimming facilities outside of those in recreation centers, such as a public beach, this account classification may be expanded to include them.

451.25 **Golf courses** is charged with expenditures for the construction, maintenance and operation of golf courses and related facilities. A separate account should be established for each golf course.

451.26 **Tennis courts** is charged with expenditures for the construction, maintenance and operation of tennis courts and related facilities.

451.27 **Other recreational facilities** is charged with expenditures for all other participant recreational facilities and areas other than those listed in the foregoing accounts. A separate account should be provided for each type of facility or area.

451.3 **Spectator recreation** is charged with expenditures for cultural and scientific recreational activities benefiting the public as spectators. These expenditures should be charged to one of the following accounts.

451.31 **Botanical gardens**
451.32 **Museums**
451.33 **Art galleries**
451.34 **Zoos**

451.4 **Special recreational facilities** is charged with expenditures for special recreational facilities not included in the foregoing accounts and maintained as separate recreational facilities. Examples include auditoriums, stadiums, camping areas and marinas. When more than one type of special facility is maintained, a separate account should be established for each one.

452. **Parks** is charged with expenditures for public parks, public squares and similar ornamental areas. Excluded from this account classification are grounds surrounding public buildings, land encompassed in other recreational facilities such as zoos and incidental landscaping and maintenance of areas elsewhere classified under recreation.

452.1 **Supervision** is charged with expenditures for supervising two or more park activities or facilities.

452.2 **Park areas** is charged with all expenditures for acquiring, operating and maintaining park areas and related facilities. These include land used for a park: planting and care of park lawns, trees, shrubs and flowers; park roads, walks and paths; park waterways and park structures and equipment. When more than one park is operated, a separate account should be established for each park.

452.3 **Parkways and boulevards** is charged with expenditures for landscaped areas with traffic lanes running through or adjacent to them. These parkways and boulevards are constructed primarily for beautification and recreation and must be distinguished from so-called boulevards routinely maintained by the street or highway department.

452.4 **Forestry and nursery** is charged with expenditures for growing trees and other plants and transplanting them along streets, in parks, in parkways or other public areas. Other activities whose expenditures should be included in this account include removal and disposal of undesirable trees and other plants, supervision of tree trimming on public property and granting of permits to plant trees in parks and other public areas.

452.5 **Park policing** is charged with expenditures for special policing in parks, whether under the direction of the police department or special park police.

452.6 **Park lighting** is charged with expenditures for lighting parks, whenever such expenditures can be separated from the cost of street lighting.

455. **Libraries**

455.1 **Library administration** is charged with expenditures for general administration of the library or the library system when more than one library is maintained.

455.2 **Circulation** is charged with expenditures incurred in the circulation of library books, periodicals and other materials. Circulation activities include the registration of borrowers, maintenance of loan records, notification to borrowers of delinquencies, collection of fines for overdue or lost books, assistance to library patrons in the use of the card catalog, and provision of information about library circulation policies, resources and schedules.

455.3 **Catalog** is charged with expenditures incurred in the classification and cataloging of library materials, the preparation and filing of catalog cards and other acquisition records, and the processing and distribution of cataloged materials to various library divisions and/or branch libraries.

455.4 **Reference** is charged with expenditures for all reference services. These services include maintaining special files of clippings and pamphlets to supplement books and periodicals, answering reference questions, assisting library patrons in their search for information and the use of indexes and finding aids, processing interlibrary loans and supervising rare book collections.

455.5 **Order** is charged with expenditures incurred in ordering books and periodicals, checking materials upon receipt, processing gift materials and forwarding materials to the catalog division for further processing.

455.6 **Periodicals** is charged with expenditures incurred in ordering, receiving and maintaining magazines and periodicals; maintaining records of periodical holdings and furnishing information and assistance to library patrons in the use of periodicals.

455.7 **Extension** is charged with expenditures incurred in the selection, maintenance and circulation of books and other library materials from bookmobiles.

455.8 **Special collections** is charged with expenditures made for special collections or clientele sections within the library. Examples of such special collections are children's and young adults' divisions, art, music, science and technology, local history and culture, and newspapers. When more than one special collection of this type is maintained, a separate account should be established for each one.

455.9 **Branch libraries** is charged with expenditures for the construction, maintenance and operation of branch libraries located away from the central library or library headquarters of a library system.

461. **Conservation,** a major function of government, includes activities designed to conserve and develop such natural resources as water, soil, forests and minerals. Expenditures for conservation should be classified according to the specific type of resource.

461.1 **Water resources**

461.2 **Agricultural resources** (including soil conservation)

461.3 **Forest resources**

461.4 **Mineral resources**

461.5 **Fish and game resources**

463. **Urban redevelopment and housing,** a major function of government, is concerned with the planning and provision of adequate housing and the redevelopment of substandard and blighted physical facilities in urban areas.

463.1 **Urban redevelopment and housing administration** is charged with expenditures for general administration of all urban redevelopment and housing activities when these are combined under a single administrative head.

463.2 **Urban redevelopment** is charged with expenditures for activities involved in the government's conservation, rehabilitation and clearance of designated portions of urban areas. It also is charged with expenditures involved in the relocation of individuals, families and businesses from clearance areas to new neighborhoods.

463.21 **Redevelopment administration** is charged with expenditures for planning and administering all redevelopment activities and projects carried out by the government.

463.22 **Conservation projects** is charged with expenditures for conservation of existing neighborhood structures and facilities to prolong their usable life and to prevent subsequent deterioration and blight. If more than one project of this type is carried on, a separate account should be established for each project.

463.23 **Rehabilitation projects** is charged with expenditures for renovation of deteriorated neighborhoods that still are capable of renovation without total clearance and complete redevelopment. If more than one project of this type is carried on, a separate account should be established for each project.

463.24 **Clearance projects** is charged with expenditures for complete demolition, clearance and redevelopment. If more than one project of this type is carried on, a separate account should be established for each project.

463.25 **Relocation** is charged with expenditures incurred in the relocation and rehousing of persons displaced by redevelopment projects.

463.3 **Public housing** is charged with expenditures for the acquisition, furnishing, maintenance and operation of the government's public housing for low-income persons. When more than one project of this type is carried on, a separate account should be established for each project.

463.4 **Other urban redevelopment** is charged with expenditures for urban redevelopment and housing projects not included under the foregoing accounts. Included are all intergovernmental expenditures for urban redevelopment and housing activities administered by other governments.

465. **Economic development and assistance** is a function whose activities are directed toward economically developing the area encompassed by the government and providing assistance to and opportunity for economically disadvantaged persons and businesses.

465.1 **Economic development and assistance administration** is charged with expenditures for the general supervision and administration of all development and assistance activities performed by the government.

465.2 **Economic development** is charged with expenditures made to foster economic growth and development of the area over which the government exercises jurisdiction. These development activities include economic and industrial surveys, financial assistance to new industries and businesses, acquisition of industrial sites, contact activities of industrial development agencies and promotional advertising.

465.3 **Employment security** is charged with expenditures for the administration of unemployment compensation programs, public employment offices and related activities.

466. **Economic opportunity** is charged with expenditures for various programs designed to eliminate or ameliorate poverty and its causes. Expenditures should be classified according to the specific type of program and/or project and in accordance with current federal grants made for such programs.

466.1 **Job corps**
466.11 **Men's urban training centers**
466.12 **Women's urban training centers**
466.13 **Rural conservation centers**
466.14 **Youth camps**
466.2 **Youth work-training programs**
466.21 **In-school projects**
466.22 **Out-of-school projects**
466.3 **Community action programs**
466.31 **Preschool readiness instruction**
466.32 **Study centers**
466.33 **Day-care centers**
466.34 **Remedial instruction for elementary school students**

466.35 **Family health education**
466.36 **Other projects**
466.4 **Adult basic education**
466.5 **Assistance to migrant agricultural workers and families**
466.6 **Work experience programs for needy persons**

470. **Debt service** includes interest and principal payments on general long-term debt.
471.1 **Bond principal** is charged with expenditures for periodic principal maturities of general obligation bonds.
471.2 **Other debt principal** is charged with payment of principal on general long-term debt other than bonds.
472.1 **Interest—bonds** is charged with periodic interest payments on general obligation bonds.
472.2 **Interest—other debt** is charged with interest payments on general long-term debt other than bonds.

475. **Fiscal agent's fees** is charged with payments made to financial institutions for services rendered in paying interest and redeeming debt at maturity.

476. **Issuance costs** is charged with payments to bond underwriters, legal fees and other costs associated with bond issuance.

477. **Advance refunding escrow** is charged with payments made to an escrow agent from sources other than refunding bond proceeds.

480. **Intergovernmental expenditures** includes expenditures made by one level or unit of government to another government in support of government activities administered by the recipient unit. Excluded from this classification are matching employer contributions by a government to a pension or retirement system administered by another government. Such contributions should be allocated to the specific functions in which employees are compensated.

490. **Other financing uses** include financial outflows classified separately from expenditures.

491. **Operating transfers out** (specify fund) are financial outflows to other funds of the government reporting entity that are not classified as quasi-external transactions, reimbursements, loans, advances or residual equity transfers out.

492. **Payments to refunded bond escrow agent** are payments to an escrow agent from advance refunding bond proceeds that are to be placed in irrevocable trust.

Object Classifications. This classification is used to describe the service or commodity obtained as the result of a specific expenditure. There are nine major object categories, each of which is further subdivided. The following are definitions of the object classes and selected subject categories:

Code   *Description*

100.   **Personal services—salaries and wages.** Amounts paid to both permanent and temporary government employees, including personnel substituting for those in permanent positions. This category includes gross salary for personal services rendered while on the payroll of the government. The third position in this number series has not been used so that a job classification code can be inserted by the government if desired.

    110.   **Regular employees.** Full-time, part-time and prorated portions of the costs for work performed by employees of the government.

    120.   **Temporary employees.** Full-time, part-time and prorated portions of the costs for work performed by employees of the government who are hired on a temporary or substitute basis.

    130.   **Overtime.** Amounts paid to employees of the government in either temporary or permanent positions for work performed in addition to the normal work period for which the employee is compensated.

200.   **Personal services—employee benefits.** Amounts paid by the government on behalf of employees; these amounts are not included in the gross salary, but are in addition to that amount. Such payments are fringe benefit payments and, although not paid directly to employees, are part of the cost of personal services. The third position in this number series has not been used so that a job classification code can be inserted by the government if desired.

    210.   **Group insurance.** Employer's share of any insurance plan.

    220.   **Social security contributions.** Employer's share of social security paid by the government.

    230.   **Retirement contributions.** Employer's share of any state or local employee retirement system paid by the government, including the amount paid for employees assigned to federal programs.

    240.   **Tuition reimbursements.** Amounts reimbursed by the government to any employee qualifying for tuition reimbursement, based upon government policy.

    250.   **Unemployment compensation.** Amounts paid by the government to provide unemployment compensation for its employees. These charges may be distributed to functions in accordance with the budget.

    260.   **Workers' compensation.** Amounts paid by the government to provide workers' compensation insurance for its employees. These charges may be distributed to functions in accordance with the budget.

    290.   **Other employee benefits.** Employee benefits other than those classified above. Government may establish subcodes locally for various accrued amounts, such as unused compensated absences. Such amounts may be distributed to the functions according to the employee's assignment.

300.   **Purchased professional and technical services.** Services that by their nature can be performed only by persons or firms with specialized skills and knowledge. Although a product may or may not result from the transaction, the primary reason for the purchase is the service provided. Included are the services of architects, engineers, auditors, dentists, physicians, lawyers and consultants. A separate account should be established for each type of service provided to the government.

    310.   **Official/administrative.** Services in support of the government's various policy-making and managerial activities. These services include management consulting activities directed toward general governance or business and financial management of the government, school management support activities, election, and tax-assessing and collecting services.

    320.   **Professional.** Services supporting the instructional program and its administration. These services include curriculum improvement services, counseling and guidance services, library and media support and contracted instructional services.

    330.   **Other professional.** Professional services, other than educational, supporting the operation of the government. These professionals include physicians, lawyers, architects, auditors, therapists, systems analysts and planners.

    340.   **Technical.** Services to the government that are not regarded as professional but that require basic scientific knowledge, manual skills, or both. These services include data processing, purchasing and warehousing, and graphic arts.

400.   **Purchased property services.** Services purchased to operate, repair, maintain and rent property owned or used by the government. These services are performed by persons other than government employees. Although a product may or may not result from the transaction, the primary reason for the purchase is the service provided.

    410.   **Utility services.** Expenditures for utility services, other than energy services, supplied by public or private organizations. Telephone and telegraph are classified under object 530.

        411.   **Water/sewerage.** Expenditures for

water/sewage utility services from a private or public utility company.

420. **Cleaning services.** Services purchased to clean buildings (apart from services provided by government employees).

421. **Disposal.** Expenditures for garbage pickup and handling not provided by government personnel.

422. **Snow plowing.** Expenditures for snow removal not provided by government personnel.

423. **Custodial.** Expenditures to an outside contractor for custodial services.

424. **Lawn care.** Expenditures for lawn and grounds upkeep, minor landscaping and nursery service not provided by government personnel.

430. **Repair and maintenance services.** Expenditures for repair and maintenance services not provided directly by government personnel. These expenditures include contracts and agreements covering the upkeep of buildings and equipment. Costs for renovating and remodeling are not included here, but are classified under object 450.

440. **Rentals.** Costs for renting or leasing land, buildings, equipment and vehicles.

441. **Rental of land and buildings.** Expenditures for leasing or renting land and buildings for both temporary and long-range use by the government.

442. **Rental of equipment and vehicles.** Expenditures for leasing or renting equipment or vehicles for both temporary and long-range use by the government. These expenditures include bus and other vehicle rental when operated by a local government, capital lease arrangements and other rental agreements.

450. **Construction services.** Includes amounts for constucting, renovating and remodeling paid to contractors.

500. **Other purchased services.** Amounts paid for services rendered by organizations or personnel not on the payroll of the government (separate from professional and technical services or property services). Although a product may or may not result from the transaction, the primary reason for the purchase is the service provided.

520. **Insurance other than employee benefits.** Expenditures for all types of insurance coverage, including property, liability and fidelity. Insurance for group health is not charged here, but is recorded under object 210.

530. **Communications.** Services provided by persons or businesses to assist in transmitting and receiving messages or information. This category includes telephone and telegraph services.

540. **Advertising.** Expenditures for announcements in professional publications, newspapers or broadcasts over radio and television. These expenditures include advertising for such purposes as personnel recruitment, legal ads, new and used equipment and sale of property. Costs for professional advertising or public relations services are not recorded here, but are charged to object 330.

550. **Printing and binding.** Expenditures for job printing and binding, usually according to specifications of the government. This category includes designing and printing forms and posters, as well as printing and binding government publications. Preprinted standard forms are not charged here, but are recorded under object 610.

580. **Travel.** Expenditures for transportation, meals, hotel and other expenses associated with staff travel for the government. Payments for per diem in lieu of reimbursements for subsistence (room and board) also are charged here.

600. **Supplies.** Amounts paid for items that are consumed or deteriorated through use or that lose their identity through fabrication or incorporation into different or more complex units or substances.

610. **General supplies.** Expenditures for all supplies (other than those listed below) for the operation of a government, including freight.

620. **Energy.** Expenditures for energy, including gas, oil, coal, gasoline and services received from public or private utility companies.

621. **Natural gas.** Expenditures for gas utility services from a public or private utility company.

622. **Electricity.** Expenditures for electric utility services from a private or public utility company.

623. **Bottled gas.** Expenditures for bottled gas, such as propane gas received in tanks.

624. **Oil.** Expenditures for bulk oil normally used for heating.

625. **Coal.** Expenditures for raw coal normally used for heating.

626. **Gasoline.** Expenditures for gasoline purchased in bulk or periodically from a gasoline service station.

630. **Food.** Expenditures for food used in the school food service program. Food used in instructional programs is charged under object 610.

640. **Books and periodicals.** Expenditures for books, textbooks and periodicals available

for general use, including reference books. These expenditures include the cost of workbooks, textbook binding or repairs, as well as textbooks that are purchased to be resold or rented.

700.   **Property.** Expenditures for acquiring fixed assets, including land or existing buildings, improvements of grounds, initial equipment, additional equipment and replacement of equipment.

    710.   **Land.** Expenditures for the purchase of land.

    720.   **Buildings.** Expenditures for acquiring existing buildings. These expenditures include the principal amount of capital lease payments resulting in the acquisition of buildings, except payments to building authorities or similar agencies. Expenditures for the contracted construction of buildings, for major permanent structural alterations and for the initial or additional installation of heating and ventilating systems, fire protection systems and other service systems in existing buildings are recorded under object 450. Buildings constructed and alterations performed by the government's own staff are charged to objects 100, 200, 610 and 730, as appropriate.

    730.   **Improvements other than buildings.** Expenditures for acquiring improvements not associated with buildings. These improvements include fences and retaining walls. Also included are special assessments against the government for capital improvements, such as streets, curbs and drains. Not included here, but generally charged to objects 450 or 340 as appropriate, are expenditures for improving sites and adjacent ways after acquisition by the government.

    740.   **Machinery and equipment.** Expenditures for the initial, additional and replacement items of equipment such as machinery, furniture, and fixtures and vehicles.

        741.   **Machinery.** Expenditures for equipment usually composed of a complex combination of parts (excluding vehicles). Examples are lathes, drill presses and printing presses.

        742.   **Vehicles.** Expenditures for equipment used to transport persons or objects. Examples include automobiles, trucks and buses.

        743.   **Furniture and fixtures.** Expenditures for furniture and fixtures including office furniture and building fixtures.

800.   **Other objects.** Amounts paid for goods and services not previously classified.

Common Uses of Balance Sheet Accounts

	Governmental Funds			Account Groups		Proprietary Funds		Fiduciary Funds			
	General and Special Revenue	Debt Service	Capital Projects	General Fixed Assets	General Long-Term Debt	Enterprise	Internal Service	Expendable Trust	Nonexpendable Trust	Pension Trust	Agency
101 Cash (including cash equivalents)	X	X	X	—	—	X	X	X	X	X	X
101.1 Petty cash	X	—	—	—	—	X	X	—	—	—	—
102 Cash with fiscal agent	X	X	—	—	—	X	—	X	X	X	X
103 Investments—current	X	X	X	—	—	X	X	X	X	X	X
104 Interest receivable—investments	X	X	X	—	—	X	X	X	X	X	X
105 Taxes receivable—current	X	X	—	—	—	—	—	—	—	—	—
105.1 Allowance for uncollectible current taxes (credit)	X	X	—	—	—	—	—	—	—	—	—
107 Taxes receivable-delinquent	X	X	—	—	—	—	—	—	—	—	—
107.1 Allowance for uncollectible delinquent taxes (credit)	X	X	—	—	—	—	—	—	—	—	—
109 Interest and penalties receivable—taxes	X	X	—	—	—	—	—	—	—	—	—
109.1 Allowance for uncollectible interest and penalties (credit)	X	X	—	—	—	—	—	—	—	—	—
111 Tax liens receivable	X	X	—	—	—	—	—	—	—	—	—
111.1 Allowance for uncollectible tax liens (credit)	X	X	—	—	—	—	—	—	—	—	—
115 Accounts receivable	X	X	—	—	—	X	X	—	—	—	—
115.1 Allowance for uncollectible accounts receivable (credit)	X	—	—	—	—	X	X	—	—	—	—
117 Unbilled accounts receivable	X	—	—	—	—	X	X	—	—	—	—
117.1 Allowance for uncollectible unbilled accounts receivable (credit)	X	—	—	—	—	X	X	—	—	—	—
121 Special assessments receivable—current	X	X	—	—	—	X	—	—	—	—	—
121.1 Allowance for uncollectible current special assessments (credit)	X	X	—	—	—	X	—	—	—	—	—
122 Special assessments receivable—noncurrent	X	X	—	—	—	X	—	—	—	—	—
122.1 Allowance for uncollectible noncurrent special assessments (credit)	X	X	—	—	—	X	—	—	—	—	—
123 Special assessments receivable—delinquent	X	X	—	—	—	X	—	—	—	—	—

No.	Account	1	2	3	4	5	6	7	8	9	10	11
123.1	Allowance for uncollectible delinquent special assessments (credit)	—	—	—	—	—	×	—	—	—	×	×
124	Special assessment liens receivable	—	—	—	—	—	×	—	—	—	×	×
124.1	Allowance for uncollectible special assessment liens (credit)	—	—	—	—	—	×	—	—	—	×	×
125	Interest receivable—special assessments	—	—	—	—	—	×	—	—	—	×	×
125.1	Allowance for uncollectible special assessment interest (credit)	—	—	—	—	—	×	—	—	×	×	×
126	Intergovernmental receivable	—	—	—	—	—	×	—	—	×	×	×
127	Taxes levied for other governments	—	—	—	—	—	—	—	—	—	—	—
128	Notes receivable	×	×	×	×	×	×	—	—	—	—	—
128.1	Allowance for uncollectible notes (credit)	—	—	—	—	—	×	—	—	—	—	—
129	Loans receivable	—	—	—	—	×	×	—	—	—	—	×
129.1	Allowance for uncollectible loans (credit)	—	—	—	—	×	×	—	—	—	—	×
130	Due from other funds—_____ fund	—	—	—	—	×	×	—	—	—	—	—
131	Interfund receivable—_____ fund	×	×	×	×	×	×	—	—	×	×	×
136	Rent receivable	—	—	—	—	×	×	—	—	—	×	×
136.1	Allowance for uncollectible rent (credit)	—	—	—	—	×	×	—	—	—	—	—
141	Inventories—materials and supplies	—	—	—	—	—	×	—	—	—	×	×
142	Inventories—stores for resale	—	×	×	×	×	×	—	—	—	×	×
143	Prepaid items	—	×	×	×	×	×	—	—	—	×	×
149	Deferred charges	—	×	×	×	—	×	—	—	—	—	—
151	Investments—noncurrent	—	—	—	—	×	×	—	—	—	—	×
151.1	Unamortized premiums—investments	—	×	×	×	×	×	—	—	—	—	—
151.2	Unamortized discounts—investments (credit)	—	×	×	—	×	×	—	—	—	—	—
152	Advance to other funds—_____ fund	—	×	×	×	×	×	—	—	—	×	×
153	Investments—joint ventures	—	—	—	—	—	×	—	×	—	—	—
161	Land	—	×	×	—	×	×	—	×	—	—	—
162	Buildings	—	×	×	—	×	×	—	×	—	—	—
162.1	Accumulated depreciation—buildings (credit)	—	×	×	×	×	×	—	×	—	—	—
163	Improvements other than buildings	—	×	×	—	×	×	—	×	—	—	—

Common Uses of Balance Sheet Accounts—(Continued)

	Governmental Funds			Account Groups		Proprietary Funds		Fiduciary Funds			
	General and Special Revenue	Debt Service	Capital Projects	General Fixed Assets	General Long-Term Debt	Enterprise	Internal Service	Expendable Trust	Nonexpendable Trust	Pension Trust	Agency
163.1 Accumulated depreciation—improvements other than buildings (credit)	—	—	—	X	—	X	X	—	X	X	—
164 Machinery and equipment	—	—	—	X	—	X	X	—	X	X	—
164.1 Accumulated depreciation—machinery and equipment (credit)	—	—	—	X	—	X	X	—	X	X	—
165 Construction in progress	—	—	—	X	—	X	X	—	X	X	—
170 Other assets	X	—	—	—	—	X	X	—	—	—	—
B. Other Debits											
181 Amount available	—	—	—	—	X	—	—	—	—	—	—
182 Amount to be provided	—	—	—	—	X	—	—	—	—	—	—
C. Liabilities and Equities											
201 Vouchers payable	X	—	X	—	—	X	X	X	X	X	X
202 Accounts payable	X	—	X	—	—	X	X	X	X	X	X
203 Compensated absences payable	X	—	—	—	X	X	X	—	—	—	—
204 Claims and judgments payable	X	—	—	—	X	X	X	—	—	—	—
205 Contracts payable	X	—	X	—	—	X	X	—	—	—	—
206 Retainage payable	X	—	X	—	—	X	X	—	—	—	—
207 Intergovernmental payable	X	—	—	—	—	X	—	—	—	—	—
208 Due to other funds—____ fund	X	X	X	—	—	X	X	X	X	X	X
209 Interfund payable—____ fund	X	X	X	—	—	X	X	—	—	—	—
212 Matured bonds payable	X	X	—	—	—	X	—	—	—	—	—
213 Matured interest payable	X	X	—	—	—	X	—	—	—	—	—
214 Accrued interest payable	X	—	—	—	—	X	X	—	—	—	—
222 Deferred revenue	X	—	—	—	—	X	X	—	—	—	—
223 Notes payable—current	X	—	—	—	X	X	—	—	—	—	—
225 Bonds payable—current	X	—	—	—	—	X	—	—	—	—	—
225.1 General obligation bonds payable	—	—	—	—	X	X	—	—	—	—	—
225.2 Special assessment bonds payable	—	—	—	—	X	X	—	—	—	—	—
225.3 Special assessment debt with government commitment	—	—	—	—	X	X	—	—	—	—	—
225.4 Revenue bonds payable	—	—	—	—	X	X	—	—	—	—	—

Account	Description	C1	C2	C3	C4	C5	C6	C7	C8	C9
225.5	Other bonds payable					X				
226	Capital leases payable—current	X		X	X	X				X
227	Other current liabilities	X			X					X
229	Customer deposits									
230	Advance from other funds—____ fund				X	X				X
231	Bonds payable—long-term				X	X				
231.1	General obligation bonds payable					X				
231.2	Special assessment bonds payable	X				X				
231.3	Special assessment debt with government commitment									
231.4	Revenue bonds payable				X	X				
231.5	Other bonds payable				X	X				
232	Unamortized premiums on bonds									
233	Unamortized discounts on bonds (debit)					X			X	
234	Notes payable—noncurrent				X	X				
237	Capital leases payable—noncurrent				X	X				
238	Deferred compensation benefits payable									
239	Other noncurrent liabilities				X	X				
241	Fund balance—reserved for debt service							X		X
242	Fund balance—reserved for endowments									X
244	Fund balance—reserved for encumbrances									X
245	Fund balance—reserved for inventories			X			X			X
246	Fund balance—reserved for prepaid items									X
247	Fund balance—reserved for noncurrent loans receivable	X								X
248	Fund balance—reserved for advance to other funds									X
249	Fund balance—reserved for fixed assets held for resale									X
251	Fund balance—reserved for employees' retirement system									
251.1	Fund balance—reserved for member contributions		X							X
251.2	Fund balance—reserved for employer contributions		X							
251.3	Fund balance—reserved for benefits		X							X

215

Common Uses of Balance Sheet Accounts—(Continued)

		Governmental Funds			Account Groups		Proprietary Funds		Fiduciary Funds			
		General and Special Revenue	Debt Service	Capital Projects	General Fixed Assets	General Long-Term Debt	Enterprise	Internal Service	Expendable Trust	Nonexpendable Trust	Pension Trust	Agency
251.4	Fund balance—reserved for disability	—	—	—	—	—	—	—	—	—	X	—
251.5	Fund balance—reserved for undistributed investment earnings	—	—	—	—	—	—	—	—	—	X	—
253	Fund balance—unreserved	—	—	—	—	—	—	—	—	—	—	—
253.1	Fund balance—unreserved, designated for____	X	X	X	—	—	—	—	—	—	—	—
253.2	Fund balance—unreserved, undesignated	X	X	X	—	—	—	—	X	X	X	—
261	Contributed capital—government	—	—	—	—	—	X	X	—	—	—	—
262	Contributed capital—customers	—	—	—	—	—	X	—	—	—	—	—
263	Contributed capital—developers	—	—	—	—	—	X	—	—	—	—	—
264	Contributed capital—intergovernmental	—	—	—	—	—	X	X	—	—	—	—
271	Retained earnings—reserved for revenue bond operations and maintenance	—	—	—	—	—	X	—	—	—	—	—
272	Retained earnings—reserved for revenue bond current debt service	—	—	—	—	—	X	—	—	—	—	—
273	Retained earnings—reserved for revenue bond renewal and replacement	—	—	—	—	—	X	—	—	—	—	—
279	Retained earnings—unreserved	—	—	—	—	—	X	X	—	—	—	—
280	Investment in general fixed assets	—	—	—	X	—	—	—	—	—	—	—

Appendix D
ILLUSTRATIVE COMPREHENSIVE ANNUAL FINANCIAL REPORT

NAME OF GOVERNMENT
Comprehensive Annual Financial Report
For the fiscal year ended December 31, 19X8

Prepared by:

Department of Finance

INTRODUCTORY SECTION

Name of Government
Comprehensive Annual Financial Report
For the Fiscal Year Ended December 31, 19X8

TABLE OF CONTENTS

LETTERHEAD OF GOVERNMENT

May 1, 19X9

To the citizens of NAME OF GOVERNMENT:

The comprehensive annual financial report of the NAME OF GOVERNMENT (government) for the fiscal year ended December 31, 19X8, is hereby submitted. Responsibility for both the accuracy of the data, and the completeness and fairness of the presentation, including all disclosures, rests with the government. To the best of our knowledge and belief, the enclosed data are accurate in all material respects and are reported in a manner designed to present fairly the financial position and results of operations of the various funds and account groups of the government. All disclosures necessary to enable the reader to gain an understanding of the government's financial activities have been included.

The comprehensive annual financial report is presented in four sections: introductory, financial, statistical and single audit. The introductory section includes this transmittal letter, the government's organizational chart and a list of principal officials. The financial section includes the general purpose financial statements and the combining and individual fund and account group financial statements and schedules, as well as the auditor's report on the financial statements and schedules. The statistical section includes selected financial and demographic information, generally presented on a multiyear basis.

The government is required to undergo an annual single audit in conformity with the provisions of the Single Audit Act of 1984 and U.S. Office of Management and Budget Circular A–128, *Audits of State and Local Governments*. Information related to this single audit, including the schedule of federal financial assistance, findings and recommendations, and auditor's reports on the internal control structure and compliance with applicable laws and regulations, are included in the single audit section of this report.

This report includes all funds and account groups of the government. The government provides a full range of services. These services include police and fire protection; sanitation services; the construction and maintenance of highways, streets, and infrastructure; recreational activities and cultural events. In addition to general government activities, the governing body exercises, or has the ability to exercise, oversight of the Water and Sewer Authority and the Public Safety Employees Retirement System; therefore, these activities are included in the reporting entity. However, the Name of Government Airport Authority, the Name of Government School District, the Name of Government Hospital District and the Name of Government Flood Control District have not met the established criteria for inclusion in the reporting entity, and accordingly are excluded from this report.

ECONOMIC CONDITION AND OUTLOOK

The government is located in the southwestern part of the state, which ranks as one of the top growth areas in the country. The economic condition and outlook of the government have substantially improved during the past two

1

years, following several years of slower economic growth attributable to a general decline in manufacturing activity. This year alone, for example, a number of computer manufacturing and software firms have started or expanded activities in the area. In addition, substantial increases in service-related industries also were noted. This growth has had a positive effect on employment and the government's tax base. The community currently has a 3.1 percent unemployment rate as compared to a statewide rate of 4.3 percent and a national average of 5.7 percent. During the past two years, housing and commercial property values have risen 23 percent. The financial impact of these events is presented later in this letter.

Based on current projections, this trend is expected to continue through the end of the century. While having a positive impact, this growth also presents significant challenges for the government. If the present high level of services is to be maintained, the government, in the future, will need to explore new methods of obtaining financial resources.

MAJOR INITIATIVES

For the Year. In preparing the 19X8 budget, the government identified several major programs needed to meet citizens' needs for services and to safeguard the environment, in conformity with applicable federal and state standards. These programs included the improvement of the police department's communication system, the expansion of wastewater treatment facilities and the construction of additional pipelines to serve the water and sewer needs of new housing, office and industrial developments.

During the year, the government acquired a new, technically advanced, police vehicle-monitoring system. This system provides police dispatch personnel with the ability to immediately identify all available uniformed personnel in a precinct from which a request for assistance has been received. Since the installation of this system, response time to requests for assistance has been reduced by 20 percent.

Also during the year, the government began planned expansion on its wastewater treatment facilities to meet the needs of a population that has increased by 40 percent since the original facility was first constructed. The original system currently is operating at an average 85 percent of capacity, and is overtaxed during peak periods of usage. Based on recent studies, without this plant expansion, the maximum capacity of the plant would be reached on a daily basis by 19Y2. These projections led the governing body to approve the Water and Sewer Authority's request for an ambitious two-phase project to enhance the service capacity of the wastewater treatment facilities. The first phase, expansion of the existing facility, was completed this year. The second phase, the construction of additional facilities, is expected to be completed by 19Y0. The project will provide the Water and Sewer Authority with the ability to meet the needs of current and projected system users through 19Z9.

In addition, the government created a new special assessment district to partially finance the construction of sewer pipeline extensions. These extensions will provide service to new developments currently under construction. General government resources and state grant revenues also are being used to finance this project. Construction, begun during the period, is now already more than half complete and should be fully completed in 19X9.

For the Future. A recent state study concluded that the portion of the state within which the government is located possesses great potential for tourist and convention development. Accordingly, the government is actively exploring the feasibility of constructing a regional convention facility. If constructed, this facility is expected to have a favorable impact on tourism. This effect, in turn, should result in increased hotel construction and a corresponding expansion of the government's tax base. A major hotel corporation, which owns a large local hotel, has agreed in principal to expand its current facilities if the regional convention facility project proves feasible. In addition, several other hotel corporations have expressed interest in building local facilities if this project is approved.

The government also has taken steps to capitalize on the recent resurgence of industrial activity with plans to create several industrial parks. The government intends that such expansion of the area's industrial infrastructure should further stimulate industrial expansion.

Maintenance and expansion of the community's general infrastructure (such as roads, bridges and sidewalks) remain a major concern of the government. To address this concern, the government has developed a five-year capital projects plan that provides a framework for the development and maintenance of infrastructure to meet current and future needs. This plan calls for the replacement or repair of 15 percent of the government's 205 miles of water mains. In addition, the government has undertaken an aggressive program to repair and replace its streets and bridges. During the next five years, the government plans to replace three bridges and to reconstruct 10 of its 215 miles of streets. A major repavement project also has been included in this plan. By the end of the five-year period, 25 percent of the government's streets are expected to be repaved.

Department Focus. Each year the government selects a department to highlight for its efforts and accomplishments. In 19X8, the government's police department has been selected for review.

The 74-person force has been the focal point of great civic pride over the past five years. During this period, the government has placed a high priority on improving the quality of its crime prevention efforts. This effort has resulted in the reduction of several key crime statistics and a significant increase in the conviction rate of those arrested. For example, in 19X8 the number of violent crimes dropped 11 percent and the number of persons arrested and convicted of those crimes increased by 15 percent as compared to the previous year. These statistics are significantly better than those of other governments with similar demographic characterics and the national averages. These improvements in crime prevention efforts can be traced to several programs implemented by the police department during the year. These programs include a revised neighborhood watch program and a 5 percent increase in patrol activities in areas that have been identified as potentially high crime locations.

3

Traffic safety is another high priority of the police department. In 19X8, the police department purchased three additional moving radar units. The use of these units resulted in the issuance of 1,437 additional traffic citations. An ongoing state study of traffic movement and patterns has identified a 5 miles per hour reduction in the average vehicle speed throughout the area. In addition, reports reflect a 7 percent reduction from the previous year in the number of traffic accidents in the year ended December 31, 19X8.

The police department's efforts have not only been recognized by the citizens of the community, but the department also has been recognized by its peers. During the past five years, the police department, or individuals within the department, have received 25 awards from national and state organizations. This total includes nine awards received in 19X8. With the installation of the new police-vehicle monitoring system, the positive trends experienced during the past five years are expected to continue.

FINANCIAL INFORMATION

Management of the government is responsible for establishing and maintaining an internal control structure designed to ensure that the assets of the government are protected from loss, theft or misuse and to ensure that adequate accounting data are compiled to allow for the preparation of financial statements in conformity with generally accepted accounting principles. The internal control structure is designed to provide reasonable, but not absolute, assurance that these objectives are met. The concept of reasonable assurance recognizes that: (1) the cost of a control should not exceed the benefits likely to be derived; and (2) the valuation of costs and benefits requires estimates and judgments by management.

Single Audit. As a recipient of federal, state and county financial assistance, the government also is responsible for ensuring that an adequate internal control structure is in place to ensure compliance with applicable laws and regulations related to those programs. This internal control structure is subject to periodic evaluation by management and the internal audit staff of the government.

As a part of the government's single audit, described earlier, tests are made to determine the adequacy of the internal control structure, including that portion related to federal financial assistance programs, as well as to determine that the government has complied with applicable laws and regulations. The results of the government's single audit for the fiscal year ended December 31, 19X8 provided no instances of material weaknesses in the internal control structure or significant violations of applicable laws and regulations.

Budgeting Controls. In addition, the government maintains budgetary controls. The objective of these budgetary controls is to ensure compliance with legal provisions embodied in the annual appropriated budget approved by the government's governing body. Activities of the general fund, special revenue funds and debt service fund are included in the annual appropriated budget. Project-length financial plans are adopted for the capital projects funds. The level of budgetary control (that is, the level at which expenditures cannot legally exceed the appropriated amount) is established by function and activity within an individual fund. The government also maintains an encumbrance accounting system as one technique of accomplishing budgetary control. Encumbered amounts lapse at year end. However, encumbrances generally are reappropriated as part of the following year's budget.

As demonstrated by the statements and schedules included in the financial section of this report, the government continues to meet its responsibility for sound financial management. As with the financial section, all amounts presented in the remainder of this letter are expressed in thousands.

General Government Functions. The following schedule presents a summary of general fund, special revenue funds and debt service fund revenues for the fiscal year ended December 31, 19X8 and the amount and percentage of increases and decreases in relation to prior year revenues.

Revenues	Amount	Percent of Total	Increase (Decrease) from 19X7	Percent of Increase (Decrease)
Taxes	$28,181	68.43%	$3,910	16.12%
Licenses and permits	2,041	4.96	221	12.14
Intergovernmental	5,870	14.25	401	7.33
Charges for services	2,300	5.59	(35)	(1.50)
Fines	808	1.96	287	55.09
Special assessments	470	1.14	470	100.00
Interest	1,019	2.47	473	78.83
Miscellaneous	494	1.20	(59)	(10.67)
Total	$41,183	100.00%	$5,668	

The most significant increase in actual continued revenue sources was derived from taxes. Tax revenues are a combination of three distinct resources: property tax, sales tax and franchise tax. A large portion of the tax revenue increase was the result of a quarter of a cent increase in the local sales tax. This increase is estimated to have generated an additional $1,127 of sales tax revenues.

The largest actual revenue increase came from property taxes. Even with a substantial increase ($1,832) in property tax revenue, the government's 4.465 millage rate remains well within the 10 mill rate limit established by the state.

An additional source of revenue was reintroduced this year with the establishment of the new special assessment district. A special assessment levy for the new pipeline construction was imposed on benefiting property owners. This revenue is recorded in the debt service fund.

The following schedule presents a summary of general fund, special revenue funds and debt service fund expenditures for the fiscal year ended December 31, 19X8 and the percentage of increases and decreases in relation to prior year amounts.

Expenditures	Amount	Percent of Total	Increase (Decrease) from 19X7	Percent of Increase (Decrease)
Current:				
General government	$ 4,244	11.18%	423	11.07%
Public safety	13,438	35.39	1,288	10.60
Highways and streets	4,477	11.79	1,088	32.10
Sanitation	3,726	9.81	322	9.46
Culture and recreation	6,883	18.13	911	15.15
Debt service:				
Principal	2,045	5.38	575	39.12
Interest and fiscal charges	3,143	8.28	1,278	68.53
Other	15	.04	15	100.00
Total	$37,971	100.00%	$5,900	

The significant increase in debt service expenditures associated with the capital projects has been previously addressed in this letter. Other expenditure variances from the prior year that warrant discussion include highways and streets and public safety functions. The costs of maintaining the government's roadways have increased in all expenditure categories. Labor costs in 19X8 outpaced the average salary increases given the remaining government employees by 5 percent. In addition, the costs of materials used in street patching and repaving increased 15 percent.

In the discussion of the police department, several enhancements to the department's equipment were mentioned. Expenditures for these items contributed to the increased costs of providing police protection to the community. Another factor that influenced 19X8 public safety expenditures was the addition of three new firefighters. This staff addition represents a 5 percent increase in fire department personnel.

General Fund Balance. The fund balance of the general fund increased by 73 percent in 19X8. The $1,328 increase provides the government with a fund balance that is the equivalent of 26 working days of expenditures. This increase should significantly reduce the likelihood of the government entering the short-term debt market to pay for current operating expenditures.

Enterprise Operations. The government's enterprise operations are comprised of two separate and distinct activities: the Water and Sewer Authority and the community golf course. Several of the government's major initiatives directly relate to the Water and Sewer Authority. As mentioned earlier, improvements in progress should provide its users with quality services through the end of this century. To provide the necessary resources for the repayment of debt issued to make these improvements, the government approved a Water and Sewer Authority proposal to increase water rates and sewer charges by 15 percent. This increase, plus charges generated through increased usage and tap fees from new customers, provided the Water and Sewer Authority with $3,332 in additional resources in 19X8.

The $1,570 increase in operating expenses was proportional to the increase in services provided to customers during the year. A 24 percent increase in interest expense is a direct result of the additional debt incurred to finance the expansion of the wastewater facilities.

Although the advance refunding of outstanding revenue bonds resulted in the recognition of a $547 accounting gain based on debt removed from the balance sheet versus the new debt added, as discussed in the next section this transaction does not represent an economic gain to the Water and Sewer Authority.

The golf course operations continue to grow at a steady pace with activities resulting in net income for the second consecutive year. Based on the continuation of this trend, the golf course should be in the position to generate revenues in an amount sufficient to cover debt service and operating costs without additional support from the government's general fund.

Pension Trust Fund Operations. The operations of the Public Safety Employees Retirement System (PSERS) remained relatively stable in 19X8. The PSERS' revenue increase of 12 percent was tied primarily to an adjustment in the employee contribution ceiling. The 10 percent increase in expenses was the result of the early retirement of several firefighters. The annual actuarial valuation continues to reflect a positive trend in the government's and employees' funding of the PSERS.

Debt Administration. At December 31, 19X8, the government had a number of debt issues outstanding. These issues included $67,179 of general obligation bonds, $4,700 of special assessment debt with government commitment and $34,600 of revenue bonds. The government has maintained its Aa rating from Standard & Poor's Corporation and a AA from Moody's Investors Service on general obligation bond issues. Under current state statutes, the government's general obligation bonded debt issuances are subject to a legal limitation based on 10 percent of total assessed value of real and personal property. As of December 31, 19X8, the government's net general obligation bonded debt of $70,327 was well below the legal limit of $408,974 and debt per capita equaled $586.

During the year, the government issued $3,365 of general obligation refunding bonds. The proceeds of these bonds were placed in an irrevocable escrow account in an amount sufficient to meet all principal and interest payments on $3,000 of general obligation bonds refunded. This advance refunding gave rise to an economic gain of $105 resulting from reduced future interest payments on the refunding bonds.

Also, the government issued $7,060 of revenue refunding bonds to bring about the advance refunding of $8,560 of revenue bonds. Although this transaction resulted in no economic gain, it enabled the government to eliminate a number of restrictive bond convenants that would have hindered the government's ability to continue expansion of the wastewater treatment facilities.

In addition, on July 15, 19X9, the government issued $34,600 of revenue serial bonds. The bonds' average effective interest rate was 8.025 percent.

Cash Management. Cash temporarily idle during the year was invested in demand deposits, certificates of deposit, obligations of the U.S. Treasury, repurchase agreements and commercial paper. The pension trust fund's investment portfolio also includes corporate bonds. The average yield on investments, except for the pension trust fund, was 8.1 percent. The pension trust fund achieved a yield rate of 9.5 percent for this same period. This higher rate of return on pension fund investments is attributable to the long-term nature of most holdings in its portfolio. The government's investment performance ranks favorably when compared to average yield rates of 6.87 percent for U.S. Treasury bills and 8.05 percent for U.S. Treasury notes in 19X8. The government earned interest revenue of $4,235 on all investments for the year ended December 31, 19X8.

The government's investment policy is to minimize credit and market risks while maintaining a competitive yield on its portfolio. Accordingly, deposits were either insured by federal depository insurance or collateralized. All collateral on deposits was held either by the government, its agent or a financial institution's trust department in the government's name. Over two-thirds of investments held by the government during the year and at December 31, 19X8, are classified in the category of lowest credit risk as defined by the Governmental Accounting Standards Board. Remaining investments were held in the government's name either by the counterparty financial institution's trust department or by a Securities and Exchange Commission-registered brokerage firm.

Risk Management. During 19X8, the government initiated a limited risk management program for workers' compensation. As part of this comprehensive plan, resources are being accumulated in the general fund to meet potential losses. In addition, various risk control techniques, including employee accident prevention training, have been implemented during the year to minimize accident-related losses. Third-party coverage is currently maintained for workers' compensation claims greater than $100 and all other potential losses. However, future plans include the assumption of additional risk of loss by the government.

OTHER INFORMATION

Independent Audit. State statutes require an annual audit by independent certified public accountants. The accounting firm of Russum, Siegert, Fucone & Co., CPAs, was selected by the government's audit committee. In addition to meeting the requirements set forth in state statutes, the audit also was designed to meet the requirements of the federal Single Audit Act of 1984 and related OMB Circular A–128. The auditor's report on the general purpose financial statements and combining and individual fund statements and schedules is included in the financial section of this report. The auditor's reports related specifically to the single audit are included in the Single Audit Section.

Awards. The Government Finance Officers Association (GFOA) awarded a Certificate of Achievement for Excellence in Financial Reporting to the government for its comprehensive annual financial report for the fiscal year ended December 31, 19X7. This was the eighth consecutive year that the government has received this prestigious award. In order to be awarded a Certificate of Achievement, the government published an easily readable and efficiently organized comprehensive annual financial report. This report satisfied both generally accepted accounting principles and applicable legal requirements.

A Certificate of Achievement is valid for a period of one year only. We believe that our current comprehensive annual financial report continues to meet the Certificate of Achievement Program's requirements and we are submitting it to the GFOA to determine its eligibility for another certificate.

In addition, the government also received the GFOA's Award for Distinguished Budget Presentation for its annual appropriated budget dated December 15, 19X7. In order to qualify for the Distinguished Budget Presentation Award, the government's budget document was judged to be proficient in several categories including policy documentation, financial planning and organization.

Acknowledgments. The preparation of the comprehensive annual financial report on a timely basis was made possible by the dedicated service of the entire staff of the finance department. Each member of the department has our sincere appreciation for the contributions made in the preparation of this report.

In closing, without the leadership and support of the governing body of the government, preparation of this report would not have been possible.

Sincerely,

Charles W. Rose
Manager

Wayne W. Barndt
Finance Director

Certificate of Achievement for Excellence in Financial Reporting

Presented to

Name of Government

For its Comprehensive Annual
Financial Report
for the Fiscal Year Ended
December 31, 19X8

A Certificate of Achievement for Excellence in Financial
Reporting is presented by the Government Finance Officers
Association of the United States and Canada to
government units and public employee retirement
systems whose comprehensive annual financial
reports (CAFRs) achieve the highest
standards in government accounting
and financial reporting.

President

Executive Director

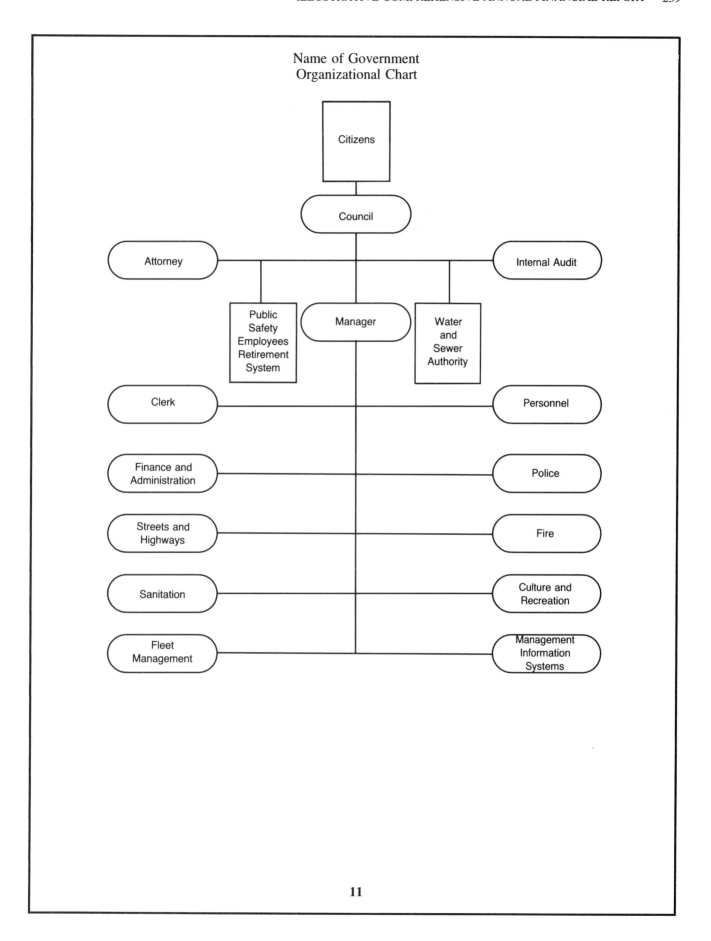

11

Name of Government
List of Principal Officials
December 31, 19X8

Title	Name
Chief Executive Officer	Thomas E. Hanstedt
Deputy Chief Executive Officer	Carol A. Sommer
Council Member	Barbara J. McCown
Council Member	Mary L. O'Brien
Council Member	John L. Walker
Public Safety Employees Retirement System President	Byron Kemmerling
Water and Sewer Authority Chair	Josephine Paquette
Manager	Charles W. Rose
Assistant Manager	David A. Schaefer
Attorney	Velma R. Metzger
Clerk	Margaret A. May
Culture and Recreation Director	Marie Desmarais
Finance Director	Wayne W. Barndt
Fire Chief	Ralph Amateis
Fleet Management Director	Dwight Omi
Internal Audit Director	Sharon Y. White
Management Information Systems Director	Florence Marker
Personnel Director	Christine A. Fair
Police Chief	David Linn
Sanitation Director	James Rinn
Streets and Highways Director	Stephen B. Michael

FINANCIAL SECTION

OFFICIAL LETTERHEAD OF
INDEPENDENT AUDITOR

INDEPENDENT AUDITOR'S REPORT

April 7, 19X9

To the governing body and audit committee of the Name of Government:

We have audited the accompanying general purpose financial statements of the Name of Government, and the combining, individual fund and account group financial statements of the Name of Government as of and for the year ended December 31, 19X8, as listed in the table of contents. These financial statements are the responsibility of the Name of Government's management. Our responsibility is to express an opinion on these financial statements based on our audit.

We conducted our audit in accordance with generally accepted auditing standards. Those standards require that we plan and perform the audit to obtain reasonable assurance about whether the financial statements are free of material misstatement. An audit includes examining, on a test basis, evidence supporting the amounts and disclosures in the financial statements. An audit also includes assessing the accounting principles used and significant estimates made by management, as well as evaluating the overall financial statement presentation. We believe that our audit provides a reasonable basis for our opinion.

In our opinion, the general purpose financial statements referred to above present fairly, in all material respects, the financial position of the Name of Government at December 31, 19X8, and the results of its operations and the changes in financial position of its proprietary and similar trust fund types for the year then ended, in conformity with generally accepted accounting principles. Also, in our opinion, the combining, individual fund, and account group financial statements referred to above present fairly, in all material respects, the financial position of each of the individual funds and account groups of the Name of Government at December 31, 19X8, and the results of operations of such funds and the changes in financial position of individual proprietary and similar trust funds for the year then ended, in conformity with generally accepted accounting principles.

Our audit was made for the purpose of forming an opinion on the general purpose financial statements taken as a whole and on the combining, individual fund and account group financial statements. The accompanying financial information listed as schedules in the table of contents is presented for purposes of additional analysis and is not a required part of the financial statements of the Name of Government. The information in these schedules has been subjected to the auditing procedures applied in the audit of the general purpose, combining, individual fund and account group financial statements and, in our opinion, is fairly stated in all material respects in relation to the financial statements of each of the respective individual funds and account groups, taken as a whole.

Russum, Siegert, Fucone & Co.
Certified Public Accountants

13

General Purpose Financial Statements

Exhibit 1

Name of Government
Combined Balance Sheet—All Fund Types and Account Groups
December 31, 19X8
(With comparative totals for December 31, 19X7)
(amounts expressed in thousands)

	Governmental Fund Types				Proprietary Fund Types		Fiduciary Fund Type	Account Groups		Totals (Memorandum Only)	
	General	Special Revenue	Debt Service	Capital Projects	Enterprise	Internal Service	Trust and Agency	General Fixed Assets	General Long-term Debt	19X8	19X7
Assets and other debits											
Assets:											
Cash	$1,369	$ 211	$ 10	$ 552	$ 1,164	$ 100	$ 293	—	—	$ 3,699	$ 1,893
Investments	2,091	1,577	1,513	11,051	15,523	50	17,327	—	—	49,132	36,301
Receivables (net of allowances for uncollectibles):											
Interest	92	2	30		420	2	434	—	—	1,391	1,014
Taxes	952	—	10	—	—	—	—	—	—	962	897
Accounts	72	—	—	—	2,622	—	—	—	—	2,694	2,386
Special assessments	—	—	4,230	—	—	—	—	—	—	4,230	—
Intergovernmental	215	—	—	199	—	4	—	—	—	418	422
Due from other funds	73	—	—	335	39	126	—	—	—	573	382
Interfund receivables	32	—	—	—	—	—	—	—	—	32	—
Inventories	39	—	—	—	308	23	—	—	—	370	498
Prepaid items	—	—	—	—	—	38	—	—	—	38	—
Advances to other funds	78	—	—	—	—	—	—	—	—	78	50
Restricted assets	—	—	—	—	27,454	—	—	—	—	27,454	5,290
Deferred charges	—	—	—	—	651	—	—	—	—	651	581
Fixed assets (net, where applicable, of accumulated depreciation)	—	—	—	—	120,053	2,904	—	$58,912	—	181,869	167,074
Other debits:											
Amount available in debt service fund	—	—	—	—	—	—	—	—	$ 1,384	1,384	10
Amount to be provided for retirement of general long-term debt	—	—	—	—	—	—	—	—	41,473	41,473	39,256
Total assets	$5,013	$1,790	$5,793	$12,548	$168,234	$ 3,247	$18,054	$58,912	$42,857	$316,448	$256,054

16

cont.

Exhibit 1, cont.

Liabilities, equity and other credits

	Governmental Fund Types				Proprietary Fund Types		Fiduciary Fund Type	Account Groups		Totals (Memorandum Only)	
	General	Special Revenue	Debt Service	Capital Projects	Enterprise	Internal Service	Trust and Agency	General Fixed Assets	General Long-Term Debt	19X8	19X7
Liabilities:											
Vouchers payable	$ 705	$ 340	—	—	$ 933	—	—	—	—	$ 1,978	$ 1,378
Accounts payable	165	76	—	$ 502	336	$ 242	$ 38	—	—	1,359	1,001
Compensated absences payable	225	—	—	—	390	28	—	—	2,022	2,665	2,414
Claims and judgments payable	—	—	—	—	—	—	—	—	220	220	—
Contracts payable	67	—	—	—	—	—	—	—	—	67	151
Retainage payable	—	—	—	282	536	—	—	—	—	818	11
Intergovernmental payable	—	—	—	—	—	—	—	—	—	—	11
Due to other funds	476	—	—	—	87	10	—	—	—	573	382
Interfund payables	—	—	—	—	—	32	—	—	—	32	—
Matured bonds payable	—	—	$ 5	—	68	—	—	—	—	73	—
Matured interest payable	—	—	3	—	55	—	—	—	—	58	—
Accrued interest payable	240	—	4,240	—	1,201	—	—	—	—	1,201	1,261
Deferred revenue					1,641					4,480	230
General obligation bonds payable—current	—	—	—	—	1,641	—	—	—	—	1,641	1,523
Capital leases—current	—	—	—	—	23	—	—	—	—	23	—
Liabilities payable from restricted assets	—	—	—	—	4,358	—	—	—	—	4,358	2,177
Advances from other funds	—	—	—	—	—	78	—	—	—	78	50
General obligation bonds payable	—	—	—	—	32,934	—	—	—	35,790	68,724	65,000
Special assessment debt with government commitment	—	—	—	—	—	—	—	—	4,700	4,700	—
Revenue bonds payable	—	—	—	—	32,828	—	—	—	—	32,828	8,580
Capital leases payable	—	—	—	—	78	—	—	—	125	203	900
Deferred compensation benefits payable	—	—	—	—	—	—	1,216	—	—	1,216	—
Total liabilities	1,878	416	4,248	784	75,468	390	1,254	—	42,857	127,295	85,069
Equity and other credits:											
Investment in general fixed assets	—	—	—	—	—	—	—	$58,912	—	$58,912	59,377
Contributed capital	—	—	—	—	59,395	2,486	—	—	—	61,881	52,152
Retained earnings:											
Reserved	—	—	—	—	3,817	—	—	—	—	3,817	2,590
Unreserved	—	—	—	—	29,554	371	—	—	—	29,925	28,252
Fund balances:											
Reserved for encumbrances	320	361	—	6,563	—	—	—	—	—	7,244	840
Reserved for advances	78	—	—	—	—	—	—	—	—	78	50
Reserved for debt service	—	—	1,545	—	—	—	—	—	—	1,545	10
Reserved for perpetual care	—	—	—	—	—	—	1,193	—	—	1,193	1,102
Reserved for employees retirement system	—	—	—	—	—	—	16,670	—	—	16,670	14,248
Unreserved, undesignated	2,737	1,013	—	5,201	—	—	(1,063)	—	—	7,888	12,364
Total equity and other credits	3,135	1,374	1,545	11,764	92,766	2,857	16,800	58,912	—	189,153	170,985
Total liabilities, equity and other credits	$5,013	$1,790	$5,793	$12,548	$168,234	$ 3,247	$18,054	$58,912	$42,857	$316,448	$256,054

The notes to the financial statements are an integral part of this statement.

17

Exhibit 2

Name of Government
Combined Statement of Revenues, Expenditures and Changes in Fund Balances
All Governmental Fund Types and Expendable Trust Fund
For the fiscal year ended December 31, 19X8
(With comparative totals for the fiscal year ended December 31, 19X7)
(amounts expressed in thousands)

		Governmental Fund Types			Fiduciary Fund Type	Totals (Memorandum Only)	
	General	Special Revenue	Debt Service	Capital Projects	Expendable Trust	19X8	19X7
Revenues:							
Taxes	$25,068	$1,528	$ 1,585	—	—	$28,181	$24,271
Licenses and permits	2,041	—	—	—	—	2,041	1,820
Intergovernmental	5,770	100	—	$ 462	—	6,332	5,674
Charges for services	2,300	—	—	—	—	2,300	2,335
Fines	808	—	—	—	—	808	521
Special assessments	—	—	470	—	—	470	—
Interest	623	116	280	844	$ 6	1,869	807
Miscellaneous	345	149	—	—	82	576	605
Total revenues	36,955	1,893	2,335	1,306	88	42,577	36,033
Expenditures:							
Current:							
General government	4,244	—	—	—	86	4,330	3,850
Public safety	13,438	—	—	—	—	13,438	12,150
Highways and streets	3,735	742	—	—	—	4,477	3,389
Sanitation	3,726	—	—	—	—	3,726	3,404
Culture and recreation	5,882	1,001	—	—	—	6,883	5,972
Capital outlay	—	—	—	5,461	—	5,461	2,501
Debt service:							
Principal	15	—	2,030	—	—	2,045	1,470
Interest and fiscal charges	150	—	2,993	—	—	3,143	1,865
Advance refunding escrow	—	—	15	—	—	15	—
Total expenditures	31,190	1,743	5,038	5,461	86	43,518	34,601
Excess (deficiency) of revenues over (under) expenditures	5,765	150	(2,703)	(4,155)	2	(941)	1,432
Other financing sources (uses):							
Operating transfers in	—	—	4,173	1,210	—	5,383	6,154
Operating transfers out	(4,537)	—	—	(846)	—	(5,383)	(6,154)
General obligation bond proceeds	—	—	—	—	—	—	7,500
Special assessment bond proceeds	—	—	—	4,690	—	4,690	—
Proceeds of refunding bonds	—	—	3,365	—	—	3,365	—
Payment to refunded bond escrow agent	—	—	(3,300)	—	—	(3,300)	—
Other	145	—	—	—	—	145	—
Total other financing sources (uses)	(4,392)	—	4,238	5,054	—	4,900	7,500
Excess of revenues and other financing sources over expenditures and other financing uses	1,373	150	1,535	899	2	3,959	8,932
Fund balances, January 1	1,807	1,224	10	10,865	49	13,955	5,023
Residual equity transfers out	(45)	—	—	—	—	(45)	—
Fund balances, December 31	$ 3,135	$1,374	$ 1,545	$11,764	$51	$17,869	$13,955

The notes to the financial statements are an integral part of this statement.

Exhibit 3

Name of Government
Combined Statement of Revenues, Expenditures and Changes in Fund Balances—
Budget and Actual - General, Special Revenue and Debt Service Funds
For the fiscal year ended December 31, 19X8
(amounts expressed in thousands)

	General Fund			Special Revenue Funds			Debt Service Fund		
	Budget	Actual	Variance Favorable (Unfavorable)	Budget	Actual	Variance Favorable (Unfavorable)	Budget	Actual	Variance Favorable (Unfavorable)
Revenues:									
Taxes	$25,566	$25,068	$ (498)	$ 1,307	$1,528	$ 221	$ 1,500	$ 1,585	$ 85
Licenses and permits	1,827	2,041	214	—	—	—	—	—	—
Intergovernmental	5,661	5,770	109	100	100	0	—	—	—
Charges for services	2,158	2,300	142	—	—	—	—	—	—
Fines	810	808	(2)	—	—	—	—	—	—
Special assessments	—	—	—	—	—	—	470	470	0
Interest	555	623	68	73	116	43	220	280	60
Miscellaneous	345	345	0	23	149	126	—	—	—
Total revenues	36,922	36,955	33	1,503	1,893	390	2,190	2,335	145
Expenditures:									
Current:									
General government	4,628	4,244	384	—	—	—	—	—	—
Public safety	13,645	13,453	192	—	—	—	—	—	—
Highways and streets	3,866	3,735	131	1,437	742	695	—	—	—
Sanitation	3,848	3,726	122	—	—	—	—	—	—
Culture and recreation	5,950	5,882	68	1,095	1,001	94	—	—	—
Capital outlay	—	—	—	—	—	—	—	—	—
Debt service:									
Principal	—	—	—	—	—	—	2,054	2,030	24
Interest and fiscal charges	150	150	0	—	—	—	3,006	2,993	13
Advance refunding escrow	—	—	—	—	—	—	15	15	0
Total expenditures	32,087	31,190	897	2,532	1,743	789	5,075	5,038	37
Excess (deficiency) of revenues over (under) expenditures	4,835	5,765	930	(1,029)	150	1,179	(2,885)	(2,703)	182
Other financing sources (uses):									
Operating transfers in	—	—	—	—	—	—	3,500	4,173	673
Operating transfers out	(4,700)	(4,537)	163	—	—	—	—	—	—
Proceeds of refunding bonds	—	—	—	—	—	—	3,365	3,365	0
Payment to refunded bond escrow agent	—	—	—	—	—	—	(3,300)	(3,300)	0
Other	34	145	111	—	—	—	—	—	—
Total other financing sources (uses)	(4,666)	(4,392)	274	—	—	—	3,565	4,238	673
Excess (deficiency) of revenues and other financing sources over (under) expenditures and other financing uses	169	1,373	1,204	(1,029)	150	1,179	680	1,535	855
Fund balances, January 1	1,807	1,807	0	1,224	1,224	0	10	10	0
Residual equity transfers out	(60)	(45)	15	—	—	—	—	—	—
Fund balances, December 31	$ 1,916	$ 3,135	$1,219	$ 195	$1,374	$1,179	$ 690	$ 1,545	$855

The notes to the financial statements are an integral part of this statement.

19

Exhibit 4

Name of Government
Combined Statement of Revenues, Expenses and Changes in Retained Earnings/Fund Balances
All Proprietary Fund Types and Similar Trust Funds
For the fiscal year ended December 31, 19X8
(With comparative totals for the fiscal year ended December 31, 19X7)
(amounts expressed in thousands)

| | Proprietary Fund Types | | Fiduciary Fund Types | | Totals (Memorandum Only) | |
	Enterprise	Internal Service	Non-expendable Trust	Pension Trust	19X8	19X7
Operating revenues:						
Charges for sales and services	$17,676	$1,857	—	—	$19,533	$14,729
Interest	—	—	$ 41	$ 774	815	867
Employer contributions	—	—	—	1,051	1,051	1,047
Employee contributions	—	—	—	729	729	511
Total operating revenues	17,676	1,857	41	2,554	22,128	17,154
Operating expenses:						
Costs of sales and services	7,797	1,145	13	—	8,955	7,127
Administration	3,148	134	—	160	3,442	3,048
Benefits	—	—	—	455	455	380
Refunds	—	—	—	15	15	34
Depreciation	2,507	511	—	—	3,018	2,415
Total operating expenses	13,452	1,790	13	630	15,885	13,004
Operating income	4,224	67	28	1,924	6,243	4,150
Nonoperating revenues (expenses):						
Interest revenue	1,823	8	—	—	1,831	1,944
Interest expense	(3,734)	—	—	—	(3,734)	(3,098)
Other	(35)	—	138	—	103	47
Total nonoperating revenues (expenses)	(1,946)	8	138	—	(1,800)	(1,107)
Net income before extraordinary items	2,278	75	166	1,924	4,443	3,043
Extraordinary gain (loss) on advance refunding	547	—	—	—	547	(76)
Net income	2,825	75	166	1,924	4,990	2,967
Retained earnings/fund balances, January 1	30,546	296	1,887	12,772	45,501	42,534
Retained earnings/fund balances, December 31	$33,371	$ 371	$2,053	$14,696	$50,491	$45,501

The notes to the financial statements are an integral part of this statement.

Exhibit 5

Name of Government
Combined Statement of Changes in Financial Position
All Proprietary Fund Types and Similar Trust Funds
For the fiscal year ended December 31, 19X8
(With comparative totals for the fiscal year ended December 31, 19X7)
(amounts expressed in thousands)

	Proprietary Fund Types		Fiduciary Fund Types		Totals (Memorandum Only)	
	Enterprise	Internal Service	Nonexpendable Trust	Pension Trust	19X8	19X7
Cash flows from operating activities:						
Cash received from customers and users	$ 17,467	$ 1,839	—	—	$ 19,306	$ 14,799
Cash received from pension contributions	—	—	—	$ 1,780	1,780	1,558
Cash paid to suppliers and employees	(10,950)	(1,166)	$ (18)	(628)	(12,762)	(10,486)
Interest received	807	6	—	547	1,360	2,759
Interest paid	(3,258)	—	—	—	(3,258)	(3,217)
Net cash provided (used) by operating activities	4,066	679	(18)	1,699	6,426	5,413
Cash flows from investing activities:						
Proceeds from sales of investments	1,930	31	1,788	3,056	6,805	3,137
Purchase of investments	(24,259)	(81)	(1,555)	(4,777)	(30,672)	(12,136)
Proceeds from sales of fixed assets	5	—	—	—	5	—
Purchase of fixed assets	(55)	(639)	—	—	(694)	(327)
Capital lease obligation down payment	(6)	—	—	—	(6)	—
Earnings on invested proceeds	550	—	—	—	550	—
Construction (including capitalized interest costs)	(10,759)	—	—	—	(10,759)	—
Net cash provided (used) by investing activities	(32,594)	(689)	233	(1,721)	(34,771)	(9,326)
Cash flows from financing activities:						
Proceeds from issuance of long-term debt	41,155	—	—	—	41,155	3,617
Principal payments - bonds	(9,945)	—	—	—	(9,945)	(4,885)
Principal payments - capital leases	(12)	—	—	—	(12)	—
Capital contributions and advances	4,294	105	—	—	4,399	6,744
Net cash provided by financing activities	35,492	105	—	—	35,597	5,476
Noncash transactions affecting financial position:						
Borrowing under capital lease obligations	101	—	—	—	101	—
Acquisition of fixed assets through capital leases	(101)	—	—	—	(101)	—
Contributions of fixed assets from government	3,230	2,160	—	—	5,390	—
Acquisition of fixed assets through government capital contributions	(3,230)	(2,160)	—	—	(5,390)	—
Borrowing from suppliers on account	374	—	—	—	374	—
Acquisition of fixed assets on account	(374)	—	—	—	(374)	—
Acquisition of fixed assets through trade-in	—	48	—	—	48	—
Value of traded fixed assets	—	(48)	—	—	(48)	—
Net effect of noncash transactions	0	0	—	—	0	—
Net increase (decrease) in cash	6,964	95	215	(22)	7,252	1,563
Cash, January 1	2,811	5	16	55	2,887	1,324
Cash, December 31	$ 9,775	$ 100	$ 231	$ 33	$ 10,139	$ 2,887

cont.

21

Exhibit 5, cont.

Reconciliation of Net Income to
Net Cash Provided (Used) by Operating Activities

	Enterprise	Internal Service	Nonexpendable Trust	Pension Trust	Totals (Memorandum Only) 19X8	19X7
Net income	$ 2,825	$ 75	$ 166	$ 1,924	$ 4,990	$ 2,966
Adjustments to reconcile net income to net cash provided (used) by operating activities:						
Extraordinary (gain) loss	(547)	—	—	—	(547)	76
Loss on sales of fixed assets	10	—	—	—	10	—
Gain on sales of investments	—	—	(138)	—	(138)	(57)
Depreciation expense	2,507	511	—	—	3,018	2,415
Amortization of bond discounts	25	—	—	—	25	—
Amortization of bond issuance costs	19	—	—	—	19	17
(Increase) decrease in interest receivable	(94)	(2)	(41)	(227)	(364)	62
(Increase) in accounts receivable	(508)	—	—	—	(508)	(59)
Increase in allowance for uncollectible accounts	213	—	—	—	213	110
(Increase) in intergovernmental receivables	—	(4)	—	—	(4)	—
(Increase) in due from other funds	—	(14)	—	—	(14)	(11)
(Increase) decrease in inventories	153	(23)	—	—	130	(47)
(Increase) in prepaid items	—	(38)	—	—	(38)	—
Net increase in customer deposits	292	—	—	—	292	109
(Increase) in interest receivable—restricted assets	(372)	—	—	—	(372)	(112)
Increase in vouchers payable	77	—	—	—	77	6
Increase (decrease) in accounts payable	76	154	(5)	2	227	17
Increase in compensated absences payable	6	10	—	—	16	8
Increase (decrease) in intergovernmental payables	(11)	—	—	—	(11)	4
Increase (decrease) in due to other funds	(138)	10	—	—	(128)	23
Increase in matured interest payable	55	—	—	—	55	—
Increase (decrease) in accrued interest payable	(60)	—	—	—	(60)	6
Increase (decrease) in accrued interest payable from restricted accounts	883	—	—	—	883	(120)
(Increase) in accounts payable related to equipment purchase	(374)	—	—	—	(374)	—
Interest capitalization	(978)	—	—	—	(978)	—
Net cash flow related to interest capitalization (reported as investing activity)	7	—	—	—	7	—
Total adjustments	1,241	604	(184)	(225)	1,436	2,447
Net cash provided (used) by operating activities	$ 4,066	$ 679	$ (18)	$ 1,699	$ 6,426	$ 5,413

The notes to the financial statements are an integral part of this statement.

NAME OF GOVERNMENT
Notes to the Financial Statements
December 31, 19X8
(amounts expressed in thousands)

Note 1. Summary of Significant Accounting Policies

The financial statements of the NAME OF GOVERNMENT (government) have been prepared in conformity with generally accepted accounting principles (GAAP) as applied to government units. The Governmental Accounting Standards Board (GASB) is the accepted standard-setting body for establishing governmental accounting and financial reporting principles. The more significant of the government's accounting policies are described below.

A. Reporting Entity

In evaluating how to define the government, for financial reporting purposes, management has considered all potential component units. The decision to include a potential component unit in the reporting entity was made by applying the criteria set forth in GAAP. The basic—but not the only—criterion for including a potential component unit within the reporting entity is the governing body's ability to exercise oversight responsibility. The most significant manifestation of this ability is financial interdependency. Other manifestations of the ability to exercise oversight responsibility include, but are not limited to, the selection of governing authority, the designation of management, the ability to significantly influence operations, and accountability for fiscal matters. A second criterion used in evaluating potential component units is the scope of public service. Application of this criterion involves considering whether the activity benefits the government and/or its citizens, or whether the activity is conducted within the geographic boundaries of the government and is generally available to its citizens. A third criterion used to evaluate potential component units for inclusion or exclusion from the reporting entity is the existence of special financing relationships, regardless of whether the government is able to exercise oversight responsibilities. Based upon the application of these criteria, the following is a brief review of each potential component unit addressed in defining the government's reporting entity.

Included within the reporting entity:

NAME OF GOVERNMENT Water and Sewer Authority. The Name of Government Water and Sewer Authority's (the Water and Sewer Authority) governing board is appointed by the government's governing body. The rates for user charges and bond issuance authorizations also are approved by the government's governing body and the legal liability for the general obligation portion of the Water and Sewer Authority's debt remains with the government.

NAME OF GOVERNMENT Public Safety Employees Retirement System. The government's public safety employees participate in the Public Safety Employees Retirement System (PSERS). PSERS functions for the benefit of these employees and is governed by a seven-member pension board. The government's manager and finance officer, and five elected public safety employees constitute the pension board. The government and PSERS participants are obligated to fund all PSERS costs based upon actuarial valuations. The government is authorized to establish benefit levels and to approve the actuarial assumptions used in the determination of contribution levels.

Excluded from the reporting entity:

NAME OF GOVERNMENT Airport Authority. The NAME OF GOVERNMENT Airport Authority (the Airport Authority) was established by a special state act in 19X2. The Airport Authority's governing board (appointed jointly by the government's governing body, the County Board and the Pilots Association), selects management staff, sets user charges, establishes budgets and controls all aspects of general aviation, airport management and development. The government provides no funding to the Airport Authority. Additionally, the government does not hold title to any of the Airport Authority's assets, nor does it have any right to the Airport Authority's surpluses.

NAME OF GOVERNMENT Hospital District, NAME OF GOVERNMENT Flood Control District and NAME OF GOVERNMENT School District. These potential component units have separate elected boards and provide services to residents, generally within the geographic boundaries of the government. These potential component units are excluded from the reporting entity because the government does not have the ability to exercise influence over their daily operations, approve budgets or provide funding.

B. Fund Accounting

The government uses funds and account groups to report on its financial position and the results of its operations. Fund accounting is designed to demonstrate legal compliance and to aid financial management by segregating transactions related to certain government functions or activities.

A fund is a separate accounting entity with a self-balancing set of accounts. An account group, on the other hand, is a financial reporting device designed to provide accountability for certain assets and liabilities that are not recorded in the funds because they do not directly affect net expendable available financial resources.

Funds are classified into three categories: governmental, proprietary and fiduciary. Each category, in turn, is divided into separate "fund types."

Governmental funds are used to account for all or most of a government's general activities, including the collection and disbursement of earmarked monies (special revenue funds), the acquisition or construction of general fixed assets (capital projects funds), and the servicing of general long-term debt (debt service funds). The general fund is used to account for all activities of the general government not accounted for in some other fund.

Proprietary funds are used to account for activities similar to those found in the private sector, where the determination of net income is necessary or useful to sound financial administration. Goods or services from such activities can be provided either to outside parties (enterprise funds) or to other departments or agencies primarily within the government (internal service funds).

Fiduciary funds are used to account for assets held on behalf of outside parties, including other governments, or on behalf of other funds within the government. When these assets are held under the terms of a formal trust agreement, either a pension trust fund, a nonexpendable trust fund or an expendable trust fund is used. The terms "nonexpendable" and "expendable" refer to whether or not the government is under an obligation to maintain the trust principal. Agency funds generally are used to account for assets that the government holds on behalf of others as their agent.

C. Basis of Accounting

The accounting and financial reporting treatment applied to a fund is determined by its measurement focus. All governmental funds and expendable trust funds are accounted for using a current financial resources measurement focus. With this measurement focus, only current assets and current liabilities generally are included on the balance sheet. Operating statements of these funds present increases (i.e., revenues and other financing sources) and decreases (i.e., expenditures and other financing uses) in net current assets.

All proprietary funds, nonexpendable trust funds and pension trust funds are accounted for on a flow of economic resources measurement focus. With this measurement focus, all assets and all liabilities associated with the operation of these funds are included on the balance sheet. Fund equity (i.e., net total assets) is segregated into contributed capital and retained earnings components. Proprietary fund-type operating statements present increases (e.g., revenues) and decreases (e.g., expenses) in net total assets.

The modified accrual basis of accounting is used by all governmental fund types, expendable trust funds and agency funds. Under the modified accrual basis of accounting, revenues are recognized when susceptible to accrual (i.e., when they become both measurable and available). "Measurable" means the amount of the transaction can be determined and "available" means collectible within the current period or soon enough thereafter to be used to pay liabilities of the current period. The government considers property taxes as available if they are collected within 60 days after year end. A one-year availability period is used for revenue recognition for all other governmental fund revenues. Expenditures are recorded when the related fund liability is incurred. Principal and interest on general long-term debt are recorded as fund liabilities when due or when amounts have been accumulated in the debt service fund for payments to be made early in the following year.

Those revenues susceptible to accrual are property taxes, franchise taxes, special assessments, licenses, interest revenue and charges for services. Sales taxes collected and held by the state at year end on behalf of the

25

government also are recognized as revenue. Fines, permits and parking meter revenues are not susceptible to accrual because generally they are not measurable until received in cash.

The accrual basis of accounting is utilized by proprietary fund types, pension trust funds and nonexpendable trust funds. Under this method, revenues are recorded when earned and expenses are recorded at the time liabilities are incurred.

The government reports deferred revenue on its combined balance sheet. Deferred revenues arise when a potential revenue does not meet both the "measurable" and "available" criteria for recognition in the current period. Deferred revenues also arise when resources are received by the government before it has a legal claim to them, as when grant monies are received prior to the incurrence of qualifying expenditures. In subsequent periods, when both revenue recognition criteria are met, or when the government has a legal claim to the resources, the liability for deferred revenue is removed from the combined balance sheet and revenue is recognized.

D. Budgets

Budgets are adopted on a basis consistent with generally accepted accounting principles. Annual appropriated budgets are adopted for the general, special revenue and debt service funds. All annual appropriations lapse at fiscal year end. Project-length financial plans are adopted for all capital projects funds.

Encumbrances represent commitments related to unperformed contracts for goods or services. Encumbrance accounting—under which purchase orders, contracts and other commitments for the expenditure of resources are recorded to reserve that portion of the applicable appropriation—is utilized in the governmental funds. Encumbrances outstanding at year end are reported as reservations of fund balances and do not constitute expenditures or liabilities because the commitments will be honored during the subsequent year.

E. Cash and Investments

Cash includes amounts in demand deposits as well as short-term investments with a maturity date within three months of the date acquired by the government.

State statutes authorize the government to invest in obligations of the U.S. Treasury, commercial paper, corporate bonds and repurchase agreements.

Investments are stated at cost or amortized cost, except for investments in the deferred compensation agency fund which are reported at market value.

F. Short-term Interfund Receivables/Payables

During the course of operations, numerous transactions occur between individual funds for goods provided or services rendered. These receivables and payables are classified as "due from other funds" or "due to other funds'' on the balance sheet. Short-term interfund loans are classified as ''interfund receivables/payables.''

G. Advances to Other Funds

Noncurrent portions of long-term interfund loan receivables are reported as advances and are offset equally by a fund balance reserve account which indicates that they do not constitute expendable available financial resources and therefore are not available for appropriation.

H. Inventories

Inventories are valued at cost, which approximates market, using the first-in/first-out (FIFO) method. The costs of governmental fund-type inventories are recorded as expenditures when consumed rather than when purchased.

I. Prepaid Items

Payments made to vendors for services that will benefit periods beyond December 31, 19X8, are recorded as prepaid items.

J. Restricted Assets

Certain proceeds of enterprise fund revenue bonds, as well as certain resources set aside for their repayment, are classified as restricted assets on the balance sheet because their use is limited by applicable bond covenants. The ''revenue bond operations and maintenance'' account is used to report resources set aside to subsidize potential deficiencies from the enterprise fund's operation that could adversely affect debt service payments. The ''revenue bond construction'' account is used to report those proceeds of revenue bond issuances that are restricted for use in construction. The ''revenue bond current debt service'' account is used to segregate resources accumulated for debt service payments over the next twelve months. The ''revenue bond future debt service'' account is used to report resources set aside to make up potential future deficiencies in the revenue bond current debt service account. The ''revenue bond renewal and replacement'' account is used to report resources set aside to meet unexpected contingencies or to fund asset renewals and replacements.

K. Fixed Assets

General fixed assets are not capitalized in the funds used to acquire or construct them. Instead, capital acquisition and construction are reflected as expenditures in governmental funds, and the related assets are reported in the general fixed assets account group. All purchased fixed assets are valued at cost where historical records are available and at an estimated historical cost where no historical records exist. Donated fixed assets are valued at their estimated fair market value on the date received.

The costs of normal maintenance and repairs that do not add to the value of the asset or materially extend asset lives are not capitalized. Improvements are capitalized and depreciated over the remaining useful lives of the related fixed assets, as applicable.

Public domain ("infrastructure") general fixed assets consisting of roads, bridges, curbs and gutters, streets and sidewalks, drainage systems and lighting systems are not capitalized, as these assets are immovable and of value only to the government.

Assets in the general fixed assets account group are not depreciated. Depreciation of buildings, equipment and vehicles in the proprietary fund types is computed using the straight-line method.

Interest is capitalized on proprietary fund assets acquired with tax-exempt debt. The amount of interest to be capitalized is calculated by offsetting interest expense incurred from the date of the borrowing until completion of the project with interest earned on invested proceeds over the same period.

L. Compensated Absences

Vested or accumulated vacation leave that is expected to be liquidated with expendable available financial resources is reported as an expenditure and a fund liability of the governmental fund that will pay it. Amounts of vested or accumulated vacation leave that are not expected to be liquidated with expendable available financial resources are reported in the general long-term debt account group. No expenditure is reported for these amounts. Vested or accumulated vacation leave of proprietary funds is recorded as an expense and liability of those funds as the benefits accrue to employees. In accordance with the provisions of Statement of Financial Accounting Standards No. 43, *Accounting for Compensated Absences*, no liability is recorded for nonvesting accumulating rights to receive sick pay benefits. However, a liability is recognized for that portion of accumulating sick leave benefits that it is estimated will be taken as "terminal leave" prior to retirement.

M. Long-term Obligations

Long-term debt is recognized as a liability of a governmental fund when due, or when resources have been accumulated in the debt service fund for payment early in the following year. For other long-term obligations, only that portion expected to be financed from expendable available financial resources is reported as a fund liability of a governmental fund. The remaining portion of such obligations is reported in the general long-term debt account group. Long-term liabilities expected to be financed from proprietary fund operations are accounted for in those funds.

N. Fund Equity

Contributed capital is recorded in proprietary funds that have received capital grants or contributions from developers, customers or other funds. Reserves represent those portions of fund equity not appropriable for expenditure or legally segregated for a specific future use. Designated fund balances represent tentative plans for future use of financial resources.

O. Bond Discounts/Issuance Costs

In governmental fund types, bond discounts and issuance costs are recognized in the current period. Bond discounts and issuance costs for proprietary fund types are deferred and amortized over the term of the bonds using the bonds-outstanding method, which approximates the effective interest method. Bond discounts are presented as a reduction of the face amount of bonds payable whereas issuance costs are recorded as deferred charges.

P. Interfund Transactions

Quasi-external transactions are accounted for as revenues, expenditures or expenses. Transactions that constitute reimbursements to a fund for expenditures/expenses initially made from it that are properly applicable to another fund, are recorded as expenditures/expenses in the reimbursing fund and as reductions of expenditures/expenses in the fund that is reimbursed.

All other interfund transactions, except quasi-external transactions and reimbursements, are reported as transfers. Nonrecurring or nonroutine permanent transfers of equity are reported as residual equity transfers. All other interfund transfers are reported as operating transfers.

Q. Memorandum Only - Total Columns

Total columns on the general purpose financial statements are captioned "memorandum only" to indicate that they are presented only to facilitate financial analysis. Data in these columns do not present financial position, results of operations or changes in financial position in conformity with generally accepted accounting principles. Neither are such data comparable to a consolidation. Interfund eliminations have not been made in the aggregation of this data.

R. Comparative Data

Comparative total data for the prior year have been presented in the accompanying financial statements in order to provide an understanding of changes in the government's financial position and operations. However, comparative data have not been presented in all statements because their inclusion would make certain statements unduly complex and difficult to understand.

Note 2. Legal Compliance—Budgets

On or before the last Tuesday in August of each year, all agencies of the government submit requests for appropriation to the government's manager so that a budget may be prepared. The budget is prepared by fund, function and activity, and includes information on the past year, current year estimates and requested appropriations for the next fiscal year.

Before October 31, the proposed budget is presented to the government's council for review. The government's council holds public hearings and may add to, subtract from or change appropriations, but many not change the form of the budget. Any changes in the budget must be within the revenues and reserves estimated as available by the government's manager or the revenue estimates must be changed by an affirmative vote of a majority of the government's council.

Expenditures may not legally exceed budgeted appropriations at the activity level. During the year, several supplementary appropriations were necessary.

Note 3. Deposits and Investments

Deposits. At year end, the carrying amount of the government's deposits was $25,994 and the bank balance was $23,533. Of the bank balance, $17,212 was covered by federal depository insurance or by collateral held by the government's agent in the government's name. The balance was covered by collateral held in the pledging financial institutions' trust departments in the government's name.

Investments. The government's investments are categorized as either (1) insured or registered or for which the securities are held by the government or its agent in the government's name, (2) uninsured and unregistered for which the securities are held by the broker's or dealer's trust department or agent in the government's name or (3) uninsured and unregistered for which the securities are held by the broker or dealer, or by its trust department or agent but not in the government's name.

	Categories			Carrying Amount	Market Value
	1	2	3		
U.S. Government securities	$ 4,300	$1,074	—	$ 5,374	$ 5,546
Commercial paper	3,515	—	—	3,515	3,468
Corporate bonds	9,932	—	—	9,932	9,277
Repurchase agreements	1,654	5,790	$827	8,271	8,271
	$19,401	$6,864	$827	27,092	26,562
Investment in deferred compensation mutual fund				1,198	1,198
Total investments				$28,290	$27,760

Statutes require collateral pledged for deposits to be held in the government's name by the trust department. However, the pledged collateral was held in the counterparty's name rather than in the government's name on four days during the year, but no losses were incurred.

Due to higher cash flows at certain times during the year, the government's investment in overnight repurchase agreements for which the underlying securities were held by the dealer increased significantly. As a result, the amounts that were in category 3 at those times were substantially higher than at year end.

Note 4. Receivables

Receivables at December 31, 19X8 consist of the following:

	General	Special Revenue	Debt Service	Capital Projects	Enterprise	Internal Service	Trust and Agency	Total
Receivables:								
Interest	$ 92	$2	$ 30	$411	$ 420	$2	$433	$ 1,390
Taxes	991	—	10	—	—	—	—	1,001
Accounts	74	—	—	—	3,094	—	—	3,168
Special assessments	—	—	4,230	—	—	—	—	4,230
Intergovernmental	215	—	—	199	—	4	—	418
Gross receivables	1,372	2	4,270	610	3,514	6	433	10,207
Less: allowance for uncollectibles	(41)	—	—	—	(472)	—	—	(513)
Net total receivables	$1,331	$2	$4,270	$610	$3,042	$6	$433	$ 9,694

The delinquent taxes receivable account represents the past four years of uncollected tax levies. The allowance for estimated uncollectibles is 4 percent of the total delinquent taxes receivable at December 31, 19X8.

Property taxes are levied as of January 1 on property values assessed as of the same date. The tax levy is divided into two billings: the first billing is an estimate of the current year's levy based on the prior year's taxes; the second billing reflects adjustments to the current year's actual levy. The first billing is mailed on February 1 and the second billing is mailed on August 1. The billings are considered due upon receipt by the taxpayer; however, the actual due date is based on a period ending 60 days after the tax bill mailing. On these dates (April 2 and September 29), the bill becomes delinquent and penalties and interest may be assessed by the government.

Note 5. Fixed Assets

The following is a summary of changes in the general fixed assets account group during the fiscal year:

	Balance January 1, 19X8	Additions	Retirements	Completed Construction	Transfers to Other Funds	Balance December 31, 19X8
Land	$38,775	$ 558	—	—	—	$39,333
Buildings	7,875	31	—	$ 472	$ (87)	8,291
Improvements other than buildings	4,604	—	—	—	—	4,604
Machinery and equipment	7,401	1,205	$(64)	—	(4,166)	4,376
Construction in progress	722	2,058	—	(472)	—	2,308
Total general fixed assets	$59,377	$3,852	$(64)	$ 0	$(4,253)	$58,912

31

The government has entered into contracts for the construction or renovation of various facilities as follows:

	Project Authorization	Expended To Date	Commitment	Required Further Financing
Hunting Ridge building restoration	$ 280	$ 250	$ 25	None
Government building	2,250	2,058	3,175	None
Total	$2,530	$2,308	$3,200	

The following is a summary of proprietary fund-type fixed assets at December 31, 19X8:

	Enterprise Funds	Internal Service Funds
Land	$ 1,073	—
Buildings	21,512	$ 87
Improvements other than buildings	3,640	—
Machinery and equipment	104,509	5,283
Less: accumulated depreciation	(17,799)	(2,466)
Construction in progress	7,118	—
Net fixed assets	$120,053	$ 2,904

In proprietary funds, the following estimated useful lives are used to compute depreciation:

Buildings	50 years
Equipment	10–20 years
Vehicles	4–5 years

Note 6. Risk Management

The government established a limited risk management program for workers' compensation in 19X8. Premiums are paid into the general fund by all other funds and are available to pay claims, claim reserves and administrative costs of the program. During fiscal year 19X8, a total of $351 was paid in benefits and administrative costs. An excess coverage insurance policy covers individual claims in excess of $100. Incurred but not reported claims of $220 have been accrued as a liability based primarily upon an actuary's estimate. Interfund premiums are based primarily upon the insured funds' claims experience and are reported as quasi-external interfund transactions.

Note 7. Operating Leases

The government is committed under various leases for building and office space and data processing equipment. These leases are considered for accounting purposes to be operating leases. Lease expenditures for the year

32

ended December 31, 19X8 amounted to $123. Future minimum lease payments for these leases are as follows:

Year Ending	Amount
19X9	$123
19Y0	123
19Y1	123
19Y2	63
19Y3	63
Thereafter	252
Total	$747

Note 8. Capital Leases

The government has entered into a lease agreement as lessee for financing the acquisition of police communication equipment with a down payment of $15. The government also has financed the acquisition of certain trucks for its Water and Sewer Authority by means of leases with a down payment of $6. These lease agreements qualify as capital leases for accounting purposes (titles transfer at the end of the lease terms) and, therefore, have been recorded at the present value of the future minimum lease payments as of the date of their inception. The following is an analysis of equipment leased under capital leases as of December 31, 19X8:

	General Fixed Assets	Enterprise Fund
Machinery and equipment	$140	$119
Less: accumulated depreciation	—	(24)
Carrying value	$140	$ 95

The following is a schedule of the future minimum lease payments under these capital leases, and the present value of the net minimum lease payments at December 31, 19X8:

Fiscal year ending December 31	General Long-term Debt	Enterprise Fund
19X9	$ 49	$ 40
19Y0	49	40
19Y1	48	39
Total minimum lease payments	146	119
Less: amount representing interest	(21)	(18)
Present value of future minimum lease payments	$125	$101

Note 9. Long-term Debt

General Obligation Bonds. The government issues general obligation bonds to provide funds for the acquisition and construction of major capital facilities. General obligation bonds have been issued for both general government and proprietary activities. These bonds therefore are reported in the propri-

33

etary funds if they are expected to be repaid from proprietary revenues. In addition, general obligation bonds have been issued to refund both general obligation and revenue bonds.

General obligation bonds are direct obligations and pledge the full faith and credit of the government. These bonds generally are issued as 25-year serial bonds, except for refunding issues, with equal amounts of principal maturing each year. General obligation bonds currently outstanding are as follows:

Purpose	Interest rates	Amount
General government	7.0–8.5%	$32,425
General government—refunding	8.0	3,365
Proprietary	7.0–8.5	23,798
Proprietary—refunding	8.0	10,777
		$70,365

Annual debt service requirements to maturity for general obligation bonds, including interest of $59,371, are as follows:

Fiscal Year Ending December 31	Enterprise Funds	General Long-Term Debt Account Group	Total
19X9	$ 4,432	$ 4,572	$ 9,004
19Y0	4,306	4,444	8,750
19Y1	4,179	4,318	8,497
19Y2	4,054	4,190	8,244
19Y3	3,926	4,064	7,990
Thereafter	42,820	44,431	87,251
Total	$63,717	$66,019	$129,736

Revenue Bonds. The government also issues bonds where the government pledges income derived from the acquired or constructed assets to pay debt service. Revenue bonds outstanding, net of unamortized discount of $288, at December 31, 19X8, are as follows:

Purpose	Interest Rates	Amount
Wastewater treatment—Water and Sewer Authority	7.5–9.0%	$34,312

Revenue bond debt service requirements to maturity, including $37,506 of interest, are as follows:

Fiscal Year Ending December 31	Amount
19X9	$ 4,152
19Y0	4,049
19Y1	3,946
19Y2	3,843
19Y3	3,740
Thereafter	52,088
Total	$71,818

Special Assessment Debt. The government issued $4,700 of special assessment bonds in 19X8 to provide funds for the construction of a sewer pipeline to serve new residential and commercial developments. The bonds have a stated rate of interest of 8.0 percent and are payable in equal installments of principal over the next 10 years.

Special assessment bond debt service requirements to maturity, including $2,068 of interest, are as follows:

Fiscal Year Ending December 31	Amount
19X9	$ 846
19Y0	808
19Y1	771
19Y2	733
19Y3	696
Thereafter	2,914
	$6,768

Advance Refunding. In 19X8, the government advance refunded a general obligation bond issue and a revenue bond issue with two separate general obligation refundings. The government issued $3,365 of general obligation refunding bonds to provide resources to purchase U.S. Government State and Local Government Series securities that were placed in an irrevocable trust for the purpose of generating resources for all future debt service payments of the refunded debt. As a result, the refunded bonds are considered to be defeased and the liability has been removed from the general long-term debt account group. This advance refunding was undertaken to reduce total debt service payments over the next 20 years by $182 and to obtain an economic gain (difference between the present value of the debt service payments of the refunded and refunding bonds) of $105.

In addition, the government issued $7,060 of general obligation bonds to advance refund $8,580 of revenue bonds presented in the Water and Sewer Authority fund. The refunding was undertaken to remove restrictive bond covenants associated with the revenue bonds. Although the financial statements present a $547 accounting gain, the transaction resulted in neither a reduction of debt service payments nor an economic gain or loss.

At December 31, 19X8, $14,380 of outstanding general obligation bonds and revenue bonds (including prior year's refundings) are considered defeased.

Changes in Long-Term Liabilities. During the year ended December 31, 19X8, the following changes occurred in liabilities reported in the general long-term debt account group:

	Balance January 1	Additions	Reductions	Balance December 31
Compensated absenses	$ 1,811	$ 857	$ (646)	$ 2,022
Claims and judgments	—	220	—	220
General obligation debt	37,455	3,365	(5,030)	35,790
Special assessment debt	—	4,700	—	4,700
Capital leases	—	140	(15)	125
	$39,266	$9,282	$(5,691)	$42,857

35

Note 10. Interfund Assets/Liabilities

Due From/To Other Funds:

Receivable fund	Payable fund	Amount
General	Water and sewer	$ 65
	Fleet management	8
Pipeline construction	General	335
Water and sewer	General	37
	Fleet management	2
Fleet management	General	47
	Water and sewer	17
Management information systems	General	57
	Water and sewer	5
Total		$573

Interfund Receivable/Payable:

Receivable fund	Payable fund	Amount
General	Fleet management	$ 8
	Management information systems	24
Total		$32

Advances From/To Other Funds:

Receivable fund	Payable fund	Amount
General	Fleet management	$32
	Management information systems	46
Total		$78

Note 11. Segment Information—Enterprise Funds

The government maintains two enterprise funds which are intended to be self-supporting through user fees charged for services to the public. Financial segment information as of and for the year ended December 31, 19X8 is presented below.

	Water and Sewer	Golf Course	Total
Operating revenues	$ 16,419	$1,257	$ 17,676
Depreciation expense	2,436	71	2,507
Operating income	3,849	375	4,224
Net income	2,693	132	2,825
Current capital contributions	7,524	—	7,524
Property, plant and equipment additions	17,154	55	17,209
Net working capital	14,221	585	14,806
Total assets	163,768	4,466	168,234
Bonds payable	65,170	3,717	68,887
Total equity	92,221	545	92,766

Note 12. Contributed Capital

During the year, contributed capital increased by the following amounts:

Source	Water and Sewer	Golf Course	Fleet Management	Management Information Systems
Customers—tap fees	$ 208	—	—	—
Developers—tap fees	4,086	—	—	—
Government—pipeline construction	3,230	—	—	—
Government—initial capital	—	—	$ 45	—
Government—general fixed assets	—	—	2,160	—
Total additions	7,524	—	2,205	—
Contributed capital, January 1	51,400	$471	—	$281
Contributed capital December 31	$58,924	$471	$2,205	$281

Note 13. Contingent Liabilities

Amounts received or receivable from grantor agencies are subject to audit and adjustment by grantor agencies, principally the federal government. Any disallowed claims, including amounts already collected, may constitute a liability of the applicable funds. The amount, if any, of expenditures which may be disallowed by the grantor cannot be determined at this time although the government expects such amounts, if any, to be immaterial.

The government is a defendant in various lawsuits. Although the outcome of these lawsuits is not presently determinable, in the opinion of the government attorney the resolution of these matters will not have a material adverse effect on the financial condition of the government.

Note 14. Subsequent Events

On January 21, 19X9, the government issued $18,000 of general obligation bonds dated February 1, 19X9 to finance infrastructure improvements. The bonds' effective interest rate was 6.025% and they mature January 19Y1 through January 19Z5.

On February 3, 19X9 the government's governing body approved a settlement with one of the government's insurance carriers in which the government received $1,569 less certain legal fees.

Note 15. Joint Ventures

Pursuant to an interlocal agreement authorized by state statutes, the government joined GOVERNMENT X to establish and operate a sanitary landfill operation for the mutual advantage of the governments. Three members of the board of directors for the joint venture are appointed by each government. The operating and capital budgets are funded by equal contributions from each government. The government's share of assets, liabilities and fund equity is 50 percent. Summary financial information as of, and for the fiscal year ended December 31, 19X8, is presented on the next page:

Cash and investments	$ 36
Other assets	1,377
Total assets	$1,413
Total liabilities	$1,331
Total equity	82
Total liabilities and equity	$1,413
Total revenues	$1,345
Total expenses	877
Net increase in equity	$ 468

Revenue bonds were issued in 19X8 to purchase the site for the landfill operation. These variable-rate bonds, with interest rates between 3.5 percent and 5.0 percent, are payable from net revenues of the operation. The debt service requirements to maturity, excluding interest, are presented below:

Year Ending	Amount
19X9	$ 300
19Y0	300
19Y1	300
19Y2	300
19Y3	100
Total outstanding	$1,300

Note 16. Deferred Compensation Plan

The government offers its employees a deferred compensation plan created in accordance with Internal Revenue Code Section 457. The plan, available to all government employees, permits them to defer a portion of their salary until future years. Participation in the plan is optional. The deferred compensation is not available to employees until termination, retirement, death or unforeseeable emergency. All amounts of compensation deferred under the plan, all property and rights purchased with those amounts, and all income attributable to those amounts, property or rights are (until paid or made available to the employee or other beneficiary) solely the property and rights of the government subject only to the claims of the government's general creditors. Participants' rights under the plan are equal to those of general creditor of the government in an amount equal to the fair market value of the deferred account for each participant.

It is the opinion of the government's legal counsel that the government has no liability for losses under the plan but does have the duty of due care that would be required of an ordinary prudent investor. The government believes that it is unlikely that it will use the assets to satisfy the claims of general creditors in the future.

Investments are managed by the plan's trustee under one of four investment options, or a combination thereof. The choice of the investment option(s) is made by the participants.

Note 17. Post-Employment Health Care Benefits

In addition to providing pension benefits, the government provides certain health care and life insurance benefits for retired public safety employees. Substantially all of the government's public safety employees may become eligible for those benefits if they reach normal retirement age while working for the government. The cost of retiree health care and life insurance benefits is recognized as an expenditure as claims are paid. For 19X8, those costs total $42.

Note 18. Employee Retirement Systems

The government maintains a single-employer, defined benefit pension plan (Public Safety Employees Retirement System) which covers all of its public safety employees, and participates in the statewide local government retirement system, a multiple-employer, cost-sharing public employee pension plan which covers substantially all of the government's general employees and the Water and Sewer Authority's employees.

Public Safety Employees Retirement System (PSERS)

Plan description and provisions:

All of the government's full-time police and fire employees participate in the PSERS, a single-employer, defined benefit pension plan. The payroll for employees covered by the PSERS for the year ended December 31, 19X8, was $5,684; the government's total payroll was $21,042. Current membership in the PSERS is comprised of the following:

Group	December 31, 19X8
Retirees and beneficiaries currently receiving benefits	37
Vested terminated employees	18
Active employees:	
Fully vested	48
Nonvested	91

Employees attaining the age of 52 who have completed 20 or more continuous years of service are entitled to annual benefits of 2.5 percent of their average monthly earnings for each year of continuous service up to a maximum of 75 percent of average monthly earnings. Minimum benefit at retirement for members as of the effective date is 50 percent of average monthly earnings. The PSERS permits early retirement at the completion of 20 years of continuous service. Active employees who become disabled receive 75 percent of their monthly earnings. As of January 1, 19X5, police members of the PSERS are allowed normal retirement benefits at age 50 with 20 or more continuous years of service.

Disability benefits are paid until the earlier of death or recovery from disability. If an active employee dies, his or her beneficiary receives a $5,000 lump-sum benefit payment plus a maximum monthly benefit equal to 90 percent of the member's average monthly earnings until the beneficiary's death or remarriage.

If an employee terminates his or her employment with the police or fire departments and is not eligible for any other benefits under the PSERS, the employee is entitled to the following:
— with less than 10 years of continuous service, a refund of member contribution plus 3 percent interest.
— with 10 or more years of continuous service, the pension accrued to the date of termination, payable commencing at his or her normal retirement date or at the option of the employee a lump-sum refund of member contribution plus 3 percent interest.

Police and fire employees are required to contribute 5 percent of their annual salary to the PSERS. The government is required to contribute the remaining amounts necessary to fund the PSERS, using the entry age-normal actuarial method as specified by ordinance.

Funding Status and Progress:

The amount shown below as the "pension benefit obligation" is a standardized disclosure measure of the present value of pension benefits, adjusted for the effects of projected salary increases, estimated to be payable in the future as a result of employee service to date. This measure is the actuarial present value of credited projected benefits and is intended to (i) help users assess the PSERS' funding status on a going-concern basis, (ii) assess progress being made in accumulating sufficient assets to pay benefits when due and (iii) allow for comparisons among public employee retirement plans. The measure is independent of the actuarial funding method used to determine contributions to the PSERS. The pension benefit obligation was determined as part of an actuarial valuation of the plan as of January 1, 19X8. Significant actuarial assumptions used in determining the pension benefit obligation include: (a) a rate of return on the investment of present and future assets of 7.5 percent per year compounded annually, (b) projected salary increases of 5.5 percent per year compounded annually, attributable to inflation, (c) additional projected salary increases ranging up to 3.0 percent per year, depending on age, attributable to seniority/merit and (d) the assumption that benefits will not increase after retirement.

Pension Benefit Obligation	January 1, 19X8
Retirees and beneficiaries currently receiving benefits	$ 5,367
Terminated employees not yet receiving benefits	413
Current employees:	
Accumulated employee contributions including allocated investment income	2,333
Employer financed—vested	9,118
Employer financed—nonvested	2,467
Total pension benefit obligation	19,698
Net assets available for benefits, at market value	17,183
Unfunded pension benefit obligation	$ 2,515

During the year ended December 31, 19X8, the PSERS experienced a net change of $2,311 in the pension benefit obligation. None of that change was attributable to plan amendments.

Contributions Required and Contributions Made:

40

The government's funding policy is to provide for periodic employer contributions at actuarially determined rates that, expressed as percentages of annual covered payroll, are designed to accumulate sufficient assets to pay benefits when due. The required contributions are determined using an entry age actuarial funding method. Unfunded actuarial accrued liabilities are being amortized as a level percent of payroll over a period of 13 to 30 years.

During the year ended December 31, 19X8, contributions—totaling $1,051 employer and $729 employee—were made in accordance with contribution requirements determined by an actuarial valuation of the PSERS as of January 1, 19X8. The employer contributions consisted of $752 for normal cost and $299 for amortization of the unfunded actuarial accrued liability. Employer contributions represented 18.49 percent of current year covered payroll.

There were no changes in actuarial assumptions during the valuation year ended January 1, 19X8.

Significant actuarial assumptions used to compute contribution requirements were the same as those used to compute the standardized measure of the pension benefit obligation.

Trend Information:

Trend information for the three years ended December 31, 19X6, 19X7 and 19X8, respectively, is as follows: available assets were sufficient to fund 73.7 percent, 82.5 percent and 87.2 percent of the pension benefit obligation. The unfunded pension benefit obligation represented 76.5 percent, 53.6 percent and 30.6 percent of the annual payroll for employees covered by the PSERS for 19X6, 19X7 and 19X8, respectively. Presenting the unfunded pension benefit obligation as a percentage of annual covered payroll approximately adjusts for the effects of inflation for analysis purposes. In addition, for the three years ended December 31, 19X6, 19X7 and 19X8, the government's contributions to the system, all made in accordance with actuarially determined requirements, were 18.89 percent, 18.52 percent and 18.49 percent, respectively, of annual covered payroll.

Statewide Local Government Retirement System (SLGRS)

Plan Description and Provisions:

All of the government's full-time general employees participate in the SLGRS, a multiple-employer, cost-sharing pension plan. The payroll for employees covered by the SLGRS for the year ended December 31, 19X8 was $12,140; the government's total payroll was $17,824.

Group	December 31, 19X8
Retirees and beneficiaries currently receiving benefits	128
Vested terminated employees	5
Active employees:	
Fully vested	145
Nonvested	350

41

Employees attaining the earlier of age 65 or 57 completing 20 or more continuous years of service, are entitled to a monthly benefit of 2 percent of their average monthly earnings as defined in the plan for each year of continuous service. The plan permits early retirement at the age of 52 and the completion of 10 years of continuous service. Active employees who become disabled receive 60 percent of their monthly earnings in effect at the time of disability, reduced by any public disability benefits to which the member is entitled. Disability benefits are paid until the earlier of death, recovery from disability or attainment of normal retirement age. If an active employee dies, his designated beneficiary receives payments, not to exceed 3½ times the member's annual earnings at date of death. The beneficiary receives an initial lump sum followed by monthly payments until the designated amount is paid in full.

If a member's employment is terminated before the member is eligible for any other benefits under SLGRS, the member shall receive a refund of his member contributions of 4 percent plus interest credited at 3 percent per year compounded annually.

Description of Funding Policy:

Covered employees are required by state statute to contribute 4.7 percent of their salary to SLGRS. The government is required by this statute to contribute the remaining amounts necessary to pay benefits when due. The contribution requirement for the year ended December 31, 19X8, was $1,887 which consisted of $1,165 (7.6 percent of covered payroll) from the government and $722 (4.7 percent of covered payroll) from employees.

The amount reported below as ''pension benefit obligation'' is a standardized disclosure measure of the present value of pension benefits, adjusted for the effects of projected salary increases, estimated to be payable in the future as a result of employee service to date. The measure is the actuarial present value of credited projected benefits and is intended to assist users assess the plan's funding status on a going-concern basis, assess progress made in accumulating sufficient assets to pay benefits when due, and make comparisons among government pension plans and employers. The SLGRS does not conduct separate measurements of assets and pension benefit obligations for individual employers. The pension benefit obligation at December 31, 19X8 for the SLGRS as a whole, determined through an actuarial valuation performed as of that date, was $98.7 million. The SLGRS net assets available for benefits on that date (valued at market) were $74.7 million, resulting in an unfunded pension benefit obligation of $14 million. The government's contribution represented 1.3 percent of total contributions required of all participating employers.

Trend Information

Ten-year historical trend information presenting the PSERS' and SLGRS' progress in accumulating sufficient assets to pay benefits when due is presented in the PSERS December 31, 19X8, component unit financial report and the SLGRS' December 31, 19X8, comprehensive annual financial report, respectively.

General Fund

The general fund is used to account for resources traditionally associated with government which are not required legally or by sound financial management to be accounted for in another fund.

Name of Government
General Fund
Comparative Balance Sheets
December 31, 19X8 and 19X7
(amounts expressed in thousands)

Exhibit A–1

	19X8	19X7
Assets		
Cash	$1,369	$ 557
Investments	2,091	1,226
Receivables (net of allowances for uncollectibles):		
Interest	92	48
Taxes:		
Property—delinquent	86	74
Property—delinquent—interest and penalties	11	4
Liens	25	19
Sales	830	800
Accounts	72	59
Intergovernmental:		
Federal	—	150
County	215	127
Due from other funds:		
Transportation fund	—	38
Water and sewer fund	65	193
Fleet management fund	8	—
Interfund receivables:		
Fleet management fund	8	—
Management information systems fund	24	—
Inventories	39	37
Advances to other funds:		
Fleet management fund	32	—
Management information systems fund	46	50
Total assets	$5,013	$3,382
Liabilities and fund balances		
Liabilities:		
Vouchers payable	$ 705	$ 454
Accounts payable	165	420
Compensated absences	225	201
Contracts payable	67	151
Due to other funds:		
Pipeline construction fund	335	—
Water and sewer fund	37	21
Fleet management fund	47	—
Management information systems fund	57	98
Deferred revenue:		
Interest	—	48
Delinquent property taxes	24	75
Interest and penalties—delinquent property taxes	10	3
Tax liens	25	19
Federal government	181	85
Total liabilities	1,878	1,575
Fund balances:		
Reserved for encumbrances	320	211
Reserved for advances	78	50
Unreserved, undesignated	2,737	1,546
Total fund balances	3,135	1,807
Total liabilities and fund balances	$5,013	$3,382

The notes to the financial statements are an integral part of this statement.

44

Exhibit A–2

Name of Government
General Fund
Comparative Statements of Revenues, Expenditures and
Changes in Fund Balances
For the fiscal years ended December 31, 19X8 and 19X7
(amounts expressed in thousands)

	19X8	19X7
Revenues:		
Taxes:		
Property	$14,133	$13,886
Sales	6,642	5,253
Franchise	4,293	4,126
Licenses and permits	2,041	1,820
Intergovernmental	5,770	5,469
Charges for services	2,300	2,335
Fines	808	521
Interest	623	476
Miscellaneous	345	314
Total revenues	36,955	34,200
Expenditures:		
Current:		
General government	4,244	3,821
Public safety	13,438	12,150
Highways and streets	3,735	3,389
Sanitation	3,726	3,404
Culture and recreation	5,882	5,367
Debt service:		
Principal	15	—
Bond issuance costs	150	—
Total expenditures	31,190	28,131
Excess of revenues over expenditures	5,765	6,069
Other financing sources (uses):		
Operating transfers out:		
Debt service fund	(3,327)	(3,331)
Pipeline construction fund	(1,210)	—
Five-year capital improvement fund	—	(2,823)
Sales of general fixed assets	5	—
Capital leases	140	—
Total other financing sources (uses)	(4,392)	(6,154)
Excess (deficiency) of revenues and other financing sources over (under) expenditures and other financing uses	1,373	(85)
Fund balances, January 1	1,807	1,892
Residual equity transfers out—fleet management fund	(45)	—
Fund balances, December 31	$ 3,135	$ 1,807

The notes to the financial statements are an integral part of this statement.

45

Name of Government
General Fund
Comparative Statements of Revenues, Expenditures and
Changes in Fund Balances—Budget and Actual
For the fiscal years ended December 31, 19X8 and 19X7
(amounts expressed in thousands)

Exhibit A–3

	19X8			19X7		
	Budget	Actual	Variance Favorable (Unfavorable)	Budget	Actual	Variance Favorable (Unfavorable)
Revenues:						
Taxes:						
Property	$14,487	$14,133	$ (354)	$13,844	$13,886	$ 42
Sales	6,767	6,642	(125)	5,198	5,253	55
Franchise	4,312	4,293	(19)	4,124	4,126	2
Licenses and permits	1,827	2,041	214	1,503	1,820	317
Intergovernmental	5,661	5,770	109	5,395	5,469	74
Charges for services	2,158	2,300	142	2,095	2,335	240
Fines	810	808	(2)	487	521	34
Interest	555	623	68	520	476	(44)
Miscellaneous	345	345	0	314	314	0
Total revenues	36,922	36,955	33	33,480	34,200	720
Expenditures:						
Current:						
General government:						
Council	98	92	6	94	90	4
Commissions	70	64	6	71	63	8
Manager	521	505	16	426	414	12
Attorney	391	387	4	216	206	10
Clerk	264	250	14	247	237	10
Personnel	325	304	21	274	249	25
Finance and administration	904	880	24	846	830	16
Other—unclassified	2,055	1,762	293	1,884	1,732	152
Total general government	4,628	4,244	384	4,058	3,821	237
Public safety:						
Police	6,513	6,369	144	6,026	5,801	225
Fire	6,040	6,031	9	5,521	5,415	106
Inspection	1,092	1,053	39	970	934	36
Total public safety	13,645	13,453	192	12,517	12,150	367
Highways and streets:						
Engineering	814	796	18	777	762	15
Maintenance	3,052	2,939	113	2,681	2,627	54
Total highways and streets	3,866	3,735	131	3,458	3,389	69
Sanitation	3,848	3,726	122	3,426	3,404	22
Culture and recreation	5,950	5,882	68	5,477	5,367	110
Debt service:						
Bond issuance costs	150	150	0	—	—	—
Total expenditures	32,087	31,190	897	28,936	28,131	805
Excess of revenues over expenditures	4,835	5,765	930	4,544	6,069	1,525
Other financing sources (uses):						
Operating transfers out:						
Debt service fund	(3,400)	(3,327)	73	(3,350)	(3,331)	19
Pipeline construction fund	(1,300)	(1,210)	90	—	—	—
Five-year capital improvement fund	—	—	—	(2,850)	(2,823)	27
Sales of general fixed assets	—	5	5	—	—	—
Capital leases	34	140	106	—	—	—
Total other financing sources (uses)	(4,666)	(4,392)	274	(6,200)	(6,154)	46
Excess (deficiency) of revenues and other financing sources over (under) expenditures and other financing uses	169	1,373	1,204	(1,656)	(85)	1,571
Fund balances, January 1	1,807	1,807	0	1,892	1,892	0
Residual equity transfers out—fleet management fund	(60)	(45)	15	—	—	—
Fund balances, December 31	$ 1,916	$ 3,135	$1,219	$ 236	$ 1,807	$1,571

The notes to the financial statements are an integral part of this statement.

Special Revenue Funds

Special revenue funds are used to account for specific revenues that are legally restricted to expenditure for particular purposes.

Transportation Fund—This fund is used to account for the government's share of motor fuel tax revenues and special state grants that are legally restricted to the maintenance of state highways within the government's boundaries.

Parks Maintenance Fund—This fund is used to account for private donations and alcoholic beverage tax revenues (approved by voters in 19X7) that are specifically restricted to the maintenance of the government's parks.

Name of Government
Special Revenue Funds
Combining Balance Sheet
December 31, 19X8
(With comparative totals for December 31, 19X7)
(amounts expressed in thousands)

	Transportation	Parks Maintenance	Totals 19X8	Totals 19X7
Assets				
Cash	$ 65	$146	$ 211	$ 188
Investments	1,174	403	1,577	1,144
Interest receivable	1	1	2	12
Total assets	$1,240	$550	$1,790	$1,344
Liabilities and fund balances				
Liabilities:				
Vouchers payable	$ 332	$ 8	$ 340	$ 68
Accounts payable	—	76	76	14
Due to other funds—general fund	—	—	—	38
Total liabilities	332	84	416	120
Fund balances:				
Reserved for encumbrances	353	8	361	154
Unreserved, undesignated	555	458	1,013	1,070
Total fund balances	908	466	1,374	1,224
Total liabilities and fund balances	$1,240	$550	$1,790	$1,344

The notes to the financial statements are an integral part of this statement.

48

Exhibit B–2

Name of Government
Special Revenue Funds
Combining Statement of Revenues, Expenditures and
Changes in Fund Balances
For the fiscal year ended December 31, 19X8
(With comparative totals for the fiscal year ended
December 31, 19X7)
(amounts expressed in thousands)

	Transportation	Parks Maintenance	Totals 19X8	Totals 19X7
Revenues:				
Motor fuel tax	$729	—	$ 729	$ 355
Alcoholic beverage tax	—	$ 799	799	651
Intergovernmental	100	—	100	—
Interest	77	39	116	70
Donations	—	149	149	239
Total revenues	906	987	1,893	1,315
Expenditures:				
Current:				
Highways and streets	742	—	742	—
Culture and recreation	—	1,001	1,001	605
Total expenditures	742	1,001	1,743	605
Excess (deficiency) of revenues over (under) expenditures	164	(14)	150	710
Fund balances, January 1	744	480	1,224	514
Fund balances, December 31	$908	$ 466	$1,374	$1,224

The notes to the financial statements are an integral part of this statement.

Exhibit B–3

Name of Government
Transportation Special Revenue Fund
Comparative Balance Sheets
December 31, 19X8 and 19X7
(amounts expressed in thousands)

	19X8	19X7
Assets		
Cash	$ 65	$ 70
Investments	1,174	706
Interest receivable	1	6
Total assets	$1,240	$782
Liabilities and fund balances		
Liabilities:		
Vouchers payable	$ 332	—
Due to other funds—general fund	—	38
Total liabilities	332	38
Fund balances:		
Reserved for encumbrances	353	—
Unreserved, undesignated	555	$744
Total fund balances	908	744
Total liabilities and fund balances	$1,240	$782

The notes to the financial statements are an integral part of this statement.

Exhibit B–4

Name of Government
Transportation Special Revenue Fund
Comparative Statements of Revenues, Expenditures and
Changes in Fund Balances
For the fiscal years ended December 31, 19X8 and 19X7
(amounts expressed in thousands)

	19X8	19X7
Revenues:		
Motor fuel tax	$729	$355
Intergovernmental	100	—
Interest	77	44
Total revenues	906	399
Expenditures:		
Current:		
Highways and streets	742	—
Excess of revenues over expenditures	164	399
Fund balances, January 1	744	345
Fund balances, December 31	$908	$744

The notes to the financial statements are an integral part of this statement.

Exhibit B–5

Name of Government
Transportation Special Revenue Fund
Comparative Statements of Revenues, Expenditures and
Changes in Fund Balances—Budget and Actual
Fiscal years ended December 31, 19X8 and 19X7
(amounts expressed in thousands)

	19X8			19X7		
	Budget	Actual	Variance Favorable (Unfavorable)	Budget	Actual	Variance Favorable (Unfavorable)
Revenues:						
Motor fuel tax	$ 625	$729	$104	$312	$355	$ 43
Intergovernmental	100	100	0	100	—	(100)
Interest	42	77	35	37	44	7
Total revenues	767	906	139	449	399	(50)
Expenditures:						
Current:						
Highways and streets—maintenance	1,437	742	695	670	—	670
Excess (deficiency) of revenues over (under) expenditures	(670)	164	834	(221)	399	620
Fund balances, January 1	744	744	0	345	345	0
Fund balances, December 31	74	$908	$834	$124	$744	$620

The notes to the financial statements are an integral part of this statement.

Name of Government
Parks Maintenance Special Revenue Fund
Comparative Balance Sheets
December 31, 19X8 and 19X7
(amounts expressed in thousands)

	19X8	19X7
Assets		
Cash	$146	$118
Investments	403	438
Interest receivable	1	6
Total assets	$550	$562
Liabilities and fund balances		
Liabilities:		
Vouchers payable	$ 8	$ 68
Accounts payable	76	14
Total liabilities	84	82
Fund balances:		
Reserved for encumbrances	8	154
Unreserved, undesignated	458	326
Total fund balances	466	480
Total liabilities and fund balances	$550	$562

The notes to the financial statements are an integral part of this statement.

Exhibit B–7

Name of Government
Parks Maintenance Special Revenue Fund
Comparative Statements of Revenues, Expenditures and
Changes in Fund Balances
For the fiscal years ended December 31, 19X8 and 19X7
(amounts expressed in thousands)

	19X8	19X7
Revenues:		
Alcoholic beverage tax	$ 799	$651
Interest	39	26
Donations	149	239
Total revenues	987	916
Expenditures:		
Current:		
Culture and recreation	1,001	605
Excess (deficiency) of revenues over (under) expenditures	(14)	311
Fund balances, January 1	480	169
Fund balances, December 31	$ 466	$480

The notes to the financial statements are an integral part of this statement.

Name of Government
Parks Maintenance Special Revenue Fund
Comparative Statements of Revenues, Expenditures and
Changes in Fund Balances—Budget and Actual
Fiscal years ended December 31, 19X8 and 19X7
(amounts expressed in thousands)

	19X8			19X7		
	Budget	Actual	Variance Favorable (Unfavorable)	Budget	Actual	Variance Favorable (Unfavorable)
Revenues:						
Alcoholic beverage tax	$ 682	$ 799	$117	$575	$651	$ 76
Interest	31	39	8	39	26	(13)
Donations	23	149	126	—	239	239
Total revenues	736	987	251	614	916	302
Expenditures:						
Current:						
Culture and recreation	1,095	1,001	94	759	605	154
Excess (deficiency) of revenues over (under) expenditures	(359)	(14)	345	(145)	311	456
Fund balances, January 1	480	480	0	169	169	0
Fund balances, December 31	$ 121	$ 466	$345	$224	$480	$456

The notes to the financial statements are an integral part of this statement.

Debt Service Fund

The debt service fund is used to account for the accumulation of resources and payment of general obligation bond principal and interest from governmental resources and special assessment bond principal and interest from special assessment levies when the government is obligated in some manner for the payment.

Exhibit C–1

Name of Government
Debt Service Fund
Comparative Balance Sheets
December 31, 19X8 and 19X7
(amounts expressed in thousands)

	19X8	19X7
Assets		
Cash	$ 2	$ 2
Cash with fiscal agent	8	—
Investments	1,513	8
Interest receivable	30	—
Taxes receivable—delinquent	10	—
Special assessments receivable	4,230	—
Total assets	$5,793	$10
Liabilities and fund balances		
Liabilities:		
Matured bonds payable	$ 5	—
Matured interest payable	3	—
Deferred revenue:		
Property taxes—delinquent	10	—
Special assessments	4,230	—
Total liabilities	4,248	—
Fund balances:		
Reserved for debt service	1,545	$10
Total liabilities and fund balances	$5,793	$10

The notes to the financial statements are an integral part of this statement.

Exhibit C–2

Name of Government
Debt Service Fund
Comparative Statements of Revenues, Expenditures and
Changes in Fund Balances
For the fiscal years ended December 31, 19X8 and 19X7
(amounts expressed in thousands)

	19X8	19X7
Revenues:		
Property taxes	$1,585	—
Special assessments	470	—
Interest	280	—
Total revenues	2,335	—
Expenditures:		
Debt service:		
Principal	2,030	$1,470
Interest	2,928	1,865
Refunding bond issuance costs	65	—
Advance refunding escrow	15	—
Total expenditures	5,038	3,335
Deficiency of revenues under expenditures	(2,703)	(3,335)
Other financing sources (uses):		
Operating transfers in:		
General fund	3,327	3,331
Pipeline construction fund	846	—
Proceeds of refunding bonds	3,365	—
Payment to refunded bond escrow agent	(3,300)	—
Total other financing sources (uses)	4,238	3,331
Excess (deficiency) of revenues and other financing sources over (under) expenditures and other financing uses	1,535	(4)
Fund balances, January 1	10	14
Fund balances, December 31	$1,545	$ 10

The notes to the financial statements are an integral part of this statement.

59

Exhibit C–3

Name of Government
Debt Service Fund
Comparative Statements of Revenues, Expenditures and
Changes in Fund Balances—Budget and Actual
For fiscal years ended December 31, 19X8 and 19X7
(amounts expressed in thousands)

	19X8			19X7		
	Budget	Actual	Variance Favorable (Unfavorable)	Budget	Actual	Variance Favorable (Unfavorable)
Revenues:						
Property taxes	$1,500	$1,585	$ 85	—	—	—
Special assessments	470	470	0	—	—	—
Interest	220	280	60	—	—	—
Total revenues	2,190	2,335	145	—	—	—
Expenditures:						
Debt service:						
Principal	2,054	2,030	24	$1,500	$1,470	$ 30
Interest	2,941	2,928	13	2,000	1,865	135
Advance refunding escrow	15	15	0	—	—	—
Refunding bond issuance costs	65	65	0	—	—	—
Total expenditures	5,075	5,038	37	3,500	3,335	165
Deficiency of revenues under expenditures	(2,885)	(2,703)	182	(3,500)	(3,335)	165
Other financing sources (uses):						
Operating transfers in	3,500	4,173	673	3,500	3,331	(169)
Proceeds of refunding bonds	3,365	3,365	0	—	—	—
Payment to refunded bond escrow agent	(3,300)	(3,300)	0	—	—	—
Total other financing sources (uses)	3,565	4,238	673	3,500	3,331	(169)
Excess (deficiency) of revenues and other financing sources over (under) expenditures and other financing uses	680	1,535	855	—	(4)	(4)
Fund balances, January 1	10	10	0	14	14	0
Fund balances, December 31	$ 690	$1,545	$855	$ 14	$ 10	$ (4)

The notes to the financial statements are an integral part of this statement.

Capital Projects Funds

Capital projects funds are used to account for the acquisition and construction of major capital facilities other than those financed by proprietary funds and trust funds.

Pipeline Construction Fund—This fund is used to account for the construction of sewer line extensions. Special assessments, governmental resources and state grant revenues are used to finance this two-year expansion project for the Water and Sewer Authority.

Five-Year Capital Improvement Fund—This fund is used to account for capital asset (including intrastructure) acquisition and construction from general government resources and intergovernmental grants, as outlined in the government's five-year capital budget.

Name of Government
Capital Projects Funds
Combining Balance Sheet
December 31, 19X8
(With comparative totals for December 31, 19X7)
(amounts expressed in thousands)

	Pipeline Construction	Five-Year Capital Improvement	Totals 19X8	19X7
Assets				
Cash	$ 323	$ 229	$ 552	$ 118
Investments	1,835	9,216	11,051	10,331
Interest receivable	64	347	411	465
Intergovernmental receivable	—	199	199	145
Due from other funds—general fund	335	—	335	—
Total assets	$2,557	$9,991	$12,548	$11,059
Liabilities and fund balances				
Liabilities:				
Accounts payable	$ 251	$ 251	$ 502	$ 183
Retainage payable	149	133	282	11
Total liabilities	400	384	784	194
Fund balances:				
Reserved for encumbrances	1,944	4,619	6,563	475
Unreserved, undesignated	213	4,988	5,201	10,390
Total fund balances	2,157	9,607	11,764	10,865
Total liabilities and fund balances	$2,557	$9,991	$12,548	$11,059

The notes to the financial statements are an integral part of this statement.

Exhibit D–2

Name of Government
Capital Projects Funds
Combining Statement of Revenues, Expenditures and
Changes in Fund Balances
For the fiscal year ended December 31, 19X8
(With comparative totals for the fiscal year ended
December 31, 19X7)
(amounts expressed in thousands)

	Pipeline Construction	Five-Year Capital Improvement	Totals 19X8	19X7
Revenues:				
Intergovernmental	$ 124	$ 338	$ 462	$ 205
Interest	209	635	844	259
Total revenues	333	973	1,306	464
Expenditures:				
Capital outlay:				
Public safety	—	1,687	1,687	1,454
Public works	1,005	253	1,258	548
Culture and recreation	—	291	291	499
Special assessments	2,225	—	2,225	—
Total expenditures	3,230	2,231	5,461	2,501
Deficiency of revenues under expenditures	(2,897)	(1,258)	(4,155)	(2,037)
Other financing sources (uses):				
Operating transfers in—general fund	1,210	—	1,210	2,823
Operating transfers out—debt service fund	(846)	—	(846)	—
General obligation bond proceeds	—	—	—	7,500
Special assessment bond proceeds	4,690	—	4,690	—
Total other financing sources (uses)	5,054	—	5,054	10,323
Excess (deficiency) of revenues and other financing sources over (under) expenditures and other financing uses	2,157	(1,258)	899	8,286
Fund balances, January 1	—	10,865	10,865	2,579
Fund balances, December 31	$2,157	$9,607	$11,764	$10,865

The notes to the financial statements are an integral part of this statement.

Exhibit D–3

Name of Government
Five-Year Capital Improvement Capital Projects Fund
Comparative Balance Sheets
December 31, 19X8 and 19X7
(amounts expressed in thousands)

	19X8	19X7
Assets		
Cash	$ 229	$ 118
Investments	9,216	10,331
Interest receivable	347	465
Intergovernmental receivable	199	145
Total assets	$9,991	$11,059
Liabilities and fund balances		
Liabilities:		
Accounts payable	$ 251	$ 183
Retainage payable	133	11
Total liabilities	384	194
Fund balances:		
Reserved for encumbrances	4,619	475
Unreserved, undesignated	4,988	10,390
Total fund balances	9,607	10,865
Total liabilities and fund balances	$9,991	$11,059

The notes to the financial statements are an integral part of this statement.

Name of Government
Five-Year Capital Improvement Capital Projects Fund
Comparative Statements of Revenues, Expenditures and
Changes in Fund Balances
For the fiscal years ended December 31, 19X8 and 19X7
(amounts expressed in thousands)

	19X8	19X7
Revenues:		
Intergovernmental	$ 338	$ 205
Interest	635	259
Total revenues	973	464
Expenditures:		
Capital outlay:		
Public safety	1,687	1,454
Public works	253	548
Culture and recreation	291	499
Total expenditures	2,231	2,501
Deficiency of revenues under expenditures	(1,258)	(2,037)
Other financing sources:		
Operating transfers in—general fund	—	2,823
General obligation bond proceeds	—	7,500
Total other financing sources	—	10,323
Excess (deficiency) of revenues and other financing sources over (under) expenditures	(1,258)	8,286
Fund balances, January 1	10,865	2,579
Fund balances, December 31	$9,607	$10,865

The notes to the financial statements are an integral part of this statement.

Enterprise Funds

Enterprise funds are used to account for operations that are financed and operated in a manner similar to private business enterprises—where the intent of the government's council is that the costs of providing goods or services to the general public on a continuing basis be financed or recovered primarily through user charges; or where the government's council has decided that periodic determination of net income is appropriate for accountability purposes.

Water and Sewer Authority Fund—This fund is used to account for the activities of the Water and Sewer Authority (a component unit of the Name of Government).

Golf Course Fund—This fund is used to account for the operations of the government's public golf course.

Exhibit E–1

Name of Government
Enterprise Funds
Combining Balance Sheet
December 31, 19X8
(With comparative totals for December 31, 19X7)
(amounts expressed in thousands)

	Water and Sewer Authority	Golf Course	Totals 19X8	Totals 19X7
Assets				
Current assets:				
Cash	$ 1,016	$ 25	$ 1,041	$ 936
Cash with fiscal agent	123	—	123	—
Investments	14,610	913	15,523	8,198
Interest receivable	409	11	420	326
Accounts receivable (net of allowance for uncollectibles)	2,621	1	2,622	2,327
Due from other funds:				
General fund	37	—	37	21
Golf course fund	—	—	—	18
Fleet management fund	2	—	2	—
Inventories	308	—	308	461
Total current assets	19,126	950	20,076	12,287
Restricted assets:				
Customer deposits	1,543	—	1,543	1,199
Revenue bond operations and maintenance account	1,294	—	1,294	1,023
Revenue bond construction account	18,542	—	18,542	—
Revenue bond current debt service account	3,706	—	3,706	1,380
Revenue bond future debt service account	737	—	737	523
Revenue bond renewal and replacement account	1,632	—	1,632	1,165
Total restricted assets	27,454	—	27,454	5,290
Deferred charges	546	105	651	581
Fixed assets:				
Land	604	469	1,073	1,073
Buildings	20,928	584	21,512	13,679
Accumulated depreciation—buildings	(2,476)	(46)	(2,522)	(1,998)
Improvements other than buildings	1,250	2,390	3,640	3,596
Accumulated depreciation—improvements other than buildings	(342)	(194)	(536)	(328)
Machinery and equipment	104,283	226	104,509	104,045
Accumulated depreciation—machinery and equipment	(14,723)	(18)	(14,741)	(12,986)
Construction in progress	7,118	—	7,118	—
Fixed assets (net of accumulated depreciation)	116,642	3,411	120,053	107,081
Total assets	$163,768	$4,466	$168,234	$125,239

cont.

Exhibit E–1, cont.

	Water and Sewer Authority	Golf Course	Totals 19X8	Totals 19X7
Liabilities and fund equity				
Current liabilities:				
Vouchers payable	$ 907	$ 26	$ 933	$ 856
Accounts payable	330	6	336	260
Compensated absences payable	374	16	390	384
Retainage payable	536	—	536	—
Due to other funds:				
General fund	65	—	65	193
Water and sewer fund	—	—	—	18
Fleet management fund	17	—	17	—
Management information systems fund	5	—	5	14
Intergovernmental payable	—	—	—	11
Matured bonds payable	68	—	68	—
Matured interest payable	55	—	55	—
Accrued interest payable	1,045	156	1,201	1,261
General obligation bonds payable—current	1,480	161	1,641	1,523
Capital leases payable—current	23	—	23	—
Total current liabilities	4,905	365	5,270	4,520
Current liabilities payable from restricted assets:				
Customer deposits payable	1,543	—	1,543	1,199
Revenue bonds payable	1,484	—	1,484	530
Accrued interest payable	1,331	—	1,331	448
Total current liabilities payable from restricted assets	4,358	—	4,358	2,177
Noncurrent liabilities:				
General obligation bonds payable (net of unamortized discounts)	29,378	3,556	32,934	27,545
Revenue bonds payable (net of unamortized discounts)	32,828	—	32,828	8,580
Capital leases payable	78	—	78	—
Total noncurrent liabilities	62,284	3,556	65,840	36,125
Total liabilities	71,547	3,921	75,468	42,822
Fund equity:				
Contributed capital:				
Government	4,033	471	4,504	1,274
Customers	14,062	—	14,062	13,854
Developers	35,241	—	35,241	31,155
Intergovernmental	5,588	—	5,588	5,588
Total contributed capital	58,924	471	59,395	51,871
Retained earnings:				
Reserved for revenue bond operations and maintenance	1,294	—	1,294	1,023
Reserved for revenue bond current debt service	891	—	891	402
Reserved for renewal and replacement	1,632	—	1,632	1,165
Unreserved	29,480	74	29,554	27,956
Total retained earnings	33,297	74	33,371	30,546
Total fund equity	92,221	545	92,766	82,417
Total liabilities and fund equity	$163,768	$4,466	$168,234	$125,239

The notes to the financial statements are an integral part of this statement.

Exhibit E–2

Name of Government
Enterprise Funds
Combining Statement of Revenues, Expenses and Changes in Retained Earnings
For the fiscal year ended December 31, 19X8
(With comparative totals for the fiscal year ended December 31, 19X7)
(amounts expressed in thousands)

	Water and Sewer Authority	Golf Course	Totals	
			19X8	19X7
Operating revenues:				
Charges for sales and services:				
Water sales	$ 9,227	—	$ 9,227	$ 7,588
Sewer charges	5,671	—	5,671	4,344
Tap fees	1,521	—	1,521	1,155
Golf course fees and charges	—	$1,257	1,257	1,190
Total operating revenues	16,419	1,257	17,676	14,277
Operating expenses:				
Costs of sales and services	6,997	800	7,797	6,642
Administration	3,137	11	3,148	2,831
Depreciation	2,436	71	2,507	2,332
Total operating expenses	12,570	882	13,452	11,805
Operating income	3,849	375	4,224	2,472
Nonoperating revenues (expenses):				
Interest revenue	1,753	70	1,823	1,943
Interest expense	(3,421)	(313)	(3,734)	(3,098)
Bond issuance costs	(25)	—	(25)	(10)
Loss on sale of fixed assets	(10)	—	(10)	—
Total nonoperating revenues (expenses)	(1,703)	(243)	(1,946)	(1,165)
Net income before extraordinary items	2,146	132	2,278	1,307
Extraordinary gain (loss) on advance refundings	547	—	547	(76)
Net income	2,693	132	2,825	1,231
Retained earnings, January 1	30,604	(58)	30,546	29,315
Retained earnings, December 31	$33,297	$ 74	$33,371	$30,546

The notes to the financial statements are an integral part of this statement.

70

Exhibit E–3

Name of Government
Enterprise Funds
Combining Statement of Changes in Financial Position
For fiscal year ended December 31, 19X8
(With comparative totals for the fiscal year ended December 31, 19X7)
(amounts expressed in thousands)

	Water and Sewer Authority	Golf Course	Totals 19X8	Totals 19X7
Cash flows from operating activities:				
Cash received from customers	$16,210	$1,257	$17,467	$14,347
Cash paid to suppliers and employees	(10,132)	(818)	(10,950)	(9,399)
Interest received	738	69	807	1,815
Interest paid	(2,947)	(311)	(3,258)	(3,217)
Net cash provided by operating activities	3,869	197	4,066	3,546
Cash flows from investing activities:				
Proceeds from sales of investments	1,568	362	1,930	710
Purchase of investments	(23,860)	(399)	(24,259)	(7,940)
Proceeds from sales of fixed assets	5	—	5	—
Purchase of fixed assets	—	(55)	(55)	(237)
Capital lease obligation down payment	(6)	—	(6)	—
Earnings on invested proceeds	550	—	550	—
Construction (including capitalized interest costs)	(10,759)	—	(10,759)	—
Net cash used in investment activities	(32,502)	(92)	(32,594)	(7,467)
Cash flows from financing activities:				
Proceeds from general obligation bonds	7,005	—	7,005	—
Proceeds from revenue bonds	34,150	—	34,150	—
Proceeds from refunding bonds	—	—	—	3,617
Principal payments—bonds	(9,752)	(193)	(9,945)	(4,885)
Principal payments—capital leases	(12)	—	(12)	—
Capital contributions	4,294	—	4,294	6,744
Net cash provided by financing activities	35,685	(193)	35,492	5,476
Noncash transactions affecting financial position:				
Borrowing under capital lease obligations	101	—	101	—
Acquisition of fixed assets through capital leases	(101)	—	(101)	—
Contributions of fixed assets from government	3,230	—	3,230	—
Acquisition of fixed assets through government capital contributions	(3,230)	—	(3,230)	—
Borrowing from suppliers on account	374	—	374	—
Acquisition of fixed assets on account	(374)	—	(374)	—
Net effect of noncash transactions	0	—	0	—
Net increase (decrease) in cash	7,052	(88)	6,964	1,555
Cash, January 1	2,698	113	2,811	1,256
Cash, December 31	$ 9,750	$ 25	$ 9,775	$ 2,811

71

cont.

Exhibit E–3, cont.

Reconciliation of Net Income to Net Cash Provided by
Operating Activities

	Water and Sewer Authority	Golf Course	Totals 19X8	Totals 19X7
Net income	$2,693	$132	$2,825	$1,231
Adjustments to reconcile net income to net cash from operating activities:				
Extraordinary (gain) loss	(547)	—	(547)	76
Loss on sales of fixed assets	10	—	10	—
Depreciation expense	2,436	71	2,507	2,332
Amortization of bond discounts	25	—	25	—
Amortization of bond issuance costs	12	7	19	17
(Increase) in interest receivable	(93)	(1)	(94)	(16)
(Increase) in accounts receivable	(508)	—	(508)	(59)
Increase in allowance for uncollectible accounts	213	—	213	110
(Increase) in due from other funds	—	—	—	(11)
(Increase) decrease in inventories	153	—	153	(47)
Net increase in customer deposits	292	—	292	109
(Increase) in interest receivable—restricted assets	(372)	—	(372)	(112)
Increase in vouchers payable	56	21	77	6
Increase (decrease) in accounts payable	77	(1)	76	(9)
Increase (decrease) in compensated absences	15	(9)	6	6
Increase (decrease) in intergovernmental payables	(11)	—	(11)	4
Increase (decrease) in due to other funds	(120)	(18)	(138)	23
Increase in matured interest payable	55	—	55	—
Increase (decrease) in accrued interest payable	(55)	(5)	(60)	6
Increase (decrease) in accrued interest payable from restricted accounts	883	—	883	(120)
(Increase) in accounts payable related to equipment purchase	(374)	—	(374)	—
Interest capitalization	(978)	—	(978)	—
Net cash flow related to interest capitalization (reported as investing activity)	7	—	7	—
Total adjustments	1,176	65	1,241	2,315
Net cash provided by operating activities	$3,869	$197	$4,066	$3,546

The notes to the financial statements are an integral part of this statement.

Exhibit E–4

Name of Government
Comparative Balance Sheets
Water and Sewer Authority Enterprise Fund
December 31, 19X8 and 19X7
(amounts expressed in thousands)

	19X8	19X7
Assets		
Current assets:		
Cash	$ 1,016	$ 823
Cash with fiscal agent	123	—
Investments	14,610	7,322
Interest receivable	409	316
Accounts receivable (net of allowance for uncollectibles)	2,621	2,326
Due from other funds:		
General fund	37	21
Golf course fund	—	18
Fleet management fund	2	—
Inventories	308	461
Total current assets	19,126	11,287
Restricted assets:		
Customer deposits	1,543	1,199
Revenue bond operations and maintenance account	1,294	1,023
Revenue bond construction account	18,542	—
Revenue bond current debt service account	3,706	1,380
Revenue bond future debt service account	737	523
Revenue bond renewal and replacement account	1,632	1,165
Total restricted assets	27,454	5,290
Deferred charge	546	469
Fixed assets:		
Land	604	604
Buildings	20,928	13,100
Accumulated depreciation—buildings	(2,476)	(1,964)
Improvements other than buildings	1,250	1,250
Accumulated depreciation—improvements other than buildings	(342)	(188)
Machinery and equipment	104,283	103,825
Accumulated depreciation—machinery and equipment	(14,723)	(12,973)
Construction in progress	7,118	—
Fixed assets (net of accumulated depreciation)	116,642	103,654
Total assets	$163,768	$120,700

cont.

Exhibit E–4, cont.

	19X8	19X7
Liabilities and equity		
Current liabilities:		
Vouchers payable	$ 907	$ 851
Accounts payable	330	253
Compensated absences payable	374	359
Retainage payable	536	—
Due to other funds:		
General fund	65	193
Fleet management fund	17	—
Management information systems fund	5	14
Intergovernmental payable	—	11
Matured bonds payable	68	—
Matured interest payable	55	—
Accrued interest payable	1,045	1,100
General obligation bonds payable—current	1,480	1,360
Capital leases payable—current	23	—
Total current liabilities	4,905	4,141
Current liabilities payable from restricted assets:		
Customer deposits payable	1,543	1,199
Revenue bonds payable	1,484	530
Accrued interest payable	1,331	448
Total current liabilities payable from restricted assets	4,358	2,177
Noncurrent liabilities:		
General obligation bonds payable (net of unamortized discounts)	29,378	23,798
Revenue bonds payable (net of unamortized discounts)	32,828	8,580
Capital leases payable	78	—
Total noncurrent liabilities	62,284	32,378
Total liabilities	71,547	38,696
Equity:		
Contributed capital:		
Government	4,033	803
Customers	14,062	13,854
Developers	35,241	31,155
Intergovernmental	5,588	5,588
Total contributed capital	58,924	51,400
Retained earnings:		
Reserved for revenue bond operations and maintenance	1,294	1,023
Reserved for revenue bond current debt service	891	402
Reserved for revenue bond renewal and replacement	1,632	1,165
Unreserved	29,480	28,014
Total retained earnings	33,297	30,604
Total equity	92,221	82,004
Total liabilities and equity	$163,768	$120,700

The notes to the financial statements are an integral part of this statement.

Name of Government
Water and Sewer Authority Enterprise Fund
Comparative Statements of Revenues, Expenses and Changes
in Retained Earnings
For the fiscal years ended December 31, 19X8 and 19X7
(amounts expressed in thousands)

	19X8	19X7
Operating revenues:		
Charges for sales and services:		
Water sales	$ 9,227	$ 7,588
Sewer charges	5,671	4,344
Tap fees	1,521	1,155
Total operating revenues	16,419	13,087
Operating expenses:		
Costs of sales and services	6,997	5,886
Administration	3,137	2,824
Depreciation	2,436	2,290
Total operating expenses	12,570	11,000
Operating income	3,849	2,087
Nonoperating revenues (expenses):		
Interest revenue	1,753	1,884
Interest expense	(3,421)	(2,765)
Bond issuance costs	(25)	(10)
Loss on sales of fixed assets	(10)	—
Total nonoperating revenues (expenses)	(1,703)	(891)
Net income before extraordinary item	2,146	1,196
Extraordinary gain on advance refunding	547	—
Net income	2,693	1,196
Retained earnings, January 1	30,604	29,408
Retained earnings, December 31	$33,297	$30,604

The notes to the financial statements are an integral part of this statement.

Exhibit E–6

Name of Government
Water and Sewer Authority Enterprise Fund
Comparative Statements of Changes in Financial Position
For the fiscal years ended December 31, 19X8 and 19X7
(amounts expressed in thousands)

	19X8	19X7
Cash flows from operating activities:		
Cash received from customers	$16,210	$13,157
Cash paid to suppliers and employees	(10,132)	(8,661)
Interest received	738	1,758
Interest paid	(2,947)	(2,887)
Net cash provided by operating activities	3,869	3,367
Cash flows from investing activities:		
Proceeds from sales of investments	1,568	710
Purchase of investments	(23,860)	(7,435)
Proceeds from sales of fixed assets	5	—
Capital lease obligation down payment	(6)	—
Earnings on invested proceeds	550	—
Construction (including capitalized interest costs)	(10,759)	—
Net cash used in investment activities	(32,502)	(6,725)
Cash flows from financing activities:		
Proceeds from general obligation bonds	7,005	—
Proceeds from revenue bonds	34,150	—
Principal payments—bonds	(9,752)	(1,885)
Principal payments—capital leases	(12)	—
Capital contributions	4,294	6,744
Net cash provided by financing activities	35,685	4,859
Noncash transactions affecting financial position:		
Borrowing under capital lease obligations	101	—
Acquisition of fixed assets through capital leases	(101)	—
Contributions of fixed assets from government	3,230	—
Acquisition of fixed assets through government capital contributions	(3,230)	—
Borrowing from suppliers on account	374	—
Acquisition of fixed assets on account	(374)	—
Net effect of noncash transactions	0	—
Net increase in cash	7,052	1,501
Cash, January 1 (including $1,875 and $574 in restricted accounts in 19X8 and 19X7)	2,698	1,197
Cash, December 31 (including $8,611 and $1,875 in restricted accounts in 19X8 and 19X7)	$ 9,750	$ 2,698

cont.

Reconciliation of Net Income to Net
Cash Provided by Operating Activities

	19X8	19X7
Net income	$2,693	$1,196
Adjustments to reconcile net income to net cash provided by operating activities:		
Extraordinary gain	(547)	—
Loss on sales of fixed assets	10	—
Depreciation expense	2,436	2,290
Amortization of bond discount	25	—
Amortization of bond issuance costs	12	10
(Increase) in interest receivable	(93)	(14)
(Increase) in accounts receivable	(508)	(59)
Increase in allowance for uncollectible accounts	213	110
(Increase) decrease in due from general fund	(16)	7
(Increase) decrease in due from golf course fund	18	(18)
(Increase) in due from fleet management fund	(2)	—
(Increase) decrease in inventories	153	(47)
Net increase in customer deposits	292	109
(Increase) in interest receivable—restricted assets	(372)	(112)
Increase in vouchers payable	56	10
Increase (decrease) in accounts payable	77	(11)
Increase (decrease) in compensated absences	15	(3)
Increase (decrease) in intergovernmental payables	(11)	4
Increase (decrease) in due to general fund	(128)	5
Increase in due to fleet management fund	17	—
(Decrease) in due to management information systems fund	(9)	—
Increase in matured interest payable	55	—
Increase (decrease) in accrued interest payable	(55)	10
Increase (decrease) in accrued interest payable from restricted accounts	883	(120)
(Increase) in accounts payable related to equipment purchase	(374)	—
Interest capitalization	(978)	—
Net cash flow related to interest capitalization (reported as investing activity)	7	—
Total adjustments	1,176	2,171
Net cash provided by operating activities	$3,869	$3,367

The notes to the financial statements are an integral part of this statement.

77

Exhibit E–7

Name of Government
Golf Course Enterprise Fund
Comparative Balance Sheets
December 31, 19X8 and 19X7
(amounts expressed in thousands)

	19X8	19X7
Assets		
Current assets:		
Cash	$ 25	$ 113
Investments	913	876
Interest receivable	11	10
Accounts receivable (net of allowance for uncollectibles)	1	1
Total current assets	950	1,000
Deferred charges	105	112
Fixed assets:		
Land	469	469
Buildings	584	579
Accumulated depreciation—buildings	(46)	(34)
Improvements other than buildings	2,390	2,346
Accumulated depreciation—improvements other than buildings	(194)	(140)
Machinery and equipment	226	220
Accumulated depreciation—machinery and equipment	(18)	(13)
Fixed assets (net of accumulated depreciation)	3,411	3,427
Total assets	$4,466	$4,539
Liabilities and equity		
Current liabilities:		
Vouchers payable	$ 26	$ 5
Accounts payable	6	7
Compensated absences payable	16	25
Due to other funds—water and sewer fund	—	18
Accrued interest payable	156	161
General obligation bonds payable—current	161	163
Total current liabilities	365	379
Noncurrent liabilities:		
General obligation bonds payable	3,556	3,747
Total liabilities	3,921	4,126
Equity:		
Contributed capital—government	471	471
Retained earnings, unreserved	74	(58)
Total equity	545	413
Total liabilities and equity	$4,466	$4,539

The notes to the financial statements are an integral part of this statement.

Exhibit E–8

Name of Government
Golf Course Enterprise Fund
Comparative Statements of Revenues, Expenses and Changes
in Retained Earnings
For the fiscal years ended December 31, 19X8 and 19X7
(amounts expressed in thousands)

	19X8	19X7
Operating revenues:		
Charges for sales and services	$1,257	$1,190
Operating expenses:		
Costs of sales and services	800	756
Administration	11	7
Depreciation	71	42
Total operating expenses	882	805
Operating income	375	385
Nonoperating revenues (expenses):		
Interest revenue	70	59
Interest expense	(313)	(333)
Total nonoperating revenues (expenses)	(243)	(274)
Net income before extraordinary item	132	111
Extraordinary loss on advance refunding	—	(76)
Net income	132	35
Retained earnings, January 1	(58)	(93)
Retained earnings, December 31	$ 74	$ (58)

The notes to the financial statements are an integral part of this statement.

Exhibit E–9

Name of Government
Golf Course Enterprise Fund
Comparative Statements of Changes in Financial Position
For the fiscal years ended December 31, 19X8 and 19X7
(amounts expressed in thousands)

	19X8	19X7
Cash flows from operating activities:		
Cash received from customers	$1,257	$1,190
Cash paid to suppliers and employees	(818)	(738)
Interest received	69	57
Interest paid	(311)	(330)
Net cash provided by operating activities	197	179
Cash flows from investing activities:		
Proceeds from sales of investments	362	—
Purchase of investments	(399)	(505)
Purchase of fixed assets	(55)	(237)
Net cash used in investing activities	(92)	(742)
Cash flows from financing activities:		
Proceeds from refunding bonds	—	3,617
Bond payments—principal	(193)	(3,000)
Net cash from financing activities	(193)	617
Net increase (decrease) in cash	(88)	54
Cash, January 1	113	59
Cash, December 31	$ 25	$ 113

Reconciliation of Net Income to Net Cash
Provided by Operating Activities

	19X8	19X7
Net income	$132	$ 35
Adjustments to reconcile net income to		
net cash provided by operating activities:		
Extraordinary loss	—	76
Depreciation expense	71	42
Amortization of bond issuance costs	7	7
(Increase) in interest receivable	(1)	(2)
Increase (decrease) in vouchers payable	21	(4)
Increase (decrease) in accounts payable	(1)	2
Increase (decrease) in compensated absences	(9)	9
Increase (decrease) in due to other funds—water and sewer fund	(18)	18
(Decrease) in accrued interest payable	(5)	(4)
Total adjustments	65	144
Net cash provided by operating activities	$197	$179

The notes to the financial statements are an integral part of this statement.

Internal Service Funds

Internal service funds are used to account for the financing of goods or services provided by one department or agency to other departments or agencies of the government and to other government units, on a cost reimbursement basis.

Fleet Management Fund—This fund is used to account for the rental of motor vehicles to other departments and related costs.

Management Information Systems Fund—This fund is used to account for the accumulation and allocation of costs associated with electronic data processing.

Name of Government
Internal Service Funds
Combining Balance Sheet
December 31, 19X8
(With comparative totals for December 31, 19X7)
(amounts expressed in thousands)

	Fleet Management	Management Information Systems	Totals 19X8	19X7
Assets				
Current assets:				
Cash	$ 36	$ 64	$ 100	$ 5
Investments	17	33	50	—
Interest receivable	2	—	2	—
Intergovernmental receivable	4	—	4	—
Due from other funds:				
General fund	47	57	104	98
Water and sewer fund	17	5	22	14
Inventories	23	—	23	—
Prepaid items	38	—	38	—
Total current assets	184	159	343	117
Fixed assets:				
Buildings	87	—	87	—
Accumulated depreciation—buildings	(8)	—	(8)	—
Machinery and equipment	4,334	949	5,283	882
Accumulated depreciation—machinery and equipment	(2,100)	(358)	(2,458)	(266)
Fixed assets (net of accumulated depreciation)	2,313	591	2,904	616
Total assets	$2,497	$750	$3,247	$733
Liabilities and equity				
Current liabilities:				
Accounts payable	$ 227	$ 15	$ 242	$ 88
Compensated absences payable	5	23	28	18
Due to other funds:				
General fund	8	—	8	—
Water and sewer fund	2	—	2	—
Interfund payable—general fund	8	24	32	—
Total current liabilities	250	62	312	106
Noncurrent liabilities:				
Advance from other funds—general fund	32	46	78	50
Total liabilities	282	108	390	156
Equity:				
Contributed capital—government	2,205	281	2,486	281
Retained earnings—unreserved	10	361	371	296
Total equity	2,215	642	2,857	577
Total liabilities and equity	$2,497	$750	$3,247	$733

The notes to the financial statements are an integral part of this statement.

Name of Government
Internal Service Funds
Combining Statement of Revenues, Expenses and Changes in Retained Earnings
For the fiscal year ended December 31, 19X8
(With comparative totals for the fiscal year ended December 31, 19X7)
(amounts expressed in thousands)

	Fleet Management	Management Information Systems	Totals 19X8	Totals 19X7
Operating revenues:				
Charges for sales and services	$1,264	$593	$1,857	$452
Operating expenses:				
Costs of sales and services	771	374	1,145	341
Administration	70	64	134	58
Depreciation	419	92	511	83
Total operating expenses	1,260	530	1,790	482
Operating income (loss)	4	63	67	(30)
Nonoperating revenues:				
Interest	6	2	8	1
Net income (loss)	10	65	75	(29)
Retained earnings, January 1	—	296	296	325
Retained earnings, December 31	$ 10	$361	$ 371	$296

The notes to the financial statements are an integral part of this statement.

Name of Government
Internal Service Funds
Combining Statement of Changes in Financial Position
For the fiscal year ended December 31, 19X8
(With comparative totals for the fiscal year ended December 31, 19X7)
(amounts expressed in thousands)

Exhibit F–3

	Fleet Management	Management Information Systems	Totals 19X8	Totals 19X7
Cash flows from operating activities:				
Cash received from users	$1,196	$643	$1,839	$452
Cash paid to suppliers and employees	(660)	(506)	(1,166)	(385)
Interest received	4	2	6	1
Net cash provided by operating activities	540	139	679	68
Cash flows from investing activities:				
Proceeds from the sale of investments	31	—	31	—
Purchase of investments	(48)	(33)	(81)	—
Purchase of fixed assets	(572)	(67)	(639)	(90)
Net cash used in investing activities	(589)	(100)	(689)	(90)
Cash flows from financing activities:				
Advance from other funds—general fund	40	20	60	—
Contributions	45	—	45	—
Net cash provided by financing activities	85	20	105	—
Noncash transactions affecting financial position:				
Contributions of fixed assets from government	2,160	—	2,160	—
Acquisition of fixed assets through government capital contributions	(2,160)	—	(2,160)	—
Acquisition of fixed assets through trade-in	48	—	48	—
Value of traded fixed assets	(48)	—	(48)	—
Total effect of noncash transactions	0	—	0	—
Net increase (decrease) in cash	36	59	95	(22)
Cash, January 1	—	5	5	27
Cash, December 31	$ 36	$ 64	$ 100	$ 5

Reconciliation of Net Income to Net Cash Provided by
Operating Activities

	Fleet Management	Management Information Systems	Totals 19X8	Totals 19X7
Net income (loss)	$ 10	$ 65	$ 75	$(29)
Adjustment to reconcile net income to net cash provided by operating activities:				
Depreciation expense	419	92	511	83
(Increase) in interest receivable	(2)	—	(2)	—
(Increase) in intergovernmental receivables	(4)	—	(4)	—
(Increase) decrease in due from other funds	(64)	50	(14)	—
(Increase) in inventories	(23)	—	(23)	—
(Increase) in prepaid items	(38)	—	(38)	—
Increase (decrease) in accounts payable	227	(73)	154	12
Increase in compensated absences payable	5	5	10	2
Increase in due to other funds	10	—	10	—
Total adjustments	530	74	604	97
Net cash provided by operating activities	$540	$139	$679	$ 68

The notes to the financial statements are an integral part of this statement.

84

Name of Government
Comparative Balance Sheets
Management Information Systems Internal Service Fund
December 31, 19X8 and 19X7
(amounts expressed in thousands)

	19X8	19X7
Assets		
Current assets:		
Cash	$ 64	$ 5
Investments	33	—
Due from other funds:		
General fund	57	98
Water and sewer fund	5	14
Total current assets	159	117
Fixed assets:		
Machinery and equipment	949	882
Accumulated depreciation	(358)	(266)
Fixed assets (net of accumulated depreciation)	591	616
Total assets	$750	$733
Liabilities and equity		
Current liabilities:		
Accounts payable	$ 15	$ 88
Compensated absences payable	23	18
Interfund payable—general fund	24	—
Total current liabilities	62	106
Noncurrent liabilities:		
Advances from other funds—general fund	46	50
Total liabilities	108	156
Equity:		
Contributed capital—government	281	281
Retained earnings—unreserved	361	296
Total equity	642	577
Total liabilities and equity	$750	$733

The notes to the financial statements are an integral part of this statement.

Exhibit F–5

Name of Government
Management Information Systems Internal Service Fund
Comparative Statements of Revenues, Expenses and Changes
in Retained Earnings
For the fiscal years ended December 31, 19X8 and 19X7
(amounts expressed in thousands)

	19X8	19X7
Revenues:		
Charges for services	$593	$452
Operating expenses:		
Costs of services	374	341
Administration	64	58
Depreciation	92	83
Total operating expenses	530	482
Operating income (loss)	63	(30)
Nonoperating revenues:		
Interest	2	1
Net income (loss)	65	(29)
Retained earnings, January 1	296	325
Retained earnings, December 31	$361	$296

The notes to the financial statements are an integral part of this statement.

Exhibit F–6

Name of Government
Management Information Systems Internal Service Fund
Comparative Statement of Changes in Financial Position
For the fiscal years ended December 31, 19X8 and 19X7
(amounts expressed in thousands)

	19X8	19X7
Cash flows from operating activities:		
Cash received from users	$643	$452
Cash paid to suppliers and employees	(506)	(385)
Interest received	2	1
Net cash provided by operating activities	139	68
Cash flows from investing activities:		
Purchase of investments	(33)	—
Purchase of fixed assets	(67)	(90)
Net cash used in investing activities	(100)	(90)
Cash flows from financing activities:		
Advance from other funds—general fund	20	—
Net cash provided by financing activities	20	—
Net increase (decrease) in cash	59	(22)
Cash, January 1	5	27
Cash, December 31	$ 64	$ 5

Reconciliation of Net Income to Net Cash Provided by
Operating Activities

	19X8	19X7
Net income (loss)	$ 65	$(29)
Adjustments to reconcile net income to net cash provided by operating activities:		
Depreciation expense	92	83
Decrease in due from general fund	41	—
Decrease in due from water and sewer fund	9	—
Increase in compensated absences	5	2
Increase (decrease) in accounts payable	(73)	12
Total adjustments	74	97
Net cash provided by operating activities	$139	$ 68

The notes to the financial statements are an integral part of this statement.

Trust and Agency Funds

Trust funds are used to account for assets held by the government in a trustee capacity. Agency funds are used to account for assets held by the government as an agent for individuals, private organizations, other governments and/or other funds.

Senior Citizens' Transportation Fund—This fund is used to account for donations that are received pursuant to a trust agreement that restricts the use of those donations to providing subsidies for senior citizens' transportation to special government sponsored events.

Perpetual Care Fund—This fund is used to account for principal trust amounts received and related interest income. The interest portion of the trust can be used to maintain the community cemetery.

Public Safety Employees Retirement System Fund—This fund is used to account for the accumulation of resources for pension benefit payments to qualified public safety employees.

Deferred Compensation Fund—This fund is used to account for assets held for employees in accordance with the provisions of Internal Revenue Code Section 457.

Exhibit G–1

Name of Government
Trust and Agency Funds
Combining Balance Sheet
December 31, 19X8
(With comparative totals for December 31, 19X7)
(amounts expressed in thousands)

	Expendable Trust	Non-expendable Trust	Pension Trust	Agency	Totals	
	Senior Citizens' Trans-portation	Perpetual Care	Public Safety Employees	Deferred Compen-sation	19X8	19X7
Assets						
Cash	$11	$ 231	$ 33	$ 18	$ 293	$ 89
Investments	41	1,753	14,335	1,198	17,327	15,394
Interest receivable	6	82	346	—	434	163
Total assets	$58	$2,066	$14,714	$1,216	$18,054	$15,646
Liabilities and fund balances						
Liabilities:						
Accounts payable	$ 7	$ 13	$ 18	—	$ 38	$ 36
Deferred compensation benefits payable	—	—	—	$1,216	1,216	902
Total liabilities	7	13	18	1,216	1,254	938
Fund balances:						
Reserved for perpetual care	—	1,193	—	—	1,193	1,102
Reserved for employees retirement system	—	—	16,670	—	16,670	14,248
Unreserved, undesignated	51	860	(1,974)	—	(1,063)	(642)
Total fund balances	51	2,053	14,696	—	16,800	14,708
Total liabilities and fund balances	$58	$2,066	$14,714	$1,216	$18,054	$15,646

The notes to the financial statements are an integral part of this statement.

90

Name of Government
Senior Citizens' Transportation Expendable Trust Fund
Comparative Balance Sheets
December 31, 19X8 and 19X7
(amounts expressed in thousands)

	19X8	19X7
Assets		
Cash	$11	$16
Investments	41	33
Interest receivable	6	2
Total assets	$58	$51
Liabilities and fund balances		
Liabilities:		
Accounts payable	$ 7	$ 2
Fund balances:		
Unreserved, undesignated	51	49
Total liabilities and fund balances	$58	$51

The notes to the financial statements are an integral part of this statement.

Exhibit G–3

Name of Government
Senior Citizens' Transportation Expendable Trust Fund
Comparative Statements of Revenues, Expenditures and
Changes in Fund Balances
For the fiscal years ended December 31, 19X8 and 19X7
(amounts expressed in thousands)

	19X8	19X7
Revenues:		
Interest	$ 6	$ 2
Donations	82	52
Total revenues	88	54
Expenditures:		
Current:		
General government	86	29
Excess of revenues over expenditures	2	25
Fund balances, January 1	49	24
Fund balances, December 31	$51	$49

The notes to the financial statements are an integral part of this statement.

Name of Government
Perpetual Care Nonexpendable Trust Fund
Comparative Balance Sheets
December 31, 19X8 and 19X7
(amounts expressed in thousands)

	19X8	19X7
Assets		
Cash	$ 231	$ 16
Investments	1,753	1,848
Interest receivable	82	41
Total assets	$2,066	$1,905
Liabilities and fund balances		
Liabilities:		
Accounts payable	$ 13	$ 18
Fund balances:		
Reserved for perpetual care	1,193	1,102
Unreserved, undesignated	860	785
Total fund balances	2,053	1,887
Total liabilities and fund balances	$2,066	$1,905

The notes to the financial statements are an integral part of this statement.

Name of Government
Perpetual Care Nonexpendable Trust Fund
Comparative Statements of Revenues, Expenses and
Changes in Fund Balances
For the fiscal years ended December 31, 19X8 and 19X7
(amounts expressed in thousands)

	19X8	19X7
Operating revenues:		
Interest	$ 41	$ 141
Operating expenses:		
Costs of sales and services	13	144
Operating income (loss)	28	(3)
Nonoperating revenues:		
Gain on the sale of investments	138	57
Net income	166	54
Fund balances, January 1	1,887	1,833
Fund balances, December 31	$2,053	$1,887

The notes to the financial statements are an integral part of this statement.

Exhibit G–6

Name of Government
Perpetual Care Nonexpendable Trust Fund
Comparative Statements of Changes in Financial Position
For the fiscal years ended December 31, 19X8 and 19X7
(amounts expressed in thousands)

	19X8	19X7
Cash flows from operating activities:		
Cash paid to suppliers and employees	$ (18)	$(132)
Interest received	—	100
Net cash used by operating activities	(18)	(32)
Cash flows from investing activities:		
Proceeds from sales of investments	1,788	814
Purchase of investments	(1,555)	(768)
Net cash provided by investing activities	233	46
Net increase in cash	215	14
Cash, January 1	16	2
Cash, December 31	$ 231	$ 16

Reconciliation of Net Income to Net Cash Used by
Operating Activities

	19X8	19X7
Net income	$ 166	$ 54
Adjustments to reconcile net income to net cash used by operating activities:		
Gain on sales of investments	(138)	(57)
(Increase) in interest receivable	(41)	(39)
Increase (decrease) in accounts payable	(5)	10
Total adjustments	(184)	(86)
Net cash used by operating activities	$ (18)	$ (32)

The notes to the financial statements are an integral part of this statement.

Exhibit G–7

Name of Government
Public Safety Employees Pension Trust Fund
Comparative Balance Sheets
December 31, 19X8 and 19X7
(amounts expressed in thousands)

	19X8	19X7
Assets		
Cash	$ 33	$ 55
Investments	14,335	12,615
Interest receivable	346	118
Total assets	$14,714	$12,788
Liabilities and fund balances		
Liabilities:		
Accounts payable	$ 18	$ 16
Fund balances:		
Reserved for:		
Member contributions	6,905	5,893
Employer contributions	7,427	6,142
Benefits	1,200	1,129
Disability	884	842
Undistributed investment earnings	254	242
Total reserved for employees retirement system	16,670	14,248
Unreserved, undesignated	(1,974)	(1,476)
Total fund balances	14,696	12,772
Total liabilities and fund balances	$14,714	$12,788

The notes to the financial statements are an integral part of this statement.

Exhibit G–8

Name of Government
Public Safety Employees Pension Trust Fund
Comparative Statements of Revenues, Expenses and
Changes in Fund Balances
For the fiscal years ended December 31, 19X8 and 19X7
(amounts expressed in thousands)

	19X8	19X7
Operating revenues:		
Employer contributions	$ 1,051	$ 1,047
Employee contributions	729	511
Interest	774	726
Total operating revenues	2,554	2,284
Operating expenses:		
Benefits	455	380
Refunds	15	34
Administration	160	159
Total operating expenses	630	573
Net income	1,924	1,711
Fund balances, January 1	12,772	11,061
Fund balances, December 31	$14,696	$12,772

The notes to the financial statements are an integral part of this statement.

Exhibit G–9

Name of Government
Public Safety Employees Pension Trust Fund
Comparative Statements of Changes in Financial Position
For the fiscal years ended December 31, 19X8 and 19X7
(amounts expressed in thousands)

	19X8	19X7
Cash flows from operating activities:		
Employer contributions	$1,051	$1,047
Employee contributions	729	511
Benefits paid	(455)	(380)
Refunds paid	(15)	(34)
Administrative cost paid	(158)	(156)
Interest received	547	843
Net cash provided by operating activities	1,699	1,831
Cash flows from investing activities:		
Proceeds from sales of investments	3,056	1,613
Purchase of investments	(4,777)	(3,428)
Net cash used in investing activities	(1,721)	(1,815)
Net increase (decrease) in cash	(22)	16
Cash, January 1	55	39
Cash, December 31	$ 33	$ 55

Reconciliation of Net Income to Net Cash Provided by
Operating Activities

	19X8	19X7
Net income	$1,924	$1,711
Adjustments to reconcile net income to net cash provided by operating activities:		
(Increase) decrease in interest receivable	(227)	117
Increase in accounts payable	2	3
Total adjustments	(225)	120
Net cash provided by operating activities	$1,699	$1,831

The notes to the financial statements are an integral part of this statement.

Name of Government
Deferred Compensation Agency Fund
Statement of Changes in Assets and Liabilities
For the fiscal year ended December 31, 19X8
(amounts expressed in thousands)

	Balance January 1, 19X8	Additions	Deletions	Balance December 31, 19X8
Assets				
Cash	—	$347	$329	$ 18
Investments	$898	300	—	1,198
Interest receivable	2	—	2	—
Total assets	$900	$647	$331	$1,216
Liabilities				
Deferred compensation benefits payable	$900	$345	$ 29	$1,216

The notes to the financial statements are an integral part of this statement.

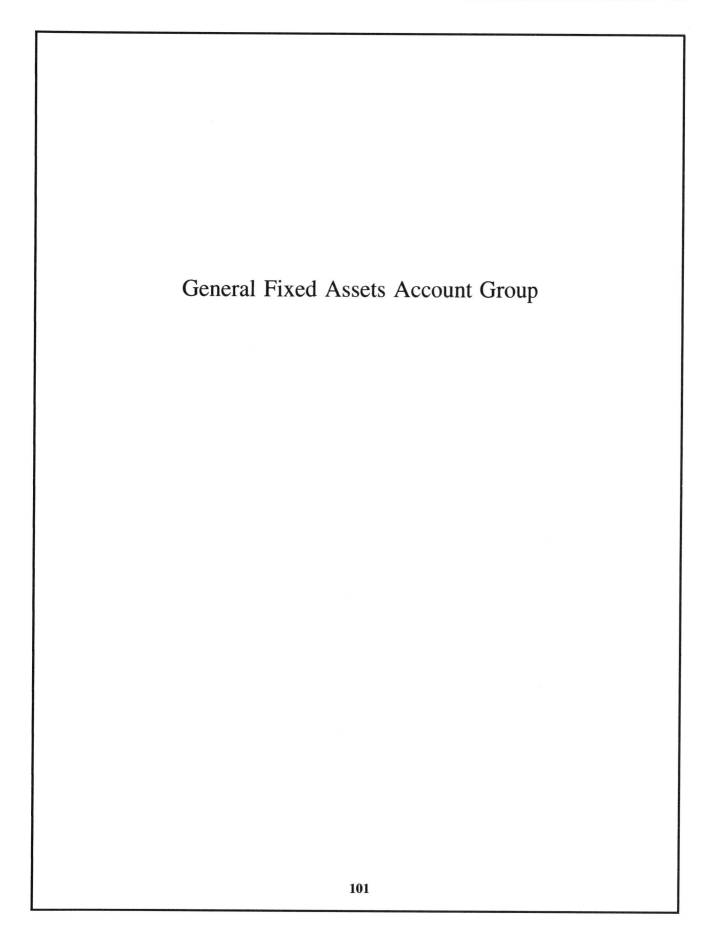

General Fixed Assets Account Group

Name of Government
Comparative Schedules of General Fixed Assets
By Source
December 31, 19X8 and 19X7
(amounts expressed in thousands)

	19X8	19X7
General fixed assets:		
Land	$39,333	$38,775
Buildings	8,291	7,875
Improvements other than buildings	4,604	4,604
Machinery and equipment	4,376	7,401
Construction in progress	2,308	722
Total general fixed assets	$58,912	$59,377
Investment in general fixed assets by source:		
General fund	$ 8,801	$11,744
Special revenue funds	3,873	3,497
Capital projects funds	44,531	42,442
Donations	1,707	1,694
Total investment in general fixed assets	$58,912	$59,377

Name of Government
Schedule of General Fixed Assets—By Function and Activity
December 31, 19X8
(amounts expressed in thousands)

Function and Activity	Land	Buildings	Improvements Other Than Buildings	Machinery and Equipment	Construction in Progress	Total
General government:						
Council	—	$ 276	—	$ 4	—	$ 280
Committees	—	—	—	2	—	2
Manager	—	3,615	$ 562	252	—	4,429
Attorney	—	—	—	60	—	60
Clerk	—	—	—	20	—	20
Personnel	—	—	—	15	—	15
Finance and administration	—	148	—	154	—	302
Other—unclassified	$ 588	15	25	458	—	1,086
Total general government	588	4,054	587	965	—	6,194
Public safety:						
Police	1,489	216	21	557	—	2,283
Fire	—	1,070	7	396	—	1,473
Inspection	—	—	—	36	—	36
Total public safety	1,489	1,286	28	989	—	3,792
Highways and streets:						
Engineering	—	—	—	88	—	88
Maintenance	—	107	—	251	—	358
Total highways and streets	—	107	—	339	—	446
Sanitation	—	—	66	557	—	623
Culture and recreation	37,256	2,844	3,923	1,526	—	45,549
Construction in progress	—	—	—	—	$2,308	2,308
Total general fixed assets	$39,333	$8,291	$4,604	$4,376	$2,308	$58,912

103

Name of Government
Schedule of Changes in General Fixed Assets—By Function and Activity
For the fiscal year ended December 31, 19X8
(amounts expressed in thousands)

Function and Activity	General Fixed Assets January 1, 19X8	Additions	Deductions*	General Fixed Assets December 31, 19X8
General government:				
Council	$ 275	$ 5	—	$ 280
Committees	2	—	—	2
Manager	4,370	59	—	4,429
Attorney	52	14	$ 6	60
Clerk	20	—	—	20
Personnel	15	—	—	15
Finance and administration	297	6	1	302
Other	712	374	—	1,086
Total general government	5,743	458	7	6,194
Public safety:				
Police	2,903	633	1,253	2,283
Fire	1,325	167	19	1,473
Inspection	145	1	110	36
Total public safety	4,373	801	1,382	3,792
Highways and streets:				
Engineering	14	74	—	88
Maintenance	1,874	91	1,607	358
Total highways and streets	1,888	165	1,607	446
Sanitation	1,895	1	1,273	623
Culture and recreation	44,756	807	14	45,549
Construction in progress	722	2,058	472	2,308
Total general fixed assets	$59,377	$4,290	$4,755	$58,912

* Includes $4,253 transfer of fixed assets to fleet management internal service fund.

STATISTICAL SECTION

Table 1

Name of Government
General Governmental Expenditures by Function (1)
Last Ten Fiscal Years
(amounts expressed in thousands)

Fiscal Year	General Government	Public Safety	Highways and Streets	Sanitation	Culture and Recreation	Debt Service	Total
19W9	$2,547	$ 4,251	$1,144	$1,297	$1,977	$2,640	$13,856
19X0	2,726	4,824	1,199	1,490	2,207	2,731	15,177
19X1	2,923	5,060	1,248	1,543	2,402	2,893	16,069
19X2	3,735	5,906	1,550	2,128	2,922	2,911	19,152
19X3	4,089	6,775	1,914	2,109	3,386	2,881	21,154
19X4	4,030	8,770	2,353	2,892	3,919	3,073	25,037
19X5	4,150	9,783	2,556	2,951	4,620	3,612	27,672
19X6	4,772	10,431	2,751	3,040	4,931	3,331	29,256
19X7	3,821	12,150	3,389	3,404	5,972	3,335	32,071
19X8	4,244	13,438	4,477	3,726	6,883	5,203	37,971

(1) Includes general, special revenue and debt service funds.

Table 2

Name of Government
General Governmental Revenues by Source (1)
Last Ten Fiscal Years
(amounts expressed in thousands)

Fiscal Year	Taxes	Licenses and Permits	Inter-governmental	Charges for Services	Fines	Interest	Special Assessments (2)	Miscellaneous	Total
19W9	$10,072	$ 658	$3,399	$ 580	$169	$ 185	—	$ 1	$15,064
19X0	10,957	957	3,565	879	177	277	—	571	17,383
19X1	11,702	1,043	4,193	918	212	639	—	348	19,055
19X2	12,976	1,018	5,533	1,316	185	916	—	119	22,063
19X3	15,207	1,359	4,535	1,642	182	1,343	—	109	24,377
19X4	16,879	1,105	4,487	1,745	306	1,091	—	—	25,613
19X5	17,472	1,461	5,689	2,483	331	542	—	—	27,978
19X6	19,175	1,759	6,607	1,996	358	652	—	11	30,558
19X7	24,271	1,820	5,469	2,335	521	546	—	243	35,205
19X8	28,181	2,041	5,870	2,300	808	1,019	$470	494	41,183

(1) Includes general, special revenue and debt service funds.
(2) Special assessment collections previously recorded in the special assessment fund type have been excluded.

Table 2A

Name of Government
General Governmental Tax Revenues By Source
Last Ten Fiscal Years
(amounts expressed in thousands)

Fiscal Year	Property Tax	Sales Tax	Franchise Tax	Motor Fuel Tax	Alcoholic Beverage Tax	Total
19W9	$ 6,874	$1,752	$1,446	—	—	$10,072
19X0	7,679	2,047	1,231	—	—	10,957
19X1	8,107	2,216	1,379	—	—	11,702
19X2	8,766	2,437	1,773	—	—	12,976
19X3	10,279	2,713	2,215	—	—	15,207
19X4	10,910	3,242	2,727	—	—	16,879
19X5	11,039	3,629	2,804	—	—	17,472
19X6	11,435	4,294	3,446	—	—	19,175
19X7	13,886	5,253	4,126	$355 (1)	$651 (1)	24,271
19X8	15,718	6,642	4,293	729	799	28,181

(1) First year of tax

Table 3

Name of Government
Property Tax Levies and Collections
Last Ten Fiscal Years
(amounts expressed in thousands)

Fiscal Year	Total Tax Levy	Current Tax Collections	Percent of Current Taxes Collected	Delinquent Tax Collections	Total Tax Collections	Ratio of Total Tax Collections to Total Tax Levy	Outstanding Delinquent Taxes	Ratio of Delinquent Taxes to Total Tax Levy
19W9	$ 6,881	$ 6,841	99.4%	$ 22	$ 6,863	99.7%	$105	.15%
19X0	7,717	7,632	98.9	41	7,673	99.4	149	.19
19X1	8,162	8,089	99.1	65	8,154	99.9	157	.19
19X2	8,825	8,754	99.2	91	8,845	100.2	137	.16
19X3	10,400	10,264	98.7	104	10,368	99.7	169	.16
19X4	11,158	10,901	97.7	82	10,983	98.4	344	.31
19X5	11,567	11,012	95.2	75	11,087	95.9	824	.71
19X6	11,439	11,405	99.7	492	11,897	104.0	366	.32
19X7	12,823	12,733	99.3	395	13,128	102.4	61	.05
19X8	15,692	15,585	99.3	72	15,657	99.8	126	.08

Table 4

Name of Government
Assessed and Estimated Actual Value of Property (1)
Last Ten Fiscal Years
(amounts expressed in thousands)

| Fiscal Year | Real Property | | Personal Property | | Exemptions | Total | | Ratio of Total Assessed Value To Total Estimated Actual Value |
	Assessed Value	Estimated Actual Value	Assessed Value	Estimated Actual Value	Real Property	Assessed Value	Estimated Actual Value	
19W9	$ 721,787	$ 974,071	$ 78,879	$106,450	$ 18,189	$ 782,477	$1,080,521	72.42%
19X0	778,648	1,038,197	88,779	118,372	24,443	842,984	1,156,569	72.89
19X1	889,651	1,152,398	104,542	135,417	26,223	967,970	1,287,815	75.16
19X2	1,069,040	1,377,629	105,846	136,400	41,812	1,133,074	1,514,029	74.84
19X3	1,693,146	2,165,148	176,779	226,061	23,907	1,846,018	2,391,209	77.20
19X4	2,120,772	2,743,560	192,590	249,146	260,537 (2)	2,052,825	2,992,706	68.59
19X5	2,738,332	3,475,041	250,865	318,357	496,559	2,492,638	3,793,398	65.71
19X6	2,994,479	3,743,099	282,422	353,027	528,607	2,748,294	4,096,126	67.09
19X7	3,575,321	4,206,260	377,583	444,215	556,446	3,396,458	4,650,475	73.03
19X8	3,682,831	4,282,362	406,909	473,150	569,311	3,520,429	4,755,512	74.03

(1) Total assessed value based on approximately 75 percent of estimated actual value.
(2) Homestead exemption increased to $25,000 per household.

108

Table 5

Name of Government
Property Tax Rates
Direct and Overlapping Governments
Last Ten Fiscal Years

	Name of Government			County			School District				
Fiscal Year	Operating Millage	Debt Service Millage	Total City Millage	Operating Millage	Debt Service Millage	Total County Millage	Operating Millage	Debt Service Millage	Total School Millage	Other	Total
19W9	5.411	3.374	8.785	6.382	.133	6.515	9.000	.970	9.970	2.519	27.789
19X0	6.869	2.240	9.109	6.264	.114	6.378	8.930	.820	9.750	2.260	27.497
19X1	5.384	2.991	8.375	6.136	.335	6.471	8.000	.300	8.300	2.174	25.320
19X2	5.167	2.569	7.736	6.568	.371	6.739	6.750	.270	7.020	1.995	23.490
19X3	4.007	1.561	5.568	6.891	.432	7.323	8.404	.226	8.630	2.790	24.311
19X4	3.817	1.498	5.315	4.653	.284	4.937	6.796	.123	6.919	2.288	19.459
19X5	2.979	1.450	4.429	3.979	.203	4.182	6.031	.102	6.133	1.736	16.480
19X6	2.950	1.211	4.161	3.827	.422	4.249	6.825	.108	6.933	1.637	16.980
19X7	3.102	.986	4.088	3.835	.349	4.184	7.172	*	7.172	1.826	17.270
19X8	3.028	1.437 (1)	4.465	4.195	.332	4.527	7.228	*	7.228	1.838	18.058

* County School District retired its debt on 12/31/X6.
(1) A portion of the property taxes are reported as revenues in the debt service fund beginning in 19X8.

Table 6

Name of Government
Principal Taxpayers
December 31, 19X8
(amounts expressed in thousands)

Taxpayer	Type of Business	19X8 Assessed Valuation	Percentage of Total Assessed Valuation
XYZ Corporation	Computer manufacturer	$ 325,197	9.2%
Beatle Corporation	Computer software manufacturer	300,339	8.5
Southwest Mutual Corporation	Insurance	164,692	4.7
1st Interstate Bank of Name of Government	Financial institution	131,233	3.7
Spark Electrical	Electrical controls	83,753	2.4
ABC Development	Shopping mall	82,811	2.4
Name of State Power and Light Company	Electrical and gas utility	73,945	2.1
PAW Parts, Inc.	Automobile component manufacturer	57,612	1.6
EFG Development	Industrial park development	44,623	1.3
Who Corporation	Hotel	41,179	1.2
Totals		$1,305,384	37.1%

Table 7

Name of Government
Special Assessment Billings and Collections
Last Ten Fiscal Years
(amounts expressed in thousands)

Fiscal Year	Special Assessment Billings	Special Assessments Collected (1)
19W9	$501	$519
19X0	629	756
19X1	236	260
19X2	222	335
19X3	263	411
19X4	229	159
19X5	294	506
19X6	—	253
19X7	—	—
19X8	470	470

(1) Includes prepayments and foreclosures.

Table 8

Name of Government
Computation of Legal Debt Margin
December 31, 19X8
(amounts expressed in thousands)

Assessed valuations:		
Assessed value		$3,520,429
Add back: exempt real property		569,311
Total assessed value		$4,089,740
Legal debt margin:		
Debt limitation—10 percent of total assessed value		$ 408,974
Debt applicable to limitation:		
Total bonded debt	$109,377	
Less: Special assessment bonds	4,700	
Revenue bonds	34,312	
Amount available for repayment of general obligation bonds	38	
Total debt applicable to limitation		70,327
Legal debt margin		$ 338,647

112

Table 9

Name of Government
Ratio of Net General Obligation Bonded Debt
To Assessed Value and Net General Obligation Bonded Debt Per Capita
Last Ten Fiscal Years

Fiscal Year	Population (1)*	Assessed Value (2)*	Gross Bonded Debt (3)*	Less Debt Service Fund (4)*	Debt Payable from Enterprise Revenues (5)*	Net Bonded Debt*	Ratio of Net Bonded Debt to Assessed Value	Net Bonded Debt per Capita
19W9	48	$ 782,477	$48,395	$ 484	$15,765	$32,146	4.10%	$670
19X0	49	842,984	46,915	549	15,280	31,086	3.69	634
19X1	52	967,970	46,995	699	14,755	31,541	3.26	607
19X2	53	1,133,074	45,198	525	14,190	30,483	2.69	575
19X3	55	1,846,018	70,130	525	40,405	29,200	1.58	531
19X4	57	2,052,825	76,445	846	42,075	33,524	1.63	588
19X5	56	2,492,638	72,955	257	40,150	32,548	1.31	561
19X6	56	2,748,294	70,435	9	39,010	31,416	1.14	542
19X7	60	3,396,458	66,523	10	29,068	37,445	1.10	624
19X8	61	3,520,429	70,365	38	34,575	35,752	1.02	586

* Amounts expressed in thousands.
(1) Annual government census.
(2) From Table 4.
(3) Amount does not include special assessment bonds and revenue bonds.
(4) Amount available for repayment of general obligation bonds.
(5) These amounts include the general obligation bonds that are being repaid from the water and sewer authority and golf course revenues.

113

Table 10

Name of Government
Ratio of Annual Debt Service Expenditures
For General Obligation Bonded Debt (1)
to Total General Governmental Expenditures
Last Ten Fiscal Years
(amounts expressed in thousands)

Fiscal Year	Principal	Interest (2)	Total Debt Service	Total General Governmental Expenditures (3)	Ratio of Debt Service to General Governmental Expenditures
19W9	$ 845	$1,795	$2,640	$13,856	19.1%
19X0	994	1,737	2,731	15,177	18.0
19X1	1,165	1,728	2,893	16,069	18.0
19X2	1,232	1,679	2,911	19,152	15.2
19X3	1,283	1,598	2,881	21,154	13.6
19X4	1,355	1,718	3,073	25,037	12.3
19X5	1,565	2,047	3,612	27,672	13.0
19X6	1,380	1,951	3,331	29,256	11.4
19X7	1,470	1,865	3,335	32,071	10.4
19X8	2,030	2,928	4,958	37,971	13.1

(1) General obligation bonds reported in the enterprise funds and special assessment debt with government commitment have been excluded.
(2) Excludes bond issuance and other costs.
(3) Includes general, special revenue and debt service funds.

Table 11

Name of Government
Computation of Direct and Overlapping Bonded Debt
General Obligation Bonds
December 31, 19X8
(amounts expressed in thousands)

Jurisdiction	Net General Obligation Bonded Debt Outstanding	Percentage Applicable to Government	Amount Applicable to Government
Direct:			
Name of Government	$ 35,790 (1)	100.00%	$35,790
Overlapping:			
County	72,240	13.80	9,969
Total	$108,030		$45,759

(1) Excluding general obligation bonds reported in the enterprise funds.

Table 12

Name of Government
Revenue Bond Coverage
Water and Sewer Authority
Last Ten Fiscal Years
(amounts expressed in thousands)

Fiscal Year	Gross Revenues (1)	Operating Expenses (2)	Net Revenue Available for Debt Service	Debt Service Requirements (3)			Coverage
				Principal	Interest	Total	
19W9	$ 4,728	$ 2,466	$2,262	$ 154	$ 840	$ 994	2.28
19X0	5,111	2,745	2,366	166	828	994	2.38
19X1	6,090	3,576	2,514	180	814	994	2.53
19X2	7,353	4,537	2,816	194	800	994	2.83
19X3	10,131	5,269	4,862	210	784	994	4.89
19X4	10,974	6,203	4,771	226	768	994	4.80
19X5	11,522	6,939	4,583	244	750	994	4.61
19X6	13,103	6,938	6,165	263	731	994	6.20
19X7	13,816	8,710	5,106	285	709	994	5.14
19X8	16,651	10,134	6,517	1,484	1,888	3,372	1.93

(1) Total revenues (including interest) exclusive of tap fees.
(2) Total operating expenses exclusive of depreciation.
(3) Includes principal and interest of revenue bonds only. It does not include the general obligation bonds reported in the water and sewer authority fund or debt defeasance transactions.

116

Table 13

Name of Government
Demographic Statistics
Last Ten Fiscal Years

Fiscal Year	(1) Population	(2) Per Capita Income	(3) Median Age	(4) Education Level In Years Of Formal Schooling	(4) School Enrollment	(2) Unemployment Rate
19W8	47,663	$ 8,147	27.7	14.9	9,590	4.1%
19W9	49,481	9,020	27.9	14.9	8,790	4.1
19X0	51,662	10,767	28.1	15.0	8,220	3.2
19X1	53,343	11,862	28.3	15.1	7,683	5.5
19X2	54,874	12,957	28.5	15.3	7,093	5.9
19X3	57,100	13,436	28.7	15.4	6,813	7.7
19X4	56,252	13,416	28.9	15.5	7,146	8.4
19X5	56,340	14,033	29.1	15.7	6,991	7.3
19X6	59,534	14,563	29.3	15.8	6,723	6.1
19X7	61,434	15,206	29.5	15.9	6,703	3.1

Data Sources
(1) Bureau of the Census/County Regional Planning Commission
(2) State Department of Labor
(3) State Department of Commerce
(4) School District

Table 14

Name of Government
Property Value, Construction and Bank Deposits
Last Ten Fiscal Years

Fiscal Year	Property Value (1)*				Commercial Construction (3)		Residential Construction		Bank Deposits (4)*
	Commercial	Residential	Exemptions	Total	Number of units	Value*	Number of units	Value*	
19W9	$ 447,414	$ 544,846	$ 18,189	$ 974,071	267	$129,637	810	$ 24,300	$ 920,430
19X0	494,037	568,603	24,443	1,038,197	147	86,758	556	16,680	1,081,506
19X1	556,128	622,493	26,223	1,152,398	185	123,495	783	27,405	1,199,150
19X2	721,967	697,474	41,812	1,377,629	175	128,625	698	27,920	1,354,109
19X3	915,577	1,273,478	23,907	2,165,148	200	158,600	718	39,310	1,480,206
19X4	1,773,869	1,230,228	260,537 (2)	2,743,560	85	57,195	652	35,340	1,738,172
19X5	2,677,119	1,294,481	496,559	3,475,041	50	43,250	569	35,605	1,769,951
19X6	2,865,811	1,405,895	528,607	3,743,099	271	143,631	652	42,600	1,938,258
19X7	3,105,601	1,657,105	556,446	4,206,260	281	151,985	939	70,425	2,264,582
19X8	3,146,581	1,705,092	569,311	4,282,362	339	164,749	1,254	106,590	2,433,050

* Amounts expressed in thousands
(1) Estimated assessed value from Table 4
(2) Increase in homestead exemption
(3) Source: County Clerk
(4) Source: Federal Deposit Insurance Corporation and Federal Savings and Loan Insurance Corporation

118

Table 15

Name of Government
Miscellaneous Statistics
December 31, 19X8

Date of Incorporation	1853
Form of Government	Council/Manager
Number of employees (excluding police and fire):	
Classified	333
Exempt	65
Area in square miles	17
Name of Government facilities and services:	
Miles of streets	215
Number of street lights	3,400
Culture and Recreation:	
Community centers	5
Parks	25
Park acreage	625
Golf courses	1
Swimming pools	4
Tennis courts	45
Fire Protection:	
Number of stations	3
Number of fire personnel and officers	65
Number of calls answered	1,030
Number of inspections conducted	4,750
Police Protection:	
Number of stations	1
Number of police personnel and officers	74
Number of patrol units	33
Number of law violations:	
Physical arrests	3,091
Traffic violations	9,575
Parking violations	25,909
Sewerage System:	
Miles of sanitary sewers	225
Miles of storm sewers	205
Number of treatment plants	1
Number of service connections	16,075
Daily average treatment in gallons	3,232,875
Maximum daily capacity of treatment plant in gallons	3,715,948
Water System:	
Miles of water mains	205
Number of service connections	16,915
Number of fire hydrants	1,150
Daily average consumption in gallons	4,684,184
Maximum daily capacity of plant in gallons	5,570,805
Facilities and services not included in the reporting entity:	
Education:	
Number of elementary schools	12
Number of elementary school instructors	234
Number of secondary schools	2
Number of secondary school instructors	85
Number of community colleges	1
Number of universities	1
Hospitals:	
Number of hospitals	2
Number of patient beds	672

119

SINGLE AUDIT SECTION

OFFICIAL LETTERHEAD OF INDEPENDENT AUDITOR

INDEPENDENT AUDITOR'S REPORT ON SUPPLEMENTARY INFORMATION SCHEDULE OF FEDERAL FINANCIAL ASSISTANCE

April 7, 19X9

To the governing body and audit committee of the Name of Government:

We have audited the general purpose financial statements of the Name of Government, and the combining, individual fund and account group financial statements of the Name of Government as of and for the year ended December 31, 19X8, and have issued our report thereon dated April 7, 19X9. These financial statements are the responsibility of the Name of Government's management. Our responsibility was to express an opinion of these financial statements based on our audit.

We conducted our audit in accordance with generally accepted auditing standards and the standards for financial audits contained in the *Standards for Audit of Governmental Organizations, Programs, Activities, and Functions,* issued by the U.S. General Accounting Office. Those standards required that we plan and perform the audit to obtain reasonable assurance about whether the financial statements are free of material misstatement. An audit includes examining, on a test basis, evidence supporting the amounts and disclosures in the financial statements. An audit also includes assessing the accounting principles used and significant estimates made by management, as well as evaluating the overall financial statement presentation. We believe that our audit provided a reasonable basis for our opinion.

Our audit was made for the purpose of forming an opinion on the general purpose financial statements taken as a whole and on the combining, individual fund and account group financial statements. The accompanying Schedule of Federal Financial Assistance is presented for purposes of additional analysis and is not a required part of the financial statements of the Name of Government. The information in this schedule has been subjected to the auditing procedures applied in the audit of the general purpose, combining, individual fund and account group financial statements and, in our opinion, is fairly stated in all material respects in relation to the financial statements of each of the respective individual funds and account groups, taken as a whole.

Russum, Siegert, Fucone & Co.
Certified Public Accountants

123

Name of Government
Schedule of Federal Financial Assistance
For the fiscal year ended December 31, 19X8
(amounts expressed in thousands)

Program Name	CFDA Number	Grantor	Balance* Jan. 1	Cash Receipts	Expenditures	Balance* Dec. 31
Childcare Food Program	10.558	Dept. of Agriculture	$(20)	$ (222)	$ 194	$ (48)
Community Service Block Grant	13.665	Dept. of Health & Human Service	(31)	(359)	314	(76)
Community Development Block Grant	14.218	Dept. of Housing & Urban Development	95	(1,053)	922	(36)
Rental Rehabilitation Program	14.156	Dept. of Housing & Urban Development	55	(610)	534	(21)
Air Pollution Control Grant	66.001	Environmental Protection Agency	(29)	(361)	390	0
Senior Community Service Grant	17.235	Dept. of Labor	(5)		5	0
Total Federal Financial Assistance			$ 65	$(2,605)	$2,359	$(181)

* Credit balances represent deferred revenue—federal government. Debit balances represent intergovernmental receivables—federal government.

NOTE: The following additional columns could be added to the schedule, as needed:

- Transfers in—funds received or "transferred in" from other grants. If used, this column should tie to a parallel transfers out column.
- Transfers out—funds distributed or "transferred out" from the grant to another grant. If used, this column should tie to a parallel transfers in column.
- Other Additions—amounts received during the period from sources other than those included in cash receipts and transfers in, such as refunds from subgrantee agencies.
- Other Deductions—payments of grant funds during the period that are not included in expenditures, transfers out or paid to grantor.
- Paid to Grantor—amounts paid to grantor agencies during the period for unexpended funds of grants terminated (i.e., no further funding) on or before fiscal year end. These amounts should not include the payment of questioned costs.

Any transactions included in one of the above categories should be noted and explained at the bottom of the schedule.

OFFICIAL LETTERHEAD OF INDEPENDENT AUDITOR

INDEPENDENT AUDITOR'S REPORT ON COMPLIANCE BASED ON AN EXAMINATION OF THE GENERAL PURPOSE FINANCIAL STATEMENTS AND THE COMBINING, INDIVIDUAL FUND AND ACCOUNT GROUP FINANCIAL STATEMENTS

April 7, 19X9

To the governing body and audit committee of the Name of Government:

We have examined the general purpose financial statements of the Name of Government, and the combining, individual fund and account group financial statements of the Name of Government as of and for the year ended December 31, 19X8, and have issued our report thereon dated April 7, 19X9. Our examination was made in accordance with generally accepted auditing standards and the standards for financial audits contained in the *Standards for Audit of Governmental Organizations, Programs, Activities, and Functions*, issued by the U.S. General Accounting Office (1988 revision), and accordingly included such tests of the accounting records and such other auditing procedures as we considered necessary in the circumstances.

The management of the Name of Government is responsible for the government's compliance with laws and regulations. In connection with our examination referred to above, we selected and tested transactions and records to determine the government's compliance with laws and regulations noncompliance with which could have a material effect on the general purpose financial statements of the Name of Government, or on the combining, individual fund and account group financial statements.

The results of our tests indicate that for the transactions tested the Name of Government complied with those laws and regulations referred to above, except as described in the accompanying findings and recommendations. Those instances of noncompliance were considered by us in evaluating whether the general purpose financial statements and the combining, individual fund and account group financial statements are presented fairly in conformity with generally accepted accounting principles. With respect to the transactions not tested, nothing came to our attention to indicate that the Name of Government had not complied with laws and regulations other than those laws and regulations for which we noted violations in our testing referred to above.

Russum, Siegert, Fucone & Co.
Certified Public Accountants

NOTE: This letter is based on a model provided in the AICPA's *Audits of State and Local Governmental Units* (1986). As a result of certain new auditing standards released in 1988, the AICPA is expected to review this letter and suggest appropriate changes to adapt it to the requirements of the new standards.

125

OFFICIAL LETTERHEAD OF INDEPENDENT AUDITOR

INDEPENDENT AUDITOR'S REPORT ON COMPLIANCE WITH LAWS AND REGULATIONS RELATED TO MAJOR AND NONMAJOR FEDERAL FINANCIAL ASSISTANCE PROGRAMS

April 7, 19X9

To the governing body and audit committee of the Name of Government:

We have examined the general purpose financial statements of the Name of Government, and the combining, individual fund and account group financial statements of the Name of Government as of and for the year ended December 31, 19X8, and have issued our report thereon dated April 7, 19X9. Our examination was made in accordance with generally accepted auditing standards; the standards for financial audits contained in the *Standards for Audit of Governmental Organizations, Programs, Activities, and Functions,* issued by the U.S. General Accounting Office (1988 revision); the Single Audit Act of 1984; and the provisions of OMB Circular A-128, *Audits of State and Local Governments* and, accordingly, included such tests of the accounting records and such other auditing procedures as we considered necessary in the circumstances.

The management of the Name of Government is responsible for the government's compliance with laws and regulations. In connection with the examination referred to above, we selected and tested transactions and records from each major federal financial assistance program and certain nonmajor federal financial assistance programs. The purpose of our testing of transactions and records from those federal financial assistance programs was to obtain reasonable assurance that the Name of Government had, in all material respects, administered major programs, and executed the tested nonmajor program transactions, in compliance with laws and regulations, including those pertaining to financial reports and claims for advances and reimbursements, noncompliance with which we believe could have a material effect on the allowability of program expenditures.

Our testing of transactions and records selected from major federal financial assistance programs disclosed instances of noncompliance with those laws and regulations. All instances of noncompliance that we found and the programs to which they relate are identified in the accompanying findings and recommendations. The ultimate resolution of these instances of noncompliance however, could not have a material effect on the allowability of expenditures of the identified programs.

In our opinion, for the year ended December 31, 19X8, the Name of Government administered each of its major federal financial assistance programs in compliance, in all material respects, with laws and regulations, including those pertaining to financial reports and claims for advances and reimbursements, noncompliance with which we believe could have a material effect on the allowability of program expenditures.

126

The results of our testing of transactions and records selected from nonmajor federal financial assistance programs indicate that for the transactions and records tested the Name of Government complied with the laws and regulations referred to in the second paragraph of our report except as noted in the accompanying findings and recommendations. Our testing was more limited than would be necessary to express an opinion on whether the Name of Government administered those programs in compliance in all material respects with those laws and regulations noncompliance with which we believe could have a material effect on the allowability of program expenditures; however, with respect to the transactions and records that were not tested by us, nothing came to our attention to indicate that the Name of Government had not complied with laws and regulations other than those laws and regulations for which we noted violations in our testing referred to above.

Russum, Siegert, Fucone & Co.
Certified Public Accountants

NOTE: This letter is based on a model provided in the AICPA's *Audits of State and Local Governmental Units* (1986). As a result of certain new auditing standards released in 1988, the AICPA is expected to review this letter and suggest appropriate changes to adapt it to the requirements of the new standards.

OFFICIAL LETTERHEAD OF INDEPENDENT AUDITOR

INDEPENDENT AUDITOR'S REPORT ON INTERNAL ACCOUNTING CONTROLS BASED SOLELY ON A STUDY AND EVALUATION MADE AS PART OF AN EXAMINATION OF THE GENERAL PURPOSE FINANCIAL STATEMENTS AND THE COMBINING, INDIVIDUAL FUND AND ACCOUNT GROUP FINANCIAL STATEMENTS

April 7, 19X9

To the governing body and audit committee of the Name of Government:

We have examined the general purpose financial statements of the Name of Government, and the combining, individual fund and account group financial statements of the Name of Government as of and for the year ended December 31, 19X8, and have issued our report thereon dated April 7, 19X9. As part of our examination, we made a study and evaluation of the system of internal accounting control of the Name of Government to the extent we considered necessary to evaluate the system as required by generally accepted auditing standards and the standards for financial audits contained in the U.S. General Accounting Office *Standards for Audit of Governmental Organizations, Programs, Activities, and Functions* (1988 revision). For the purpose of this report, we have classified the significant internal accounting controls in the following categories: financing, receipts, disbursements and external financial reporting. Our study included all of the control categories listed above. The purpose of our study and evaluation was to determine the nature, timing and extent of the auditing procedures necessary for expressing an opinion on the Name of Government's financial statements. Our study and evaluation was more limited than would be necessary to express an opinion on the system of internal accounting control taken as a whole or on any of the categories of controls identified above.

The management of Name of Government is responsible for establishing and maintaining a system of internal accounting control. In fulfilling this responsibility, estimates and judgments by management are required to assess the expected benefits and related costs of control procedures. The objectives of a system are to provide management with reasonable, but not absolute, assurance that assets are safeguarded against loss from unauthorized use or disposition, and that transactions are executed in accordance with management's authorization and recorded properly to permit the preparation of financial statements in accordance with generally accepted accounting principles. Because of inherent limitations in any system of internal accounting control, errors or irregularities may nevertheless occur and not be detected. Also, projection of any evaluation of the system to future periods is subject to the risk that procedures may become inadequate because of changes in conditions or that the degree of compliance with the procedures may deteriorate.

Our study and evaluation made for the limited purpose described in the first paragraph would not necessarily disclose all material weaknesses in the system. Accordingly, we do not express an opinion on the system of internal accounting control of Name of Government taken as a whole or on any of the categories of controls identified in the first paragraph. However, our study and evaluation disclosed no condition that we believe to be a material weakness.

This report is intended solely for the use of management and federal grantor agencies and should not be used for any other purpose. This restriction is not intended to limit the distribution of this report which, upon acceptance by the governing body of the Name of Government, is a matter of public record.

Russum, Siegert, Fucone & Co.
Certified Public Accountants

NOTE: This letter is based on a model provided in the AICPA's *Audits of State and Local Governmental Units* (1986). As a result of certain new auditing standards released in 1988, the AICPA is expected to review this letter and suggest appropriate changes to adapt it to the requirements of the new standards.

OFFICIAL LETTERHEAD OF INDEPENDENT AUDITOR

**INDEPENDENT AUDITOR'S REPORT ON INTERNAL CONTROLS
(ACCOUNTING AND ADMINISTRATIVE)—BASED ON A STUDY
AND EVALUATION MADE AS PART OF AN EXAMINATION OF
THE GENERAL PURPOSE FINANCIAL STATEMENTS AND THE
COMBINING, INDIVIDUAL FUND AND ACCOUNT GROUP
FINANCIAL STATEMENTS AND ADDITIONAL TESTS REQUIRED
BY THE SINGLE AUDIT ACT**

April 7, 19X9

To the governing body and the audit committee of the Name of Government:

We have examined the general purpose financial statements of the Name of Government, and the combining, individual fund and account group financial statements of the Name of Government as of and for the year ended December 31, 19X8, and have issued our report thereon dated April 7, 19X9. As part of our examination, we made a study and evaluation of the internal control systems, including applicable internal administrative controls, used in administering federal financial assistance programs to the extent we considered necessary to evaluate the systems as required by generally accepted auditing standards, the standards for financial audits contained in the *Standards for Audit of Governmental Organizations, Programs, Activities, and Functions,* issued by the U.S. General Accounting Office (1988 revision), the Single Audit Act of 1984, and the provisions of OMB Circular A-128, *Audits of State and Local Governments.* For the purpose of this report, we have classified the significant internal accounting and administrative controls used in administering federal financial assistance programs in the following categories: general compliance, eligibility, other specific compliance, and grantor reporting.

The management of the Name of Government is responsible for establishing and maintaining internal control systems used in administering federal financial assistance programs. In fulfilling that responsibility, estimates and judgments by management are required to assess the expected benefits and related costs of control procedures. The objectives of internal control systems used in administering federal financial assistance programs are to provide management with reasonable, but not absolute, assurance that, with respect to federal financial assistance programs, resource use is consistent with laws, regulations, and policies; resources are safeguarded against waste, loss and misuse; and reliable data are obtained, maintained and fairly disclosed in reports.

Because of inherent limitations in any system of internal accounting and administrative controls used in administering federal financial assistance programs, errors or irregularities may nevertheless occur and not be detected. Also, projection of any evaluation of the systems to future periods is subject to the risk that procedures may become inadequate because of changes in conditions or that the degree of compliance with the procedures may deteriorate.

130

Our study included all of the applicable control categories listed above. During the year ended December 31, 19X8, the Name of Government expended 92 percent of its total federal financial assistance under major federal financial assistance programs. With respect to internal control systems used in administering major federal financial assistance programs, our study and evaluation included considering the types of errors and irregularities that could occur, determining the internal control procedures that should prevent or detect such errors and irregularities, determining whether the necessary procedures are prescribed and are being followed satisfactorily, and evaluating any weaknesses.

With respect to the internal control systems used solely in administering the nonmajor federal financial assistance programs of the Name of Government, our study and evaluation was limited to a preliminary review of the systems to obtain an understanding of the control environment and the flow of transactions through the accounting system. Our study and evaluation of the internal control systems used solely in administering the nonmajor federal financial assistance programs of the Name of Government did not extend beyond this preliminary review phase.

Our study and evaluation was more limited than would be necessary to express an opinion on the internal control systems used in administering the federal financial assistance programs of the Name of Government. Accordingly, we do not express an opinion on the internal control systems used in administering the federal financial assistance programs of the Name of Government. Further we do not express an opinion on the internal control systems used in administering the major federal financial assistance programs of the Name of Government.

Also, our examination, made in accordance with the standards mentioned above, would not necessarily disclose material weaknesses in the internal control systems used solely in administering nonmajor federal financial assistance programs. However, our study and evaluation and our examination disclosed no condition that we believe to be a material weakness in relation to a federal financial assistance program of the Name of Government.

This report is intended solely for the use of management and federal grantor agencies and should not be used for any other purpose. This restriction is not intended to limit the distribution of this report, which, upon acceptance by the governing body of the Name of Government, is a matter of public record.

Russum, Siegert, Fucone & Co.
Certified Public Accountants

NOTE: This letter is based on a model provided in the AICPA's *Audits of State and Local Governmental Units* (1986). As a result of certain new auditing standards released in 1988, the AICPA is expected to review this letter and suggest appropriate changes to adapt it to the requirements of the new standards.

FINDINGS AND RECOMMENDATIONS

FINDING 1: TIMELINESS OF GRANTEE PERFORMANCE REPORTS NEEDS TO BE IMPROVED

The terms of community development block grants require that recipients submit grantee performance reports (GPR) within two months after the end of each program year. The Name of Government's GPR for the most recent program year, however, was submitted 17 days later than required. Illness of the employee chiefly responsible for submission of the report was the cause of the delay. No costs were questioned as a result of the late submission of the GPR.

Recommendation: Management of the Name of Government should establish alternative procedures to ensure that its GPR will be submitted within the period prescribed by the terms of the grant agreement regardless of employee turnover or unforeseen absence.

Management's Response: We concur. Steps have been taken to ensure that at least two staff members share responsibility for the timely submission of all grant reports to avoid the possibility that employee turnover or unforeseen absence could delay their submission.

FINDING 2: DOCUMENTATION OF MATCHING REQUIREMENTS NEEDS IMPROVEMENT

The Name of Government's air pollution control grant from the Environmental Protection Agency (EPA) requires the Name of Government to match certain stated percentages of development and ongoing project costs. Several of the amounts claimed as matching share on reports to grantors, however, were not adequately documented. Inexperienced new personnel were the cause of the lack of adequate documentation. Although not all of the costs on the reports to grantors were adequately documented, sufficient documentation was found for other qualifying costs of the government to demonstrate that matching requirements were met. Accordingly, no costs were questioned.

Recommendation: Management of the Name of Government should take steps to ensure that new personnel are trained on the need to provide adequate documentation for all costs, including those that will be reported to grantors to meet matching requirements.

Management's Response: We concur. In future, all new personnel involved with grants administration will receive basic training on grant compliance procedures, including the documentation of matching share, as part of their initial employee orientation.

FINDING 3: MONITORING OF REENTERED PARTICIPANTS NEEDS IMPROVEMENT

The U.S. Department of Labor's senior community service grant requires that:

all participants be 55 or older and either from a family receiving regular cash welfare payments or with an annual income no greater than 125 percent of the OMB-defined poverty level. Reentered participants' income may exceed the poverty level by no more than $500 annually (29 CFR 89.19)

Although eligibility for first-time participants was established adequately by program staff, reentered participants were mistakenly judged for eligibility using the 125 percent criterion rather than the separate $500 criterion applicable to reentered participants. Program staff were unaware of the separate provision for determining the eligibility of reentered participants. However, because all reentered participants met both critieria, no costs were questioned.

Recommendation: Management of the Name of Government should ensure that program staff charged with the administration of the senior community service grant use the proper criteria to establish the eligibility of reentered participants.

Management's Response: We concur. Program staff have been alerted to the difference in criteria relative to first-time and reentered participants in the senior community service program.

GENERAL INDEX

INDEX TO JOURNAL ENTRIES

The following index provides references to each of the more than two hundred journal entries that appear in the 1988 *GAAFR*. As a general principle, journal entries are *not* referenced by each of the balance sheet or operating statement accounts that appear in them. Instead, entries are indexed by the term that best describes the transaction as a whole, be it a general term (e.g., ''advance refunding'') or an account title (e.g., ''accounts payable''). This allows for an index that is sufficiently brief so that a reader can easily review all entries when in doubt as to how a given transaction may have been classified.

1. The first number that appears refers to the chapter in which the journal entry occurs. The number in parentheses is the number of the journal entry itself. For example, the reference ''7 (4)'' indicates journal entry number 4 in chapter 7.

2. The fund in which a journal entry is recorded is indicated by one of the following abbreviations:

af	agency fund
cpf	capital projects fund
dsf	debt service fund
ef	enterprise fund
etf	expendable trust fund
gf	general fund
gfaag	general fixed assets account group
gltdag	general long-term debt account group
isf	internal service fund
ntf	nonexpendable trust fund
ptf	pension trust fund
srf	special revenue fund